9,000
WORDS

9,000
WORDS

A Supplement to
Webster's Third
New International Dictionary

A Merriam-Webster®
MERRIAM-WEBSTER INC. *Publishers*
Springfield, Massachusetts, U.S.A.

CONTENTS

Library of Congress Cataloging in Publication Data
Main Entry under title:

9,000 words

   1. English language—Dictionaries. 2. Words, New—
English—Dictionaries. I. Merriam-Webster, Inc.
II. Webster's third new international dictionary of the
English language, unabridged. III. Title: Nine thousand words.
PE1630.A16   423   83-13071

ISBN 0-87779-107-4

MADE IN THE UNITED STATES OF AMERICA
    123 RRD 868483

Preface

A dictionary begins to go out-of-date as soon as it is published. When Webster's Third New International Dictionary appeared in 1961, it provided as complete a coverage of contemporary American English as was then available. But the editing of the Third had begun more than a decade earlier; the language did not stand still during the editing, nor has it since. To try to keep abreast of the living language, Merriam-Webster editors added an eight-page Addenda section to Webster's Third in 1966, increased it to sixteen pages in 1971, to thirty-two in 1976, and to forty-eight in 1981.

The Addenda section serves two purposes: to record as many as space will permit of the new words and meanings that have become established since Webster's Third was edited and to enter those older words that for various reasons had been passed over in the earlier editing. 9,000 Words is essentially the most recent Addenda section of Webster's Third New International Dictionary; it contains most of the entries of its predecessor, 6,000 Words, and the new material added for 1981. It differs from the Addenda proper in that it has added a number of newer terms for which the Addenda section is physically too small. In addition the somewhat larger compass of a separate book has permitted the inclusion of a more generous selection of quoted illustrations than is possible in the Addenda proper. Still, 9,000 Words has one disadvantage of an Addenda section. It cannot be self-contained; the reader will find it necessary to consult another dictionary for terms—especially technical terms—which are unfamiliar. Every word used in 9,000 Words can be found in Webster's Third or in 9,000 Words; most can be found in a good desk dictionary like Webster's Ninth New Collegiate Dictionary.

In order to get such satisfaction and pleasure as a dictionary affords, one must learn how to use it—that is, how to interpret the information contained in each entry. This knowledge involves mainly an ability to recognize different typefaces, a number of abbreviations that occur over and over, and a few traditional dictionary devices. Every reader is therefore urged to read the Explanatory Notes that follow this preface carefully. After these the reader will find an informative section on the recent growth of English vocabulary, the fields which yield new words, the processes of word-formation, and the means by which Merriam-Webster editors record and define new words and meanings, then a list of pronunciation symbols and a list of abbreviations.

In addition to present members of the staff, the contributions of the following former members of the staff deserve acknowledgment: William C. Hale, Elizabeth A. Johnson, Hubert P. Kelsey, and Amy L. Liston.

Editorial Staff

Editorial Director
Frederick C. Mish

Senior Editors
E. Ward Gilman • James G. Lowe • Roger W. Pease, Jr.

Associate Editors
John K. Bollard • Julie A. Collier • Robert D. Copeland
Kathleen M. Doherty • Grace A. Kellogg • John M. Morse

Assistant Editors
Michael G. Belanger • Eileen M. Haraty • Peter D. Haraty
Daniel J. Hopkins • Karen J. Langridge
Madeline L. Novak • Stephen J. Perrault

Editorial Assistant
Robin L. Easson

Librarian
Francine A. Roberts

Department Secretary
Helene Gingold

Head of Typing Room
Gloria J. Afflitto

Senior General Clerk
Ruth W. Gaines

Clerks and Typists
Georgette B. Boucher • Karen L. Cormier
Jean M. Fitzgerald • Patricia M. Jensen
Theresa M. Klewin • Ardelia L. Thomas
Barbara A. Winkler

ENTRIES

A boldface letter or a combination of such letters set flush with the left-hand margin of each column of type is a main entry. The main entry may consist of letters set solid (as **anchorperson**), of letters joined by a hyphen (as **pro–life**), or of letters separated by one or more spaces (as **angel dust**).

The main entries follow one another in alphabetical order letter by letter. Those containing an Arabic numeral are alphabetized as if the numeral were spelled out.

A main entry marked with an asterisk (as **bad***) is not a new word, but a new sense of a word already entered in Webster's Third New International Dictionary.

When one new main entry has exactly the same written form as another, the two are distinguished by superscript numerals preceding each word (as **¹photochromic** *adj* and **²photochromic** *n*). Main entries marked with asterisks are not given such superscript numerals.

The centered periods within entry words indicate points at which a hyphen may be put at the end of a line of print or writing. They are not shown at the second and succeeding homographs of a word or for asterisked entries. There are acceptable alternative end-of-line divisions just as there are acceptable variant spellings and pronunciations, but for reasons of space no more than one division is shown for any entry in this dictionary. Without being dogmatic, we simply offer these divisions as a guide for writers, typists, and printers aiming at a consistency of end-of-line division in their work.

A double hyphen ⸗ at the end of a line in this dictionary stands for a hyphen that belongs at that point in a hyphened word and that is retained when the word is written as a unit on one line.

When a main entry is followed by the word *or* and another form (as *or* **Chomskian** at **Chomskyan**), the two forms are equal variants. Both are standard, and either one may be used according to personal inclination. When another form is joined to the main entry by the word *also*, the form after *also* is a secondary variant and occurs less frequently than the first. Secondary variants belong to standard usage and may be used according to personal inclination. If there are two secondary variants, the second is joined to the first by *or*.

Variants whose spelling puts them alphabetically more than a column away from the main entry are entered at their own alphabetical places.

A main entry may be followed by one or more derivatives (as **cablecaster** *n* at **cablecast** *vt*) or by a homograph with a different functional label (as **cablecast** *n* at **cablecast** *vt*). These are run-on entries. Each is introduced by a lightface dash and each has a functional label. They are not defined, however, since their meanings are readily derivable from the meaning of the root word.

A few main entries may be followed by one or more phrases (as **hang five** and **hang loose** at **hang***) containing the entry word or an inflected form of it. These are also run-on entries. Each is introduced by a lightface dash but there is no functional label. They are, however, defined since their meanings are more than the sum of the meanings of their elements.

Boldface words that appear within parentheses (as **angiotensin II** at **angiotensin**) are run-in entries. They are related to the entry word in an obvious way and their meaning should be clear from the context in which they occur.

A guide word is printed at the top of each page. On a left-hand page the guide word is usually the alphabetically first entry on the page; on a right-hand page it is usually the alphabetically last entry on the page. Thus the guide words on a two-page spread indicate that the entries falling alphabetically between them may be found on those pages. Any boldface word—a main entry with definition, a variant, an inflected form, a defined or undefined run-on—may be used as a guide word.

PRONUNCIATION

The matter between a pair of reverse slant lines \ \ following the entry word indicates the pronunciation. The symbols used are explained in the chart printed on pages 18a and 19a.

Pronunciation is shown for most entries in this book. Some entries, however, are common words for which new senses have developed in recent years. No pronunciation is shown for words which have been found to occur commonly in their earlier senses in textbooks and supplementary reading in the elementary school curriculum and which therefore may be considered as belonging to the current general vocabulary, e.g. **country, estimate, into.** Similarly, no pronunciation is normally shown for common elements of open compounds, e.g. **American dream, beef Wellington** \-'weliŋtən\, **blue stellar object** \-;stelər-\, **command module** \-;mäj(,)ü(ə)l\, **line judge.**

All the pronunciation variants shown for entries or parts of entries may be considered acceptable in educated English speech. Variation in pronunciation falls into two main categories, predictable and unpredictable. Predictable variants are those for which one speaker's pronunciation differs from another's because their dialects or speech patterns are different. This type of variation may be predicted from the speaker's pronunciation of other words. One type of predictable variation often recorded in this book is the so-called "loss" of \r\ before a consonant or pause in the speech of many Americans from New England, New York City, and much of the South and in that of most southern British speakers. Unpredictable variation, on the other hand, may occur in any dialect, and there is no certain way of telling from a speaker's treatment of other words which variant he might use for a particular utterance of a word with unpredictable variants. For instance, some speakers put more stress on the first syllable of **acadamese** than on the second; others stress the second syllable more than the first. The order of pronunciation variants in this book does not mean that the first is to be preferred over the second or even that it is more frequent; with two equally acceptable variants one of them must be printed before the other. Variants preceded by *also* are appreciably less frequent than unlabeled variants, and those preceded by *sometimes* are infrequent; however, no variant with either of these labels should be considered unacceptable simply on the basis of relative infrequency.

Entries labeled *abbr* are not normally given a pronunciation respelling in this work; the pronunciation may be assumed to be that of its individual constituent letters: **EFTS** *abbr*, **CPR** *abbr*. However, abbreviations are given a pronunciation respelling if evidence of a pronunciation other than that of the constituent letters appears in the Merriam-Webster pronunciation files: **gox** \'gäks\ *abbr*, **TEFL** \'tefəl\ *abbr*. For these it can be assumed that some people may pronounce the constituent letters, even though such a pronunciation is not shown. Some abbreviations are not initialisms but are shortened forms of words or parts of words. Many of these are automatically expanded in speech; for instance, **kbar** is probably most often pronounced like **kilobar**, though it may possibly also be pronounced in a way analogous to the pronunciation of the noun **krad** \'kā,rad\. In entries of this class no pronunciation is shown unless evidence appears in our pronunciation files.

Words of foreign origin whose pronunciations have not been anglicized are shown with a transcription approximating the pronunciation of the original language. In French, vowel duration is phonemic, and some French pronunciations in this book indicate greater duration by doubling the appropriate vowel symbol, as at **dacquoise** \dȧkwȧȧz\ and **fièvre boutonneuse** \fyeevrᵊbütȯn̄ēȫēz\. Similarly, consonantal lengthening or gemination is phonemic in Italian, and this is indicated by doubling the appropriate consonant symbol, as at **agnolotti** \,änyə'lȯttē\.

The following devices are used in the pronunciation transcriptions in addition to the character symbols:

\, ;\ A comma separates pronunciation variants, e.g. **fentanyl** \fen'tanᵊl, 'fentᵊn-,il\. A semicolon separates groups of variants, as at **medullin** \mə'dələn, me-; 'medᵊlən, 'mejəl-\ where the variants transcribed in full would be \mə'dələn, me-'dələn, 'medᵊlən, 'mejələn\.

\( ), (\ Parentheses indicate that the enclosed symbols are present in some utterances and not in others; for example, \'eb(y)ə,lizəm\ indicates two pronunciation variants for **ebullism,** \'ebyə‚lizəm\ and \'ebə‚lizəm\. In entries such as **lekvar** \'lek‚vär, -‚vȧ(r\ where the pronunciation of so-called "*r*-droppers" is distinguished from that of "*r*-keepers," \(r\ with no closing parenthesis indicates that the *r*-dropper may pronounce the \r\ when a vowel initial word or suffix follows without pause.

\-\ A hyphen is used at the beginning or end of a pronunciation respelling to show that not all of the boldface entry is transcribed. The missing part may be supplied from another entry, from a preceding variant within the same pair of reversed slants, or in the case of open compounds, from the pronunciation of a common word which is not entered separately in this dictionary.

\'‚‚\ Three levels of stress are indicated in this dictionary: primary stress \'\ as in **granola** \grə'nōlə\, secondary stress \‚\ as in the first syllable of **kung fu** \‚kəŋ'fü\, and no stress at all, as in the second syllable of **lexis** \'leksəs\. The stress marks stacked together \'‚\ mean "either \'\ or \‚\." Items with a stress pattern like that of **laid–back** \'‚lād'‚bak\ should be interpreted as indicating that when one of the stressed syllables has primary stress the other has secondary, or that both may have secondary stress, as is common in running speech for adjectives and even nouns in attributive position where the primary stress may fall on the word being modified. Thus the transcription for **laid–back** represents \‚lād'bak, 'lād‚bak, ‚lād‚bak\. Stress is especially variable in compounds, depending on context, emphasis, and personal preference. Fully French pronunciations are shown without any stress marks, as in the usual practice of transcribers of French. Heaviest stress generally falls on the last syllable of French words pronounced in isolation, though no such precise rule can be given for French pronunciation in running speech. The placement of stress marks in this book is not intended to indicate syllable division; see the section on \·\ following.

\·\ Syllable division is not regularly indicated in the pronunciation transcriptions. However, we have found it desirable to indicate what we will here call syllable division in some cases where confusion might arise otherwise. This is shown by the use of a centered dot \·\. It occurs, for instance, between the third and fourth syllables of the plural of **corpus allatum, corpora allata** \‚kȯrpərə·ə'lād·ə, . . . \, to indicate that the two adjacent vowels are in separate syllables. In the entry **FOR-TRAN** \'fȯr·‚tran, . . . \ the centered dot indicates that the variety of \t\ used in this word is that heard at the beginning of a word or syllable as in *tan* or *train*, and not that heard at the end of a word or syllable as in *foot* or *fort*. That is to say, the centered dot shows that the *tr* in **FORTRAN** is pronounced as in *four transoms*, not as in *Fort Ransom*. The centered dot following the character in the symbol \d·\ is not meant to represent syllable division. The use of this symbol is explained in some more detail in the Pronunciation Guide to Webster's Third. \d·\ should be thought of as a single character representing a sound heard in the speech of most Americans in both *madder* and *matter*.

\÷\ The symbol \÷\ preceding a variant indicates that although the variant occurs in educated speech many people consider it unacceptable. For example, at the entry for **escalate** the variant \÷-kyə-\ is included because it has been heard from a number of educated speakers including highly placed government officials, members of Congress, and journalists or news commentators with nationwide radio and television exposure. The absence of a representative in the spelling for the \y\ in this pronunciation variant may have given rise to the objections to its acceptability, but spelling should not overly influence the transcription of the spoken language.

FUNCTIONAL LABELS

An italic label indicating a part of speech or some other functional classification follows the pronunciation or, if no pronunciation is given, the main entry. The eight traditional parts of speech are abbreviated thus: *adj* (adjective), *adv* (adverb), *conj* (conjunction), *interj* (interjection), *n* (noun), *prep* (preposition), *pron* (pronoun), *vb* (verb).

Other italicized labels used to indicate functional classifications that are not traditional parts of speech include these: *vi* (verb intransitive), *vt* (verb transitive), *abbr* (abbreviation), *comb form* (combining form), *prefix, service mark, suffix, symbol, trademark.* Functional labels are sometimes combined.

INFLECTED FORMS

NOUNS

The plurals of nouns are shown in this dictionary when suffixation brings about a change of final *-y* to *-i-*, when the noun ends in a consonant plus *-o* or in *-ey*, when the noun has an irregular plural or a zero plural or a foreign plural, when the noun is a compound that pluralizes any element but the last, when the noun has variant plurals, and when it is believed that the dictionary user might have reasonable doubts about the spelling of the plural.

heavy* *n, pl* **heavies**	**granum** . . . *n, pl* **grana**
²hetero *n, pl* **-eros**	**halala** . . . *n, pl* **halala** *or* **halalas**
bogey* . . . *n, pl* **bogeys**	**bialy** . . . *n, pl* **bialys**
dong . . . *n, pl* **dong**	**goofy–foot** . . . *n, pl* **goofy–foots**

Cutback inflected forms are frequently used when the noun has three or more syllables:

helicity . . . *n, pl* **-ties**

The plurals of nouns are usually not shown when the base word is unchanged by suffixation, when the noun is a compound whose second element is readily recognizable as a regular free form, or when the noun is unlikely to occur in the plural.

Nouns that are plural in form and that regularly occur in plural construction are labeled *n pl*:

granny glasses *n pl*

Nouns that are plural in form but that do not always take a plural verb are appropriately labeled:

macrobiotics* . . . *n pl but sing in constr*

VERBS

The principal parts of verbs are shown in this dictionary when suffixation brings about a doubling of a final consonant or an elision of a final *-e* or a change of final *-y* to *-i-*, when the verb ends in *-ey*, when the inflection is irregular, when there are variant inflected forms, and when it is believed that the dictionary user might have reasonable doubts about the spelling of an inflected form.

grab* *vt* **grabbed; grabbing**
goose* *vt* **goosed; goosing**
gussy up . . . *vt* **gussied up; gussying up**
hang* *vb* **hung; hanging**
input . . . *vt* **inputted** *or* **input; inputting**

Inflected forms are usually cut back when the verb has three or more syllables or when it is a compound whose second element is readily recognized as an irregular verb:

habituate* . . . *vi* **-ated; -ating**

The principal parts of verbs are usually not shown when the base word is unchanged by suffixation or when the verb is a compound whose second element is readily recognizable as a regular free form.

ADJECTIVES & ADVERBS

The comparative and superlative forms of adjectives and adverbs are shown in this dictionary when suffixation brings about a doubling of a final consonant or an elision of a final *-e* or a change of final *-y* to *-i-*, when the word ends in *-ey,* when the inflection is irregular, and when there are variant inflected forms. The superlative forms of adjectives and adverbs of two or more syllables are usually cut back:

> **grungy** . . . *adj* **grun·gi·er; -est**

The inclusion of inflected forms in *-er* and *-est* at adjective and adverb entries does not mean that *more* and *most* cannot be used with these adjectives and adverbs; their comparative and superlative degrees may be expressed in either way.

The comparative and superlative forms of adjectives and adverbs are usually not shown when the base word is unchanged by suffixation or when the word is a compound whose second element is readily recognizable as a regular free form. Inflected forms are not shown at undefined run-ons.

CAPITALIZATION

Most entries in this dictionary begin with a lowercase letter. A few of these have an italicized label *often cap*, which indicates that the word is as likely to be capitalized as not, that it is as acceptable with an uppercase initial as it is with one in lowercase. Some entries begin with an uppercase letter, which indicates that the word is usually capitalized. The absence of an initial capital or of an *often cap* label indicates that the word is not ordinarily capitalized.

> **icekhana** . . . *n*
> **joual** . . . *n, often cap*
> **Sasquatch** . . . *n*

The capitalization of entries that are open or hyphened compounds is similarly indicated by the form of the entry or by an italicized label:

> **fruit leather** *n*
> **fourth world** *n, often cap F&W*
> **Denver boot** *n*
> **oysters Rockefeller** . . . *n pl*
> **Hardy–Weinberg** . . . *adj*

For a word that is capitalized in some senses and lowercase in others, variation from the form of the main entry is shown by the use of an italicized label at the appropriate sense:

> **Lacombe** . . . *n* . . . **2** *often not cap*

ETYMOLOGY

The matter in square brackets preceding the definition is the etymology. Meanings given in roman type within these brackets are not definitions of the entry, but are meanings of the italicized words within the brackets.

The etymology gives the language from which a word borrowed into English has come. It also gives the form or a transliteration of the word in that language, if the form in that language differs from that in English.

Whenever a language name appears in an etymology without an expressed form or without an expressed meaning, the form or meaning of the etymon in that language is the same as that of the word immediately preceding. If a language name which begins an etymology has no expressed form or meaning, the form of the word in that language is the same as the form of the entry word, or the meaning is the same as that of the first definition of the entry.

When an italicized word appears in an etymology with no language label, that word belongs to the same language as the word immediately preceding. When no language label at all appears ahead of it, the word is assumed to be English.

In some cases the expression "deriv. of" replaces the more usual "fr." This indicates that one or more intermediate steps have been omitted in tracing the derivation.

Small superscript numerals following words or syllables in an etymology refer to the tone of the word or syllable which they follow. They are, therefore, used only with forms cited from tone languages.

An etymology is usually not given for a word formed in English by compounding, affixation, or functional shift. Such an absence indicates that the etymology is expected to be self-evident. When several words formed from the same English prefix are entered, only the first is etymologized.

USAGE

Two types of status labels are used in this dictionary—regional and stylistic—to signal that a word or a sense of a word is not part of the standard vocabulary of English.

A word or sense limited in use to one of the other countries of the English-speaking world has an appropriate regional label:

clanger . . . *n, Brit*

The stylistic label *slang* is used with words or senses that are especially appropriate in contexts of extreme informality:

scag . . . *n* . . . *slang*

There is no satisfactory objective test for slang, especially with reference to a word out of context. No word, in fact, is invariably slang, and many standard words can be given slang applications.

When the application of a word or sense is very limited, the definition may be preceded by an italic guide phrase that points out the limitation:

scramble* *vi* . . . *of a football quarterback*

Definitions are sometimes followed by usage notes that give supplementary information about such matters as idiom, syntax, and semantic relationship. A usage note is introduced by a lightface dash:

schmear . . . *n* . . . —usu. used in the phrase *the whole schmear*
plastic* *adj* . . . —often used as a generalized term of disapproval
performance* *n* . . . —contrasted with *competence*

Definitions are frequently followed by illustrative quotations and verbal illustrations that show a typical use of the word in context. These illustrations are enclosed in angle brackets, and the word being illustrated is set in italic.

SENSE DIVISION

A boldface colon is used in this dictionary to introduce a definition; it is also used to separate two or more definitions of a single sense.

Boldface Arabic numerals separate the senses of a word that has more than one sense and boldface letters separate subsenses.

A particular semantic relationship between senses is sometimes suggested by the use of one of the italic sense dividers *esp, specif, also,* or *broadly.*

The sense divider *esp* (for *especially*) is used to introduce the most common meaning included in the more general preceding definition. The sense divider *specif* (for *specifically*) is used to introduce a common but highly restricted meaning subsumed in the more general preceding sense.

The sense divider *also* is used to introduce a meaning that is closely related to the preceding sense but that may be considered less important. The sense divider *broadly* is used to introduce an extended or wider meaning of the preceding definition.

The order of senses is basically historical: the sense our evidence shows to have been first used in English is usually entered first.

When an italicized label follows a boldface numeral, the label applies only to that specific numbered sense. It does not apply to any other boldface numbered senses.

CROSS-REFERENCES

Three different kinds of cross-references are used in this dictionary: directional, synonymous, and cognate. In each instance the cross-reference is readily recognized by the lightface small capitals in which it is printed. Every occurrence of small capitals refers the reader to another entry in 9,000 Words.

A cross-reference following a lightface dash and beginning with either *compare* or *see* is a directional cross-reference. It directs the dictionary user to look elsewhere for further information:

> **plateglass** . . . *adj* . . . —compare OXBRIDGE, REDBRICK
> **diazepam** . . . *n* . . . —see VALIUM

A cross-reference following a boldface colon is a synonymous cross-reference:

> **apocynthion** . . . *n* . . . : APOLUNE

A synonymous cross-reference indicates that a definition at the entry in this dictionary cross-referred to can be substituted as a definition for the entry or the sense in which the cross-reference appears. A lightface numeral following a synonymous cross-reference refers to a sense number at the entry cross-referred to:

> **magnetoplasmadynamic** . . . *adj* : HYDROMAGNETIC 1

A cross-reference following an italic *var of* (for *variant of*) is a cognate cross-reference:

> **schtick** *var of* SHTICK

ABBREVIATIONS & SYMBOLS

Abbreviations and symbols are included as main entries in the vocabulary:

> **ICU** *abbr* intensive care unit
> **p*** *symbol*. . .

Abbreviations have been normalized to one form. In practice, however, there is considerable variation in the use of periods and in capitalization (as *bpi, b.p.i., BPI, B.P.I.*), and stylings other than those given in this dictionary are often acceptable.

The vocabulary of English, like that of every other living language, is constantly growing. This growth is certainly not new. Always, as people have met with new objects and new experiences and have developed new ideas, they have needed new words to describe them. New words and new meanings for old words are the reason for this book. In the sections that follow, we will indicate some of the areas that produce new words, the ways in which new words are formed, and how new words get into the dictionary.

Where Do They All Come From?

Science and technology are probably the most prolific providers of new words today. Most spectacularly, perhaps, they have combined to make flights of *space shuttles* almost routine, to take men to the moon and bring them back, and to send robot craft even farther into space and to planets. The exploration of the moon has given us words for novel experiences: *moonwalk, earthrise.*

Extraterrestrial exploration has brought changes in our conception of more familiar experiences. Consider the moon. We have long been familiar with the moon's maria, those large dark areas which appear to the naked eye of the earthbound observer to be the features of the man in the moon. We long ago borrowed the Latin word *mare* "sea" to refer to these dark patches. We now know that the moon has highlands, too, contrasting with the low-lying maria. These we call *terrae*, contrasting Latin *terra* "land" with *mare* "sea." And we have long been aware that the earth and the other planets orbit the sun. We have referred to a planet's greatest distance from the sun as its *aphelion*, the least distance as its *perihelion.* Now that we are able to orbit the moon we speak analogously of a moon satellite's *apolune* and *perilune.* But we have not yet settled down with these words; we have created variants, borrowing from both Greek and Latin, even from mythology. We base *apolune* and *perilune* on the Latin word for the moon, *luna; aposelene, aposelenium, periselene,* and *periselenium* on the Greek *selēnē.* And we use the name of *Cynthia*, goddess of the moon, in *apocynthion* and *pericynthion.*

It is not only the more direct exploration of *deep space* which adds to our extraterrestrial vocabulary. Earthbound astronomers continue to make new discoveries and formulate new theories. We hear about *quasars, pulsars, neutron stars*, and the mysterious *black hole.* The *big bang theory* and the *steady state theory* offer us alternative explanations of the origin of the universe. We learn that the earth moves in a mysterious way, *Chandler's wobble*, not yet explained. And on a more terrestrial scale, we find *plate tectonics* gaining increasing acceptance on the basis of geological observations.

Other fields of scientific study are also adding to the English vocabulary. For all the years men have lived on the earth, they have not exhausted the study of the earth's natural history. It is true that discoveries of undescribed and uncataloged animals and plants are not as frequent as they were in earlier ages, when whole continents were being opened up for scientific exploration. Nor have we yet discovered living things in our exploration of outer space. But we shall probably never feel confident that we know all the forms of life. Few new discoveries are as striking or as controversial as that, as yet unconfirmed, of a large nonhuman primate in the Pacific Northwest. Whether or not he exists, the animal's names, *Sasquatch* and *bigfoot*, are now a part of our language. Other animals, although not new to science, are new to America. For example, two immigrants from abroad, the *walking catfish* and the *imported fire ant*, are making their presence felt in the southeastern United States, and their names have become established in American English.

The discovery of the mechanism of protein synthesis has made genetics a fertile provider of new terms, giving us the *Watson-Crick model* of DNA, the *genetic code*, *messenger RNA*, and a new meaning for *template* among many others. And as physicists pry deeper and deeper into the atomic nucleus they have discovered more subatomic particles: *kaon, lambda*, and *muon*, for example. They have discovered *antiparticles*, studied *isospin*, and used *spark chambers.* Medicine too is a major contributor of new terms such as *busulfan, open-heart* surgery, the *sudden infant death syndrome*, and the famous *pill.* Mathematics has become more noticeable especially since the revising of the subject as taught in school. *Fourier transform, open sen-*

tence, onto, and *truth set* are among the mathematical terms that will be found herein.

Technological sophistication always seems to make things faster or smaller, as such terms as *computerize* and *microminiaturization* attest. Programmers communicate with computers in *FORTRAN, COBOL,* or *BASIC* and computers talk to each other in *ASCII* or *EBCDIC.* Technical improvement in *microforms* has made possible the business of *micropublishing.* Tiny *integrated circuits* make the pocket calculator and the *microcomputer* possible. And in even more familiar applications technology has supplied the *flashcube,* the *microwave oven,* the *videocassette,* and the *solar cell.*

Some technological advances are less benevolent than these, however. Our capacity for military destructiveness is constantly increasing, and with it our military vocabulary. We have *ABMs, SAMs,* and *MIRVs.* We have *overkill.* We can talk almost casually about the possibility of nuclear war, and we have a new unit of measurement to use in such discussions, the *megadeath.* Our long military involvement in Vietnam also increased our vocabulary. We sought to justify our actions by the *domino theory.* We disparaged the *Cong* by calling them *dinks.* The *Green Berets* became a household word, and the common foot soldier became a *grunt.* The division of American opinion on our undeclared war gave us *doves* and *hawks.* And the words we brought out of the war were not only military: the appearance in American English of such words as *ao dai* and *hootch* was a by-product of our military involvement in Southeast Asia.

But science and technology are not the only sources of new words. The two decades since the publication of Webster's Third has seen considerable political and social ferment, and this ferment has left its mark on the language. Besides *hippies, teenyboppers,* and *flower people* we have *preppies, pro-lifers,* and *whistle-blowers, Hare Krishnas* and *Moonies.* We have been exposed to *Watergate* and *ayatollah,* to *white flight* and *gentrification,* to *redlining* and *supply-side* economics.

So many people have become involved with the drug subculture that the jargon of drugs has won a prominent place in the consciousness of contemporary America. We talk of *uppers* and *downers, acid, free base, jays, dexies,* and *smack,* of people who have *OD'd,* and of people *busted* for trying to smuggle in a couple of *keys.*

Minorities have also made themselves heard. The civil rights movement that began with *freedom rides* has made us all more aware of black culture. Black culture itself has given us many new words. A new academic subject, *black studies,* has been added to the curriculum of many schools. And *Afro, dashiki,* the *Black Panthers,* the *Black Muslims,* and *soul* are familiar to most of us. Other minorities have also become more politically active and more visible: we are now familiar with both *Chicanos* and *Native Americans.* From the women's movement we get such terms as *Ms., sexism,* and *chairperson.* Rounding out the group are politically active *golden≈ agers* who call themselves *Gray Panthers* and fight *ageism.*

The changing attitude of Americans toward sexual matters and materials has also contributed to the language. Movies are now rated *G, PG, R,* or *X,* and people may be *AC/DC.* The homosexual subculture has become more open, bringing into general use such terms as *homophile, gay, butch,* and *camp.*

Education is another source of new vocabulary, giving us *underachiever, open classroom, TA, grade-point average, CAI,* and *pass-fail* grading. Increasing interest in the consumer has given us *consumerism, callback, unit pricing,* and *generic.*

Entertainment has always been a source of new words. We have *sitcoms* and *shoot-'em-ups* on television and *call-in* programs on radio; at the neighborhood movie theater we might watch a *spaghetti western.* We might see *guerrilla theater* or listen to *salsa, punk rock, rhythm and blues,* or *zydeco.* Sports continues its steady production of vocabulary with new sports such as *roller hockey* and new ways of playing old ones, such as baseball's *designated hitter.* Television coverage of football fills weekends with *blitzes, play-action passes, square outs,* and *squib kicks.* Those who care *zilch* about football may go to the track and play the *perfecta, superfecta,* or *trifecta.* The *martial arts* of the Far East have given us *aikido* and *kung fu* along with *dan, dojo,* and *black belt.*

Cooking too has added to the English vocabulary. From *aioli* to *zuppa inglese* English has borrowed a host of terms from foreign cuisines, including *caldo verde, frijoles refritos, tabbouleh,* and *wok.* The vocabulary of food has also been increased by such domestic contributors as the *corn chip, lane cake,* and *green goddess dressing.*

How Are They Formed?

English gets its new vocabulary from many fields, some very new. But these new words are, for the most part, created or derived in a number of time-honored ways. Not all new words, in fact, are really new. Old words are frequently given new meanings to fit new situations. *Angel,* for example, is the name of a spiritual being believed by many to be able to exert an influence on humans without their being aware of his presence. Now the word *angel* is used also for a radar echo whose cause is not visually discernible. Because the dove is a traditional symbol of peace and the hawk is a predatory bird, *dove* has come to be used for a conciliatory person, *hawk* for one who is militant. We have long been familiar with the *Mafia* as a secret criminal society; now the use of the word has been extended so that any clique may be called a *mafia.*

Some new words are new not in form but in function. By functional shift an old noun, for example, may come to be used as a new verb. The noun *clone* means "an aggregate of the progeny of an individual, reproduced asexually." *Clone* has now been made into a verb, meaning "to propagate a clone from." The noun *update,* meaning "an updating", comes by functional shift from the verb *update.* Similarly, the adjective *soul* comes from the noun, the noun *commute* from the verb, the verb *format* from the noun.

Of course the words most obviously new are those whose forms have not been used before, whether in earlier senses or in other functions. One common method of forming new words is compounding, combining two (or more) old words to form a new one. Typical compounds are such words as *fake book, pantsuit, uptight, goof-off, acidhead, strawberry jar, end-of-day glass, floating decimal, water bed, litterbag, splashdown.* Some of these occur in more than one styling—closed (*acidhead*), hyphenated (*acid-head*), or open (*acid head*)—but only the most common styling will appear in the dictionary. Some new words are compounds of parts of older words. *Gravisphere,* for example, adds *sphere* to the *gravi-* of *gravity. Underwhelm* is formed from *under* and the *-whelm* of *overwhelm.*

Sometimes words which are combined seem to overlap. Two words which have letters or sounds in common may be blended. Typical blends are such new words as *cremains,* from *cremated* and *remains, gasohol,* from *gasoline* and *alcohol,* and *Franglais,* blended in French of *français* (French) and *anglais* (English).

Many word elements occur only in combinations, never alone. These are affixes (prefixes and suffixes) and combining forms. Many old affixes and combining forms are very prolific. The prefix *anti-,* for example, has given us *antihero, antiheroine, antiparticle, antipollution, antismog,* and a host of other new words. From *non-* we derive such words as *nonbook, nondiscrimination, nonnegative,* and *nonperson.* The suffix *-ese,* which denotes a jargon, has formed *academese, computerese, educationese.* The combining form *-logy* has been especially prolific in recent years, yielding terms for such studies as *erotology, Pekingology,* and *planetology.* Nor is the English language content with its already large hoard of affixes and combining forms; it creates or borrows new ones like the suffix *-manship,* taken from *sportsmanship* and used to form such words as *grantsmanship;* like the suffix *-nik,* borrowed from Yiddish and used in *peacenik, computernik,* and their relatives; like the combining form *-in,* which we find not only in the original *sit-in,* but very widespread, as in *love-in, teach-in,* and *smoke-in,* and like the very frequently used new combining form *mini-,* in *minibike, minibus, minicomputer, miniskirt,* and *ministate.*

Many new words are simply shortened forms, or clippings, of older words. By shortening we derive *deli* from *delicatessen, mayo* from *mayonnaise, mod* from *modern, narc* from *narcotics agent.* Some words are formed as acronyms from the initial letters of the parts of a compound term. In this way we have created *COBOL* from *common business oriented language*, *PG* from *parental guidance*, and *WASP* from *white Anglo-Saxon Protestant*.

A process somewhat similar to clipping is known as back-formation. A back-formation is formed from an already existing word by subtracting a real or supposed affix. *Gangling*, for example, looks as if it ought to be the present participle of a verb, so we create a new verb *gangle*, removing the supposed derivative suffix *-ing*. *Laser*, although it is an acronymic formation from *light amplification by stimulated emission of radiation*, looks like an agent noun formed from a verb. So we remove the apparent agent suffix and form the verb *lase*. In like manner, we have created the back-formations *free-associate* from *free association* and *one-up* from *one-upmanship*.

Many new English words are not products of English word formation at all. They are borrowed from other languages. For much of its history English has been a great borrower, building its vocabulary by culling languages all over the world for new and useful terms. From the French, English has taken such words as *après-ski, extraordinaire, bidonville*, and *yé-yé* (the last borrowed earlier by French from English *yeah-yeah*). We have borrowed Italian *autostrada* and *ciao*, Portuguese *favela*, German *gemütlich* and *gemütlichkeit*, Swedish *ombudsman*, Mexican Spanish *machismo*, Hindi *tabla*, Sanskrit *tala*, Chinese *wok*, Japanese *ikebana*, Tahitian *mai tai*.

We have borrowed such words as *flokati* from modern Greek and gone back to classical Greek for *lexis*. One language from which English has borrowed extensively is in a unique position. Yiddish is a language foreign to English, but it is spoken by many English-speaking American Jews, who often lard their English with Yiddish words. And many Yiddish words have passed into the speech of non-Yiddish-speaking Americans. Especially prominent among these borrowings are pejorative terms like *klutz, nebbish, schlepp*, and *schlock*. But also from Yiddish come *chutzpah* (perhaps pejorative), *bialy*, and *maven*.

Sometimes English compounds are borrowed from other languages, but their components are translated into English. These are called loan translations. *Black humor* is a loan translation from French *humour noir*. French *objet trouvé* has entered English both as a straight borrowing and as a loan translation (*found object*). Occasionally we translate only part of a compound we are borrowing. *Auteur theory*, for example, is a part translation of French *politique des auteurs*.

Some new words come from the names of people or places. The *Alfvén wave*, for instance, was named for Swedish astrophysicist Hannes Alfvén, *Chandler's wobble* for American astronomer Seth Carlo Chandler. A jacket of eastern appearance is called either *Mao*, after Mao Tse-tung, or *Nehru*, after Jawaharlal Nehru. *A-go-go* comes from a café and discotheque in Paris, the Whisky à Gogo.

Trademarks are another source of new words. Although a trademark is owned by a particular company and used for a specific class of products, some trademarks become so familiar that they are used by many people for similar products. Of course a company that owns a trademark will try to protect its property and maintain the association of the trademarked name with its product alone. But occasionally a trademark does become generic. *Granola*, formerly a trademark, is now a generic name for a cereal mixture whose basic component is rolled oats. Sometimes a trademark for one product is borrowed and used as a general word for something else. *STP* is a trademark for a motor fuel additive, but it is commonly applied to a psychedelic drug. Other trademarks, although they do not become generic, do produce derivatives by functional shift. The trademark *Mace*, for example, has given us the verb *mace*. Some trademarks which have not become generic occur so often in speech and writing that they deserve a place in a dictionary, even though they cannot really be considered a part of the general vocabulary of English. Those entries known to be trademarks or service marks are so labeled and are treated in accordance with a formula approved by the United States Trademark Association. No entry in this dictionary, however, should be regarded as affecting the validity of any trademark or service mark.

Many new words are onomatopoeic, imitative of sounds. *Chugalug* imitates the sound of swallowing liquid, *bleep* a high-pitched sound of electronic equipment, *zap* the sound of a gun. Some words are simply coined ex nihilo, but these are relatively rare. One such is *grok*, which was coined by the American author Robert A. Heinlein in his 1961 science fiction novel *Stranger in a Strange Land.*

How Do They Get Into Merriam-Webster Dictionaries?

It is one thing for a word to get into the language and quite another for it to get into a dictionary. The definitions in this book, as in all Merriam-Webster dictionaries, are based upon our voluminous files of citations. The editorial staff regularly reads a variety of periodicals, as well as fiction and nonfiction books in many fields. Every editor spends a part of each working day reading and marking. When he comes across a word that is not in our dictionaries or that is used in a new or striking way, he underlines the word and brackets enough of its context to make the word's meaning clear. (Sometimes, it is true, a word's meaning will not be clear no matter how much context surrounds it. When this happens, the only thing an editor can do is mark it anyway, simply for its occurrence, and hope that the word will turn up elsewhere, more intelligibly used.) The passages marked in this manner are put on 3x5 slips of paper, called citation slips, and filed alphabetically. When a new dictionary is being written, a definer will take all the citations for a particular word, sort them according to grammatical function (such as noun or verb) and possible separable segments of meaning, read them carefully to determine the meaning of the word as it is used, and write a definition. The definitions, then, are based not on an editor's idea of what words ought to mean but rather on the meanings actually given to words by the speakers and writers of English who use them.

Not every word that is represented in the citation files will be entered in a dictionary. A single citation or two is not normally considered evidence of a word's establishment as part of the general vocabulary. We look for the use of a word in a variety of sources, and for its occurrence over several years. Some words enjoy a brief vogue, when they are on practically every tongue, then disappear. The division of British youth a few years ago into *Mods* and *Rockers* seemed destined to add these terms to the general vocabulary. But after a couple of years the division faded away and with it the words. Such words as *Mod* and *Rocker* are items of interest for a historical dictionary, but are unlikely to enter a general dictionary.

Some of our 9,000 Words are older than the 1960s. They appear here because, for one reason or another, they were not entered in Webster's Third New International Dictionary. Some words, although they had been in the spoken language for years, did not appear in print until recently or appeared so rarely as to be caught only once or twice, or not at all, by our reading and marking program. *Mayo* has probably been heard at lunch counters for forty years or more, but it was only in the early 1960s that we began to see it in print. Another word, *frog* "a spiked or perforated holder used to keep flowers in position in a vase", is quite old. Even now it has been cited only very rarely by our readers and markers. But after the appearance of Webster's Third, a number of correspondents questioned its absence from that book, so it was entered in the addenda.

In some fields, our reading and marking program was fairly weak in the past. In mathematics, for example, such words as *counterexample* and *Fibonacci number,* although they are not new, have only recently caught the attention of the markers and definers. Some older words did not appear in Webster's Third because they were rejected by outside consultants. One such is *sprechstimme*, which was rejected by the music consultant with the note "The time will come . . . when this word will or must, be entered". His note is dated 1957 and the citational evidence, now more than three times what it was in 1957, shows that *sprechstimme* deserves entry.

Some words have an air of antiquity not because they themselves are old but because the objects with which they are associated are old. The controversial *Homo habilis*, for example, although he is a fossil about two million years old, was not discovered until 1964. And though typists have been taught for years with the aid of such sentences as "The quick brown fox jumps over the lazy dog", we knew of no word for such sentences until 1964, when we first met *pangram* in print.

ə . . . in unstressed syllables as in b**a**nan**a**, c**o**llide, **a**but, mak**e**r; in stressed syllables as in h**u**mdr**u**m, **a**but, and by *r*-keepers in b**i**rd

ə̇ . . . two-value symbol meaning \ə\ or \i\ in unstressed syllables only

ᵊ . . . immediately preceding \l\, \n\, \m\ as in batt**le**, cott**on**, and one pronunciation of **open** \'ōpᵊm\; immediately following \l\, \m\, \r\ as often in French tab**le**, pris**me**, tit**re**

ə̄, ə̇i . . . alternative pronunciations used by *r*-droppers in stressed positions where *r*-keepers have \ər\ as in b**i**rd

a . . . m**a**t, m**a**p, m**a**d, m**a**n, p**a**ss, st**a**mp

ā . . . d**a**y, f**a**de, **a**orta, dr**a**pe, c**a**pe, d**a**te

ä . . . b**o**ther, c**o**t, and with most Americans f**a**ther, c**a**rt

ȧ . . . f**a**ther as pronounced by speakers who do not rhyme it with *bother*; **au**nt as pronounced by speakers who do not rhyme it with *pant* or *font*; f**a**rther, c**a**rt as pronounced by *r*-droppers; French p**a**tte

au̇ . . . n**ow**, l**ou**d, **ou**t, some pronunciations of t**a**lcum (see \u̇\)

b . . . **b**a**b**y, ri**b**

ch . . . **ch**in, na**t**ure \'nāchə(r)\ (actually, this sound is \t\ + \sh\)

d . . . el**d**er, un**d**one, gla**d**

d· . . . as in the usual American pronunciation of du**t**y, la**tt**er; \t\ is always to be understood as an alternative

e . . . b**e**d, p**e**t

ē . . . in stressed syllables as in b**ea**t, nosebl**ee**d, **e**venly, sl**ee**py; in un-stressed syllables as in one pronunciation of even**ly**, sleep**y**, env**i**ous, ign**e**ous (alternative \i\)

f . . . **f**i**f**ty, cu**ff**

g . . . **g**o, bi**g**

h . . . **h**at, a**h**ead

hw . . . **wh**ale as pronounced by those who do not have the same pronuncia-tion for both *whale* and *wail*

i . . . b**i**d, t**i**p, one pronunciation of act**i**ve, even**ly** (alternative unstressed \ē\)

ī . . . s**i**te, s**i**de, b**uy** (actually, this sound is \ä\ + \i\ or \ȧ\ + \i\)

j . . . **j**ob, **g**em, ju**dg**e (actually, this sound is \d\ + \zh\)

k . . . **k**in, **c**ook, a**ch**e

k̲ . . . as in one pronunciation of lo**ch** (altenative \k\); German i**ch**, bu**ch**

l . . . **l**i**l**y, poo**l**, co**l**d

m . . . **m**ur**m**ur, di**m**, ny**m**ph

n . . . **n**o, ow**n**

ⁿ . . . indicates that a preceding vowel or diphthong is pronounced with open nasal passages as in French *un bon vin blanc* \œ̃ⁿbō̃ⁿvaⁿblä̃ⁿ\

ŋ . . . si**ng** \'siŋ\, si**ng**er \'siŋə(r)\, fi**ng**er \'fiŋgə(r)\, i**nk** \'iŋk\

ō . . . bone, know, beau

ȯ . . . saw, all, gnaw

œ . . . French bœuf, German Hölle

ō̄e . . . French feu, German Höhle

ȯi . . . coin, destroy, sawing

p . . . pepper, lip

r . . . rarity, read; car and card as pronounced by r-keepers

s . . . source, less

sh . . . with nothing between, as in shy, mission, machine, special (actually this is a single sound, not two)

t . . . tie, attack; one pronunciation of latter (alternative \d·\)

th . . . with nothing between, as in thin, ether (actually this is a single sound, not two)

<u>th</u> . . . then, either, this (actually this is a single sound, not two)

ü . . . rule, youth, union \'yünyən\, few \'fyü\

u̇ . . . pull, wood, took, curable \'kyu̇rəbəl\, some pronunciations of milk \'miu̇k\, talcum \'tau̇kəm\

ue . . . German füllen, hübsch

ūe . . . French rue, German fühlen

v . . . vivid, give

w . . . we, away; in some words having final \(͵)ō\ or \(͵)yü\ variant \əw\ occurs before vowels as in following \'faləwiŋ\, covered by the variant \ə(w)\ at the entry word

y . . . yard, young, cue \'kyü\, union \'yünyən\

z . . . zone, raise

zh . . . with nothing between, as in vision, azure \'azhə(r)\ (actually this is a single sound, not two)

\ . . . slant line used to mark the beginning and end of a transcription

, ; . . . a comma separates pronunciation variants; a semicolon separates groups of variants (see page 7a)

(), (. . . indicate that what is symbolized between or after is present is some utterances but not in others (see page 7a)

- . . . used at the beginning or end of a partially transcribed pronunciation (see page 8a)

'͵ ͵ . . . \'\ precedes a syllable with primary (strongest) stress; \͵\ precedes a syllable with secondary (next-strongest) stress; combined marks \͵\ precede a syllable whose stress may be either primary or secondary (see page 8a)

· . . . used to indicate syllable division where confusion might otherwise arise (see also \d·\ above and page 8a)

÷ . . . indicates that many regard as unacceptable the one pronunciation immediately following, as in escalate \'eskə͵lāt, ÷-kyə-\ (see page 8a)

AAUP	American Association of University Professors	F	French	NL	New Latin
		fem	feminine	Norw	Norwegian
		fl	flourished	obs	obsolete
		Fla	Florida	OE	Old English
ab	about	fr	from	OF	Old French
abbr	abbreviation	Fr	French	OHG	Old High German
adj	adjective	freq	frequentative		
adv	adverb	G, Ger	German	OIt	Old Italian
advt	advertisement	Gk	Greek	ON	Old Norse
alter	alteration	Heb	Hebrew	orig	originally
Am, Amer	American	Hung	Hungarian	part	participle
AmerSp	American Spanish	Icel	Icelandic	Pek	Pekingese
		Ill	Illinois	perh	perhaps
Ar	Arabic	imit	imitative	Pg	Portuguese
b	born	interj	interjection	pl	plural
B.C.	before Christ	Introd	Introduction	Pol	Polish
Biog	Biography	irreg	irregular	prep	preposition
Biol	Biological	ISV	International Scientific Vocabulary	prob	probably
Brit	British			pron	pronoun
Bull	Bulletin			Prov	Provençal
C	centigrade	It, Ital	Italian	Russ	Russian
cal	caliber	Jp	Japanese	Sat	Saturday
Canad	Canadian	Jour	Journal	Sc	Scots
CanF	Canadian French	Jr.	Junior	Scand	Scandinavian
		L	Latin	Scot	Scottish
Cant	Cantonese	LHeb	Late Hebrew	sing	singular
cent	century	lit	literally	Skt	Sanskrit
Chem	Chemical	Lit	Literary	Slav	Slavic
Chin	Chinese	LL	Late Latin	So	South
Co	Company	Mag	Magazine	Sp	Spanish
comb	combining	Mass	Massachusetts	specif	specifically
conj	conjunction	MD	Middle Dutch	Supp	Supplement
constr	construction	MexSp	Mexican Spanish	Sw, Swed	Swedish
contr	contraction			trans	translation
Dan	Danish	MF	Middle French	U.S.	United States
D.C.	District of Columbia	MHG	Middle High German	U.S.S.R.	Union of Soviet Socialist Republics
deriv	derivative	MLG	Middle Low German		
dial	dialect			usu	usually
dim	diminutive	modif	modification	v, vb	verb
Du	Dutch	n	noun	var	variant
E, Eng	English	NE	northeast	vi	verb intransitive
Esk	Eskimo	neut	neuter	VL	Vulgar Latin
esp	especially	Nev	Nevada	vt	verb transitive
et al	and others	NGk	New Greek	Vt	Vermont
Eve	Evening	NHeb	New Hebrew		

A Supplement to
Webster's Third New
International Dictionary

A

a*abbr atto-
A and R *abbr* artists and repertory
A band *n* [anisotropic *band*] **:** one of the cross striations of striated muscle that contains myosin filaments and appears dark under the light microscope and light in polarized light
ABC art *n* **:** MINIMAL ART
ABD \‚ā(‚)bē'dē\ *n* [all *b*ut *d*issertation] **:** a doctoral candidate who has completed the required course work and examinations but not the dissertation
Abe·lian \ə¦bēlyən, -lēən\ *adj* [Niels *Abel* †1829 Norw. mathematician] **:** combining elements or having elements that combine in such a manner that the result is independent of the order in which elements are taken **:** commutative ⟨*Abelian* ring⟩ ⟨the real numbers under addition comprise an *Abelian* group⟩
ab·la·tor \a'blād-ə(r)\ *n* [LL, one that removes, fr. *ablatus*, suppletive past part. of *auferre* to remove] **:** a material that provides thermal protection (as to the outside of a spacecraft on reentry) by ablating
ABM \‚ā(‚)bē'em\ *n* **:** ANTIBALLISTIC MISSILE
abort*\ə'bȯ(ə)rt, -ȯət\ *n* **:** the premature termination of an action, procedure, or mission relating to a rocket or spacecraft ⟨a launch *abort*⟩
ab·scis·ic acid \(‚)ab‚sizik-, -‚sis-\ *n* [*abscis*ion (var. of *abscission*) + -*ic*, adj. suffix] **:** a growth-inhibiting plant hormone widespread in nature and made synthetically that promotes leaf abscission and dormancy and has an inhibitory effect on cell elongation — called also *abscisin II, dormin*
ab·scis·in *also* **ab·scis·sin** \'absəsən, ab'sis³n\ *n* [*abscis*ion, *abscis*sion + -*in* chemical compound] **:** any of a group of plant hormones (as abscisic acid) that tend to promote leaf abscission and inhibit various growth processes
ab·seil \'äp‚zīl, -īəl\ *vi, chiefly Brit* **:** to rappel — **ab·seil·er** \-ə(r)\ *n*

absurd*adj* **1 :** having no rational or orderly relationship to man's life **:** meaningless; *also* **:** lacking order or values ⟨adults have condemned them to live in what must seem like an *absurd* universe —Joseph Featherstone⟩ **2 :** dealing with the absurd or with absurdism
absurd *n* **:** the state or condition in which man exists in an irrational and meaningless universe and in which man's life has no meaning outside his own existence ⟨no . . . existential *Absurd* to perplex us —Dwight Macdonald⟩ ⟨the black humor of the *absurd* —Mark Phillips⟩
ab·surd·ism \əb'sərd‚izəm, ab-, -'z-, -ȯd-, -ȯid-\ *n* **:** a philosophy based on the belief that man exists in an irrational and meaningless universe and that his search for order brings him into conflict with his universe
¹ab·surd·ist \-dəst\ *n* **:** a proponent or adherent of absurdism; *esp* **:** a writer who deals with absurdist themes
²absurdist *adj* **:** of, relating to, or dealing with absurdism
-ac \‚ak, *in a few words* ik *or* ək\ *n suffix* [NL -*acus* of or relating to, fr. Gk -*akos*] **:** one affected with ⟨nostalgi*ac*⟩
aca·de·mese \ə¦kadə¦mēz, ¦akəd-, -ēs\ *n* [*academ*ic + -*ese* jargon] **:** a style of writing held to be characteristic of those in academic life ⟨the usual scholarly biography, written in barbarous *academese* —Dwight Macdonald⟩
Aca·pul·co gold \‚äkə¦púl(‚)kō-, ‚ak-, -úl-\ *n, often cap G* [*Acapulco*, Mexico] **:** marijuana grown in Mexico that is held to be very potent
acathisia *var of* AKATHISIA
acceptable*adj* **:** capable of being endured **:** supportable, tolerable ⟨maximum *acceptable* damage from nuclear attack⟩ ⟨concluded that environmental damage caused by the line could be held to an "*acceptable* minimum" —Robert Gillette⟩
ac·cess \'ak‚ses *also* ik's- *or* ak's-\ *vt* **:** to get at **:** gain access to ⟨accumulator and index registers can be *accessed* by the programmer —*Datamation*⟩

access time *n* **1 :** the lag between the time stored information (as in a computer) is requested and the time it is delivered **2 :** television airtime during prime viewing hours that is reserved for exclusive use by local broadcasters

ac·com·mo·da·tion·ist \ə‚kämə'dāsh(ə)nəst\ *n* **:** one who adapts to or compromises with an opposing viewpoint; *specif* **:** a black who adapts to the ideals or attitudes of whites ⟨making Uncle Toms, compromisers, and *accommodationists* . . . ashamed of the urbane and smiling hypocrisy we practice —Ossie Davis⟩

AC/DC \‚ā(‚)sē‚dē(‚)sē\ *adj* [fr. the likening of a bisexual person to an electrical appliance which can operate on either alternating or direct current] **:** sexually oriented to both sexes **:** bisexual ⟨help the *A.C./D.C.* youngster to shape his actions in a heterosexual direction —R.H. Kuh⟩

ace*vt* **aced; ac·ing 1 :** to earn the grade of A on (an examination) **2 :** to defeat, displace, or dispose of **:** gain a decisive advantage over — usu. used with *out* ⟨a beautiful, compelling cover can *ace* out much of the visual competition —Geraldine Rhoads⟩

ac·e·tab·u·lo·plas·ty \‚asə‚tabyə(‚)lō‚plastē, -i\ *n, pl* **-ties** [*acetabulum* + *-plasty* plastic surgery] **:** a plastic operation on the acetabulum intended to restore its normal state (as by repairing or enlarging its cavity)

ac·et·amin·o·phen \‚asəd-ə'minəfən, ə‚sēd--\ *n* [*acetic* + *amino-* containing an amino group + *phenol*] **:** a crystalline compound $C_8H_9NO_2$ that is a hydroxy derivative of acetanilide and is used in chemical synthesis and in medicine to relieve pain and fever

ac·e·to·hex·amide \‚asəd-ō‚heksəməd, ə‚sē-, -‚heks-‚aməd, -‚mīd\ *n* [N-(p-*acetyl*phenylsulfonyl)-N'-cyclo*hexyl*urea + *amide*, chemical family name for ureas] **:** a sulfonylurea drug $C_{15}H_{20}N_2O_4S$ used in the oral treatment of some of the milder forms of diabetes to lower the level of glucose in the blood

ace·tyl–coA \ə'sēd-ºl'kō'ā; 'asəd‚ºl-, -ə‚tēl-\ *n* [*acetyl* coenzyme *A*] **:** a compound $C_{25}H_{38}N_7O_{17}P_3S$ formed as an intermediate in metabolism and active as a coenzyme in biological acetylations

ace·tyl·cys·te·ine \ə‚sēd-ºl'sis‚tēn, 'asəd‚ºl-, -ə‚tēl-, -‚sistē‚ēn, -stə‚ēn\ *n* [*acetyl* + *cysteine*] **:** a mucolytic agent $C_5H_9NO_3S$ used esp. to reduce the viscosity of abnormally viscid respiratory tract secretions

acid*n* **:** a hallucinogenic drug lysergic acid diethylamide **:** LSD

acid·head \'asəd‚hed\ *n* **:** a person who frequently uses LSD

acid precipitation *n* **:** precipitation (as rain or snow) whose increased acidity is caused by environmental factors (as sulfur dioxide and nitrogen oxides from the combustion of fossil fuels)

acid rain *n* **:** acid precipitation in the form of rain

acid rock *n* **:** rock music with lyrics and sound relating to or suggestive of drug-induced experiences

acid·uria \‚asə'd(y)ùrēə\ *n* [*acid* + *-uria* presence in urine] **:** the condition of having acid in the urine esp. in abnormal amounts — see AMINOACIDURIA

acoustic*adj* **1** *also* **acoustical* :** of, relating to, or being a musical instrument whose sound is not electronically modified ⟨an *acoustic* guitar⟩ **2 a :** being a musical group or performer that uses acoustic instruments **b**

: being or involving a musical performance on acoustic instruments ⟨an *acoustic* LP⟩

acoustic *n* **:** an acoustic musical instrument (as a guitar)

acous·to·elec·tric \ə‚küstō-ə‚'lektrik\ *adj* **:** of or relating to electroacoustics **:** electroacoustic

acquire*vt* **ac·quired; ac·quir·ing :** to locate and hold (a desired object) in a detector ⟨*acquire* a target by radar⟩

acquired immunodeficiency syndrome *n* **:** AIDS

ac·ra·sin \'akrəsən\ *n* [*Acrasia*, a genus of fungi related to the slime molds + *-in* chemical compound] **:** a substance and esp. cyclic AMP that is secreted by the individual cells of a slime mold and that causes them to aggregate into a multicellular mass

ac·ro·lect \'akrə‚lekt, -rō-\ *n* [*acro-* top (fr. Gk *akro-*, fr. *akros* topmost, extreme) + *-lect* (as in *dialect*)] **:** the most prestigious dialect of a community — compare BASILECT

acro·mio·cla·vic·u·lar \ə‚krōmē(‚)ōklə‚'vikyələ(r), a‚-, -kla-\ *adj* [*acromio-* acromial and + *clavicular*] **:** relating to or being the joint connecting the acromion and the clavicle ⟨*acromioclavicular* arthritis⟩

acrylic*n* **:** a paint in which the vehicle is an acrylic resin; *also* **:** a painting done in an acrylic resin

ac·ti·no·my·cin D \‚aktə(‚)nō‚mīs²n'dē\ *n* **:** DACTINOMYCIN

ac·ti·no·spec·ta·cin \‚aktənō'spektəsən\ *n* [*actino*mycete + NL *spectabilis* (specific epithet of *Streptomyces spectabilis*, species of actinomycete) + E *-mycin* substance obtained from a fungus, fr. *streptomycin*] **:** a broad-spectrum antibiotic from a soil bacterium of the genus *Streptomyces* (*S. spectabilis*) that is esp. effective against penicillin-resistant venereal infections

action*n* **:** the most vigorous, productive, or exciting activity in a particular field, area, or group ⟨go where the *action* is⟩ ⟨obvious to women in the office ghetto that they are not getting the *action*, but only the crumbs — Margaret Dawson⟩ ⟨kids could act like kids and look forward to growing up because that's where the *action* was —Margot Hentoff⟩

action painting *n* **:** nonrepresentational painting marked esp. by thickly textured surfaces and by the use of improvised techniques (as dribbling, splattering, or smearing) to create apparently accidental pictorial effects — **action painter** *n*

action potential *n* **:** a momentary change in electrical potential (as between the inside of a nerve cell and the extracellular medium) that occurs when a cell or tissue has been activated by a stimulus

ac·ti·va·tion analysis \‚aktə'vāshən-\ *n* **:** a method of analyzing a material for chemical elements by bombarding it with nuclear particles or gamma rays to produce radioactive atoms whose radiations indicate the identity and quantity of the parent elements

active transport *n* **:** a movement of a chemical substance by the expenditure of energy through a gradient (as across a cell membrane) in concentration or electrical potential and opposite to the direction of normal diffusion

acu·pres·sure \'akyù‚preshə(r)\ *n* [*acu-* (as in *acupuncture*) + *pressure*] **:** SHIATSU — **acu·pres·sur·ist** \‚akyù‚preshərəst\ *n*

ACV *abbr* **1** actual cash value **2** air-cushion vehicle

add*n **:** an instance of addition ⟨the computer does an *add* in 7 microseconds⟩

additive identity *n* **:** an identity element (as 0 in the group of whole numbers under the operation of addition) that in a given mathematical system leaves unchanged any element to which it is added

additive inverse *n* **:** a number of opposite sign with respect to a given number so that addition of the two numbers gives zero ⟨the *additive inverse* of 4 is –4⟩

add–on \ˈadˌȯn, -ˌän\ *n* **:** something added as a supplement; *esp* **:** a component (as of a hi-fi or computer system) that increases capability

ad·dress·able \əˈdresəbəl\ *adj* **:** accessible through an address (as in the memory of a computer) ⟨*addressable* registers in a computer⟩

ad·e·no·ac·an·tho·ma \ˌadᵊn(ˌ)ōˌaˌkanˈthōmə, -ˌakən-\ *n, pl* **-mas** *or* **-ma·ta** \-mədˌə\ [*aden-* glandular + *acanthoma*] **:** an adenocarcinoma with epithelial cells differentiated and proliferated into squamous cells

ad·e·no·ma·toid \ˌadᵊnˈōməˌtȯid\ *adj* [*adenomat-* (as in *adenomatosis*), fr. *adenoma* + *-oid* having the form of] **:** relating to or resembling an adenoma ⟨*adenomatoid* tumors of the fallopian tube⟩

aden·o·sine mo·no·phos·phate \əˈdenəˌsen,mänəˈfäsˌfāt, -əsˈn-, -ˌmōn-\ *n* **:** AMP

adenosine 3′,5′-monophosphate *n* **:** CYCLIC AMP

ad·e·no·sis \ˌadᵊnˈōsəs\ *n, pl* **-no·ses** \-ˌōˌsēz\ [NL, fr. Gk *aden-* gland + *-osis* condition, disease] **:** a disease of glandular tissue; *esp* **:** one involving abnormal proliferation or occurrence of glandular tissue ⟨vaginal *adenosis*⟩

ade·no·syl·me·thi·o·nine \əˌdenəsˌəlməˌthīəˌnēn, ˌadᵊnˈōs-, -ˌsil-, -ənən\ *n* [*adenosine* + *-yl* chemical radical + *methionine*] **:** the active sulfonium form of methionine which gives up a methyl group in various metabolic reactions; *S*-adenosylmethionine

ad·e·no·vi·rus \ˌadᵊnōˈvīrəs\ *n* [*aden*oid + connective *-o-* + *virus*] **:** any of a group of DNA-containing icosahedral animal viruses orig. identified in human adenoid tissue, causing respiratory diseases (as catarrh), and including some capable of inducing malignant tumors in experimental animals — **ad·e·no·vi·ral** \-rəl\ *adj*

ad·e·nyl·ate cy·clase \ˌadᵊnˈilətˈsīˌklās, -lˌāt-, -āz\ *n* [*adenylate* fr. *adenyl* + *-ate* derivative compound; cyclase fr. *cyclic* AMP + *-ase* enzyme] **:** an enzyme that catalyzes the formation of cyclic AMP from ATP

ad·e·nyl cyclase \ˌadᵊnˌil-\ *n* **:** ADENYLATE CYCLASE

ad·ho·cra·cy \(ˈ)adˈhäkrəsē, -ōk-, -si\ *n, pl* **-cies** [*ad hoc* + *-cracy* form of government] **:** a temporary organization or committee set up to accomplish a specific task; *also* **:** a system of government comprised of such organizations

adipocyte*n **:** a fat-containing cell of adipose tissue

adip·sia \āˈdipsēə, ə′-\ *n* [NL, fr. Gk *a-* without + *dipsa* thirst + *-ia* pathological condition] **:** loss of thirst; *also* **:** abnormal and esp. prolonged abstinence from the intake of fluids

¹ad·mass \ˈadˌmas\ *n* [*advertising* + *mass*] *chiefly Brit* **:** a system of commercial marketing that attempts to influence great masses of consumers by mass-media advertising; *also* **:** a society thus influenced

²admass *adj, chiefly Brit* **:** of, characterized by, or influenced by admass

ado·bo \əˈdōbō, *Sp* äˈthōbō\ *n, pl* **-bos** \-ōz\ [Sp] **:** a dish of Spanish origin consisting of meat (as chicken or pork)

marinated in a spicy sauce, browned, and then simmered in the marinade

ADP*abbr automatic data processing

ad·re·no·cor·ti·co·ste·roid \əˌdrēnōˌkȯrdˌəkōˈsti(ə)-ˌrȯid, -ren-, -ˈste(ə)ˌ-\ *n* [*adrenocortical* + connective *-o-* + *steroid*] **:** a steroid (as cortisone or hydrocortisone) obtained from, resembling, or having physiological effects like those of the adrenal cortex

ad·re·no·cor·ti·co·tro·pin \-ˈtrōpən, -äp-\ *or* **ad·re·no·cor·ti·co·tro·phin** \-ˈtrōfən, -äf-\ *n* [*adrenocorticotrop*ic or *adrenocorticotroph*ic + *-in* chemical compound] **:** a protein hormone of the anterior lobe of the pituitary gland that stimulates the adrenal cortex **:** ACTH

ad·re·no·med·ul·lary \əˌdrēnōˌmedᵊlˌere, -ren-, -ˌmejəˌlere, -məˌdələre, -ri\ *adj* [*adren-* adrenal glands + *medullary*] **:** relating to or derived from the medulla of the adrenal glands ⟨*adrenomedullary* extracts⟩

adri·a·my·cin \ˌādrēəˈmīsᵊn\ *n* [*adriatic* + *-mycin* substance obtained from a fungus, fr. *streptomycin*] **:** an antibiotic with antitumor activity that is obtained from a bacterium of the genus *Streptomyces* (*S. peucetius*) and is administered as the hydrochloride $C_{27}H_{29}NO_{11}$·HCl — called also *doxorubicin*

adult*adj **:** dealing in or with explicitly sexual material **:** pornographic ⟨*adult* bookstore⟩ ⟨*adult* movie⟩

advance man*n **:** an aide (as of a political candidate) who makes a security check or handles publicity in advance of personal appearances by his employer

ad·vect \(ˈ)adˈvekt\ *vt* [back-formation fr. *advection*] **1** **:** to convey by atmospheric convection ⟨*advect* heat⟩ **2** **:** to transport by convection ⟨*advect* water⟩ ⟨*advect* plankton⟩

advection*n **:** the vertical or usu. horizontal flow of a current of water (as in the sea)

ad·ver·bi·al \(ˈ)adˈvərbēəl, ad′v-, -ˌ ōb-\ *n* **:** a word or phrase that functions as an adverb

ad·ver·sar·i·al \ˌadvə(r)ˈsereəl\ *adj* [*adversary* + *-al*, adj. suffix] **:** of, relating to, or characteristic of an adversary or adversary procedures **:** adversary ⟨want them to be genuinely supportive, not litigious or *adversarial* in temperament —Shirley Hufstedler⟩ ⟨the report adopts the lawyer's *adversarial* stance to build up a case —*Chem. & Engineering News*⟩

advocacy journalism *n* **:** journalism that advocates a cause or expresses a viewpoint

aeon*n **:** a unit of geologic time equal to one billion years

ae·quo·rin \ēˈkwȯrən, -ōr-\ *n* [*Aequore*a + *-in* chemical compound] **:** a bioluminescent protein of jellyfish (genus *Aequorea*) that emits light in response to the addition of calcium or strontium and is used to demonstrate the presence and distribution of calcium in cells

aer·o·bics \ˌa(ə)ˈrōbiks, ˈe(ə)-, ˌāə-\ *n pl but sing or pl in constr* [fr. *aerobic,* after such pairs as *calisthenic: calisthenics*] **:** a system of physical conditioning designed to improve respiratory and circulatory function by exercises (as running, walking, or swimming) that increase oxygen consumption

aer·on·o·my \aˈ(ə)ˈränəme, e(ə)′-, ˌāə′-\ *n* [*aero-* air (deriv. of Gk *aēr* air) + *-nomy* sum of knowledge regarding a field, deriv. of Gk *nemein* to distribute] **:** a science that deals with the physics and chemistry of the upper atmosphere — **aer·on·o·mer** \-mə(r)\ *n* — **aer·o·nom·ic** \ˌa(ə)rəˈnämik, ˌe(ə)r-, ˌāər-\ *adj*

aero·plank·ton \ˌa(ə)rəˈplaŋ(k)tən, ˌe(ə)rə-, ˈāərə-, -rō-, -ˌtän\ *n* **:** small airborne organisms (as flying insects)

¹aero·space \ˈa(ə)rəˌspās, ˈe(ə)r-, ˈāər-\ *n* **1 :** space comprising the earth's atmosphere and the space beyond **2 :** a branch of physical science that deals with aerospace **3 :** the industry involved in the manufacture of aerospace vehicles

²aerospace *adj* **:** of or relating to aerospace, to vehicles used in aerospace or the manufacture of such vehicles, or to travel in aerospace ⟨*aerospace* research⟩ ⟨*aerospace* medicine⟩

aero·train \-rəˌträn\ *n* **:** a propeller-driven vehicle that rides on a cushion of air astride a single rail

AFDC *abbr* aid to families with dependent children

affirmative action *n* **:** an active effort to improve employment or educational opportunities for members of minority groups and women

af·ford·able \əˈfō(ə)rdəbəl, -ˈo(ə)rd-, -ˈōəd-, -ˈo(ə)d-\ *adj* **:** that can be afforded ⟨*affordable* prices⟩ ⟨the *affordable* single-family home —William Safire⟩ — **af·ford·abil·i·ty** \əˌfō(ə)rdəbiləd-ē, -ˈo(ə)rd-, -ˈōəd-, -ˈo(ə)d-, -ətē, -i\ *n*

Af·ghan·i·stan·ism \afˈganəˌstaˌnizəm, -stə-\ *n* [fr. the remoteness of Afghanistan from America] **:** the practice (as by a journalist) of concentrating on problems in distant parts of the world while ignoring controversial local issues

af·la·tox·in \ˌafləˈtäksən\ *n* [NL *Aspergillus flavus*, species of mold + E *toxin*] **:** any of several carcinogenic mycotoxins that are produced esp. in agricultural crops (as peanuts) by molds (as *Aspergillus flavus*)

A–frame* \ˈāˌfrām\ *n* [fr. the resemblance of the shape of the facade to a capital A] **:** a building (as a house) that typically has a triangular front and rear wall and a roof reaching to or nearly to the level of the ground floor

Af·ri·cana \ˌafrəˈkänə, -ˈkanə\ *n pl* [*Africa* + *-ana* collected items] **:** materials (as books, documents, or artifacts) relating to African history and culture

Af·ri·can·i·ty \-ˈkanəd-ē, -ətē, -i\ *n* [*African* + *-ity* quality, state] **:** the cultural heritage of black Africa

¹Af·ro \ˈa(ˌ)frō\ *adj* [*Afro-* African] **:** having the hair shaped into a round bushy mass ⟨bouffant *Afro* hairstyles —*N.Y. Times*⟩

²Afro *n, pl* **Afros** **:** an Afro hairstyle — **Af·roed** \ˈa(ˌ)frōd\ *adj*

Af·ro·phile \ˈafrəˌfil, -rō-\ *n* [*afr-* African + *-phil* one that loves] **:** a person who has strong interest in African life and culture

af·ter·burn·er* \ˈaftə(r)ˌbərnə(r), -ˌbōn-, -ˌbəin-\ *n* **:** a device for burning or catalytically destroying unburned or partially burned carbon compounds in exhaust (as from an automobile)

af·ter·tax \ˈaftə(r)ˌtaks\ *adj* **:** remaining after payment of taxes and esp. of income tax ⟨*aftertax* earnings⟩

agar·ose \ˈägəˌrōs, -ōz\ *n* [*agar* + *-ose* carbohydrate] **:** a polysaccharide obtained from agar that is used esp. as a supporting medium in chromatography

age·ism *also* **agism** \ˈā(ˌ)jizəm\ *n* [*age* + *-ism* (as in *racism*)] **:** prejudice or discrimination against a particular age-group and esp. against the elderly ⟨fighting *ageism* through . . . a group of elderly activists —Mary Ann Meyers⟩ — **age·ist** *also* **agist** \-əst\ *adj*

Agent Orange *n* [so called fr. the identifying color stripe on its container] **:** an herbicide widely used as a defoliant in the Vietnam War that is composed of 2,4-D and 2,4,5-T and contains dioxin as a contaminant

Age of Aquar·i·us \-əˈkwareəs, -wer-, -wär-\ **:** an astrological age of freedom and brotherhood

ag·gior·na·men·to \əˌjó(r)nəˈmen(ˌ)tō\ *n* [It, fr. *aggiornare* to bring up to date, fr. *a* to (fr. L *ad*) + *giorno* day, fr. LL *diurnum*, fr. L, neut. of *diurnus* of the day, fr. *dies* day] **:** a bringing up to date ⟨the enthusiasts of *aggiornamento* and the defenders of older, stricter ways —*Time*⟩

ag·grieve·ment \əˈgrēvmənt *also* a'-\ *n* **:** the quality or state of being aggrieved

ag·gro *also* **ag·ro** \ˈag(ˌ)rō\ *n, pl* **aggros** *also* **agros** [by shortening & alter. of *aggravation*] **1** *Brit* **:** exasperation, irritation ⟨in any case it is not worth the *aggro* it causes — *The Sun* (*London*)⟩ **2** *Brit* **:** a rivalry or grievance esp. public in nature marked by mistrust, rancor, and often violence ⟨the railwaymen could cause trouble again in May . . . even if their *aggro* about inter-union differentials is resolved —*Economist*⟩ ⟨a lot of Town-versus-Gown *aggro*: bricks flew . . . the atmosphere was edgy —Ann Leslie & Geoffrey Dickinson⟩ **3** *Brit* **:** violence against persons and property that is usu. deliberate but not specific in its aims ⟨shots fired and tyres let down as the *aggro* flares —Gilbert Johnson⟩

agin·ner \əˈginə(r)\ *n* [*agin* against + *-er*, n. suffix] *slang* **:** one who opposes change ⟨government officials eye him suspiciously as an *aginner* who opposes change — *Newsweek*⟩

ag·no·lot·ti \ˌänyəˈlòttē\ *n, pl* **agnolotti** [It *agnellotto*, fr. *agnello* lamb, fr. LL *agnellus*, dim. of L *agnus* lamb] **:** a crescent-shaped dumpling usu. filled with meat

¹a–go–go \äˈgō(ˌ)gō, əˈg-\ *n, pl* **a–go–gos** [*Whisky à Gogo*, café and discotheque in Paris, France, fr. F *whisky whiskey* + *à gogo* galore, fr. MF] **:** a nightclub for dancing to live or recorded pop music **:** DISCOTHEQUE

²a–go–go *adj* **1 :** of, relating to, or being an a-go-go or the music or dances performed there ⟨*a-go-go* dancers⟩ **2 :** being in the latest style ⟨psychiatry *a-go-go* —Charles Schulz⟩

agonist* *n* **:** a chemical substance capable of combining with a nervous receptor and initiating a reaction

ag·o·nis·tic* \ˌagəˈnistik\ *adj* **:** of, relating to, or being aggressive or defensive social interaction (as fighting, fleeing, or submitting) between individuals usu. of the same species ⟨*agonistic* behavior⟩ ⟨*agonistic* encounters between warblers⟩

ago·ra \ˌägəˈrä\ *n, pl* **ago·rot** \-ˈrōt\ [NHeb *āgōrāh*, fr. Heb, a small coin] **1 :** a monetary unit of Israel representing $1/100$ of a pound **2 :** a coin representing one agora

agrav·ic \(ˈ)āˌgravik\ *adj* [*a-* not (fr. Gk) + *gravity* + *-ic*, adj. suffix] **:** of or relating to a theoretical condition of no gravitation

ag·ri·pow·er \ˈagrəˌpaú(ə)r, -aùə, *esp in southern US* -aùwə(r\ *n* [*agriculture* + *power*] **:** the economic and political power of an agriculturally productive nation

ag·ro–in·dus·tri·al \ˌa(ˌ)grō-ənˈdəstrēəl\ *adj* [*agriculture* + connective *-o-* + *industrial*] **1 :** of or relating to production for both industrial and agricultural purposes ⟨a nuclear-powered *agro-industrial* complex for producing cheap electric power and desalted seawater⟩ **2 :** of or relating to an industry (as the production of farm tools

or fertilizer) directly related to agriculture — **ag·ro–in·dus·try** \-ˌin(ˌ)dəstrē, -i\ *n*

ag·ro·nome \'agrəˌnōm\ *n* [Russ or F; Russ *agronom*, fr. F *agronome*, after such pairs as F *astronomie* astronomy: *astronome* astronomer] **:** an agronomist

AI*abbr artificial intelligence

AIDS \'ādz\ *n* [*a*cquired *i*mmuno*d*eficiency *s*yndrome] **:** a condition of acquired immunological deficiency associated esp. with male homosexuality and intravenous drug abuse and recognized by the presence of a life-threatening infection (as pneumonia or candidiasis) or of Kaposi's sarcoma in individuals under 60 years of age who have not been subjected to immunosuppressive drugs or disease

ai·ki·do \ˈīkēˌdō, -kə-\ *n* [Jp *aikidō*, fr. *ai-* match, coordinate + *ki* breath, spirit + *dō* art, way] **:** a Japanese art of self-defense employing locks and holds and utilizing the principle of nonresistance to cause an opponent's own momentum to work against him

ai·o·li \(')ī̩ˌōlē, (')ä̩ˌ-, -li, F äyōlē\ *n* [Prov, fr. *ai* garlic (fr. L *allium*) + *oli* oil, fr. L *oleum*] **:** a sauce made of crushed garlic, egg yolks, olive oil, and lemon juice and usu. served with fish, cold meat, or vegetables **:** garlic mayonnaise

air bag *n* **:** a bag designed to inflate automatically in front of riders in an automotive vehicle in case of accident to protect them from pitching forward into solid parts (as the dashboard or windshield) — called also *air cushion*

air battery *n* [fr. the oxidation's being produced by exposure to pressurized air] **:** a rechargeable battery in which current is generated as a result of oxidation of a metal

air·bus \'a(ə)rˌbəs, 'e(ə)rˌ-, 'aə-, 'eə-\ *n* **:** a short-range or medium-range subsonic jet passenger airplane

air cavalry *or* **air cav** \-ˈkav\ *n* **1 :** an army unit that is transported in air vehicles and carries out the traditional cavalry missions of reconnaissance and security **2 :** an army unit that is esp. equipped and adapted for transportation in air vehicles but is organized for sustained ground combat

air–cush·ion \-ˈküshən *sometimes* -shin\ *also* **air–cushioned** *adj* **:** of, relating to, or being a vehicle that is used for transporting material or traveling over land or water and that is supported a short distance above the surface on a cushion of air produced by downwardly directing fans

air·date \-ˈdāt\ *n* **:** the scheduled date of a radio or television broadcast

air door *n* **:** a temperature-controlled strong usu. upward current of air used instead of a door (as at a store)

air·er \'e(ə)rə(r), 'a(ə)-\ *n, Brit* **:** a frame on which clothes are aired or dried

air·fare \ˈa(ə)rˌfa(ə)r, ˈe(ə)rˌfe(ə)r; ˈaəˌfaə(r, ˈeəˌfeə(r\ *n* **:** fare for travel by airplane

air·mo·bile \ˈa(ə)rˌmōbəl, ˌa(ə)rˈmōˌbēl, ˈe(ə)rˌ-, ˈaəˌ-, ˈeəˌ-, -ˌbīl\ *adj* **:** of, relating to, or being a military unit whose members are transported to combat areas usu. by helicopter

air piracy *n* **:** the hijacking of an airplane **:** SKYJACKING ⟨held . . . on a charge of *air piracy* in the plot to hijack the plane for $502,000 ransom —*Springfield (Mass.) Union*⟩ — **air pirate** *n*

air·play \'a(ə)rˌplā, 'e(ə)rˌ-, 'aə-, 'eə-\ *n* **:** the playing of a phonograph record on the air by a radio station

air·shed \-ˌshed\ *n* [*air* + *-shed* (as in *watershed*)] **:** the air supply of a given region; *also* **:** the geographical area covered by such an air supply

air taxi *n* **:** a small commercial airplane that makes short trips to localities not served by regular airlines

air·tel \'a(ə)rˌtel, 'e(ə)rˌ-, 'aə-, 'eə-\ *n* [*air* + *hotel*] **:** a hotel situated at or close to an airport

air·time \-ˌtīm\ *n* **:** the time or any part thereof that a radio or television station is on the air

aka *abbr* also known as

aka·thi·sia *or* **aca·thi·sia** \ˌākə'thizh(ē)ə, ˌa-, -ēzh-\ *n* [*a-* without + Gk *kathisis* a sitting down + *-ia* pathological condition] **:** a condition characterized by uncontrollable motor restlessness

albatross*n [fr. the albatross killed by the ancient mariner and subsequently hung about his neck in the poem *The Rime of the Ancient Mariner* (1798) by S. T. Coleridge †1834 Eng. poet] **1 :** something that causes persistent deep concern or anxiety ⟨an *albatross* of guilt that he has volunteered to carry —Jack Holland⟩ **2 :** something that makes accomplishment particularly difficult **:** an encumbrance ⟨this regulatory *albatross* inhibits any marketing scheme that might lure commuters —Charles Luna⟩

al den·te \(ˌ)äl'den-(ˌ)tā, -äl-, -al-\ *adj* [It, lit., to the tooth] *of food* **:** cooked just enough to retain a somewhat firm texture ⟨fresh pasta cooked *al dente* —*Vogue*⟩ ⟨hosannahs for precisely *al dente* carrots —Gael Green⟩

al·do·ste·ron·ism \al'dästəˌrōˌnizəm, ˌal(ˌ)dōstəˈr-\ *n* **:** a condition that is characterized by excessive production and excretion of aldosterone and typically by loss of body potassium, muscular weakness, and elevated blood pressure

ale·a·tor·ic \ˌālēəˈtórik, -tär-\ *adj* [L *aleator* dice player, gambler (fr. *alea* dice game) + E *-ic*, adj. suffix] **:** characterized by chance or random elements ⟨*aleatoric* music⟩

ale·a·to·ry*\'ālēəˌtōrē, -ˌtór-, -ri\ *adj* **:** ALEATORIC

Alf·vén wave \ˌal(f)ˌvän-, -ˌven-\ *n* [Hannes *Alfvé b*1908 Swed. astrophysicist] **:** a transverse electroma netic wave that propagates along the lines of force ir magnetized plasma

ALG *abbr* antilymphocyte globulin; antilymphoc globulin

al·ge·bra*\'aljəbrə\ *n* **:** LINEAR ALGEBRA 2

AL·GOL *or* **Al·gol** \'alˌgäl, -ˌgól\ *n* [*algorithmic langu* **:** an algebraic and logical language for programmi computer

al·go·rithm*\'algəˌrithəm, -th-\ *n* **:** a procedure for ing a mathematical problem (as finding the greatest mon divisor) in a finite number of steps that freqr involves repetition of an operation; *broadly* **:** a st step procedure for solving a problem or accomplish end ⟨the *algorithm* used by the computer in com footprints —*Technical News Bull.*⟩ — **al·g mic***\'algəˌrithmik, -th-\ *adj* — **al·go·rith·m** \-mək(ə)lē, -mēk-, -li\ *adv*

al·gor mor·tis \ˌalgó(ə)rˈmórtəs\ *n* [NL, fr. L, li ness of death] **:** the gradual cooling of the body f death

Al·ice–in–Won·der·land \ˌaləsənˈwəndə(r)ˌla [fr. *Alice's Adventures in Wonderland* (1865) Carroll †1898 Eng. storywriter] **:** suitable to a

fantasy or illusion ⟨the *Alice-in-Wonderland* realm of unorthodox scientific claims —J.S. Trefil⟩

ali·es·ter·ase \ˌălēˈestəˌrās, -āz\ *n* [*ali*phatic + *esterase*] **:** an esterase that promotes the hydrolysis of ester links esp. in aliphatic esters of low molecular weight

A–line \ˈāˌlīn\ *adj* [fr. the resemblance of such a garment's outline to that of a capital A] **:** having a flared bottom and a close-fitting top — used of a garment ⟨an *A-line* skirt⟩

alin·gual \(ˈ)āˌliŋgwəl *sometimes* -gyəwəl\ *adj* [*a-* not + *lingual*] **:** not fluent in any language

ali·yah*or* **ali·ya** \ˌälēˈ(y)ä, äˈlē\)(-, əˈlē(y)ə\ *n* **:** immigration of Jews into Israel ⟨their *aliyah* was voluntary; they did not have to come to Israel —Sandra Stencel⟩

all–night·er \(ˌ)ȯlˈnīd-ə(r)\ *n* **:** something (as a party or a study session) that lasts throughout the night ⟨classes, meetings, eye-straining hours in the library, and *all-nighters* over last-minute papers —Nora Peck⟩

al·lo·an·ti·body \ˌalōˈantəˌbädē, -dì\ *n* [*allo-* other, different (fr. Gk, fr. *allos* other) + *antibody*] **:** an antibody against an antigen sometimes present in members of a species that is produced by a member of a species lacking that antigen when exposed to it **:** an isoantibody

al·lo·an·ti·gen \-ˈantəjən, -ˌjen, -in\ *n* [*allo-* + *antigen*] **:** an antigen capable of inducing the production of an antibody **:** an isoantigen — **al·lo·an·ti·gen·ic** \-ˌantəˈjenik\ *adj*

al·lo·ge·ne·ic \ˌaləjəˈnēik, -lō-\ *also* **al·lo·gen·ic** \-ˈjenik\ *adj* [*allogeneic* fr. *allo-* + *-geneic* (as in *syngeneic*); *allogenic* fr. *allo-* + *genic*] **:** sufficiently unlike genetically to interact antigenically but of the same species ⟨*allogeneic* skin grafts⟩ — compare SYNGENEIC, XENOGENEIC

al·lo·graft \ˈalōˌgraft, ˈaləˌ\ *n* [*allo-* + *graft:* fr. its being a graft from another individual] **:** a homograft between genetically dissimilar individuals of the same species — **allograft** *vt*

al·lo·im·mune \ˌalōəˈmyün\ *adj* [*allo-* + *immune*] **:** of, relating to, or characterized by isoimmunization ⟨*alloimmune* reactivity⟩

al·lo·pu·ri·nol \ˌalōˈpyürəˌnȯl, -ˌnōl\ *n* [*allo-* + *purine* + *-ol* compound containing hydroxyl] **:** a drug $C_5H_4N_4O$ used to promote excretion of uric acid esp. in the treatment of gout

al·lo·ste·ric \ˌaləˈsterik, -ti(ə)r-\ *adj* [*allo-* + *steric* relating to the arrangement of atoms in space] **:** of, relating to, or being alteration of the activity of a protein (as an enzyme) by combination with another substance at a point other than the chemically active site — **al·lo·ste·ri·cal·ly** \-rək(ə)lē, -rēk-, -li\ *adv*

al·lo·trans·plan·ta·tion \ˌal(ˌ)ō·tran(t)sˌplanˈtāshən, -ˌtranzˌ-, -splən-\ *n* [*allo-* + *transplantation*] **:** transplantation of tissue between genetically different individuals of the same species — **al·lo·trans·plant** \ˌalōˈtran(t)s-ˌplant, ˌalə-, -nzˌ-\ *vt* — **allo·trans·plant** \ˈalōˌ-, ˈaləˌ-\ *n*

al·lo·type*\ˈaləˌtīp\ *n* **:** an isoantigenic immunoglobulin — **al·lo·typ·ic** \ˌaləˈtipik\ *adj* — **al·lo·typ·i·cal·ly** \-ək(ə)lē, -ēk-, -li\ *adv* — **al·lo·typy** \ˈaləˌtīpē, -pi\ *n*

al·lo·zyme \ˈalōˌzīm, ˈalə-\ *n* [*allo-* + *-zyme* enzyme] **:** any of the variants of an enzyme that are determined by alleles at a single genetic locus

all–ter·rain vehicle \ˈȯlˌtəˌrān-\ *n* **:** a small amphibious motor vehicle that has a boatlike bottom, rides on four or more soft rubber tires or on endless rubber belts, and is designed to travel over all types of terrain

à l'orange \àlȯränⁿzh\ *adj* [F] **:** prepared or served with oranges

alpha*n* **:** an alpha rhythm of the brain

alpha*adj* **:** socially dominant esp. in a group of animals

al·pha \ˈalfə, ˈaùfə\ *adj* [short for *alphabetic*] **:** being or done in the order of the alphabet **:** alphabetic ⟨an *alpha* sort done by computer⟩

al·pha–ad·ren·er·gic \ˌalfəˌadrəˈnərjik\ *adj* **:** of, relating to, or being an alpha-receptor ⟨*alpha-adrenergic* blocking action⟩

alphabet soup*n* **:** a hodgepodge esp. of initials (as of the names of organizations) ⟨an *alphabet soup* of Government agencies, commissions and departments, the I.C.C., the F.A.A., H.E.W., H.U.D., I.R.S. —Alice Shabecoff⟩

alpha decay *n* **:** the radioactive decay of an atomic nucleus by emission of an alpha particle

al·pha–he·lix \-ˈhēliks\ *n* **:** the coiled structural arrangement of many proteins consisting of a single amino-acid chain that is stabilized by hydrogen bonds — compare DOUBLE HELIX — **al·pha–he·li·cal** \ˌalfəˈheləkəl, -hēl-\ *adj*

al·pha–ke·to·glu·tar·ic acid \ˌalfəˌkedˌōglüˈtarik-\ *n* **:** the alpha keto isomer of ketoglutaric acid formed in various metabolic processes (as the Krebs cycle)

al·pha·met·ic \ˌalfəˈmedˌik\ *n* [*alphabetic* + *arithmetic*] **:** a mathematical puzzle consisting of a numerical computation with letters substituted for numbers which are to be restored through mathematical reasoning

al·pha–1–an·ti·tryp·sin \ˌalfəˈwənˌantəˈtripsən, -ˌanˌtī-\ *n* **:** a trypsin-inhibiting serum protein whose deficiency has been implicated as a factor in emphysema

al·pha–re·cep·tor \ˈalfəˌrəˌseptə(r), -rēˌ-\ *n* **:** any of a group of receptors on cell membranes that are postulated to exist and to mediate esp. vasoconstriction, relaxation of intestinal muscle, and contraction of myometrium, nictitating membrane, iris dilator muscle, and splenic smooth muscle primarily on the basis of experimental evidence that chemical antagonists of norepinephrine and epinephrine are relatively effective in blocking these functions and that those of isoproterenol are relatively ineffective in blocking them — compare BETA-RECEPTOR

Al·pine*\ˈalˌpīn, *also* ˈalpən\ *adj* **:** of or relating to competitive ski events consisting of slalom and downhill racing — compare NORDIC

alternative*adj* **:** existing or functioning outside the established cultural, social, or economic system ⟨an *alternative* newspaper⟩ ⟨reporters from both the straight and the *alternative* (nee underground) press —Playboy⟩

alternative school *n* **:** an elementary or secondary school with a nontraditional curriculum

al·ve·o·lo·plas·ty \alˈvēə(ˌ)lōˌplastē, -i\ *or* **al·veo·plas·ty** \ˈalvē(ˌ)ō-\ *n, pl* **-ties** [*alveoloplasty* fr. *alveolo*-alveolus + *-plasty* plastic surgery; *alveoplasty* fr. L *alveus* cavity + connective *-o-* + E *-plasty*] **:** surgical shaping of the dental alveoli and alveolar processes esp. after extraction of several teeth or in preparation for dentures

am·a·ni·tin \ˌaməˈnētˌ°n\ *n* [ISV *amanit-* (fr. *Amanita*, genus of mushrooms) + *-in* chemical compound; orig. formed in G] **:** a highly poisonous cyclic peptide produced by the death cup that selectively inhibits RNA polymerase in mammalian cells

aman·ta·dine \ə'mantə,dēn\ *n* [*amantad*- (fr. anagram of *adamantane*) + *amine*] **:** a drug used esp. as the hydrochloride $C_{10}H_{17}N \cdot HCl$ to prevent infection (as by an influenza virus) by interfering with virus penetration into host cells

am·a·ret·to \,amə'red-ō, -etō\ *n, often cap* [It, dim. of *amaro* bitter, fr. L *amarus* bitter] **:** an almond-flavored liqueur

am·bi·plas·ma \'ambə,plazmə, -bē-\ *n* [*ambi*- both (fr. L) + *plasma*] **:** a hypothetical plasma that is held to consist of matter and antimatter

am·bi·po·lar \-,'pōlə(r)\ *adj* **:** relating to or consisting of both electrons and positive ions moving in opposite directions ⟨an *ambipolar* diffusion⟩

am·bi·sex·trous \-,'sekstrəs\ *adj* [*ambi*- + *sex* + -*trous* (as in *ambidextrous*)] **:** UNISEX

Am·er·asian \,amər'āzhən, -,'āshən\ *n* **:** a person of mixed American and Asian descent

Americana**n pl** **1 :** things typical of America ⟨a veritable emporium of gastronomic *Americana* —James Villas⟩ **2 :** American culture ⟨freak shows are a vanishing item of *Americana* —Edward Hoagland⟩

American dream *n, often cap D* **:** an American social ideal that stresses egalitarianism and esp. material prosperity ⟨the notions of progress and perfectibility, without which there can be no *American dream* —Jerome Charyn⟩

Amer·i·can·o·pho·bia \ə,merəkənə'fōbēə, -,kan- *also* -rē-\ *n* **:** hatred of the U.S. or American culture — **Amer·i·cano·phobe** \ə'merəkənə,fōb, ə,merə'kanə,fōb\ *n*

American Shorthair *n* **:** a domestic cat with a relatively short close coat in which the guard hairs are not notably elongated **:** shorthair

American Sign Language *n* **:** a sign language for the deaf in which meaning is conveyed by a system of articulated hand gestures and their placement relative to the upper body

Amer·i·ka \ə'merəkə *also* -rē-\ *n* [G *Amerika;* fr. the likening of the U.S. to Nazi Germany] **:** the fascist or racist aspect of American society

Ameslan \'am(ə),slan\ *n* **:** AMERICAN SIGN LANGUAGE

am·e·thop·ter·in \,amə'thäpt(ə)rən\ *n* [*amino*- containing an amino group + *metho*- methyl + *pter*oyl the radical $(C_{13}H_{11}N_6O)CO$ + -*in* pharmaceutical product] **:** METHOTREXATE

ami·no·ac·id·uria \ə,mēnō,asə,'dyürēə, -ür-\ *n* [NL, fr. *amino acid* + -*uria* presence in urine] **:** a condition in which one or more amino acids are excreted in excessive amounts

ami·no·trans·fer·ase \-,'tran(t)s(,)fər,ās, -nz,f-, -,āz\ *n* **:** an enzyme promoting transamination

ami·no·tri·a·zole \-,'trīə,zōl, -,(,)trī,a,zōl\ *n* **:** AMITROLE

am·i·trip·ty·line \,amə-'triptə,lēn, -ələn\ *n* [*amino*- + *tript*- (alter. of *trypt*- — as in *tryptophan*, an amino acid) + -*yl* chemical radical + -*ine* chemical substance] **:** an antidepressant drug $C_{20}H_{23}N$

am·i·trole \'amə,trōl\ *n* [*amino*- + *triazole* $C_2H_3N_3$] **:** a systemic herbicide $C_2H_4N_4$ used in areas other than food croplands

am·nio·cen·te·sis \,amnēō(,)sen·'tēsəs\ *n, pl* -**te·ses** \-'tēsēz\ [*amnion* + *centesis*] **:** the surgical insertion of a hollow needle through the abdominal wall and uterus of a pregnant female and into the amnion esp. to obtain amniotic fluid for the determination of sex or chromosomal abnormality in the fetus

am·ni·og·ra·phy \,amnē'ägrəfē\ *n, pl* -**phies** [*amnion* + *radiography*] **:** radiographic visualization of the outlines of the uterine cavity, placenta, and fetus after injection of a radiopaque substance into the amniotic sac

am·ni·os·co·py \-'äskəpē\ *n, pl* -**pies** [*amnion* + -*scopy* observation, fr. Gk -*skopia*, fr. *skeptesthai* to watch, look at] **:** visual examination of the amniotic cavity and its contents by means of an endoscope — **am·nio·scope** \'amnēə,skōp\ *n*

amp \'amp\ *n* **:** an amplifier

AMP \,ā,em'pē\ *n* [adenosine *monophosphate*] **:** a mononucleotide of adenine $C_{10}H_{12}N_5O_3H_2PO_4$ that was orig. isolated from mammalian muscle and is reversibly convertible to ADP and ATP in metabolic reactions — called also *adenosine monophosphate;* see CYCLIC AMP

am·pho·ter·i·cin \,amfə'terəsən\ *n* [*amphoteric* capable of reacting chemically either as an acid or as a base (fr. Gk *amphoteros* each of two, fr. *amphō* both) + -*in* chemical compound] **:** either of two antibiotic drugs obtained from a soil actinomycete of the genus *Streptomyces* (*S. nodosus*); *esp* **:** the clinically useful one (**amphotericin B**) that is used against deep-seated and systemic fungal infections

am·pi·cil·lin \,ampə,'silən\ *n* [*amino*- + *penicillin*] **:** an antibiotic of the penicillin group that is effective against gram-negative and gram-positive bacteria and is used to treat various infections of the urinary, respiratory, and intestinal tracts

amyg·da·lot·o·my \ə,migdə'lätəmē\ *n, pl* -**mies** [*amygdala* + connective -*o*- + -*tomy* incision] **:** destruction of part of the amygdala (as for the control of epilepsy) esp. by surgical incision

am·y·lo·bar·bi·tone \,amolō'bärbə,tōn\ *n* [*amyl* + *barbitone*] Brit **:** a crystalline compound $C_{11}H_{18}N_2O_3$ used as a sedative and hypnotic **:** amobarbital

amyo·tro·phic lateral sclerosis \,ā,mīə,trōfik-\ *n* **:** a rare progressive degenerative fatal disease that affects pyramidal motor neurons, usu. begins in middle age, and is characterized esp. by increasing and spreading muscular weakness

an·a·bo·lic steroid \,anə,bälik-\ *n* **:** any of a group of usu. synthetic hormones that increase constructive metabolism and are sometimes taken by athletes in training to temporarily increase the size of their muscles

an·a·dama bread \,anə,damə, -,dàm-\ *n* [origin unknown] **:** a leavened bread made with flour, cornmeal, and molasses

ana·gen·e·sis*\,anə'jenəsəs\ *n* **:** linear evolutionary change in which one group replaces another without branching into distinct forms **:** phyletic evolution — **ana·ge·net·i·cal·ly** \,anəjə,'ned·ək(ə)lē\ *adv*

an·a·log *also* **an·a·logue** \'an²l,ȯg, -,äg\ *adj* **1 :** of, relating to, or being an analogue **2 a :** of or relating to the representation of data by continuously variable physical quantities **b :** being a watch having both hour and minute hands **c :** of or relating to an analog computer

analogue*also **analog****n :** a chemical compound that is similar in structure to another but differs in composition in the matter of one element

analyst**n :** SYSTEMS ANALYST

an·am·nes·tic* \ˌanəmˈnestik, -ˌam-\ adj : of or relating to a second rapid increased production of antibodies in response to an immunogenic substance after serum antibodies from a first response can no longer be detected in the blood

an·a·tom·i·co- \ˌanəˈtämə(ˌ)kō\ or **anat·o·mo-** \əˈnadˌə(ˌ)mō\ comb form : anatomical and : anatomical ⟨anatomicopathological⟩ ⟨anatomoclinical⟩

an·au·tog·e·nous \ˌan(ˌ)ȯˈtäjənəs, ˌanəˈt-\ adj [an- not (fr. Gk) + autogenous] : requiring a meal esp. of blood to produce eggs ⟨anautogenous mosquitoes⟩

anchor* n **1** anchors pl, slang : the brakes of a motor vehicle **2** : an anchorman or anchorwoman ⟨pictures of six of the most prominent Chicago TV news anchors — Bill O'Hallaren⟩

anchor* vt : to act or serve as anchorman or anchorwoman for ⟨anchor the evening news⟩ ⟨was anchoring the . . . network's election coverage —J.R. Dickenson⟩

an·chor·man \ˈaŋkə(r)ˌman, -kə(r)mən\ n **1** : a broadcaster (as on a newscast) who introduces reports by other broadcasters and usu. reads the news **2** : the moderator of a discussion group (as on radio or television)

an·chor·peo·ple \ˈaŋkə(r)ˌpēpəl\ n pl : ANCHORPERSONS

an·chor·per·son \-ˌpərsᵊn, -ˌpȯs-, -ˌpȯis-\ n : an anchorman or anchorwoman

an·chor·wom·an \-ˌwùm-ən\ n : a woman who anchors a broadcast

AND \ˈand\ n : a logical operator equivalent to the sentential connective and ⟨AND gate in a computer⟩

an·dra·go·gy \ˈandrəˌgäjē, -ˌgōjē, -ˌgägē, -i\ n [andrman, male + -agogy (as in pedagogy)] : the art or science of teaching adults

an·dro·gen·ize \anˈdräjəˌnīz\ vt -ized; -iz·ing [androgen + -ize, vb. suffix] : to treat or influence with male sex hormone esp. in excessive amounts ⟨neonatally androgenized female rats⟩

androgynous* adj **1 a** : neither specifically feminine or masculine ⟨the androgynous pronoun them⟩ ⟨the themes cross the sexual divide to the darkest place of our androgynous soul —Anne Roiphe⟩ **b** : suitable to or for either sex ⟨an androgynous school of clothing design — Angelo d'Arcangelo⟩ ⟨the best fiction is androgynous: designed by a writer . . . for a reader of either sex —Doris Grumbach⟩ **2** : having traditional male and female roles obscured or reversed ⟨the possibility of a new androgynous way of life —Gerda Lerner⟩

an·dro·stene·di·one \ˌandrəˈstēnˌdīˌōn, -ˈstēndē-\ n [androsterone, a male sex hormone + -ene unsaturated carbon compound + -dione chemical compound with two carbonyl groups] : a steroid sex hormone that is secreted by the testis, ovary, and adrenal cortex and acts more strongly in the production of male characteristics than testosterone

angel* n : a radar echo caused by something not visually discernible

angel dust n : PHENCYCLIDINE

an·gi·op·a·thy \ˌanjēˈäpəthē, anˈjäp-\ n, pl -thies [angioblood and lymph vessels + -pathy disease] : a disease of the blood or lymph vessels

an·gio·sar·co·ma \ˌanj(ē)ōsärˈkōmə, -jēə-\ n [angio- + sarcoma] : a rare malignant tumor affecting esp. the liver

an·gio·ten·sin \-ˈten(t)sən\ n [blend of angiotonin and hypertensin] : either of two forms of a kinin of which one

(angiotensin II) is an octapeptide with vasoconstrictive activity; also : a synthetic amide of the physiologically active form used to treat some forms of hypotension

an·gio·ten·sin·ase \-səˌnās, -āz\ n : any of several enzymes in the blood that hydrolyze angiotensin

¹An·glo·phone \ˈaŋ(ˌ)glōˌfōn, -glə-\ or **An·glo·phon·ic** \ˌaŋglōˈfänik, -glə-, -ēk\ adj [Anglophone fr. F, fr. anglo- English + -phone (as in francophone French-speaking); Anglophonic fr. Anglophone + -ic, adj. suffix] : having or belonging to an English-speaking population esp. in a country where two or more languages are spoken

²Anglophone n : an English-speaking person esp. in a country where two or more languages are spoken

angry young man n [Angry Young Man, autobiography (1951) of Leslie A. Paul b1905 Eng. journalist] **1** : one of a group of mid-20th century British writers whose works express the bitterness of the lower classes toward the established sociopolitical system and toward the mediocrity and hypocrisy of the middle and upper classes **2** : an outspoken critic of or protester against a social or economic condition or injustice

angular perspective n : linear perspective in which parallel lines along the width and depth of an object are represented as meeting on two separate points on the horizon that are 90 degrees apart as measured from the common intersection of the lines of projection : two≈point perspective

an·ky·los·ing spon·dy·li·tis \ˌaŋkəˌlōsiŋˌspändəˈlīdˌəs\ n : rheumatoid arthritis of the spine : rheumatoid spondylitis

anneal* vt : to heat and then cool (nucleic acid) in order to separate strands and introduce combination at lower temperatures esp. with complementary strands of a different species ~ vi : to be capable of combining with complementary nucleic acid by a process of heating and cooling ⟨some bacterial nucleic acid anneals well with eucaryotic DNA⟩

annihilate* vi -lat·ed; -lat·ing : to undergo annihilation ⟨an elementary particle and its antiparticle annihilate when they meet⟩

annual percentage rate n : a measure of the annual percentage cost of consumer credit (as in installment buying or a charge account) that is required by law to appear on statements of credit accounts and is variously computed but always takes into consideration the amount financed, the amount of the finance charges, and the schedule of repayment

anod·al \ˈaˌnōdᵊl, ˌaˈ-\ adj [anode + -al, adj. suffix] : of, relating to, or attracted to an anode ⟨anodal potentials⟩ — used esp. in the life sciences — **anod·al·ly** \-ē, -i\ adv

¹an·o·rex·ic \ˌanəˈreksik, -nōˈ-\ adj [anorexia + -ic, adj. suffix] **1** : having diminished appetite or anorexia nervosa **2** : causing loss of appetite

²anorexic n : one affected with anorexia nervosa

an·ovu·lant \aˈnävyələnt, -ōv-\ n [an- not (fr. Gk) + ovulation + -ant thing that promotes] : an anovulatory drug — **anovulant** adj

an·ovu·la·tion \(ˈ)anˌävyəˈläshən, -ˌōv-\ n : failure or absence of ovulation

an·ovu·la·to·ry* \(ˈ)anˈävyələˌtōrē, -ˈōv-, -ˌtȯr-, -ri\ adj : suppressing ovulation ⟨anovulatory drugs⟩

answer*n **:** one that imitates, matches, or corresponds to another ⟨picture books — the book business's *answer* to the movies —Edward Hoagland⟩

answering service n **:** a commercial service that answers telephone calls for its clients

an·tero·lat·er·al \ˌantə(ˌ)rōˈlad-ərəl, -atərəl, -aˈtrəl\ *adj* [*antero-* anterior and + *lateral*] **:** situated or occurring in front and to the side ⟨*anterolateral* wall of the left ventricle of the heart⟩

an·tero·pos·te·ri·or \-(ˈ)päˈstirēə(r), -(ˈ)pōˈ-, -ˈstēr-\ *adj* [*antero-* + *posterior*] **:** concerned with or extending along a direction or axis from front to back or from anterior to posterior — **an·tero·pos·te·ri·or·ly** *adv*

an·thro·po·nym \anˈthräpəˌnim, ˈan(t)thrəpə-\ n [*anthrop-* human (deriv. of Gk *anthrōpos* human being) + *-onym* name] **:** a person's name; *esp* **:** the name borne in common by members of a family as distinguished from an individualizing forename **:** surname — **an·thro·po·nym·ic** \ˌan₁thräpəˈnimik, ˌan(t)thrəpə-\ *adj*

an·thro·po·sere \anˈthräpəˌsi(ə)r, ˈan(t)thrəpə-, -ˌsiə\ n [*anthropo-* human + *sere* series of ecological communities, fr. L *series* series] **:** NOOSPHERE

an·thro·sphere \ˈan(t)thrəˌsfi(ə)r, -ˌsfiə\ n [*anthropo-* + *sphere*] **:** NOOSPHERE

an·ti·abor·tion \ˌan₁tiəˈbórshən, ˌantē-, ˌantə-, -ˌbó(ə)sh-\ *adj* [*anti-* against + *abortion*] **:** opposed to abortion ⟨*antiabortion* lobbyists⟩ — **an·ti·abor·tion·ist** \-əst\ n

an·ti·al·ler·gic \-əˈlərjik, -ˈläj-, -ˈläij-\ *also* **an·ti·al·ler·gen·ic** \-ˌalə(r)ˈjenik\ *adj* **:** tending to relieve or control allergic symptoms — **antiallergic** *also* **antiallergenic** n

an·ti·an·dro·gen \-ˈandrəjən\ n **:** a substance that tends to inhibit the production, activity, or effects of male sex hormone

an·ti·an·gi·nal \-(ˈ)anˈjīn²l, -ˌanjən²l\ *adj* **:** used or tending to prevent or relieve angina pectoris ⟨*antianginal* drugs⟩

an·ti·anx·i·ety \-aŋˈzīəd-ē, -ət-, -i\ *adj* **:** tending to prevent or relieve anxiety ⟨*antianxiety* drugs⟩

an·ti·ar·rhyth·mic \-(ˌ)āˈrithmik\ *adj* **:** counteracting or preventing cardiac arrhythmia ⟨an *antiarrhythmic* agent⟩ ⟨*antiarrhythmic* therapy⟩

an·ti·art \ˌan₁tīˌärt, ˈantē-, ˈantə-, -ˌát\ n **:** art (as dada) based on premises antithetical to traditional or popular art forms

an·ti·ar·thrit·ic \-ˈärthrid·ik\ *adj* **:** tending to relieve or prevent arthritic symptoms — **antiarthritic** n

an·ti·at·om \-ˌad-əm, -ˌatəm\ n **:** an atom comprised of antiparticles

an·ti·au·thor·i·tar·i·an \ˌan₁tiöˌthärəˈterēən, ˈantē-, ˈantə-, -ə₁th-, -thór-\ *adj* **:** opposed or hostile to authoritarians or authoritarianism ⟨the individualistic, *antiauthoritarian* nature of science —E.B. Wilson⟩ — **an·ti·au·thor·i·tar·i·an·ism** \-ēə₁nizəm\ n

an·ti·aux·in \-ˈöksən\ n **:** a plant substance that opposes or suppresses the natural effect of an auxin

an·ti·bal·lis·tic missile \-bəˈlistik-\ n **:** a missile for intercepting and destroying a ballistic missile

an·ti·bary·on \-ˈbarē₁än\ n **:** an antiparticle of a baryon (as an antiproton or antineutron)

an·ti·black \-ˈblak\ *adj* **:** opposed or hostile to people belonging to the Negro race — **an·ti·black·ism** \-ˌizəm\ n

an·ti·bus·ing \-ˈbəsiŋ\ *adj* **:** opposed to the busing of schoolchildren ⟨*antibusing* parents⟩ ⟨*antibusing* campaign⟩

an·ti·can·cer \-ˈkan(t)sə(r)\ *also* **an·ti·can·cer·ous** \-sərəs\ *adj* **:** used or effective against cancer ⟨*anticancer* drugs⟩ ⟨*anticancer* treatments⟩

an·ti·car·ci·no·gen·ic \-ˈkärs²n(ˌ)ōˈjenik\ *adj* **:** tending to inhibit or prevent the activity of a carcinogen or the development of carcinoma ⟨an *anticarcinogenic* substance counteracting the carcinogenic potential of estrogens in birth control pills⟩

an·ti·car·ies \-ˈka(ə)rēz, -ˈke(ə)r-\ *adj* **:** tending to inhibit the formation of caries ⟨*anticaries* effects⟩ ⟨an *anticaries* toothpaste additive⟩

an·ti·co·ag·u·late \ˌan₁ti(ˌ)kōˈagyəˌlāt, ˌantē-, ˌantə-\ *vt* **:** to hinder the clotting of the blood of esp. by treatment with an anticoagulant — **an·ti·co·ag·u·la·tion** \-ˌagyə-ˈlāshən\ n — **an·ti·co·ag·u·la·tive** \-ˈagyələd·iv, -ətiv\ *adj*

an·ti·co·don \-ˈkō₁dän\ n **:** a triplet of nucleotide bases in transfer RNA that identifies the amino acid carried and binds to a complementary codon in messenger RNA during protein synthesis at a ribosome

an·ti·com·pet·i·tive \-kəmˈped·əd·iv\ *adj* **:** tending to reduce or discourage competition ⟨bank mergers that . . . could have serious *anticompetitive* effects —*Wall St. Jour.*⟩

an·ti·con·vul·sant \-kənˈvəlsənt\ *or* **an·ti·con·vul·sive** \-ˈvəlsəv, -sēv\ *adj* **:** used or tending to control or ward off convulsions (as in epilepsy) — **anticonvulsant** *or* **anticonvulsive** n

an·ti·crop \-ˈkräp\ *adj* **:** destructive to or directed against crops ⟨*anticrop* chemical weapons⟩

¹an·ti·de·pres·sant \-dəˈpres²nt, -de-\ *or* **an·ti·de·pres·sive** \-ˈpresəv, -sēv \ *adj* **:** used or tending to relieve psychic depression

²antidepressant n **:** an antidepressant drug — called also *psychic energizer*

an·ti·deu·ter·on \-ˈd(y)üdə₁rän\ n **:** the antimatter counterpart of deuteron

an·ti·di·a·bet·ic \-ˌdīəˈbed·ik\ *adj* **:** tending to relieve diabetes ⟨*antidiabetic* drugs⟩ — **antidiabetic** n

an·ti·di·ure·sis \-ˌdī(y)əˈrēsəs\ n **:** reduction in or suppression of the excretion of urine

an·ti·di·uret·ic hor·mone \-ˌdī(y)əˌred·ikˈhòr₁mōn, -ˌhó(ə)ˌ-\ n **:** a polypeptide hormone secreted by the posterior lobe of the pituitary that increases blood pressure and decreases urine flow **:** vasopressin

an·ti·dump·ing \ˌan₁tiˈdəmpiŋ, ˌantē-, ˌantə-\ *adj* **:** designed to discourage the importation and sale of foreign goods at prices substantially lower than domestic prices ⟨*antidumping* tariffs⟩ ⟨rash of U.S. *antidumping* actions against Japanese television sets and other goods —*Chem. & Engineering News*⟩

an·ti·elec·tron \-əˈlek₁trän\ n **:** the antiparticle of the electron **:** positron

an·ti·emet·ic \-əˈmed·ik\ *adj* **:** used or tending to prevent or check vomiting ⟨*antiemetic* drugs⟩ — **antiemetic** n

an·ti·en·vi·ron·ment \-ənˈvīrənmənt, -ˈvī(ə)r(n)-\ n **:** something (as a work of art) that points up aspects of the actual environment by contrast — **an·ti·en·vi·ron·men·tal** \-ən,vīrən¦men²l, -,vī(ə)r(n)-\ *adj*

an·ti·ep·i·lep·tic \-,epə¦leptik\ *adj* : tending to suppress or prevent epilepsy ⟨*antiepileptic* treatment⟩

an·ti·es·tab·lish·ment \-ə¦stablishmənt\ *adj* : opposed or hostile to the social, economic, and political principles of a ruling class (as of a nation) ⟨*antiestablishment* candidates with long records of opposition to various national policies —N.C. Miller⟩

an·ti·es·tab·lish·men·tar·i·an \-ə,stablishmən·¦tarēən\ *adj* [*antiestablishment* + *-arian* (as in *establishmentarian*, adj.)] : ANTIESTABLISHMENT — **antiestablishmentarian** *n*

an·ti·es·tro·gen \-¦estrəjən\ *n* : a substance that inhibits the physiological action of an estrogen — **an·ti·es·tro·gen·ic** \-,estrə¦jenik\ *adj*

an·ti·fem·i·nist \-¦femənəst\ *adj* : opposed to feminism ⟨the *antifeminist* view that intensity of purpose in a woman is unnatural and therefore unladylike —Elizabeth L. Cless⟩ — **an·ti·fem·i·nism** \-,nizəm\ *n* — **antifeminist** *n*

an·ti·fer·til·i·ty \-fə(r)¦tiləd·ē, -ətē, -i\ *adj* : having the capacity or tending to reduce or destroy fertility : contraceptive ⟨*antifertility* agents⟩ ⟨*antifertility* action⟩

an·ti·flu·o·ri·da·tion·ist \¦an,tī¦flùrə¦dāsh(ə)nəst, ¦antē-, ¦antə-, -ōr-, -òr-\ *n* : one opposed to the fluoridation of public water supplies

an·ti·foul·ant \-¦faùlənt\ *n* : a substance (as paint for use on the bottom of a boat) designed to prevent, reduce, or eliminate fouling

an·ti·fun·gal \-¦fəngəl\ *adj* : used or effective against fungi : fungicidal ⟨*antifungal* drugs⟩ ⟨*antifungal* activity⟩ ⟨*antifungal* properties⟩ — **antifungal** *n*

an·ti·glob·u·lin \-¦gläbyələn\ *n* : an antibody that combines with and precipitates globulin

¹an·ti·grav·i·ty \-¦gravəd·ē, -i\ *adj* : reducing, canceling, or protecting against the effect of gravity ⟨an *antigravity* suit⟩ ⟨tracheophytes developed an *antigravity* and a water-conducting mechanism —P.B. Weisz⟩

²antigravity *n* : a hypothetical effect resulting from cancellation or reduction of a gravitational field

an·ti·he·li·um \¦an,tī¦hēlēəm, ¦antē-, ¦antə-\ *n* : the antimatter counterpart of helium

an·ti·he·mo·phil·ic factor \-¦hēmə¦filik-\ *n* : FACTOR VIII

antihemophilic globulin *n* : FACTOR VIII

an·ti·he·ro \-¦hē(,)rō, -¦hi(ə)r(,)ō\ *n* : a protagonist who is notably lacking in heroic qualities ⟨the quintessential *antihero* of the Age of Anxiety, a textbook case of contemporary alienation with whom intellectuals could easily identify —J.W. Aldridge⟩ ⟨an *antihero* who scorned law and morality in his lust for money —*Current Biog.*⟩ — **an·ti·he·ro·ic** \-hə¦rōik, -he-, -hē-\ *adj*

an·ti·her·o·ine \-¦herəwən, -¦hir-\ *n* : a female antihero ⟨his *antiheroine*, Christy, is fearful and compliant to the point of lacking personal dignity —Phil Frankfeld⟩

an·ti·hu·man \-¦(h)yümən\ *adj* : acting or being against man; *esp* : reacting strongly with human antigens

an·ti·hy·dro·gen \-¦hīdrəjən, -rēj-\ *n* : the antimatter counterpart of hydrogen

an·ti·hy·per·tens·ive \-¦hīpə(r)¦ten(t)səv\ *adj* [*anti-* + *hypertens*ion high blood pressure + *-ive* tending toward]

: used or effective against high blood pressure — **antihypertensive** *n*

an·ti–im·mu·no·glob·u·lin \-,imyənō¦gläbyələn\ *adj* : acting against specific antibodies ⟨*anti-immunoglobulin* sera⟩ — **anti–immunoglobulin** *n*

an·ti–in·fec·tive \-ən¦fektiv\ *adj* : used against or tending to counteract or prevent infection ⟨*anti-infective* agents⟩ — **anti–infective** *n*

an·ti–in·flam·ma·to·ry \¦an,tiən¦flamə,tōrē, ¦antē-, ¦antə-, -tòr-, -ri\ *adj* : counteracting inflammation ⟨*anti-inflammatory* drugs⟩ ⟨*anti-inflammatory* effects⟩ — **anti–inflammatory** *n*

an·ti–in·tel·lec·tu·al \-¦int²l¦ekch(əw)əl, -ksh-\ *adj* : opposing or hostile to intellectuals or to an intellectual view or approach ⟨an *anti-intellectual* know-nothingism: forget politics, forget art, forget history —Samuel Hynes⟩ — **anti–intellectual** *n*

an·ti·lep·ton \-¦lep,tän\ *n* : an antiparticle (as a positron or an antineutrino) of a lepton

an·ti·leu·ke·mic \-lü¦kēmik\ *also* **an·ti·leu·ke·mia** \-¦kēmēə\ *adj* : counteracting the effects of leukemia ⟨*antileukemic* effect of a drug⟩

an·ti·life \-¦līf\ *adj* : antipathetic to normal, full, or healthy life; *also* : favoring birth control

an·ti·lit·ter \-¦lid·ə(r), -itə-\ *adj* : serving to prevent or discourage the littering of public areas ⟨*antilitter* laws⟩

an·ti·lym·pho·cyte glob·u·lin \-¦lim(p)fə,sit'gläbyələn\ *n* : serum globulin containing antibodies against lymphocytes that is used similarly to antilymphocyte serum

antilymphocyte serum *n* : a serum containing antibodies against lymphocytes that is used for suppressing graft rejection caused by lymphocyte-controlled immune responses in organ or tissue transplant recipients

an·ti·lym·pho·cyt·ic globulin \-,lim(p)fə¦sid·ik-\ *n* : ANTILYMPHOCYTE GLOBULIN

antilymphocytic serum *n* : ANTILYMPHOCYTE SERUM

¹an·ti·mis·sile \¦an,ti¦misəl, ¦antē-, ¦antə-, *chiefly Brit* -¦mis,īl\ *adj* : designed as a defense against missiles ⟨an *antimissile* system⟩

²antimissile *n* : ANTIMISSILE MISSILE

antimissile missile *n* : a missile for intercepting another missile in flight; *esp* : ANTIBALLISTIC MISSILE

an·ti·mi·tot·ic \-,mi¦täd·ik\ *adj* : inhibiting or disrupting mitosis ⟨*antimitotic* drugs⟩ ⟨*antimitotic* activity⟩ — **antimitotic** *n*

an·ti·mu·ta·gen·ic \-,myüd·ə¦jenik\ *adj* : reducing the rate of mutation ⟨*antimutagenic* substances⟩

an·ti·my·cot·ic \-mi¦käd·ik, -ätik\ *adj or n* : ANTIFUNGAL

an·ti·na·tal·ist \-¦nād·²l·əst, -āt²l-\ *n* : an advocate of population control

an·ti·neo·plas·tic \-,nēə¦plastik\ *adj* : inhibiting or preventing the growth and spread of neoplasms or malignant cells — **antineoplastic** *n*

an·ti·noise \-¦nòiz\ *adj* : designed or acting to reduce noise level ⟨an *antinoise* ordinance⟩

an·ti·nov·el \¦an,ti¦nävəl, ¦antē-, ¦antə-\ *n* : a work of fiction that lacks most or all of the traditional features (as coherent structure or character development) of the novel — **an·ti·nov·el·ist** \-ləst\ *n*

an·ti·nu·cle·ar \-¦n(y)üklēə(r), ÷ -kyələ(r)\ *adj* **1** : tending to react with cell nuclei or their components (as

DNA) ⟨*antinuclear* antibodies⟩ **2 :** opposing the use or production of nuclear power plants ⟨a strong *antinuclear* movement demanding that the U.S. close down all existing nuclear power plants —*Newsweek*⟩

an·ti·nuke \-ʲn(y)ük\ *adj* [by shortening & alter.] **:** ANTINUCLEAR 2

an·ti·ob·scen·i·ty \-ˌäbʲsenəd-ē, -əb-, *also* -sēn-\ *adj* **:** designed to prevent or restrict the dissemination of obscene materials ⟨*antiobscenity* laws⟩

an·ti·ozon·ant \-ʲō̱ˌzōnənt\ *n* **:** a substance that opposes ozonization or protects against it

an·ti·par·a·sit·ic \-ˌparəʲsid·ik\ *adj* **:** acting against parasites ⟨*antiparasitic* drugs⟩

an·ti·par·kin·so·ni·an \-ˌpärkənʲsōnēan\ *adj* **:** tending to relieve parkinsonism ⟨*antiparkinsonian* drugs⟩

an·ti·par·ti·cle \ʲan,tīˌpärtəkəl, ʹantē-, ʹantə-, -ˌpád-\ *n* **:** an elementary particle identical to another elementary particle in mass but opposite to it in electric and magnetic properties that when brought together with its counterpart produces mutual annihilation

an·ti·po·lit·i·cal \ʲan,tīpəʲlid·əkəl, ʹantē-, ʹantə-\ *adj* **:** opposing or reacting against traditional political policies and principles

an·ti·pol·i·ti·cian \-ˌpälōʲtishən\ *n* **:** a politician who appears to be antipolitical

an·ti–pol·i·tics \-ʲpälə-ˌtiks\ *n pl but sing or pl in constr* **:** reaction against or rejection of the practices or attitudes associated with traditional politics

an·ti·pol·lu·tion \-pəʲlüshən\ *adj* **:** intended to prevent, reduce, or eliminate pollution ⟨*antipollution* devices on automobiles⟩ ⟨*antipollution* regulations⟩ — **an·ti·pol·lu·tion·ist** \-əst\ *n*

an·ti·pov·er·ty \-ʲpävə(r)d·ē, -i\ *adj* **:** of or relating to action designed to relieve poverty ⟨*antipoverty* programs⟩

an·ti·psy·chot·ic \-(ˌ)sīʲkäd·ik\ *adj* **:** tending to alleviate psychosis or psychotic states ⟨an *antipsychotic* drug⟩ — **antipsychotic** *n*

an·ti·quark \ʲan,tīʲkwärk, ʹantē-, ʹantə-, -ʲkwȯrk\ *n* **:** the antiparticle of the quark

antique*vb* **an·tiqued; an·tiqu·ing :** to shop around for antiques ⟨an afternoon of *antiquing* and browsing in the dozen or so shops and restaurants that make up this quaint . . . community —Jane L. Gregory⟩

an·ti·rac·ism \ʲan,tīˌrāˌsizəm, ʹantē-, ʹantə-, *also* -ˌshizəm\ *n* **:** adherence to the view that racism is a social evil — **an·ti·rac·ist** \-ʲrāsəst, *also* -shəst\ *n or adj*

an·ti·rad·i·cal \-radəkəl, -dēk-\ *adj* **:** opposed to radicals or radicalism ⟨the thoroughly *antiradical* sheriff —H.F. May⟩

an·ti·rheu·mat·ic \-(ˌ)rüʲmad·ik, -rə-\ *adj* **:** alleviating or preventing rheumatism — **antirheumatic** *n*

an·ti·sci·ence \-ʲsīən(t)s\ *n* **:** a system or attitude or cult that rejects scientific methods or the value of science to man; *also* **:** one that denies the value of basic scientific research — **an·ti·sci·en·tif·ic** \-ˌsīənʲtifik\ *adj*

an·ti·sci·en·tism \-ʲsīən,tizəm\ *n* **:** ANTISCIENCE

an·ti·sex \-ʲseks, *or* **an·ti·sex·u·al** \-ʲseksh(ə)wəl, -shəl\ *adj* **:** antagonistic toward sex; *esp* **:** tending to reduce or eliminate the sex drive or sexual activity

an·ti·sex·ist \-ʲseksəst\ *adj* **:** opposed to sexism

an·ti·skid \ʲan,tīʲskid, ʹantē-, ʹantə-\ *adj* **:** designed to prevent skidding ⟨*antiskid* braking systems⟩

an·ti·smog \-ʲsmäg, *also* -ʲsmȯg\ *adj* **:** designed to reduce pollutants that contribute to the formation of smog ⟨*antismog* devices on automobiles⟩

an·ti·stat \ʲan,tiʲstat, ʹantē-, ʹantə-\ *or* **an·ti·stat·ic** \-ʲstad·ik\ *adj* [*antistat* short for *antistatic*] **:** reducing, removing, or preventing the buildup of static electricity ⟨the can't-be-copied *antistat* nylon crepe the women's wear industry is mad for —*advt*⟩ ⟨an *antistatic* coating⟩ — **antistatic** *n*

an·ti·strep·to·coc·cal \-ʲstreptəʲkäkəl\ *or* **an·ti·strep·to·coc·cic** \-ʲkäk(s)ik\ *adj* [*anti-* + *streptococcal* or *streptococcic*] **:** tending to destroy or inhibit the growth and reproduction of streptococci ⟨*antistreptococcal* antibodies⟩

an·ti·throm·bot·ic \-ʲthrämʲbäd·ik\ *adj* **:** used against or tending to prevent thrombosis ⟨*antithrombotic* agents⟩ ⟨*antithrombotic* therapy⟩

an·ti·tu·ber·cu·lous \-t(y)ùʲbərkyələs, -tə-ʲ-\ *or* **an·ti·tu·ber·cu·lo·sis** \-ˌbərkyə-ʲlōsəs\ *or* **an·ti·tu·ber·cu·lar** \-ʲbərkyələr\ *adj* **:** used or effective against tuberculosis ⟨*antituberculous* drugs⟩ ⟨*antituberculous* activity⟩

an·ti·tu·mor \-ʲt(y)ümə(r)\ *also* **an·ti·tu·mor·al** \-mərəl \ *adj* **:** ANTICANCER ⟨*antitumor* agents⟩ ⟨*antitumor* activity⟩

an·ti·tus·sive \-ʲtəsiv\ *n* **:** an antitussive agent

an·ti·ul·cer \-ʲəlsə(r)\ *adj* **:** tending to prevent or heal ulcers ⟨*antiulcer* drug research⟩

an·ti–uto·pia \-yùʲtōpēə\ *n* **1 :** DYSTOPIA **2 :** a work describing an anti-utopia — **an·ti–uto·pi·an** \-pēən\ *adj or n*

an·ti·war \-ʲwȯ(ə)r, -ʲwȯ(ə)\ *adj* **:** opposed to war ⟨*antiwar* protests⟩

an·ti·white \-ʲ(h)wit\ *adj* **:** opposed or hostile to people belonging to a light-skinned race — **an·ti·whit·ism** \-ʲ(h)wīd·ˌizəm\ *n*

an·ti·world \ʲan,tī,wər(ə)ld, ʹantē-, ʹantə-, -ˌwȯld, -ˌwȯild\ *n* **:** the hypothetical antimatter counterpart of a world

anx·io·lyt·ic \ˌaŋzēōʹlid·ik, ˌaŋ(k)sē-, -itik\ *n* [*anxiety* + connective *-o-* + *-lytic* (perh. influenced by *analytic, catalytic*)] **:** an agent that relieves anxiety — **anxiolytic** *adj*

ao dai \ʲäōˌdī, ʲa-\ *n, pl* **ao dais** [Vietnamese *áo dái*, fr. *áo* jacket, tunic (of Chinese origin — akin to Chin (Pek) *ao³* jacket) + *dai* long] **:** the traditional dress of Vietnamese women that consists of a long tunic with slits on either side and wide trousers

A–OK \ˌā(ˌ)ōˌkā\ *adj* **:** very definitely OK ⟨the fuses were all *A-OK* —John Gould⟩

aor·to·il·i·ac \ˌāˌȯrd-ō̱ʹilē̱ak, -rtō-\ *adj* [*aorto-* aorta + *iliac*] **:** of, relating to, or joining the abdominal aorta and the iliac arteries

ape \ʲāp\ *adj* **:** being beyond restraint **:** crazy, wild ⟨it's driving me *ape* with that goony noise —*Datamation*⟩ — usu. used in the phrase *go ape* ⟨went *ape* over another girl —*Boston Sunday Globe Mag.*⟩

aperture card *n* **:** a punch card for data processing in which one or more frames of a microfilmed document are mounted

Ap·gar score \ʲap,gär-, -ˌgá(r-\ *n* [Virginia *Apgar* †1974 Am. anesthesiologist] **:** an index used to evaluate the condition of a newborn infant based on a rating of 0, 1, or 2 for each of the five characteristics of color, heart rate, response to stimulation of the sole of the foot, muscle tone, and respiration with 10 being a perfect score

apha·si·ol·o·gy \ə'fāz(h)ē'äləjē, -ji\ n [aphasia + connective -o- + -logy science] **:** the study of aphasia including its linguistic, psychological, and neurological aspects — **apha·si·ol·o·gist** \-jəst\ n

aph·ox·ide \(')a'fäk,sīd, also -ksəd\ n [prob. fr. aziridinyl + phospine, a chemical compound + oxide] **:** TEPA

apo·ap·sis \apō,apsəs\ n, pl **-ap·si·des** \-,apsə,dēz\ [NL, fr. apo- away from (deriv. of Gk apo away from) + apsis] **:** the apsis that is the greatest distance from the center of attraction

apo·cyn·thi·on \apə'sin(t)thēən\ n [NL, fr. apo- + Cynthia, goddess of the moon (fr. Gk Kynthia) + -on (as in aphelion)] **:** APOLUNE

apo·li·po·pro·tein \apə'līpō'prō,tēn, 'apō-, -'lipō-, -'prōd·ēən\ n [apo- + lipoprotein] **:** a protein that combines with a lipid to form a lipoprotein

apo·lune \'apə,lün\ n [apo- away from + L luna moon] **:** the point in the path of a body orbiting the moon that is farthest from the center of the moon

apo·pro·tein \apə'prō,tēn, 'apō-, -'prōd·ēən\ n [apo- + protein] **:** a protein that combines with a prosthetic group to form a conjugated protein

apo·se·lene \'apəsə,lēn\ n [ISV apo- + -selene, fr. Gk selēnē moon] **:** APOLUNE

apo·se·le·ni·um \apəsə'lēnēəm\ n [NL, fr. apo- + Gk selēnē moon + NL -ium, alter. of -ion (as in aphelion)] **:** APOLUNE

Ap·pa·la·chian \apə'lāchən, -'lach-, -'läsh-, -chēən\ n **:** a white native or resident of the Appalachian mountain area ⟨blacks and Appalachians competing for the same scarce jobs, housing, and recreational facilities —James Adams⟩

ap·ple–pie*\apəl'pī\ adj [fr. the tradition that apple pie is a quintessentially American dish] **:** of, relating to, or characterized by traditionally American values ⟨concerned with the recovery of a lot of apple-pie virtues after an era of turmoil and flux —E. B. Fiske⟩

approach–approach conflict n **:** psychological conflict that results when a choice must be made between two desirable alternatives — compare APPROACH-AVOIDANCE CONFLICT, AVOIDANCE-AVOIDANCE CONFLICT

approach–avoidance conflict n **:** psychological conflict that results when a goal is both desirable and undesirable — compare APPROACH-APPROACH CONFLICT, AVOIDANCE-AVOIDANCE CONFLICT

¹après–ski \ä,prä'skē, ,a-\ n [F, fr. après after + ski ski, skiing] **:** social activity (as at a ski lodge) after a day's skiing

²après–ski adj **:** of, relating to, or suitable for après-ski ⟨appear on slopes and around crackling fires in their newest ski and après-ski clothes —Women's Wear Daily⟩ ⟨offers its typically cosmopolitan clientele . . . unsurpassed accommodations, diverse après-ski pastimes and calculated Alpine charm —Playboy⟩

aqua·naut \'akwə,nòt, 'äk-, -nät\ n [aqua water (fr. L) + -naut (as in astronaut)] **:** a scuba diver who lives beneath the surface of water for an extended period and carries on activities both inside and outside his underwater shelter

aquaplane*vi **:** HYDROPLANE

Aquarian*n **:** AQUARIUS

Aquar·i·an \ə'kwarēən, -wer-, -wär-\ adj **1 :** relating to or characteristic of an Aquarius ⟨that little bit of Aquarian perversity —Annabel⟩ **2 :** of or relating to the Age of Aquarius ⟨their Aquarian dream of peace, freedom and brotherhood —P.D. Zimmerman⟩

Aquarian Age n **:** AGE OF AQUARIUS

Aquarius*n **:** one born under the astrological sign Aquarius

ar·a·besque*\arə'besk, 'er-\ n **:** a contrived intricate pattern of verbal expression ⟨arabesques of alliteration — C.E. Montague⟩

ara·chid·o·nate \arə'kid°n,āt\ n [arachidonic + -ate chemical compound] **:** a salt or ester of arachidonic acid

ar·bo·vi·rol·o·gy \ärbə,vī'räləjē, -ji\ n [arbovirus + connective -o- + -logy science] **:** a branch of virology that deals with the arboviruses

ar·bo·vi·rus \'ärbə,vīrəs\ n [arthropod-borne virus] **:** any of various viruses transmitted by arthropods and including the causative agents of encephalitis, yellow fever, and dengue

arcade*n **:** an amusement center having coin-operated devices (as video games) for entertainment

ar·chaeo·as·tron·o·my \ärkē,()ōə'stränəmē, är'kēō-, -mi\ n [archaeo- ancient + astronomy] **:** the astronomy of ancient cultures — **ar·chaeo·as·tron·o·mer** \-nəmər\ n

ar·cho·saur \'ärkə,sò(ə)r\ n **:** a member of the reptilian subclass Archosauria

arc·jet \'ärk,jet, 'äk-\ n **:** ARC-JET ENGINE

arc–jet engine n **:** a rocket engine in which the propellant gas is heated by an electric arc

ar·cu·ate nucleus \ärkyəwət-, -,wät-\ n **:** any of several cellular masses in the thalamus or medulla oblongata

area code n [fr. its designation of major subdivisions of the territory of the United States] **:** a 3-digit code used in dialing long-distance telephone calls

area rug n **:** a rug designed to cover a limited area within a room

arena stage n **:** a theater stage surrounded or nearly surrounded by audience; specif **:** the stage of an arena theater

ar·eo·cen·tric \arēō'sen·trik, -ēə'-\ adj [areo- the planet Mars (fr. Gk Areios of Ares, the Greek god of war, fr. Arēs Ares) + -centric having as a center] **:** having or relating to the planet Mars as a center

AR 15 \'ā'är(')fif,tēn, 'ā'á(-\ or **AR 15 rifle** n [fr. Armalite, the manufacturer] **:** a .223 caliber gas-operated semi-automatic rifle that is essentially a civilian version of the M16

Ar·gy·rol \'ärjə,ròl, -,röl\ trademark — used for a silver=protein compound whose aqueous solution is used as a local antiseptic esp. for mucous membranes

arhyth·mic \ā'rithmik\ also **arhyth·mi·cal** \-məkəl\ adj [a- not + rhythmic or rhythmical] **:** marked by the absence of rhythm ⟨struck by the arhythmic quality of their reading —Charles Drake⟩

Ar·i·an \'arēən, 'er-, 'är-\ n [fr. Aries + E -an one belonging to] **:** ARIES

Aries*n **:** one born under the astrological sign Aries

arm and a leg n **:** an exorbitant price ⟨have fun without shelling out an arm and a leg —Genevieve Stuttaford⟩

arm–twist·ing \'ärm,twistiŋ, 'äm-\ n **:** the use of direct personal pressure in order to achieve a desired end ⟨for all the *arm-twisting,* the . . . vote on the measure was unexpectedly tight —*Newsweek*⟩

arm wrestling *n* **:** a form of wrestling in which two opponents sit face to face gripping usu. their right hands and setting corresponding elbows firmly on a surface (as a tabletop) in an attempt to force each other's arm down **:** Indian wrestling

around the world *n* **:** the action of orally stimulating many parts of the body for sexual gratification

array*n **:** an arrangement of computer memory elements (as magnetic cores) in a single plane

ar·res·tant \ə'restənt\ *n* **:** a substance or stimulus that causes an insect to stop locomotion

art de·co \ˌär(t)dā'kō; (')är(t)'dā(ˌ)kō, -de-; -à(t)-\ *n, often cap A&D* [F *Art Déco,* fr. *Exposition Internationale des Arts Décoratifs et Industriels Modernes,* an exposition of modern decorative and industrial arts held in Paris, France, in 1925] **:** a popular decorative style of the 1920s and 1930s characterized esp. by bold outlines and colors and by streamlined and geometric forms

ar·thro·gry·po·sis \ˌärˌthrōgrə'pōsəs, ˌàˌth-\ *n* [NL, fr. *arthr-* joint + *gryposis*] **:** permanent flexure of a joint

ar·throl·o·gy \är'thräləjē, à'th-, -ji\ *n* [*arthr-* + *-logy* science] **:** a science concerned with the study of joints

ar·thros·co·py \-'thräskəpē, -pl\ *n* [ISV *arthr-* + *-scope* + *-y* activity] **:** visual examination of the interior of a joint (as the knee) with a special surgical instrument — **ar·thro·scope** \'ärthrəˌskōp, 'àth-\ *n*

ar·throt·o·my \är'thrätəmē, à'-, -mi\ *n, pl* **-mies** [ISV *arthr-* + *-tomy* incision] **:** incision into a joint

ar·tic \à'tik\ *n* [short for *articulated lorry*] *Brit* **:** a trucking rig made up of a tractor and semitrailer

artificial intelligence *n* **:** the capability of a machine to imitate intelligent human behavior (as reasoning, learning, or the understanding of speech)

art·mo·bile \'ärtmōˌbēl, 'àt-\ *n* **:** a trailer that houses an art collection designed for exhibition on road tours

art mo·derne \ˌär(t)mō'de(ə)rn\ *n, often cap A & M* [F, lit., *modern art*] **:** ART DECO

art·sy \'ärtsē, 'àt-, -i\ *adj* [*art* + *-sy* (as in *folksy*)] **:** pretentiously artistic **:** arty ⟨a pretentious mix of mod-pop doo-dads and *artsy* effects —Judith Crist⟩ ⟨a very rich, social, *artsy* New York crowd —Sally Quinn⟩

aru·gu·la \ə'rüg(y)ələ\ *n* [prob. from It dial. *arugula,* fr. L *ērūca* colewort; akin to Sp *ruqueta,* Cat *oruga,* F *roquette*] **:** a yellowish flowered European herb (*Eruca sativa*) of the mustard family that is sometimes grown for salad

ary·te·noi·dec·to·my \ˌarə-ˌtēˌnòi'dektəmē, ə-ˌritⁿˌòi-\ *n, pl* **-mies** [*arytenoid,* n. + *-ectomy* excision] **:** excision of an arytenoid cartilage

ASAP *abbr* as soon as possible

ascending colon *n* **:** the part of the large intestine that extends from the cecum to the bend on the right side below the liver — compare DESCENDING COLON

ASCII \'as(ˌ)kē\ *n* [American *S*tandard *C*ode for *I*nformation *I*nterchange] **:** a code for representing alphanumeric information (as in a data processing system)

asexual*adj **:** devoid of sexuality ⟨why speak of friendship as pure when all you mean is that it is *asexual* —E.R. Bentley⟩

as far as *prep* **:** with reference to **:** as for — not often in formal use; used in speech and speechlike prose ⟨*as far as*

being mentioned in the Ten Commandments, I think it is —Billy Graham⟩

ash*n [OE *æsc,* lit., ash tree, name of the corresponding runic letter] **:** the ligature æ used in Old English to represent a low front vowel

ASL *abbr* American Sign Language

as·par·tame \'aspə(r)ˌtām, ə'spärˌtām, -àˌt-\ *n* [*aspartic* acid + *-ame* (of unknown origin)] **:** a noncarbohydrate sweetener $C_{14}H_{18}N_2O_5$ that is formed from the amino acids phenylalanine and aspartic acid

as·par·to·kinase \əˌspärd-ō'kīˌnāz, -às-\ *n* [*aspartic* acid + connective *-o-* + *kinase,* an enzyme] **:** an enzyme that catalyzes the phosphorylation of aspartic acid by ATP

asphalt jungle *n* **:** a big city or a specified part of a big city ⟨the *asphalt jungle* around Times Square —E.R. Bentley⟩

¹-ass \ˌas, *also* ˌàs\ *adj or adv comb form* [*ass* buttocks] — used as a derogatory intensive ⟨a fancy-*ass* limited edition at ten bucks a throw —*East Village Other*⟩ ⟨a story that's dead-*ass* wrong —J.D. Ehrlichman⟩; often considered vulgar

²-ass *n comb form* **:** a contemptible person ⟨smart-*ass*⟩ ⟨my son is a wise*ass.* He answers the telephone with cracks —Richard Reeves⟩ — often considered vulgar

as·sem·blage*\ə'semblij, -lēj; ˌaˌsä(ⁿ)m'bläzh, ˌàˌs-, -sänⁿb-, -làzh\ *n* **1 :** an artistic composition made from scraps, junk, and odds and ends (as of paper, cloth, wood, stone, or metal) **2 :** the art of making assemblages — **as·sem·blag·ist** \-jəst, -zhəst\ *n*

assembler*n **1 :** a computer program that automatically converts instructions written in a symbolic code into the equivalent machine code **2 :** ASSEMBLY LANGUAGE

assembly*n **:** the translation of symbolic code to machine code by an assembler

assembly language *n* **:** a symbolic language for programming a computer that is a close approximation of machine language

ass·hole \'as,(h)ōl, *also* 'às-\ *n* [*ass* buttocks + *hole*] **1 :** anus — usu. considered vulgar **2 :** a stupid or incompetent person **:** blockhead — usu. considered vulgar **3 :** the least attractive or desirable part or area — usu. considered vulgar

assist*n **:** a mechanical device that provides assistance

ass·kiss·ing \-ˌkisin\ *n* **:** obsequious flattery or attentiveness — usu. considered vulgar

associative neuron *n* **:** a neuron that conveys nerve impulses from one neuron to another

As·ti spu·man·te \ˌästē(ˌ)spü'män(ˌ)tā, ˌas-, ˌàs-, -sti-, -spə'-, -tē\ *n* [It, lit., sparkling Asti] **:** a sweet sparkling white wine made in and around the village of Asti in Piedmont

astral projection *n* **:** out-of-body travel

as·tri·on·ics \ˌastrē'äniks\ *n pl but sing or pl in constr* [*astro*nautics + *-ionics* (as in *avionics*)] **:** electronics applied to astronautics

as·tro·bi·ol·o·gy \ˌas(ˌ)trō,bī'äləjē, -ji\ *n* [*astro-* star, outer space (deriv. of Gk *astron* star) + *biology*] **:** EXOBIOLOGY — **as·tro·bi·o·log·i·cal** \-ˌbīə'läjəkəl\ *adj* — **as·tro·bi·ol·o·gist** \-ˌbī'äləjəst\ *n*

as·tro·bleme \'astrəˌblēm\ *n* [*astro-* + Gk *blēma* throw, missile, wound from a missile, fr. *ballein* to throw] **:** a scar on the earth's crust made by the impact of a meteorite

as·tro·chem·is·try \ˌastrōˈkeməstrē, -tri\ *n* **:** the chemistry of the stars and interstellar space — **as·tro·chem·ist** \-ˈkeməst\ *n*

as·tro·dy·nam·ics \ˌas(ˌ)trōˌdīˈnamiks, *sometimes* -də-\ *n pl but sing or pl in constr* **:** dynamics that deals with objects in outer space — **as·tro·dy·nam·ic** \-ˈnamik\ *adj* — **as·tro·dy·nam·i·cist** \-ˈnaməsəst\ *n*

as·tro·ge·ol·o·gy \ˌas(ˌ)trō(ˌ)jēˈäləjē, -ji\ *n* **:** a branch of geology that deals with celestial bodies — **as·tro·geo·log·ic** \-ˌjēəˈläjik\ *adj* — **as·tro·ge·ol·o·gist** \-(ˌ)jēˈäləjəst\ *n*

atem·por·al \(ˈ)äˌtemp(ə)rəl\ *adj* [*a-* not + *temporal*] **:** independent of or unaffected by time **:** timeless

athe·o·ret·i·cal \ˌäˌthēəˈredˌəkəl, -etə-\ *adj* **:** not based on or concerned with theory

ath·ero·gen·e·sis \ˌathərōˈjenəsəs\ *n* [*athero-* atheroma + *genesis*] **:** the production of atheroma

ath·ero·gen·ic \ˌathərōˈjenik\ *adj* [*athero-* + *-genic* producing] **:** relating to or tending to produce degenerative changes in arterial walls — **ath·ero·ge·nic·i·ty** \ˌathə(ˌ)rōjəˈnisədˌē, -ət-, -i\ *n*

athymic \(ˈ)äˌthīmik\ *adj* [*a-* + *thymic*] **:** lacking a thymus ⟨congenitally *athymic* babies⟩

At·lan·ti·cism \ətˈlantəˌsizəm, at-\ *n* **:** a policy of military, political, and economic cooperation between European and North American powers — **At·lan·ti·cist** \-əsəst\ *n*

at·mo·sphe·ri·um \ˌatməˈsfirēəm\ *n* [*atmosphere* + *-ium* (as in *planetarium*)] **1 :** an optical device for projecting images of meteorological phenomena (as clouds) on the inside of a dome **2 :** a room housing an atmospherium

atox·ic \(ˈ)äˌtäksik\ *adj* [*a-* + *toxic*] **:** not toxic ⟨*atoxic* antibiotics⟩

ATPase \ˌäˌtēˈpēˌās, -ˌāz\ *n* [*ATP* + *-ase* enzyme] **:** an enzyme that hydrolyzes ATP; *esp* **:** one that hydrolyzes ATP to ADP and inorganic phosphate

at·ra·zine \ˈaˌtrəˌzēn\ *n* [ISV *atr-* (perh. fr. L *atr-, ater* black, dark) + *triazine*] **:** a photosynthesis-inhibiting persistent herbicide $C_8H_{14}ClN_5$ used esp. to kill annual weeds and quack grass

atrium*n, *pl* **-ums :** a many-storied court in a building (as a hotel) usu. with a skylight

at·ro·pin·iza·tion \ˌaˌtrəpənəˈzāshan, -ˌpēn-, -ˌiˈz-\ *n* [*atropine* + *-ization* action, result] **:** the physiological condition of being under the influence of atropine

at·tack·man \əˈtakˌman, -kmən\ *n* **:** a player (as in lacrosse) assigned to an offensive zone or position

at·to- \ˈadˌ(ˌ)ō, -dˌə\ *comb form* [ISV, fr. Dan or Norw *atten* eighteen, fr. ON *āttjān*] **:** one quintillionth (10^{-18}) part of

at·trite \əˈtrit, aˈ-\ *or* **at·trit·ed** \-ˈtrīt\ *vt* **at·trit·ed; at·trit·ing** [back-formation fr. *attrition*] **:** to weaken or reduce by attrition ⟨had little success in *attriting* the enemy⟩

attrition*n **:** a usu. gradual loss of personnel from causes normal or peculiar to a given situation (as death, retirement, and resignation in a labor force or failure and dropout among students) often without filling the vacancies ⟨the total number of employees was reduced . . . through normal *attrition* and adjustments based on business con-siderations —*Annual Report E.I. DuPont De Nemours & Co.*⟩ ⟨student *attrition* rate is very high —J.M. Ziegler⟩

au bleu \(ˌ)ōˈblœ, -ˈblə, -ˈblü\ *adj or adv* [F, lit., to the blue; fr. the fact that the skin of fish cooked in this manner turns blue] **:** cooked by boiling in acidulated water immediately after being killed and cleaned but without being washed or scaled — used esp. of trout

au·di·al \ˈodēəl\ *adj* [*audio-* hearing (fr. L *audire* to hear) + *-al* (as in *visual*)] **:** of, relating to, or affecting the sense of hearing **:** aural

audible *n* [*audible,* adj.] **:** a substitute offensive play or defensive formation called at the line of scrimmage in football

au·dio–lin·gual \ˌodē(ˌ)ōˈliŋg(yə)wəl\ *adj* [*audio-* + *lingual*] **:** involving the use of listening and speaking drills in language learning

au·dio·tape \ˈodēōˌtāp\ *n* [*audio,* adj. + *tape*] **:** a tape recording of sound

au·dio·typ·ist \ˈodēˌōˈtīpəst\ *n* **:** one who types directly from a tape recording — **au·dio·typ·ing** \-piŋ\ *n*

au·dio·vi·su·als \ˌodēōˈvizh(ə)wəlz, -zhəlz\ *n pl* **:** instructional materials (as filmstrips accompanied by recordings) that make use of both hearing and sight

au gra·tin \ōˈgratˈⁿ, oˈ-, -rat-\ *n, pl* **au gratins :** a container in which au gratin dishes may be cooked and served

auntie*n **:** a usu. middle-aged male homosexual who seeks the companionship of younger men

Aunt Sally**n, pl* **Aunt Sallies** *or* **Aunt Sallys** *Brit* **:** an object of criticism or contention; *esp* **:** a person, condition, or argument set up to invite criticism or be easily refuted ⟨the old *Aunt Sallys* of imperialism —Clive Barnes⟩ ⟨who, as a liberal pacifist, provides a convenient *Aunt Sally* —*Times Lit. Supp.*⟩

au pair \(ˈ)ōˈpa(ə)r, -ˈpe(ə)r\ *or* **au pair girl** *n* [F *au pair* on equal terms] **:** a foreign girl who does domestic work for a family in return for room and board and the opportunity to learn the family's language

aus·form \ˈosˌfo(ə)rm, -ō(ə)m\ *vt* [*austenitic* + de*form;* fr. the deformation's taking place while the steel is still in the austenitic form] **:** to subject (steel) to deformation and then to quenching and tempering in order to increase the strength, ductility, and resistance to fatigue failure

Aus·tra·li·ana \ȯˌstrālēˈänə, ä-, -ə,-, -ˈanə\ *n pl* [*Australia* + *-ana* collected items] **:** collected material (as books) relating to Australia

au·teur \ōˈtər, -tœœr\ *n* **:** a film director whose practice accords with the auteur theory

au·teur·ism \-ˌizəm\ *n* **:** AUTEUR THEORY — **au·teur·ist** \-əst\ *n or adj*

auteur theory *n* [part trans. of F *politique des auteurs,* fr. *auteur* author; fr. the view that the director is the true author of a film] **:** a view of film making in which the director is considered the primary creative force in a motion picture

au·to·ci·dal \ˌodˌəˈsīdᵊl, -ōˌs-\ *adj* [*auto-* self, same + *-cide* killing + *-al,* adj. suffix] **:** controlling or eradicating populations of noxious insects (as the screwworm) by reducing their capacity to produce viable or fertile offspring (as by the introduction of sterile males) ⟨*autocidal* procedures⟩ ⟨*autocidal* effects⟩

au·to·cide \-ˌsīd\ *n* [*auto-* automobile + *-cide* (as in suicide)] **:** suicide by crashing one's automobile

au·to·clav·able \ˌȯd·ə¦klāvəbəl, -d·ō¦-\ *adj* **:** able to withstand the action of an autoclave ⟨*autoclavable* laboratory equipment⟩

au·to·cross \ˈȯd·ə‚krȯs, -d·ō-, ˈäd-‚ *also* -‚kräs\ *n* [*auto* + *cross*-country, n.] **:** an automobile gymkhana

au·to·drome \-‚drōm\ *n* [*auto* + *-drome* racecourse, deriv. of Gk *dromos;* akin to Gk *dramein* to run] **:** an automobile racetrack

au·tog·e·nous*\(ˈ)ȯ¦täjənəs, ə¦-\ *or* **au·to·gen·ic*** \ˌȯd·ō¦jenik\ *adj* **:** not requiring a meal of blood to produce eggs ⟨*autogenous* mosquitoes⟩

au·to·ges·tion \ˌȯd·ō¦jes(h)chən\ *n* [F *autogestion*, fr. Gk *autos* self + F *gestion* administration, fr. L *gestio* managing, performing, fr. *gerere* to perform, accomplish] **:** control and management of an enterprise (as a factory) by representatives of the workers

au·to·im·mune \ˌȯd·ōə¦myün\ *adj* [back-formation fr. *autoimmunization*] **:** of, relating to, or caused by autoantibodies or lymphocytes that attack molecules, cells, or tissues of the organism producing them ⟨*autoimmune* diseases⟩ — **au·to·im·mu·ni·ty** \-ə¦myünəd·ē, -i\ *n* — **au·to·im·mu·ni·za·tion** \-‚imyənə¹zāshən, -əm‚yünə-\ *n* — **au·to·im·mu·nize** \-¦imyə‚nīz\ *vt*

au·to·ma·nia \ˌȯd·ə¦mänyə, -ō¦m-, -nēə\ *n* [*auto-* automobile + *mania*] **:** undue dependence on or concern with having an automobile esp. for recreation

au·to·ma·nip·u·la·tion \-mə‚nipyə¦läshən\ *n* [*auto-* self, same (fr. Gk, fr. *autos* same, self) + *manipulation*] **:** physical stimulation of the genital organs by oneself — **au·to·ma·nip·u·la·tive** \-mə¦nipyələd·iv\ *adj*

automatic*n **:** AUDIBLE

au·toph·a·gy \ȯ¹täfəjē\ *n* [*auto-* self, same + *-phagy* eating, fr. Gk *-phagia,* fr. *phagein* to eat] **:** digestion of cellular constituents by enzymes of the same cell — **au·toph·a·gic** \-jik\ *adj*

au·to·reg·u·la·tion \ˌȯd·ō‚regyə¦läshən\ *n* [*auto-* self + *regulation*] **:** the maintenance of relative constancy of a physiological process under varying conditions by an organ or tissue; *esp* **:** the maintenance of a constant supply of blood to an organ in spite of varying arterial pressure ⟨the influence of vasoactive agents on *autoregulation* of renal flow —P.C. Johnson *et al*⟩ — **au·to·reg·u·la·tive** \-¦regyə‚lād·iv, -yələd--, -ēv\ *adj* — **au·to·reg·u·la·to·ry** \-¦regyələ‚tȯrē, -‚tȯr-, -i\ *adj*

au·to·route \ˈȯd·ə‚rüt, -d·ō-, ˈäd--; F ȯtȯrüt, ō-\ *n* [F, fr. *auto* automobile (fr. *automobile*) + *route* road] **:** a high‐speed multilane motor road in France

au·to·stra·da \‚aùd·ō¹strädə, ‚ȯd--\ *n, pl* **-stra·das** *or* **-stra·de** \-äd(‚)ā\ [It, fr. *auto*mobile automobile (fr. F) + *strada* street, fr. LL *strata* paved road] **:** a high-speed multilane motor road first developed in Italy

au·to·work·er \ˈȯd·ə‚wərkər, -‚wōkə(r, -‚wȯik-\ *n* [*auto* automobile + *worker*] **:** a person employed in the automobile manufacturing industry

auxo·troph \ˈȯksə‚trȯf, -äf\ *n* **:** an auxotrophic strain or individual

auxo·tro·phic \ˌȯksə¹trȯfik, -äf-\ *adj* [*auxo-* growth (fr. Gk, fr. *auxein* to increase) + *-trophic* relating to nutrition, deriv. of Gk *trephein* to nourish] **:** requiring a specific growth substance beyond the minimum required for normal metabolism and reproduction of the parental or wild-type strain ⟨*auxotrophic* mutants of bacteria⟩ — **aux·ot·ro·phy** \ȯk¹sätrəfē\ *n*

avale·ment \ávál(ə)mäⁿ\ *n* [F, lit., swallowing, fr. *avaler* to lower, swallow, fr. MF] **:** the technique of allowing the knees to flex and thus absorb bumps when skiing and turning at high speed so that the skis will remain in constant contact with the snow

aversion*n **:** a tendency to extinguish a behavior or to avoid a thing or situation and esp. a usu. pleasurable one because it is or has been associated with a noxious stimulus ⟨conditioning of food *aversions* by drug injection⟩

aversion therapy *n* **:** therapy intended to change habits or antisocial behavior by inducing a dislike for them through association with a noxious stimulus

aver·sive*\ə¹vərsiv, -¹vōs-, -¹vəis-, -ziv\ *adj* **:** tending to avoid or causing avoidance of a noxious or punishing stimulus ⟨behavior modification by *aversive* stimulation⟩ — **aver·sive·ly** \-lē, -li\ *adv*

av·go·lem·o·no \‚ävgō¹lemə(‚)nō\ *n* [NGk *augolemono,* fr. *augon* egg + *lemonion* lemon] **:** a soup made of chicken stock, rice, egg yolks, and lemon juice

aviator glasses *n pl* **:** eyeglasses having a lightweight metal frame and usu. tinted lenses

avoidance*n **:** an anticipatory response undertaken to avoid a noxious stimulus ⟨conditioned *avoidance* in mice⟩

avoidance–avoidance conflict *n* **:** psychological conflict that results when a choice must be made between two undesirable alternatives — compare APPROACH‐APPROACH CONFLICT, APPROACH-AVOIDANCE CONFLICT

avoid·ant \ə¹vȯid^ənt\ *adj* **:** characterized by turning away or by withdrawal or defensive behavior ⟨the *avoid‐ant* detached schizophrenic patient —Norman Cameron⟩

AWACS \ˈā‚waks\ *n, pl* **AWACS** [*airborne warning and control system*] **:** a long-range military surveillance system contained in an airplane

ax*or **axe***n **:** any of several musical instruments (as a guitar or a saxophone) ⟨these cats were blowing their horns, their *axes,* whatever they had —Claude Brown⟩

aya·tol·lah \‚īə¹tōlə, -¹tälə, -¹tələ, ¹īə‚t-; ‚īə·tə¹lä\ *n* [Per, lit., sign of God, fr. Ar *ayat* sign, miracle + *allāh* God] **:** a religious leader among Shiite Muslims — used as a title of respect esp. for one who is not an imam

aza·thi·o·prine \‚azə¹thīə‚prēn, -əprən\ *n* [*aza-* containing nitrogen in place of carbon + *thio-* containing sulfur + *purine*] **:** a purine antimetabolite $C_9H_7N_7O_2S$ that is used esp. to suppress antibody production

azin·phos·meth·yl \‚āz^ən(‚)fäs¹methəl, ‚az-\ *n* [*azine* + *phos*phorus + *methyl*] **:** an organophosphorus pesticide $C_{10}H_{12}N_3O_3PS_2$ used against insects and mites

azy·gog·ra·phy \ˈā(‚)zī¹gägrəfē, ə‚zī¹gäg-\ *n* [ISV *azygo*azygous + *-graphy* representation] **:** roentgenographic visualization of the azygous system of veins after injection of a radiopaque medium

B

bab·ka \'bäbkə, 'bab-\ *n* [Pol *babka* old woman, grandmother] **:** a glazed sweet bread made with dried fruit (as raisins)

baby boom *n* **:** a marked rise in birthrate (as in the U.S.) immediately following the end of World War II

baby–sit*vi **-sat; -sit·ting :** to stay with and care for any offspring ⟨the male *baby-sits,* uncovering the eggs if the mound gets too hot —*Nat'l Geographic World*⟩ ~ *vt* **:** to stay with and look after the welfare of ⟨*baby-sit* the children⟩

bach·e·lor·ette \ˌbach(ə)lə'ret\ *n* [*bachelor* + *-ette,* fem. dim. suffix] **:** a young unmarried woman

back*vt **:** to provide a musical accompaniment for ⟨hired a band to *back* him for his dates⟩ — often used with *up* ⟨a song is categorized as "country" if it is *backed* up with a steel guitar —Robert Windeler⟩

back·beat \'bak,bēt\ *n* [*background* + *beat*] **:** a steady pronounced rhythm that is the characteristic driving force esp. of rock music ⟨using the band to construct a heavy *backbeat* dance pattern to complement the vocalist —Gary Von Tersch⟩

back burner *n* [fr. the custom of allowing food to simmer on the back burner of a stove] **:** the condition of being out of active consideration or development ⟨directed the board to put on a *back burner* follow-up studies —Dan Berger⟩ ⟨*back burner* projects⟩

back forty *n* **:** a remote and uncultivated or undeveloped piece of land of indefinite size (as on a farm)

back·ground·er \'bak,graùndə(r)\ *n* **:** an informal off-the-record news conference in which a government official provides reporters with background information on a particular government policy or action ⟨detailed *backgrounders* . . . a useful tool for informally clarifying policy —*Newsweek*⟩

back judge *n* **:** a football official whose duties include keeping the official time and identifying eligible pass receivers

back·lash\'bak,lash\ *n* **:** a strong adverse reaction (as to a recent political or social development) ⟨a national white *backlash* in which the aspirations of blacks are meeting increased resistance —Wayne King⟩ ⟨the threat of an "English *backlash*" against the Quebec people — Bruce Hutchison⟩ ⟨a major American involvement could have stirred new *backlashes* of anti-Semitism —J.A. Wechsler⟩

back·mark·er \'bak,märkər, -,màkə(r\ *n* **:** an also-ran

back of beyond *chiefly Brit* **:** an extremely remote place; *esp* **:** the outback of Australia

back·pack·er \'bak,pakə(r)\ *n* **:** a person who backpacks

back–street \,bak(,)strēt\ *adj* **:** done or made surreptitiously ⟨the terror, abuse and loneliness of her *back-street* abortion —Mary F. Hoyt⟩ ⟨*back-street* amours⟩

back·up\'bak,əp\ *n* **:** one that serves as a substitute or alternative ⟨the second spacecraft would be a *backup* in case of failure⟩

back·up \,bak,əp\ *adj* **1 :** serving as a backup ⟨most systems in the Apollo spacecraft have *backup* systems in case of failure —*Science News*⟩ ⟨present the *backup* data for inspection upon request —*Area Development*⟩ **2 :** serving as an accompaniment ⟨records as a soloist with *backup* musicians —Ellen Sander⟩

back·wrap \'bak,rap\ *n* **:** a wraparound garment (as a skirt) designed so that the ends of the garment are at the back

bac·te·rio·cin \bak'tirēəsən\ *n* [ISV *bacteri*um + connective *-o-* + *-cin* (as in *colicin*)] **:** an antibacterial agent (as colicin) produced by bacteria

bac·te·rio·rho·dop·sin \bak,tirēərō'däpsən\ *n* [ISV *bacterio-* + *rhodopsin*] **:** a purple-pigmented protein that is found in the outer membrane of a bacterium (*Holobacterium halobium*) and converts light energy into chemical energy in the synthesis of ATP

bad*adj **bad·der; bad·dest** *slang* **:** very good **:** great ⟨one of the *baddest* songwriters to be found anywhere — *Black Collegian*⟩

bad·ass \,bad,as\ *adj* [*bad* + *-ass,* an intensive] *slang* **:** ready and willing to cause or get into trouble ⟨down on the ground in a great big ring lived a *badass* lion who knew he was king —*The Signifying Monkey*⟩ ⟨pretending to be a *badass* gunslinger —L.L. King⟩ — sometimes used as a term of approval — **badass** *n, slang*

bad–mouth \'bad,maùth, -,th\ *vt* **:** to criticize severely **:** make disparaging remarks about ⟨a former patient *bad-mouthing* him in an office across town —M. L. Stein⟩

bad news *n pl but sing in constr* **:** a troublesome situation or person ⟨a roll-over accident in a topless car is . . . *bad news* —W. K. Stevens⟩ ⟨a loner, and *bad news* for the women who find him attractive —Vance Bourjaily⟩

baf·fle·gab \'bafəl,gab\ *n* [*baffle,* n. + *gab* talk] **:** pretentiously unintelligible language **:** gobbledygook ⟨solemn gibberish in the approved educationist *bafflegab* — Douglas Form⟩ ⟨that bastion of *bafflegab,* the federal bureaucracy —Joan Melloan⟩

bag*n **1 :** frame or state of mind ⟨when a person acts stupidly, he is "in his stupid *bag*" —Junius Griffin⟩ **2 :** something suited to one's taste **:** something one likes or does well **:** specialty ⟨hasn't been my *bag* so far, but I'm a very dedicated actor —Dick Van Dyke⟩ **3 a :** an individual's typical way of life ⟨can't expect people who are in another *bag* to accept my *bag* —Jerry Rubin⟩ **b :** a characteristic manner of expression ⟨more than any other singer in the soul *bag* — Albert Goldman⟩ **4 :** something that frustrates or impedes **:** HANG-UP **5 :** a small packet of a narcotic drug (as heroin or marijuana)

bag lady *n* **:** SHOPPING-BAG LADY

bag·wash \'bag,wäsh\ *n, Brit* **:** clothes or linens to be washed; *esp* **:** wet wash

Ba·ha·sa In·do·ne·sia \bə,häsə,ində'nēzhə, -ēshə, -ēzēə, -ēsēə\ *n* [Indonesian *bahasa indonésia,* fr. *bahasa* lan-

guage (fr. Skt *bhāsā,* fr. *bhāsate* he speaks; akin to Gk *phanai* to say) + *indonésia* Indonesian, fr. *Indonesia,* republic in Malay archipelago) : the Malay dialect that is the national language of the Republic of Indonesia
bailout*n* : the rescue of a business and esp. a large corporation from financial difficulty by government aid ⟨massive Government *bailouts* of big businesses —*Time*⟩
bail out *vi* [*bail* escape + *out*] **1** : to back away from a pitch in baseball **2** : to jump off a surfboard or skis in order to avoid an accident **3** : to go away : leave, depart ⟨some guests *bailed out* early —Laura Stevenson⟩
bait and switch *n* : a sales tactic in which a customer is attracted by the advertisement of a low-priced item but is then encouraged to buy a higher-priced one
Ba·jan \'bājən\ *n* [fr. *Barbadian,* by shortening & alter.] : a native or inhabitant of Barbados
Ba·ker–Nunn camera \,bākə(r)'nən-\ *n* [James G. *Baker* b1914 & Joseph *Nunn,* Am. optical designers] : a large camera for tracking earth satellites
bake sale *n* : a fund-raising event at which homemade foods (as cakes and cookies) are offered for sale
BAL \,be,ā'el\ *n* [basic assembly *l*anguage] : a generalized assembly language for programming a computer with a small memory
Balinese*n* : a domestic cat of a breed that originated as a spontaneous mutation of the Siamese and is identical to it in type and in coat and eye color but has a long silky coat and plumelike tail
ball*vt* [*ball* testis] : to have sexual intercourse with ⟨bachelor who wanders through life *balling* various chicks —Gene Lees⟩ ⟨she was inevitably treated as a high-class groupie and was expected to *ball* visiting dignitaries —William Kloman⟩ — often considered vulgar
ball control *n* : an offensive strategy (as in football or basketball) in which a team tries to maintain possession of the ball for extended periods of time
ball game*n* **1** : a set of circumstances : situation ⟨letter answering is a whole new *ball game* —Goodman Ace⟩ **2** : a contest or competition ⟨the big powers will have to play the decisive role.... It's a U.S.-Soviet *ball game* — G.S. Wills⟩
ball of wax : a vaguely specified set of objects or circumstances ⟨will you go to the file safe, please, get the whole *ball of wax,* and lay it out here —*New Yorker*⟩ ⟨knows who's having troubles, who's sleeping with who, the whole *ball of wax* —Grover Lewis⟩
¹ball·park \'bȯl,pärk, -,påk\ *n* : a range (as of prices, views, or capabilities) within which comparison or compromise is possible ⟨the views of the two sides are being brought closer.... We are in the same general *ballpark* —H.A. Kissinger⟩ ⟨price of $3500 puts it in the same *ballpark* —*Datamation*⟩ —**in the ballpark** : approximately correct
²ballpark *adj* : approximately correct ⟨a 20 percent increase would be a good *ballpark* figure —H. L. Mac Odrum⟩
balls *n pl* : courage, guts —often considered vulgar ⟨don't have enough *balls* to try out their new material in front of a real audience —*East Village Other*⟩
ballsy \'bȯlzē, -zi\ *adj* **balls·i·er; -est** [*balls* (pl. of *ball* testis) + -*y,* adj. suffix] : aggressively tough : gutsy ⟨a *ballsy* little guy, and ... the most perfect writer of my generation —Norman Mailer⟩ ⟨movie where I play a

sexy, *ballsy,* gutsy adventuress who makes her way any way she can —Elizabeth Ashley⟩
bal·lute \bə'lüt, 'ba,lüt\ *n* [*bal*loon + para*chute*] : a small inflatable parachute for stabilization and deceleration of a jumper or object before the conventional parachute opens
bal mu·sette \,bȧlmūēzet\ *n* [F, bagpipe dance] : a French dance hall with an accordion band
Bal·ti·more chop \'bȯltə,mō(ə)r-, -,mȯ(ə)r-, -mər-\ *n* [so called fr. its perfection by the Baltimore baseball team of the 1890s] : a batted ball in baseball that usu. bounces too high for an infielder to make a putout at first base
ba·nal·ize \bə'näl,īz, -'nȧl-; bə'nal, ba-, bā-; 'bān°l-\ *vt* -**ized; -iz·ing** [*banal* + -*ize,* vb. suffix] : to make banal ⟨*banalized* the art ... by mass-producing a few popular designs —Bernard Leach⟩
ba·nan·as \bə'nanəz\ *adj* : crazy ⟨spelling the English language drives everyone *bananas* —G. H. Poteet⟩
banana seat *n* : an elongated bicycle saddle that often has an upward-curved back
bananas Fos·ter \-'fȯstə(r), -'fȧs-\ *n pl but sing in constr* [prob. fr. the name *Foster*] : a dessert of bananas flamed (as with rum) and served with ice cream
band–aid \'ban,dād\ *adj* [fr. *Band-Aid,* a trademark] : serving as a temporary or expedient remedy or solution ⟨lawyers were ... engaged in a *band-aid* operation, but even on a remedial basis were frequently unable to give effective representation —J.E. Carlin⟩
B and B *abbr* bed and breakfast
B and D *n* [bondage *and d*iscipline] : sadomasochistic practices
B and E *abbr* breaking and entering
band razor *n* : a safety razor with a cartridge that contains a narrow single-edged band of steel which may be advanced just enough to expose a new surface
bang·er \'baŋə(r)\ *n* **1** [prob. fr. the noise sausages often make while frying] *Brit* : a sausage ⟨*bangers* and mash⟩ **2** *Brit* : a firecracker **3** *Brit* : a noisy dilapidated automobile
bankable*adj* : sure to bring in a profit ⟨only one *bankable* female star whose name can guarantee financing of a movie —Judy Klemesrud⟩
bank·card \'baŋk,kärd, -,kȧd\ *n* : a credit card issued by a bank
bankers' hours *n pl* : short working hours
banquet lamp *n* : a tall elaborate kerosene table lamp
Ban·tu·stan \,ban-(,)tü,stan, 'bantə,s-, ,bän-(,)tü,stän\ *n* [*Bantu* + -*stan* land (as in *Hindustan*)] : an all-black enclave in the Republic of South Africa with a limited degree of self-government
barb \'bärb, 'bȧb\ *n, slang* : a barbiturate
Bar·ce·lo·na chair \'bärsə,lōnə-\ *n* [*Barcelona,* Spain, site of the 1929 International Exposition for which the chair was designed] : an armless chair with leather-covered cushions on a stainless steel frame
bar code *n* : a code made up of a group of printed and variously patterned bars and spaces and sometimes numerals that is designed to be scanned and read into computer memory as identification for the object it labels — see UNIVERSAL PRODUCT CODE
Bar·do·li·no \,bärd°l'ēnō, -də'lē-\ *n* [*Bardolino,* village on Lake Garda, Italy] : a light dry red Italian wine

barf \'bärf, 'báf\ *vi* [origin unknown] **:** to throw up **:** vomit — **barf** *n*

bar·gel·lo \bär'jelō\ *n* [fr. the *Bargello*, museum in Florence, Italy; fr. the use of this stitch in the upholstery of 17th cent. chairs at the Bargello] **:** a needlepoint stitch that produces a zigzag pattern

bar girl *n* **1 :** a barmaid **2 :** a prostitute who frequents bars **3 :** a B-girl

bar·iat·rics \‚barē'a·triks\ *n pl but sing in constr* [*bar-* weight (fr. Gk *baros*) + *-iatrics* medical treatment, deriv. of Gk *iatros* physician] **:** a branch of medicine that deals with the treatment of obesity — **bar·iat·ric** \-ik\ *adj* — **bar·ia·tri·cian** \-ēə-'trishən\ *n*

bar mitz·vah \(')bär'mitsvə, (')bá'm-, -(‚)vä\ *vt* **bar mitz·vahed; bar mitz·vah·ing** *often cap B&M* **:** to administer the ceremony of bar mitzvah to

barn sale *n* **:** GARAGE SALE

Ba·ro·lo \bä'rō(‚)lō, bə-\ *n* [*Barolo*, village in the Piedmont region, Italy] **:** a dry red Italian wine

baro·re·cep·tor \‚barōrə‚'septə(r), -ōrē‚-\ *also* **bar·o·cep·tor** \'barō‚s-\ *n* [*baro-* weight, pressure + *receptor*] **:** a neural receptor (as of the arterial walls) sensitive to changes in pressure

Barr body \'bär-, 'bá-\ *n* [Murray Llewellyn *Barr* b1908 Canad. anatomist] **:** material from the inactivated X chromosome that is present in each somatic cell of most mammals and is used as a test of genetic femaleness (as in a fetus or an athlete) — called also *sex chromatin*

Bar·tók·ian \‚bär'täkyən, -tók-, -kēən\ *adj* [Béla *Bartók* †1945 Hung. composer] **:** of, relating to, or suggestive of Béla Bartók or his musical compositions ⟨stressing a flowing line rather than the usual *Bartókian* percussiveness —D.J. Henahan⟩

bar·ware \'bär‚wa(ə)r, -‚we(ə)r; 'bá‚waə(r, -weə(r\ *n* **:** glassware or utensils used in serving alcoholic beverages

bary·on \'barē‚än, -ēən\ *n* [ISV *bary-* (fr. Gk *barys* heavy) + *-on* elementary particle, fr. *ion*] **:** any of a group of elementary particles (as nucleons) that undergo strong interactions and are held to be a combination of three quarks — **bary·on·ic** \‚barē'änik\ *adj*

baryon number *n* **:** a number equal to the number of baryons minus that of antibaryons in a system of elementary particles

base* *n* **1 :** a number that is calculated by a rate or of which a percentage or fraction is calculated ⟨to find the interest on $90 at 10% multiply the *base* 90 by .10⟩ **2 :** a price level at which a security previously actively declining in price resists further price decline **3 :** a point to be considered ⟨is covering . . . detailed material and is trying to touch every *base* —R.L. Tobin⟩

base exchange *n* **:** a post exchange on a naval or an air force base

base pair *n* **:** one of the pairs of chemical bases composed of a purine on one strand of DNA joined by hydrogen bonds to a pyrimidine on the other that hold together the two complementary strands much like the rungs of a ladder and include adenine linked to thymine, adenine linked to uracil, and guanine linked to cytosine

BA·SIC \'bāsik, -zik\ *n* [*B*eginner's *A*ll-purpose *S*ymbolic *I*nstruction *C*ode] **:** a simplified language for programming and interacting with a computer

basi·lect \'bazə‚lekt, 'bāzə-, -sə-\ *n* [*basi-* base, lower part (fr. L *basis*) + *-lect* (as in *dialect*)] **:** the least prestigious dialect of a community — compare ACROLECT

basis* *n* **:** a set of linearly independent vectors in a vector space such that any vector in the vector space can be expressed as a linear combination of them with appropriately chosen coefficients

basket* *n* **1** *slang* **:** male genitalia **2 :** a ring around the lower end of a ski pole that keeps the pole from sinking too deep in snow

basket case* *n* **:** one that is totally worn-out, incapacitated, or inoperable ⟨dad's a *basket case* by the time he gets out to Yellowstone from the East —Harold Graham⟩ ⟨reveal the Northeast to be an economic *basket case* —Michael Kramer⟩ ⟨many models end up emotional *basket cases* —Gwen Kinkead⟩

bass–ack·ward \‚bas‚akwə(r)d, *sometimes in NE* -əs-\ *or* **bass–ack·wards** \-dz\ *adv (or adj)* [anagram for *ass≠ backward*] **:** in a backward or inept way ⟨you're looking at it all *bass-ackwards* —James Jones⟩

batch* *n* **:** a group of jobs to be run on a computer at one time with the same program ⟨*batch* processing⟩

ba·tracho·tox·in \bə-‚trakə'täksən, ‚ba-trəkō-\ *n* [ISV *batracho-* (fr. Gk *batrachos* frog) + *toxin*] **:** a very powerful steroid venom $C_{31}H_{42}N_2O_6$ extracted from the skin of a South American frog (*Phyllobates aurotaenia*)

battered child syn·drome \-'sin‚drōm, *also* -'sindɪəm\ *n* **:** the complex of grave physical injuries (as fractures, hematomas, and contusions) that results from gross abuse (as by a parent) of a young child

baud* \'bȯd, 'bod\ *n, pl* **baud** *also* **bauds :** a variable unit of data transmission speed usu. equal to one bit per second

Baud·e·lair·ean *also* **Baud·e·lair·ian** \‚bōd'lerēən, ‚bōdᵊl'er-\ *adj* [Charles Pierre *Baudelaire* †1867 Fr. poet] **:** of, relating to, or characteristic of Baudelaire or his writings

Bayes·ian \'bāzēən, 'bäzhən\ *adj* [Thomas *Bayes* †1761 Eng. mathematician] **:** being or relating to a theory (as of decision or of statistical inference) in which probabilities are associated with individual events or statements and not merely with sequences of events (as in frequency theories)

ba·zoom \bə'züm\ *n* [prob. alter. of *bosom*] **:** a woman's breast

BBA \‚bē(‚)bē'ā\ *n* **:** a bachelor of business administration

BCD \‚bē(‚)sē'dē\ *n* [*b*inary *c*oded *d*ecimal] **:** a code for representing alphanumeric information (as on magnetic tape)

B cell *n* [*b*one-marrow-derived *cell*] **:** a lymphocyte that reacts to an antigen by producing antibodies against it — compare T CELL

beach bag *n* **:** a capacious bag for carrying articles used at the beach

beach bunny *n* **:** a girl who joins a surfing group but does not engage in surfing

beach·wear \'bēch‚wa(ə)r, -‚we(ə)r, -‚waə, -‚weə\ *n* **:** clothing for wear at the beach

beam·width \'bēm‚width, -‚witth\ *n* **:** the angular diameter of the region adjoining an antenna through which the reception of the signal is best

beans *n pl* **:** exuberance — used in the phrase *full of beans* ⟨we were all pretty full of *beans* about this program — D.P. Moynihan⟩

beat off*vi **:** to masturbate — usu. considered vulgar

beautiful people *n pl, often cap B&P* **:** people who are identified with high society ⟨to this festival came the stars, the magnates, the *beautiful people,* and the crowds of onlookers —Roland Gelatt⟩ ⟨an audience aglow with *Beautiful People,* in their colorful dress and creamy affluence —Irving Howe⟩

beauty contest*n **:** a presidential primary election in which the popular vote does not determine the number of convention delegates a candidate receives

beaver*n [perh. fr. its similarity to a man's beard] **:** the pudenda of a woman — often considered vulgar

bea·ver \'bēvə(r)\ *vi* **bea·vered; bea·ver·ing** \-v(ə)riŋ\ [fr. the proverbial energy of the animal] *chiefly Brit* **:** to work diligently — usu. used with *away* ⟨my subconscious, *beavering* away independently, suddenly came up with that dazzlingly brilliant punch line —*Yorkshire Post*⟩

bed–and–breakfast *adj* **:** offering lodging and breakfast ⟨a *bed-and-breakfast* inn⟩

bed·da·ble \'bedəbəl\ *adj* **:** suitable for taking to bed **:** sexually attractive ⟨tolerated brains in women who were too old to be *beddable* —Peter Quennell⟩

¹bed·dy-bye \'bede'bi\ *n* [baby talk, fr. *bed*] **:** bed, sleep

²beddy–bye *adv* **:** to bed or sleep ⟨the best way to go *beddy-bye* since flannel —*advt*⟩

bed–sit \'bed,sit\ *n, Brit* **:** a bed-sitting-room

bed·so·nia \,bed'sōnēə\ *n* [NL, fr. Samuel P. *Bedson* †1969 Brit. bacteriologist] **1** — used as a taxonomic synonym of the genus *Chlamydia* **2** *pl* **bed·so·ni·ae** \-nē,ī\ **:** any of a group of rickettsias including the causative agents of psittacosis, lymphogranuloma venereum, and trachoma that are now classified in the genus *Chlamydia* of the family Chlamydiaceae

bed·wor·thy \'bed,wərthē, -,wȯth-, -i\ *adj, chiefly Brit* **:** BEDDABLE

beef·alo \'bēfə,lō\ *n, pl* **-alos** *or* **-aloes** [*beef* + buff*alo*] **:** a hybrid between the American buffalo and domestic cattle that is hardier and heavier than the latter and thrives on range grass

beef Bour·gui·gnon \-;'bùr(,)gēn'yōⁿ\ *n* [part trans. of F *boeuf bourguignon,* lit., Burgundian beef] **:** chunks of beef cooked with vegetables in burgundy and often cognac

beef Wel·ling·ton \-'weliŋtən\ *n* [prob. fr. the name *Wellington*] **:** a fillet of beef covered with pâté de foie gras and enclosed in pastry

beehive*n **1 :** a scene of often noisy activity ⟨the sleepy little town is transformed into a *beehive* of hoopla and chaos —Liz Smith⟩ **2 :** a woman's hairdo in a conical shape

beeper*n **:** a portable electronic device used to page the person carrying it that beeps when it receives a special radio signal

beeswax*n **:** business — used chiefly by children in the phrases *mind your own beeswax, none of your beeswax*

beggar's chicken *n* **:** a traditional Chinese dish of marinated and stuffed chicken wrapped in lotus leaves and roasted in a shell of clay

be·hav·ior·al scientist \bə'hāvyərəl-, bē-\ *n* **:** a specialist in behavioral science

behavior therapy *n* **:** psychotherapy that emphasizes the application of the principles of learning to substitute desirable responses and behavior patterns for undesirable ones — called also *behavior modification* — **behavior therapist** *n*

Belgian Ma·li·nois \-,malən'wä\ *n* **:** any of a breed of squarely built working dogs closely related to the Belgian sheepdog and having relatively short straight hair with a dense undercoat

Belgian Ter·vu·ren \-(,)tər'vyùrən, -(,)ter-\ *n* [*Tervuren,* commune in Brabant, Belgium] **:** any of a breed of working dogs closely related to the Belgian sheepdog but having abundant long straight fawn-colored hair with black tips

belle epoque *or* **belle époque** \,belā'pòk\ *n* [F *belle époque* beautiful age] **:** a period that represents the height of artistic or cultural development (as for a society); *specif* **:** the period in France around the turn of the century

bells \'belz\ *n pl* [short for *bell bottoms*] **:** pants with wide flaring bottoms

bel·ly·board \'belē,bō(ə)rd, -li-, -,bȯ(ə)rd, -ōəd, -ȯəd\ *n* [fr. the prone position of the rider] **:** a small buoyant board usu. less than three feet long that is used in surf riding

belly dancer *n* **:** one who performs a belly dance — **belly dance** *vi*

bel·ly-up \,belē'əp, -li-\ *adj* **:** done for; *esp* **:** bankrupt ⟨twelve thousand businesses have gone *belly-up* this year — L. A. Iacocca⟩

belt·ed–bi·as tire \,beltəd'bīəs-\ *n* **:** a pneumatic tire with a hooplike belt of cord or steel around the tire underneath the tread and on top of the ply cords laid at an acute angle to the center line of the tread

be·me·gride \'bemə,grīd, -ēm-\ *n* [*be*ta + *e*thyl + *m*ethyl + *g*lutaric acid + im*ide*] **:** an analeptic drug $C_8H_{13}NO_2$ used esp. to counteract the effect of barbiturates

¹bench·mark \'bench,märk, -,màk\ *n* **:** something that serves as a standard by which others may be measured ⟨economic *benchmarks,* including business loans, auto, steel and oil production and the money supply — *Newsweek*⟩; *esp* **:** a standardized problem by which computer systems or programs may be compared

²benchmark *vt* **:** to test (as a computer system) by a benchmark problem

Benedict's solution \,benə,dik(t)(s)-\ *n* [Stanley Rossiter *Benedict* †1936 Am. chemist] **:** a blue solution containing sodium carbonate, sodium citrate, and cupric sulfate which yields a red, yellow, or orange precipitate upon warming with a reducing sugar (as glucose or maltose)

Be·nin \bə'nin, -'nēn; 'benən\ *adj* **:** of or relating to Benin **:** of the kind or style prevalent in Benin

Ben·ning·ton \'beniŋtən\ *or* **Bennington ware** *also* **Bennington pottery** *n* **:** ceramic ware including earthenware, stoneware, and Parian ware produced at Bennington, Vt.; *esp* **:** earthenware with brown or mottled glaze

ben·o·myl \'benə,mil, -nō,-\ *n* [*benz*- containing benzine + connective *-o-* + *-myl* (by shortening & alter. fr. *methyl*)] **:** a derivative $C_{14}H_{18}N_4O_3$ of carbamate and benzimidazole used as a systemic fungicide on agricultural crops and ornamental plants

bent*adj **1** *slang* **:** different from what is normal or usual: as **a** *chiefly Brit* **:** dishonest, corrupt ⟨[the] role is wider than that of a basically straight guy making it in an unrepentantly *bent* world —*Times Lit. Supp.*⟩ **b :** eccentric, crazy ⟨she was so out of line, she was so *bent* that she's probably a woman who ought to be locked up somewhere —Robert Redford⟩ **c :** homosexual **2** *slang* **:** extremely upset or angry — often used in the phrase *bent out of shape*

ben·zo·di·az·e·pine \ˌbenzō͵dīˈazəˌpēn, -əpən\ *n* [*benzo-* containing a benzene ring + *diazep*am + *-ine* chemical substance] **:** any of a group of aromatic lipophilic amines (as diazepam and chlordiazepoxide) that are used as tranquilizers

ben·zo·mor·phan \ˌbenzōˈmȯrˌfan\ *n* [*benzo-* + *-morph*ine + *-an* chemical compound] **:** any of a group of synthetic compounds whose best-known members are analgesics (as phenazocine or pentazocine)

be·rim·bau \bāˈrēⁿ(m)ˌbau̇\ *n* [Pg *berimbau* Jew's harp] **:** a musical instrument of the Indians of Brazil that consists of a gourd resonator and a single string which is struck with a stick

Bering time \ˈbi(ə)riŋ-, ˈbe(ə)r-\ *n* [*Bering* (*sea*)] **:** the time of the 11th time zone west of Greenwich that includes western Alaska and the Aleutian islands

Ber·mu·da petrel \bə(r)ˈmyüdə-, *South also* -müd-\ *n* **:** a brown-and-white earth-burrowing nocturnal bird (*Pterodroma cahow*) formerly abundant in Bermuda but now nearly extinct

Ber·noul·li trial \bə(r)ˈnülē-; ͵bər̄ˈnü(ˌ)ē-, -ˌnü͵yē-\ *n* [Jacques *Bernoulli* †1705 Swiss mathematician] **:** a statistical experiment that has two mutually exclusive outcomes each of which has a constant probability of occurrence

be·som \ˈbēzəm, ˈbiz-, ˈbis-, ˈbəz-\ *n* [origin unknown] **:** a welting or edging around a pocket opening

best boy *n* **:** the chief assistant to the gaffer in motion-picture or television production

best–ef·forts \ˈbestˌefə(r)ts\ *adj, of security underwriting* **:** not involving a firm commitment on the part of an underwriter to take up any unsold shares or bonds of an issue being underwritten

be·ta–ad·ren·er·gic \ˌbād-ə͵adrəˈnərjik, -ˌnōj-, *also* ͵bē-\ *adj* **:** of, relating to, or being a beta-receptor ⟨*beta-adrenergic* blocking action⟩

beta–adrenergic receptor *n* **:** BETA-RECEPTOR

be·ta–block·er \ˈbād-ə͵bläkə(r), *also* ͵bē-\ *n* **:** an agent (as propranolol) that combines with and blocks the activity of a beta-receptor

beta decay *n* **1 :** a radioactive transformation of an atomic nucleus in which the atomic number is increased or decreased by 1 by the simultaneous emission of a beta particle and a neutrino or antineutrino without change in the mass number **2 :** the decay of an unstable elementary particle in which an electron or positron is emitted

beta–en·dor·phin \-enˈdȯrfən\ *n* [*beta* + *endorphin*] **:** an endorphin of the pituitary gland with much greater analgesic potency than morphine that occurs free and as the terminal sequence of 31 amino acids in the polypeptide chain of beta-lipotropin

be·ta–li·po·tro·pin \-͵lipəˈtrōpən, -͵lī-\ *n* [*beta* + *lipotropin*] **:** a lipotropin of the anterior pituitary that contains beta-endorphin as the terminal sequence of 31 amino acids in its polypeptide chain

be·ta·meth·a·sone \-ˈmethə͵zōn, -͵sōn\ *n* [*beta* + *meth*ylprednisolone + *-a-* (arbitary infix)] **:** a potent glucocorticoid $C_{22}H_{29}FO_5$ that is isomeric with dexamethasone and has anti-inflammatory activity

be·ta–ox·i·da·tion \ˈbād-ə-͵äksəˈdāshən, *also* ͵bē-\ *n* **:** stepwise catabolism of fatty acids in which two-carbon fragments are successively removed from the carboxyl end of the chain

beta particle*n **:** an electron or positron ejected from the nucleus of an atom during beta decay; *also* **:** a high-speed electron or positron

be·ta–re·cep·tor \ˈbād-ərə͵septə(r), *also* ˈbē-\ *n* **:** any of a group of receptors on cell membranes that are postulated to exist and to mediate esp. positive cardiac chronotropic and inotropic effects, vasodilation, and inhibition of smooth muscle in the bronchi, myometrium, and intestine primarily on the basis of experimental evidence that chemical antagonists of isoproterenol and epinephrine are relatively effective in blocking these functions and that those of norepinephrine are not — compare ALPHA-RECEPTOR

be·tha·ne·chol \bəˈthānəˌkȯl, -ōl\ *n* [*beth-* (blend of *beta* and *methyl*) + *-ane* carbon compound + *cho*line] **:** a parasympathomimetic agent administered in the form of its chloride $C_7H_{17}ClN_2O_2$ and used esp. to treat gastric and urinary retention

beurre blanc \ˈbər̄ˈblän\ *n* [F, lit., white butter] **:** a butter sauce flavored with vinegar or lemon juice that is usu. served hot with fish

BFA *abbr* bachelor of fine arts

bi \ˈbī\ *adj* **:** bisexual — **bi** *n*

Bi·a·fran \bēˈafrən, bi-, -äf-, -äf-\ *n* [*Biafra,* name assumed by seceding region of Nigeria (1967–1970)] **:** a native or inhabitant of the onetime secessionist Republic of Biafra — **Biafran** *adj*

bi·aly \bēˈälē\ *n, pl* **bialys** [Yiddish, short for *bialystoker,* fr. *bialystoker* of Bialystok, fr. *Białystok,* city in northeast Poland] **:** a flat roll that has a depressed center and is usu. covered with onion flakes

bi·as–belt·ed tire \ˈbīəsˌbeltəd-\ *n* **:** BELTED-BIAS TIRE

biased*adj **1 :** tending to yield or select one outcome more frequently or less frequently than others in a statistical experiment ⟨a *biased* coin⟩ ⟨a *biased* sample⟩ **2 :** having an expected value different from the quantity or parameter estimated ⟨a *biased* estimate⟩ **3 :** not having minimum probability of rejecting the null hypothesis when it is true ⟨a *biased* statistical test⟩

bi·as–ply tire \ˈbīəsˌplī-\ *n* **:** a pneumatic tire having crossed layers of ply cord set diagonally to the center line of the tread

bi·ath·lon \bīˈathlən, -ˌlän \ *n* [*bi-* two (fr. L) + *-athlon* (as in *pentathlon*)] **:** a composite athletic contest consisting of cross-country skiing and rifle sharpshooting

Bibb lettuce \ˈbib-\ *n* [Major John *Bibb,* 19th cent. Am. grower] **:** lettuce of a variety that has a small head and dark green color

Bi·chon Fri·se \bēˈshōⁿfrēˈzā\ *n* [modif. of F *bichon à poil frisé* curly-furred lap dog] **1 :** a breed of small sturdy white dogs of Mediterranean origin having a thick wavy coat and tail curving over the back   **2** *pl* **bichons frises** \-ōⁿ(z)frē'zā(z)\ *often not cap* **:** a dog of the Bichon Frise breed

bi·cu·cul·line \(')bĭ̠'k(y)ükyə̠lēn, -yələn\ *n* [*bi-* + *cucull-* (fr. *Dicentra cucullaria,* species of fungus in which the substance occurs) + *-ine* chemical substance] **:** a convulsant alkaloid $C_{20}H_{17}NO_6$ obtained esp. from plants of the family Fumariaceae and having the capacity to antagonize the action of gamma-aminobutyric acid in the central nervous system

bi·cul·tur·al \'bĭ̠'kəlch(ə)rəl\ *adj* **:** of, relating to, or including two distinct cultures ⟨*bicultural* education⟩ — **bi·cul·tur·al·ism** \-(͵)lizəm\ *n*

bi·di·a·lec·tal \'bī͵dīə̠'lektəl\ *adj* **:** fluent in the use of two dialects of the same language — **bidialectal** *n*

bi·di·a·lec·tal·ism \-tə͵lizəm\ *or* **bi·di·a·lect·ism** \(!)bĭ̠'dīə͵lekt(͵)izəm\ *n* **:** facility in using two dialects of the same language

bi·di·a·lec·tal·ist \'bī͵dīə̠'lektələst\ *n* **:** a person who favors the promotion and development of bidialectalism by schools esp. for speakers whose primary dialects are not standard

bi·don·ville \͵bē͵dōⁿ'vē(ə)l\ *n* [F, fr. *bidon* tin can (fr. MF, canteen, fr. OF, prob. fr. —assumed— ON *bidha* milk jug) + *ville* city, fr. OF, village] **:** a settlement of jerry-built dwellings on the outskirts of a city (as in France or Africa)

big bang *n* **:** the cosmic explosion that marked the beginning of the universe according to the big bang theory

big bang theory *n* **:** a theory in astronomy: the universe originated billions of years ago from the explosion of a single mass of compressed material —compare STEADY STATE THEORY

big beat *n, often cap both Bs* **:** music (as rock 'n' roll) characterized by a heavy persistent beat

Big C *n* **:** cancer ⟨don't believe in the *Big C* . . . don't believe that smoking is bad for you —John Lennon⟩

big deal *n* **:** one that is of special importance ⟨athletics are always a *big deal* on campus —Patricia Linden⟩

big·foot \'big͵fu̇t\ *n, often cap* [fr. the size of the footprints ascribed to it] **:** SASQUATCH

big one*n **:** a thousand dollars ⟨pulling down 30 *big ones* as an "up-and-coming" vice-president —Howard Anderson⟩

bi·jec·tion \bī'jekshən\ *n* [*bi-* + *-jection* (as in *injection*)] **:** a mathematical function that is a one-to-one and onto mapping — compare INJECTION, SURJECTION — **bi·jec·tive** \-ktiv\ *adj*

bike*n **:** a 2-wheeled automotive vehicle (as a motorcycle or motor bicycle)

biker*n **:** a motorcyclist; *esp* **:** one who belongs to an organized gang

bike·way \'bī͵kwā\ *n* **:** a thoroughfare for bicycles

bi·lay·er \'bĭ̠'lāə(r), -'le(ə)r, -'leə(r\ *n* **:** a film or membrane with two molecular layers ⟨a *bilayer* of phospholipid molecules⟩

bi–lev·el \'bĭ̠'levəl\ *n* **:** a two-story house with the first floor beginning below ground level and divided into two areas by a ground-level entry situated between the stories of the adjoining areas

bil·li·bi *also* **bil·ly–bi** \'bilē͵bē, -lĭ̠'-\ *n* [F, alter. of *Billy B.,* William B. Leeds, Jr. †1972 Am. industrialist; fr. his

partiality for it] **:** a soup made of mussel stock, white wine, and cream and served hot or cold

bi·lo·qui·al·ism \(')bī͵lōkwēə͵lizəm\ *also* **bi·lo·quil·ism** \-kwə̠-\ *n* [*bi-* + *-loquial* (as in *colloquial*) + *-ism*] **:** BIDIALECTALISM

bi·lo·qui·al·ist \-kwēələst\ *n* **:** BIDIALECTALIST

bi·na·ry*\'bīnərē, -ri, *sometimes* -͵ner-\ *adj*   **1** **:** involving a choice or condition of two alternatives only (as on= off or yes-no)   **2** **:** involving binary notation

binary notation *n* **:** expression of a number with a base of 2 using only the digits 0 and 1 with each digital place representing a power of 2 instead of a power of 10 as in decimal notation

bio- \'bīō\ *comb form* [*biological*] **:** being such biologically ⟨the *bio*mother gave up her baby for adoption⟩

bio·ac·cu·mu·la·tion \'bīoə͵kyümyə̠'lāshən\ *n* [*bio-* life, living organisms (fr. Gk, fr. *bios* mode of life) + *accumulation*] **:** the accumulation of a substance (as a pesticide) in a living organism

bio·ac·tiv·i·ty \'bīō(͵)ak͵tivəd·ē, -d·i\ *n* **:** the effect (as of an insecticide) on a living organism — **bio·ac·tive** \'bīō-'aktiv\ *adj*

bio·as·tro·nau·tics \-͵astrə̠'nȯd·iks, -näd--\ *n pl but sing or pl in constr* **:** the medical and biological aspect of astronautics — **bio·as·tro·nau·ti·cal** \-lkəl\ *adj*

bio·au·tog·ra·phy \͵bīōȯ'tägrəfē\ *n* **:** the identification or comparison of organic compounds separated by chromatography by means of their effect on living organisms and esp. microorganisms — **bio·au·to·graph** \-'ȯd--ə͵graf\ *n* — **bio·au·to·graph·ic** \'bīō͵ȯd-ə̠'grafik\ *adj*

bio·avail·abil·i·ty \'bīōə͵vālə̠'biləd·ē, -d·i\ *n* **:** the degree and rate at which a substance (as a drug) is absorbed into a living system or is made available at the site of physiological activity

bio·cid·al \'bīə̠'sīd^l\ *adj* [*bio-* + *-cidal* killing, deriv. of L *caedere* to cut, kill] **:** destructive to life ⟨*biocidal* temperature effects⟩ ⟨*biocidal* compounds⟩

bio·clean \'bīō͵klēn\ *adj* **:** free or almost free of harmful or potentially harmful organisms (as bacteria) ⟨a *bioclean* room⟩

bio·crit·i·cal \'bīō͵krid·ikəl\ *adj* **:** of, relating to, or being a study of the life and work of someone (as a writer or moviemaker)

bio·de·grad·able \'bīōdə̠'grādəbəl\ *adj* **:** capable of being broken down esp. into innocuous products by the action of living beings (as microorganisms) ⟨*biodegradable* detergents⟩ — **bio·de·grad·abil·i·ty** \-͵grā-də̠'biləd-ē\ *n* — **bio·deg·ra·da·tion** \-͵degrə̠'dāshən\ *n* — **bio·de·grade** \-də̠'grād, -dē̠'-\ *vb*

bio·elec·tro·gen·e·sis \'bīōə̠͵lektrə̠'jenəsəs, -ōē͵l-\ *n* **:** the production of electricity by living organisms

bio·elec·tron·ics \'bīōə̠(͵)lek'träniks\ *n pl but sing in constr*   **1** **:** a branch of the life sciences that deals with electronic control of physiological function esp. as applied in medicine to compensate for defects of the nervous system   **2** **:** a branch of science that deals with the role of electron transfer in biological processes — **bio·elec·tron·ic** \-ik\ *adj*

bio·en·gi·neer·ing*\'bīō͵enjə̠'ni(ə)riŋ\ *n* **:** the application to biological or medical science of engineering principles (as the theory of control systems in models of the nervous system) or engineering equipment (as in the construction of artificial organs) — **bio·en·gi·neer** \-ˌni(ə)r, -iə(r\ *n*

bio·en·vi·ron·men·tal \ˌbīōənˈvīrənˌmentᵊl, -(ˌ)enˈv-, -ī(ə)rnˈ-\ *adj* **:** concerned with the environment and esp. with deleterious factors in the environment of living beings

bio·eth·ics \-ˈethiks\ *n pl but usu sing in constr* **:** the discipline dealing with the ethical implications of biological research and applications esp. in medicine — **bio·eth·ic** \-ik\ *n* — **bio·eth·i·cal** \-əkəl\ *adj* — **bio·eth·i·cist** \-əsəst\ *n*

bio·feed·back \-ˈfēdˌbak\ *n* **:** the technique of making unconscious or involuntary bodily processes (as heartbeat or brainwaves) perceptible to the senses (as by use of an oscilloscope) in order to manipulate them by conscious mental control

bio·gas \-ˈgas\ *n* **:** a mixture of gases that is composed mostly of methane and carbon dioxide and is produced by the bacterial decomposition of animal and vegetable wastes

bio·ce·nose or **bio·geo·coe·nose** \ˌbīōˈjēōsəˌnōz, -nōs\ *n* [Russ *biogeotsenoz*, fr. NL *bio-* + *geo-* earth (deriv. of Gk *gē*) + *-coenosis*, deriv. of Gk *koinōsis* sharing, fr. *koinos* common] **:** BIOGEOCOENOSIS

bio·geo·coe·no·sis or **bio·geo·ce·no·sis** \-ˈjēōsəˌnōsəs, -ˌnōˌsēz\ *n, pl* **-no·ses** \-ˌnōˌsēz\ **:** the complex of a community and its environment functioning as an ecological unit in nature **:** ecosystem — **bio·geo·coe·not·ic** \-ˈnädˌik\ *adj*

bio·haz·ard \ˈbīōˌhazə(r)d\ *n* **:** a biological agent or condition (as an infectious organism or insecure laboratory procedures) that constitutes a hazard to man or his environment; *also* **:** a hazard posed by such an agent or condition — **bio·haz·ard·ous** \-əs\ *adj*

bio·in·stru·men·ta·tion \ˈbīōˌin(t)strəmənˈtāshən, -ˌmen-\ *n* **:** the development and use of instruments for recording and transmitting physiological data (as from astronauts in flight); *also* **:** the instruments themselves

biological clock *n* **:** an inherent timing mechanism responsible for various cyclical behaviors and physiological activities of living beings

biomass*n **:** plant materials and animal waste used as a source of fuel

bio·ma·te·ri·al \ˈbīōməˌtirēəl, -ˈtēr-\ *n* **:** material used for or suitable for use in prostheses that come in direct contact with living tissues

bio·med·i·cal \-medəkəl\ *adj* **1 :** of or relating to biomedicine ⟨*biomedical* studies⟩ **2 :** of, relating to, or involving biological, medical, and physical science

biomedical engineering *n* **:** BIOENGINEERING

bio·med·i·cine \-ˈmedəsən, *Brit usu* -ˈmedsən\ *n* **:** a branch of medical science concerned esp. with the capacity of human beings to survive and function in abnormally stressful environments and with the protective modification of such environments

bio·mem·brane \-ˈmemˌbrān\ *n* **:** a membrane either on the surface or in the interior of a cell that is composed of protein and lipid and limits the diffusion and transport of materials

bio·mo·lec·u·lar \-məˈlekyələr\ *adj* **:** of or relating to organic molecules and esp. macromolecules in living organisms

bi·on·ic \(ˈ)bīˈänik\ *adj* [*bio-* + *-onic* (as in *electronic*)] **1 :** of or relating to bionics **2 a :** having natural biological capability or performance enhanced by or as if by electronic or electromechanical devices ⟨our future may lie not with the *bionic* man but with natural man —Susan Schiefelbein⟩ ⟨the canines possess no *bionic* or other superpowers —*Variety*⟩ **b :** better than ordinary **:** super ⟨the developer of this *bionic* tuber . . . admits that it's not the perfect potato —*Saturday Rev.*⟩

bi·on·ics \bīˈäniks\ *n pl but sing in constr* [*bio-* + *-onics* (as in *electronics*)] **:** a branch of science concerned with the application of data about the functioning of biological systems to the solution of engineering problems

bio·or·gan·ic \ˈbīōˌȯ(r)ˈganik\ *adj* **:** of, relating to, or concerned with the organic chemistry of biologically significant substances

bio·phar·ma·ceu·tics \-ˌfärməˈsüdˌiks\ *n pl but sing in constr* **:** the study of the relationships between the physical and chemical properties, the dosage, and the form of administration of a drug and its activity in the living animal — **bio·phar·ma·ceu·ti·cal** \-əkəl\ *adj*

bio·poly·mer \-ˈpäləmə(r)\ *n* **:** a polymeric substance (as a protein or a polysaccharide) formed in a biological system

bio·re·search \-rəˈsərch, -ˈrēˌs-, -sōch, -səich\ *n* **:** research in biological science

bio·rhythm \ˈbīōˌrithəm\ *n* **:** an innately determined rhythmic biological process or function (as sleep behavior); *also* **:** an innate rhythmic determiner of such a process or function — **bio·rhyth·mic** \ˈbīōˌrithmik\ *adj* — **bio·rhyth·mic·i·ty** \-thmisədˈē\ *n*

bio·sat·el·lite \ˈbīōˌsad-ᵊlˌīt, -atᵊlˌit\ *n* **:** an artificial satellite for carrying a living human being, animal, or plant

bio·sci·ence \ˈbīōˌsīən(t)s\ *n* **:** biological science **:** biology; *also* **:** LIFE SCIENCE — **bio·sci·en·tif·ic** \ˈbīōˌsīənˈtifik\ *adj* — **bio·sci·en·tist** \ˈbīōˌsīəntəst\ *n*

bio·sen·sor \ˈbīōˌsenˌsȯ(ə)r, -ˌsen(t)sə(r)\ *n* **:** a device sensitive to a physical stimulus (as heat or a particular motion) and transmitting information about a life process (as of an astronaut)

bio·spe·le·ol·o·gy \ˈbīōˌspēlēˈäləjē, -ˌspel-\ *n* **:** the biological study of cave-dwelling organisms — **bio·spe·le·ol·o·gist** \-əjəst\ *n*

bio·syn·the·size \-ˈsin(t)thəˌsīz\ *vt* **:** to produce by biosynthesis

bio·te·lem·e·try \-təˈlemə·trē\ *n* **:** the remote detection and measurement of a biological function, activity, or condition of a man or animal — **bio·tele·met·ric** \-ˌteləˈmeˌtrik\ *adj*

bio·trans·for·ma·tion \-ˌtran(t)sfə(r)ˈmāshən, -(ˌ)fȯ(r)-\ *n* **:** the transformation of a chemical compound into another compound in a living system

bio·tron \ˈbīəˌträn\ *n* [*bio-* + *-tron* (as in *cyclotron*)] **:** a climate control chamber used to study the effect of specific environmental factors on living organisms

bipolar*adj **:** characterized by the alternation of manic and depressive states ⟨a *bipolar* affective disorder⟩

bi·qui·na·ry \(ˈ)bīˈkwīnərē, -win-\ *adj* [*bi-* two + *quinary* quintuple] **:** of, based on, being, or relating to a mixed-base system of numbers in which each decimal digit *n* is represented as a pair of digits *xy* where *n* = 5*x* + *y* and *x* is written in base 2 as 0 or 1 and *y* is written in base 5 as 0, 1, 2, 3, or 4 〈decimal 9 is represented by *biquinary* 14〉

Birch·er \'bərchər, 'bāchə(r, 'bəichə(r\ *n* [the John *Birch* Society, ultraconservative political organization] **:** a member or adherent of the John Birch Society — **Birch·ism** \-,chizəm\ *n* — **Birch·ist** \-chəst\ *or* **Birch·ite** \-,chīt\ *n or adj*

bird*n **1 :** one that flies (as an airplane, a rocket, a satellite, or a spacecraft) **2 :** an obscene gesture of contempt made by pointing the middle finger upward while keeping the other fingers down — usu. used with *the* 〈some . . . gave the peace sign out of classroom windows, and others gave the *bird* —L.K. Truscott IV〉; called also *finger*

birdy·back also **bird·ie·back** \'bərdē,bak, -əd-, -əid-, -di-\ *n* [*bird* + *-yback* (as in *piggyback*)] **:** the movement of loaded truck trailers by airplane

Birman*n **:** a long-haired domestic cat of a breed originating in Burma and resembling the Siamese in eye color and coat pattern but much stockier in build and with paws symmetrically marked with white

birr \'bi(ə)r\ *n, pl* **birr** also **birrs** [native name in Ethiopia] **1 :** the basic monetary unit of Ethiopia **2 :** a note representing one birr

birth defect *n* **:** a physical or biochemical defect (as cleft palate or phenylketonuria) that is present at birth and may be inherited or environmentally induced

bir·ya·ni also **bir·ia·ni** \bi(ə)r'yänē, ,birē'änē, -i\ *n* [origin unknown] **:** an Indian dish of meat (as lamb or chicken) or vegetables cooked with rice flavored esp. with saffron or turmeric

bis·cot·to \bə'skäd-ō, -ä(,)tō\ *n, pl* **-ti** \-äd-ē, -ä(,)tē, -i\ [It] **:** a crisp cookie or biscuit of Italian origin flavored usu. with anise and filberts

bi·sta·ble \(')bi',stābəl\ *adj* **:** having two stable states 〈a *bistable* electrical element〉 — **bi·sta·bil·i·ty** \',bistə-',hiläd·ē\ *n*

bi·stat·ic \(')bi',stad·ik, -ēk\ *adj* [*bi-* two + *static* stationary] **:** involving the use of a transmitter and receiver at separate locations 〈*bistatic* radar〉

bi·swing \',bi',swiŋ\ *adj* [*bi-* + *swing;* perh. because of the freedom allowed by this garment] *of a coat or jacket* **:** made with a pleat or gusset at the back of the arms to permit more freedom of movement

¹bit*n [*bit* small quantity] **1 :** a characteristic situation, appearance, behavior, or action 〈book burning, unless it's an embassy library, is strictly a Fascist *bit* —Gene Williams〉 〈I never have dates or call up a girl and meet her and take her out, that whole *bit* —Arthur Garfunkle〉 **2 :** an action or mode of behavior likened to a theater role or sketch 〈starts in with one of her crazy lunatic *bits* — Judith Rossner〉 **3 :** subject under consideration **:** matter 〈as for the *bit* about marriage being a woman's be-all and end-all —Letty C. Pogrebin〉 — often used as a general indirect reference to something specified or implied 〈the blouson top . . . matches exactly. The blouson *bit* is piped in suede —Lois Long〉

²bit*n [*bit* unit of computer information] **:** the physical representation (as in a computer tape or memory) of a bit by an electrical pulse, a magnetized spot, or a hole whose presence or absence indicates data

bitch box *n, slang* **:** an intercom

bite*vb — **bite the bullet :** to enter with resignation upon a difficult or distressing course of action 〈someone finally had to *bite the bullet*, and . . . the decision properly went out over my name —R. D. Wood〉

bite plate *n* **:** a dental appliance that is usu. made of plastic and wire, is worn in the palate or sometimes on the lower jaw, and is used in orthodontics and prosthodontics to assist in therapy and diagnosis

bi·unique \',biyü',nēk\ *adj* **:** being a correspondence between two sets that is one-to-one in both directions 〈the *biunique* correspondence between the points on a straight line and the real numbers〉 〈a phonemic transcription should be *biunique*〉 — **bi·unique·ness** \-knəs\ *n*

Bi·zen ware \bē'zen-\ *n* [part trans. of Jp *bizen-yaki*, fr. *Bizen*, former province in Japan, where it was made + Jp *yaki* pottery] **:** a Japanese ceramic ware produced since the 14th century that is typically a dark bronzy stoneware often with smears of natural ash glaze

black*adj **1 :** of or relating to covert intelligence operations **2 :** employed in covert intelligence operations

black**vt, chiefly Brit* **:** to declare (as a business or industry) subject to boycott by trade-union members

¹black belt *n* **1 :** an area characterized by rich black soil **2** *often cap both Bs* **:** an area densely populated by blacks

²black belt *n* [fr. the color of the belt of the uniform worn by the holder of the rating] **1 :** a rating of expert in various arts of self-defense (as judo and karate) **2 :** one who holds a black belt

blackboard jungle *n* **:** an urban school whose students are generally belligerent and disorderly

black box *n* **1 :** a usu. complicated electronic device (as a radar set) that can be inserted in or removed as a unit from a particular place in an assembly (as a spacecraft) **2 :** a usu. electronic device (as a control for a computer) which operates on an input to produce an output but whose internal mechanism is hidden from or mysterious to the user

black comedy *n* [trans. of F *comédie noire*] **:** comedy that employs black humor

Black English *n* **:** the nonstandard dialect of English held to be spoken by many American blacks

black hole *n* **1 :** a hypothetical celestial body with a small diameter and intense gravitational field that is held to be a collapsed star **2 :** one that resembles a black hole (as in absence of light or in invisibility)

black humor *n* [trans. of F *humour noir*] **:** humor marked by the use of usu. morbid, ironic, grotesquely comic episodes — **black–hu·mored** \',blak-',(h)yümə(r)d\ *adj* — **black humorist** *n*

black·light trap \'blak',lit-,trap\ *n* **:** an insect trap using a form of black light for attraction

black lung *n* **:** a disease of the lungs caused by habitual inhalation of coal dust (as by miners) — called also *black lung disease*

black money *n* **:** income (as from gambling) that is not reported to the government for tax purposes 〈the country is full of *black money* in hiding from the tax collectors — Alexander Campbell〉

Black Muslim *n* **:** a member of a chiefly black group that professes Islamic religious belief

black nationalist *n, often cap B&N* **:** one of a group of militant blacks who advocate separatism from whites and the formation of self-governing black communities — **black nationalism** *n, often cap B&N*

blackness*n   **1 :** the aggregate of qualities characteristic of the Negro race   **2 :** NEGRITUDE

Black Panther *n* **:** a member of an organization of militant American blacks

black power *n, often cap B&P* **:** the power of American blacks esp. as applied to the achieving of their political and economic rights

black studies *n pl* **:** studies (as in history and literature) relating to the culture of American blacks

black·town \'blak͵taủn\ *n* **:** the predominantly black section of a city

blahs \'bläz, -ȧz\ *n pl* **:** a feeling of boredom, discomfort, or general dissatisfaction — usu. used with *the* ⟨you're moribund from the late-winter *blahs*. And you feel you must get away for a weekend —Richard Curtis⟩

blast*n   **1 :** an enjoyably exciting occasion or event ⟨have a *blast*⟩; *esp* **:** a party ⟨great beer *blasts* were held on the mountain —Peter Range⟩   **2 :** a home run in baseball ⟨second *blast* into the left centerfield bleachers came with one out in the sixth inning —*Springfield (Mass.) Union*⟩

blast *n* [-*blast* formative unit, deriv. of Gk *blastos* bud, shoot] **:** an immature or imperfectly developed cell — **blastic** *also* **blast** *adj*

blast cell *n* **:** a precursor of a blood cell in the earliest stage of development in which it is recognizably committed to development along a particular cell lineage

blastogenesis*n **:** the transformation of lymphocytes into larger cells capable of undergoing mitosis

blas·to·my·cin \͵blastō'mīs²n\ *n* [*Blastomyces,* genus name + -*in* chemical compound] **:** a preparation of growth products of the causative agent (*Blastomyces dermatitidis*) of No. American blastomycosis that is used esp. to test for this disease

blax·ploi·ta·tion \͵blak͵splói͵tāshǝn\ *n* [blend of *blax* (alter. of *blacks*) and *exploitation*] **:** the exploitation of blacks by producers of black-oriented films

¹bleep \'blēp\ *n* [imit.] **:** a short high-pitched sound (as from electronic equipment)

²bleep *vt* **:** BLIP ⟨a nerve-racking session. We had to keep *bleeping* every other sentence —P.B. Benchley⟩

³bleep *interj* — used in place of an expletive

bleep·er \-ǝ(r)\ *n, chiefly Brit* **:** a device that emits bleep signals

bleo·my·cin \͵blēō'mis²n\ *n* [*bleo*- (of unknown origin) + -*mycin*] **:** a mixture of polypeptide antibiotics derived from a streptomyces (*Streptomyces verticillus*) and used in the form of its sulfate as an antineoplastic agent

bleph·a·ro·plas·ty \'blefǝrō͵plastē, -i\ *n, pl* -ties [*blepharo*- eyelid + -*plasty* plastic surgery] **:** a plastic operation on an eyelid

blind side*\(¹)blīn(d)͵sīd\ *n* **:** the side away from which one is looking

blind·side \'blīn(d)͵sīd\ *vt*   **1 :** to hit from the blind side   **2 :** to strike suddenly and unexpectedly **:** surprise unpleasantly ⟨was *blindsided* by the news of his colleague's disloyalty⟩

blind trust *n* **:** an arrangement by which a person in a sensitive position protects himself from possible conflict of interest charges by placing his financial affairs in the hands of a fiduciary and giving up all right to know about or intervene in their handling

blip*\'blip\ *vt* **blipped; blip·ping :** to remove (recorded sound) from a videotape so that in the received television program there is an interruption in the sound ⟨swearwords *blipped* by a censor⟩ ⟨her dialogue is studded with the kind of language that is *blipped* on TV —Louise A. Sweeney⟩

blister pack *n* **:** a package holding and displaying merchandise in a clear plastic case sealed to a sheet of cardboard

blitz*\'blits\ *n* **:** a rush on a passer in football by the linebackers or safetymen

blitz*vt   **1 :** to rush (a passer) in football from a position as a linebacker or defensive back   **2 :** to order (as a linebacker) to blitz ~ *vi, of a linebacker or defensive back* **:** to make a rush on the passer in football — **blitz·er** \-sǝ(r)\ *n*

block*vt **:** to work out (as the principal positions and movements) for the performers (as of a play) ⟨spent three hours painstakingly reading and rereading lines while *blocking* their stage movements —Melodie Bowsher⟩; *also* **:** to work out the players' positions and movements for (as a scene or play) ⟨*blocked* the play, meticulously moving the characters around the room and through the lines —Mel Gussow⟩ — often used with *out*

block·bust·ing \'bläk͵bǝstiŋ\ *n* **:** profiteering by first inducing white property owners to sell hastily and often at a loss by appeals to fears of depressed values because of threatened minority encroachment and then reselling at inflated prices — **block·bust·er** \'bläk͵bǝstǝ(r)\ *n*

block club *n* **:** an organized group of residents in an urban neighborhood

block grant*n **:** an unrestricted federal grant

block·ing*\'bläkiŋ\ *n* **:** the planning and working out of the principal positions and movements of stage performers (as for a play) ⟨camera shots, musical cues, *blocking,* makeup, costumes and the rest were run through — Robert Jacobson⟩

blood*n **:** a black American — used esp. among blacks

blood–brain barrier *n* **:** a barrier postulated to exist between brain capillaries and brain tissue to explain the relative inability of many substances to leave the blood and cross the capillary walls into the brain tissues

bloom*n **:** an abundant or excessive growth of plankton

bloop*vt **:** to hit (a fly ball) usu. just beyond the infield in baseball ⟨*blooped* a single to center field⟩

bloop \'blüp\ *adj, of a baseball* **:** hit in the air just beyond the infield

blouse*vt **bloused; blous·ing :** to cause to blouse ⟨trousers are *bloused* over the boots⟩ ⟨big, loose shapes (which the fainthearted may *blouse* over a belt) —Anne͌ Marie Shiro⟩

blou·son \'blaủ͵zän, -͵sän, -s²n; 'blü͵zän\ *n* [F, dim. of *blouse* blouse] **:** a woman's garment (as a dress or blouse) having a close waistband with a blousing of material over it

blow*vt **blew; blown; blow·ing**   **1 :** FELLATE— usu. considered vulgar   **2 :** to consume by smoking ⟨a few had started *blowing* grass in their early teens —Daniel Greene⟩ — **blow one's cool :** to lose one's composure — **blow one's cover :** to reveal one's real identity **:** give one's cover away — **blow one's mind**   **1 :** to affect one with intense emotional excitement ⟨a grand guignol floor show that's guaranteed to *blow your mind* —Foster Hirsch⟩ **2 :** to take one by surprise ⟨did *blow my mind* and forced me to think —C.M. Mahon⟩ **3 :** to undergo or cause to undergo a psychedelic experience ⟨heroin really *blew my mind* —Joe Eszterhas⟩

blow*n [perh. fr. *blow* a hit or punch] *slang* **:** cocaine

blow away*vt **1 :** to kill by gunfire **:** shoot dead ⟨death squads would *blow away* a few reporters —Ike Seamans⟩ **2 :** to overwhelm emotionally **:** stun ⟨was *blown away* by her beauty —Fred Bernstein⟩

blow–dry \(')blōˌdrī\ *vt* **:** to dry and usu. style (hair) with a hand-held dryer — **blow–dry** \'blōˌdrī\ *n*

blower**n, Brit* **:** telephone

blow·job \'blōˌjäb\ *n* **:** the act of stimulating the penis orally usu. to orgasm — usu. considered vulgar

BLS \ˌbē(ˌ)el'es\ *n* **1 :** a bachelor of liberal studies **2 :** a bachelor of library science

BLT \ˌbē(ˌ)el'tē\ *n* **:** a bacon, lettuce, and tomato sandwich

blue flu *n* [fr. the color of a police uniform] **:** a sick-out staged by policemen; *broadly* **:** SICK-OUT

bluegrass*n [fr. the *Blue Grass Boys*, performing group, fr. *Bluegrass State*, nickname of Kentucky] **:** country music played on unamplified stringed instruments (as banjo, fiddle, guitar, and mandolin) and characterized by free improvisation and close usu. high-pitched harmony

blue heaven *n, slang* **:** amobarbital or its sodium derivative in a blue tablet or capsule

blue shift *n* **:** the displacement of the spectrum of an approaching celestial body toward shorter wavelengths

blues·man \'blüzmən, -ˌman\ *n* **:** one who plays or sings the blues

blues–rock \'blüzˌräk\ *n* **:** blues sung to a rock 'n' roll background

blue stellar object \-ˌstelər-\ *n* **:** any of various blue celestial bodies that do not emit appreciable radio waves

bluesy \'blüzē, -i\ *adj* [*blues* + *-y* characteristic of] **:** characterized by the musical patterns of the blues

blush·er*n \'bləshə(r)\ *n* **:** a cosmetic applied to the face to give a usu. pink color or to accent the cheekbones

B lym·pho·cyte \'bēˌlim(p)fəˌsīt\ *n* [bone-marrow-derived *lymphocte*] **:** B CELL

BM*n **:** a bachelor of music

BME \ˌbē(ˌ)em'ē\ *n* **1 :** a bachelor of mechanical engineering **2 :** a bachelor of mining engineering **3 :** a bachelor of music education

board*n **1 :** a blackboard **2 a boards** *pl* **:** the low wooden wall enclosing a hockey rink **b :** a basketball backboard — usu. used in pl. **c :** a surfboard **3 :** a sheet of insulating material carrying circuit elements and terminals so that it can be inserted in an electronic apparatus — **on board*:** in or into a working relationship — **on the boards :** in or into stage production

boa·tel \(')bō'tel\ *n* [blend of *boat* and *hotel*] **:** a waterside hotel equipped with docks to accommodate persons traveling by boat

boat people *n pl* **:** refugees fleeing by boat

bob*n **:** SKIBOB

bob·bing \'bäbiŋ\ *n* [*bob* bobsled] **:** the act or sport of riding a bobsled or skibob

bo·cage*\bō'käzh\ *n* **:** a supporting and ornamental background (as of shrubbery and flowers) for a ceramic figure

bod*\'bäd\ *n* **:** the body of a human being ⟨you can't even figure out what to put on your *bod* —Cyra McFadden⟩ ⟨various means to unkink the *bod* —Catherine Breslin⟩ ⟨this great-looking doll with a fine *bod* —F.P. Tullius⟩ ⟨in Rome let it be brain over *bod* —Roberta Ashley⟩

body bag *n* **:** a zippered bag (as of rubber) in which a human corpse is placed (as for transportation)

body builder *n* **:** one who engages in body building

body building *n* **:** the developing of the body through physical exercises and diet; *specif* **:** the developing of the physique for competitive exhibition

body checker *n* **:** one that body checks

body-clothes \'bädēˌklō(th)z, -di-\ *n pl* **:** close-fitting garments (as shirts or dresses)

body count *n* **:** a count of or as if of the bodies of killed enemy soldiers ⟨the *body count* by which the Vietnam war is officially and journalistically reported —Ramsey Clark⟩ ⟨the disgraceful *body count* from auto accidents — Lewis Mumford⟩ ⟨firing 120 employees and raising the industry *body count* to 600 —*Rolling Stone*⟩

body language *n* **:** the bodily gestures and mannerisms by which a person communicates with others

body mechanics *n pl but sing or pl in constr* **:** systematic exercises designed esp. to develop coordination, endurance, and poise

body shirt *n* **1 :** a woman's close-fitting top made with a sewn-in or snapped crotch **2 :** a close-fitting shirt or blouse

body stocking *n* **:** a sheer close-fitting one-piece garment for the torso that often has sleeves and legs

body·suit \'bädēˌs(y)üt\ *n* **:** a close-fitting one-piece garment for the torso

body·surf \-ˌsərf, -ˌsȯf, -ˌsȯif\ *vi* **:** to ride on a wave without a surfboard by planing on the chest and stomach — **body·surf·er** \-fə(r)\ *n*

bof·fo \'bäf(ˌ)ō\ *adj* [*boffo*, n., short for *boffola*] **:** extraordinarily successful **:** sensational ⟨we're a *boffo* smash! —Tom Eyen⟩ ⟨should be *boffo* for boating biz —H.D. Whall⟩

bog**n, Brit* **:** toilet, loo

bo·gey*\'bügē, 'bōgē, 'bügē\ *n, pl* **bogeys** *slang* **:** an unidentified flying object ⟨on Gemini 7 the crew reported a *bogey* . . . in the sky —Neal Stanford⟩

Bohr effect \'bō(ə)r-, 'bȯ(ə)r-\ *n* [Christian *Bohr* †1911 Dan. physiologist] **:** the decrease in oxygen affinity of hemoglobins and some invertebrate respiratory pigments (as hemocyanin) in response to increased carbon dioxide concentration and consequent increased acidity of the blood

boil·off \'bȯilˌȯf, *also* -ˌäf\ *n* **:** the vaporization of a liquid (as liquid oxygen)

bok choy \'bäk'chȯi, -'jȯi\ *n* [modif. of *pakchoi*] **:** a Chinese cabbage (*Brassica chinensis*)

Bok·mål \'bükˌmȯl, 'bōk-\ *n* [Norw, fr. *bok* book (fr. ON *bōk*) + *mål* language, fr. ON *māl*] **:** a literary form of Norwegian developed by the gradual reform of written Danish **:** Riksmål — compare NYNORSK

bol·li·to mis·to \bȯˌlēd-ō'mē(ˌ)stō, -ētō'-\ *n, pl* **bol·li·ti mis·ti** \-ēd-ē'mēstē, -ētē'-\ [It, fr. *bollito*, past part. of *bollire* boil + *misto* mixed] **:** a dish of mixed meats (as lamb, veal, beef, and sausage) boiled with vegetables

bo·lo tie \'bō(ˌ)lō-\ *or* **bo·la tie** \'bōlə-\ *n* [prob. fr. *bola*] **:** a cord fastened around the neck with an ornamental clasp and worn as a necktie

bomb*n **1 :** the atom bomb; *also* **:** nuclear weapons in general — usu. used with *the* ⟨when the *bomb* has taken the place of God . . . as the ultimate disposer of the earth —H. C. Schonberg⟩ **2 :** an unsuccessful performance or production **:** a flop ⟨a terrible *bomb* of a movie —Paul Newman⟩; *broadly* **:** a failure **3** *chiefly Brit* **:** an old car **4** *Brit* **:** a lot of money ⟨demonstrating how to avoid the flu and save a *bomb* on the central heating —Richard Gordon⟩ **5** *Brit* **:** a great success **:** a hit — often used in the phrases *go a bomb* or *go like a bomb* **6 :** a long pass in football

bomb*vi **1 :** to be a failure ⟨if I *bomb* in the movies . . . I could always join the Peace Corps —R.G. Goulet⟩; *esp* **:** to fail to win audience approval ⟨will not be the first show to seem great in Philadelphia and then to *bomb* in New York —Clive Barnes⟩ **2** *slang* **:** to move rapidly ⟨realized there was more to [ski] racing than *bombing* down her native hill —Adam Shaw⟩

Bom·bay \bäm'bā\ *n* [fr. *Bombay,* India] **:** a domestic cat of a breed originating as a cross between the American Shorthair and the Burmese that is characterized by a shiny black short-haired coat and gold or copper eyes

bombed \'bämd\ *adj, slang* **:** affected by alcohol or drugs **:** drunk, high

bomb·let \'bämlət\ *n* [*bomb* + *-let,* dim. suffix] **:** a small bomb

bonce**n, Brit* **:** head, noggin ⟨respect for the brain inside his *bonce* —Grundy⟩

bond·ed*\'bändəd\ *adj* **:** composed of two or more layers of the same or different fabrics held together by an adhesive ⟨*bonded* jersey⟩

bonding*n **:** the formation of a close personal relationship (as between a mother and child) esp. through frequent or constant association

bone·head \'bōn‚hed\ *adj* **:** being a college course intended for students lacking fundamental skills **:** remedial ⟨teaches *bonehead* English⟩

bong \'bȯŋ, 'bäŋ\ *n* [origin unknown] **:** a simple water pipe for smoking marijuana that consists of a bottle or vertical tube partially filled with a liquid (as water or liqueur) and a smaller offset tube ending in a bowl

bonk \'bäŋk, 'bȯŋk\ *vt* [imit.] **:** to hit ⟨baseball players getting *bonked* on the head by routine fly balls —Gary Cartwright⟩

bon·kers \'bäŋkə(r)z, 'bȯŋ-\ *adj* [origin unknown] **:** out of one's mind **:** crazy, mad ⟨if I don't work, I go *bonkers* —Zoe Caldwell⟩

boo \'bü\ *n* [origin unknown] **:** marijuana

boob**n, Brit* **:** a mistake or blooper

boob tube \'büb‚t(y)üb\ *n* [fr. the belief that a taste for television viewing indicates stupidity] **:** a television set ⟨spending weekends at various motels and deftly removing their *boob tubes* —F.A. Tinker⟩; *also* **:** the medium of television or the watching of television ⟨if you don't think your family is addicted to the television habit, try doing without the *boob tube* for a few days and see what happens —Harold Hudson⟩ ⟨the role of advertising in man-

aging the *boob tube's* coverage of complex problems — Bill Cutler⟩

boogie*n [*boogie* boogie-woogie] **:** earthy and strongly rhythmic rock music conducive to dancing ⟨their thundering fusion of barroom *boogie* and Western swing — Barbara Graustark⟩

boog·ie *also* **boogy** *vi* **boog·ied; boogy·ing :** to dance to rock music ⟨quartets that play soft rock and remind people to *boogie* —*Chicagoan*⟩ ⟨who has been seeming about to *boogie* out of her jeans all evening —Stu Werbin⟩

book**vt, Brit, of a referee* **:** to note the name or number of (as a soccer player) because of a flagrant foul

boon·ies \'bünēz, -iz\ *n pl* [by shortening and alter. fr. *boondocks*] *slang* **:** rural backcountry **:** sticks, boondocks ⟨out in the *boonies,* where bright city distractions are hours away —Jesse Kornbluth⟩

boot·strap*\'büt‚strap\ *n* **:** a computer routine consisting of a few initial instructions by means of which the rest of the instructions are brought into the computer

bootstrap*adj **:** designed to function independently of outside direction **:** capable of using one internal function or process to control another ⟨a *bootstrap* operation to load a computer⟩ ⟨use of inside sources of heat has made *bootstrap* heat-pump systems competitive with conventional systems —*Technical Survey*⟩

bootstrap *vt* **1 :** to enter (a program) into a computer by a bootstrap **2 :** to work or develop by individual initiative and effort with minimum or no assistance ⟨the junior-grade professional woman may face stiff opposition when she tries to *bootstrap* her way up —Lisa C. Wohl⟩

borderline*adj **:** characterized by psychological instability in several areas (as interpersonal relations, behavior, mood, and identity) often with impaired social and vocational functioning but with brief or no psychotic episodes ⟨a *borderline* personality disorder⟩

Bor·de·tel·la \‚bȯrdā'telə\ *n* [Jules *Bordet* †1961 Belg. bacteriologist] **:** a genus of uncertain affiliation comprising short gram-negative bacilli resembling cocci and including the causative agent (*B. pertussis*) of whooping cough

born–again \‚bȯ(ə)rnə‚gen, ‚bȯ(ə)n-, -‚gin, -‚gän\ *adj* [fr. the biblical injunction in John 3:3] **1 :** of, relating to, or being a Christian who has made a renewed or confirmed commitment of faith esp. after an intense religious experience **2 :** having returned recently or suddenly to a belief, interest, or occupation ⟨a *born-again* humanist out to defy the computer establishment —Lee Smith⟩

borough*n **:** a civil division of the state of Alaska corresponding to a county in other states

Bor·sa·li·no \‚bȯrsə'lē(ˌ)nō\ *or* **Borsalino hat** *n* [It, fr. *Borsalino,* the manufacturer] **:** a wide-brimmed soft felt hat for men

bos·sa no·va \‚bäsə'nōvə, ‚bȯs-\ *n* [Pg, lit., new trend, fr. *bossa* hump, bump, trend (fr. F *bosse* hump, fr. OF *boce*) + *nova,* fem. of *novo* new, fr. L *novus*] **1 :** a Brazilian dance characterized by the sprightly step pattern of the samba and a subtle bounce **2 :** music resembling the samba with jazz interpolations

Bos·ton arm \‚bȯstən-, *sometimes* ‚bäs-, *in rapid speech also* -sᵊn-\ *n* [fr. its development by four institutions in Boston, Mass.] **:** an artificial arm that is activated by an amputee's nerve impulses which are electrically amplified and transmitted to a motor operating the arm

bo·ta \'bōd-ə, -ōtə\ n [Sp, fr. LL *buttis* cask, flask] **:** a leather pouch for carrying wine

bo·tan·i·ca \bə'tanikə, bō-\ n [Sp *botánica* botanical] **:** a shop that specializes in articles (as herbs, charms, and statues) relating esp. to voodoo or the occult

Bot·ti·cel·lian \ˌbäd-ə'chelēən, -ätə-, -lyən\ adj [Alessandro *Botticelli* †1510 Ital. painter] **:** of, relating to, or having the characteristics of the painter Botticelli or his work

bot·tle-feed \'bäd-ᵊl,fēd, 'bätᵊl-\ vt **-fed; -feed·ing :** to feed (as an infant) with a bottle

bottleneck*or* **bottleneck guitar** n **:** a style of guitar playing in which an object (as a metal bar or the neck of a bottle) is pressed against the strings for a glissando effect

bottling*n* **:** a bottled beverage; esp **:** wine

bottom*n* **1 :** the bass or baritone instruments of a band **2 :** a quantum characteristic ascribed to certain massive quarks and fundamental particles that accounts for the existence and lifetime of upsilon particles and has a value of zero for most known particles

bot·tomed \'bäd-əmd, -ätə-\ adj **:** having a bottom esp. of a specified kind — usu. used in combination ⟨a broad≈ *bottomed* boat⟩

bottomless*adj* **1 :** nude **2 :** featuring nude entertainers ⟨a *bottomless* bar⟩

bottom line \'bäd-əm'līn\ n **1 a :** the line at the bottom of a financial report that shows the net profit or loss ⟨estimates that only $350,000 was brought down to the *bottom line* —Gwen Kinkead⟩ **b :** financial considerations (as cost or profit or loss) ⟨most corporate buildings . . . appear to have been built, above all, with an eye to the *bottom line* —Paul Goldberger⟩ ⟨known for its aggressiveness in advertising and promotion and its sharp eye on the *bottom line* —Tom Buckley⟩ **c :** the final result **:** outcome, upshot ⟨merger . . . caused surprise. But the *bottom line* is a stronger energy-minerals company —P.J. Stanton⟩ **2 a :** the essential or salient point **:** crux ⟨the *bottom line* is . . . what legal right do the politicians have to keep cameras out of a public meeting —Dale Spencer⟩ **b :** the primary or most important consideration ⟨getting clear was the *bottom line* —Cyra McFadden⟩

bot·tom-line \ˌbäd-əm,līn, -ätə-\ adj **1 :** concerned only with cost or profits ⟨*bottom-line* publishing, with little real concern for editorial values —Newsweek⟩ **2 :** pragmatic, realistic ⟨a realist, dealing in facts, in *bottom≈ line* emotions —Allene Talmey⟩

bottom out vi **1** *of a security market* **:** to decline to a point where demand begins to exceed supply and a rise in prices is imminent **2 :** to reach a point where a decline is halted or reversed ⟨signs that the recession has *bottomed* out⟩ ⟨his streak of bad luck seems to be *bottoming* out — Barbara Howar⟩

bottom woman n, slang **:** a pimp's favorite or most dependable prostitute

bou·bou \'bü,bü\ n [native name in Mali] **:** a long flowing garment worn in parts of Africa

bouillabaisse*n* **:** potpourri ⟨a weekend *bouillabaisse* of jazz, rock, reggae and salsa —Tony Schwartz⟩

boul·der·ing \'bōld(ə)riŋ\ n **:** practice in the techniques of rock climbing or mountaineering

boulevard*adj* **:** produced primarily to entertain ⟨*boulevard* farce⟩

bounce*vt* **bounced; bounc·ing :** to write (a check) on an account having insufficient funds

bouque·tière \ˌbük(ə)'tye(ə)r, -k(ə)tē'e(ə)r\ adj [F, woman who sells flowers, fem. of *bouquetier* flower seller, fr. *bouquet* bouquet] **:** garnished with vegetables ⟨rack of lamb *bouquetière*⟩

bour·ride \bu'rēd, bə-\ n [Prov *bourrido, boulido* something boiled; akin to *bouillon*] **:** a fish stew similar to bouillabaisse that is usu. thickened with egg yolks and strongly flavored with garlic

bou·zou·ki also **bou·sou·ki** \bu'zükē, bə'-\ n, pl **-kia** \-kēə\ also **-kis** [NGk *mpouzouki*] **:** a long-necked stringed musical instrument of Greek origin

box*n* **1 :** vagina — usu. considered vulgar **2 :** television **:** a television set **:** BOOB TUBE

BP \ˌbē'pē\ n **:** BEAUTIFUL PEOPLE

bpi abbr bits per inch; bytes per inch

braces n pl **:** wire fastened to teeth to correct irregularities in their position

brachio·ce·phal·ic artery \ˌbrakē(ˌ)ōsə'falik-\ n [*brachio-* arm and + *-cephalic* directed to the head] **:** the innominate artery

brachiocephalic trunk n **:** the innominate artery

brachiocephalic vein n **:** the innominate vein

bra·ci·o·la \ˌbräch(ē)'ōlə\ or **bra·ci·o·le** \-lä\ n [*braciola* fr. It, fr. *brace* live coal, fr. OIt *bragia; braciole* fr. It, pl. of *braciola*] **:** a thin slice of meat (as steak) that is usu. wrapped around a filling of meat, chopped vegetables, and seasonings and often cooked in wine

bra·dy·ki·nin \ˌbrädə'kīnən\ n [*brady-* slow (fr. Gk *bradys*) + *kinin*] **:** a kinin that is formed locally in injured tissue, acts in vasodilation of small arterioles, is held to play a part in inflammatory processes, and is composed of a chain of nine amino acids

brain*n* **:** an automatic device (as a computer) that performs one or more of the functions of the human brain for control, guidance, or computation ⟨the *brain* of a missile⟩

brain death n **:** final cessation of activity in the central nervous system esp. as indicated by a flat electroencephalogram for a predetermined length of time

brain drain n **:** the migration of professional people (as scientists, professors, or physicians) from one country to another usu. for higher salaries or better living conditions

brain–drain \'brän'drän\ vt **:** to entice (as a scientist) to emigrate for a higher salary or better working conditions

brain hor·mone \-'hór,mōn, -'hó(ə),-\ n **:** a hormone that is secreted by neurosecretory cells of the insect brain and that stimulates the prothoracic glands to secrete ecdysone

bra·less \'bräləs, -rä-, sometimes -rō-\ adj, of a woman **:** wearing no bra — **bra·less·ness** \-nəs\ n

branch*n* **:** a part of a computer program executed as a result of a program decision

branch*vi* **:** to follow one of two or more branches (as in a computer program)

bran·dade \brän'däd\ n [F, fr. Prov *brandado,* past part. of *branda* shake, agitate, fr. Gmc *brand* sword] **:** a seasoned puree of fish and esp. of salt cod

Bran·gus \'braŋgəs\ trademark — used for registered polled solid black beef cattle that are ³⁄₈ Brahman and ⁵⁄₈ Angus, for the offspring of crosses between such animals which conform to breed specifications, and for registered purebred Brahman and Angus used to produce such stock

brass·ware \'bras,wa(ə)r, -,we(ə)r, -,waə(r, -,weə(r\ *n* **:** articles made of brass

bread·board \'bred,bō(ə)rd, -,bó(ə)rd, -ōəd, -ȯəd\ *vt* **:** to make an experimental arrangement of (an electronic circuit) on a flat surface

Brecht·ian \'brektēən, -ḵ-\ *adj* [Bertolt *Brecht* †1956 Ger. dramatist] **:** of, relating to, or suggestive of Bertolt Brecht or his writings ⟨the production ... is coarse in spirit and with no gloss at all on its rendering of the *Brechtian* view of a materialistic society —Irving Kolodin⟩

brick**n, slang* **:** a one-kilogram package of marijuana

bride's basket *n* [so called fr. such bowls' frequently being given as wedding presents in the late 19th century] **:** an ornate, handled, usu. colored, and often cased glass bowl fitted with a silver-plated base

bring·down \'briŋ,daún\ *n* **:** a comedown or letdown

British Shorthair *n* **1 :** a breed of domestic cats resembling the American Shorthair but stockier in build with a closer-lying coat **2** *often not cap S* **:** a cat of the British Shorthair breed

broad·band \'bród,band\ *adj* **:** of, having, or involving operation with uniform efficiency over a wide band of frequencies ⟨a *broadband* radio antenna⟩

broken*adj **:** disunited by divorce, separation, or desertion of one parent ⟨children from *broken* homes⟩ ⟨a *broken* family⟩

broker*n **:** POWER BROKER

broker*vt **:** to arrange, settle, or control as a broker ⟨*broker* a convention⟩ ⟨could *broker* his renomination with other party leaders —Hedrick Smith⟩

bro·kered \'brōkə(r)d\ *adj* **:** arranged or controlled by power brokers ⟨a *brokered* political convention⟩

bro·mo·de·oxy·uri·dine \,brōmō(,)dē'äksē,yùrə,dēn\ *n* [*bromo-* containing bromine + *deoxy-* containing less oxygen than related compounds + *uridine*] **:** a mutagenic analogue $C_9H_{11}O_5NBr$ of thymidine that induces chromosomal breakage esp. in heterochromatic regions and has been used to selectively destroy actively dividing cells — abbr. *BUdR*

bro·mo·ura·cil \,brōmō'yùrə,sil, -mə'-, -əsəl\ *n* [*bromo-* containing bromine + *uracil*] **:** a mutagenic uracil derivative $C_4H_3N_2O_2Br$ that is an analogue of thymine and pairs readily with adenine and sometimes with guanine during bacterial or phage DNA synthesis

bron·cho·con·stric·tion \,bräŋ(,)kōkən,strikshən, -än(-\ *n* [*broncho-* bronchial + *constriction*] **:** constriction of the bronchial air passages

bron·cho·con·stric·tor \-'striktə(r)\ *adj* **:** causing or involving bronchoconstriction ⟨*bronchoconstrictor* effects⟩ ⟨*bronchoconstrictor* responses⟩

bron·cho·pul·mo·nary \-'pulmə,nere, -,pál-, -i\ *adj* **:** of, relating to, or affecting the bronchi and the lungs ⟨arterial branches that supply the *bronchopulmonary* segments of the lungs⟩

bronzer*n **:** a cosmetic esp. for men that makes the skin look tanned

brown bag·ging \'braún'bagiŋ\ *n* [fr. the brown paper bag used] **1 :** the practice of carrying a bottle of liquor into a restaurant or club where setups are available but where the sale of liquor by the drink is illegal **2 :** the practice of carrying one's lunch (as to work) usu. in a brown paper bag — **brown–bag** \-,bag\ *vb or adj* — **brown bag·ger** \-gə(r)\ *n*

brown fat *n* **:** a mammalian heat-producing tissue occurring esp. in hibernators

brownie point *n, often cap B* **:** a credit regarded as earned esp. by currying favor with a superior ⟨a new chance to gain those *Brownie points* so essential to promotion and tenure —Theodore Sturgeon⟩ ⟨must make this kind of scholarship respectable, give *brownie points* for it —G.E. Forsythe⟩

brown lung disease *n* **:** a chronic industrial disease associated with the inhalation of cotton dust over a long period of time **:** byssinosis

brown recluse spider *also* **brown recluse** *n* [*recluse* prob. fr. NL *reclusa*, specific epithet, fr. LL, fem. of *reclusus* shut up; fr. its living chiefly in dark corners] **:** a venomous spider (*Loxosceles reclusa*) introduced into the southern U.S. that has a violin-shaped mark on the cephalothorax and produces a dangerous neurotoxin

brown·ware \'braún,wa(ə)r, -,we(ə)r, -,waə(r, -,weə(r\ *n* **1 :** a brown-glazed earthenware formerly widely used for utility pottery **2 :** typically primitive pottery that fires to a brown or reddish color

browser*n **:** an open case for holding phonograph records that is designed for ease in browsing

brush back \'brəsh'bak\ *vt* **:** to throw a brushback to ⟨hard to set up a hitter if you can't *brush* him *back* —Red Schoendienst⟩

brush·back \'brəsh,bak\ *n* **:** a fastball thrown near the batter's head in baseball in an attempt to make him move back from home plate

bru·tal·ism \'brüd-ᵊl,izəm, -ütᵊl-\ *n* **:** a style in art and esp. architecture using exaggeration and distortion to create its effect (as of massiveness or power) — **bru·tal·ist** \-ᵊləst\ *adj or n*

BSEE \,bē,es,ē'ē\ *n* **1 :** a bachelor of science in electrical engineering **2 :** a bachelor of science in elementary education

B side *n* **:** the flip side of a phonograph record; *also* **:** a song on that side

bubble*n **1 :** something (as a plastic structure) that is more or less semicylindrical or dome-shaped **2 :** MAGNETIC BUBBLE

bubble car *n* **:** an automobile having a transparent bubble top

bub·ble·gum \'bəbəl,gəm\ *n* [fr. the fact that bubble gum is chewed chiefly by children] **:** rock music characterized by simple repetitive phrasing and intended esp. for young teenagers

buc·co·lin·gual \,bəkō'liŋ(g)(yə)wəl\ *adj* [*bucco-* buccal and + *lingual*] **1 :** relating to or affecting the cheek and the tongue **2 :** of or relating to the buccal and lingual aspects of a tooth ⟨the *buccolingual* width of a molar⟩ — **buc·co·lin·gual·ly** \-ē\ *adv*

bu·do \'büd(,)ō\ *n* [Jp *budō* martial arts] **:** the Japanese martial arts (as karate, aikido, and kendo)

BUdR *abbr* bromodeoxyuridine

bug off \'bəg'óf, *also* -äf\ *vi* [short for *bugger*] **:** to go away **:** leave, scram ⟨the body's immune system, nature's way of telling foreign substances to *bug off* —Philip Nobile⟩ — usu. used as a command ⟨you'll get your forecast. Now *bug off* —P.B. Benchley⟩

building society *n, Brit* **:** a savings and loan association

bul·bo·spon·gi·o·sus muscle \ˈbəl(ˌ)bō-spənjēˈōsəs-, -spän-\ *n* [NL, fr *bulbo-* bulb + L *spongiosus* spongy] **:** the bulbocavernosus muscle

bull dyke *n* **:** an aggressively masculine lesbian

bull·shot \ˈbul̩shät\ *n* [shortening and alter. of *bouillon* + *shot*] **:** a drink made of vodka and bouillon

bum·mer \ˈbəmə(r)\ *n* [*bum* not good] **1 :** an unpleasant drug-induced hallucinatory experience; *broadly* **:** an unpleasant event or situation ⟨people seem to realize that this war is a *bummer* —Arthur Moses⟩ **2 :** something that fails **:** a flop ⟨the book is a *bummer* —Albert Goldman⟩

bumper sticker *n* **:** a strip of adhesive paper or plastic bearing a printed message (as a slogan or a candidate's name) and designed to be stuck on a vehicle's bumper

BUN \ˌbē,yüˈen\ *n* [*b*lood *u*rea *n*itrogen] **:** the concentration of nitrogen in the form of urea in the blood

bunny* *n* [fr. *Bunny,* a service mark used for a waitress whose minimal attire includes a tail and ears resembling those of a rabbit] **:** a pretty girl esp. considered as an object of sexual desire ⟨those ads, where the hirsute hero struts off with a bikinied *bunny* —Chris Welles⟩

Bun·ra·ku \ˈbün'rä(ˌ)kü, 'bün(ˌ)r-\ *n* [Jp] **:** Japanese puppet theater featuring large costumed wooden puppets, onstage puppeteers, and a chanter who speaks all the lines

buns \ˈbənz\ *n pl* **:** the human buttocks

buq·sha \ˈbüksha, 'bȯk-\ *n, pl* **buqsha** *or* **buqshas** [Ar] **1 :** a monetary unit of the Yemen Arab Republic equal to $^1/_{40}$ rial **2 :** a note or coin representing one buqsha

bu·reau·cra·tese \ˌbyüra'krad-ˌēz, 'byü-, -rō-, -a'tēz; byüˌräkra'tēz, byü-, byə-; -ēs\ *n* [*bureaucrat* + *-ese* jargon] **:** an impersonal style of language typically used by bureaucrats and marked by the prevalence of abstractions, jargon, euphemisms, and circumlocutions ⟨the style is heavy, cliché-ridden, *bureaucratese* at its very worst —A.H. Marckwardt⟩ ⟨even in its original, carefully hedged *bureaucratese* the warning was ominous —*Newsweek*⟩

Bur·kitt's lym·pho·ma \ˈbərkəts(ˌ)lim̩fōma, 'bāk-\ *or* **Burkitt lymphoma** \-kət-\ *n* [Denis Parsons *Burkitt* b1911 Brit. surgeon] **:** a malignant lymphoma that affects primarily the upper and lower jaws, orbit, retroperitoneal tissues situated near the pancreas, kidneys, ovaries, testes, thyroid, adrenal glands, heart, and pleura, that occurs esp. in children of central Africa, and that is associated with Epstein-Barr virus

Burkitt's tu·mor *or* **Burkitt tumor** \-ˈt(y)ümə(r)\ *n* **:** BURKITT'S LYMPHOMA

burn* *n* **1 :** the firing of a spacecraft rocket engine in flight **2** *slang* **:** an instance of dishonest dealing **:** a swindle or gyp

burn bag *n* **:** a bag for holding classified papers that are to be destroyed by burning

burn·out* \ˈbərn̩aut, 'bən-, 'bain-\ *n* **1 a :** the process or an instance of burning out **b :** the cessation of operation of a jet engine as the result of exhaustion of or shutting off of fuel **2 :** the point in the trajectory of a rocket engine at which burnout occurs **3 :** exhaustion of physical or emotional strength ⟨*burnout* is almost entirely due

to stress inherent in a job —J. E. Bishop⟩ **4 :** a person showing the results of drug abuse

burrito* \bə'rēd·(ˌ)ō\ *n, pl* **-tos :** a flour tortilla rolled or folded around a filling (as of meat, beans, or cheese) and usu. baked

bur·sec·to·my \ˌbər'sektəmē, bā'-, bəi'-, bə(r)'-, -mi\ *n, pl* **-mies** [*bursa* + *-ectomy* cutting out] **:** excision of a bursa (as the bursa of Fabricius of a chicken)

burster* *n* **:** the celestial source of an outburst of radiation (as X rays)

bush \ˈbush\ *adj* [short for *bush-league*] **:** of an inferior class or group of its kind **:** bush-league, unprofessional, amateurish ⟨the travesty was not that the speedway went the show-business route, but that the execution was so *bush* —J.S. Radosta⟩

bush hat *n* [*bush* backcountry] **:** a broad-brimmed hat worn esp. as part of an Australian military uniform

businessman's risk *n* **:** an investment (as a stock) with a moderately high risk factor that is bought with an eye to growth potential and capital gains or sometimes tax advantages rather than for income

bus·ing *or* **bus·sing** \ˈbəsiŋ\ *n* **:** the act of transporting by bus; *specif* **:** the transporting of children to a school outside their residential area as a means of establishing racial balance in the school

bust* *vt* **1 :** to put under arrest ⟨was *busted* for running a Baltimore stock swindle —*Newsweek*⟩ **2 :** to make a raid on ⟨since her brothel was *busted* —Diana Davenport⟩ — **bust one's ass** *slang* **:** to make an all-out effort to do something

bust* *n* **1** *slang* **:** a police raid ⟨the night the club was raided . . . he was rushed into the kitchen, fitted with a white jacket, and disguised as a waiter until the *bust* was completed —David Butwin⟩ **2** *slang* **:** an act or instance of arresting or of being arrested ⟨the biggest *bust* of top narcotics dealers ever —Mary P. Nichols⟩

bust·out \ˈbə,staut\ *n* [*bust* go broke + *out*] *slang* **:** a confidence scheme in which an established business is taken over, a large stock of merchandise is purchased on credit and quickly sold, and the business is then abandoned or bankruptcy is declared

bust–up* \ˈbə,stəp\ *n, chiefly Brit* **:** an outbreak of dissension or hostility **:** an altercation; *also* **:** a rough argument or fight **:** a scuffle

bu·sul·fan \byü'səlfən\ *n* [*butane* + *sulf*onyl] **:** an antineoplastic agent $C_6H_{14}O_6S_2$ used in the treatment of chronic myelogenous leukemia

busway* *n* **:** an expressway or a lane of one that is reserved for the exclusive use of commuter buses

butch* \ˈbuch\ *n* **:** one who is butch

1butch *adj* [prob. fr. *Butch,* a nickname for boys, esp. tough boys] **1** *of a homosexual* **:** playing the male role in a homosexual relationship **2 :** very masculine in appearance or manner

2butch *n* [by shortening] **:** a vendor esp. on trains or in theaters **:** butcher

but·ter·fly·er \ˈbəd·ər,flī(ə)r, 'bəd·ə,flīə(r, -ətə-\ *n* **:** a swimmer who specializes in the butterfly

butter pat* *n* **:** an individual dish for a pat of butter

button* *n* **:** a mescal button chewed for its hallucinogenic effect

but·ton–down* *also* **but·toned–down** \ˈbət²n̩daun\ *adj* [fr. the fact that buttondown shirts are felt to be conservative] **:** lacking originality and imagination and adhering to conventional standards esp. in dress and behavior ⟨*button-down* minds who want to know about the paper's pension plan rather than what beat is open — *Newsweek*⟩

but·ton·down \'bət³n͵daùn\ *n* **:** a shirt with a button‑down collar

button man *n* [earlier *button boy* page, errand boy; fr. the buttons on a page's uniform] **:** a low-ranking member of an underworld organization who is given disagreeable and often dangerous assignments

bu·tut \'bü͵tüt\ *n* [native name in Gambia] **1 :** a monetary unit of Gambia equal to $^1/_{100}$ dalasi **2 :** a coin representing one butut

butylated hy·droxy·an·is·ole \-hi͵dräksē͵anȯ͵sōl\ *n* [ISV *hydroxy-* hydroxyl, containing hydroxyl + *anisole*] **:** a phenolic antioxidant $C_{11}H_{16}O_2$ used to preserve fats and oils in food, some cosmetics, and pharmaceuticals

butylated hy·droxy·tol·u·ene \-(͵)hī͵dräksē͵tälyə͵wēn\ *n* [ISV *hydroxy-* + *toluene*] **:** a crystalline phenolic antioxidant $C_{15}H_{24}O$ used esp. to preserve fats and oils in food, some cosmetics, and pharmaceuticals

buy–in \'bī͵in\ *n* **:** the act or process of buying in to cover a short on a stock or commodity exchange

buzz off *vi* **:** to leave forthwith **:** go away **:** scram — usu. used as a command ⟨he sits down, shoving away —

"*Buzz off ! Buzz off !*" — the cat that occupies his chair —Gerald Clarke⟩

buzz session *n* **:** a small informal group discussion ⟨the PTA meeting will be opened to informal *buzz sessions* — *Fallon (Nev.) Eagle-Standard* ⟩

buzz word *n* **:** an important-sounding and often technical word or phrase that frequently has little meaning and is used chiefly to impress laypersons ⟨it is obvious those *buzz words* were used to draw attention to an otherwise somewhat trivial article —T.W. Bryan⟩

BX \(')bē͵eks\ *n* **:** BASE EXCHANGE

BY *abbr, usu not cap* billion years

BYOB *abbr* bring your own booze; bring your own bottle

byte \'bīt\ *n* [perh. alter. of *bite* morsel] **:** a group of adjacent binary digits often shorter than a word that a computer processes as a unit ⟨an 8-bit *byte*⟩

Byz·an·tine*\'biz³n͵tēn, *sometimes* 'bī-, -͵tīn; *sometimes* bə'zan-͵tēn, bī-, -͵tīn, -ntən\ *adj* **1 :** of, relating to, or characterized by a devious and usu. surreptitious manner of operation ⟨the government, with its own *Byzantine* sources of intelligence —Wesley Pruden⟩ **2 :** intricately involved **:** labyrinthine ⟨searching in the *Byzantine* complexity of the record for leads, defenses, and . . . evidence of perjured testimony —B.L. Collier⟩

BZ \(')bē͵zē\ *n* [*BZ*, army code name] **:** a gaseous benzilic acid ester $C_{21}H_{23}NO_3$ that when breathed produces incapacitating physical and mental effects

C

C\\'sē\ *n, slang* **:** cocaine

cabana set *n* **:** a two-piece beachwear ensemble for men consisting of loosely fitting shorts and a short-sleeved jacket

cab·er·net sau·vi·gnon \,kabə(r),nesōvēn'yōⁿ\ *n* [F] **:** a dry red wine made from a single variety of black grape that is widely cultivated (as in France, California, and Argentina) — called also *cab·er·net* \,kabə(r)'ne, -'nä\

ca·ble·cast \'kābəl,kast\ *vt* **-cast** *also* **-cast·ed; -cast·ing :** to telecast by cable television — **cablecast** *n* — **ca·ble·cast·er** \-ə(r)\ *n*

cable television *or* **cable TV** *n* **:** a system of television reception in which signals from distant stations are picked up by a tall or elevated antenna and sent by cable to the individual receivers of paying subscribers

ca·ble·vi·sion \'kabəl,vizhən\ *n* **:** CABLE TELEVISION

cack–hand·ed \'kak,handėd\ *adj* [prob. fr ON *keikr* bent backwards; akin to Dan *keite* left-handed] **1** *Brit* **:** being left-handed **2** *Brit* **:** clumsy, awkward

CAD *abbr* computer-aided design

Caer·phil·ly \ke(ə)r'filē, kär-, kī(ə)r-, kə(r)-\ *n* [*Caerphilly,* urban district in Wales] **:** a mild white friable cheese of Welsh origin

Cae·sar salad \'sēzə(r)-\ *n* [fr. *Caesar's,* restaurant in Tijuana, Mexico, where it originated] **:** a tossed salad made typically with romaine, garlic, anchovies, and croutons and served with a dressing of olive oil, coddled egg, lemon juice, and grated cheese

ca·fé filtre \'ka,fä'filtə(r), *F* kàfäfiltr(ᵊ)\ *n* [F] **:** coffee made by passing hot water through ground coffee and a filter

caff \'kaf\ *n* [by shortening and alter. fr. *café*] *Brit* **:** a small restaurant serving light meals **:** café

cage*n **:** a sheer one-piece dress that has no waistline, is often gathered at the neck, and is worn over a close-fitting underdress or slip

CAGS *abbr* certificate of advanced graduate study

CAI *abbr* computer-aided instruction; computer-assisted instruction

cal·ci·phy·lax·is \,kalsəfə'laksəs\ *n, pl* **-lax·es** \-ak,sēz\ [NL, fr. *calci-* calcium + *-phylaxis* (as in *prophylaxis*)] **:** an adaptive response that follows systemic sensitization by a calcifying factor (as a D-vitamin) and a challenge (as with a metallic salt) and involves local inflammation and sclerosis with calcium deposition — **cal·ci·phy·lac·tic** \,kalsəfə'laktik\ *adj* — **cal·ci·phy·lac·ti·cal·ly** \-tək(ə)lē, -li\ *adv*

cal·ci·to·nin \,kalsə'tōnən\ *n* [*calci-* + *tonic* + *-in* chemical compound] **:** a polypeptide hormone esp. from the thyroid gland that tends to lower the level of calcium in the blood plasma — called also *thyrocalcitonin*

cal·do ver·de \,kaldō've(ə)rdä, ,käl-, ,kòl-, -dē\ *n* [Pg, green soup] **:** a soup made of potatoes, chopped greens, and sausage

calibrate*vt **-brat·ed; -brat·ing :** to adjust or tune ⟨neither do they listen to polls, nor *calibrate* their responses to the urgings of public-relations men — Eugene Kennedy⟩

Cal·i·for·ni·ana \,kalə,fórnē'änə, -,fò(ə)n-, -'anə\ *n pl* [*California* + *-ana* collected items] **:** materials concerning or characteristic of California, its history, or its culture

caliper*n **:** a device consisting of two plates lined with a frictional material that press against the sides of a rotating wheel or disk in some brake systems

call*vt **1 :** to indicate and keep track of balls and strikes in (a baseball game) **2 :** to manage (as an offensive game) by giving the signals or orders ⟨that catcher *calls* a good game⟩ — **call forth :** to bring into being or action **:** elicit ⟨these events *call forth* great emotions⟩ — **call on**\ **:** to elicit a response from (as a student) ⟨the teacher always *called on* her first⟩

¹cal·la·loo *also* **cal·a·loo** *or* **calalu**\ *or* **cal·la·lou** \,kalə'lü\ *n* [*calalu*] **:** a soup or stew made with greens (as calalu or spinach), onions, and crabmeat

²callaloo *n* **:** a tropical American plant (*Xanthosoma hastifolium*) **:** calalu

call·back \'kòl,bak\ *n* **:** a recall by a manufacturer esp of a recently sold product (as an automobile) for correction of a defect

cal·li·graph \'kalə,graf\ *vt* [back-formation fr. *calligraphy*] **:** to produce or reproduce in a calligraphic style ⟨the pages were some of them printed, some *calligraphed,* some illuminated, some painted —Francis Meynell⟩

call in**vb** — **call in sick :** to report by telephone that one will be absent because of illness

call–in \'kòl(,)in\ *adj, of a radio program* **:** allowing listeners to engage in on-the-air telephone conversations with the host ⟨a constant guest on radio *call-in* shows — Playboy⟩

cal·zo·ne \kal'zó(,)nä, -'zō(-\ *n, pl* **-zone** *or* **-zones** [It, sing. back-formation fr. *calzoni* trousers; fr. its shape] **:** a turnover filled with cheese and ham

CAM *abbr* computer-aided manufacturing

Cam·e·lot \'kamə,lät\ *n* [fr. the musical *Camelot* by Alan J. Lerner *b*1918 Am. playwright and Frederick Loewe *b* 1901 Ger. composer which portrayed an ideal world in the Arthurian setting] **:** a time, place, or atmosphere of idyllic happiness

cam·eo**\'kamē,ō\ *n* **:** a small theatrical role performed by a well-known actor or actress and often limited to a single scene ⟨a neat *cameo* performance as a fifth-columnist butler —Michael Billington⟩

cam·era·work \'kam(ə)rə,wərk, -;wōk, -;waik\ *n* **:** work done by a camera ⟨special *camerawork,* such as instant replay —New Yorker⟩

¹camp \'kamp\ *n* [origin unknown] **1 :** a homosexual **2 :** exaggerated effeminate mannerisms (as of speech or gesture) exhibited esp. by homosexuals **3 :** something

that is so outrageously artificial, affected, inappropriate, or out-of-date as to be considered amusing — **camp·i·ly** \-pəlē, -li\ *adv* — **camp·i·ness** *n* — **campy** *adj*
²**camp** *adj* **1 :** of, relating to, or displaying camp ⟨specializing in *camp* send-ups of the songs of the Fifties and Sixties —John Elsom⟩ **2 :** of, relating to, or being a camp ⟨loose-limbed sensuality, which was sometimes macho and sometimes *camp* —Jane Margold⟩
³**camp** *vi* **:** to engage in camp **:** exhibit the qualities of camp ⟨he ... was *camping*, hands on hips, with a quick eye to notice every man who passed by —R. M. McAlmon⟩
camper*n **:** a portable dwelling (as a collapsible structure folded into a small trailer or a specially equipped automotive vehicle) for use during casual travel and camping
camphor glass *n* **:** glass with a cloudy white appearance resembling gum camphor in lump form
can*n, *slang* **:** an ounce of marijuana
Cancer*n **:** one born under the astrological sign Cancer
Can·cer·ian \kan'sərēən, -'si(ə)r-\ *n* [*Cancer* + E *-ian*] **:** CANCER
C and W *abbr* country and western
candy ass *n* **:** a timid or cowardly person **:** sissy — usu. considered vulgar — **candy-assed** *adj*
candy strip·er \-ˌstrīpə(r)\ *n* [fr. the red and white stripes of her uniform] **:** a teenage volunteer nurse's aide
cannibalize*vb **-ized; -iz·ing :** to use or draw on material of (as another writer or an earlier work) ⟨a volume ... that not only *cannibalizes* previous publications but is intended itself to be *cannibalized* —R.M. Adams⟩
can·no·li \kə'nōlē, ka-\ *n pl but sing or pl in constr* [It, pl. of *cannolo* small cylinder, tube, dim. of *canna* tube, fr. *canna* reed, fr. Gk *kanna* pole, reed — more at CANE] **:** a roll of fried pastry stuffed with creamy often sweetened filling (as of whipped ricotta cheese)
cannon net *n* **:** a net that is left in wait on the ground until birds or mammals are in position and then is spread over them by the simultaneous firing of several projectiles
can of worms : something that presents one problem after another **:** a source of continuing difficulty **:** an unpleasant mess ⟨to suggest Washington bureaucracy should determine the circumstances under which any public instrumentality can borrow opens up a new *can of worms* —J.J. Fogarty⟩
ca·non·i·cal form \kə'nänəkəl-\ *n* **:** the simplest form of a matrix; *specif* **:** the form of a square matrix that has zero elements everywhere except along the principal diagonal
Can·ton china \'kan-ˌtän-, kan-'tän-\ *n* **:** porcelain Canton ware esp. when blue and white
Canton enamel *n* [*Canton, China*] **:** Chinese enamelware of Limoges type
cap*n [*cap* covering] **1** *Brit* **:** DUTCH CAP **2 :** the symbol ∩ indicating the intersection of two sets — compare CUP
ca·pac·i·tate*\kə'pasəˌtāt\ *vt* **-tat·ed; -tat·ing :** to cause (sperm) to undergo capacitation
ca·pac·i·ta·tion*\kəˌpasə'tāshən\ *n* **:** change undergone by sperm in the female reproductive tract which enables them to penetrate and fertilize an egg
capital gains distribution *n* **:** the part of the payout of an investment company to its shareholders that con-

sists of realized profits from the sale of securities and technically is not income
capital–intensive *adj* **:** having a high capital cost per unit of output; *esp* **:** requiring greater expenditure in the form of capital than of labor
capital structure *n* **:** the makeup of the capitalization of a business in terms of the amounts and kinds of equity and debt securities **:** the equity and debt securities of a business together with its surplus and reserves
cap·i·tate \'kapəˌtāt\ *n* **:** the largest bone of the wrist **:** capitatum
ca·po \'kä(ˌ)pō, 'ka-, 'kà-\ *n, pl* **capos** [It, head, chief, fr. L *caput*] **:** the head of a branch of a crime syndicate
ca·po·na·ta \ˌkäpə'näd-ə, -ätə\ *n* [It (Sicilian dial.)] **:** a relish of chopped eggplant and assorted vegetables
cap·puc·ci·no \ˌkäp(y)ə'chēnō, ˌka-, ˌkà-, -(y)ù'-\ *n* [It, lit., Capuchin; fr. the likeness of its color to that of a Capuchin's habit] **:** espresso coffee topped with frothed hot milk or cream and often flavored with cinnamon
cap·reo·my·cin \ˌkaprēəˌmīsᵊn\ *n* [NL, fr. L *capreolus* + ISV *-mycin* substance obtained from a fungus, fr. *streptomycin*] **:** an antibiotic obtained from a bacterium of the genus *Streptomyces* (*S. capreolus*) that is used to treat tuberculosis
Capricorn*n **:** one born under the astrological sign Capricorn
Cap·ri·cor·ni·an \ˌkaprəˌkòrnēən, -rēˌk-, -ò(ə)n-\ *n* [*Capricorn* + E *-ian*] **:** CAPRICORN
ca·pri pants \ka'prē-, kə-; 'kä(ˌ)prē-, 'ka-\ *n pl, often cap* C [*Capri,* island in the Bay of Naples, Italy] **:** close-fitting women's pants that end above the ankle — called also *capris*
cap·sid \'kapsəd\ *n* [L *capsa* case + E *-id* structure, particle] **:** the outer protein shell of a virus particle — **cap·sid·al** \-dᵊl\ *adj*
cap·so·mere \'kapsəˌmi(ə)r\ *n* [*caps*id + connective *-o- + -mere* part, segment, deriv. of Gk *meros* part] **:** one of the subunits making up a viral capsid
cap·su·li·tis \ˌkaps(y)ə'līd-əs, -ītəs\ *n* [*capsule* + *-itis* inflammation] **:** inflammation of a capsule (as that of the crystalline lens)
cap·su·lot·o·my \ˌkaps(y)ə'läd-əmē, -ätə-, -mi\ *n* [*capsule* + connective *-o-* + *-tomy* incision] **:** incision of a capsule esp. of the crystalline lens (as in a cataract operation)
cap·tan \'kapˌtan\ *n* [perh. fr. *mercaptan*] **:** a fungicide $C_9H_8Cl_3NO_2S$ that is used on agricultural crops and as a bacteriostat in soaps
car·a·van·eer \ˌkarə(ˌ)va'ni(ə)r, -əvəˌ-, -niə(r\ *n* **:** CARAVANNER 1
car·a·van·ner \'karəˌvanə(r), *also* 'ker-, *esp Brit* ˌkarə'vanə(r)\ *n* **1** *or* **car·a·van·er :** one that travels in a caravan **2** *Brit* **:** one that goes camping with a trailer
car·ba·maz·e·pine \ˌkärbə'mazəˌpēn\ *n* [*carb-* carboxyl + *amide* + *-azepine* (chemical designation)] **:** a tricyclic anticonvulsant $C_{15}H_{12}N_2O$ used in the treatment of trigeminal neuralgia
car·ba·ryl \'kärbəˌril, -ərəl\ *n* [*carb*amate + *aryl* radical derived from an aromatic hydrocarbon] **:** a nonpersistent carbamate insecticide $C_{12}H_{11}O_2N$ effective against numerous crop, forage, and forest pests
car bed *n* **:** a portable bed for an infant that is designed for use in an automobile

car·ben·i·cil·lin \,kär(,)benə'silən\ *n* [*carb*oxybenzyl-pen*icillin*] **:** a broad-spectrum semisynthetic penicillin that is effective against gram-negative bacteria (as pseudomonas) and that acts esp. by inhibiting cell-wall synthesis

car·bo·line \'kärbə,lēn\ *n* [*carb*-+ ind*ole* + pyrid*ine*] **:** any of various isomers $C_{11}H_8N_2$ having a tricyclic structure which is related to indole and pyridine and which is found in many alkaloids

car·bo·na·ra \,kärbə'närə\ *n* [It, fr. *alla carbonara* from the charcoal grill] **:** a pasta dish made with a white cheese sauce that incorporates bits of bacon and ham ⟨spaghetti *carbonara*⟩

carbon dating *n* **:** determination of age (as of an archaeological find) by means of the content of carbon 14 — called also *carbon 14 dating, radiocarbon dating* —

car·bon–date \'kärbən,dāt, 'kàb-\ *vt*

car·bon·nade \,kärbə,näd\ *n* [F, lit., grilled meat, fr. It *carbonata*, fr. *carbone* carbon] **:** a stew usu. of beef cooked in beer

carbon spot*n **:** a small black spot on a coin

carbon star *n* **:** a reddish star of low surface temperature composed in part of carbon compounds

car·bo·rane \'kärbə,ran\ *n* [blend of *carbon* and *borane*] **:** any of a class of thermally stable compounds $B_nC_2H_{n+2}$ that are used in the synthesis of polymers and lubricants

car·ci·no·em·bry·on·ic an·ti·gen \,kärs°n(,)ō,embrē-'änik,antəjən\ *n* [*carcino*- tumor, cancer + *embryonic*] **:** a glycoprotein present in fetal gut tissues during the first two trimesters of pregnancy and in peripheral blood of patients with cancer of the digestive system

car coat *n* **:** a three-quarter-length overcoat

card–car·ry·ing \'kärd,karēiŋ, 'kàd-, *also* -,kerē-\ *adj* [fr. the assumption that such a member carries a membership card] **1 :** being a full-fledged member esp. of a Communist party **2 :** being strongly identified with a group (as of people with a common interest) ⟨*card-carrying* members of the ecology movement —Richard Neuhaus⟩

car·di·nal·i·ty \,kärd°n'aləd·ē\ *n* **:** the number of elements in a given mathematical set

cardinal number*n **:** the property that a mathematical set has in common with all sets that can be put into one=to-one correspondence with it

cardinal's hat *n* **:** GALERO

car·dio·ac·cel·er·a·tor \,kärdē(,)ōāk,selə,rād·ər, -ak,-\ *also* **car·dio·ac·cel·er·a·to·ry** \-,selərə,tōrē, -,tòr-, -i\ *adj* [*cardio*- heart (fr. Gk *kardia* heart) + *accelerator* or *acceleratory*] **:** speeding up the action of the heart — **car·dio·ac·cel·er·a·tion** \-,selə,rāshən\ *n*

car·dio·ac·tive \'kärdēō,aktiv\ *adj* [*cardio*- + *active*] **:** having an influence on the heart ⟨*cardioactive* drugs⟩ — **car·dio·ac·tiv·i·ty** \-ak'tivəd·ē, -i\ *n*

car·dio·cir·cu·la·to·ry \-,sərkyələ,tōrē, -,tòr-, -i\ *adj* [*cardio*- + *circulatory*] **:** of or relating to the heart and circulatory system ⟨temporary *cardiocirculatory* assist⟩

car·dio·dy·nam·ics \-dī'namiks\ *n pl but sing or pl in constr* [*cardio*- + *dynamics*] **:** the dynamics of the heart's action in pumping blood — **car·dio·dy·nam·ic** \-ik\ *adj*

car·dio·gen·ic \'kärdēə,jenik, *also* -jēn-\ *adj* [*cardio*- + -*genic* produced by] **:** originating in the heart **:** caused by a cardiac condition ⟨*cardiogenic* shock⟩

car·dio·meg·a·ly \,kärdēō'megəlē\ *n* [*cardio*- + -*megaly* enlargement, deriv. of Gk *megal*-, *megas* large, great] **:** enlargement of the heart

car·dio·my·op·a·thy \'kärdēō,mī'äpəthē\ *n* [*cardio*- + *myopathy* disorder of muscle tissue] **:** a typically chronic disorder of heart muscle that may involve hypertrophy and obstructive damage to the heart

car·dio·pul·mo·nary \-',pùlmə,nerē, -,pəl-\ *adj* [*cardio*- + *pulmonary* relating to the lungs] **:** of or relating to the heart and lungs ⟨a *cardiopulmonary* bypass that diverts blood from the entrance to the right atrium through an oxygenator directly to the aorta⟩

cardiopulmonary resuscitation *n* **:** a procedure designed to restore normal breathing after cardiac arrest that includes the clearance of air passages to the lungs, heart massage by the exertion of pressure on the chest, and the use of drugs

car·dio·scle·ro·sis \'kärdē(,)ōsklə',rōsəs\ *n*, *pl* **-scle·ro·ses** \-,ō,sēz\ [*cardio*- + *sclerosis* hardening of tissues] **:** induration of the heart caused by formation of fibrous tissue in the cardiac muscle

car·dio·tox·ic \-',täksik\ *adj* [*cardio*- + *toxic*] **:** having a toxic effect on the heart — **car·dio·tox·ic·i·ty** \-,täk-'sisəd·ē, -i\ *n*

car·dio·ver·sion \-',vərzhən, -,vēzh-, -,vaizh-, *also* -shən\ *n* [*cardio*- + -*version*, fr. L *version*-, *versio* action of turning] **:** application of an electric shock in order to restore normal heartbeat

cargo pocket *n* **:** a large pocket usu. with a flap and a pleat

car·hop \'kär,häp, ,kà,-\ *vi* **:** to work as a carhop

car·io·stat·ic \'karēō,stad·ik\ *adj* [*cario*- caries + *static* stable, unchanging] **:** tending to inhibit the formation of dental caries ⟨the *cariostatic* action of fluorides⟩

ca·ri·so·pro·dol \,kə,rīsə'prō,dòl, -īzə-, -dòl\ *n* [*car*- (prob. fr. *carbamate*) + *isopropyl* + *diol* compound with two hydroxyl groups] **:** a drug $C_{12}H_{24}N_2O_4$ related to meprobamate that is used to relax muscle and relieve pain

carnet*n **:** a booklet of postage stamps

carnival glass, *often cap C* [fr. its frequent use for prizes at carnival booths] **:** pressed glass with an iridescent finish mass-produced in a variety of colors (as frosty white or deep purple) in the U. S. in the early 20th century

carp \'kärp, 'kàp\ *n* [*carp*, vb.] **:** complaint

car·pac·cio \kär'päch(ē)ō\ *n* [It *filetto Carpaccio* fillet Carpaccio, after Vittore *Carpaccio* †1525 Venetian painter known for his use of reds and whites] **:** slices of raw beef served with a sauce

carpal tunnel *n* **:** a passage between the flexor retinaculum of the hand and the carpal bones that is sometimes a site of compression of the median nerve

carpal tunnel syndrome *n* **:** a condition caused by compression of the median nerve in the carpal tunnel and characterized esp. by discomfort and disturbances of sensation in the hand

carpetbag steak *n* **:** a thick piece of steak in which a pocket is cut and stuffed with oysters

carpool \'kär,pùl, 'kà,p-\ *vb* [*car* + *pool*] *vt* **:** to take turns driving ⟨*carpooled* their way from New Mexico —

Reader's Digest⟩ ⟨*carpool* children to school⟩ ~ *vi* **:** to participate in a car pool — **car pool·er** \-ˌpülə(r)\ *n*
carrier bag *n, Brit* **:** SHOPPING BAG
carrot–and–stick *adj* [fr. the traditional alternatives of driving a donkey on by either holding out a carrot or by whipping it with a stick] **:** characterized by use of alternating reward and punishment ⟨*carrot–and–stick* foreign policy⟩
carry*vb — **carry the can** *chiefly Brit* **:** to bear alone and in full an often hazardous responsibility ⟨in good democratic theory, Ministers are responsible to the people for the miscalculation of Arab intentions and potential. They ought to *carry the can* —Eric Silver⟩
carry**n, pl* **carries :** a quantity that is transferred in addition from one number place to the adjacent one of higher place value
car·ry·cot \ˈkareˌkät\ *n, Brit* **:** a portable bed for an infant
car·ry·on \ˈkareˌón, -ˌän, *also* ˈker-\ *n* **:** a piece of luggage suitable for being carried aboard an airplane by a passenger — **carry–on** *adj*
car·ry·out \ˈkareˌaút, *also* ˈker-\ *adj* **:** TAKE-OUT — **car·ry·out** \ˈkare-, *also* ˈker-\ *n*
Car·te·sian plane \(ˈ)kärˌtēzhən-, (ˈ)käˌ-\ *n* **:** a plane whose points are labeled with Cartesian coordinates
Cartesian product *n* **:** a set that is constructed from two given sets and comprises all pairs of elements such that one element of the pair is from the first set and the other element is from the second set
car·top·per \ˈkärˌtäpər; ˈkäˌ-, -pə(r)\ *n* **:** a small boat that may be transported on top of a car
case*n **:** one of a set of relational semantic categories in the deep structure of a sentence that help determine the meaning of the sentence
case·book*\ˈkäsˌbúk\ *n* **:** a compilation of primary and secondary documents relating to a central topic together with scholarly comment, exercises, and study aids that is often designed to serve as a source book for short papers (as in a course in composition) or as a point of departure for a research paper
case grammar *n* **:** a grammar that describes the deep structure of sentences in terms of the relation of a verb to a set of semantic cases
ca·sette \kəˈset, ka-\ *n* [alter. of *cassette*] **1 :** a cassette photographic film **2 :** a cassette for magnetic tape
cash bar *n* **:** a bar (as at a wedding reception) at which drinks are sold — compare OPEN BAR
cash desk *n, Brit* **:** a counter at which a cashier works
cash flow *n* **1 :** a measure of an organization's liquidity that usu. consists of net income after taxes plus noncash charges (as depreciation) against income **2 :** a flow of cash ⟨maintaining an international *cash flow* —C. H. Stern⟩ ⟨the faster the speed of *cash flow*, the better the fiscal health of the publishing company —*Book Production Industry*⟩; *esp* **:** one that provides solvency ⟨colleges obtained short loans in July to maintain a *cash flow* until tuition money came in —L. B. Mayhew⟩
cas·sa·ta \kəˈsäd-ə, ka-, -ätə\ *n* [It dial. (Sicilian) *cassata*, perh. fr. L *caseus* cheese] **:** a cake filled with ricotta cheese, candied fruit, and chocolate
cas·sette*\kəˈset, ka-\ *n* **:** a usu. plastic cartridge containing magnetic tape with the tape on one reel passing to the other without having to be threaded

Cas·tro·ism \ˈkas(ˌ)trōˌizəm, *sometimes* -äs-\ *n* [Fidel *Castro b*1927 Cuban political leader] **:** the political, economic, and social principles and policies of Fidel Castro — **Cas·tro·ist** \-ōˌist, -ōəst\ *n or adj* — **Cas·tro·ite** \-ōˌīt\ *n or adj*
CAT *abbr* **1 :** clear-air turbulence **2 :** computerized axial tomography
catalytic converter *n* **:** a device in the exhaust system of an automobile that contains a catalyst for converting gases into harmless or less harmful products (as water and carbon dioxide)
catchment area*n **:** the geographical area served by an institution ⟨describe the *catchment areas* and social backgrounds of the various schools she examined —*Times Lit. Supp.*⟩
catch–22 \ˈkachˌtwentēˈtü, ˈkech-, -tiˈt-\ *n, pl* **catch–22's** *or* **catch–22s** *often cap C* [fr. *Catch-22*, the paradoxical rule found in the novel *Catch-22* (1961) by Joseph Heller *b* 1923 Am. author, fr. *catch* a hidden difficulty + 22] **1 :** a problematic situation for which the only solution is denied by a circumstance inherent in the problem or by a rule ⟨the show-business *catch-22* — no work unless you have an agent, no agent unless you've worked — Mary Murphy⟩; *also* **:** the circumstance or rule that denies a solution ⟨this *Catch-22* principle of the tax code: . . . any transaction which has no substantive object other than to reduce one's taxes — does not qualify to reduce one's taxes —Andrew Tobias⟩ **2 a :** an illogical, unreasonable, or senseless situation ⟨continuing the *Catch-22* logic, he explained that the agents busted in with guns drawn "to reduce the potential for violence" —Michael Drosnin⟩ **b :** a measure or policy whose effect is the opposite of what was intended ⟨a medical *catch-22:* some experts now believe that the examination . . . may actually cause more cases of breast cancer than it helps to cure —*Newsweek*⟩ **c :** a situation presenting two equally undesirable alternatives **:** dilemma ⟨"*catch-22*" If I don't jog, it's bad. If I jog in polluted city air, it's bad —Jim Berry⟩ **3 :** a hidden difficulty **:** catch ⟨the puritanical *Catch-22* that runs through our society — pleasure, it warns, must be paid for —Janet S. King⟩
catch–up *adj* **:** intended to catch up to a theoretical norm or a competitor's accomplishments
catechism*n **:** something resembling a catechism esp. in being a rote response or formulaic statement
cat·e·chol·amine \ˌkad·əˈchóləˌmēn, -əˈsh-, -əˈk-, -ōl-, -əmən\ *n* [*catechol* pyrocatechol + *amine*] **:** any of various substances (as epinephrine, norepinephrine, and dopamine) that contain a benzene ring with two adjacent hydroxyl groups and a side chain of ethylamine and that function as hormones or neurotransmitters or both
cat·e·chol·amin·er·gic \ˌkad·əˈchólə(ˌ)mēˈnərjik, -əˈsh-, -əˈk-, -ōl-, -əməˈn-\ *adj* [ISV *catecholamine* + *-ergic* exhibiting or stimulating activity] **:** involving, liberating, or mediated by catecholamine ⟨*catecholaminergic* neurons in the brain⟩ ⟨*catecholaminergic* transmission in the nervous system⟩
cat·e·na·tive \ˈkad·əˌnād·iv, ˈkatᵊnˌād·iv, -atə-, -ātiv\ *or* **catenative verb** *also* **catenative auxiliary** *n* [*catenate* connect, link + *-ive*, adj. suffix] **:** a verb often followed by a function word (as *to* or *on*) that occupies a position other than final in a succession of two or more verbs together forming the main part of the predicate of a

sentence (as *ought* in "I ought to go home now" and *try* and *keep* in "they tried to keep on working")

cathedral**adj, of women's formal apparel* **:** having a length that reaches the floor and trails behind ⟨*cathedral* veil⟩

ca·tho·dal \'kath,ōd⁰l, kath'-\ *adj* [*cathode* + *-al*, adj. suffix] **:** of, relating to, or attracted to a cathode ⟨*cathodal* potentials⟩ ⟨*cathodal* hemoglobins⟩ — used esp. in the life sciences — **ca·tho·dal·ly** \kath'ōd⁰lē, -i\ *adv*

CAT scan \,sē,ā,tē-, ,kat-\ *n* **:** a sectional view of the body constructed by computerized axial tomography

CAT scanner *n* **:** a medical instrument consisting of integrated X-ray and computing equipment and used for computerized axial tomography

cattle call *n* **:** a mass audition (as of actors)

CATV *abbr* community antenna television

Cau·chy sequence \kō'shē-\ *n* [Augustin-Louis Cauchy †1857 Fr. mathematician] **:** a sequence of elements in a metric space such that for any positive number no matter how small there exists a term in the sequence for which the distance between any two consecutive or nonconsecutive terms beyond this term is less than the arbitrarily small positive number ⟨the sequence 1, $\frac{1}{2}$, $\frac{1}{3}$, $\frac{1}{4}$, ..., $\frac{1}{n}$, ... is a *Cauchy sequence*⟩

CB \(')sē'bē\ *n* **:** CITIZENS BAND

CB-er \(,)sē'bē(r)\ *n* [*CB* + *-er*, n. suffix] **:** one that operates a CB radio

CBW *abbr* chemical and biological warfare

CCTV *abbr* closed-circuit television

CDP *abbr* certificate in data processing

ce·co·pexy \'sēkə,peksē, -kō-\ *n* [*ceco-* cecum + *-pexy* fixation] **:** a surgical operation to fix the cecum to the abdominal wall

ce·di \'sādē\ *n* [Akan *sedie* cowrie] **1 :** the basic monetary unit of Ghana **2 :** a note representing one cedi

cell*n **:** a basic subdivision of a computer memory that is addressable and can hold one basic operating unit (as a word)

cell cycle *n* **:** the complete series of events from one cell division to the next — see G₁PHASE, G₂PHASE, M PHASE, S PHASE

cel·lu·lite \'selyə,līt\ *n* [F, fr. *cellule* cell + *-ite* constituent part of the body] **:** lumpy fat found in the thighs, hips, and buttocks of some women

center*n **:** the center of the circle inscribed in a regular polygon

cen·ter·fold \'sentə(r),fōld\ *n* **1 :** a foldout that is the center spread of a magazine **2 :** a picture (as of a nude model) on a centerfold

cen·ter–of–mass system*\,sentərə(v)'mas-\ *n* **:** a frame of reference in which the center of mass is at rest

centime*n **:** a monetary unit of Equatorial Guinea equivalent to $\frac{1}{100}$ ekuele

cen·ti·sec·ond \'sentə,sekənd, *also* -ənt, *esp before a pause or consonant* -ən, -⁹ŋ\ *n* [ISV *centi-* hundredth (deriv. of L *centum* hundred) + *second*] **:** one hundredth of a second

central angle *n* **:** an angle formed by two radii of a circle

central dogma *n* **:** a theory in genetics and molecular biology subject to several exceptions that genetic information is coded in self-replicating DNA and undergoes unidirectional transfer to messenger RNAs in transcrip-

tion which act as templates for protein synthesis in translation

central limit the·o·rem \-,thēərəm, -,thi(ə)rəm\ *n* **:** any of several fundamental theorems of probability and statistics giving the conditions under which the distribution of a sum of independent random variables can be found approximately by using the normal distribution; *esp* **:** a special case of the central limit theorem which is much applied in sampling: the distribution of the mean of a sample from a population with finite variance approaches the normal distribution as the number in the sample becomes large

central processing unit *n* **:** PROCESSOR 1b

central tendon *n* **:** a 3-lobed aponeurosis located near the central portion of the diaphragm caudal to the pericardium and composed of intersecting planes of collagenous fibers

cen·tri·lob·u·lar \,sen·trə,läbyələ(r)\ *adj* [*centri-* center + *lobular*] **:** relating to or affecting the center of a lobule ⟨*centrilobular* necrosis in the liver⟩; *also* **:** affecting the central parts of the secondary pulmonary lobules of the lung ⟨*centrilobular* emphysema⟩

cen·trism \'sen,trizəm\ *n* [*centr-* + *-ism*] **:** a political philosophy of avoiding extremes of right or left

ceph·a·lex·in \,sefə'leksən\ *n* [NL, tr. *cephalosporin* + *-ex-* (arbitrary infix) + *-in* chemical compound] **:** a semisynthetic cephalosporin $C_{16}H_{17}N_3O_4S$ with a spectrum of antibiotic activity similar to the penicillins

ceph·a·lo·pel·vic disproportion \,sefə(,)lō,pelvik-\ *n* [*cephalo-* head and + *pelvic*] **:** a condition in which a maternal pelvis is small in relation to the size of the fetal head

ceph·a·lor·i·dine \,sefə'lòrə,dēn, -'lär-\ *n* [prob. fr. *cephalosporin* + *-idine* chemical compound] **:** a broad-spectrum antibiotic $C_{19}H_{17}N_3O_4S_2$ derived from cephalosporin

ceph·a·lo·spo·rin \,sefələ'spōrən, -'spòr-\ *n* [*Cephalosporium*, genus name + *-in* chemical compound] **:** any of several antibiotics produced by an imperfect fungus of the genus *Cephalosporium*

ceph·a·lo·thin \'sefələ(,)thin\ *n* [*cephalo*sporin + *thio* containing sulfur + *-in* chemical compound] **:** a semisynthetic broad-spectrum antibiotic $C_{16}H_{15}N_2NaO_6S_2$ that is an analogue of a cephalosporin and is effective against penicillin-resistant staphylococci

cer·amide \'se(ə)rə,mīd, 'si(ə)r-, -əməd; sə'ram,īd, -məd\ *n* [*cerebroside* + *amide*] **:** any of a group of amides formed by linking a fatty acid to sphingosine and found widely but in small amounts in plant and animal tissue

cereal leaf beetle *n* **:** a small reddish brown black‹ headed Old World chrysomelid beetle (*Oulema melanopa*) that feeds on cereal grasses and is a serious threat to U. S. grain crops

ce·re·bral–pal·sied \sə'rēbrəl'pólzēd, 'serəbrəl-\ *adj* **:** affected with cerebral palsy

ce·ru·lo·plas·min \sə,rülō,plazmən, ,ser(y)əl-\ *n* [ISV *cerulo-* (fr. L *caeruleus* dark blue) + *plasma* + *-in* chemical compound; prob. orig. formed in Sw] **:** an alpha globulin active in the biological storage and transport of copper

cer·vico·tho·rac·ic \,sərvə(,)kōthə,rasik\ *adj* [*cervico-* cervical and + *thoracic*] **:** of or relating to the neck and thorax ⟨*cervicothoracic* sympathectomy⟩

cer·vi·co·vag·i·nal \-ˌvajənᵊl\ *adj* [*cervico-* + *vaginal*] **:** of or relating to the uterine cervix and the vagina ⟨*cervicovaginal* flora⟩ ⟨*cervicovaginal* carcinoma⟩

ce·si·um clock \'sēzēəm-, -zh(ē)əm-\ *n* **:** an atomic clock regulated by the natural vibration frequency of cesium atoms

cesium 137 *n* **:** a radioactive isotope of cesium that has the mass number 137 and a half-life of about 12 months and that is present in fallout

ce·tri·mide \'sē·trəˌmid, 'se·t-\ *n* [fr. *cetyl* + *tri-* containing three atoms, radicals, or groups + *methyl* + *-ide* chemical compound] **:** a mixture of bromides of ammonium used esp. as a detergent and antiseptic

CFA *abbr* certified financial analyst

chain printer *n* **:** a line printer in which the printing element is a continuous chain

chain rule *n* **:** a mathematical rule concerning the differentiation of a function of a function (as $f[u(x)]$) by which under suitable conditions of continuity and differentiability one function is differentiated with respect to the second considered as an independent variable and then the second function is differentiated with respect to the independent variable ⟨if $v = u^2$ and $u = 3x^2 + 2$ the derivative of v by the *chain rule* is $2u(6x)$ or $12x(3x^2 + 2)$⟩

chain·wheel \'chānˌ(h)wēl\ *n* **:** a sprocket wheel of a bicycle

chair·per·son \'che(ə)rˌpərs²n, 'cha(ə)r-; 'cheəˌpās²n, 'chaə-, -ˌpəis-\ *n* **1 :** the presiding officer of a meeting or an organization or a committee ⟨pocket reference handbook provides the *chairperson* of any meeting with a concise summary of parliamentary procedures —*Henry Regnery Co. Catalog*⟩ **2 :** the administrative officer of a department of instruction (as in a college) ⟨an opening now exists for *chairperson* of the Department of Oral Surgery at the School of Dentistry —*advt*⟩

chair·side \-ˌsīd\ *adj* [*chair* + *side* (as in *bedside*)] **:** relating to, performed in the vicinity of, or assisting in the work done on a patient in a dentist's chair ⟨a dental *chairside* assistant⟩ ⟨a good *chairside* manner⟩

chak·ra* \'chəkrə, 'shäk-\ *n* **:** any of several points of physical or spiritual energy in the human body according to yoga philosophy

chamberlain* *n* **:** an often honorary papal attendant; *specif* **:** a priest having a rank of honor below domestic prelate

Chan·dler's wobble \ˌchandlə(r)z-, -nl-\ *n* [Seth Carlo Chandler †1913 Am. astronomer] **:** an elliptical oscillation of the earth's axis of rotation with a period of 14 months whose cause has not been determined

changing room *n, Brit* **:** a room where one may change clothes; *esp* **:** one for use by sports participants **:** a locker room

channel* *n* **1 :** a path along which information passes or an area (as of magnetic tape) on which it is stored **2 :** a transition passage in jazz **:** a bridge

chan·nery \'chan(ə)rē, -ri\ *adj* [Sc, gravelly, fr. *channer* gravel, alter. of *channel* gravel, channel; fr. gravel's being a major constituent of the channel of a river] **:** containing more than 15 percent but less than 90 percent fragments of thin flat sandstone, limestone, or schist up to 6 inches along the longer axis ⟨*channery* soil⟩

character* *n* **:** a symbol (as a letter or number) that represents information; *also* **:** a representation (as by a series of ones and zeros) of such a character that may be accepted by a computer

characteristic* *n* **:** the smallest positive integer n which for an operation in a ring, integral domain, or field yields 0 when any element is used n times with the operation and which is taken as 0 when no such integer exists

characteristic equation *n* **:** an equation in which the characteristic polynomial of a matrix is set equal to 0

characteristic poly·no·mi·al \-ˌpälᵊˌnōmēəl\ *n* **:** the determinant of a square matrix in which an arbitrary variable (as x) is subtracted from each of the elements along the principal diagonal

characteristic root *n* **:** a scalar associated with a given linear transformation of a vector space and having the property that there is some nonzero vector which when multiplied by the scalar is equal to the vector obtained by letting the transformation operate on the vector ⟨if $T(v) = \lambda v$, where T is a linear transformation, v is a nonzero vector, and λ is a scalar, then λ is a *characteristic root* of T, and v is an eigenvector of T corresponding to λ⟩ ; *specif* **:** a root of the characteristic equation of a matrix

characteristic value *n* **:** CHARACTERISTIC ROOT

characteristic vector *n* **:** EIGENVECTOR

char·ac·to·nym \'karəktəˌnim *also* 'ker-\ *n* [*character* + *-onym* name] **:** a name esp. for a fictional character (as Mistress Quickly or Caspar Milquetoast) that suggests a distinctive trait of the character

char·broil \'chärˌbröil, 'chȧ-, *esp before a pause or consonant* -öiəl\ *vt* [*charcoal* + *broil*] **:** to broil on a rack over hot charcoal **—** **char·broil·er** \-öilə(r)\ *n*

charge con·ju·ga·tion \-ˌkänjəˈgäshən\ *n* **:** an operation in mathematical physics in which each particle in a system is replaced by its antiparticle

charismatic* *adj* **:** of or relating to the religious movement that emphasizes the extraordinary power (as of healing) given a Christian by the Holy Spirit

char·is·mat·ic \ˌkarəzˈmadˈik\ *n* **:** a member of a charismatic religious group or movement

charm* *n* **:** a quantum characteristic of a quark or fundamental particle that accounts for the unexpectedly long lifetime of the J particle, explains various difficulties in the theory of weak interactions, and has a value of zero for most known particles

charmed* *adj* **:** having charm ⟨a *charmed* antiquark⟩

char·mo·ni·um \chärˈmōnēəm\ *n, pl* **charmonium** [*charm* + *-onium* (as in *positronium*)] **:** any of a group of fundamental particles that are held to consist of a charmed quark-antiquark pair

chart·bust·er \'chärtˌbəstər, 'chȧtˌbəstə(r\ *n* **:** one that is a best seller; *esp* **:** a best-selling phonograph record

charter* *n* **:** a travel arrangement in which transportation (as a bus or plane) is hired by and for a specific group of people **—** **charter** *adj*

Char·treux* \(')shärˈtrüs, -ȧˌt-, -üz, *sometimes* -ärˌtrərs *or* -ȧˌtrās\ *n, pl* **Chartreux** **:** any of a breed of short-haired domestic cats of French origin having a bluish gray coat and gold or orange eyes

chau·vin·ism* \'shōvəˌnizəm\ *n* **:** an attitude of superiority toward members of the opposite sex; *also* **:** behavior expressive of such an attitude ⟨maintain that it is a sexist fallacy to fight male *chauvinism* with female *chauvinism* —Lynn Z. Bloom⟩

cheapo \'chē(,)pō\ *adj* [alter. of *cheap*] **:** cheap

cheap shot *n* **1 :** an act of deliberate roughness against a defenseless opponent esp. in a contact sport **2 :** an unfair statement that takes advantage of a known weakness of the target

checkbook journalism *n* **:** journalism in which a person is paid for granting an interview

check off*vi **:** to change a play at the line of scrimmage in football by calling an audible

checkoff*n **:** designation by a taxpayer of a dollar of income tax to be used for public financing of political campaigns

checkout \'chek,aút\ *n* **1 :** the process of examining and testing something as to readiness for intended use ⟨facilities for the manufacture, testing, assembly, and *checkout* of launch vehicles and spacecraft —G. E. Mueller⟩ **2 :** the process of familiarizing oneself with the operation of a mechanical thing (as an airplane) ⟨training that must include *checkout* on several types of multiengine airplanes —*Plane Talk*⟩

Che·diak–Hl·ga·shi syndrome \shäd¦yükhē¦gäshē-\ *n* [Moises *Chediak fl* 1952 Fr. physician and Ototaka *Higashi fl* 1954 Jp. physician] **:** a genetic disorder inherited as an autosomal recessive and characterized by partial albinism, abnormal granules in the white blood cells, and marked susceptibility to bacterial infections

ohef's sal·ad \¦shef¦saləd\ *n* **:** a meal-size salad that usu. includes lettuce, tomatoes, celery, hard-boiled eggs, and julienne strips of meat and cheese

che·la·tor \'kē,lād-ə(r)\ *n* **:** a binding agent that suppresses chemical activity by forming chelates

che·mo·nu·cle·ar \¦kemō¦n(y)üklēə(r), ¦kēmō-, ÷-kyələ(r)\ *adj* [*chemo-* chemical + *nuclear*] **:** being or relating to a chemical reaction induced by nuclear radiation or fission fragments

che·mo·nu·cle·ol·y·sis \-,n(y)üklē¦äləsəs\ *n* **:** treatment of a slipped disk by the injection of chymopapain to dissolve the displaced nucleus pulposus

che·mo·sen·so·ry \-¦sen(t)s(ə)rē, -ri\ *adj* **:** related to or involved in the sensory reception of chemical stimuli ⟨*chemosensory* hairs⟩ ⟨*chemosensory* responses⟩

che·mo·sphere \'kemə,sfi(ə)r, 'kēmə-, -,sfiə\ *n* **:** a stratum of the upper atmosphere in which photochemical reactions are prevalent and which begins about 20 miles above the earth's surface

che·mo·ster·il·ant \¦kemō¦sterələnt, ¦kēmō-\ *n* **:** a substance that produces irreversible sterility (as of an insect) without marked alteration of mating habits or life expectancy — **che·mo·ster·il·iza·tion** \-,sterələ¦zāshən, -,lī¦z-\ *n* — **che·mo·ster·il·ize** \-¦sterə,līz\ *vb*

che·mo·sur·gery \-¦sərj(ə)rē, -¦sōj-, -¦sōij-, -ri\ *n* **:** removal by chemical means of diseased or unwanted tissue — **che·mo·sur·gi·cal** \-¦jəkəl\ *adj*

che·mo·tax·on·o·my \-,tak¦sänəmē, -mi\ *n* **:** the classification of plants and animals based on similarities and differences in biochemical composition — **che·mo·tax·o·nom·ic** \-,taksə¦nämik\ *adj* — **che·mo·tax·o·nom·i·cal·ly** \-k(ə)lē, -li\ *adv* — **che·mo·tax·on·o·mist** \-,tak¦sänəməst\ *n*

cheong·sam \'cheün¦säm, 'chòn-\ *n* [Chin (Cant) *ch'eung shaam*, lit., long gown] **:** a dress with a slit skirt and a mandarin collar worn esp. by Oriental women

chet·rum \'chē-trəm, 'che-\ *n* [native name in Bhutan] **1 :** a monetary unit of Bhutan equal to $^{1}/_{100}$ ngultrum **2 :** a coin representing one chetrum

chiao \'jaù\ *n, pl* **chiao** [Chin (Pek) *chiao[3]*] **1 :** a monetary unit of China equal to $^{1}/_{10}$ yuan **2 :** a coin or note representing one chiao

Chi·ca·na \chi'känə, shi-, -kän-\ *n* [Chicano + -*a* (fr. Sp, fem. ending)] **:** an American woman or girl of Mexican descent — **Chicana** *adj*

chi·cane*\shə'kän, chə-\ *n* **:** a series of tight turns in opposite directions in an otherwise straight stretch of a road-racing course

chi·ca·nis·mo \chi¦kä¦niz(,)mō, shi-, -kä-, -is(,)mō\ *n, often cap* [*Chicano* + -*ismo*, fr. Sp, -ism (characteristic trait)] **:** strong ethnic pride exhibited by Chicanos

Chi·ca·no \chi'kän(,)ō, shi-, -kän-\ *n, pl* **-nos** [modif. of Sp *mejicano* Mexican, fr. *Méjico* Mexico] **:** an American of Mexican descent — **Chicano** *adj*

chick·en–and–egg \,chik(ə)nən¦(d)eg, -¦(d)äg\ *adj* [fr. the proverbial question of whether the chicken or the egg first came into being] **:** of, relating to, or being a dilemma of cause and effect or of priority ⟨a *chicken-and-egg* affair: it isn't easy to say which came first, the parts or the boys with the ability to play them —Christopher Ford⟩ ⟨my problem is a *chicken-and-egg* one. To provide the goodies that will interest people, I need money and I don't like to hit people for money unless I can provide services that they need —P.J. Rich⟩

chicken Ki·ev \-'kē,ef, -,(y)ef, -,(y)ev, -,(y)əf\ *n* [*Kiev*, U.S.S.R.] **:** a boneless chicken breast that is stuffed with seasoned butter and deep fried

Chi·com \'chi¦käm\ *n* [Chinese + communist] **:** a communist Chinese

Chien ware \chē'en,-\ *also* **Chien yao** \-n¦yaù\ *n* [Chin (Pek) *ch'ien yao[2]*, fr. *Ch'ien an*, locality in China where it was first made + Chin (Pek) *yao[2]* pottery] **:** a dark Chinese stoneware dating from the Sung period that usu. has a black brown-mottled glaze and is used esp. for tea wares

child·proof \'chil(d),prüf\ *adj* **:** designed to prevent tampering by children ⟨a *childproof* door lock⟩ ⟨unable to open *childproof* pill bottles —Geoffrey Wolff⟩

chili·bur·ger \'chilē,bərgər, -li-; -,bōgə(r, -,bəig-\ *n* **:** a hamburger topped with chili

chili dog *n* **:** a hot dog topped with chili

chill factor *n* **:** WINDCHILL

Chil·tern Hundreds \,chiltə(r)n-\ *n pl* [*Chiltern Hundreds*, three hundreds in the Chiltern hills of England appointment to the stewardship of which is a disqualification for membership in Parliament] **:** a nominal appointment granted by the British crown that serves as a legal fiction to enable a member of Parliament to relinquish his seat

chi·me·rism \ki'mi(ə)r,izəm, kə-, 'kīmə,riz-\ *n* **:** the state of being a genetic chimera

chinaman*n **:** an off-break in cricket bowled by a left-handed bowler to a right-handed batsman

China syndrome *n* [so called fr. the notion that the molten reactor contents could sink through the earth to reach China] **:** the accidental melting of the core of a nuclear reactor so that it passes through the bottom of its container and down into the earth

Chinese fire drill *n* **1 :** a state of great confusion or disorder ⟨we had a *Chinese fire drill* here. Pandemonium broke loose. Everybody was running around calling everybody he knew asking for help —Nareid Maxey⟩ **2 :** a prank in which a number of people jump out of an automobile stopped at a red light, run around to the opposite side, and jump back in often in a different seat before the light changes to green

Chinese restaurant syndrome *n* **:** a group of symptoms that may include numbness of the neck, arms, and back with headache, dizziness, and palpitations and that is held to affect susceptible persons ingesting monosodium glutamate often used to season Chinese food

chip***n** **1 :** INTEGRATED CIRCUIT **2 a :** a soft high pass or shot over a defender's head in soccer **b :** a return shot in tennis made by hitting down on the ball to give it backspin

chip***vt** **1 :** to hit (a return in tennis) with backspin **2 :** to kick (a soccer ball) in a soft high arc ~ *vi* **:** to make a chip (as in soccer or tennis)

chi·ral \'kī(ə)rəl\ *adj* [*chir-* hand (deriv. of Gk *cheir*) + *-al*, adj. suffix] **:** of or relating to a molecule that is nonsuperimposable on its mirror image — **chi·ral·i·ty** \kī'raləd·ē, kə'-\ *n*

chi–square distribution \'kī;skwa(ə)r-, -;skwe(ə)r-\ *n* **:** a probability density function that gives the distribution of the sum of the squares of a number of independent random variables each having a normal distribution with zero mean and unit variance, that has the property that the sum of two random variables with such a distribution also has one, and that is widely used in testing statistical hypotheses esp. about the theoretical and observed values of a quantity and about population variances and standard deviations

chit·lin circuit \'chitlən-\ *n* [fr. the assumption that chitterlings are eaten chiefly by blacks] **:** a group of theaters and nightclubs that cater to black audiences and feature black entertainers

chlor·am·bu·cil \klór'ambyə₃sil, klòr-\ *n* [*chlor*oethyl + *amino* + *butyric* + *-il* related substance] **:** an anticancer drug $C_{14}H_{19}Cl_2NO_2$ that is a derivative of nitrogen mustard and is used esp. to treat leukemias and Hodgkin's disease

chlor·di·az·epox·ide \₃klórdī₃azə'päk₃sīd, ₃klòr-\ *n* [*chlor-* containing chlorine + *diaz-* containing the group N_2 + *epoxide*] **:** a benzodiazepine $C_{16}H_{14}ClN_3O$ structurally and pharmacologically related to diazepam that is used in the form of its hydrochloride esp. as a tranquilizer and to treat the withdrawal symptoms of alcoholism — see LIBRIUM

chlor·hex·i·dine \klōr'hexə₃dīn, klór-, -₃dēn\ *n* [ISV *chlor-* chlorine + *hex-* containing six atoms or groups + *-idine* chemical compound] **:** a biguanide derivative $C_{22}H_{30}Cl_2N_{10}$ used as a local antiseptic esp. in the form of its hydrochloride or acetate

chlor·mer·o·drin \klōr'merədrən, klòr-\ *n* [*chlor-* + *mer*cury + connective *-o-* + *-hydrin* chemical compound containing halogen or cyanogen] **:** a mercurial diuretic $C_5H_{11}ClHgN_2O_2$ used in the treatment of some forms of edema, ascites, and nephritis

chlo·ro·flu·o·ro·car·bon \₃klōrə;flú(ə)(₃)rō;kärbən, ;klór-, -;flōr(₃)ō-, ;flò(₃)rō-, -;káb-\ *n* [ISV *chloro-* chlorine + *fluorocarbon*] **:** CHLOROFLUOROMETHANE

chlo·ro·flu·o·ro·meth·ane \-;meth₃än\ *n* [ISV *chloro-* + *fluoro-* fluorine + *methane*] **:** any of several gaseous compounds that are derivatives of methane, contain chlorine and fluorine, and are used esp. as aerosol propellants and refrigerants

chlo·ro·thi·a·zide \-;'thīə₃zīd, -əzəd\ *n* [*chloro-* + *thiazide*] **:** a thiazide diuretic $C_7H_6ClN_3O_4S_2$ used esp. to treat edema and to increase the effectiveness of antihypertensive drugs

chlo·ro·tri·anis·ene \-(₃)trī;anə₃sēn\ *n* [*chloro-* containing chlorine in place of hydrogen + *tri-* containing three atoms, radicals, or groups + *anisyl* (alcohol) + *ethylene*] **:** a synthetic compound $C_{23}H_{21}ClO_3$ that is converted to a potent estrogenic substance in the living system and is used esp. orally to treat menopausal symptoms

chlor·prop·amide \-'präpə₃mīd, -prōp-, -əməd\ *n* [*chlor-* + *prop*ane + *amide*] **:** a sulfonylurea compound $C_{10}H_{13}ClN_2O_3S$ used to reduce blood sugar in the treatment of mild diabetes

chlor·thal·i·done \klōr'thalə₃dōn, klór-\ *n* [*chlor-* + *thalidone*, fr. ph*thal*imide + *ketone*] **:** a sulfonamide $C_{14}H_{11}ClN_2O_4S$ that is a long-acting diuretic used esp. in the treatment of edema and sometimes against hypertension

choke***vi** **choked; chok·ing :** to lose one's composure and fail to perform effectively in a critical situation ⟨but they did lose . . . . Why? Overconfident? Maybe. Peaked too soon? Maybe. Got behind and *choked* ? Maybe. —Dan Jenkins⟩ ⟨we *choked*, we made a lot of errors. . . . I think we felt the pressure today —Bill North⟩

cho·le·cyst·agogue \₃kōlə;sistə₃gäg, ₃käl-, -òg\ *n* [*cholecyst* + *-agogue* substance that promotes secretion or expulsion] **:** an agent (as cholecystokinin) that causes the gallbladder to discharge bile

cho·le·cyst·ec·to·mized \₃kōlə(₃)sis'tektə₃mīzd, ₃käl-\ *adj* [*cholecystectomy* + *-ize*, vb. suffix + *-ed*] **:** having had the gallbladder removed

¹cho·le·cys·to·ki·net·ic \₃kōlə;sistōkə;ned·ik, ;käl-, -kī;n-\ *adj* [*cholecyst* + connective *-o-* + *kinetic*] **:** tending to cause the gallbladder to contract and discharge bile

²cholecystokinetic *n* **:** CHOLECYSTAGOGUE

cho·le·sta·sis \₃kōlə'stäsəs, ₃käl-\ *n, pl* **-sta·ses** \-'stä₃sēz\ [NL, fr. *chol-* bile, gall (deriv. of Gk *cholē, cholos* gall) + *-stasis* stoppage, deriv. of Gk *stasis* standing, stopping] **:** a checking or failure of bile flow — **cho·le·stat·ic** \₃kōlə;stad·ik, ;käl-\ *adj*

cho·li·no·lyt·ic \₃kōlənō;lid·ik, ₃käl-\ *adj* [ISV acetyl*choline* + *-o-* + *-lytic* of decomposition, fr. Gk *lytikos* able to loose, fr. *lyein* to loose] **:** interfering with the action of acetylcholine or cholinergic agents — **cholinolytic** *n*

cho·li·no·mi·met·ic \-mə;med·ik, -(₃)mī;-\ *adj* [ISV acetyl*choline* + *-o-* + *mimetic*] **:** resembling acetylcholine or simulating its physiologic action — **cholinomimetic** *n*

cho·li·no·re·cep·tor \-rə;septə(r)\ *n* [acetyl*choline* + *-o-* + *receptor*] **:** a receptor for acetylcholine in a postsynaptic membrane

Chom·skyan *or* **Chom·skian** \'chäm(p)skēən, -òm-, -kyən\ *adj* [Avram Noam *Chomsky b*1928 Am. linguist]

: of, relating to, or based on the linguistic theories of Noam Chomsky ⟨the applicability of a *Chomskian* transformation is determined by comparison of two syntactic structures —D.G. Hays⟩

chopper**n 1 :** a high-bouncing batted baseball **2 :** a customized motorcycle

chop·per \'chäpə(r)\ *vb* [*chopper* helicopter] *vi* **:** to travel by helicopter ⟨they *choppered* up from the Pentagon's helicopter pad —*Newsweek*⟩ ~ *vt* **:** to transport by helicopter ⟨were daringly *choppered* into a North Vietnamese prison —Burr Snider⟩

chor·do·ma \kōr'dōmə, kȯr-\ *n, pl* **-mas** *or* **-ma·ta** \-mədə, -ətə\ [noto*chord* + -*oma* tumor] **:** a malignant tumor that is derived from remnants of the embryonic notochord and occurs along the spine attacking esp. the bones at the base of the skull or near the coccyx

chord organ *n* **:** an electronic or reed organ with buttons for producing simple chords

cho·ri·on fron·do·sum \ˌkōrēˌänfrän'dōsəm, ˌkȯr-, -ōon-\ *n* [NL, fr. *chorion* + L *frondosum* leafy, fr. *frond-, frons* foliage + -*osum* -ose (adj. suffix)] **:** the part of the chorion that has persistent villi and that with the attached portions of the endometrium forms the placenta

cho·roi·de·re·mia \ˌkōrˌȯidəˌrēmēə, ˌkȯr-\ *n* [*choroid* + Gk *ēremia* desolation] **:** progressive degeneration of the choroid that is controlled by a sex-linked gene

chrome*'krōm\ *n* **:** something plated with an alloy of chromium

chro·mo·dy·nam·ics \ˌkrōmō(ˌ)dī'namiks\ *n pl but sing in constr* [*chromo*- color + *dynamics*] **:** a theory of fundamental particles based on the assumption that quarks are distinguished by differences in color and are held together by an exchange of gluons

chro·no·bi·ol·o·gy \ˌkränəbī'äləjē, ˌkrō-, -nō-, -ji\ *n* [*chrono*- time + *biology*] **:** the study of biological rhythms — **chron·no·bi·o·log·ic** \-ˌbīə'läjik\ *or* **chro·no·bi·o·log·i·cal** \-jəkəl\ *adj* — **chro·no·bi·ol·o·gist** \-bī-'äləjəst\ *n*

chuffed \'chəft\ *adj* [*chuff* proud + -*ed*] *Brit* **:** proud of or satisfied with oneself

chug·a·lug \'chəgəˌləg\ *vb* **-lugged; -lug·ging** [imit.] *vt* **:** to drink a whole container of without pause ⟨*chugalugged* his beer, and . . . called out for another draft — M.J. Bosse⟩; *also* **:** to drink quickly or copiously **:** guzzle ⟨chain-smoking cigarettes and *chugalugging* tea — Melvin Maddox⟩ ~ *vi* **:** to drink a whole container (as of beer) without pause

church key *n* **:** a can opener with a triangular pointed head for piercing the tops of cans (as of beer) ⟨killed the six-pack, two cans apiece, opening them with a *church key* and drinking right out of the cans —Kay Martin⟩

churn*vt* **:** to subject (a client's security account) to excessive numbers of purchases and sales primarily to generate additional commissions ⟨revoked the registration of several firms which have *churned* the accounts —*Frauds & Quackery Affecting the Older Citizen*⟩

churn out *vt* **:** to produce mechanically or copiously **:** grind out ⟨the usual pap which has been *churned out* about this superstar —W.S. Murphy⟩ ⟨computers *churn out* gaudy parlay cards at peak efficiency —Pete Axthelm⟩

chutz·pah *also* **chutz·pa** *or* **hutz·pah** *or* **hutz·pa** \'kùtspə, 'hù-, -(ˌ)spä\ *n* [Yiddish, fr. LHeb *ḥuṣpāh*] **:** supreme self-confidence **:** nerve, gall ⟨flaunted her newfound grooviness with characteristic *chutzpah* by smoking a joint onstage —Ed McCormack⟩

Chvos·tek's sign \(kə)ˌvös,tek(s)-\ *or* **Chvostek sign** \-ˌtek-\ *n* [Franz *Chvostek* †1884 Austrian surgeon] **:** a twitch of the facial muscles following gentle tapping over the facial nerve in front of the ear that indicates hyperirritability of the facial nerve

chy·lo·mi·cro·ne·mia \ˌkīlə,mīkrəˈnēmēə, -ˌmik-\ *n* [*chylomicron* + -*emia* blood condition] **:** an excessive number of chylomicrons in the blood ⟨postprandial *chylomicronemia*⟩

chy·lo·tho·rax \ˌkīlə'thō(ə)rˌaks, -ˌthó(ə)r-\ *n* [*chylochyle* + *thorax*] **:** an effusion of chyle or chylous fluid into the thoracic cavity

chy·mo·pa·pa·in \ˌkīmōpə'pāən, -ˌpīən\ *n* [*chyme* + connective -*o*- + *papain*] **:** a proteolytic enzyme from the latex of the papaya that is used in meat tenderizer and has been used medically in chemonucleolysis

ciao \'chaù\ *interj* [It, fr. It dial., alter. of *schiavo* (I am your) slave, fr. ML *sclavus* slave] — used conventionally as an utterance at meeting or parting

ci·lan·tro \sə'läntrō, lan-\ *n* [Sp, coriander, fr. LL *coliandrum*, alter. of L *coriandrum*] **:** leaves of coriander used as a flavoring or garnish

ci·met·i·dine \sī'medəˌdēn, -ctə-\ *n* [*ci*- (alter. of *cyan*-cyanogen) + *methyl* + -*idine* chemical compound] **:** an analogue of histamine $C_{10}H_{16}N_6S$ that has been used in the short-term treatment of duodenal ulcers and in the treatment of pathological hypersecretory disorders

cine·an·gio·car·di·og·ra·phy \ˌsinēˌanjēōˌkärdēˈägrəfē\ *n* [*cine*- motion picture (fr. *cinema*) + *angiocardiography*] **:** motion-picture photography of a fluoroscopic screen recording passage of a contrasting medium through the chambers of the heart and large blood vessels — **cine·an·gio·car·dio·graph·ic** \-dēōˈgrafik\ *adj*

cine·an·gi·og·ra·phy \-ˌanjēˈägrəfē\ *n* **:** motion-picture photography of a fluorescent screen recording passage of a contrasting medium through the blood vessels — **cine·an·gio·graph·ic** \-ˌanjēōˈgrafik\ *adj*

cin·e·ma·theque \ˌsinəməˈtek\ *n* [F *cinémathèque* film library, fr. *cinéma* cinema + -*thèque* (as in *bibliothèque* library)] **:** a small movie house specializing in avant-garde films

cinéma vé·ri·té\-ˌverəˈtā\ *n* [F *cinéma-vérité* truth cinema] **:** the art or technique of filming a motion picture (as a documentary) so as to convey candid realism

cine·phile \'sinəˌfil\ *n* [*cine*- + -*phile* lover, deriv. of Gk *philos* beloved, loving] **:** a devotee of motion pictures

cin·gu·late gyrus \ˌsingyələt-, -ˌlāt-\ *n* **:** a medial gyrus of each cerebral hemisphere that partly surrounds the corpus callosum

cin·gu·lec·to·my \ˌsingyəˈlektəmē, -mi\ *n, pl* **-mies** [*cingulum* + -*ectomy* cutting out] **:** CINGULOTOMY

cin·gu·lot·o·my \-ˈläd-əmē, -ätə-, -mi\ *n, pl* **-mies** [*cingulum* + connective -*o*- + -*tomy* incision] **:** surgical removal of all or part (as the cingulum) of the cingulate gyrus

CIP *abbr* cataloging in publication

cir·ca·di·an \(ˌ)sər'kādēən, 'sərkəˌdēən\ *adj* [L *circa* about + *dies* day + E -*an*, adj. suffix] **:** being, having, characterized by, or occurring in approximately 24 hour periods or cycles (as of biological activity or function)

⟨*circadian* oscillations⟩ ⟨*circadian* periodicity⟩ ⟨*circadian* rhythms in hatching⟩ ⟨*circadian* leaf movements⟩ — **cir·ca·di·an·ly** *adv*

circ·an·nu·al \(ˈ)sərˈkanyə(wə)l\ *adj* [L *circa* about + E *annual*] **:** having, characterized by, or occurring in approximately yearly periods or cycles (as of biological activity or function) ⟨*circannual* rhythmicity⟩

circle*n **:** a residential street that curves and typically loops back on itself — used chiefly in the names of streets

circuit breaker*n **:** a provision (as in an insurance contract or tax law) that limits financial obligations beyond a specified amount for covered individuals

circular di·chro·ism \-ˈdīˌkrōˌizəm\ *n* **1 :** the property (as of an optically active medium) of unequal absorption of right and left circularly plane-polarized light so that the emergent light is elliptically polarized **2 :** a spectroscopic technique that makes use of circular dichroism

circular file *n* [fr. its shape] **:** wastebasket

cir·cum·plan·e·tary \ˌsərkəmˈplanəˌterē, ˌsȯk-, ˌsȯik-\ *adj* [*circum*- around, about (fr. L, fr. *circum*, fr. *circus* circle) + *planetary*] **:** surrounding and relatively close to a planet ⟨*circumplanetary* space⟩

cir·cum·so·lar \-ˈsōlə(r), -ˌlär, -ˌlȧ(r\ *adj* **:** revolving about or surrounding the sun ⟨a *circumsolar* orbit⟩

cir·cum·stel·lar \-ˈstelə(r)\ *adj* **:** surrounding or occurring in the vicinity of a star ⟨*circumstellar* dust⟩

cir·cum·ter·res·tri·al \-təˌrest(r)ēəl, -ˌres(h)chəl\ *adj* **:** revolving about or surrounding the earth ⟨a *circumterrestrial* orbit⟩

cir·cus·iana \ˌsərkəsēˈänə, ˌsȯk-, ˌsȯik-, -ˈanə\ *n pl* [*circus* + connective *-i-* + *-ana* collected items] **:** materials or objects relating to circuses or circus life

cis·lu·nar \(ˈ)sisˈlünə(r), -ˌnär, -ˌnȧ(r\ *adj* [*cis* on this side (fr. L) + *lunar*] **:** of or relating to the space between the earth and the moon or the moon's orbit

cis·ter·na*\sisˈtərnə\ *n, pl* **-nae** \-ˌnē\ **:** one of the interconnected flattened vesicles or tubules comprising the endoplasmic reticulum

cis·tron \ˈsiˌsträn\ *n* [*cis-trans* + *-on* basic hereditary component] **:** a segment of DNA which specifies a single functional unit (as a protein or enzyme) and within which two heterozygous and closely linked recessive mutations are expressed in the phenotype when on different homologous chromosomes but not when on the same chromosome — compare OPERON — **cis·tron·ic** \siˈstränik\ *adj*

citizen's arrest *n* **:** an arrest made by a citizen who derives his authority from the fact that he is a citizen

citizens band *n* **:** a range of radio-wave frequencies allocated by the Federal Communications Commission for private radio use

citrus red mite *n* **:** a comparatively large mite (*Panonychus citri*) that is a destructive pest on the foliage of citrus — called also *citrus red spider*

city·bil·ly \ˈsidˌē,bilē, -dˌiˌ-, -li\ *n, pl* **-bil·lies** [*city* + hill*billy*] **:** a musician or singer brought up in a city who performs country music

clad *n* **1 :** a composite material formed by cladding; *specif* **:** a clad coin **2 :** cladding; *specif* **:** the outer layer of a clad coin

cla·dis·tic \kləˈdistik, klaˈ-\ *adj* [*clad*- (fr. Gk *klados* branch) + *-istic*, adj. suffix] **:** based on phylogenetic relationships ⟨a *cladistic* system of classification⟩ — compare PHENETIC — **cla·dis·ti·cal·ly** \-təˌk(ə)lē, -li\ *adv*

cla·dis·tics \-iks\ *n pl but sing in constr* **:** biological systematics based on phylogenetic relationships

clado·gen·e·sis \ˌkladəˈjenəsȯs\ *n* [NL, fr. Gk *klados* branch + *genesis*] **:** evolutionary change characterized by treelike branching of lines of descent — **clado·ge·net·ic** \ˌkladōjəˈnedˌik\ *adj* — **clado·ge·net·i·cal·ly** \-k(ə)lē, li\ *adv*

clams casino *n pl but sing or pl in constr, often cap 2d C* **:** clams on the half shell usu. topped with green pepper and bacon and baked or broiled

clang·er \ˈklaŋə(r)\ *n, Brit* **:** a conspicuous blunder — often used in the phrase *drop a clanger* ⟨the Inland Revenue dropped an outsize *clanger*. It sent an income tax form to Samuel Pepys, the diarist who died in 1703 — Nicholas Holmes⟩

clapped–out \ˈklapˈdaùt\ *adj, Brit* **:** exhausted or worn out esp. from hard use or hard work ⟨many flights, sometimes in *clapped-out* aircraft —*Times Lit. Supp.*⟩ ⟨they start in slaving . . . at crack of dawn and by the time I get there for dinner, everybody's *clapped-out* —Patrick Ryan⟩

class*n **1 :** a group of adjacent and discrete or continuous values of a random variable **2 :** a mathematical set

class action *n* **:** a legal action undertaken by one or more plaintiffs on behalf of themselves and all other persons having an identical interest in the alleged wrong

clath·rate \ˈklaˌthrāt, ˈklathrȯt\ *n* **:** a clathrate compound

clath·ra·tion \klaˈthrāshən\ *n* **:** the process of clathrate formation

claus·tro·phil·ia \ˌklòstrəˈfilēə\ *n* [NL, fr. *claustro*- (fr. L *claustrum* bar, bolt) + *-philia* abnormal liking] **:** an abnormal desire for confinement in an enclosed space

clean*adj **1** *slang* **:** smartly dressed **2 :** free from drug addiction ⟨an addict's baby is often born addicted; these children were born *clean* —Gertrude Samuels⟩ **3 :** having no contraband (as drugs) in one's possession ⟨the severe lack of drugs, since . . . everybody seemed to have come up to New Haven *clean* —*East Village Other*⟩

clean*vb — **clean one's clock :** to beat or whip one in a fight or competition ⟨I've got a father and two brothers at home who can *clean my clock* —Duane Bobick⟩

clean room \ˈklēnˌrüm, -ˌrùm\ *n* **:** a room for the manufacture or assembly of objects (as precision parts) that is maintained at a high level of cleanliness by special means

clean up*vt — **clean up one's act :** to behave in a more acceptable manner (as by discarding questionable practices) ⟨find himself a decent job and start *cleaning up his act* —Tim O'Brien⟩

clear–air tur·bu·lence \ˌkli(ə)rˈa(ə)rˈtərbyələn(t)s, -ˈe(ə)r-\ *n* **:** sudden severe turbulence occurring in cloudless regions that causes violent jarring or buffeting of aircraft passing through

clear·way \ˈkli(ə)rˌwā, ˈkliə-\ *n, Brit* **:** an expressway with fully controlled access **:** a freeway

cleaver*n **:** a rock ridge protruding from a glacier or snowfield

cleft sentence *n* **:** a sentence produced by a transformation which adds *what* to the beginning and a form of the verb *be* to the end of the original sentence and removes a noun phrase from its original position to follow *be* ⟨the sentence "George likes gin" yields the *cleft sentence* "What George likes is gin"⟩

client state *n* **:** a country that is economically, politically, or militarily dependent on another country ⟨Congress is going to cut back on military aid to *client states* and raise barriers against new military involvement — Tris Coffin⟩

clin·da·my·cin \ˌklində'mīsᵊn\ *n* [chlor- (chlorine) + *lindamycin*, alter. (influenced by *deoxy-*) of *lincomycin*] **:** a semisynthetic antibacterial antibiotic $C_{18}H_{33}ClN_2O_5S$ chemically related to lincomycin and used esp. against gram-positive organisms

Clio \'klē(ˌ)ō\ *n* [L *Clio*, the Greek muse of history, fr. Gk *Kleiō*] **:** any of several statuettes awarded annually by a professional organization for notable achievement in radio and television commercials

clio·met·rics \ˌklīə'me·triks\ *n pl but sing in constr* [*Clio*, muse of history + *-metric* relating to a science or process of measuring + *-s*, plural ending] **:** the application of methods developed in other fields (as economics, statistics, and data processing) to the study of history — **clio·met·ric** \-ik\ *adj* — **clio·met·ri·cian** \-me·'trishən, -mə·-\ *n*

clip art *n* **:** ready-made illustrations sold in books from which they may be cut and pasted as artwork

clock***n* **:** a synchronizing device (as in a computer) that produces pulses at regular intervals — **kill the clock** *or* **run out the clock :** to use up as much as possible of the playing time remaining in a game (as football) while retaining possession of the ball or puck esp. to protect a lead

clock in *vi, Brit* **:** to punch in

clock off *vi, Brit* **:** to punch out

clock on *vi, Brit* **:** to punch in

clock out *vi, Brit* **:** to punch out

clock radio *n* **:** a combination clock and radio device in which the clock can be set to turn on the radio at a designated time

clo·fi·brate \klō'fīˌbrāt, -'fib-\ *n* [perh. fr. *chlorine* + *fibr-* fiber + *propionate*] **:** a compound $C_{12}H_{15}ClO_3$ used esp. in the treatment of hypercholesterolemia

clo·mi·phene \'kläməˌfēn, 'klōm-\ *n* [*chlorine* + *amine* + *-phene* (fr. *phenyl*)] **:** a synthetic drug $C_{26}H_{28}ClNO$ used in the form of its citrate to induce ovulation

clone***n** **1 :** an individual grown from a single somatic cell of its parent and genetically identical to it **2 :** one that appears to be a copy of an original form ⟨the perfect *clone* of some... tune —Tony Trischka⟩

clone \'klōn\ *vb* **cloned; clon·ing** *vt* **1 :** to propagate a clone from ⟨frogs have been successfully *cloned* by transplanting nuclei from body cells to enucleated eggs⟩ **2 :** to make a copy of ⟨fast-food franchises, *cloned* burger dispensaries —Jay Jacobs⟩ ~ *vi* **:** to produce a clone

clo·ni·dine \'klänəˌdēn, 'klōn-, -ˌdīn\ *n* [*chlor-* chlorine + *-nidine*, alter. fr. *imidazoline*] **:** an antihypertensive drug $C_9H_9Cl_2N_3$ used to treat essential hypertension and to prevent migraine headache

closed***adj* **1 :** traced by a moving point that returns to an arbitrary starting point ⟨*closed* curve⟩; *also* **:** so formed that every plane section is a closed curve ⟨*closed* surface⟩ **2 a :** containing all the limit points of every subset ⟨a *closed* set⟩ **b** *of an interval* **:** containing its endpoints **3 :** characterized by mathematical elements that when subjected to an operation produce only elements of

the same set ⟨the set of whole numbers is *closed* under addition and multiplication⟩

closed–captioned *adj, of a television program* **:** broadcast so that captions appear only on the screen of a receiver equipped with a decoder

closed loop *n* **:** an automatic control system for an operation or process in which feedback in a closed path or group of paths acts to maintain the output at the desired level

closet***n* **:** a state or condition of secrecy, privacy, or obscurity ⟨he comes out of the *closet* and unabashedly urges socialism —*New Times*⟩

closet***adj* **:** being so in private **:** secret ⟨a *closet* racist⟩ ⟨pretending to be a tough-minded naturalist when he's really a *closet* transcendentalist —J.R. Frakes⟩

closet queen *n* **:** one who is a latent or a covert homosexual

closing***n* **:** a meeting between parties to a real-estate deal usu. together with their attorneys and interested parties (as a mortgagor) for the purpose of formally transferring title

closing costs *n pl* **:** expenses (as for appraisal, title search, and title insurance) connected with the purchase of real estate that usu. constitute a charge against the purchaser additional to the cost of the property purchased

closure***n** **1 :** the property that a number system or a set has when it is mathematically closed under an operation **2 :** a set that contains a set and all limit points of the set

clothesline***n** **:** a tackle in football in which a defensive player's outstretched arm catches the ballcarrier by the neck unawares — **clothesline** *vt*

clotting factor *n* **:** any of several plasma components (as fibrinogen, prothrombin, and thromboplastin) that are involved in the clotting of blood

cloud nine *n* [perh. fr. *cloud* the ninth and highest heaven of Dante's Paradise, whose inhabitants are most blissful because nearest to God] **:** a state of feeling extreme elation — usu. used with *on* ⟨was on *cloud nine* after his victory⟩ ⟨the A-flat major Ballade which lifted the body of listeners out of their collective seats and gave them a ride on *cloud nine* —L.I. Snyder⟩

clout***n** **:** ability or power to affect something (as a political decision) **:** influence, pull ⟨the oil lobby, the labor lobby, the doctors' lobby, the postal lobby, the people with the money and the *clout* again and again exercise undue influence upon the nation's legislators —*Parade Mag.*⟩

clox·a·cil·lin \ˌkläksə'silən\ *n* [*chlorophenol* + *isoxazole* + *penicillin*] **:** a synthetic oral penicillin $C_{19}H_{17}$-ClN_3NaO_5S esp. effective against staphylococci because of resistance to their penicillinases

cloze \'klōz\ *adj* [by shortening & alter. fr. *closure*] **:** of, relating to, or being a test of reading comprehension that involves having the person being tested supply words which have been systematically deleted from a text

clunker***n** **:** someone or something notably unsuccessful ⟨the album has its... *clunkers* and unmemorable bits — Lester Bangs⟩

cluster***n** **:** a group of buildings and esp. houses built close together on a sizable tract in order to preserve open spaces larger than the individual yard for common recreation

cluster college *n* **:** a small residential college constituting a semiautonomous division of a university and usu. specializing in one branch of knowledge (as history and the social sciences)

Clut·ton's joints \'klət°nz-\ *n pl* [Henry Hugh *Clutton* †1909 Eng. surgeon] **:** symmetrical hydrarthrosis esp. of the knees or elbows that occurs in congenital syphilis

CMA *abbr* certified medical assistant

CN*abbr chloroacetophenone

co·adapt·ed \¦kōə¦daptəd\ *adj* [co- with, together (fr. L) + *adapted*] **:** mutually adapted esp. by natural selection ⟨*coadapted* gene complexes⟩

co·ag·u·lop·a·thy \(ˌ)kō¸agyə'läpəthē, -i\ *n* [*coagul*ation + connective -o- + -*pathy* disease] **:** a disease affecting blood coagulation

co–anchor \('kō¦aŋkə(r)\ *n* [co- + *anchor*] **:** a newscaster who shares the duties of anchoring a news broadcast — **co–anchor** *vt*

Co·an·da effect \kō¦andə-, -än-\ *n* [Henri *Coanda* †1972 Romanian engineer] **:** the tendency of a jet of fluid emerging from an orifice to follow an adjacent flat or curved surface and to entrain fluid from the surroundings so that a region of lower pressure develops

cobblers \'käblə(r)z\ *n pl* [fr. *cobblers' awls,* rhyming slang for *balls*] *Brit* **:** foolish or insincere talk **:** nonsense, bunk ⟨I'll bet he gives them that spiel at every house he goes to — he was word perfect. It was all a load of *cobblers* —Bill Naughton⟩

CO·BOL \'kō¸bòl\ *n* [*common business oriented language*] **:** a standardized business language for programming a computer

co·chro·mat·o·graph \¸kō(ˌ)krō'mad·ə¸graf\ *vi* **:** to undergo separation out of a mixed sample by cochromatography ⟨a compound that *cochromatographs* with farnesol⟩ ~ *vt* **:** to subject to cochromatography

co·chro·ma·tog·ra·phy \¸kō¸krōmə'tägrəfē, -fi\ *n* **:** chromatography of two or more samples together; *esp* **:** identification of an unknown substance by chromatographic comparison with a known substance

cock·a·ma·my *or* **cock·a·ma·mie** \'käkə¸māmē\ *adj* [prob. fr. *cockamamie* decal, alter. of *decalcomania*] **:** being ridiculous or unbelievable **:** absurd ⟨of all the *cockamamy* excuses I ever heard —Leo Rosten⟩ ⟨if you ever bring us a *cockamamie* script like this again we'll ban you from the studio for life —Art Buchwald⟩

cock·a·poo \'käkə¸pü\ *n* [*cocka-,* shortening and alter. of *cocker* spaniel + *poodle*] **:** a dog that is a cross between a cocker spaniel and a poodle

cock·suck·er \'käk¸səkə(r)\ *n* **:** one who fellates — usu. considered obscene; often used as a generalized term of abuse — **cocksucking** \¦käk¦səkiŋ\ *adj*

cock·teas·er \'käk¦tēzə(r)\ *n* **:** a female who excites a male sexually and then refuses intercourse — usu. considered obscene

code*n **:** GENETIC CODE

code*vi **:** to specify the genetic code ⟨the DNA sequence of the gene that *codes* for that protein —Gina B. Kolata⟩

code–switch·ing \'kōd¦swichiŋ\ *n* **:** the switching from the linguistic system of one language or dialect to that of another

code word*n **:** a euphemism ⟨interpreting "compatability" as a *code word* for stifling dissent, the faculty denounced the memorandum —Robert Griffith⟩

co·di·col·o·gy \¸kōdi'käləjē, ¸käd-, -ji\ *n* [L *codic-, codex* book + E connective -o- + -*logy* science] **:** the study of manuscripts as cultural artifacts for historical purposes — **co·di·co·log·i·cal** \-ikə'läjikəl\ *adj*

co·dom·i·nant**('kō¦dämənənt\ *adj* **:** being fully expressed in the heterozygous condition ⟨the alleles controlling blood groups A and B are *codominant* since an individual with both alleles belongs to blood group AB⟩

co·don \'kō¸dän\ *n* [*code* + -*on* basic hereditary component] **:** a triplet of adjacent nucleotides that is part of the genetic code and that specifies a particular amino acid in a protein or starts or stops protein synthesis

cods·wal·lop \'kädz¸wäləp, -wòl-\ *n* [origin unknown] *chiefly Brit* **:** foolish or worthless talk or writing **:** nonsense, drivel ⟨from which the author manages to soar sympathetically above his own fuzzy *codswallop* — Mordecai Richler⟩ ⟨shall continue to attack their philosophy for the dangerous *codswallop* that it is —*The People* ⟩

co·en·zy·mat·ic \¸kō¸enzə¦mad·ik, *also* -¸zī¦-\ *adj* **:** of or relating to a coenzyme ⟨*coenzymatic* activity⟩ — **co·en·zy·mat·ical·ly** \-mad·ək(ə)lē\ *adv*

co·en·zyme Q \(')kō¸en¸zīm'kyü\ *n* [Q prob. fr. *quinone*] **:** UBIQUINONE

coes·ite \'kō¸zit\ *n* [Loring *Coes,* Jr., *b*1915 Am. chemist] **:** a dense crystalline silica formed from quartz under great heat and pressure and found in meteorite craters

coffee lightener *or* **coffee whit·en·er** \-¦(h)wīt-(ə)nə(r)\ *n* **:** a nondairy product used as a substitute for cream in coffee

co·gen·er·a·tion \¦kō¸jenə¦rāshən\ *n* [co- + *generation*] **:** the utilization of wasted heat generated in an industrial process for a special purpose (as supplying domestic hot water); *also* **:** the use of fuel for dual purposes (as steam heating and the generation of electricity)

cog·ni·tive dissonance \¦kägnəd·iv-\ *n* **:** internal psychological conflict resulting from incongruous beliefs and attitudes (as a fondness for smoking and a belief that it is harmful) held simultaneously

co·he·sion·less \kō¦hēzhənləs, -¸les\ *adj* **:** composed of particles or granules that tend not to cohere ⟨*cohesionless* soils⟩

co·in·ci·dent**\kō¦in(t)sədənt, -d°nt, -¸dent\ *or* **coincident indicator** *n* **:** an economic indicator (as level of personal income or of retail sales) that more often than not correlates directly with the state of the economy

co·in·sti·tu·tion·al \¦kō¸instə¦t(y)üshnəl, -shən°l\ *adj* **:** of, relating to, or being a high school having separate class or activity areas for boys and girls

CO·LA \'kōlə\ *abbr* cost-of-living adjustment

cold call *n* **:** a sales call made directly to a potential customer without prior contact or without a lead

cold duck *n* [trans. of G *kalte ente,* a drink made of a mixture of fine wines] **:** a beverage that consists of a blend of sparkling burgundy and champagne

cold weld *vi* **:** to adhere on contact without application of pressure or heat — used of metals in the vacuum of outer space

col·i·ci·no·ge·nic \¦käləsənə¦jenik, -¸sēn-, -jēn-\ *adj* [*colicin* + connective -o- + -*genic* producing] **1 :** producing or having the capacity to produce colicins ⟨*colicino-*

genic bacteria⟩ **2 :** conferring the capacity to produce colicins ⟨*colicinogenic* genetic material⟩ — **col·i·ci·no·ge·nic·i·ty** \-nəjə'nis(ə)d·ē, -i\ *n*

col·i·ci·nog·e·ny \ˌkäləsə'näjənē, -ni\ *n* **:** the capacity to produce colicins

co·lin·ear\(')kō'linēə(r)\ *adj* **:** having corresponding parts arranged in the same linear order ⟨good evidence is accumulating that the gene and its polypeptide product are *colinear* —J.D. Watson⟩ — **co·lin·ear·i·ty** \(ˌ)kō-ˌlinē'arəd·ē\ *n*

co·lis·tin \kə'listən, kō-\ *n* [NL *colistinus*, specific epithet of the bacterium producing it] **:** a polymyxin antibiotic produced by a bacterium of the genus *Bacillus* (*B. colistinus*) and used against some gram-negative pathogens esp. of the genera *Pseudomonas*, *Escherichia*, and *Aerobacter*

col·la·gen·o·lyt·ic \ˌkäləjənə'lid·ik, -ˌjen-\ *adj* [*collagen* + connective -*o-* + -*lytic* of decomposition, fr. Gk *lytikos* able to loose, fr. *lyein* to loose] **:** relating to or having the capacity to break down collagen ⟨*collagenolytic* activity⟩ ⟨*collagenolytic* enzyme⟩

col·lap·sar \kə'lapˌsär\ *n* [*collapse* + -*ar* (as in *quasar*)] **:** BLACK HOLE 1

collateral ligament *n* **:** either of two ligaments of the knee that help stabilize it by preventing lateral dislocation: **a :** one connecting the lateral condyle of the femur with the lateral side of the head of the fibula **b :** one connecting the medial condyle of the femur with the medial condyle and medial surface of the tibia

col·lect·ible or **col·lect·able** \kə'lektəbəl\ *n* [*collect* + -*ible* or -*able*] **:** an object that is collected by fanciers; *esp* **:** one other than such traditionally collectible items as art, stamps, coins, and antiques

col·le·gi·al·i·ty\kəˌlējē'aləd·ē\ *n* **:** the participation of bishops in the government of the Roman Catholic Church in collaboration with the pope

co·lon·ic \(')kō'länik, kə'l-\ *n* **:** irrigation of the colon **:** enema

co·lo·nos·co·py \ˌkōlə'näskəpē\ *n* [*colon* + connective -*o-* + -*scopy* examination] **:** endoscopic examination of the colon

color*n* **:** a hypothetical property of quarks that differentiates each type into three forms that are identical in mass, spin, electric charge, and all other measurable quantities but that have distinct roles in the strong interactions that bind quarks together

col·or-blind*\'kələ(r)ˌblīnd\ *adj* **:** not recognizing differences of race ⟨*color-blind* policy which refused to record anything about the race of welfare recipients —D.P. Moynihan⟩; *esp* **:** free from racial prejudice ⟨would become, in reality, a white man with an invisible black skin in a *color-blind* community —James Farmer⟩

col·or·cast·er \-ˌkastə(r), -äs-\ *n* [*color* picturesqueness, local color + broad*caster*] **:** a broadcaster (as of a sports contest) who supplies vivid or picturesque details and often gives statistical or analytical information

color-code \ˈkələ(r)ˌkōd\ *vt* **:** to color (as wires or pipes) according to a key designed to facilitate identification

co·lo·rec·tal \ˈkōləˌrekt³l\ *adj* [*colon* + *rectal*] **:** relating to or affecting the colon and the rectum ⟨*colorectal* cancer⟩ ⟨*colorectal* surgery⟩

color-field \ˈkələ(r)ˈfē(ə)ld\ *adj* **:** of, relating to, or being abstract painting in which color is emphasized and form and surface are correspondingly de-emphasized ⟨*color-field* abstractionists⟩

color painting *n* **:** color-field painting — **color painter** *n*

Col·or·point \'kələ(r)ˌpoint\ *n* [*color* + *point*] **:** any of a variety of domestic short-haired cats of Siamese type and coat pattern but with different colors

Col·our·point Longhair \ˈkələˌpoint-\ *n*, *Brit* **:** HIMALAYAN

col·por·rha·phy \käl'pôrəfē, -òr-\ *n* [Gk *kolpos* vagina + *rhaphē* suture] **:** surgical repair of the vaginal wall

column chromatography *n* **:** chromatography in which the substances to be separated are absorbed in layers as they pass in solution through a column packed with the absorbing medium (as silica gel or alumina) — compare THIN-LAYER CHROMATOGRAPHY

COM *abbr* computer-output microfilm; computer-output microfilmer

com·bi·na·to·ri·al\kəmˌbīnə'tōrēəl, ˌkämbənə-, -'tòr-\ *adj* **:** of or relating to the arrangement, operation, and selection of mathematical elements within finite or discrete sets or states (as the set of possible states of a digital computer)

combinatorial to·pol·o·gy \-tə'päləjē\ *n* **:** a study that deals with geometric forms based on their decomposition into combinations of the simplest geometric figures

com·bi·na·to·rics \ˌkämbənə'tōriks, kəmˌbīn-, -'tòr-\ *n pl but sing in constr* [*combinatorial* mathematics] **:** combinatorial mathematics

comb-out*\'kōˌmaut\ *n* **:** the combing of hair into a desired hairdo

come*vb* — **come off*** **:** to return to a regular activity after (a particular condition, experience, or performance) ⟨an injury-prone wide receiver *coming off* his only good season in five —D.P. Anderson⟩

come*n* **1 :** an orgasm — usu. considered vulgar **2 :** semen — usu. considered vulgar

come·back·er \'kamˌbakə(r)\ *n* **:** a grounder in baseball hit directly to the pitcher

come on*vi* **1 :** to project an indicated personal image ⟨*comes on* gruff and laconic ... on the telephone — Robert Craft⟩ **2 :** to show sexual interest in someone; *also* **:** to make sexual advances — usu. used with *to* or *with* ⟨didn't get the feeling that [she] was interested in him or that he was *coming on* strong to her —Ellen J. Willis⟩ ⟨in his own inept way was trying to *come on* to her —*East Village Other*⟩ **3 —** used to express astonishment, incredulity, or recognition of an obvious put-on

come up*vi* **:** to turn out to be ⟨he *came up* hoarse for opening day —Jack Schiffman⟩ — **come up roses :** to turn out far better than expected **:** turn out extremely well ⟨would be disingenuous in the extreme to conclude that everything is *coming up roses* —C.G. Spiegler⟩

comfort letter *n* **:** a formal statement by a company's auditors made usu. before a merger or the sale of securities indicating no apparent change in the company's financial situation since the last audit or financial report

comix \'kämiks\ *n pl* [by alter.] **:** comic books or comic strips

command*n* **1 :** an electrical or electronic signal that actuates a device (as a control mechanism in a spacecraft or one step in a computer) **2 :** the activation of a device in or the control of a vehicle (as a spacecraft) by means of a command

command mod·ule \-'mäj(ˌ)ü(ə)l\ *n* **:** a space vehicle module designed to carry the crew, the chief communication equipment, and the equipment for reentry

commentator*n* **:** a layman who leads a congregation in prayer at Mass or explains the rituals performed by the priest

common market *n* **:** an economic association (as of nations) formed to remove trade barriers among members

common si·tus picketing \-'sīd·əs-\ *n* [fr. L *situs* site] **:** picketing of an entire construction site by a trade union having a grievance with only a single subcontractor working at the site

common trust fund *n* **:** a fund which is managed by a bank or trust company and in which the assets of many small trusts are handled as a single portfolio with individual beneficiaries receiving returns proportionate to their share of the principal

communication theory *or* **communications theory** *n* **:** a theory that deals with the technology of the transmission of information (as in the printed word or a computer) between men or men and machines or machines and machines

community antenna television *n* **:** CABLE TELEVISION

com·mu·ta·tiv·i·ty \kəˌmyüd·ə'tivəd·ē, ˌkämyəd·ə'ti-\ *n* **:** the property of being commutative ⟨the *commutativity* of a mathematical operation⟩

com·mu·ta·tor*\'kämyəˌtäd·ə(r)\ *n* **:** an element of a mathematical group that when multiplied by the product of two given elements yields the product of the elements in reverse order

commute*vi* **com·mut·ed; com·mut·ing :** to yield the same result regardless of order — used of two mathematical elements undergoing an operation or of two operations on elements

com·mute \kə'myüt\ *n* **1 :** an act or instance of commuting ⟨his usual morning *commute* to work — *Newsweek*⟩ **2 :** the distance covered in commuting ⟨about an hour's *commute* from the university —*College Composition & Communication*⟩

¹comp \'kämp, 'kəmp\ *vi* [short for *accompany*] **:** to play an irregular rhythmic chord accompaniment for jazz

²comp \'kämp\ *n* [by shortening] **:** a complimentary ticket; *broadly* **:** something provided free of charge ⟨flying them here free on charters and supplying them with other *comps* — a room, meals and liquor —Hal Lancaster⟩

com·pact·ible \kəm'paktəbəl\ *adj* **:** capable of being compacted ⟨*compactible* soils⟩

comparative advertising *n* **:** advertising in which a competitor's product is named and compared with the advertiser's product

comparison shop *vi* **:** to compare prices on competing brands or in competing stores in order to find the best value

compensatory education *n* **:** educational programs intended to make up for cultural experiences or educational stimulation lacked by disadvantaged children

competence*n* **1 :** readiness of bacteria to undergo genetic transformation **2 :** the knowledge that enables a person to speak and understand a language — contrasted with *performance*

competent*adj* **:** having the capacity to respond (as by producing an antibody) to an antigenic determinant ⟨immunologically *competent* cells⟩

competitive*adj* **:** depending for effectiveness on the relative concentration of two or more substances ⟨*competitive* inhibition of an enzyme⟩

com·pil·er*\kəm'pīlə(r)\ *n* **:** a computer program that automatically converts instructions written in a higher-level symbolic language (as FORTRAN) into machine language

complement*n* **:** the set of all elements that do not belong to a given set and are contained in a particular mathematical set containing the given set

com·ple·men·tar·i·ty* \ˌkämplə(ˌ)men·'tarəd·ē, -lə-mən-·\ *n* **:** the correspondence between complementary strands or nucleotides of DNA or sometimes RNA that permits their precise pairing

com·ple·men·ta·ry* \ˌkämpləˌmentərē, -n·trē, -ri\ *adj* **:** characterized by molecular complementarity; *esp* **:** characterized by the capacity for precise pairing of purine and pyrimidine bases between strands of DNA and sometimes RNA such that the structure of one strand determines the other

com·ple·men·ta·tion* \ˌkämpləmən·'tāshən, -lə-(ˌ)men-\ *n* **1 :** the determination of the complement of a given mathematical set **2 :** production of normal phenotype in an individual heterozygous for two closely related mutations with one on each homologous chromosome and at a slightly different position

complex con·ju·gate \-'känjəgət, -jēg-, -jəˌgät\ *n* **1 :** one of two complex numbers (as $a + bi$ and $a - bi$) differing only in the sign of the imaginary part **2 :** a matrix whose elements and the corresponding elements of a given matrix form pairs of conjugate complex numbers

com·plex·om·e·try \ˌkämˌplek'sämə·trē, kəm-, -ri\ *n* [*complex* + connective -o- + -*metry* measuring, deriv. of Gk *metron* measure] **:** a titrimetric technique involving the use of a complexing agent (as EDTA) as the titrant — **com·plex·o·met·ric** \(ˌ)käm,pleksə'me·trik, kəm-\ *adj*

com·plic·it \(ˌ)kəm'plisət\ *adj* [back-formation fr. *complicity*] **:** having complicity ⟨who, having abjured killing in revulsion against the war, finds himself guiltily *complicit* in it in the revolution —C.E. Schorske⟩

com·plic·i·tous \(ˌ)kəm'plisəd·əs, -ətəs\ *adj* [*complicit* + -*ous*, adj. suffix] **:** COMPLICIT

com·po·nent*\kəm'pōnənt, 'käm,pō-, käm'pō-\ *n* **:** a coordinate of a vector; *also* **:** either member of an ordered pair of numbers

composite*adj, of a statistical hypothesis* **:** specifying a range of values for one or more statistical parameters — compare SIMPLE

composite*or* **composite function** *n* **:** a function whose values are found from two given functions by applying one function to an independent variable and then applying the second function to the result and whose domain consists of those values of the independent variable for which the result yielded by the first function lies in the domain of the second

computation*n* **:** the use or operation of a computer

com·pu·ta·tion·al linguistics \,kämpyu̇'tāshnəl-, -shən⁴l-\ *n pl but usu sing in constr* **:** linguistic research carried out by means of a computer

compute*vb **comput·ed; comput·ing** *vt* **:** to determine or calculate by means of a computer ~ *vi* **:** to use a computer

com·put·er·ese \kəm'pyüd·ə'rēz, -ütə-, -ēs\ *n* [*computer* + *-ese* jargon] **1 :** MACHINE LANGUAGE **2 :** jargon used by computer technologists

computerise *Brit var of* COMPUTERIZE

com·put·er·ite \-'pyüd·ə,rīt, -ütə-\ *n* **:** COMPUTERNIK

com·put·er·ize \kəm'pyüd·ə,rīz, -ütə-\ *vb* **-ized; -iz·ing** *vt* **1 :** to carry out, control, or produce by means of a computer ⟨*computerized* typesetting⟩ ⟨planning to *computerize* their entire accounting systems —*Data Processing Mag.*⟩ **2 :** to equip with computers ⟨getting the rights but not the skills of a modern *computerized* society —J.B. Reston⟩ **3 :** to put into a computer ⟨will soon *computerize* all available information on the buyers and sellers of property —Ward Morehouse III⟩ ~ *vi* **:** to use computers ⟨another advantage of *computerizing* is that the automatic printout virtually eliminated human error in transcribing data —*Consumer Reports*⟩ — **com·put·er·iz·able** \-'pyüd·ə,rīzəbəl\ *adj* — **com·put·er·iza·tion** \-,pyüd·ərə'zāshən, -,rīz-\ *n*

com·put·er·ized \kəm'pyüd·ə,rīzd, -ütə-\ *adj* **:** run or produced as if by computer — used as a generalized term of disapproval ⟨arguments against *computerized* America with its *computerized* language —T.L. Gross⟩

computerized axial tomography *n* **:** radiography in which a three-dimensional image of a body structure is constructed by computer from a series of plane cross-sectional images made along an axis

com·put·er·like \-'pyüd·ə(r),līk, -ütə-\ *adj* **:** resembling or characteristic of a computer ⟨handled with *computerlike* impersonality in anonymous offices —D.W. Harding⟩

com·put·er·nik \-'pyüd·ə(r),nik, -ütə-\ *n* [*computer* + *-nik* one connected with, fr. Yiddish] **:** a person who works with or has a deep interest in computers

Com·sat \'käm,sat\ *service mark* — used for communications services involving an artificial satellite

com·symp \'käm,simp\ *n, often cap* [*communist* + *sympathizer*] **:** a person who sympathizes with communist causes — usu. used disparagingly

conative*adj **:** of or relating to the function of a message to influence the one receiving it — **conatively** *adv*

concave*n **:** a concave line or surface

con·cep·tu·al\kən'sepchə(wə)l, kän-, -'sepshwəl\ *adj* **:** of, relating to, or being conceptual art

conceptual art *n* **:** an art form in which the artist's intent is to convey a concept rather than to create an art object — **conceptual artist** *n*

con·cord \kən'kȯ(ə)rd, kän-, -ȯ(ə)d\ *vt* [back-formation fr. *concordance*] **:** to prepare a concordance of

con·crete\'kän,krēt, kän'krēt, -än-\ *adj* **:** of or relating to concrete poetry ⟨a *concrete* poet⟩

concrete*n **1 :** CONCRETE POETRY **2 :** a concrete poet

concrete jungle *n* **:** ASPHALT JUNGLE

concrete poetry *n* **:** poetry in which the poet's intent is conveyed by the graphic patterns of letters, words, or symbols rather than by the conventional arrangement of words

con·cret·ism*\-ēd·,izəm\ *n* **:** the theory or practice of concrete poetry — **con·cret·ist** \-ēd·əst\ *n*

conditional*adj **1 :** involving or yielding values that are conditional probabilities ⟨a *conditional* distribution⟩ **2 :** eliciting a conditional response ⟨a *conditional* stimulus⟩ **3 :** permitting survival only under special growth or environmental conditions ⟨*conditional* lethal mutations⟩

conditional probability *n* **:** the probability that a given event will occur if it is certain that another event has taken place or will take place

conditioned*adj **:** CONDITIONAL 2 ⟨a *conditioned* stimulus⟩

con·do \'kän(,)dō\ *n, pl* **condos** [short for *condominium*] **:** an individually owned unit in a multi-unit structure (as an apartment house) or complex **:** a condominium

conference call *n* **:** a telephone call by which a caller can speak to several people at the same time

con·fig·u·ra·tion*\kən,fig(y)ə'rāshən, ,kän-\ *n* **:** something (as a figure, contour, pattern, or apparatus) that results from a particular arrangement of parts or components; *esp* **:** a set of interconnected equipment forming a computer system

conflagration*n **:** something like a large disastrous fire ⟨the neon *conflagrations* of the downtown casinos still assault the senses —Les Ledbetter⟩; *esp* **:** a war

con·for·ma·tion·al \,kän(,)fȯ(r)'māshnəl, -nfə(r)-, -shən⁴l\ *adj* **:** of, relating to, or being molecular conformation ⟨*conformational* changes in proteins⟩ — **con·for·ma·tion·al·ly** \-lē, -li\ *adv*

Cong \'käŋ, 'kȯŋ\ *n, pl* **Cong** [short for *Vietcong*] **:** a member of the Vietcong

conglomerate*n **:** a widely diversified company; *esp* **:** a corporation that acquires other companies whose activities are unrelated to the corporation's primary activity

con·glom·er·a·tor \kən'glämə,rād·ə(r)\ *n* **:** one who forms or heads a conglomerate

con·gru·ence*\kən'grüən(t)s, 'käŋgrəwən(t)s\ *n* **:** a statement that two numbers or mathematical expressions (as polynomials) are congruent with respect to a modulus

congruent *adj* **:** related in such a way that the difference is divisible by a given modulus ⟨12 is *congruent* to 2 (modulo 5) since $12 - 2 = 2 \times 5$⟩

conjugate*adj **:** relating to or being conjugate complex numbers ⟨complex roots occurring in *conjugate* pairs⟩

con·ju·gate\'känjəgət, -jēg-, -jə,gāt\ *n* **1 :** one of two complex numbers differing only in the sign of the imaginary part (as $a + bi$ and $a - bi$) **2 :** an element of a mathematical group that is equal to a given element of the group multiplied on the right by another element and on the left by the inverse of the latter element

con·ju·ga·tion*\,känjə'gāshən\ *n* **:** the one-way transfer of DNA between bacteria in cellular contact

¹conk \'käŋk, 'kȯŋk\ *vt* [prob. by shortening and alter. fr. *congolene*, a preparation used for straightening hair, prob. fr. *congolene*, a hydrocarbon produced from Congo copal, fr. *Congolese* + *-ene* unsaturated carbon compound] **:** to treat (as kinky hair) so as to straighten

²conk *n* **:** a hairstyle in which kinky hair is straightened out and flattened down or lightly waved

consciousness–raising *n* **:** an increasing of concerned awareness esp. of some social or political issue ⟨*consciousness-raising* groups, formed . . . to heighten women's awareness of sex discrimination —Georgia Dullea⟩

conservation of angular momentum : a principle in physics: the total angular momentum of a system free of external torque remains constant irrespective of transformations and interactions within the system

conservation of bary·ons \-'barēənz, -,änz\ **:** a principle in physics: the number of baryons in an isolated system of elementary particles remains constant irrespective of transformations or decays

conservation of charge : a principle in physics: the total electric charge of an isolated system remains constant irrespective of whatever internal changes may take place

conservation of lep·tons \-'lep,tänz\ **:** a principle in physics: the number of leptons in an isolated system of elementary particles remains constant irrespective of transformations or decays

conserve* *vt* **con·served; con·serv·ing :** to maintain (a quantity) constant during a process of chemical, physical, or evolutionary change ⟨*conserve* angular momentum⟩ ⟨a DNA sequence that has been *conserved*⟩

consistent* *adj* **:** tending to be arbitrarily close to the true value of the parameter estimated as the sample becomes large ⟨a *consistent* statistical estimator⟩

console* *n* **:** the part of a computer used for communication between the operator and the computer

con·sol·i·da·tion*\kən,sälə'dāshən\ *n* **:** a period of backing and filling in a security or commodity market usu. following a strong run-up of prices and typically preceding a further active advance

con·sta·tive \kənz'tād·iv, -n'st-, -ātiv\ *adj* [constate + -ive, adj. suffix] **:** making an assertion and thus capable of being judged as to truth ⟨*constative* utterance⟩ — **con·stative** *n*

constituent structure *n* **:** a formal representation of the grammatical structure of a sentence in terms of its individual constituents; *also* **:** the structure which such a representation describes

consumer* *n* **:** an organism requiring complex organic compounds for food which it obtains by preying on other organisms or by eating particles of organic matter — compare PRODUCER

con·sum·er·ism \kən'sümə,rizəm\ *n* **1 :** the promotion of the consumer's interests ⟨*consumerism* is undoubtedly a needed corrective to corporate excesses —L.E. Sissman⟩ **2 :** the theory that an increasing consumption of goods is economically desirable; *also* **:** a preoccupation with and an inclination toward the buying of consumer goods ⟨our addiction to the concept of unlimited growth, the promotion of blatant *consumerism*, and the direction of much social and economic energy into frivolous aspects of society —F.H. Borman *et al* ⟩ — **con·sum·er·ist** \-ərəst\ *n*

con·sum·ma·to·ry*\kən'səmə,tōrē, -,tȯr-, -i\ *adj* **:** of, relating to, or being a response or act (as eating or copulating) that terminates a period of usu. goal-directed behavior

contact in·hi·bi·tion \-,in(h)ə̇'bishən\ *n* **:** cessation of cellular undulating movements upon contact with other cells with accompanying cessation of cell growth and division

con·tain·er·iza·tion \kən,tānərə'zāshən, -,rī'z-\ *n* **:** a method of shipping whereby a considerable amount of material (as merchandise) is packed in large containers for more efficient handling

con·tain·er·ize \kən'tānə,rīz\ *vt* **-ized; -iz·ing 1 :** to ship by containerization ⟨*containerized* freight⟩ **2 :** to pack in containers ⟨having garden wastes *containerized* rather than dumped in the streets —W.B. Mueller⟩

con·tain·er·port \kən'tānər,pó(ə)rt, -nə,pó(ə)t\ *n* **:** a shipping port specially equipped to handle containerized cargo

con·tain·er·ship \-nə(r),ship\ *n* **:** a ship esp. designed or equipped for carrying containerized cargo

con·tex·tu·al·ize \kən'tekschə(wə),līz, kän-\ *vt* **-ized; -iz·ing :** to place (as a word or activity) in a context — **con·tex·tu·al·iza·tion** \-,tekschə(wə)lə'zāshən, -,lī\ *n*

continental seating *n, often cap C* **:** theater seating with no center aisle and with room enough between rows to allow easy passage

continuing education *n* **:** formal courses of study for part-time students **:** adult education

continuous creation theory *n* **:** STEADY STATE THEORY

con·toid \'kän-,tȯid\ *n* [consonant + -oid resembling] **:** a speech sound of a phonetic rather than phonemic classification that includes most sounds traditionally treated as consonants and that excludes those (as English \y\, \w\, \r\, and \h\) which like vowels are characterized by the escape of air from the mouth over the center of the tongue without oral friction

contract* *n* **:** an arrangement whereby an assassin is paid to murder a particular person ⟨the mob put out a *contract* on the man's life —Patricia Burstein⟩

con·tra·cy·cli·cal \'kän-trə'sīkləkəl, -'sik-\ *adj* [contra against (fr. L) + cyclical] **:** being or acting in opposition to an economic cycle ⟨*contracyclical* fiscal policies⟩

con·tra·test \'kän-trə,test\ *adj* [contra- + test] **:** of, relating to, or serving as an experimental control

con·tre·fi·let \kōⁿ-trəfēlä; ¡kōn-trəfə¡lā, ¡kän-, -'fi(,)lā\ *n* [F] **:** a small steak cut from the end of the short loin **:** a club steak

control chart *n* **:** a chart kept to determine whether the number of defectives in a daily industrial operation exceeds reasonable expectation **:** quality control chart

controlled* *adj* **:** having the capacity to affect behavior and regulated by law with regard to possession and use ⟨*controlled* drugs⟩

co·nus med·ul·lar·is \'kōnə,smed⁹l'erəs, -ejə'ler-\ *n* [NL, lit., cone situated in the pith] **:** a tapering lower part of the spinal cord at the level of the first lumbar segment

convection oven *n* **:** an oven having a fan that circulates hot air uniformly and continuously around food

con·ve·nience \kən'vēnyən(t)s\ *adj* **:** designed for quick and easy preparation or use ⟨*convenience* food⟩

convenience store *n* **:** a small often franchised market that is open long hours

conventional* *adj* **:** not making use of nuclear weapons ⟨*conventional* warfare⟩

con·ver·gent lady beetle \kən'vərjənt-, -'vōj-, -'vəij-\ *also* **convergent** *n* [fr. the two converging white lines on its prothorax] **:** a periodically migratory beneficial ladybug (*Hippodamia convergens*) that feeds on various crop pests (as aphids)

conversation*n **:** an exchange similar to conversation; *esp* **:** real-time interaction with a computer esp. through a keyboard

conversation pit n **:** a usu. sunken area (as in a living room) with intimate seating that facilitates conversation

converse*vi **conversed; con·vers·ing :** to carry on an exchange similar to a conversation; *esp* **:** to interact with a computer

cook*vi [*cook* develop] **1 :** to play music extremely well and entertainingly; *specif* **:** to play or sing with a lively compelling rhythm **2 :** to go or do well **:** proceed successfully ⟨suffused with a happy glow because his party was really *cooking* —Cyra McFadden⟩

cookbook***:** a book of detailed instructions

cooker*n **:** a small and often makeshift container (as a bottlecap) in which a drug (as heroin) is heated and dissolved in water

cooking top n **:** a built-in cabinet-top cooking apparatus consisting of usu. four heating units for gas or electricity

cook·off \'kúk,óf\ n [*cook* + *-off* (as in *playoff*)] **:** an organized cooking competition

cook·top \'kúk,täp\ n **:** the flat top of a range

cool*adj **:** employing understatement and a minimum of detail to convey information and usu. requiring the listener, viewer, or reader to complete the message ⟨another indication of the very *cool* . . . character of this medium —H.M. McLuhan⟩

cool*vb — **cool it :** to keep or regain control of one's emotions ⟨everything would be much nearer to being all right if only everybody would *cool it* — get the mind back in tune with the body —*Times Lit. Supp.*⟩

Coombs test \'kümz-\ n [R. R. A. *Coombs* ♭1921 Brit. immunologist] **:** an agglutination test used to detect proteins and esp. antibodies on the surface of red blood cells

co-opt*\(')kö'äpt\ vt **:** to take in and make part of a group, movement, or culture **:** absorb ⟨the students are *co-opted* by a system they serve even in their struggle against it —A.C. Danto⟩; *also* **:** to take over **:** appropriate ⟨organized crime *co-opted* the computer —J. T. De-Weese⟩

co-optation*n **:** the act or action or an instance of co-opting

coordinate*adj **:** of, relating to, or being a system of indexing by two or more terms so that documents may be retrieved through the intersection of index terms

coordinates*n pl **:** articles (as of clothing or furniture) designed to be used together and to attain their effect through pleasing contrast (as of color, material, or texture) ⟨the shirt and the tie are color *coordinates* ⟩

cop out*\(')käp'aút\ vi **:** to back out (as of an unwanted responsibility) **:** evade — often used with *on* or *of* ⟨young Americans who *cop out* on society —*Christian Science Monitor*⟩ ⟨*copping out* of jury duty through a variety of machinations —H.F. Waters⟩

cop–out \'käp,aút\ n **1 :** an excuse for copping out **:** pretext **2 :** the means for copping out **3 :** one who cops out **4 :** the act or an instance of copping out

cop·per·ware \'käpər,wa(ə)r, -,we(ə)r; -ə,waə(r, -ə,weə(r\ n **:** articles made of copper

cop·ro·an·ti·body \'käprō,antə,bädē, -di\ n [*copro-* dung, feces + *antibody*] **:** an antibody whose presence in the intestinal tract can be demonstrated by examination of an extract of the feces

coq au vin \,kōkō'vaⁿ, ,käk-, ,kök-, -kö'v-, *F* kókōvaⁿ\ n [F, cock with wine] **:** chicken cooked in usu. red wine

coquille Saint Jacques \-saⁿ'zhäk\ n, pl **coquilles Saint Jacques** [*Saint Jacques* St. James the apostle, whose identifying token is a scallop shell] **:** a dish of scallops usu. served with a wine sauce

cor·al·ene \'kórə,lēn, 'kär-\ n [irreg. fr. *coral*] **1 :** a raised decoration of glass beading on glassware **2 :** glassware with coralene decoration

cord blood n **:** blood from the umbilical cord of a fetus or newborn

cord·less \'kó(ə)rdləs, -ó(ə)d-\ adj **:** having no cord; *esp* **:** powered by a battery ⟨*cordless* tools⟩

cor·don bleu*\,kórdōn'blœ\ adj, often cap C & B **1 a :** of, relating to, or being a cook of great skill **b :** of, relating to, or being the food prepared by such a cook **2 :** stuffed with ham and Swiss cheese ⟨veal *cordon bleu*⟩

cor·dy·cep·in \,kó(r)də'sepán\ n [*cordyceps* + *-in* chemical compound] **:** an adenosine analogue $C_{10}H_{13}N_5O_3$ with antibiotic activity used esp. to study gene regulation because of its ability to inhibit transcription

core*n **1 :** a tiny doughnut-shaped piece of magnetic material (as ferrite) used in computer memories — called also *magnetic core* **2** or **core memory** or **core storage :** a computer memory consisting of an array of cores strung on fine wires

core city n **:** INNER CITY

co·re·pres·sor \,kórə'presə(r)\ n **:** a substance that activates a particular genetic repressor by combining with it

corn chip n **:** a piece of a crisp dry snack food prepared from a seasoned cornmeal batter

cor·neo·scler·al \'kó(r)nē(,)ö,skleral\ adj [*corneo-* corneal and + *scleral*] **:** of, relating to, or affecting both the cornea and the sclera ⟨posterior to the *corneoscleral* junction⟩

corner*adj **:** of, relating to, or being a defensive football player who covers one of the flanks ⟨*corner* linebacker⟩ ⟨*corner* positions⟩

cor·ner·back \'kórnər,bak, sometimes 'kónər-; 'kó(ə)nə,bak\ n **:** a defensive back in football whose duties include defending the flank and covering a wide receiver

cor·ner·man \-,man, -mən\ n **:** one that is in a corner: as **a :** CORNERBACK **b :** a basketball forward **c :** a boxer's second

corn·hole \'kó(ə)rn,hōl, 'kó(ə)n-\ vt [perh. fr. the notion that corncobs were used instead of toilet paper] **:** to perform anal intercourse with — usu. considered vulgar

cor·ni·chon \,kórnēshōn\ n [F, gherkin] **:** a sour gherkin usu. flavored with tarragon

corn·row \'kó(ə)rn,rō, 'kó(ə)n-\ vt [fr. the fancied resemblance of the braids to rows of corn] **:** to style (hair) by dividing into sections (that are braided usu. flat to the scalp in rows — **cornrow** n

co·ro·na·virus \kə,rōnə'vīrəs\ n [*corona* + *virus*, fr. their shape as seen under an electron microscope] **:** any of a group of viruses that resemble myxoviruses, have widely spaced club-shaped projections, and usu. cause respiratory symptoms in man

co·ro·tate \(')kō͝rō͝,tāt\ *vi* **:** to rotate in conjunction with or at the same rate as another rotating body — **co·ro·ta·tion** \͝kō(͝)rō'tāshən\ *n*

cor·pus al·la·tum \͝kôrpəsə'lād·əm, -äd··\ *n, pl* **cor·po·ra al·la·ta** \͝kôrpərə-ə'lād·ə, -äd··\ [NL, lit., applied body] **:** one of a pair of separate or fused bodies in many insects that are sometimes closely associated with the corpora cardiaca and secrete hormones (as juvenile hormone)

corpus car·di·a·cum \-pəskär'dīəkəm\ *n, pl* **cor·po·ra car·di·a·ca** \-pərəkär-'dīəkə\ [NL, lit., cardiac body] **:** one of a pair of separate or fused bodies of nervous tissue in many insects that lie posterior to the brain and dorsal to the esophagus and function in the storage and secretion of brain hormone

corpus spon·gi·o·sum \-͝spənjē'ōsəm, -͝spän-\ *n* [NL, lit., spongy body] **:** the median longitudinal column of erectile tissue of the penis that contains the urethra and is ventral to the two corpora cavernosa

correction fluid *n* **:** a liquid used to paint over typing errors

cor·ti·co·tro·pin–releasing factor \͝kôrd·əkō͝trō͝pən-\ *n* **:** a substance secreted by the median eminence of the hypothalamus that regulates the release of ACTH by the anterior lobe of the pituitary gland

co–script \'kō͝skript\ *vt* **:** to collaborate in the preparation of a script for

co·set \'kō͝set\ *n* **:** a subset of a mathematical group that consists of all the products obtained by multiplying either on the right or the left a fixed element of the group by each of the elements of a given subgroup

cosmetic*adj **:** lacking in depth or thoroughness **:** superficial ⟨bought up older homes in declining neighborhoods, fixed them up with *cosmetic* repairs, and sold them at inflated values —M.W. Karmin⟩

cos·met·i·cize \käz'med·ə͝sīz\ *vt* **-cized; -ciz·ing :** to make (something unpleasant or ugly) superficially attractive ⟨saw the singer whole; this is not a flack's *cosmeticized* biography —*Playboy*⟩

cos·mo·drome \'käzmə͝drōm\ *n* [Russ *Kosmodrom*, fr. *Kosmo*navt cosmonaut + *-drom* racecourse, large specially prepared place, deriv. of Gk *dromos* racecourse, act of running] **:** a Soviet aerospace center; *esp* **:** a Soviet spacecraft launching installation

cos·mo·gen·ic \͝käzmə'jenik\ *adj* [*cosmic* (ray) + connective *-o-* + *-genic* produced by] **:** produced by the action of cosmic rays ⟨*cosmogenic* carbon 14⟩

cos·mo·nau·tics \͝käzmə'nôd·iks, -näd··\ *n pl but usu sing in constr* **:** the science of the construction and operation of vehicles for travel in space beyond the earth's atmosphere **:** Soviet astronautics — **cos·mo·nau·tic** \-d·ik\ *or* **cos·mo·nau·ti·cal** \-d·əkəl\ *adj*

cossack hat *n* **:** an oblong visorless folding cap usu. made of fur or imitation fur

cost–ben·e·fit \͝kôst͝benə͝fit\ *adj* **:** of, relating to, or being economic analysis that assigns a numerical value to the cost-effectiveness of usu. industrial operations or procedures

cost–ef·fec·tive \'kôstə'fektiv, -tē͝-, *also* 'käst-\ *adj* **:** economical in terms of tangible benefits produced by money spent — **cost–ef·fec·tive·ness** \͝kôstə'fektivnəs, -tē͝'-, *also* ͝käst-\ *n*

cost–push \'kòs(t)͝push, *also* 'käs(t)-\ *n* **:** an increase or upward trend in production costs (as wages) that tends to result in increased consumer prices irrespective of the level of demand — compare DEMAND-PULL — **cost–push** \͝kòs(t)-, *also* ͝käs(t)-\ *adj*

cot death *n, chiefly Brit* **:** SUDDEN INFANT DEATH SYNDROME

co·te·chi·no \͝kōd·ā'kē(͝)nō\ *n* [It] **:** a smoked and dried pork sausage

co·ter·mi·nal \(')kō͝tərmnəl, -mən²l\ *adj* **:** having different angular measure but with the vertex and sides identical — used of angles generated by the rotation of lines about the same point in a given line whose values differ by an integral multiple of 2π radians or of 360° ⟨*coterminal* angles measuring 30° and 390°⟩

co·trans·duc·tion \͝kō͝tran(t)s'dəkshən, -͝tranz'-\ *n* **:** transduction involving two or more genetic loci carried by a single bacteriophage

cou·chette \kü'shet\ *n* [F, berth, bunk, dim. of *couche* bed, fr. MF] **1 :** a compartment on a European passenger train so arranged that berths can be provided at night **2 :** one of the berths in a couchette

cou·li·biac \͝küleb'yäk, -âk\ *n* [F, fr. Russ *kulebyaka*] **:** fish rolled in pastry dough and baked ⟨*coulibiac* of salmon⟩

cou·lom·bic \(')kü͝läm(b)ik, kə͝l-, -lōm-\ *adj* **:** of or relating to electrostatic coulomb forces

cou·ma·phos \'kümə͝fäs, -fòs\ *n* [*couma*rin + *phospho*rus] **:** an organophosphorus systemic insecticide and anthelmintic $C_{14}H_{16}ClO_5PS$ used esp. on cattle and poultry

count·abil·i·ty \͝kaún(t)ə'biləd·ē, -i\ *n* **:** the quality or state of being countable

count·ably \'kaún(t)əblē, -li\ *adv* **:** in a way that is countable ⟨*countably* infinite sets⟩

counter*n **:** a football play in which the ballcarrier goes in a direction opposite to the flow of play

coun·ter·ad·ver·tis·ing \͝kaún(t)ə͝radvə(r)͝tīziŋ\ *n* [*counter-* contrary, opposite + *advertising*] **:** COUNTERCOMMERCIALS

coun·ter·com·mer·cial \͝kaún(t)ərkə͝mərshəl; -əkə͝māsh-, -məish-\ *n* **:** a commercial that rebuts the claims of another commercial

coun·ter·con·di·tion·ing \͝kaún(t)ə(r)kən͝dish(ə)niŋ\ *n* **:** conditioning in order to replace an undesirable response (as fear) to a stimulus (as an engagement in public speaking) by a favorable one

coun·ter·cul·ture \'kaún(t)ə(r)͝kəlchə(r)\ *n* **:** a culture with values and mores that run counter to those of established society — **coun·ter·cul·tur·al** \͝kaún(t)ə(r)͝kəlch(ə)rəl\ *adj* — **coun·ter·cul·tur·ist** \-ch(ə)rist\ *n*

coun·ter·elec·tro·pho·re·sis \͝kaún(t)ərə͝lektrōfə͝rē-səs, -rē͝l-\ *n* **:** an electrophoretic method of testing blood esp. for antigens associated with hepatitis

coun·ter·ex·am·ple \'kaún(t)ərəg͝zampəl\ *n* **:** an example that disproves a theorem or proposition; *broadly* **:** an example that is inconsistent with or contrary to what is typical or usual

coun·ter·in·sur·gen·cy \͝kaún(t)ərin͝sərjən(t)sē\ *n* **:** organized activity designed to combat insurgency — **coun·ter·in·sur·gent** \-jənt\ *n*

coun·ter·in·tu·itive \-in͝t(y)üəd·iv\ *adj* **:** contrary to intuition ⟨complex systems are *counterintuitive*. They behave in ways opposite to what most people expect — J.W. Forrester⟩

coun·ter·pho·bic \ˌkaún(t)ə(r)ˈfōbik\ *adj* **:** relating to or characterized by a preference for the seeking out of a situation that is feared ⟨*counterphobic* reaction patterns⟩

coun·ter·pro·duc·tive \-prəˈdəktiv\ *adj* **:** tending to hinder the attainment of a desired goal ⟨violence as a means to achieve an end is *counterproductive* —W.E. Brock *b*1930⟩

coun·ter·pro·gram \-ˈprō‚gram, -‚grəm\ *vi* **:** to engage in counterprogramming ~ *vt* **:** to run against (another television program)

coun·ter·pro·gram·ming \-iŋ\ *n* **:** the scheduling of programs by television networks so as to attract audiences away from simultaneously telecast programs of competitors

coun·ter·pul·sa·tion \-‚pəlˈsāshən\ *n* **:** a technique for reducing the work load on the heart by the automatic lowering of systemic blood pressure just before or during expulsion of blood from the ventricle and by the automatic raising of blood pressure during diastole

coun·ter·shock \ˈkaún(t)ə(r)‚shäk\ *n* **:** therapeutic electric shock applied to the heart for the purpose of altering a disturbed rhythm (as in chronic atrial fibrillation)

country*adj **1 :** of or relating to country music ⟨*country* singer⟩ **2 :** featuring country music ⟨*country* radio stations⟩ **3 :** of, relating to, or having the characteristics of early American rustic or informal furniture

country and western *adj, sometimes cap C&W* **:** having or using lyrics, style, or string instrumentation identified with country music of western U.S. origin

country rock *n* **:** ROCKABILLY

cou·pon·ing \ˈk(y)ü‚päniŋ\ *n* **:** the distribution or redemption of coupons

cour·gette \kü(ə)rˈzhet, kúəˈzhet\ *n* [F dial., dim. of *courge* gourd] *chiefly Brit* **:** a zucchini squash

courtesy light *n* **:** an interior automobile light that goes on automatically when a door is opened

couth \ˈküth\ *n* **:** polish, refinement ⟨I expected kindness and gentility and I found it, but there is such a thing as too much *couth* —S.J. Perelman⟩

cover–up*n **1 :** a usu. concerted effort to keep an illegal or unethical act or situation from being made public ⟨assuming of course that he was involved in the *cover-up*, he couldn't escape —J.K. Galbraith⟩ **2 :** a loose outer garment

cow·boy·ing \ˈkaú‚bòi(‚i)ŋ\ *n* **:** the work or occupation of a cowboy

cow·shed \ˈkaú‚shed\ *n* **:** a shed for the housing of cows

CPI *abbr* consumer price index

CPR *abbr* cardiopulmonary resuscitation

CPS*abbr certified professional secretary

CPU *abbr* central processing unit

crack·back \ˈkrak‚bak\ *n* **:** a blind-side block on a defensive back in football by a pass receiver who starts downfield and then cuts back toward the middle of the line

crack up \(ˈ)krakˈəp\ *vi* **:** to laugh out loud ~ *vt* **:** to cause to laugh out loud

cram·be**\ˈkram(‚)bē\ *n* **:** an annual Mediterranean herb (*Crambe abyssinica*) cultivated as an oilseed crop

cranberry glass *n* **:** clear ruby glass usu. with a blue-violet tint

cra·nio·pha·ryn·gi·oma \ˌkrānē(‚)ō‚farənjēˈōmə, -fə-‚rinjēˈōmə\ *n, pl* **-mas** *or* **-ma·ta** \-mədᵊ-ə, -ətə\ [*cranio-* cranium + *pharyng-* pharynx + connective *-i-* + *-oma* tumor] **:** a tumor of the brain near the pituitary gland that develops esp. in children or young adults and is often associated with increased intracranial pressure

crap·shoot \ˈkrap‚shüt\ *n* [*crap* craps + *shoot*] **:** a risky business venture ⟨the film business is always a *crapshoot* in which only a small percentage of films make money — H.M. Hefner⟩

crash*vi **1** *slang* **:** to experience the aftereffects (as dysphoria or depression) of drug intoxication **2** *slang* **:** to spend the night in a particular place **:** sleep ⟨sometimes we can't pay the rent and we *crash* around town, sleep in yards or at friends' houses —*East Village Other*⟩

crash pad*n **:** a place where free temporary lodging is available ⟨storefront medical clinics and *crash pads* for runaway youths —Martin Oppenheimer⟩

crash·wor·thy \ˈkrash‚wərthē, -‚wȯth-, -‚wáith-, -i\ *adj* [*crash* + *-worthy* (as in *seaworthy*)] **:** resistant to the effects of a collision ⟨the ideal *crashworthy* car would have a strong passenger compartment —*Consumer Reports*⟩

crash·wor·thi·ness \-nəs\ *n*

cra·ter·iza·tion \ˌkrādᵊrəˈzāshən, -ātə-, -ˌrᵢˈz-\ *n* [*crater* + *ize* vb. suffix + *-ation* process] **:** surgical excision of a crater-shaped piece of bone

crawl·er·way \ˈkrólə(r)‚wä\ *n* [fr. its slow-moving traffic] **:** a road built esp. for moving heavy rockets and spacecraft

crawl·way \ˌkról-\ *n* **:** a low passageway (as in a cave) that can be traversed only by crawling

cray·fish·ing \ˈkrā‚fishiŋ\ *n* **:** the occupation or pastime of catching crayfish

crazy**adj —** **like crazy :** to an extreme degree ⟨cameras whirred and clicked *like crazy* —*Rolling Stone*⟩ ⟨everyone dancing *like crazy*⟩

cra·zy \ˈkrāzē\ *n, pl* **crazies :** one who is or acts crazy ⟨he said you were a *crazy* and always had been but that he trusted you —Ernest Hemingway⟩; *esp* **:** such a one associated with a radical or extremist political cause ⟨candidates were not the *crazies* of the left but sensible and practical men —R.J. Gleason⟩ ⟨fall into the hands of . . . the right-wing *crazies* —H.S. Thompson⟩

C–re·ac·tive protein \ˌsē(‚)rēˈaktiv-\ *n* [*C-polysaccha*ride, a polysaccharide found in the cell wall of pneumococci and precipitated by this protein, fr. carbohydrate] **:** a protein present in blood serum in various abnormal states (as inflammation or neoplasia)

cream puff*n **:** a vehicle (as an automobile) that is usu. used but in good condition ⟨a clean, low-mileage *cream puff* —*Sports Illustrated*⟩

cre·a·tine ki·nase \ˈkrēə‚tēn‚kī‚nās, -ə-tən-, -‚kī-, -‚āz\ *n* **:** an enzyme of vertebrate skeletal and myocardial muscle that catalyzes the transfer of a high-energy phosphate group from phosphocreatine to ADP with the formation of ATP and creatine

creatine phosphoki·nase *n* **:** CREATINE KINASE

cre·den·tial \krəˈdenchəl, krē-\ *vt* **-tialed** *also* **-tialled; tial·ing** *also* **-tial·ling :** to furnish with credentials ⟨to *credential* adequate academic performance —K.P. Cross⟩

cre·den·tial·ism \krəˈdenchə‚lizəm, krē-\ *n* **:** undue emphasis on credentials (as college degrees) as prerequisites to employment ⟨to deemphasize *credentialism* will require that employers make greater efforts to evaluate applicants as individuals —D.L. Wolfle⟩

cred·i·bil·i·ty gap \ˌkredə'bilǝd·ē͜'gap\ *n* **1 a :** lack of trust ⟨a special *credibility gap* is likely to open between the generations —Kenneth Keniston⟩ **b :** lack of believability ⟨a *credibility gap* created by contradictory official statements —Samuel Ellenport⟩ **2 :** an instance of being discrepant **:** discrepancy ⟨the *credibility gap* between the professed ideals . . . and their actual practices — Jeanne L. Noble⟩

cred·it·wor·thy \'kredǝt,wǝrthē, -,wǎth-, -wǎith-, -i\ *adj* **:** being financially sound enough to justify the extension of credit **:** having an acceptable credit rating — **credit·wor·thi·ness** \-nǝs\ *n*

creeping*adj **:** developing or advancing slowly over a period of time ⟨*creeping* urbanization⟩ ⟨*creeping* senility⟩

cre·mains \krǝ'mānz, krē'-\ *n pl* [blend of *cremated* and *remains*] **:** the ashes of a cremated human body

crème brû·lée \ˌkrembrū͞e'lā, ˌkräm-, ˌkrēm-, -brü-\ *n* [F, lit., scorched cream] **:** a rich custard topped with caramelized sugar

crème fraîche *or* **crème fraiche** \-'fresh\ *n* [F, lit., fresh cream] **:** heavy cream thickened and slightly soured with buttermilk and often served on fruit

crew sock *n* [fr. its use by rowing crews] **:** a short bulky usu. ribbed sock

crib death *n* **:** SUDDEN INFANT DEATH SYNDROME

¹cri·co·thy·roid \ˌkrīkǝ'thī,ròid\ *adj* [crico- cricoid and + *thyroid*] **:** relating to or connecting the cricoid cartilage and the thyroid cartilage ⟨a *cricothyroid* muscle⟩

²cricothyroid *n* **:** a cricothyroid muscle

cri du chat syndrome \ˌkrēdü'shä-, -dǝ'-\ *n* [*cri du chat* fr. F, cry of the cat] **:** an inherited condition that is characterized by a mewing cry, mental retardation, physical anomalies, and the absence of part of a chromosome

crisis center *n* **:** a facility run usu. by nonprofessionals who counsel those who telephone for help in a personal crisis

cris·ta*\'kristǝ\ *n, pl* **cris·tae** \-(ˌ)tē\ **:** any of the inwardly projecting folds of the inner membrane of a mitochondrion

critical region *n* **:** the set of outcomes of a statistical test for which the null hypothesis is to be rejected

crock*n [fr. the phrase *crock of shit*] **:** a lot of insincere, pretentious, or misleading talk **:** bunkum — often used in the phrase *that's a crock*

Crock·pot \'kräk,pät\ *trademark* — used for an electric cooking pot

cro·quem·bouche \kròkän'büsh\ *n* [F] **:** a pyramid of cream puffs coated with caramelized sugar

cross·court \ˌkròs'kō(ǝ)rt, -'kò(ǝ)rt, -'kōǝt, -ˌkò(ǝ)t, *also* ˌkräs-\ *adv (or adj)* **:** to or toward the opposite side of a court (as in tennis or basketball)

cross–dis·ci·plin·ary \ˌkròs'disǝplǝ,nerē, *also* ˌkräs-, *esp Brit*-,disǝ'plinǝrē, -i\ *adj* **:** of, relating to, or involving two or more disciplines **:** interdisciplinary ⟨*cross-disciplinary* study⟩

cross–dress \-ˌdres\ *vi* **:** to dress in the clothes of the opposite sex

cross multiply *vi* [back-formation fr. *cross multiplication*] **:** to find the two products obtained by multiplying the numerator of each of two fractions by the denominator of the other

cross·over*\'krò,sōvǝ(r), *also* 'krä-\ *n* **1 :** a voter registered as a member of one political party who votes in the primary of the other party **2 :** a broadening of popular music appeal that is often the result of a change of musical style; *also* **:** a musician who has achieved a crossover

crossover*adj **1 :** of, relating to, or being a turning point or important juncture **:** critical ⟨*crossover* point⟩ ⟨*crossover* date⟩ **2 :** permitting voting by crossovers ⟨*crossover* primary⟩

cross–re·ac·tive \ˌkròs(ˌ)rē͜'aktiv, *also* ˌkräs-\ *adj* **:** capable of undergoing cross-reaction — **cross–re·act** \-(ˌ)rē͜'akt\ *vi* — **cross–re·ac·tiv·i·ty** \-(ˌ)rē,ak'tivǝd-ē, -i\ *n*

cross–train \-ˌtrān\ *vt* **:** to train (a person) to do more than one specific job

crown of thorns *or* **crown–of–thorns starfish : a** starfish (*Acanthaster planci*) of the Pacific region that is covered with long spines and is destructive to the coral of coral reefs

cru·di·tés \krü͞edētä\ *n pl* [F, pl. of *crudité* indigestibility] **:** pieces of raw vegetables (as celery and carrot sticks) served as an hors d'oeuvre often with a dip

cruise*vb **cruised; cruis·ing** *vi* **:** to search (as in public places) for a sexual partner ⟨to *cruise* for sex requires leisure —Laud Humphreys⟩ **~** *vt* **:** to search in (a public place) for a sexual partner ⟨*cruises* the singles bars for girls one night and the gay bars for homosexuals the next —A.W. Johnston⟩

cruise missile *n* **:** a guided missile that has a terrainsensing radar system and that flies at moderate speed and low altitude

crunch*n **:** a tight or critical situation: as **a :** a critical point in the buildup of pressure between opposing elements ⟨if it came to the *crunch*, the small new states would succumb —*Times Lit. Supp.*⟩ **b :** a severe economic squeeze (as on credit) ⟨a *crunch* would cripple home mortgages, slow down mergers and acquisitions, and ultimately cut employment —Walter Fedor⟩ **c :** a deficiency in amount **:** shortage ⟨when the gas *crunch* became part of the American way of life —Ray Walters⟩

cryo·bi·ol·o·gy \ˌkrīō(ˌ)bī͜'äləjē\ *n* [cryo- cold, freezing (deriv. of Gk *kryos* icy cold) + *biology*] **:** the study of the effects of extremely low temperature on biological systems (as cells or organisms) — **cryo·bi·o·log·i·cal** \-ˌbīǝ'läjǝkǝl\ *adj* — **cryo·bi·o·log·i·cal·ly** \-k(ǝ)lē, -li\ *adv* — **cryo·bi·ol·o·gist** \-(ˌ)bī͜'äläjǝst\ *n*

cryo·chem·is·try \-'kemǝstrē, -ri\ *n* **:** chemistry dealing with processes carried out at very low temperatures — **cryo·chem·i·cal** \-ˈkeməkǝl\ *adj* — **cryo·chem·i·cal·ly** \-k(ǝ)lē, -li\ *adv*

cryo·elec·tron·ics \-ǝˌlek'träniks\ *n pl but sing in constr* **:** a branch of electronics that employs cryogenic methods to bring about a desired effect (as superconductivity) — **cryo·elec·tron·ic** \-ˈtränik\ *adj*

cryo·ex·trac·tion \-ek'strakshǝn\ *n* **:** extraction of a cataract through use of a cryoprobe whose refrigerated tip adheres to and freezes tissue of the lens permitting its removal

cryo·ex·trac·tor \-ktǝ(r)\ *n* **:** a cryoprobe used for removal of cataracts

cryo·gen·ic*\ˌkrīǝ'jenik\ *adj* **1 :** being or relating to a very low temperature ⟨a *cryogenic* temperature of −50°C⟩ **2 a :** requiring or involving the use of a cryogenic temperature ⟨*cryogenic* surgery⟩ **b :** requiring cryogenic storage **c :** suitable for the storage of a cryogenic substance ⟨a *cryogenic* container⟩ — **cry·o·gen·i·cal·ly** \-nək(ə)lē\ *adv*

cryo·glob·u·li·ne·mia \ˌkrīō͵gläbyələˈnēmēə\ *n* [*cryoglobulin* + *-emia* blood condition] **:** the condition of having abnormal quantities of cryoglobulins in the blood

cry·on·ics \krīˈäniks\ *n pl but usu sing in constr* [*cryobiology* + *-onics* (as in *electronics*)] **:** the practice of freezing a dead diseased human being in hopes of bringing him back to life at some future time when a cure for his disease has been developed — **cry·on·ic** \(ʹ)krīˈänik\ *adj*

cryo·pre·cip·i·tate \ˌkrīōprəˈsipəd·ət, -ə͵tāt\ *n* **:** a precipitate that is formed by cooling a solution — **cryo·pre·cip·i·ta·tion** \-prə͵sipəˈtāshən\ *n*

cryo·pre·ser·va·tion \-͵prezə(r)ˈvāshən\ *n* **:** preservation (as of cells) by subjection to extremely low temperatures

cryo·probe \ʹkrīə͵prōb\ *n* **:** a blunt instrument used to apply cold to tissues in cryosurgery

cryo·pro·tec·tive \ˌkrīōprəˈtektiv, -(͵)prō-\ *adj* **:** serving to protect against the deleterious effects of subjection to freezing temperatures ⟨an extracellular *cryoprotective* agent⟩ — **cryo·pro·tec·tant** \-ktənt\ *n*

cryo·pump \ʹkrīō͵pəmp\ *n* **:** a vacuum pump whose operation involves the freezing and adsorption of gases on cold surfaces at very low temperatures — **cryopump** *vi*

cryo·sorp·tion \ˌkrīōˈsórpshən\ *n* **:** the adsorption of gases onto the cold surfaces of a cryopump

cryo·sur·gery \-ʹsərj(ə)rē\ *n* **:** surgery in which extreme controlled chilling (as by use of liquid nitrogen) produces the desired dissection — **cryo·sur·geon** \-ʹsərjən\ *n* — **cryo·sur·gi·cal** \-jəkəl\ *adj*

cryp·to·bi·o·sis \ˌkrip(͵)tō͵bīˈōsəs, -(͵)bē͵-\ *n, pl* **-o·ses** \-ʹō͵sēz\ [NL, fr. *crypto-* hidden, covered (deriv. of Gk *kryptos* hidden) + *-biosis* mode of life, deriv. of Gk *bios* life] **:** the reversible cessation of metabolism under extreme environmental conditions (as low temperature)

crystal*n **:** powdered methamphetamine

C–type \ʹsē͵tīp\ *adj* **:** relating to or being any of the oncornaviruses in which the structure containing the nucleic acid is spherical and centrally located

cuat·ro \ʹkwä·trō\ *n, pl* **cuatros** [Sp *cuatro* four] **:** a Puerto Rican stringed instrument similar to a small guitar

cu·chi·fri·to \ˌküchiˈfrēd·ō, -chēʹ-\ *n, pl* **-tos** [AmerSp, fr. *cuche, cuchi* hog, pig (fr. Sp *cochino*) + Sp *frito* fried, past part. of *freir* to fry, fr. L *frigere*] **:** a deep-fried cube of pork

Cui·se·naire rod *also* **Cuisenaire colored rod** \ˌkwēzᵊnˈa(ə)r-, -ʹe(ə)r-\ *n* [fr. *Cuisenaire*, a trademark] **:** any of a set of colored rods that are usu. of 1 centimeter cross section and of ten lengths from 1 to 10 centimeters and that are used for teaching number concepts and the basic operations of arithmetic

cuisine min·ceur \-maⁿsœːcer\ *n* [F, slimness cooking] **:** a low-calorie form of French cooking

cul·dot·o·my \(͵)kəlˈdäd·əmē, kùl-, -ätə-, -mi\ *n, pl* **-mies** [*culdo-* pouch of Douglas + *-tomy* incision] **:** surgical incision of the pouch of Douglas

Cu·li·coi·des \ˌkyüləˈkói͵dēz\ *n* [NL, fr. L. *culic*is, gen. of *culex* gnat + L *-oides* -oid] **:** a genus of bloodsucking

midges of the family Ceratopogonidae of which some are intermediate hosts of filarial parasites

cul·tur·a·ti \ˌkəlchəˈräd·ē, -ʹrä-, -i, *also* -ʹrä͵tī\ *n pl* [fr. *culture* + *-ati* (as in *literati*)] **:** people intensely interested in cultural affairs ⟨bookstores used to be for flush *culturati* and aunts in the afternoon —Gail Sheehy⟩

culture shock *n* **:** a sense of confusion and uncertainty sometimes with feelings of anxiety that may affect people exposed to an alien culture without adequate preparation ⟨the *culture shock* often suffered by Americans on work assignments abroad —Kenneth Goodall⟩

culture–vulture *n* **:** a person who avidly attends cultural events

Cum·ber·land sauce \ʹkəmbə(r)lənd-\ *n* [*Cumberland* county, England] **:** a cold sauce flavored with orange, lemon, currant jelly, wine, and usu. mustard that is served with game

cumulative*adj **:** summing or integrating overall data or values of a random variable less than or less than or equal to a specified value ⟨*cumulative* normal distribution⟩ ⟨*cumulative* frequency distribution⟩

cumulative distribution function *n* **:** a function that gives the probability that a random variable is less than or equal to the independent variable of the function

cup**n :** the symbol ∪ indicating the union of two sets — compare CAP 2

cup·pa \ʹkəpə\ *n* [fr. *cuppa* tea, pronunciation spelling of *cup of tea*] *chiefly Brit* **:** a cup of tea ⟨if you're trying to lose weight one of the few comforts left to you is probably a nice sweet *cuppa* —News of the World⟩

cu·pule*\ʹkyü͵p(y)ül\ *n* **:** an outer integument partially enclosing the seed of some seed ferns

cu·rate's egg \ˌkyùrəts'-\ *n* [fr. the story of a curate who was given a stale egg by his bishop and declared that parts of it were excellent] *Brit* **:** something with both good and bad parts or qualities ⟨this is a bit of a *curate's egg*, very good but spoilt by facetiousness —Times Lit. Supp.⟩

curb weight *n* **:** the weight of an automobile with standard equipment and fuel, oil, and coolant

curl**n :** a hollow arch of water formed when the crest of a breaking wave spills forward — called also *tube, tunnel*

cur·sil·lo \kùrˈsē(l)yō\ *n, pl* **-los** *often cap* [Sp, short course, dim. of *curso* course] **1 :** a movement in Roman Catholicism designed to deepen the spiritual life and bring about Christian involvement in daily activities through participation in a 3-day gathering usu. followed up by weekly or monthly meetings **2 :** a 3-day gathering of a group of individuals that is the initial stage in associating oneself with the cursillo movement

cursor**n :** a usu. manually controllable bright figure (as an underline or box) on a computer display to indicate a character to be revised or a position where data is to be entered

curve*vt **curved; curv·ing :** to throw a curve to (a batter) in baseball

custard glass *n* **:** opaque glass of creamy buff color

custom–make \ʹkəstə(m)͵māk\ *vt* **-made; -mak·ing** [back-formation from *custom-made*] **:** to make to order

cut**vb** — **cut it :** to manage or perform something successfully ⟨there's nothing worse than keeping someone on who can't *cut it* —G.R. Ford⟩

cut**n :** a single song or musical piece on a phonograph record ⟨the best *cut* in the album⟩

cut·abil·i·ty \ˌkəd·ə'biləd·ē, -i\ *n* **:** the proportion of lean salable meat yielded by a carcass

cut·back*\'kət‚bak\ *n* **:** a surfing maneuver in which a surfboard is turned back toward the crest of the wave

cute·sy *also* **cute·sie** \'kyütsē, -si\ *adj* **cute·si·er; -est** [*cute* + *-sy* (as in *folksy*)] **:** self-consciously cute ⟨tries . . . to be bright and often ends up merely *cutesy* — Newgate Callendar⟩ — **cute·sy·ness** \-nəs\ *n*

cut·offs \'kəd·ˌôfs, -ət‚-, *also* -äfs\ *n pl* [short for *cut-off blue jeans*] **:** trousers (as of blue denim) cut off at the knee or higher — **cut–off** \ˌkəd·ˌôf, -ət‚-, -ˌäf\ *adj*

cy·a·no·ac·ry·late \'sīənō'akrəˌlāt, -ələt\ *n* [*cyano-* containing the cyanogen group + *acrylate*] **:** any of several liquid acrylate monomers that readily undergo anionic polymerization and are used as adhesives in industry and on living tissue in medicine to close wounds as an adjunct to surgery

cy·ber·cul·ture \'sībə(r)ˌkəlchə(r)\ *n* [*cybernetics* + *culture*] **:** a society that is served by cybernated industry — **cy·ber·cul·tur·al** \ˌsībə(r)ˌkəlch(ə)rəl\ *adj*

cy·ber·nat·ed \'sībə(r)ˌnād·əd\ *adj* [fr. *cybernation*; after such pairs as E *automation: automated*] **:** characterized by or involving cybernation ⟨a *cybernated* factory⟩ ⟨a *cybernated* society⟩

cy·ber·na·tion \ˌsība(r)'nāshən\ *n* [*cybernetics* + *-ation* action or process] **:** the automatic control of a process or operation (as in manufacturing) by means of computers

cy·borg \'sī‚bórg, -ó(ə)g\ *n* [*cybernetic* + *organism*] **:** a human being who is linked (as for temporary adaptation to a hostile space environment) to one or more mechanical devices upon which some of his vital physiological functions depend

cy·ca·sin \'sīkəsən\ *n* [*cycas* + *-in* chemical compound] **:** a glucoside $C_8H_{16}N_2O_7$ that occurs in cycads and results in toxic and carcinogenic effects when introduced into mammals

cy·clan·de·late \ˌsī'klandᵊlˌāt, -ᵊlət\ *n* [*cyclo*hexyl + *mandelate*] **:** an antispasmodic drug $C_{17}H_{24}O_3$ used esp. as a vasodilator in the treatment of diseased arteries

cy·clase \'sī‚klās, -āz\ *n* [*cycl-* cyclic + *-ase* enzyme] **:** an enzyme (as adenyl cyclase) that catalyzes cyclization of a compound

cy·claz·o·cine \sī'klazəˌsēn, -əsən\ *n* [*cycl-* + *azocine*, a compound C_7H_7N, fr. *benzazocine*, a derivative of azobenzene, prob. irreg. fr. *azobenzene*] **:** an analgesic $C_{18}H_{25}NO$ that inhibits the effect of morphine and related addictive drugs and is used in the treatment of drug addiction

cycle*n **:** a permutation of a set of ordered elements in which each element takes the place of the next and the last becomes first

cy·cle·ry \'sīkəl(ˌ)rē, -klə(ˌ)rē, -ri\ *n, pl* **-ries** [*cycle* + *-ery* place for selling] **:** a place where bicycles are sold and serviced

cy·clic aden·o·sine mo·no·phos·phate \ˌsīklikə‚denəˌsēn‚mänə'fäs‚fāt, -əsən-, -ˌmōn-, *also* ‚sik-\ *n* [*mono-* containing a single atom, radical, or group + *phosphate*] **:** CYCLIC AMP

cy·clic AMP \ˌsīklikˌā(ˌ)em'pē, *also* ‚sik-\ *n* **:** a cyclic mononucleotide of adenosine that has been implicated as a second messenger in addition to hormones in the control of cellular processes (as lipid metabolism, membrane transport, and cell proliferation — called also *adenosine 3',5'-monophosphate*

cyclic GMP \-ˌjē(ˌ)em'pē\ *n* [guanosine *monophosphate*] **:** a cyclic mononucleotide of guanosine that has been implicated with cyclic AMP as a second messenger in addition to hormones in the control of cellular processes

cyclic group *n* **:** a mathematical group that has an element such that every element of the group can be expressed as one of its powers

cyclic gua·no·sine monophosphate \-ˌgwänəˌsēn-, -əsən-\ *n* **:** CYCLIC GMP

cy·clo \'sē(ˌ)klō, 'sik(ˌ)lō\ *n, pl* **cy·clos** [prob. fr. F, short for (assumed) *cyclotaxi*, fr. moto*cyclette* motorcycle + connective *-o-* + *taxi*] **:** a 3-wheeled motor-driven taxi

cy·clo·di·ene \ˌsīklō'dīˌēn, ‚sik-, -ˌdī'ēn\ *n* [*cyclo-* cyclic + *-diene* compound with two double bonds] **:** an organic insecticide (as aldrin, dieldrin, chlordane, or endosulfan) with a chlorinated methylene group forming a bridge across a 6-membered carbon ring

cy·clo·phos·pha·mide \ˌsīklə'fäsfəˌmīd, ‚sik-, -əməd\ *n* [prob. fr. *cyclo-* + *phosph*orus + *amide*] **:** an immunosuppressive and antineoplastic agent $C_7H_{15}Cl_2N_2O_2P$ used esp. against lymphomas and some leukemias

cy·clo·tom·ic*\ˌsīklə'tämik, ‚si-, -(ˌ)klō-\ *adj* **:** relating to, being, or containing a polynomial of the form $x^{p-1} + x^{p-2} + \ldots + x + 1$ where p is a prime number

cy·clo·tron resonance \'sīklə‚trän-\ *n* **:** the absorption of electromagnetic energy by a charged particle orbiting in a magnetic field when the electromagnetic and orbital frequencies are equal

Cym·ric*\'kəmrik, 'kim-, *sometimes* 'sim-\ *n* **:** any of a breed of domestic cats that prob. originated as a spontaneous mutation of the Manx and that differs from it only in having a long coat

cy·pro·hep·ta·dine \ˌsīprō'heptəˌdēn\ *n* [*cyclic* + *propyl* + *hepta-* seven (fr. Gk *hepta*) + piperi*dine*] **:** a drug $C_{21}H_{21}N$ that acts antagonistically to histamine and serotonin and is used esp. in the treatment of asthma

cy·prot·er·one \sī'prädəˌrōn\ *n* [prob. fr. *cyclic* + *pro*ges*terone*] **:** a synthetic steroid used in the form of its acetate to inhibit androgenic secretions (as testosterone)

cys·ta·mine \'sistəˌmēn, -əmən\ *n* [*cystine* + *amine*] **:** a cystine derivative $C_4H_{12}N_2S_2$ used in the prevention of radiation sickness (as of cancer patients)

cys·ta·thi·o·nine \ˌsistə'thīəˌnēn, -ənən\ *n* [irreg. fr. *cyst*eine, an amino acid + *methionine*, an amino acid] **:** a sulfur-containing amino acid $C_7H_{14}N_2O_4S$ formed as an intermediate in the conversion of methionine to cysteine in animals

cys·te·amine \sis'tēəmən\ *n* [*cyst*eine + *amine*] **:** a cysteine derivative C_2H_7NS used in the prevention of radiation sickness (as of cancer patients)

cys·ti·no·sis \ˌsistə'nōsəs\ *n, pl* **-no·ses** \-ō‚sēz\ [NL *cystine* + *-osis* abnormal or diseased condition] **:** a recessive autosomally inherited disease characterized esp. by cystinuria and deposits of cystine throughout the body — **cys·ti·not·ic** \-'nädik, -ätik\ *adj*

cys·to·ure·throg·ra·phy \ˌsistəˌyürə'thrägrəfē\ *n* [*cysto-* urinary bladder + *urethrograph* + *-y* action, instance] **:** roentgenography for the purpose of preparing a cystourethrogram — **cys·to·ure·thro·graph·ic** \-təyəˌrē-thrə'grafik\ *adj* cy·to·cha·la·sin \ˌsīd·ōkə'lāsən\ n [cyto- cell + Gk chalasis slackening + E -in chemical compound] : any of a group of metabolites isolated from fungi (esp. Helminthosporium dematioideum) that inhibit various cell processes

cy·to·chi·me·ra \ˌsīd·ōkə'mirə, -ˌkī'-\ n [NL, fr. cyto- cell + chimera] : an individual (as a plant, an organ, or a tissue) having cells of varied genetic constitution and esp. of various ploidy levels

cy·to·dif·fer·en·ti·a·tion \-ˌdifə,renchē'āshən\ n : the development of specialized cells (as muscle, blood, or nerve cells) from undifferentiated precursors

cy·to·ecol·o·gy \-ə'käləjē, -e'k-, -ē'k-\ n : the study of organismic adaptation at the molecular and cellular level — cy·to·eco·log·i·cal \-ˌēkə'läjəkəl, -ˌekə-\ adj

cy·to·ki·nin \-'kīnən\ n : any of various plant growth substances that are usu. derivatives of adenine

cy·to·me·gal·ic \ˌsīd·ōmə̇'galik\ adj [NL cytomegalia condition of having enlarged cells] : characterized by or causing the formation of enlarged cells ⟨a cytomegalic virus⟩

cytomegalic inclusion disease n : a severe disease esp. of newborns that is caused by a cytomegalovirus and usu. affects the salivary glands, brain, kidneys, liver, and lungs

cy·to·meg·a·lo·vi·rus \ˌsīd·ə,megəlō'vīrəs\ n [NL, fr. cytomegalia + connective -o- + virus] : any of several viruses that cause cellular enlargement and formation of eosinophilic inclusion bodies esp. in the nucleus and include the causative agent of cytomegalic inclusion disease

cy·to·mem·brane \ˌsīd·ə'mem,brān\ n : one of the cellular membranes including those of the plasmalemma, the endoplasmic reticulum, nuclear envelope, and Golgi apparatus; specif : UNIT MEMBRANE

cy·tom·e·try \sī'tämə·trē\ n [cyto- + -metry measuring, deriv. of Gk metron measure] : a technical specialty concerned with the counting of cells and esp. blood cells — cy·to·met·ric \ˌsīd·ə'me·trik\ adj

cy·to·mor·phol·o·gy \-ˌmȯ(r)'fäləjē\ n : the morphology of cells — cy·to·mor·pho·log·i·cal \-fə'läjəkəl\ adj

cy·to·patho·gen·ic \-ˌpathə'jenik\ adj : pathologic for or destructive to cells — cy·to·patho·ge·nic·i·ty \-jə-'nisəd·ē\ n

cy·to·pho·tom·e·ter \-(ˌ)fō'täməd·ə(r)\ n : a photometer for use in cytophotometry

cy·to·pho·tom·e·try \-(ˌ)fō'tämə·trē\ n : photometry applied to the study of the cell or its constituents — cy·to·pho·to·met·ric \-ˌfōd·ə'me·trik\ also cy·to·pho·to·met·ric·al \-kəl\ adj — cy·to·pho·to·met·ri·cal·ly \-k(ə)lē\ adv

cy·to·phys·i·ol·o·gy \-ˌfizē'äləjē, -i\ n : the physiology of cells — cy·to·phys·i·o·log·i·cal \-ēə'läjəkəl\ adj — cy·to·phys·i·o·log·i·cal·ly \-k(ə)lē, -i\ adv

cy·to·sine ar·a·bin·o·side \ˌsīd·ə,sēn,arə'binə,sīd, -ə,zēn-, -əsən-\ n : a synthetic cytotoxic antineoplastic agent $C_9H_{13}N_3O_5$ that is an isomer of the naturally occurring nucleoside of cytosine and arabinose and is used esp. in the treatment of acute myelogenous leukemia in adults

cy·to·sol \'sīd·ə,säl, -,sȯl\ n [cyto- + sol fluid colloidal system, fr. solution] : the fluid portion of the cytoplasm exclusive of organelles and membranes that is usu. obtained as the supernatant fraction from high-speed centrifugation of a tissue homogenate — cy·to·sol·ic \ˌsīd·ə'sälik, -'sȯl-\ adj

cy·to·spec·tro·pho·tom·e·try \ˌsīd·ō,spektrəfō-'tämə·trē, -ri\ n : the application of spectrophotometry to the study of cells and esp. to the quantitative estimation of their constituents (as DNA)

cy·to·stat·ic \ˌsīd·ə'stad·ik\ adj [cyto- + Gk statikos causing to stand] : tending to retard cellular activity and multiplication ⟨cytostatic treatment of tumor cells⟩ — cytostatic n — cy·to·stat·i·cal·ly \-ək(ə)lē\ adv

cy·to·tech \'sīd·ə,tek\ n [by shortening] : CYTOTECHNOLOGIST

cy·to·tech·nol·o·gist \ˌsīd·ō(ˌ)tek'näləjəst\ also cy·to·tech·ni·cian \-(ˌ)tek'nishən\ n : a medical technician trained in cytotechnology

cy·to·tech·nol·o·gy \-(ˌ)tek'näləjē, -ji\ n : a specialty in medical technology concerned with the identification of cells and cellular abnormalities (as in cancer)

cy·to·vi·rin \ˌsīd·ə'vi(ə)rən\ n [cyto- + virus + -in chemical compound] : a compound that is produced by a bacterium of the genus Streptomyces (S. olivochromogenes) and that is active against some plant viruses (as tobacco mosaic virus)

D

da*abbr deka-

¹DA \ˌdēˈā\ n [duck's ass; fr. its resemblance to the tail of a duck] **:** a hairstyle in which the hair is slicked back to form a vertical ridge at the back of the head

²DA \ˌdēˈā\ n **:** a doctor of arts

dab*n, slang Brit **:** fingerprint

dac·quoise \dåkwååz\ n [F Dacquoise of or relating to Dax, a town in southern France] **:** a dessert made of layers of baked nut meringue with a filling usu. of buttercream

dac·ryo·cys·to·rhi·nos·to·my \ˌdakrē(ˌ)ō͏ˌsis(ˌ)tōrī-'nästəmē\ n, pl **-mies** [dacryocyst + connective -o- + rhino- nose + -stomy surgical operation] **:** surgical creation of a passage for drainage between the lacrimal sac and the nasal cavity

dac·ti·no·my·cin \ˌdaktənōˈmīsᵊn\ n [alter. of actinomycin D] **:** a toxic antineoplastic drug $C_{62}H_{86}N_{12}O_{16}$ of the actinomycin group — called also actinomycin D

dag·wood \ˈdagˌwùd\ n, often cap [Dagwood Bumstead, character who made such sandwiches in the comic strip Blondie by M.B. Young †1973] **:** a many-layered sandwich

daisy chain*n **:** a group sexual activity in which each person attends to the one in front while being attended to by the one behind

daisy wheel n **:** a printing element of an electric typewriter or printer that consists of a disk with spokes bearing type

dal·a·pon \ˈdaləˌpän\ n [prob. fr. di- two + alpha + propionic acid] **:** an herbicide $C_4H_4Cl_2O_2$ that kills monocotyledonous plants selectively and is used esp. on unwanted grasses

da·la·si \däˈläsē, -si\ n, pl **-si** or **-sis** [native name in Gambia] **1 :** the basic monetary unit of Gambia **2 :** a coin or note representing one dalasi

Dal·mane*\ˈdalˌmān, ˈdäl-\ trademark — used for a preparation of flurazepam hydrochloride

dal·ton \ˈdòltᵊn\ n [John Dalton †1844 Eng. chemist and physicist] **:** atomic mass unit — used chiefly in biochemistry

damsel bug n **:** any of a family (Nabidae) of small brown or black predaceous bugs that feed on pest insects

dan \ˈdän, 'dan\ n [Jp, step, grade] **:** the expert level in Oriental arts of self-defense (as judo and karate) and games (as shogi)

D & C abbr dilatation and curettage

dap·sone \ˈdapˌsōn, -ˌzōn\ n [diaminodiphenyl sulfone] **:** an antimicrobial agent $C_{12}H_{12}N_2O_2S$ used esp. against leprosy

Dar·ier's disease \därˌyāz, då(r)-\ n [J. F. Darier †1938 Fr. dermatologist] **:** a genetically determined skin condition characterized by patches of keratotic papules — called also keratosis follicularis

Dar·win's finches \ˌdärwònz-, ˌdàw-\ n pl [Charles Darwin †1882 Eng. naturalist] **:** finches of a subfamily (Geospizinae) characterized by great variation in bill shape and confined mostly to the Galapagos islands

da·shi \ˈdäsh(ˌ)ē, däˈshē\ n [Jp, lit., broth] **:** a fish broth made from dried bonito

da·shi·ki \däˈshēkē, də'-\ n [alter. of Yoruba danshiki] **:** a usu. brightly colored loose-fitting tunic of African origin worn esp. by black men

data bank n **1 :** DATA BASE **2 :** an institution whose chief concern is building and maintaining a data bank

data base n **:** a collection of data organized esp. for rapid search and retrieval (as by a computer)

data processing n **:** the conversion and subsequent processing of raw data esp. by computer — **data processor** n

dating bar n **:** SINGLES BAR

dau·no·my·cin \ˌdònəˈmīsᵊn, ˌdaù-\ n [(assumed) It daunomicina, fr. Daunia, ancient region of Apulia, Italy + -o-, connective vowel + -micina (as in streptomicina streptomycin)] **:** an antibiotic $C_{27}H_{29}NO_{10}$ that is a nitrogenous glycoside and is used experimentally as an antineoplastic agent

dau·no·ru·bi·cin \-'rübəsən\ n [daunomycin + -rubi- (arbitrary infix)] **:** DAUNOMYCIN

day–care center \ˈdāˌke(ə)r-, -ˌka(ə)r-, -ˌkeə-, -ˌkaə-\ n **:** a center that provides supervision and facilities for preschool children during the day

Day–Glo \ˈdāˌglō\ trademark — used for fluorescent materials

day·glow \ˈdāˌglō\ n [day + airglow] **:** airglow seen during the day

day release n, Brit **:** a program whereby employees are permitted to spend part of the workday attending courses to develop needed job skills

day sailer n **:** a small sailboat without sleeping accommodations

day·side*\ˈdāˌsīd\ n **:** the side of a planet in daylight

day trader n **:** a speculator who seeks profit from the intraday fluctuation in the price of a security or commodity and therefore completes double trades of buying and selling or selling and covering in the course of single sessions of the market — **day–trade** \ˈdāˌtrād\ n or vb

DBA abbr doctor of business administration

DC abbr doctor of chiropractic

DDE \ˌdēˈ(ˌ)dēˈē\ n [dichlorodiphenyldichloroethylene] **:** a persistent organochlorine $C_{15}H_8Cl_4$ that is produced by the metabolic breakdown of DDT

DDVP \ˌdē(ˌ)dēˈvēˈpē\ n [dimethyl + dichlor- containing two chlorine atoms + vinyl + phosphate] **:** DICHLORVOS

de·ac·ces·sion \ˌdēək'seshən, -ˌak-\ vt **:** to remove and sell (a work of art) from a museum's collection esp. to raise funds to purchase other works of art 〈does not de-accession works or dispose of them by sale, unless it owns duplicates — D.L. Shirey〉 ~ vi **:** to de-accession a

work of art ⟨I'm sick of being told museums must *de=accession.* Of course they must —Edmund Carpenter⟩
de·ac·yl·ate \(')dē'asə,lāt\ *vt* [*de-* remove, do the opposite (deriv. of L *de* from, away) + *acylate* to introduce acyl into] **:** to remove an acyl group from (a compound) — **de·ac·yl·a·tion** \-,asə'lāshən\ *n*

dead drop *n* [fr. the absence of personal contact between the agents] **:** a prearranged hiding place for the deposit and pickup of information obtained through espionage

dead–on \(')ded'òn, -'än\ *adj* **:** precisely correct **:** extremely accurate ⟨*dead-on* timing⟩ ⟨*dead-on* in his contention that effective worker-education programs need firm intellectual . . . underpinnings —Benjamin DeMott⟩

Dear John *n* **:** a letter (as to a soldier) in which a wife asks for a divorce or a girl friend breaks off an engagement or a friendship ⟨jilted? Recipient of a *Dear John* letter? —Gore Vidal⟩

death control *n* **:** a decreasing of the natural human mortality rate and prolonging of the average life-span esp. through advances in medicine and hygiene

de·boost \(')dē,büst, də-\ *n* **:** the process of slowing down a spacecraft ⟨before *deboost* into low orbit —C.J. Sitomer⟩

debrief*\də'brēf, dē-\ *vt* **:** to instruct not to reveal classified information after release from a sensitive position

de·bug*\(,)dē'bəg, də'-\ *vt* **1 :** to remove a concealed microphone or wiretapping device from ⟨*debug* a room⟩ **2 :** to make (concealed microphones) ineffective by electronic means — **de·bug·ger** \dē'bəgə(r), də-\ *n*

deca·met·ric \,dekə;me·trik\ *adj* [fr. the wavelength range being between 1 and 10 dekameters] **:** of, relating to, or being a radio wave of high frequency

deca·pep·tide \,dekə;pep,tid\ *n* [*deca-* ten + *peptide*] **:** a polypeptide (as angiotensin I) that consists of a chain of 10 amino acids

Dec·ca \'dekə\ *n* [*Decca Co.*, British firm which developed it] **:** a system of long-range navigation utilizing the phase differences of continuous-wave signals from synchronized ground transmitters

deciding *adj* **:** having the effect of settling a contest or controversy ⟨the *deciding* run⟩ ⟨the *deciding* vote⟩

de·cid·u·o·ma \də,sijə'wōmə, dē-\ *n, pl* **-mas** *or* **-ma·ta** \-mədə, -ətə\ [NL, fr. *decidua* + *-oma* tumor] **1 :** a mass of tissue formed in the uterus following pregnancy that contains remnants of chorionic or decidual tissue **2 :** decidual tissue induced in the uterus (as by trauma) in the absence of pregnancy

decision theory *n* **:** a branch of statistical theory that attempts to quantify the process of making choices between alternatives

deck*n **:** TAPE DECK 1b

de·clin·ing–bal·ance method \də;klīniŋ;balən(t)s-, dē-\ *n* **:** a method of calculating periodic depreciation that involves the determining at regular (as annual) intervals throughout the expected life of an asset of equal percentage amounts of a cost balance which is progressively decreased by subtraction of each prior increment of depreciation from the original cost of the asset

de·clot \(')dē'klät, də-\ *vt* **:** to remove blood clots from

de·col·late*\də'käl,āt, dē'-\ *vt* **:** to separate the copies of (as a computer printout produced in multiple copies) — **de·col·la·tor** \-,äd-ə(r), -ātə(r)\ *n*

de·col·o·nize \(')dē'kälə,nīz, də-\ *vt* **:** to free from colonial status ~ *vi* **:** to grant independence to colonies — **de·col·o·ni·za·tion** \(,)dē,kälənə'zāshən, -,nī,-\ *n*

de·com·mit·ment \,dēkə;mitmənt\ *n* **:** a dropping or turning away from a prior commitment

de·com·pos·er*\,dēkəm'pōzə(r)\ *n* **:** any of various organisms (as many bacteria and fungi) that return constituents of organic substances to ecological cycles by feeding on and breaking down dead protoplasm

dec·o·ra·tive \'dek(ə)rəd·iv, -rətiv; 'dekə,rād·iv, -ātiv\ *n* **:** something used to decorate **:** something decorative

de·cou·ple \(,)dē'kəpəl, də'-\ *vt* **1 :** to reduce or eliminate the coupling of (as circuits or mechanical parts) **2 :** to decrease the seismic effect of (a nuclear explosion) by explosion in an underground cavity — **de·cou·pler** \-'kəp(ə)lə(r)\ *n*

de·crim·i·nal·ize \(')dē'krimən°l,īz, də'-, -m(ə)nəl-\ *vt* **-ized; -iz·ing :** to remove or reduce the criminal classification or status of; *esp* **:** to repeal a strict ban on while keeping under some form of regulation ⟨wanted to *decriminalize* the possession of marijuana⟩ — **de·crim·i·nal·iza·tion** \-,krimən°lə'zāshən, -mnəl-, -,lī'-\ *n*

de·cu·mu·la·tion \,dē,kyümyə;lāshən\ *n* **:** disposal of something accumulated

DEd *abbr* doctor of education

deep*adv **:** at the farther limits of the normal position of play ⟨the shortstop was playing *deep*⟩

deep space*also **deep sky** *n* **:** space well beyond the limits of the earth's atmosphere including space outside the solar system

deep structure *n* **:** a formal representation of the underlying semantic content of a sentence; *also* **:** the structure which such a representation specifies

de–es·ca·late \(')dē'eskə,lāt, ÷ -kyə-\ *vi* **:** to decrease in extent, volume, number, amount, or scope **:** diminish ⟨the rhetoric of violence has *de-escalated* —John Cogley⟩~ *vt* **:** to decrease the extent, volume, number, amount, or scope of ⟨my sister . . . tried to *de-escalate* our feud —H.A. Smith⟩ ⟨a tactical step toward *de-escalating* the Vietnamese war —Barbara Raskin⟩ — **de–es·ca·la·tion** \(')dē,eskə'lāshən, ÷ -kyə-\ *n*

de–es·ca·la·tor \(')dē,eskə,lād·ə(r), ÷-kyə-\ *n* **:** an advocate of de-escalation

de–es·ca·la·to·ry \-,ələ,tōrē, -,tòr-\ *adj* **:** of or relating to de-escalation ⟨took the first *de-escalatory* step⟩

deet \'dēt\ *n* [fr. *d. t.* (abbr. of *diethyl toluamide*)] **:** a colorless oily liquid insect repellent $C_{12}H_{17}NO$

de·fang*\(')dē'faŋ, də-\ *vt* **:** to make harmless or less powerful **:** weaken ⟨automation's role in *defanging* unions —A.H. Raskin⟩

defensive*adj **:** of, relating to, or being industries (as foods, utilities, and insurance) which provide essential needs to the ultimate consumer and in which business activity is relatively insensitive to changes in general business activity

deferred income*n **:** current income forgone to produce a later higher income (as at retirement)

de·fi·bril·late \(')dē'fibrə,lāt, də-, -'fib-\ *vt* **:** to restore the rhythm of (a fibrillating heart) — **de·fi·bril·la·tion** \(')dē,fibrə'lāshən, də-\ *n* — **de·fi·bril·la·tive** \dē'fibrə,lād·iv, də-, -'fib-, -ələd--\ *adj* — **de·fi·bril·la·tor** \-rə,lād-ə(r)\ *n* — **de·fi·bril·la·to·ry** \-rə,lād-ərē, -rələ,tōrē, -tòr-, -ri\ *adj*

¹de·fo·cus \(')dē¦fōkəs, də̇-\ *vt* **:** to cause (as a beam of radiation or a lens) to deviate from an accurate focus ⟨*defocused* his eye⟩ ⟨a *defocused* image⟩ ~ *vi* **:** to lose accuracy of focus **:** become defocused

²defocus *n* **:** a result of defocusing; *esp* **:** an image (as on motion-picture film) deliberately blurred for dramatic effect

de·fog \(')dē¦fȯg, də̇-, -¦fäg\ *vt* **:** to remove fog or condensed moisture from **:** keep free of fog ⟨defroster couldn't even keep the windshield fully *defogged* — *Consumer Reports* ⟩ — **de·fog·ger** \-ə(r)\ *n*

de·fuse*\(')dē¦fyüz\ *vt* **:** to make less dangerous, potent, or tense **:** calm ⟨the means to *defuse* explosive campus racial situations —M.L. Dillon⟩ ⟨Congress and the Administration are now seeking to *defuse* such criticism — Tom Alexander⟩

de·gen·er·a·cy*\də̇'jen(ə)rəsē, dē'-, -si\ *n* **:** the coding of an amino acid by more than one codon of the genetic code

de·gen·er·ate*\-n(ə)rət\ *adj* **1 :** being mathematically simpler (as by having a factor or constant equal to zero) than the typical case ⟨the graph of a second degree equation yielding two intersecting lines is a *degenerate* hyperbola⟩ **2 a :** having two or more states or subdivisions ⟨*degenerate* energy level⟩ **b** *of a gas* **:** having such a low temperature that quantum states of low energy are filled **c** *of a semiconductor* **:** having sufficient concentration of impurities to conduct electricity as a semimetal **3 :** having more than one codon representing an amino acid; *also* **:** being such a codon

de·grad·able \də̇'grādəbəl, dē-\ *adj* **:** capable of being chemically degraded ⟨*degradable* detergents⟩

de·gran·u·la·tion \(,)dē¸granyə'lāshən, də̇-\ *n* **:** the process of losing granules ⟨*degranulation* of leukocytes⟩

de·hire \(')dē'hī(ə)r, də̇-, -'hīə(r\ *vt* **:** to dismiss esp. from an executive position

de·hy·drase \dē'hī¸drās, -āz\ *n* [*dehydr-* dehydrogenate + *-ase* enzyme] **1 :** an enzyme that accelerates the removal of hydrogen from metabolites and its transfer to other substances **2 :** DEHYDRATASE

de·hy·dra·tase \-'hīdrə¸tās, -āz\ *n* [*dehydrate* + *-ase*] **:** an enzyme that catalyzes the removal of oxygen and hydrogen from metabolites in the proportion in which they form water

de·hy·dro·chlo·ri·nase \(¸)dē¸hīdrə'klōrə¸nās, -lȯr-, -āz\ *n* **:** an enzyme that dehydrochlorinates a chlorinated hydrocarbon (as DDT) and is found esp. in some DDT-resistant insects

de·hy·dro·chlo·ri·nate \-¸nāt\ *vt* **-nat·ed; -nat·ing :** to remove hydrogen and chlorine or hydrogen chloride from (a compound) — **de·hy·dro·chlo·ri·na·tion** \-¸klōrə-'nāshən, -lȯr-\ *n*

de·hy·dro·epi·an·dros·ter·one \(¸)dē¸hīdrō¸epēan-'drästə¸rōn\ *n* [*dehydro-* + *epi-* compound related to + *androsterone*] **:** an androgenic ketosteroid $C_{19}H_{28}O_2$ found in human urine and the adrenal cortex that is thought to be an intermediate in the biosynthesis of testosterone

de·hy·dro·iso·an·dros·ter·one \-¸ī(¸)sō-\ *n* [*dehydro-* + *iso-* isomer + *androsterone*] **:** DEHYDROEPIANDROSTERONE

de·hy·dro·tes·tos·ter·one \-(¸)te'stästə¸rōn\ *n* [*dehydro-* + *testosterone*] **:** a derivative $C_{19}H_{30}O_2$ of testosterone with similar androgenic activity

de·in·dus·tri·al·iza·tion \¸dēən¸dəstrēələ'zāshən\ *n* **:** the act or process of reducing or destroying the industrial organization and potential esp. of a defeated nation

de·in·sti·tu·tion·al·iza·tion \-¸insti̇¸t(y)üshənºlə-'zāshən, -sh(ə)nəl-\ *n* **:** the release of mental patients from care in state hospitals to care in the community — **de·in·sti·tu·tion·al·ize** \-'t(y)üshənºl¸īz, -sh(ə)nə¸līz\ *vt*

deix·is \'dīksəs\ *n* [Gk, lit., demonstrative force] **:** the pointing or specifying function of some words (as definite articles and demonstrative pronouns)

deka·gram \'dekə¸gram\ *n* [alter. of *decagram*] **:** 10 grams

deka·li·ter \-¸lid·ə(r)\ *n* [alter. of *decaliter*] **:** 10 liters

deka·me·ter \-¸mēd·ə(r)\ *n* [alter. of *decameter*] **:** 10 meters

deka·met·ric \¸dekə¦me·trik\ *adj* [by alter.] **:** DECAMETRIC

delay*n* **:** a play in football in which a ballcarrier or potential receiver delays momentarily as if to block before receiving a hand-off or running a prescribed pattern

de·le·git·i·ma·tion \¸dēlə̇¸jid·ə'māshən, -itə-\ *n* **:** a decline in or loss of prestige or authority of a dominant group or institution ⟨many young people, fearing the consequences of a full-scale *delegitimation* of authority, continue to search for a more responsive political alternative within the system —Richard Flacks⟩

deli *also* **del·ly** \'delē, -li\ *n, pl* **del·is** *also* **del·lies** [short for *delicatessen*] **:** a store where ready-to-eat food products (as cooked meats and prepared salads) are sold **:** delicatessen

delicacy*n* **:** the degree of differentiation between subcategories of linguistic categories ⟨by increase in *delicacy,* the primary class is broken down into secondary classes —M.A.K. Halliday⟩

de·lim·it·er*\də̇'liməd·ə(r), dē-\ *n* **:** a character that marks the beginning or end of a unit of data (as on a magnetic tape)

deliver*vt* **1 :** to cause (oneself) to produce as if by giving birth ⟨has *delivered* himself of half an autobiography —H.C. Schonberg⟩ **2 :** to come through with **:** produce ⟨can *deliver* the goods⟩ ⟨the new car *delivers* high gas mileage⟩ ~ *vi* **:** to produce the promised, desired, or expected results **:** come through ⟨failed to *deliver* on their promises⟩ ⟨year after year, he promised salary raises and could almost never *deliver* —John McPhee⟩

de·lo·cal·ize*\(')dē¦lōkə¸līz\ *vt* **:** to remove (electrons) from a particular position

del·ta wave \¸deltə-\ *n* **:** a high amplitude electrical rhythm of the brain with a frequency less than 6 cycles per second that occurs in deep sleep, in infancy, and in many diseased conditions of the brain — called also *delta, delta rhythm*

deltoid tuberosity *n* **:** a rough triangular bump on the outer side of the middle of the humerus that is the site of insertion of the deltoid muscle

de·mag·ni·fy \(')dē¦magnə¸fī, də̇-\ *vt* **:** to reduce the size of (as a photographic image or an electron beam) — **de·mag·ni·fi·ca·tion** \-¸magnəfə'kāshən\ *n*

de·mand–pull \də̇'mand¸pu̇l, dē-\ *n* **:** an increase or upward trend in spendable money that tends to result in increased competition for available goods and services and a corresponding increase in consumer prices — compare COST-PUSH — **demand–pull** *adj*

de·mar·ket·ing \(ˌ)dē'märkəd·iŋ, də-, -'màk-, -ətiŋ\ *n* **:** the use of advertising to decrease demand for a product that is in short supply

de·mas·cu·lin·ize \(ˌ)dē'maskyələˌnīz, də-\ *vt* **:** to remove the masculine character or qualities of ⟨prenatal stress... *demasculinizes* the behavior of males — Ingeborg L. Ward⟩ ⟨seems sensitive to women and the need to *demasculinize* society —Brenda F. Fasteau & Bonnie Lobel⟩ — **de·mas·cu·lin·iza·tion** \-ˌmaskyə-lànə'zäshən, -ˌnĭ'-\ *n*

dem·e·ton \'demə,tän\ *n* [prob. fr. *di*ethyl + *mer*captan + *thi*onate] **:** a mixture of organophosphorus insecticides used as a systemic on plants

demi–pen·sion \ˌdemē(')pän'syōⁿ, -ˌpäⁿsē'ōⁿ\ *n* [F, fr. *demi-* half + *pension* board] **:** MODIFIED AMERICAN PLAN

de·mist·er \dē'mistə(r), də-\ *n, Brit* **:** a device for freeing an automobile windshield of frost or ice **:** defroster

demo* \'dē(ˌ)mō\ *n, pl* **demos** **1 :** a demonstration ⟨gave *demos* of karate and judo during the intermission⟩; *esp* **:** a political demonstration **:** a protest ⟨workers elsewhere staged brief strikes and *demos* —Donald Kirk⟩ **2 :** something used for purposes of demonstration: as **a :** a demonstration record or tape ⟨*demos* are cut by song publishers to demonstrate their songs —*Rolling Stone*⟩ **b :** a demonstrator automobile ⟨sale on 1983 factory *demos*⟩

de·mo·graph·ics \ˌdēmə'grafiks, ˌdem-\ *n pl* [*demographic* + *-s*, pl. suffix] **:** the statistical characteristics of human populations (as age, sex, family size, and income) used esp. to identify markets

de·mo·li·tion derby \ˌdemə'lishən-, ˌdē-\ *n* **:** a contest in which drivers ram old cars into one another until only one car remains running

de·moth·ball \(')dē'mòth,bòl\ *vt* **:** to remove the preservative covering of in order to reactivate (as ships)

de·mys·ti·fy \(')dē'mistə,fī\ *vt* **:** to eliminate the mystifying features of ⟨his novels... *demystify* death, confronting us with the omnipresent reality of it —Harriet Blodgett⟩

de·ni·abil·i·ty \də,nīə'bilàd·ē, dē-, -i\ *n* **:** the ability of an official to deny something (as knowledge of covert activities) esp. on the basis of being officially uninformed ⟨the President, as befits his rank, is armed by all but impervious *deniability* —New Yorker⟩

den·som·e·ter \den'säməd·ə(r)\ *n* [ISV *dens-* (fr. L *densus* dense) + connective *-o-* + *-meter* instrument for measuring, deriv. of Gk *metron* measure] **1 :** an instrument for measuring the porosity of paper by forcing air through it **2 :** an instrument for determining density or specific gravity **:** densimeter

den·tur·ist \'dencharàst\ *n* **:** a dental technician who makes, fits, and repairs dentures directly for the public

de·nu·cle·ar·ize \(')dē'n(y)üklēə,rīz, ÷-kyələ,rīz\ *vt* **-ized; -iz·ing :** to remove nuclear arms from **:** prohibit the use of nuclear arms in ⟨both sides... agree that Germany should be *denuclearized* —Newsweek⟩ ⟨the proposed *denuclearized* zone in Latin America — H.A. Spalding⟩ — **de·nu·cle·ar·iza·tion** \(ˌ)dē,n(y)üklēèrà-'zäshən, ÷ -kyələr-, -,rī'z-\ *n*

Denver boot *n* [fr. its having been devised in Denver, Colo.] **:** a metal clamp that locks onto one of the wheels of an automobile and must be unlocked before a motorist can drive off (as after payment of a fine)

¹de·or·bit \(')dē,órbàt, -,ó(ə)b-\ *vi* **:** to go out of orbit ~ *vt* **:** to cause to deorbit ⟨*deorbit* a spacecraft⟩

²deorbit *n* **:** the process of deorbiting

de·oxy·ri·bo·nu·cle·o·tide \(ˌ)dē,äksē,rī(ˌ)bō'n(y)üklēə-,tīd\ *n* [*deoxyribose* + *nucleotide*] **:** a nucleotide that contains deoxyribose and is a constituent of DNA

de·pic·ture \də'pikchə(r), dē-, -ksh-\ *vt* [blend of *depict* and *picture*, vb.] **1 :** to depict **2 :** to imagine — **de·pic·ture·ment** \-mənt\ *n*

de·po·lit·i·cize \ˌdēpə'lid·ə,sīz\ *vt* **:** to remove the political character from **:** take out of the realm of politics ⟨failure of government measures aimed at *depoliticizing* the armed forces —Jane Monahan⟩ — **de·po·lit·i·ci·za·tion** \-,lid·əsə'zäshən\ *n*

de·pol·lute \-pə'lüt\ *vt* **:** to remove the pollution from ⟨*depollute* our rivers and streams⟩ — **de·pol·lu·tion** \-'lüshən\ *n*

Depression glass *n* **:** glassware mass-produced in a variety of colors and patterns during the late 1920s and 1930s

de·pres·sur·ize \(ˌ)dē'preshə,rīz\ *vt* **:** to release pressure from — **de·pres·sur·iza·tion** \-,preshə(ə)rə'zäshən, -,rī'-\ *n*

de·pro·gram \(')dē,prō,gram, -ōgrəm\ *vt* **:** to dissuade or try to dissuade from convictions usu. of a religious nature often with the use of force ⟨parents lure their children away from the communes so that he can *deprogram* them —Kenneth Woodward⟩ — **de·pro·gram·mer** \-,gramə(r)\ *n*

de·pro·tein·ate \(')dē'prō,tē,nāt *also* -ˌpröd·ēə,n- *or* -ōtēə,n-\ *vt* **-at·ed; -at·ing** [*de-* + *protein* + *ate*, vb. suffix] **:** to remove protein from — **de·pro·tein·ation** \(')dē,prō,tē'nāshən *also* -,pröd·ēə'n- *or* -ōtēə'n-\ *n*

de·Quer·vain's disease \dəkər'vaⁿz-\ *n* [Fritz *de Quervain* †1940 Swiss surgeon] **:** inflammation of tendons and their sheaths at the styloid process of the radius that often causes pain in the thumb side of the wrist

de·rail·leur \də'rālə(r), dē-\ *n* [F *dérailleur*, fr. *dérailler* to throw off the track (fr. *dé-* de- + *rail* rail, fr. E)] **:** a multiple-speed gear mechanism on a bicycle that involves the moving of the chain from one sprocket to another ⟨10-speed *derailleur*⟩

de·reg·u·late \(')dē'regyə,lāt, də-\ *vt* **:** to remove from regulation **:** decontrol ⟨proposals to *deregulate* natural= gas prices — *Wall Street Jour.*⟩ — **de·reg·u·la·tion** \-,regyə'lāshən\ *n*

de·repress \ˌdērə'pres\ *vt* **:** to activate (a gene) by releasing from a blocked state — **de·re·pres·sion** \-'preshən\ *n*

derm·abra·sion \ˌdərmə'brāzhən, ˌdəm-\ *n* [*derm-* skin (deriv. of Gk *derma*) + *abrasion*] **:** surgical removal of skin blemishes or imperfections (as scars or tattoos) by abrasion (as with sandpaper or wire brushes)

der·mom·e·ter \(ˌ)dər'mäməd·ər, -ətər, ˌdə'mäməd·ə(r, -ətə(r\ *n* [*dermo-* + *-meter*] **:** an instrument used to measure the electrical resistance of the skin

der·mo·ne·crot·ic \ˌdər(ˌ)mōnè'kräd·ik, ˌdə(ˌ)mō-, -ätik\ *adj* [*dermo-* + *necrotic*] **:** relating to or causing necrosis of the skin ⟨a *dermonecrotic* toxin⟩ ⟨*dermonecrotic* effects⟩

de·ro·man·ti·cize \ˌdērōˈmantəˌsīz\ *vt* **:** to remove the romance from **:** make mundane ⟨*deromanticizing* all those myths about sexuality —Joel Siegel⟩

derrick*vt **:** to remove (a pitcher) from a baseball game

DES \ˌdē(ˌ)ēˈes\ *n* [*di*ethyl*s*tilbestrol] **:** a colorless crystalline synthetic compound $C_{18}H_{20}O_2$ used as a potent estrogen

de·sa·li·nate \(ˈ)dēˈsaləˌnāt, -sā-\ *vt* **-nat·ed; -nat·ing** [*de-* + *salin-* salt (deriv. of L *sal* salt) + *-ate*] **:** to remove salt from ⟨*desalinate* seawater⟩ — **de·sa·li·na·tor** \-ˌnād-ə(r)\ *n*

de·sa·li·nize \-ˌnīz\ *vt* **-nized; -niz·ing :** DESALINATE

descending colon *n* **:** the part of the large intestine on the left side that extends from the bend below the spleen to the sigmoid flexure — compare ASCENDING COLON

de·school \ˌdēˈskül\ *vt* **:** to eliminate traditional schools from ⟨the movement to *deschool* society —John Holt⟩

de·scrip·tor*\dəˈskriptə(r), dē-\ *n* **1 :** a word or phrase (as an index term) used to identify an item (as a subject or document) esp. in an information retrieval system; *also* **:** an alphanumeric symbol so used **2 :** something (as a word or phrase or a characteristic feature) that serves to describe or identify

de·select \ˌdēsəˈlekt\ *vt* **:** to dismiss (a trainee) from a training program ⟨had been *deselected* because he was "unsuitable" for the work —*N.Y. Times*⟩

des·ert·i·fi·ca·tion \ˌdezərtəfəˈkāshən\ *n* **:** the process of becoming arid land or desert (as from land mismanagement or climate change)

designated hitter *n* **:** a baseball player designated at the start of the game to bat in place of the pitcher without causing the pitcher to be removed from the game

de·si·pra·mine \ˌdezəˈpramən, dəˈziprə-, -ˌmēn\ *n* [*des*methyl (fr. *des-* having a molecule characterized by the removal of one or more atoms + *methyl*) + *i*m*ipramine*] **:** a tricyclic antidepressant $C_{18}H_{22}N_2$ administered as the hydrochloride

des·mo·some \ˈdezməˌsōm\ *n* [*desmo-* bond, ligament (deriv. of Gk *desmos* band, bond) + *-some* body, deriv. of Gk *sōma*] **:** a specialized local thickening of the cell membrane of an epithelial cell that serves to anchor contiguous cells together

des·mos·ter·ol \dezˈmästəˌròl, -ˌrōl\ *n* [*desmo-* + *sterol*] **:** a crystalline steroid alcohol $C_{27}H_{43}OH$ **:** dehydrocholesterol

de·spin \(ˈ)dēˈspin\ *vt* **-spun; -spin·ning :** to stop the rotation of or reduce the speed of rotation of (as a satellite)

de–Sta·lin·iza·tion \(ˌ)dēˌstälənəˈzāshən, -tal-, -ˌnīˈz-\ *n* **:** the discrediting of Stalin and his policies

de·struct \ˈdēˌstrəkt, dəˈs-, dēˈs-\ *n* [short for *destruction*] **:** the deliberate destruction of a rocket after launching esp. during a test; *also* **:** such destruction of a device or material (as to prevent its falling into enemy hands)

de·syn·chro·nize \(ˈ)dēˈsiŋkrəˌnīz, də-\ *vt* **:** to put out of synchronization ⟨*desynchronize* internal biorhythms by changing your sleep pattern⟩ — **de·syn·chro·ni·za·tion** \-ˌsiŋkrənəˈzāshən\ *n*

de·ter·rence*\dəˈtərən(t)s, -ˈter-; -ˈtə-rən(t)s\ *n* **:** the maintaining of vast military power and weaponry in order to discourage war ⟨an official council blessing on the concept of nuclear *deterrence* —*Current Biog.*⟩

det·o·nate*\ˈdetᵊnˌāt, ˈdedˑəˌnāt\ *vt* **-nat·ed; -nat·ing :** to set off in a burst of activity **:** spark ⟨programs that *detonated* controversies⟩

¹de·tox \(ˈ)dēˈtäks\ *vt* [by shortening] **:** DETOXIFY 1

²detox *adj* [by shortening] **:** of or used for detoxification

de·tox·i·fy*\(ˈ)dēˈtäksəˌfī, də-\ *vb* **-fied; -fy·ing** *vt* **1 :** to free from addiction to a drug or alcohol ⟨the clinic started *detoxifying* him by gradually lowering his dosage —J.M. Markham⟩ **2 :** to counteract the activity or effect of **:** neutralize ⟨*detoxifying* tensions that arise between people of divergent tastes and goals —M. B. Duberman⟩ ∼ *vi* **:** to become free of addiction to a drug or alcohol

de·tu·mes·cent \ˌdēt(y)üˈmesᵊnt\ *adj* **:** characterized by detumescence

deu·ter·ate \ˈd(y)üdəˌrāt\ *vt* **-at·ed; -at·ing** [*deute*rium + *-ate*, vb. suffix] **:** to introduce deuterium into (a compound)

developing *adj* **:** not having attained a potential economic level of industrial production and standard of living (as from lack of capital) **:** underdeveloped ⟨a poor and *developing* nation in the early stages of modernization —A.D. Barnett⟩

de·vol·a·til·ize \(ˈ)dēˈvälətᵊlˌiz, də-, *Brit also* ˌdēvəˈlat-\ *vt* **:** to remove volatile material from (as coal) — **de·vol·a·til·iza·tion** \-ˌvälətᵊlə'zāshən, *Brit also* -vəˌlat-\ *n*

dex \ˈdeks\ *n* [short for *Dexedrine*] **:** the sulfate of dextroamphetamine

dexa·meth·a·sone \ˌdeksəˈmethəˌsōn, -ˌzōn\ *n* [perh. fr. *Dexa*myl, a trademark + *meth*yl + *-a-* (arbitrary infix) + *-sone* (as in *cortisone*)] **:** a synthetic glucocorticoid $C_{22}H_{29}FO_5$ used esp. as an anti-inflammatory and antiallergic agent

de·am·phet·amine \ˌdeksamˈfetəˌmēn, -əmən\ *n* [alter. of *dextroamphetamine*] *chiefly Brit* **:** dextroamphetamine

Dex·e·drine \ˈdeksəˌdrēn, -drən\ *trademark* — used for a preparation of the sulfate of dextroamphetamine

dex·ies \ˈdeksēz\ *n pl* **:** tablets or capsules of the sulfate of dextroamphetamine

dex·tran·ase \-strəˌnās, -ˌnāz\ *n* **:** a hydrolase that prevents tooth decay by breaking down dextran and eliminating dental plaque

dex·tro·pro·poxy·phene \ˌdekstrəprōˈpäksəˌfēn\ *n* [*dextro-* dextrorotatory + *propoxyphene*] **:** PROPOXYPHENE

DH *abbr* designated hitter

di·ag·o·nal·ize \(ˈ)dīˌag(ə)nᵊlˌīz, -gnəl-\ *vt* **-ized; -iz·ing** **:** to convert (a matrix) to a diagonal matrix — **di·ag·o·nal·iz·able** \-ˈīzəbəl\ *adj* — **di·ag·o·nal·iza·tion** \-ˌag(ə)nᵊlə'zāshən, -gnəl-\ *n*

diagonal ma·trix \-ˈmā-triks\ *n* **:** a matrix that has all the nonzero elements located along the diagonal from upper left to lower right

di·az·e·pam \dīˈazəˌpam\ *n* [*diaz-* containing the group N_2 + *epox*ide + *-am* compound related to ammonia] **:** a synthetic tranquilizer $C_{16}H_{13}ClN_2O$ used esp. to relieve anxiety and tension and as a muscle relaxant — see VALIUM

di·azo·ben·zene·sul·fon·ic acid \(ˈ)dīˌazōˈben,zēn-(ˌ)səlˈfänik-, -ˌāzō-\ *n* [*diazo-* + *benzene* + *sulfonic*] **:** a white or reddish crystalline acid derivative $C_6H_4N_2O_3S$ of sulfanilic acid that is used as the reagent in the diazo reaction

di·az·ox·ide \ˌdīˌazˈäkˌsīd\ n [diaz- + oxide] **:** an antihypertensive drug $C_8H_7ClN_2O_2S$ that has a structure similar to chlorothiazide but no diuretic activity

dice*n **:** a close contest between two racing-car drivers for position during a race

dice*vi diced; dic·ing **:** to engage in a jockeying for position (as in an automobile race) ⟨had been dicing along the road with the driver of another car —London Daily Telegraph⟩

di·cen·tric \(')dīˌsen·trik\ n **:** a dicentric chromosome

dic·ey \ˈdīsē\ adj **:** having an uncertain outcome **:** risky ⟨in the best of situations, detoxification is a dicey undertaking —J.M. Markham⟩

di·chlor·vos \(')dīˌklȯr(ə)rˌväs, -lȯ(ə)r-, -vəs\ n [dichlor- containing two atoms of cholorine + vinyl + phosphate] **:** a nonpersistent organophosphorus pesticide $C_4H_7Cl_2O_4P$ that is used esp. against insects and is of low toxicity to man — called also DDVP

dich·otic \(')dīˌkōd·ik, -käd-\ adj [dich- in two, apart (deriv. of Gk dicha in two) + -otic of the ear, fr. Gk ōtikos, fr. ōt-, ous ear] **:** affecting or relating to the two ears differently in regard to a conscious aspect (as pitch or loudness) or a physical aspect (as frequency or energy) of sound — dich·oti·cal·ly \-d·ək(ə)lē\ adv

dictionary*n, pl -nar·ies **:** a list (as of synonyms or hyphenation instructions) stored in machine-readable form for reference by an automatic system (as for information retrieval or computerized typesetting)

diddle*vi did·dled; did·dling \ˈdid(ə)liŋ\ **:** to fool around **:** fiddle, toy — usu. used with ⟨diddling around with the tape machine —Michael Stephens⟩

die·sel·ing \ˈdēz(ə)liŋ, ˈdēs(-\ n **:** the continued operation of an internal-combustion engine after the ignition is turned off

di·eth·yl tolu·amide \ˌdīˌethəlˈtäl(ˌ)yüəˌmīd, -əməd\ n [diethyl + tolu- related to toluene + amide] **:** DEET

difference*vt -enced; -enc·ing **:** to compute the difference between ⟨measuring the output and differencing this from a desired setting —Andrew St. Johnston⟩

di·func·tion·al \(')dīˌfəŋ(k)shnəl, -shnəl\ adj [di- two + functional] **:** of, relating to, or being a compound with two sites in the molecule that are highly reactive — di·func·tion·al·i·ty \(ˌ)dīˌfəŋ(k)shəˈnaləd·ē\ n

di·ges·tif \ˌdēzhesˈtēf\ n [F, lit., digestive] **:** an after-dinner drink (as a brandy or a liqueur)

digital*adj 1 **:** providing a readout in numerical digits ⟨a digital voltmeter⟩ ⟨a digital clock radio⟩ 2 **:** relating to or being a phonograph record made from a magnetic tape on which sound waves have been represented digitally as the sum of minute increments in amplitude so that wow and flutter are eliminated and background noise is greatly reduced

dig·i·tal·ize \ˈdijədˈəlˌīz\ vt -ized; -iz·ing [digital + -ize, vb. suffix] **:** to put (as data) into digital notation

di·glos·sia \(')dīˌgläsēə, -ˌglȯs-\ n [NL, fr. F diglossie, fr. di- + -glossie, fr. Gk glōssa language, tongue] **:** the use of two languages or dialects for different functions or at different social levels — di·glos·sic \-sik\ adj

di·hy·droxy·ac·e·tone \ˌdīhīˌdräksēˈasəˌtōn\ n [dihydroxy- containing two hydroxyl groups + acetone] **:** an isomer of glyceraldehyde that is used esp. to produce artificial tanning of the skin

di·hy·droxy·cho·le·cal·cif·er·ol \-ˌkōləkalˈsifəˌrȯl, -ˌkälə-, -ˌrȯl\ n [dihydroxy- + cholecalciferol] **:** a physiologically active vitamin D derivative $C_{27}H_{44}O_3$ that is synthesized in the kidney

di·hy·droxy·phe·nyl·al·a·nine \-ˌfenᵊlˈaləˌnēn, -ˌfēn-\ n [dihydroxy- + phenylalanine] 1 **:** a crystalline amino acid found in various fruits and vegetables 2 **:** L-DOPA

dike, dikey var of DYKE, DYKEY

di·lu·tive \(')dī(y)üd·iv, dəˈl-\ adj **:** reducing or involving reduction of per share income of a corporate stock ⟨the dilutive effect of stock options and convertible securities⟩

dime*n 1 slang a **:** 10 dollars b or dime bag **:** a packet containing 10 dollars worth of an illicit drug (as marijuana) 2 slang **:** a sentence of 10 years in prison

dimension*n **:** the number of elements in a basis of a vector space

di·meth·o·ate \dīˈmethəˌwāt\ n [dimethyl + -thioic having a sulfur atom in place of an oxygen atom + -ate derivative compound] **:** an organophosphorus insecticide $C_5H_{12}NO_3PS_2$ used on livestock and various crops

di·meth·yl·hy·dra·zine \ˌdīˌmethəlˈhīdrəˌzēn\ n [dimethyl + hydrazine] **:** either of two flammable corrosive isomeric liquids $C_2H_8N_2$ which are methylated derivatives of hydrazine and of which one is used in rocket fuels

di·meth·yl·ni·tros·amine \-(ˌ)nī·ˈtrōsəˌmēn\ n [dimethyl + nitrosamine] **:** a carcinogenic nitrosamine $(CH_3)_2N_2O$ that occurs esp. in tobacco smoke

di·meth·yl·sulf·ox·ide \-(ˌ)səlˈfäkˌsīd\ n [dimethyl + sulfoxide] **:** a compound $(CH_3)_2SO$ obtained as a byproduct in wood-pulp manufacture and used as a solvent and in experimental medicine — called also DMSO

dimethyl te·reph·tha·late \-ˌte·refˈthaˌlāt, -aˌlət; -təˈreftho·lāt\ n **:** a chemical $C_{10}H_{10}O_2$ used for making polyester film and fiber

di·meth·yl·tryp·ta·mine \-ˈtriptəˌmēn\ n [dimethyl + tryptamine] **:** an easily synthesized hallucinogenic drug $C_{12}H_{16}N_2$ that is chemically similar to but shorter acting than psilocybin — called also DMT

dim sum \ˈdimˈsəm\ n pl [Chin (Cant) tím sam, lit., small center] **:** traditional Chinese refreshments consisting of steamed or fried dumplings with a savory filling

dinch \ˈdinch\ vt [origin unknown] **:** to extinguish by crushing ⟨looked at his half-smoked cigar, then on his way to the cabaña he dinched it in the concrete flowerpot —John O'Hara⟩

din·er-out \ˌdīnəˈraút\ n, pl diners-out \ˌdīnə(r)ˈzaút\ **:** one that dines out ⟨an essential aspect of being a leading writer, in his opinion, was to be a leading diner-out — W.G. Rogers⟩

ding*n **:** minor surface damage (as a dent)

ding–a–ling*\ˈdiŋəˌliŋ\ n **:** a nitwit or kook

ding·bat*\ˈdiŋˌbat\ n **:** DING-A-LING

dink \ˈdiŋk\ n [origin unknown] slang **:** a Vietnamese — used disparagingly

dinner theater n **:** a restaurant in which a play is presented after the meal is over

dinosaur*n **:** one that is out-of-date or is useless or impractical because of its great size or complexity ⟨those who believe the traditional symphony orchestra is a bit of a dinosaur —Christopher Ford⟩

di·ox·in \dīˈäksən\ n [di- two + oxygen + -in chemical compound] **:** any of several heterocyclic hydrocarbons that occur esp. as persistent toxic impurities in herbicides; *esp* : a teratogenic impurity $C_{12}H_4O_2Cl_4$ in 2,4,5,-T

di·phe·nox·y·late \ˌdīˌfēn'äksəˌlāt, -ˌfen-\ *n* [fr. *diphenyl*-propyl + carb*oxylic* acid + *-ate* derivative compound] : an antidiarrheal agent chemically related to meperidine and administered as the hydrochloride $C_{30}H_{32}N_2O_2 \cdot HCl$

di·phos·pho·glyc·er·ate \(')dīˌfäsfō'glisəˌrāt\ *n* [*di-* + *phosphoglycerate*] : an isomeric ester of diphosphoglyceric acid that occurs in human erythrocytes and facilitates release of oxygen by decreasing the oxygen affinity of hemoglobin

di·phos·pho·gly·cer·ic acid \(')dīˌfäsfō(ˌ)glis'erik-\ *n* [*di-* + *phospho-* phosphate + *glyceric acid*] : a diphosphate $C_3H_8O_9P_2$ of glyceric acid that is an important intermediate in photosynthesis and in glycolysis and fermentation

dip·lo·tene \'dipləˌtēn\ *adj* : relating to or being the diplotene stage of meiotic prophase

dip·shit \'dip'shit\ *n* : a stupid or incompetent person — usu. considered vulgar

di·pyr·i·dam·ole \(')dīˌpirə'damˌōl, -ōl\ *n* [*di-* + *pyri*d*ine* + *amino* + *-ole* hydrocarbon of the benzene series] : a drug $C_{24}H_{40}N_8O_4$ used as a coronary vasodilator

di·quat \'dīˌkwät\ *n* [*di-* + *qua*ternary] : a powerful nonpersistent herbicide $C_{12}H_{12}Br_2N_2$ that has been used to control water weeds (as the water hyacinth)

director's chair *n* [fr. its use by movie directors] : a lightweight usu. folding armchair with a back and seat usu. of cotton duck

direct variation *n* : a relationship between variables in which one variable is equal to a nonzero constant times the other ⟨the function *y* = *kx* with *k* a nonzero constant is a *direct variation* in which *y* varies directly as *x*⟩ — compare INVERSE VARIATION

dir·ham*\də'ram\ *n* **1 a** : the basic monetary unit of Morocco and the United Arab Emirates **b** : a monetary unit of Iraq equal to $\frac{1}{20}$ dinar **c** : a monetary unit of Libya equal to $\frac{1}{1000}$ dinar **2** : a coin or note representing one dirham

dirt bike *n* : a usu. lightweight motorcycle designed for operation on unpaved surfaces

dirty \'dərdˌē, 'dōdˌē, 'dōidˌē, -tē, -i\ *n*, *pl* **dirt·ies** : one that is dirty

dirty old man *n* : a lecherous mature man

dirty pool *n* [*pool* pocket billiards] : underhanded or unsportsmanlike conduct ⟨none of the lawyers . . . seems to have been disturbed by the fact that all the recommended techniques were illegal. It appears that the scheme . . . was rejected not on the ground that it was *dirty pool* but on the ground of impracticality —*New Yorker*⟩

dis·ag·gre·gate*\(')dis'agrəˌgāt\ *vi* : to break up or apart ⟨the molecules of a gel *disaggregate* to form a sol⟩ — **dis·ag·gre·ga·tive** \-ˌgād·iv\ *adj*

dis·am·big·u·ate \ˌdis(ˌ)am'bigyəˌwät, -əwət\ *vt* **-at·ed; -at·ing** [*dis-* reverse, do the opposite + *ambigu*ous + *-ate*, vb. suffix] : to establish a single semantic or grammatical interpretation for — **dis·am·big·u·a·tion** \-ˌbigyə'wāshən\ *n*

dis·bound \(')dis'baund\ *adj* : no longer having a binding ⟨a *disbound* pamphlet⟩

disc brake *n* : a brake that operates by the friction of a caliper pressing against the sides of a rotating disc

¹dis·co \'dis(ˌ)kō\ *n*, *pl* **discos** [short for *discotheque*] **1** : a nightclub for dancing to live and recorded music often featuring flamboyant decor, special lighting effects, and live disc jockeys **2** : popular dance music characterized by hypnotic rhythm, repetitive lyrics, and usu. a predominance of electronically produced sounds

²disco *vi* : to dance to disco music

¹dis·co·theque \'diskəˌtek, ˌdiskə'tek\ *n* [F *discothèque* collection of phonograph records, discotheque, fr. *disque* disk (fr. L *discus*) + connective *-o-* + *thèque* (as in *bibliothèque* library, fr. L *bibliotheca*)] : a usu. small intimate nightclub for dancing to recorded music; *also* : DISCO 1

²discotheque *vi* **-thequed; -thequ·ing** : to dance at a discotheque

dis·cre·tion·ary account \dis'kreshəˌnerē-, *chiefly Brit* -'kreshən(ə)ri-\ *n* : a security or commodity market account in which an agent (as a broker) is given power of attorney allowing him to make independent decisions and buy and sell for the account of his principal

discretionary income *n* : the part of personal income left after basic necessities (as food, shelter, and taxes) have been paid for

dis·cret·iza·tion \(ˌ)disˌkrēd·ə'zāshən\ *n* : the action of making mathematically discrete

discriminant function *n* : a function of a set of variables (as measurements of taxonomic specimens) that is evaluated for samples of events or objects and used as an aid in discriminating between or classifying them

dish·ware \'dishˌwa(ə)r, -ˌwe(ə)r, -ˌwaa, -ˌwea\ *n* : tableware (as of china) used in serving food

dishy \'dishē, -i\ *adj* **dish·i·er; -est** *chiefly Brit* : being good-looking : attractive ⟨kissed and caressed by *dishy* young girls —*Daily Mirror (London)*⟩ ⟨looks *dishier* than he did when he was one of the cinema's favorite romantic heroes —Margaret Forwood⟩

dis·in·sec·tion \ˌdisən'sekshən, -ˌin's-\ *n* : removal of insects (as from an aircraft)

dis·in·ter·me·di·a·tion \(ˌ)disˌintə(r)ˌmēdē'āshən\ *n* [fr. the investor's bypassing of the intermediate institution] : diversion of savings from institutions (as savings banks) with governmentally imposed interest ceilings to direct investment in higher-yielding instruments

dis·in·tox·i·cate \ˌdisⁿn'täksəˌkāt\ *vt* : to subject (as a drug user or an alcoholic) to disintoxication

dis·joint*\(')dis'joint\ *adj* : having no elements in common ⟨*disjoint* mathematical sets⟩

disk**or disc***n **1** : a round flat plate (as of metal) coated with a magnetic substance on which data for a computer can be stored — called also *magnetic disk* **2** : a circular grid in a photocomposer

disk·ette \'disˌket, ˌdis'ket\ *n* [*disk* + *-ette*, dim. suffix] : FLOPPY DISK

disk pack *n* : a storage device for a computer that consists of a stack of magnetic disks mounted on a central hub and that are removable protective cover and that can be handled and stored as a unit

Dis·ney·esque \'diznēˌesk, ˌdiznē'-\ *adj* [Walt *Disney* †1966, Am. cartoonist] : resembling or suggestive of the films, television productions, or amusement parks made by Walt Disney or his organization

displacement*n : the substitution of another form of behavior for what is normal or expected esp. when the usual response is nonadaptive

display***n** : an electronic device (as a cathode-ray tube in a computer or in a radar receiver or a liquid-crystal watch) that presents information in visual form; *also* : the visual information

dis·pos·able \dis'pōzəbəl\ *n* : something (as a paper blanket) that is disposable ⟨returnable containers have been replaced by *disposables* —P.C. Stuart⟩

dissonance***n** : inconsistency between the beliefs one holds or between one's actions and one's beliefs : discord

dis·to·buc·cal \ˌdistö'bəkəl\ *adj* [*disto-* distal + *buccal*] : relating to or located on the distal and buccal surfaces of a molar or premolar ⟨the *distobuccal* cusp of the first molar⟩ — **dis·to·buc·cal·ly** \-k(ə)lē, -i\ *adv*

dis·to·lin·gu·al \-ˈliŋg(yə)wəl\ *adj* [*disto-* + *lingual*] : relating to or situated on the distal and lingual surfaces of a tooth ⟨the *distolingual* cusp of a tooth⟩

dis·tract·er***or** **dis·tract·or*** \dis'traktə(r)\ *n* : an incorrect answer given as a choice in a multiple-choice test

distribute***vb -ut·ed; -ut·ing** *vt* : to use in an operation or as an operation so as to be mathematically distributive ⟨addition is not *distributed* over multiplication⟩ ~ *vi* : to be mathematically distributive ⟨multiplication *distributes* over addition⟩

dis·trib·ut·ed *adj* : characterized by a statistical distribution of a particular kind ⟨independently *distributed* random variables⟩

distribution***n** 1 : an arrangement of statistical data that exhibits the frequency of the occurrence of the values of a variable : frequency distribution 2 : a function of a discrete random variable that gives the probability that a specific value will occur : probability function 3 : a function of a continuous random variable whose integral over an interval gives the probability that its value will fall within the interval : probability density function

distribution function *n* : a function that gives the probability that a random variable is less than or equal to the independent variable of the function

distributive education *n, often cap D & E* : a vocational program set up between schools and employers in which the student receives both classroom instruction and on-the-job training

di·sul·fo·ton \dī'səlfəˌtän\ *n* [*diethyl* + *sulfo-* containing sulfur + *-ton* (prob. fr. *thionate*)] : an organophosphorus systemic insecticide $C_8H_{19}O_2PS_3$ used esp. on cultivated plants

di·uron \'dīyəˌrän\ *n* [*di-* two + *urea* + *-on* chemical compound] : a persistent herbicide $C_9H_{10}Cl_2N_2O$ used esp. to control annual weeds

di·verge*\də'vərj, (')dī'v-, -vəj, -vəij\ *vi* **diverged; di·verg·ing** : to be mathematically divergent

divergence***n** : the state of being mathematically divergent

divide***vt** **divid·ed; divid·ing** : to use as a divisor — used with *into* ⟨*divide* 14 into 42⟩

divide***n** : an instance of division performed by a computer; *also* : the means for performing division

division sign *n* 1 : the symbol ÷ used to indicate division 2 : a diagonal / used to indicate a fraction

DMA \ˌdēˌē'mä\ *n* : a doctor of musical arts

DMSO \ˌdēˌemˌe'sō\ *n* [*di*methyl*s*ulf*o*xide] : DIMETHYL-SULFOXIDE

DMT \ˌdēˌem'tē\ *n* [*di*methyl*t*ryptamine] : DIMETHYL-TRYPTAMINE

DMZ *abbr* demilitarized zone

DNA polymerase *n* : a polymerase that promotes replication of DNA usu. using single-stranded DNA as a template

DN·ase \(')dēˌen'ās, -ˌāz\ *also* **DNA·ase** \(ˌ)dēˌen'āˌās, -ˌāz\ *n* [*DNase*, blend of *DNA* and *-ase* enzyme; *DNAase*, fr. *DNA* + *-ase*] : an enzyme that hydrolyzes DNA to nucleotides

DNF *abbr* did not finish

do***vt** — **do a number on** 1 : to defeat or confound thoroughly esp. by indirect or deceptive means ⟨I decided that I wasn't being excessively paranoid in concluding that one of these churls was trying to *do a number on* us —George Kimball⟩ 2 : to mock or ridicule

Do·bro \'dō(ˌ)brō\ *trademark* — used for an acoustic guitar having a metal resonator

dock***vt** : to join mechanically (as two spacecraft) while in space ~ *vi* : to become docked

docu·dra·ma \'däkyəˌdrämə, -kyü-, -amə, -āmə\ *n* [*docu*mentary + *drama*] : a television or motion-picture drama dealing freely with historical events and esp. those of a recent and controversial nature

dodgy***adj** 1 *Brit* : not sound, stable, or reliable ⟨there were thirteen planes, all brand new. And I had to pick the one with the *dodgy* engine —Susan Saggers⟩ 2 *Brit* : requiring skill or care in handling or coping with : awkward or tricky ⟨it was a little *dodgy* getting her home and into the parsonage without anyone noticing —R. F. Delderfield⟩; *also* : chancy or risky ⟨bringing out a restaurant guide is a *dodgy* business, since it has been prepared so far in advance —Alison Mitchell⟩

dog and pony show *n* : an often elaborate public relations or sales presentation

doggie bag *or* **doggy bag** *n* [fr. the original assumption that such leftovers were destined for the diner's dog] : a bag used for carrying home leftover food and esp. meat from a meal eaten at a restaurant

do–good·ing \'düˌgùdiŋ\ *n* : the activities of a do-gooder

dogs·body \'dògzˌbädē, *sometimes* 'däg-\ *n* [Brit. naval slang, midshipman, fr. slang *dog's body* pease pudding] *chiefly Brit* : one who performs menial tasks ⟨thought it would be grand to have a housekeeper and general *dogsbody* he wouldn't have to pay, and could bully — Georgette Heyer⟩

do–it–your·self \ˌdüəchə(r)ˈself, -ətyə-\ *adj* : of, relating to, or designed for use in construction, repair, or artistic work done by an amateur or hobbyist ⟨a *do-it-yourself* car model kit⟩

do–it–your·self·er \-ˈselfə(r)\ *n* : one who engages in do-it-yourself projects

do·jo \'dō(ˌ)jō\ *n, pl* **dojos** [Jp *dōjō*, fr. *dō* way, art + *-jō* ground] : a school for training in oriental martial arts

Dol·by \'dòlbē, 'dōl-, -bi\ *trademark* — used for an electronic device that eliminates noise from recorded sound or sound broadcast on FM radio

dol·ce vi·ta \ˌdōlchě'vēˌtä, -(ˌ)chä-\ *n* [It, lit., sweet life] : a life of indolence and self-indulgence ⟨introduced him to the *dolce vita* of New York's high-society bohemians —Current Biog.⟩

DOM \ˌdēˌō'em\ *n* [prob. fr. *d*imethoxy- containing two methoxy groups + *m*ethyl] : STP

dome car *n* : a railroad car with a raised glassed-in seating section

domestic prelate *n* : a priest having permanent honorary membership in the papal household and ranking above a papal chamberlain

domino effect *n* [fr. the fact that if a number of dominoes are stood on end one behind the other with a slight intervening space, a slight push on the first one will result in the toppling of all the others] : a cumulative effect produced when one event initiates a succession of similar events — compare RIPPLE EFFECT ⟨businessmen, in particular, fear the *domino effect* of an increase that tends to push up the wages of higher-paid workers to keep pace with gains legislated for lower-paid employees —J.N. Erlenborn⟩

domino theory *n* [*domino* (effect)] **1** : the theory that if one nation (as in Southeast Asia or Central America) becomes Communist-controlled the neighboring nations will also become Communist-controlled ⟨the *domino theory* was offered to prove that all Asia, or more, was at stake —A.D. Tussing⟩ **2** : the theory that if one act or event is allowed to take place a succession of similar acts or events will follow ⟨another frequently mentioned fear is the *domino theory* —that if you grant the gays a lounge, all sorts of other deviant and weird groups will demand lounges —Robert Liebert⟩

done·ness \'dənnəs\ *n* : the condition of being cooked to the desired degree ⟨test the meat for *doneness*⟩

dong \'dóŋ\ *n*, *pl* **dong** [Annamese] **1** : the basic monetary unit of Vietnam **2** : a coin or note representing one dong

do·pa·mine \'dōpə,mēn, -əmən\ *n* [*dopa* + *amine*] : a monoamine $C_8H_{11}NO_2$ that is a decarboxylated form of dopa and occurs esp. as a neurotransmitter in the brain and as an intermediate in the biosynthesis of epinephrine; *also* : dopa itself

do·pa·min·er·gic \,dōpə,mē'nərjək, -mǝ'n-\ *adj* [*dopamine* + *-ergy* work, effect + *-ic*, adj. suffix] : relating to, participating in, or activated by the neurotransmitter activity of dopamine or related substances ⟨a *dopaminergic* pathway⟩ ⟨*dopaminergic* activity⟩

dop·ant \'dōpənt\ *n* [*dope* to treat with a foreign substance + *-ant* agent] : an impurity added usu. in minute amounts to a pure substance to alter its properties

dope* *vt* **doped; dop·ing** : to treat with a dopant ⟨*doped* semiconductor⟩

doper* *n* : an habitual or frequent drug user

Dopp·ler \'däplə(r)\ *adj* : of, relating to, or utilizing a shift in frequency in accordance with the Doppler effect; *also* : of or relating to Doppler radar

Doppler radar *n* : a radar system utilizing the Doppler effect for measuring velocity

do·rag \'dü,rag\ *n* [*do* (as in *hairdo*) + *rag*] : a kerchief worn over the hair

dork \'dórk, 'dó(ə)k\ *n* [perh. alter. of *dick* penis] **1** : penis — usu. considered vulgar **2** *slang* : a stupid or foolish person : a jerk

dor·min \'dórmən\ *n* [*dorm*ancy + *-in* chemical compound] : ABSCISIC ACID

dosage compensation *n* : the genetic mechanism by which the same effect on the phenotype is produced by a pair of identical sex-linked genes in the sex (as the human female) having the two sex chromosomes of the same type as by a single gene in the sex (as the human male) having the two sex chromosomes of different types or having only one sex chromosome (as in the males of some insects)

dot matrix *n* : a pattern of dots in a grid from which alphanumeric characters can be formed (as in printing)

double bind *n* : a psychological dilemma in which a usu. dependent person (as a child) receives conflicting interpersonal communications from a single source or faces disparagement no matter what his response to a situation; *broadly* : a dilemma

dou·ble–blind \,dəbəl'blīnd\ *adj* : of, relating to, or being an experimental procedure in which neither the subjects nor the experimenters know the makeup of the test and control groups during the actual course of the experiments — compare SINGLE-BLIND

double–cov·er \-'kəvə(r)\ *vt* : to cover (a single offensive player) with two defenders

double–dig·it \-'dijət\ *adj* : of 10 percent or more ⟨*double-digit* inflation⟩ ⟨*double-digit* price increases⟩

double–dip·per \'dipə(r)\ *n* : a government employee who draws a pension from one government department while working for another — **double–dip·ping** \-piŋ\ *n*

double helix *n* : a helix or spiral consisting of two strands in the surface of a cylinder that coil around its axis; *esp* : the structural arrangement of DNA in space that consists of paired polynucleotide strands stabilized by cross-links between purine and pyrimidine bases — ALPHA-HELIX, WATSON-CRICK MODEL — **dou·ble-he·li·cal** \,dəbəl'heləkəl, -'hēl-\ *adj*

double knit *n* : a knitted fabric (as wool or polyester) made with a double set of needles to produce a double thickness of fabric with each thickness joined by interlocking stitches; *also* : an article of clothing made of such fabric

double precision *n* : the use of two computer words rather than one to represent a number

double reverse *n* : an offensive play in football consisting of a reverse with an additional handoff so that the ultimate ballcarrier is running in the direction in which the play started

dou·ble·speak \'dəbəl,spēk\ *n* : inflated, involved, and often deliberately ambiguous language ⟨the semantic nightmare of Orwellian *doublespeak* where peace means war and love means hate —Stephen Ullmann⟩

doublet* *n* **1 a** : a pair of atomic, molecular, or nuclear quantum states that are usu. close together in energy and arise from two possible orientations of spin **b** : a pair of spectral frequencies of light arising from transitions to or from such quantum states **2** : a pair of otherwise similar elementary particles (as a proton and a neutron) with different charge

Doug·las bag \'dəgləs-\ *n* [C. G. *Douglas* †1963 Eng. physiologist] : an inflatable bag used to collect expired air for the determination of oxygen consumption and basal metabolic rate

dove* *n* : one who takes a conciliatory attitude (as in a dispute) and advocates negotiations and compromise — compare HAWK — **dov·ish** \'dəvish\ *adj* — **dov·ish·ness** *n*

down–and–out* *n* : a pass pattern in football in which the receiver runs straight downfield and then cuts sharply to the outside usu. after a fake

down·er*\'daůnə(r)\ *n* **1 :** a depressant drug and esp. a barbiturate — compare UPPER **2 :** something (as an experience, situation, or person) that is depressing ⟨at least the movie is benign — it isn't a *downer* —Pauline Kael⟩ ⟨tension, she knew, was bad for you; it led to depression, which was a real *downer* —Cyra McFadden⟩

down–home \'daůn,hōm\ *adj* **:** having the simple, informal, earthy qualities that are associated with the common people esp. of the southern U.S. ⟨as *down-home* as Abe Lincoln —Seymour Krim⟩ ⟨family-style meals and informal, *down-home* hospitality —*Southern Living*⟩ ⟨the *down-home* quality of the black musical experience — Margo Jefferson⟩ ⟨funky *down-home* blues —Tony Glover⟩

down·play \'daůn,plā\ *vt* **:** to play down **:** de-emphasize ⟨government has long sought to *downplay* the reports of terrorism —J.N. Goodsell⟩

down quark *n* **:** a quark having an electric charge of − ⅓, a baryon number of ⅓, zero charm, and zero strangeness

down·range \'daůn,rānj\ *adv or adj* **:** away from a launching site and along the course of a test range

down·size \(')daůn,sīz\ *vt* **:** to design or produce in smaller size **:** reduce in size ⟨a plan to *downsize* its car fleet all across the board —C.E. Dole⟩ ⟨builders put *downsized* ... houses on the market — Gurney Breckenfeld⟩ ⟨economic realities are forcing many ... to *downsize* their vision of the American dream house —*Fortune*⟩

Down's syn·drome \'daůn,sin,drōm, -,sindrəm\ *n* [J. L. H. *Down* †1896 Eng. physician] **:** a congenital idiocy in which a child is born with slanting eyes, a broad short skull, and broad hands with short fingers **:** mongolism

downstream* *adv or adj* **:** in or toward the later stages of an industrial process ⟨improve profits *downstream*⟩ ⟨invest money *downstream*⟩ ⟨the *downstream* end of the business — refining and distribution —*Fortune*⟩

down·tick \'daůn,tik\ *n* **:** a stock market transaction at a price below the last previous transaction in the same security — compare UPTICK 1

down·time \'daůn,tīm\ *n* **:** time during which production is stopped (as in a factory or on a machine) esp. during setup for an operation or when making repairs ⟨few moving parts and, thus, low maintenance costs and *downtime* —J.C. Friedlander⟩

dox·e·pin \'däksə,pin, -əpən\ *n* [*d*imethyl + *ox*- containing oxygen + -*ep*- (arbitrary infix) + -*in* chemical compound] **:** a tricyclic antidepressant administered as the hydrochloride salt $C_9H_{21}NO·HCl$

dox·o·ru·bi·cin \,däksō,rübəsən\ *n* [fr. *doxo*-, alter. of *deoxy*- derived by removal of an oxygen atom + -*rubi*- (perh. alter. of ISV *rube*- reddish) + -*cin* (as in -*mycin*)] **:** ADRIAMYCIN

dox·y·cy·cline \,däksə,sī,klēn, -'sīklən\ *n* [*deoxy*- + *oxy*- containing oxygen + tetra*cycline*] **:** a broad-spectrum tetracycline antibiotic $C_{22}H_{24}N_2O_8$ that is administered orally and is used esp. to treat bronchial infections and gonorrhea

dozens *n pl* **:** a game that consists of exchanging often obscene insults usu. about the members of the opponent's family ⟨the real aim of the *dozens* was to get a dude so mad he'd cry —H.R. Brown⟩ — often used in the phrase *play the dozens*

D phase *n* **:** M PHASE

draft*vi **:** to drive close behind another car while racing at high speed in order to take advantage of the reduced air pressure created by the leading car

drag*n **1 :** something that is boring ⟨their work ... is a *drag* a good deal of the time —Nora Johnson⟩ **2 :** a costume or outfit ⟨dresses hundreds in full clown *drag* — Bill Cardoso⟩ **3 :** DRAG QUEEN **4 :** man's clothing worn by a woman ⟨a lesbian can also wear *drag;* that is ... clothing designed for men —Julia P. Stanley⟩

drag queen *n* **:** a male homosexual who dresses as a woman

drag racing *n* [*drag*, n.] **:** the sport of holding acceleration contests for vehicles over a straight course

draw·down*\'dró,daůn\ *n* **1 :** a lowering of the water level (as in a reservoir) **2 :** the process of depleting or reducing ⟨a substantial *drawdown* in domestic producer stocks of lead —*Minerals Yearbook*⟩ ⟨no significant *drawdown* of inventories is forecast —*World Economic Outlook*⟩

dread·locks \'dred,läks\ *n pl* [perh. fr. *dread*, adj. + *locks*] **:** long braids of hair worn by Rastafarians

dream·scape \'drēmz,kāp, -m,sk-\ *n* [*dream* + -*space* (as in *landscape*)] **:** a dreamlike usu. surrealistic scene ⟨seemed greener than he had remembered any jungle to be; a *dreamscape* out of neverland —Frank Yerby⟩; *also* **:** a painting of a dreamscape

drill·ship \'dril,ship\ *n* **:** a ship equipped for drilling (as for oil) in the ocean floor

Drink·er respirator \,drinkə(r)-\ *n* [Philip *Drinker* †1972 Am. public health engineer] **:** a device for artificial respiration **:** iron lung

drive*n **:** a device including an electric motor and heads for reading or writing a magnetic storage medium (as magnetic tape or disks)

drive·line \'drīv,līn\ *n* **:** the parts including the universal joint and the drive shaft that connect the transmission with the driving axles of an automotive vehicle

drive·train \'drīv,trān\ *n* **:** DRIVELINE

drive–up \-,əp\ *adj* **:** designed to allow patrons or customers to be served while remaining in their automobiles ⟨two *drive-up* windows at the bank⟩

drop*vt **dropped; drop·ping :** to take (a drug) through the mouth **:** swallow ⟨he *drops* acid⟩

drop–dead \,dräp,ded\ *adj* **:** sensationally striking or attractive ⟨interior decorators specializing in *drop-dead* chic —Marilyn Bethany⟩ ⟨in actual golden threads and golden slippers, waited to make the proper *drop-dead* entrance —Tom Wolfe⟩

drop–in \'drä,pin\ *n* **1 :** one who drops in **:** a casual visitor **2 :** an informal social gathering at which guests are invited to drop in

drop–in center *n* **:** an establishment designed to provide recreational, educational, and counseling services to a particular group (as teenagers)

drop out*vi **:** to withdraw from conventional society because of disenchantment with its values and mores ⟨a kind of guru for the young who were *dropping out* — George Levine⟩

dropout*n **1 :** one who drops out of conventional society **2 :** a spot on a magnetic tape from which information has disappeared

drop pass *n* **:** a pass in ice hockey in which the dribbler skates past the puck leaving it for a teammate following close behind

drown·proof·ing \'draún'prüfiŋ\ *n* **:** a technique for staying afloat in water for an extended period with minimum effort through the use of a person's natural buoyancy

drug·gie \'drəgē, -gi\ *n* [*drug* + *-ie* one having to do with] **:** one who habitually uses drugs

drug·ola \‚drəg'ōlə\ *n* [*drug* + *-ola* (as in *payola*)] **:** payola in the form of illicit drugs

drumbeat*n **:** vociferous advocacy of a cause

drum printer *n* **:** a line printer in which the printing element is a revolving drum

drunk tank *n* **:** a large detention cell for arrested drunks

dry–eyed \'drī‚īd\ *adj* **1 :** not moved to tears or to sympathy ⟨these group sessions . . . seldom leave the participants *dry-eyed* —Carl Rogers⟩ ⟨the reasons why Washington was so *dry-eyed* when the colonels seized power —Elizabeth Drew⟩ **2 :** marked by the absence of sentimentalism or romanticism ⟨a hard-boiled and *dry-eyed* age, where it is not fashionable to talk about such matters —Norman Cousins⟩

dry out *vt* **:** to subject to withdrawal from the use of alcohol or drugs **:** DETOXIFY 1 ∼ *vi* **:** to withdraw from the use of alcohol or drugs

dry sink *n* **:** a wooden cabinet with a tray top for holding a wash basin

du·al–pur·pose fund \‚d(y)üəl‚pərpəs-, -‚pāp-, -‚pəip-\ *n* **:** a closed-end investment company with two classes of shares one of which is entitled to all dividend income and the other to all gains from capital appreciation

duck's ass *n* **:** DA — often considered vulgar

duc·ti·bil·i·ty \‚dəktə'biləd·ē\ *n* **:** the quality or state of being ductile

dude*n **:** fellow, guy ⟨jive-talking West Coast *dudes* and their ladies —Roger Greenspun⟩

du·en·de \dü'en(‚)dā\ *n* [Sp dial., charm, fr. Sp, ghost, goblin, fr. *duen de casa*, prob. fr. *dueño de casa* owner of a house] **:** the power to attract through personal magnetism and charm

dulls·ville \'dəlz‚vil\ *n* **:** something or some place that is dull or boring ⟨mostly it was one teacher speaking to one camera, and *dullsville* —M.P. Mayer⟩ ⟨that long-ago summer when he decided San Diego was *dullsville* — Guy Flatley⟩; *also* **:** the state of being bored **:** boredom ⟨together, these American prototypes ought to spell *dullsville* —*Playboy*⟩

dum–dum \'dəm‚dəm\ *n* [redupl. of *dum*, alter. of *dumb*] **:** a stupid person

dummy variable *n* **:** an arbitrary mathematical symbol or variable that can be replaced by another without affecting the value of the expression in which it occurs

dump*vt **:** to copy (data in a computer's internal storage) onto an external storage medium — **dump on :** to speak disparagingly of **:** BAD-MOUTH ⟨made it a practice to . . . *dump on* . . . religious leaders —Faubion Bowers⟩

dump* *n* **:** an instance of dumping data stored in a computer

dumpy* *adj* **:** being in a dirty or shabby condition **:** GRUNGY ⟨*dumpy* hotel rooms⟩

dune buggy *n* **:** a motor vehicle with oversize tires for driving on sand beaches

dunk* *vt* **:** to make a dunk shot with

dunk shot *n* **:** a shot in basketball made by jumping high into the air and throwing the ball down through the basket

duplicate*vi **-cat·ed; -cat·ing :** to become duplicate **:** replicate ⟨DNA in chromosomes *duplicates*⟩

du·pli·ca·tion*\‚d(y)üplə'kāshən\ *n* **:** a part of a chromosome in which the genetic material is repeated; *also* **:** the process of forming a duplication

durable press *n* **:** PERMANENT PRESS — **du·ra·ble–press** \‚d(ü)ùrəbəl‚pres\ *adj*

dust·off \'dəst‚óf\ *n* [fr. the dust raised by a helicopter in landing or taking off] **:** a helicopter used to evacuate the dead and wounded from a combat area

Dutch cap*n **:** a molded contraceptive cap that fits over the uterine cervix

DWI \‚dē‚dəbə(l)yə'wī, -byə'-\ *n* [*driving while intoxicated*] **1 :** an instance of driving while intoxicated **2 :** one who is charged with driving while intoxicated

dyke *or* **dike** \'dīk\ *n* [origin unknown] **:** a female homosexual; *esp* **:** one assuming an aggressively masculine role — **dy·key** *or* **di·key** \-kē\ *adj*

dy·nap·o·lis \dī'napələs\ *n* [NGk, fr. *dynamikos* dynamic (fr. Gk, powerful) + *polis* city, fr. Gk] **:** a city planned for orderly growth along a main traffic artery by means of self-contained communities

dys·au·to·no·mia \(‚)dis‚ód·ə'nōmēə, -‚äd·-\ *n* [*dys-* abnormal, difficult (deriv. of Gk *dys-* bad, difficult) + *autonomic* + *-ia* pathological condition] **:** a familial disorder of the nervous system characterized esp. by multiple sensory deficiency (as of taste and pain) and by excessive sweating and salivation — **dys·au·to·nom·ic** \-‚nämik\ *adj*

dys·ba·rism \'disbə‚rizəm\ *n* [*dys-* + *bar-* weight, pressure (deriv. of Gk *barys* heavy) + *-ism* state, condition] **:** the complex of symptoms (as bends, headache, or mental disturbance) that accompanies exposure to excessively low or rapidly changing environmental air pressure

dys·cal·cu·lia \‚diskal'kyülēə\ *n* [NL, fr. *dys-* + L *calculare* to compute + E *-ia*] **:** impairment of mathematical ability due to an organic condition of the brain

dys·gen·e·sis \(')dis'jenəsəs\ *n* **:** defective development esp. of the gonads (as in Klinefelter's syndrome or Turner's syndrome)

dys·graph·ia \dis'grafēə\ *n* [NL, fr. *dys-* + *-graphia* writing] **:** impairment of the ability to write caused by brain damage

dys·pro·tein·emia \‚dis‚prō‚tē'nēmēə *also* -ōd·ē‚'n- *or* -ōtē‚'n-\ *n* [NL, fr. *dys-* + *protein* + *-emia* blood condition] **:** any abnormality of the protein content of the blood — **dys·pro·tein·emic** \-'nēmik\ *adj*

dys·rhyth·mia*\dis'rithmēə\ *n* **:** JET LAG

dys·to·pia \di'stōpēə\ *n* [*dys-* + *-topia* (as in *utopia*)] **:** an imaginary place which is depressingly wretched and whose people lead a fearful existence ⟨an Orwellian *dystopia* working away full blast —John Simon⟩ — **dys·to·pi·an** \-pēən\ *adj*

E

Eames chair \'ēmz-\ *n* [Charles *Eames* †1978 Am. designer] **:** a swivel armchair with a headrest and a matching ottoman having a frame of molded wood and upholstery of tufted leather mounted on a steel base

earth·rise \'ərth,rīz, 'ōth-, 'əith-\ *n* **:** the rising of the earth above the horizon of the moon as seen from the moon

earth tone *n* **:** any of various rich dark colors containing some brown

eat*vt **:** to perform fellatio or cunnilingus on — usu. considered vulgar

EBCDIC \'epsə,dik, 'ebs-\ *n* [extended binary coded decimal *i*nterchange code] **:** a code for representing alphanumeric information (as on magnetic tape)

eb·ul·lism \'eb(y)ə,lizəm\ *n* [L *ebullire* to come bubbling out + E *-ism*] **:** the formation of bubbles in body fluids under sharply reduced environmental pressure

ec·cle·si·al \ə'klēzēəl, e'k-, -zhəl\ *adj* **:** of or relating to a church esp. as a formal and established institution **:** ecclesiastical ⟨these differences of *ecclesial* belief . . . are not an absolute prohibition of intercommunion —W.M. Bassett⟩

ec·dy·sone \'ekdə,sōn\ *n* [*ecdy*sis + horm*one*] **:** any of several arthropod hormones that in insects are produced by the prothoracic gland and that trigger molting and metamorphosis

echo·car·dio·gram \e(,)kō'kärdēə,gram, -ēō,-\ *n* [*echo* + *cardiogram*] **:** a visual record made by echocardiography

echo·car·di·og·ra·phy \-,kärdē'ägrəfē, -i\ *n* **:** a noninvasive and painless diagnostic procedure for making a record of cardiac structure and functioning by means of high frequency sound waves reflected back from the heart — **echo·car·dio·graph·ic** \-ēə'grafik\ *adj*

echo·en·ceph·a·log·ra·phy \e(,)kōən,sefə'lägrəfē, -fi\ *n* [ISV, fr. L *echo* + ISV *encephalography*] **:** the use of ultrasound in the examination and measurement of internal structures (as the ventricles) of the skull and in the diagnosis of abnormalities — **echo·en·ceph·a·lo·graph·ic** \-,sefəlō'grafik\ *adj*

echog·ra·phy \e'kägrəfē\ *n* [*echo* + *-graphy* representation] **:** the use of ultrasound in the examination and measurement of internal structures and in the diagnosis of abnormalities — **echo·graph·ic** \,ekə'grafik, ,e(,)kō-\ *adj* — **echo·graph·i·cal·ly** \-ik(ə)lē, -li\ *adv*

echo·lo·cate \'ekō,lō,kāt\ *vt* **:** to find by echolocation ⟨a bat *echolocates* food⟩ ~ *vi* **:** to utilize or have the capacity for echolocation

echo·vi·rus \'e(,)kō,vīrəs\ *n* [enteric cytopathogenic *h*uman *o*rphan + *virus*] **:** any of a group of picornaviruses that are found in the gastrointestinal tract, that cause cytopathic changes in cells in tissue culture, and that are sometimes associated with respiratory ailments and meningitis

eco·ca·tas·tro·phe \,ekōkə'tastrə(,)fē, ,ēkō-\ *n* [*eco*-environment, habitat (deriv. of Gk *oikos* house) + *catastrophe*] **:** a major destructive upset in the balance of nature esp. when caused by the intervention of man

eco·cide \'ekō,sīd, 'ēkō-\ *n* [*eco*- + *-cide* killing] **:** the destruction and esp. the deliberate destruction (as in war) of large areas of the natural environment ⟨herbicides, insecticides, bulldozers, and nuclear weapons now give humanity a greatly enhanced capability to commit *ecocide* —P.R. Ehrlich & J.P. Holdren⟩

eco·geo·graph·ic \,ekō,jēə,grafik, ,ēkō-\ *or* **eco·geo·graph·ic·al** \-ə·kəl\ *adj* **:** of or relating to both ecological and geographical aspects of the environment — **eco·geo·graph·i·cal·ly** \-k(ə)lē\ *adv*

economy *adj* **:** designed to save the buyer money ⟨*economy* cars⟩

eco·phys·i·ol·o·gy \,ēkō,fizē'äləjē, ,ēkō-\ *n* **:** the science of the interrelationships between the physiology of organisms and their environment — **eco·phys·i·o·log·ic·al** \-ēə'läjəkəl\ *or* **eco·phys·i·ol·o·gist** \-e'äləjəst\ *n*

eco·sphere \'ekō,sfi(ə)r, 'ekō-, -,sfiə\ *n* **:** the parts of the universe (as the biosphere) habitable by living organisms — **eco·spher·ic** \-;'sfi(ə)rik, -,'sfer-\ *adj*

ec·to·crine \'ektəkrən; -,krin, -rīn, -rēn\ *n* [*ecto*- outside, external + *-crine* (as in *endocrine*)] **:** a metabolite produced by an organism of one kind and utilized by one of another kind

ec·to·hor·mone \,ektə'hòr,mōn, -,'hò(ə),-\ *n* **:** PHEROMONE— **ec·to·hor·mon·al** \,ektə,hò(r)'mōn°l\ *adj*

ecu·me·nop·o·lis \,ekyəmə'näpələs, e,kyüm-\ *n* [NGk *oikoumene*, fr. Gk *oikoumenē* the inhabited world (deriv. of *oikos* house) + *polis* city] **:** a single city encompassing the whole world that is held to be a possibility of the future

ed·it \'edət\ *n* **:** an instance or the result of editing ⟨had to stay up late to do the final *edit* on the CIA report — Robert Scheer⟩

EDP *abbr* electronic data processing

edro·pho·ni·um \,edrə'fōnēəm\ *n* [ethyl + hydroxy + phenyl + ammon*ium*] **:** an anticholinesterase $C_{10}H_{16}ClNO$ used esp. to stimulate skeletal muscle and in the diagnosis of myasthenia gravis — called also *edrophonium chloride*

educational park *n* **:** a large centralized educational complex of elementary and secondary schools

educational psychologist *n* **:** a specialist in educational psychology

educational television *n* **1 :** PUBLIC TELEVISION **2** **:** television that provides instructional material esp. for students sometimes by closed circuit

ed·u·ca·tion·ese \,ejə,käshə'nēz, -ēs\ *n* [education + *-ese* jargon] **:** the jargonistic language used esp. by educational theorists ⟨the faults of *educationese* are excessive abstraction and intentional vagueness —Wilson Follett⟩

⟨leads to their being "retained" (*educationese* for left back) in the first grade at least once —C.E. Silberman⟩

EEO *abbr* equal employment opportunity

EFTS *abbr* electronic funds transfer systems

egg*n — **with egg on one's face** : in a state of embarrassment or humiliation ⟨after putting up a competent job of defending the indefensible, cheerfully confided that the Government was sure to change its mind and he only hoped they didn't do it too soon and leave him *with egg on his face* —Austin Mitchell⟩

egg cream *n* : a drink consisting of milk, a flavoring syrup, and soda water

ego–dys·ton·ic \ˌēgōdis'tänik, *also* ˌegō-\ *adj* [ego + dystoni̇a + -ic, adj. suffix] : incompatible with or unacceptable to the ego ⟨*ego-dystonic* acts or thoughts —J. L. Singer⟩

ego trip *n* : an act or course of action that enhances and satisfies one's ego ⟨think that a woman is . . . on an *ego trip* if she wants to run for political office —Betty Friedan⟩

ego–trip \'ēgō,trip\ *vi* **-tripped; -trip·ping** : to behave in a self-seeking manner ⟨never overplayed, never *ego=tripped*, never grabbed the spotlight —Bob Palmer⟩ — **ego–trip·per** \-ə(r)\ *n*

Egyptian Mau \-'maů\ *n, pl* **Egyptian Maus** [*mau* of imit. origin] : any of a breed of short-haired domestic cats developed in the U.S. having a spotted coat and light green or amber eyes

EHV *abbr* extra high voltage

ei·gen·vec·tor \'īgən,vektə(r)\ *n* [ISV *eigen-* characteristic (fr. G *eigen*) + *vector*] : a nonzero vector that is mapped by a given linear transformation of a vector space onto a vector that is the product of a scalar multiplied by the original vector — called also *characteristic vector*

eight·fold way \'āt,fōl'dwā\ *n* [fr. the *Eightfold Way*, the Buddhist teaching of the means of attaining Nirvana through rightness of belief, resolve, speech, action, livelihood, effort, thought, and meditation; fr. the fact that the most common grouping contains eight interacting particles] : a unified theoretical scheme for classifying the relationship among strongly interacting elementary particles on the basis of isospin and hypercharge

eighty–six *or* **86** \ˌād-ē'siks, ˌātē-, -i̇'s-\ *vt, past & past part* **eighty–sixed** *or* **86'd** *also* **86ed** [rhyming slang for *nix*, vb.] *slang* : to refuse to serve (a customer) ⟨you are *eighty-sixed* forever. You will never get another drink here —Malcolm Braly⟩; *also* : to cause to leave : eject ⟨he'd been *86'd* out of another place . . . for tweaking a man's nose —Gilbert Millstein⟩

ekis·tics \ə'kistiks, ē'k-\ *n pl but sing in constr* [NGk *oikistikē*, fr. fem. of *oikistikos* relating to settlement, fr. Gk, fr. *oikizein* to settle, colonize, fr. *oikos* house] : a science dealing with human settlements and drawing on the research and experience of professionals in various fields (as architecture, engineering, city planning, and sociology) — **ekis·tic** \-tik\ *adj* — **ekis·ti·cian** \ˌə,ki'stishən, ˌ)ē,k-\ *n*

Ek·man dredge \'ekmən-\ *n* [prob. fr. V.W. *Ekman* †1954 Swed. oceanographer] : a dredge that has opposable jaws operated by a messenger traveling down a cable to release a spring catch and that is used in ecology for sampling the bottom of a body of water

ekt·ex·ine \(')ek'tek,sēn, -,sīn\ *n* [Gk *ekto-* outside + E *exine*] : a structurally variable outer layer of the exine

ekue·le \ā'kwä(,)lā\ *also* **ek·pwe·le** \ek'pwä(,)lā\ *n, pl* **ekuele** *also* **ekpweles** [native name in Equatorial Guinea] **1** : the basic monetary unit of Equatorial Guinea **2** : a coin or note representing one ekuele

El·a·vil \'elə,vil\ *trademark* — used for amitriptyline

el chea·po \el'chē(,)pō\ *adj* [pseudo-Spanish alter. of *cheap*] *slang* : of shoddy or inferior quality ⟨what you get for $3,330 is strictly *el cheapo* —Tony Hogg⟩

el·der·ly \'eldə(r)lē, -li\ *n, pl* **-ly** *or* **-lies** : an elderly person

elect·able \ə'lektəbəl, ē'l-\ *adj* : capable of being elected — **elect·abil·i·ty** \ə,lektə'bilə̇d-ē, ē,l-, ətē\ *n*

elective*adj : beneficial to the patient but not essential for his survival ⟨an *elective* appendectomy⟩

electric*adj : being or involving a musical performance on electric instruments ⟨*electric* blues⟩

electric broom *n* : a lightweight upright vacuum cleaner

elec·tro·cor·ti·cog·ra·phy \ə̇,lektrō,kōrtə̇'kägrəfē, ē,l-, -kȯr-, -fi\ *n* [*electro-* electric + *cortico-* cortex + *-graphy* writing] : the process of recording electrical activity in the brain by placing electrodes in direct contact with the cerebral cortex — **elec·tro·cor·ti·co·graph·ic** \-tə̇kə'grafik, -ēk\ *adj* — **elec·tro·cor·ti·co·graph·i·cal·ly** \-k(ə)lē, -li\ *adv*

elec·tro·der·mal \-'dərməl, -'dōm-, -'dəim-\ *adj* : of or relating to electrical activity in or electrical properties of the skin

elec·tro·di·ag·nos·tic \-,dīə̇g'nästik\ *adj* : involving or obtained by the recording of responses to electrical stimulation or of spontaneous electrical activity (as in electromyography) for purposes of diagnosing a pathological condition ⟨*electrodiagnostic* studies⟩ — **elec·tro·di·ag·nos·ti·cal·ly** \-ə̇k(ə)lē, -li\ *adv*

elec·tro·fish·ing \ə̇'lektrō,fishi̇ŋ, ē'l-\ *n* : the taking of fish by a system based on their tendency to respond positively to a source of direct electric current

elec·tro·gas·dy·nam·ics \ə̇,lektrə̇'gas(,)dī'namiks, ē,l-, -ēks\ *n pl but sing in constr* : a method of generating electrical energy that is based on the conversion of the kinetic energy of the flow of a high pressure charged combustion gas — **elec·tro·gas·dy·nam·ic** \-ik\ *adj*

elec·tro·gen·e·sis \ə̇,lektrə̇'jenəsə̇s, ē'l-\ *n* : the production of electrical activity esp. in living tissue

elec·tro·gen·ic \ə̇,lektrə̇'jenik, ē,l-\ *adj* : of or relating to the production of electricity in living tissue ⟨an *electrogenic* pump causing movement of sodium ions across a membrane⟩

elec·tro·hy·drau·lic \ə̇,lektrō(,)hī'drȯlik, ē,l-\ *adj* **1** : of, relating to, or involving a combination of electric and hydraulic mechanisms ⟨an *electrohydraulic* elevator⟩ **2** : involving or produced by the action of very brief but powerful pulse discharges of electricity under a liquid resulting in the generation of shock waves and highly reactive chemical species ⟨an *electrohydraulic* effect⟩ — **elec·tro·hy·drau·li·cal·ly** \-k(ə)lē, -li\ *adv*

elec·tro·hy·drau·lics \-iks\ *n pl but usu sing in constr* : the production of shock waves by electrohydraulic means

electromagnetic interaction *n* : a fundamental interaction experienced by most elementary particles that is responsible for the emission and absorption of photons and for electric and magnetic forces

electronic mail *n* : messages sent and received electronically (as between terminals linked by telephone lines or microwave relays)

electronic music *n* : music that consists of sounds electronically captured or originated, taped, and played through a loudspeaker

electron spin resonance *n* : the magnetic resonance of electrons that are either free or bound in atoms

electron transport *n* : the sequential transfer of electrons esp. by cytochromes in cellular respiration from an oxidizable substrate to molecular oxygen by a series of oxidation-reduction reactions

elec·tro·nys·tag·mog·ra·phy \ə̇ˌlektrōˌnis͟ˌtag'mägrəfē, ēᵗl-, -fi\ *n* [*electro-* + *nystagmus* + connective *-o-* + *-graphy* writing] : the use of electrooculography to study nystagmus — **elec·tro·nys·tag·mo·graph·ic** \-məˈgrafik\ *adj*

elec·tro·oc·u·lo·gram \ə̇ˌlektrōˈäkyələˌgram, ēᵗl-\ *n* [*electro-* + *oculo-* eye (deriv. of L *oculus*) + *-gram* drawing, writing, record, deriv. of Gk *gramma* letter, writing] : a record of the standing voltage between the front and back of the eye that is correlated with eyeball movement (as in REM sleep) and obtained by electrodes suitably placed on the skin near the eye

elec·tro·ocu·log·ra·phy \-ˌäkyəˈlägrəfē, -fi\ *n* [*electro-* + *oculo-* + *-graphy*] : the preparation and study of electrooculograms

elec·tro·pho·re·se \ə̇ˌlektrəfəˈrēs, ēˌl-, -ˈträfə͜-, -ēz\ *vt* **-resed; -res·ing** [back-formation fr. *electrophoresis*] : to subject to electrophoresis

elec·tro·pho·reto·gram \ə̇ˌlektrəfəˈred·ə͜ˌgram, ēˌl-\ *n* [*electrophoretic* + connective *-o-* + *-gram*] : a record that consists of the separated components of a mixture (as of proteins) produced by electrophoresis in a supporting medium (as filter paper)

elec·tro·ret·i·no·graph \ə̇ˌlektrōˈret(ᵊ)nə͜ˌgraf, ēᵗl-\ *n* [*electro-* + *retino-* retina + *-graph* recording instrument, deriv. of Gk *graphein* to write] : an instrument for recording electrical activity in the retina — **elec·tro·ret·i·no·graph·ic** \-ˌret(ᵊ)nə͜ˈgrafik\ *adj* — **elec·tro·ret·i·nog·ra·phy** \-n͜əˈägrəfē, -fi\ *n*

elec·tro·sen·si·tive \ə̇ˌlektrōˈsen(t)səd·iv, -ˈsen(t)stiv, ēᵗl-\ *adj* : being or using sensitive paper on which an image is produced by the passage of electric current through it

elec·tro·sleep \ə̇ˈlektrōˌslēp, ēᵗl-\ *n* : profound relaxation or a state of unconsciousness induced by the passage of a very low voltage electric current through the brain

elec·tro·stat·ic printing \ə̇ˌlektrəˈstad·ik-, ēᵗl-\ *n* : a process (as xerography) for printing or copying in which electrostatic forces are used to form the image (as with powder or ink) directly on a surface

el·e·doi·sin \ˌeləˈdȯisᵊn\ *n* [irreg. fr. NL *Eledone* + *-in* chemical compound] : a small protein $C_{54}H_{85}N_{13}O_{15}S$ from the salivary glands of several octopuses (genus *Eledone*) that is a powerful vasodilator and hypotensive agent

elementary particle *n* : OXYSOME

el·hi \ˈelˌhī\ *adj* [elementary school + high school] : of, relating to, or designed for use in grades 1 through 12 ⟨*elhi* students⟩ ⟨*elhi* textbook publishers⟩

emalangeni *pl of* LILANGENI

em·bat·tled \əmˈbatᵊld, em-\ *adj* [ME *embatailled*, fr. past part. of *embatailen* to battle] **1 a** : ready to fight : prepared to give battle ⟨here once the *embattled* farmers stood —R. W. Emerson⟩ **b** : engaged in battle, conflict, or controversy ⟨lends psychological support to an *embattled* president —R. J. Whalen⟩ **2 a** : being a site of battle, conflict, or controversy ⟨defending his *embattled* capital city —*Wall Street Jour.*⟩ **b** : characterized by conflict or controversy ⟨his highly diversified, often *embattled* experience as an educator —Nat Hentoff⟩

em·bat·tle·ment \əmˈbatᵊlmənt, em-\ *n* [*embattle* prepare for combat + *-ment*] : the state of being embattled

em·bour·geoise·ment \əmˈbu̇rzh,wäzmənt, äm-, em-, -u̇əzh-, -ˌmänt, Fänburzhwäzmäⁿ\ *n* [F, fr. *embourgeoiser* to make bourgeois] : the shift to bourgeois values and practices ⟨the *embourgeoisement* of the working class since World War II —Alden Whitman⟩

emic \ˈēmik\ *adj* [phonemic] : of, relating to, or involving analysis of linguistic or behavioral phenomena in terms of internal structure or functional elements of a particular system ⟨a phonemic transcription . . . is an *emic* description of speech —John Algeo⟩ — compare ETIC

em·pa·na·da \ˌ(ˌ)empəˈnädə\ *n* [Sp, fr. *empanada* breaded, fem. of *empanado*, past part. of *empanar* to bread, fr. *em-* in + *pan* bread, fr. L *panis*] : a pastry turnover stuffed esp. with a savory meat filling

EMT *abbr* emergency medical technician

emulate *vt* **-lat·ed; -lat·ing** : to imitate (a different computer system) by means of an emulator

emulation *n* : the use of or technique of using an emulator

em·u·la·tor \ˈemyəˌlād·ə(r)\ *n* : a hardware device or a combination of hardware and software that permits programs written for one computer to be run on another usu. newer computer

en·amine \ˈenəˌmēn, eˈnaˌm-\ *n* [*en-* having one double bond + *amine*] : an amine containing the double bond linkage C=C–N

en·cap·su·lant \ənˈkapsələnt, en-, *also* -syə-\ *n* : a material used for encapsulating

en·ceph·a·lo·myo·car·di·tis \enˈsefəlōˌmī͜ə(ˌ)kärˈdīd·əs\ *n* [*encephalo-* brain (deriv. of Gk *enkephalos*) + *myocarditis*] : an acute febrile virus disease characterized by degeneration and inflammation of skeletal and cardiac muscle and lesions of the central nervous system

encounter group *n* : a usu. leaderless and unstructured group that seeks to develop the capacity of the individual to express human feelings openly and to form close emotional ties by more or less unrestrained confrontation of individuals — compare T-GROUP

endangered *adj* : threatened with extinction ⟨the California condor, one of our country's most *endangered* species of birds —R.C.B. Morton⟩

end around *n* : a football play in which an offensive end comes behind the line of scrimmage to take a handoff and attempts to carry the ball around the opposite flank

end·ar·ter·ec·to·my \ˌenˌdärd·əˈrektəmē\ *n* [*endarterium* inner layer of an artery + *-ectomy* surgical removal] : surgical removal of the inner layer of an artery when thickened and atheromatous or occluded (as by intimal plaques)

end·exine \(')en¦dek,sēn, -,sīn\ *n* [*end-* within, inside (deriv. of Gk *endon*) + *exine*] **:** an inner membranous layer of the exine

en·do·cyt·ic \,endō¦sid·ək, -¦sīd--\ *adj* **:** of or relating to endocytosis **:** ENDOCYTOTIC ⟨*endocytic* vesicles⟩

en·do·cy·to·sis \,endō,sī'tōsəs\ *n, pl* **-to·ses** \-'tō,sēz\ [NL, fr. *endo-* within + *cyt-* cell (deriv. of Gk *kytos* hollow vessel) + *-osis* condition] **:** incorporation of substances into a cell by phagocytosis or pinocytosis — **en·do·cy·tot·ic** \,endō,sī'täd·ik\ *adj*

end–of–day glass \,endə(v)'dā,glas\ *n* [from its resemblance to objects made by glassblowers at the end of the day's work to use up various odds and ends of glass left over] **:** glass of various colors (as red, blue, green, and white) mixed together

en·do·gen·ic* \,endə'jenik\ *adj* **1 a :** growing from or on the inside **:** developing within the cell wall **b :** originating within the body **2 :** constituting or relating to metabolism of the nitrogenous constituents of cells and tissues

en·do·mor·phism* \,endə'mòr,fizəm\ *n* **:** a homomorphism that maps a mathematical set into itself — compare ISOMORPHISM

en·do·nu·cle·ase \,endō'n(y)üklē,ās, -āz\ *n* **:** an enzyme that breaks down a chain of nucleotides (as a nucleic acid) at points not adjacent to the end and thereby produces two or more shorter nucleotide chains — compare EXONUCLEASE

en·do·per·ox·ide \-pə'räk,sīd\ *n* [*endo-* + *peroxide*] **:** any of various biosynthetic intermediates in the formation of prostaglandins

en·do·phil·ic \,endə'filik\ *adj* [*endo-* + *-philic* loving, deriv. of Gk *philos* beloved, loving] **:** ecologically associated with man and his domestic environment ⟨mosquitoes that are *endophilic* vectors of malaria⟩ — compare EXOPHILIC — **en·doph·i·ly** \en'däfəlē\ *n*

en·do·plas·mic re·tic·u·lum \,endə¦plazmikrə'tikyələm\ *n* **:** a system of interconnected vesicular and lamellar cytoplasmic membranes that functions esp. in the transport of materials within the cell and that is studded with ribosomes in some places

en·do·ra·dio·sonde \,endō'rādēō,sänd\ *n* **:** a microelectronic device introduced into the body to record physiological data

en·dor·phin \en'dòrfən\ *n* [*end-* + *morphine*] **:** any of a group of proteins with potent analgesic properties that occur naturally in the brain — see BETA-ENDORPHIN; compare ENKEPHALIN

en·do·sul·fan \,endō'səlfən, -,fan\ *n* [perh. fr. *endrin* + connective *-o-* + *sulf-* sulfur + *-an* unsaturated carbon compound] **:** a brownish crystalline insecticide $C_9H_6Cl_6O_3S$ that is used in the control of numerous crop insects and some mites

en·do·tes·ta \'endō,testə\ *n* [*endo-* within + *testa*] **:** an inner layer of the testa in various seeds — compare SCLEROTESTA

end·point \'en(d),pòint\ *n* **:** either of two points or values that mark the ends of a line segment or interval; *also* **:** a point that marks the end of a ray

en·duro \ən'd(y)ù(ə)r(,)ō, en-\ *n, pl* **-dur·os** [irreg. fr. *endurance*] **:** a long race (as for automobiles or motorcycles) stressing endurance rather than speed

en·er·get·ics* \,enə(r)'jed·iks\ *n pl but sing in constr* **:** the total energy relations and transformations of a system (as a chemical reaction or an ecological community) ⟨*energetics* of muscular contraction⟩

en·er·giz·er* \'enə(r),jīzə(r)\ *n* **:** ANTIDEPRESSANT

energy*n* **:** usable power (as heat or electricity) ⟨urgent need for more large supplies of gas to meet growing *energy* requirements —*Annual Report Atlantic Richfield Co.*⟩; *also* **:** the resources for producing such power ⟨the global search for new *energy* sources⟩

energy budget *n* **:** an accounting of the income, use, and loss of energy in an ecosystem ⟨the sun's contribution to the *energy budget* of the earth —M. K. Hubbert⟩

en·flur·ane \en'flù(ə)r,ān\ *n* [*en-* within, inside + tri*fluo*roethane] **:** a liquid inhalational general anesthetic $C_3H_2ClF_5O$ prepared from methanol

en·ga·gé \,äⁿgä'zhä, ,eⁿ-, *F* äⁿgàzhä\ *adj* [F, fr. past part. of *engager* to engage, pledge] **:** committed to or supportive of a cause ⟨a man of devout pacifism . . . making even his art *engagé* —E. M. Yoder, Jr.⟩

English cock·er spaniel \-,käkə(r)-\ *n* **:** any of a breed of spaniels that have square muzzles, wide well-developed noses, and distinctive heads which are ideally half muzzle and half skull with the forehead and skull arched and slightly flattened

en·keph·a·lin \en'kefələn, eŋ-\ *n* [NL, fr. *enkephal-*, modif. of *encephal-* brain + *-in* chemical compound] **:** either of two pentapeptides with opiate and analgesic activity that occur naturally in the brain and have a marked affinity for opiate receptors — compare ENDORPHIN

en·tero·bac·te·ri·um \,entə(,)rō(,)bak'tirēəm\ *n* **:** a bacterium of the family Enterobacteriaceae — **en·tero·bac·te·ri·al** \-ēəl\ *adj* — **en·tero·bac·te·ri·ol·o·gist** \-(,)bak,tirē'äləjəst\ *n*

en·tero·path·o·gen·ic \-,pathə¦jenik\ *adj* [*entero-* intestine (deriv. of Gk *enteron*) + *pathogenic*] **:** tending to produce disease in the intestinal tract ⟨*enteropathogenic* bacteria⟩

en·ter·op·a·thy \,entə'räpəthē\ *n* [*entero-* + *-pathy* disease] **:** a disease of the intestinal tract

en·tero·vi·rus \'entərō'vīrəs\ *n* [NL, fr. *entero-* + *virus*] **:** any of a group of picornaviruses (as a Coxsackie virus) that typically occur in the gastrointestinal tract but may be involved in respiratory ailments, meningitis, and neurological disorders — **en·tero·vi·ral** \-rəl\ *adj*

en·ti·tle·ment* \ən'tīt³lmənt, en-\ *n* **:** a government program providing benefits to members of a specified group ⟨the refrain that we can't get control over the budget until we do something about *entitlements* . . . is a cop-out —A. F. Ehrbar⟩; *also* **:** funds supporting or distributed by such a program

en·train* \ən-'trān, en-\ *vt* **:** to determine or modify the phase or period of ⟨circadian rhythms *entrained* by a light cycle⟩

en·ven·om·ation \ən,venə'māshən, en,v-\ *n* **:** an act or instance of impregnating with a venom (as of a snake or spider); *also* **:** ENVENOMIZATION

en·ven·om·iza·tion \-əmə'zāshən, -(,)mī'zā-\ *n* **:** a poisoning caused by a bite or sting

environment*n* **:** an artistic or theatrical work that involves or encompasses the spectator **:** an instance of environmental art or theater

en·vi·ron·men·tal* \ən'vīrə(n)'men(t)ºl, -'vī(ə)r(n)-, (,)en-\ adj : involving or encompassing the spectator rather than simply facing him ⟨environmental art⟩ ⟨environmental theater⟩

en·vi·ron·men·tal·ist \-,vīrə(n)'men(t)ºlàst, -,vī(ə)r(n)-\ n : a person who is concerned about the quality of the human environment; specif : a specialist in human ecology

EP* abbr European plan

epi·an·dros·ter·one \,epēan'drästə,rōn\ n [epi- compound related to + androsterone] : an androsterone derivative C19H30O2 that occurs in normal human urine — called also isoandrosterone

epi·con·dy·li·tis \,epə,känd°l'īd·əs, -'ītəs\ n [epicondyle + -itis inflammation] : inflammation of an epicondyle or of adjacent tissues

epi·fau·na \'epə'fònə, 'epē-, -'fänə\ n [NL, fr. epi- upon (deriv. of Gk epi on, upon) + fauna] : benthic fauna living on the substrate (as a hard sea floor) or on other organisms — compare INFAUNA — epi·fau·nal \-nºl\ adj

epis·co·pal vicar \ə'piskəpəl-, -əbəl-\ n : a bishop assigned to the pastoral supervision of a part of a Roman Catholic diocese

epi·some \'epə,sōm\ n [epi- outer + -some body, deriv. of Gk sōma] : a genetic determinant (as the DNA of some bacteriophages) that can replicate either autonomously in bacterial cytoplasm or as an integral part of the chromosomes — epi·som·al \'epə'sōməl\ adj — epi·som·al·ly \-lē, -li\ adv — epi·som·ic \-ōmik\ adj

EPN \,ē(,)pē'en\ n [ethyl para-nitro-phenyl] : an organophosphorus miticide and insecticide C14H14NO4PS used esp. on cotton and orchard crops that enhances the toxicity of malathion to vertebrates

ep·oxy \ə'päksē, e'p-, (,)ē'p-, -si\ vt ep·ox·ied or ep·oxyed; ep·oxy·ing : to glue with epoxy

Ep·stein–Barr virus \,ep,stīn'bär-\ n [Michael Anthony Epstein and Y. M. Barr, 20th cent. Eng. pathologists, its discoverers] : a herpes virus that causes infectious mononucleosis and that is associated with Burkitt's lymphoma and nasopharyngeal carcinoma

equal opportunity employer n : an employer who agrees not to discriminate against any employee or job applicant because of race, color, religion, national origin, sex, physical or mental handicap, or veteran status

equiv·a·lence class \ə'kwiv(ə)lən(t)s-, ē'-\ n : a set for which an equivalence relation holds between every pair of elements

equivalence relation n : a relation (as equality) between elements of a set (as the real numbers) that is symmetric, reflexive, and transitive and for any two elements either holds or does not hold

equivalent* adj 1 : having the same solution set ⟨equivalent equations⟩ 2 : related by an equivalence relation

ER abbr emergency room

erase* vt erased; eras·ing : to delete from a computer storage device

-er·gic \ə(r)jik, ,ərj-, ,əj-, ,əij-\ adj comb form [-ergy work + -ic, adj. suffix] : exhibiting or stimulating activity ⟨synergic⟩

er·go·met·ric \,ərgə'me·trik\ adj [ergometer + -ic, adj. suffix] : relating to, obtained by, or being an ergometer

⟨ergometric investigations⟩ ⟨ergometric findings⟩ ⟨an ergometric bicycle⟩

er·gon·o·mist \(,)ər'gänəmàst\ n [fr. ergonomic biotechnological (fr. ergo- work — fr. Gk ergon — + economic) + -ist specialist] : a specialist in biotechnology

er·o·tol·o·gy \,erə'täləjē\ n [Gk erōt-, erōs sexual love + connective -o- + -logy oral or written expression, theory, science, deriv. of Gk logos word] : erotic description or literature — er·o·to·log·i·cal \,erəd-°l'äjəkəl\ adj

er·y·thor·bate \,erə'thòr,bāt\ n [erythorbic (acid) + -ate derivative compound] : a salt of erythorbic acid that is used in foods as an antioxidant

er·y·thor·bic acid \,erə'thòrbik-\ n [prob. fr. erythrose + ascorbic acid] : an optical isomer of ascorbic acid

eryth·ro·leu·ke·mia \ə,rithrō(,)lü'kēmēə\ n [NL, fr. erythro- red (deriv. of Gk erythros) + leukemia] : a malignant disorder that is marked by proliferation of erythroblastic and myeloblastic tissue and in later stages by leukemia

eryth·ro·poi·e·tin \ə,rithrə'pòiət°n\ n [erythropoietic producing red blood cells + -in chemical compound] : a hormonal glycoprotein that is prob. formed in the kidney and stimulates red blood cell formation

es·bat \'es,bat\ n [OF, esbat, diversion, blow, fr. esbatre to divert, amuse, beat, fr. (assumed) VL exbattuere, fr. L ex-, intensive prefix + battuere to beat] : a meeting of a coven of witches

es·ca·beche \,eskə'besh\ n [F escabéche, fr. past part. of escabécher to prepare fish for preserving, perh. fr. Prov escabesser to decapitate, fr. es- off + cabessa head] : fish or chicken fried in oil then marinated in a spicy sauce and served cold

es·ca·late*\'eskə,lāt, ÷-kyə-\ vb -lat·ed; -lat·ing vi : to increase in extent, volume, number, amount, or scope : expand ⟨any limited nuclear war would rapidly escalate into full-scale disaster —Sat. Eve. Post⟩ ~ vt : to increase the extent, volume, number, amount, or scope of ⟨escalated the case from a political crisis to an epic constitutional collision —Newsweek⟩

es·ca·la·tion*\,eskə'lāshən, ÷ -kyə-\ n : an increasing in extent, volume, number, amount, or scope — es·ca·la·to·ry \'eskələ,tòrē, -,tór-, ÷ -kyə-\ adj

es·ca·pol·o·gist*\ə,skā'päləjàst, e,s-\ n, chiefly Brit : an escape artist ⟨complete with sword-swallowers and escapologists wriggling in sacks and chains —Alan Brien⟩

es·cu·do*\ə'sk(y)ü(,)dō, e'-, -kü(,)thō\ n : a monetary unit of Chile equivalent to 1/1000 peso

ESL abbr English as a second language

ESOP \'ē,säp, ,ē,es(,)ō'pē\ n [employee stock ownership plan] : a program by which a company's stock is acquired by its employees

esoph·a·go·gas·tric \ə'säfə(,)gō'gastrik, ē'-\ adj [esophago- esophagus, esophagus and + gastric] : of, relating to, involving, or affecting the esophagus and the stomach ⟨esophagogastric anastomosis⟩ ⟨esophagogastric ulcers⟩

esoph·a·gos·co·py \ə,säfə'gäskəpē, -pi\ n [esophago- + -scopy examination] : examination of the esophagus by means of an esophagoscope

establishment* n, often cap 1 : a group of social, economic, and political leaders who form a ruling class (as of a nation) ⟨by them he meant not the English, but the governing classes, the Establishment —A.J.P. Taylor⟩ 2 : a controlling group ⟨the Welsh literary Establishment . . .

kept him out of everything —Keidrych Rhys⟩ ⟨the high-strung gladiators of the cookbook *establishment* . . . who are forever plunging verbal forks into each other's orange soufflés —Marcia Seligson⟩

estimate***n :** a numerical value obtained from a statistical sample and assigned to a population parameter

es·ti·ma·tor*\'estəmād·ə(r)\ *n :* ESTIMATE; *also :* a statistical function whose value for a sample furnishes an estimate of a population parameter

es·tro·ge·nic·i·ty \ˌestrəjəˈnisəd·ē\ *n* [*estrogenic* + *-ity* state, condition] **:** capacity for estrogenic action or effect

ET*abbr elapsed time

eta particle \'ād·ə-, 'ēd·ə-\ *n* [*eta,* the seventh letter in the Greek alphabet] **:** an uncharged elementary particle with zero spin that has a mass 1074 times the mass of an electron and that decays rapidly into pions or gamma rays

eth·a·cryn·ic acid \ˌethəˌkrinik-\ *n* [fr. *eth*ane + *ac*etic + *but*yr*yl* + *phe*n*ol* + *-ic,* adj. suffix] **:** a potent synthetic diuretic $C_{13}H_{12}Cl_2O_4$ used esp. in the treatment of edema

eth·am·bu·tol \eth'ambyùˌtȯl, -ˌtōl\ *n* [*eth*ylene + *am*ine + *butan*ol] **:** a synthetic drug $C_{10}H_{24}N_2O_2$ used esp. in the treatment of tuberculosis

etha·mi·van \e'thaməˌvan, ˌethə'mīvan\ *n* [*di*ethyl + *am*ide + *van*illic acid] **:** an analeptic drug and central nervous stimulant $C_{12}H_{17}NO_3$ that is related to vanillic acid and is used as a respiratory stimulant for intoxication with central nervous depressants (as barbiturates) and for chronic lung diseases

eth·e·phon \'ethəˌfän\ *n* [modif. of chloro*ethyl phosphonic* acid] **:** a synthetic plant growth regulator $C_2H_6ClO_3P$ that induces flowering and abscission by promoting the release of ethylene and has been used to cause early ripening (as of apples on the tree)

ethid·i·um bromide \e'thidēəm-\ *n* [*eth*yl + *phen*an*thridinium*] **:** a biological dye that is a phenanthridine derivative used as a trypanocide and to block nucleic acid synthesis (as in mitochondria)

eth·i·on \'ethēˌän\ *n* [blend of *ethyl* and *thion-* sulfur, fr. Gk *theion*] **:** an organophosphate $C_9H_{22}O_4P_2S_4$ used as a pesticide

eth·i·on·amide \ˌethē'änəˌmīd, ə'thīən-, -əməd\ *n* [*ethyl* + *thion-* + *amide*] **:** a compound $C_8H_{10}N_2S$ used against mycobacteria (as in tuberculosis and leprosy)

Ethiopian Orthodox *adj* **:** of or relating to the ancient Monophysite church of Ethiopia

ethnic**n :* a member of an ethnic group; *esp :* a member of a minority group who retains the customs, language, or social views of the group

eth·no·meth·od·ol·o·gy \ˌethnōˌmethə'däləjē, -ji\ *n* [*ethno-* ethnic (deriv. of Gk *ethnos* nation) + *methodology*] **:** a branch of sociology dealing with nonspecialists' commonsense understanding of the structure and organization of society — **eth·no·meth·o·dol·o·gist** \-əjəst\ *n*

eth·no·mu·si·col·o·gy \ˌethnō,myüzə'käləjē, -ji\ *n* **:** a study of the music chiefly of non-European cultures esp. in relation to the culture that produces it — **eth·no·mu·si·co·log·i·cal** \-əkə'läjəkəl\ *adj* — **eth·no·mu·si·col·o·gist** \-ə'käləjəst\ *n*

eth·no·sci·ence \'ethnōˌsīən(t)s\ *n* **:** the nature lore (as folk taxonomy of plants and animals) of primitive people

— **eth·no·sci·en·tif·ic** \ˌethnō,sīənˈtifik\ *adj* — **eth·no·sci·en·tist** \-ˈsīəntəst\ *n*

eth·o·sux·i·mide \ˌethō'səksəˌmīd, -əməd\ *n* [*ethyl* + connective *-o-* + *-suximide* (by shortening and alter. fr. *succinimide*)] **:** an antidepressant drug $C_7H_{11}NO_2$ derived from succinic acid and used to relieve epilepsy

et·ic \'ed·ik\ *adj* [*phon*etic] **:** of, relating to, or involving description of linguistic or behavioral phenomena considered in isolation from a particular system or in relation to predetermined general concepts ⟨a sound spectrogram is a good example of *etic* description —John Algeo⟩ — compare EMIC

etio·cho·lan·o·lone \ˌed·ē-(ˌ)ōkō'lan·ᵊlˌōn, *also* ed·ē-\ *n* [*etio-* formed by chemical degradation + *chol*esterol + *-ane* saturated carbon compound + *-ol* chemical compound containing hydroxyl + *-one* ket*one*] **:** a testosterone metabolite $C_{19}H_{30}O_2$ that occurs in urine

etio·patho·gen·e·sis \ˌēd·ēō,pathə'jenəsəs, *also* ˌe-\ *n* [*etio-* cause (deriv. of Gk *aitia*) + *pathogenesis* development of a disease] **:** the cause and development of a disease or abnormal condition

etor·phine \ē'tȯrˌfēn, ə't-, -ȯ(ə)ˌ-\ *n* [perh. fr. *ether* + *morphine*] **:** a synthetic narcotic drug $C_{25}H_{33}NO_4$ related to morphine but with more potent analgesic properties

ETV *abbr* educational television

eu·phen·ics \yü'feniks\ *n pl but sing in constr* [*eu-* good, well (deriv. of Gk *eys* good) + *phen-* (fr. *phen*otype); after E *geno*type: *eu*gen*ics*] **:** a science that deals with the biological improvement of human beings after birth — **eu·phen·ic** \-ik\ *adj*

Eu·ro·bond \'yùrōˌbänd\ *n* [*Euro*pe + *bond*] **:** a bond sold outside its country of origin; *esp* **:** a bond of a U.S. corporation that is sold outside the U.S. and that is denominated and paid for in dollars and yields interest in dollars

Euro·cen·tric \ˌyùrō'sen·trik\ *adj* [*Euro*pe + *centric* having such as its center] *chiefly Brit* **:** EUROPOCENTRIC

Euro·com·mu·nism \ˌyùrō'kämyə,nizəm\ [*Euro*pean + *communism*] **:** the communism esp. of western European Communist parties that is marked by a willingness to reach power through coalitions and by independence from Soviet leadership — **Euro·com·mu·nist** \-yənəst\ *n or adj*

Eu·ro·crat \'yùrəˌkrat\ *n* [*Euro*pe + *-crat* member of a class or faction, deriv. of Gk *kratos* strength, power] **:** a staff member of the administrative commission of the European Common Market — **Eu·ro·crat·ic** \ˌyùrəˈkradˌik, -atik\ *adj*

Eu·ro·cur·ren·cy \'yùrō,kər·ənsē, -,kə·rənsē\ *n* **:** moneys (as of the U.S. and Japan) held outside their countries of origin and used in the money markets of Europe

Eu·ro·dol·lar \-,dälə(r)\ *n* **:** a U.S. dollar used as Euro-currency

Eu·ro·po·cen·tric \yə,rōpə,sen·trik, ,yürəpə-\ *adj* [*Eu*rope + connective *-o-* + *-centric*] **:** centered on Europe and the Europeans ⟨the ethnocentric, or *Europocentric,* view that has been held for so long a time in the West — C.V. Woodward⟩ ⟨both [China and the United States] remained outside the *Europocentric* power politics of the 19th century —J.K. Fairbank⟩ — **Eu·ro·po·cen·trism** \-ˌsen·trizəm\ *n*

eu·than·a·tize \yü'thanəˌtīz\ *also* **eu·tha·nize** \'yüthə,nīz\ *vt* **-tized** *also* **-nized; -tiz·ing** *also* **-niz·ing**

[fr. Gk *eu*- happy + *thanatos* death + E *-ize*, vb. suffix] **:** to subject to euthanasia

EVA *abbr* extravehicular activity

even per·mu·ta·tion \-ˌpərmyu̇'tāshən\ *n* **:** a permutation that is produced by the successive application of an even number of interchanges of pairs of elements — compare ODD PERMUTATION

event*n **:** a subset of the possible outcomes of a statistical experiment ⟨7 is an *event* in the throwing of two dice⟩

ev·er·glade \'evə(r)ˌglād\ *n* [the *Everglades*, Fla.] **:** a swampy grassland esp. in southern Florida usu. containing sawgrass and at least seasonally covered by slowly moving water — usu. used in pl.

evoked potential *n* **:** recorded electrical activity esp. in the cerebral cortex following stimulation of a peripheral sense receptor

ex·ac·ta \ig'zaktə, eg-\ *n* [AmerSp *quiniela exacta* exact quiniela] **:** PERFECTA

ex·cess \ik'ses, 'ekˌses, ek'ses\ *vt* [*excess*, n.] **:** to eliminate the position of ⟨the decline in enrollment has allowed us to *excess* about 75 teachers —Stuart Binion⟩

exchange force *n* **:** a force between two elementary particles (as a neutron and a proton) arising from the continuous interchange between them of other particles (as pions)

ex·ci·mer \'cksəˌ(ˌ)mə(r)\ *n* [*excited* di*mer*] **:** an aggregate of two atoms or molecules that exists in an excited state

ex·ci·ton \'eksəˌtän\ *n* [*excitation* + *-on* elementary particle] **:** a mobile bound electron-hole pair that is produced in a solid by the absorption of a photon — **ex·ci·ton·ic** \ˌeksə'tänik\ *adj*

ex·ci·ton·ics \ˌeksə'täniks\ *n pl but sing in constr* **:** a branch of solid-state physics that deals with excitons and their behavior in semiconductors and dielectrics

ex·clu·sion·ary rule \ə̇ks'klüzhəˌnerē-, eks-\ *n* **:** a legal rule that bars any unlawfully obtained evidence from being used in court proceedings

exclusive dis·junc·tion \-dis'jəŋ(k)shən\ *n* **:** a statement of a logical proposition expressing alternatives usu. taking the form *p* + *q* meaning *p* or *q* but not both

ex–di·rec·to·ry \ˌeksdə̇'rekt(ə)rē, rapid -ˌdrek-\ *adj* [L *ex* out of] *Brit* **:** not listed in a telephone directory **:** unlisted ⟨*ex-directory* number⟩

executive privilege *n* **:** exemption from legally enforced disclosure of communications within the executive branch of government when such disclosure would adversely affect the functions and decision-making processes of the executive branch

exo·bi·ol·o·gy \ˌek(ˌ)sōbī'äləjē\ *n* [*exo*- outside (fr. Gk *exō*) + *biology*] **:** a branch of biology concerned with the search for life outside the earth and with the effects of extraterrestrial environments on living organisms — **exo·bi·o·log·i·cal** \-ˌbīəˌ'läjəkəl\ *adj* — **exo·bi·ol·o·gist** \-bī'äləjə̇st\ *n*

ex·o·cri·nol·o·gy \ˌeksōkrə̇'näləjē, -ˌkrī-, -ˌkrē-\ *n* [*exocrine* secreting externally (fr. *exo*- + *-crine*, fr. Gk *krinein* to separate) + connective *-o-* + *-logy* theory, science] **:** the study of external secretions (as pheromones) that serve an integrative function

exo·cy·clic \ˌek(ˌ)sō'sīklik, -ˌ'sik-\ *adj* **:** situated outside of a ring in a chemical structure

exo·cy·to·sis \ˌek(ˌ)sōsī'tōsə̇s\ *n, pl* **-to·ses** \-ˌō'sēz\ [NL, *exo*- outside + *cyt*- cell + *-osis* process] **:** the release of

cellular substances (as secretory products) contained in cell vesicles by fusion of the vesicular membrane with the plasma membrane and subsequent release of the contents to the exterior of the cell — **exo·cy·tot·ic** \-sī̇'täd·ik\ *adj*

ex·on \'ekˌsän\ *n* [expressed sequence + *-on* basic hereditary component or region] **:** a sequence of nucleotides in DNA or RNA that is expressed as all or part of the polypeptide chain of a protein — compare INTRON — **ex·on·ic** \ek'sänik\ *adj*

exo·nu·cle·ase \ˌeksō'n(y)ükēˌās, -ˌāz\ *n* **:** an enzyme that breaks down a nucleic acid by removing nucleotides one by one from the end of a chain — compare ENDONUCLEASE

exo·nu·mia \ˌeksə'n(y)ümēə\ *n pl* [NL, fr. *exo*- + E *numismatic* + NL *-ia* related things] **:** numismatic items (as tokens, medals, or scrip) other than coins and paper money

exo·nu·mist \ˌeksə'n(y)ümə̇st, 'eksəˌn(y)ü-\ *n* **1 :** a specialist in exonumia **2 :** a collector of exonumia

exo·phil·ic \ˌeksə'filik\ *adj* [*exo*- + *-philic* loving, deriv. of Gk *philos* beloved, loving] **:** ecologically independent of man and his domestic environment ⟨an *exophilic* species of mosquito⟩ — compare ENDOPHILIC — **ex·oph·i·ly** \ek'säfəlē\ *n*

exotic*adj **:** of or relating to striptease ⟨*exotic* dancing⟩

exotic*n **:** a dancer who performs a striptease

ex·pa·tri·a·tism \ek'spā-trēəˌtizəm *also* -rēədˌiz-, *chiefly Brit* -pa-\ *n* **:** the quality or state of being an expatriate

explosive*adj **:** done by the force of a controlled explosion ⟨*explosive* welding⟩ ⟨*explosive* forming of metal parts⟩

ex·po \'ek(ˌ)spō\ *n, pl* **ex·pos** [short for *exposition*] **:** a public exhibition or show **:** an exposition

ex·po·nence \ik'spōnən(t)s, ek's-, 'ekˌs-\ *n* [fr. *exponent*, after such pairs as E *dependent: dependence*] **:** the correlation between an abstract linguistic category and its exponents ⟨by moving towards the data within abstractions one is considered to be moving down the scale of *exponence* —R.H. Robins⟩

ex·po·nent*n **:** a specific element of a linguistic category ⟨*eat* is an *exponent* of the class 'verb'⟩

ex·po·nen·ti·a·tion \ˌekspəˌnenchē'āshən, *sometimes* -n(t)sē-\ *n* [*exponent* + *-iation* (as in *differentiation*)] **:** the act or process of raising a quantity to a power

extension*n **:** a mathematical set (as a field or group) that includes a given and similar set as a subset

ex·tern·ship \'ekˌstərnˌship, -tə̄n-, -tə̇in-\ *n* [blend of *external* and *internship*] **:** a period of temporary employment for an advanced student in a professional field (as teaching or engineering) for practical experience outside an educational institution

ex·tra·chro·mo·som·al \ˌekstrəˌkrōməˌsōməl, -ˌzō-\ *adj* [*extra*- outside, beyond (deriv. of L *extra*) + *chromosomal*] **:** situated or controlled by factors outside the chromosomes ⟨*extrachromosomal* inheritance⟩ ⟨*extrachrosomal* DNA⟩

ex·tra·cor·po·re·al \-kȯ(r)ˌpōrēəl, -ˌpȯr-\ *adj* **:** occurring or based outside the living body ⟨heart surgery employing *extracorporeal* circulation⟩ — **ex·tra·cor·po·re·al·ly** \-ēəlē\ *adv*

ex·tra·cra·ni·al \-ˌ'krānēəl\ *adj* **:** situated or occurring outside the cranium ⟨*extracranial* arterial occlusion⟩

ex·tra·mi·to·chon·dri·al \-ˌmīd·ə¦kändrēəl\ *adj* **:** situated or occurring in the cell outside the mitochondria ⟨*extramitochondrial* synthesis of fatty acids⟩

ex·tra·ne·ous*\(ʰ)ek¦strānēəs, ik's-\ *adj* **:** being a number obtained in solving an equation that is not a solution of the equation ⟨*extraneous* roots⟩

ex·tra·nu·cle·ar*\¦ekstrə'n(y)üklēə(r), ÷-kyələ(r)\ *adj* **:** situated outside the nucleus of an atom ⟨*extranuclear* electrons⟩

ex·traor·di·naire \(ˌ)ek¸strȯrdᵃn'e(ə)r, ¸ekstrə¸ȯrd-\ *adj* [F] **:** markedly exceptional **:** remarkable, extraordinary — used postpositively ⟨jazz artist *extraordinaire* and composer of more than 50 film scores —Barbara Wilkins⟩ ⟨this bathroom *extraordinaire* is the size of most people's living rooms —Lisa Hammel⟩

ex·tra·re·nal \¦ekstrə¦rēnᵒl\ *adj* **:** situated or occurring outside the kidneys ⟨*extrarenal* action of diuretics⟩

ex·tra·so·lar \-¦sōlə(r), -¸lär, -¸lá(r\ *adj* **:** originating or existing outside the solar system ⟨*extrasolar* life⟩

ex·tra·ter·res·tri·al \-tə¦restrēəl, -¦res(h)chəl\ *n* **:** an extraterrestrial being

ex·tra·ve·hic·u·lar \-vē'hikyələ(r)\ *adj* **1 :** taking place outside a vehicle (as a spacecraft) ⟨*extravehicular* activity⟩ **2 :** relating to extravehicular activity ⟨an *extravehicular* assignment⟩

eye chart *n* **:** a chart that is read at a fixed distance for purposes of testing sight; *esp* **:** one with rows of letters or objects of decreasing size

eye contact *n* **:** visual contact with another person's eyes ⟨a handbook . . . put out by one of those new nudist camps . . . which advised beginners to practice *eye contact* —W.K. Zinsser⟩

eye doctor *n* **:** a specialist (as an optometrist or ophthalmologist) in the examination, treatment, or care of the eyes

eye·lin·er \'ī¸līnə(r)\ *n* **:** makeup used to emphasize the contour of the eyes

eyes only *adj* [fr. expression *for your eyes only*] **:** to be read by only the person addressed ⟨the *eyes only* crisis memorandums prepared for Presidents —R.R. Silver⟩

F

f*abbr femto-

fab \\'fab\\ *adj* [by shortening] *chiefly Brit* **:** fabulous, marvelous, wonderful ⟨had a *fab* time last night dancing — *Punch*⟩

fab·ri·ca·ble \\'fabrəkəbəl\\ *adj* [LL *fabricabilis,* fr. L *fabricari* to fabricate] **:** capable of being shaped ⟨*fabricable* alloys⟩ — **fab·ri·ca·bil·i·ty** \\,fabrəkə'biləd·ē\\ *n*

Fa·bry's disease \\'fäbrēz-, -riz-\\ *n* [Johannes *Fabry* †1930 Ger. dermatologist] **:** a sex-linked inherited disorder of lipid catabolism characterized esp. by renal dysfunction, a rash in the inguinal, scrotal, and umbilical regions, and corneal defects

face fly *n* **:** a European fly (*Musca autumnalis*) that is similar to the housefly, is widely established in No. America, and causes great distress to livestock by clustering about the face

face–off*\\'fā,sòf\\ *n* **:** a face-to-face confrontation **:** a showdown ⟨swaggered down cattletown streets, pistols waggling dangerously on their hips as though ready for a *face-off* with any man —W.H. Forbis⟩ ⟨had avoided *face-offs* with the militants —Benjamin DeMott⟩

factor VIII \\-'āt\\ *n* **:** a glycoprotein of blood plasma that is essential for blood clotting and is absent or inactive in hemophilia — called also *antihemophilic factor, antihemophilic globulin*

factor V \\-'fiv\\ *n* **:** a globulin occurring in inactive form in blood plasma that in its active form is one of the factors accelerating the formation of thrombin from prothrombin in the clotting of blood **:** accelerator globulin

fag·got·ry \\'fagə·trē\\ *n* [*faggot* homosexual + *-ry* quality, condition] **:** male homosexuality ⟨why is *faggotry* okay, but the imputation of it discreditable? —W.F. Buckley *b*1925⟩

fag·goty *also* **fag·got·ty** \\'fagəd·ē, -əte, -i\\ *adj* [*faggot* + *-y,* adj. suffix] **:** resembling or suggesting the manner of an effeminate male homosexual — often used disparagingly

fag hag *n, slang* **:** a woman who seeks the company of male homosexuals

fail**n* **:** a failure (as by a security dealer) to deliver or receive securities within a prescribed period after a purchase or sale

¹fail–safe \\'fā(ə)l,sāf\\ *adj* **1 :** incorporating some feature for automatically counteracting the effect of an anticipated possible source of failure ⟨a *fail-safe* drive train that cannot lock up the rear wheel —*Consumer Reports*⟩ **2 :** being or relating to a safeguard that prevents continuing on a bombing mission according to a preconceived plan **3 :** having no chance of failure **:** infallibly problem-free ⟨a written guarantee that your back is in A-1, *fail-safe* condition —Fern Lebo⟩

²fail–safe *vi* **:** to counteract the effect of a malfunction automatically ~ *vt* **:** to equip with a fail-safe device

fairness doctrine *n* **:** a tenet of licensed broadcasting that ensures a reasonable opportunity for the airing of conflicting viewpoints on controversial issues of public concern

fake book \\'fāk,bùk\\ *n* [*fake* to improvise + *book*] **:** a book that contains the melody lines of popular copyrighted songs without accompanying harmonies and that is published without the permission of the copyright owners

fake·lore \\'fāk,lō(ə)r, -ȯ(ə)r, -ōə, -ȯ(ə)\\ *n* [*fake* + *lore* (as in *folklore*)] **:** imitation folklore (as tales or songs) created to pass as genuinely traditional

fa·laf·el *or* **fe·laf·el** \\fə'läfəl\\ *n, pl* **falafel** *or* **felafel** [Ar *falāfil*] **:** a spicy mixture of ground vegetables (as chick peas or fava beans) formed into balls or patties and then fried; *also* **:** a sandwich of pita bread filled with falafel

fa·lan·ga \\fə'läŋgə, -aŋ-\\ *n* [NGk] **:** a method of torture in which the soles of the feet are beaten

fallout**n* **1 :** an incidental result or product ⟨the war ... produced its own literary *fallout* — a profusion of books —*Newsweek*⟩ ⟨left behind, as *fallout,* a feeling of acute vulnerability —Daniel Yergin⟩ **2 :** particulate matter dispersed through the air and landing in a wide distribution ⟨flowers open and glowing, but on the pure yellow the *fallout* of soot already was sprinkled —Saul Bellow⟩

family**n* **:** a group constituting a unit of a crime syndicate (as the Mafia) and engaging in underworld activities within a defined geographical area ⟨was made head of one of New York's five large Mafia *families* at the age of twenty-six —Joseph Epstein⟩

family**adj* **:** designed or suitable for both children and adults ⟨*family* restaurants⟩ ⟨*family* movies⟩

family planning *n* **:** planning of the number and spacing of one's children by effective methods of birth control

family room *n* **:** a large room designed as a recreation center for members of a family

Fan·co·ni syndrome \\fän,kōnē-, fan-, -ŋ,k-\\ *n* [Guido *Fanconi b*1882 Swiss pediatrician] **:** a disorder of reabsorption in the proximal convoluted tubules of the kidney that is characterized esp. by the presence of glucose, amino acids, and phosphates in the urine

fan–jet \\'fan,jet\\ *n* **1 :** a jet engine having a ducted fan in its forward end that draws in extra air whose compression and expulsion provide extra thrust **2 :** an airplane powered by a fan-jet engine

fan·tab·u·lous \\fan-'tabyələs\\ *adj* [*fanta*stic + *fabulous*] *slang* **:** marvelously good ⟨he's only *fantabulous,* only the best pitcher in the majors —J.R. Dickenson⟩

fantasy**n, pl* **-sies :** a coin usu. not intended for circulation as currency and often issued by a dubious authority (as a government-in-exile)

Far·a·day rotation \\'farə,dā-, -ədē-\\ *n* **1 :** optical rotation of a beam of polarized light due to the Faraday effect **2 :** rotation of a beam of polarized microwaves traversing an isotropic medium along the lines of force of a magnetic field

far–out \'fär͵aút\ adj [far out (adverbial phrase), fr. ME fer oute, fr. fer far + out, oute out] **:** marked by a considerable departure from the conventional or traditional **:** extreme ⟨a small, far-out, but fervent religious sect —Joseph Alsop⟩ — **far–out** \'fär͵aút\ n — **far-out-er** \'fär͵aúd-ə(r)\ n — **far-out-ness** \-'aútnəs\ n

far–red \'fä(r)͵red\ adj **1 :** lying in the part of the infra-red spectrum farthest from the red — used of radiations with wavelengths between 30 and about 1000 microns **2 :** lying in the part of the infrared spectrum nearest to the red — used of radiations with wavelengths starting at about .8 micron

fart around vi **:** to mess around **:** waste time — often considered vulgar

fast·back n **1** \'fas(t)͵bak\ **:** a back roof on a closed passenger automobile sloping in a long unbroken line toward the rear bumper **2** \-͵bak\ **:** an automobile having a fastback

fast–breed·er reactor \'fas(t)͵brēdə(r)-\ n **:** a breeder reactor that depends on high energy neutrons to produce fissionable material

fast–food \-'füd\ adj **:** specializing in the rapid preparation and service of food (as hamburgers or fried chicken) ⟨a fast-food restaurant chain⟩ — **fast food** \͵fas(t)'füd\ n

fat* n **:** a fat person

fatal n **:** a fatal outcome; esp **:** a fatal automobile accident ⟨had 11 fatals at three spots on Interstate 610 —Dexter Jones⟩

fat city n, often cap F&C **:** an extremely comfortable situation or condition of life ⟨the one-subject whiz kid from the Bronx has finally achieved Fat City —Joe Flaherty⟩

fat depot n **:** connective tissue in which fat is stored and which has the cells distended by droplets of fat

fate* n **:** the expected result of normal development ⟨prospective fate of embryonic cells⟩

fat farm n **:** HEALTH SPA

Faulk·ner·ian \(')fók'nirēan, -'ner-\ adj [William Cuthbert Faulkner †1962 Am. novelist] **:** of, relating to, or suggestive of William Faulkner or his writings ⟨style is rather Faulknerian, skillfully handled, a pastiche of past and present, memories and fantasies —John Leonard⟩

fa·ve·la also **fa·vel·la** \fə'velə\ n [Pg favela] **:** a settlement of jerry-built shacks lying on the outskirts of a Brazilian city

favorite son* n **:** a renowned person (as an artist or celebrity) who is viewed with great favor and affection by the people of his hometown

fax \'faks\ n [by shortening and alter. fr. facsimile] **:** the transmission of graphic matter (as printing or still pictures) by wire or radio and its reproduction **:** facsimile

FDC* abbr fleur de coin

federal funds n pl **:** reserve funds lent overnight by one member bank of the Federal Reserve to another

feed·back in·hi·bi·tion \'fēd͵bak͵in(h)ə'bishən\ n **:** inhibition of an enzyme controlling an early stage of a series of biochemical reactions by the end product when it reaches a critical concentration

feed·through \'fēd͵thrü\ n **:** a conductor that connects two circuits on opposite sides of a surface

felafel var of FALAFEL

fel·late \'fel͵āt, fə'lāt\ vb **-lat·ed; -lat·ing** [L fellatus, past part. of fellare to suck] vt **:** to perform fellatio on ~ vi **:** to fellate someone — **fel·la·tor** \'fel͵ād·ə(r), fə-'lā-\ n

femme* \'fem\ n **:** a lesbian who plays the female role in a homosexual relationship

fem·to- \͵fem(p)(͵)tō\ comb form [ISV, fr. Dan or Norw femten fifteen (fr. ON fimmtān) + connective -o-] **:** one quadrillionth (10^{-15}) part of ⟨femtoampere⟩

fence–mend·ing \'fen(t)s͵mendiŋ\ n **:** the rehabilitating of a deteriorated political relationship ⟨governmental employees have spent their time and energy on political fence-mending to keep their party in power —S.H. Patterson & A.W.S. Little⟩

fender bender n **:** a minor automobile accident

fen·tan·yl \fen'tanᵊl, 'fentᵊn͵il\ n [alter. of phentanyl, fr. phen- phenyl + ethyl + aniline + -yl chemical radical, fr. Gk hylē wood, matter] **:** a narcotic analgesic $C_{22}H_{28}N_2O$ with pharmacologic action similar to morphine that is administered esp. as the citrate

fen·thi·on \'fen'thī͵än, -iən\ n [fen- (alter. of phenphenyl) + -thion sulphur-containing compound] **:** an organophosphorus insecticide $C_{10}H_{15}O_3PS_2$

fer·mi \'fer(͵)mē\ n [Enrico Fermi †1954 Ital. physicist] **:** a unit of length equal to 10^{-13} centimeter

fer·re·dox·in \͵ferə'däksən\ n [L ferrum iron + E redox + -in chemical compound] **:** any of a group of iron-containing plant proteins that function as electron carriers in photosynthetic organisms and in some anaerobic bacteria

FET \͵ef(͵)ē'tē\ n **:** FIELD-EFFECT TRANSISTOR

FET abbr federal excise tax

fe·tal hemoglobin \͵fēd-ᵊl-\ n **:** a hemoglobin variant that predominates in the blood of a newborn and persists in increased proportions in some forms of anemia (as thalassemia)

fetal position n [fr. the similar position of the fetus in the womb] **:** a resting position in which the body is curved, the legs and arms are bent and drawn toward the chest, and the head is bowed forward and which is assumed esp. in some forms of psychic regression

fe·tol·o·gy \fē'täləjē\ n [feto- fetus + -logy theory, science, deriv. of Gk logos word] **:** a branch of medical science concerned with the study and treatment of the fetus in the uterus — **fe·tol·o·gist** \-jəst\ n

fe·to·pro·tein \͵fēd-ō͵'prō͵tēn, ͵fē(͵)tō-, also -ōdēən, -ōtēən\ n **:** a fetal antigen that is also associated with some malignant conditions (as hepatoma) in the adult

fe·tos·co·py \fēd-'äskəpē, fē'täs-, -pi\ n [feto- + -scopy examination] **:** examination of the pregnant uterus by means of a fiber-optic tube

fet·tuc·ci·ne Al·fre·do \͵fed-ə'chēnē(͵)al'frä(͵)dō, -äl-, -äl-\ or **fet·tuc·ci·ne all' Al·fre·do** \-͵al(͵)al'frä(͵)dō, -͵äl(͵)äl-, -͵äl(͵)äl-\ n [Alfredo all' Augusteo, restaurant in Rome, where it originated] **:** a dish consisting of butter, fettuccine, Parmesan cheese, cream, and seasonings

Feul·gen \'fóilgən\ adj **:** of, relating to, utilizing, or staining by the Feulgen reaction ⟨positive Feulgen mitochondria⟩

FG abbr field goal

fi·ber·fill \'fībə(r)͵fil\ n **:** man-made fibers (as of polyester) used as a filling material (as for cushions)

fiber op·tics \-'äptiks\ n pl **1 :** thin transparent fibers of glass or plastic that are enclosed by material of a lower index of refraction and that transmit light throughout their length by internal reflections; also **:** a bundle of such fibers used in an instrument (as for viewing body cavities) **2** sing in constr **:** the field of or technique of using fiber optics — **fi·ber–op·tic** \'fībər,äptik\ adj

fi·ber·scope \'fībə(r),skōp\ n [fiber + -scope instrument for observing, deriv. of Gk skeptesthai to watch, look at] **:** a flexible instrument utilizing fiber optics and used esp. in medicine for examination of inaccessible areas (as the stomach)

Fi·bo·nac·ci number \,fibə'nächē-, ,fēb-\ n [Leonardo Fibonacci (Leonardo Pisano) †ab 1250 Ital. mathematician] **:** a number in the infinite sequence 1, 1, 2, 3, 5, 8, 13, . . . of which the first two terms are 1 and 1 and each succeeding term is the sum of the two immediately preceding

fi·brino·pep·tide \fī,brinō'pep,tīd\ n [fibrinogen + peptide] **:** any of the vertebrate proteins that are split off from fibrinogen by thrombin during clotting of the blood, comprise two in each species, and exhibit great interspecific variability

fi·bro·cystic \'fībrə,sistik\ adj [fibro- fiber, fibrous tissue + cystic] **:** characterized by the presence or development of fibrous tissue and cysts ⟨fibrocystic changes in the pancreas —Lancet⟩

fi·bro·elas·to·sis \,fī(,)brōə,las'tōsəs, -ē,las-\ n [fibroelastic + -osis abnormal condition] **:** a condition of the body or one of its organs (as the left ventricle of the heart) characterized by proliferation of fibroelastic tissue

fi·bro·gen·ic \,fibrə'jenik\ adj **:** promoting the development of fibers ⟨a fibrogenic agent⟩

fiche \'fēsh, also 'fish\ n, pl **fiche** also **fiches** [short for microfiche] **:** a sheet of microfilm containing rows of microimages of pages of printed matter **:** microfiche

Fick principle \'fik-\ n [Adolph Eugen Fick †1901 Ger. physiologist] **:** a generalization in physiology which states that blood flow is proportional to the difference in concentration of a substance in the blood as it enters and leaves an organ and which is used to determine cardiac output from the difference in oxygen concentration in blood before it enters and after it leaves the lungs and from the rate at which oxygen is consumed

fiddle*n [Brit. slang fiddle to cheat] **:** an illegal or dishonest transaction or one of doubtful legality or honesty **:** a dodge, swindle, or fraud ⟨the lorry driver instigated a fiddle whereby a smaller amount was put in the tank than shown on the invoice —London Times⟩ ⟨a 1967 capital gains fiddle —Peter Jenkins⟩ ⟨one of the legitimate tax fiddles —Alisdair Fairley⟩

fi·do \'fīd(,)ō\ n, pl **fidos** [freaks + irregulars + defects + oddities] **:** a coin having a minting error

fi·du·ci·ary*\fəd(y)üshē,erē, fī'-, -ri\ adj **:** being a mark or set of marks in the reticle of an optical instrument used as a point of reference or for a measure

field*n **:** a particular area (as a column on a punched card) in which the same type of information is regularly recorded

field*vt **:** to answer or respond to extemporaneously ⟨fielded the questions with ease⟩ ⟨tactfully field the numerous phone calls that came in from anxious models night and day —Peter Maas⟩

field–ef·fect transistor \'fē(ə)ldə,fekt-, -ē,f-\ n **:** a nonrectifying transistor in which the output current is controlled by a variable electric field

field ion microscope n **:** a high-magnification microscope in which an image of the atoms of a metal surface is formed on a fluorescent screen by means of usu. helium ions formed in a high-voltage electric field

field judge n **:** a football official whose duties include covering action on kicks and forward passes and timing intermission periods and time-outs

fièvre bou·ton·neuse \fyeevr⁽ᵉ⁾bütȯnōēōēz\ n [F] **:** a disease that is characterized by headache, pain in muscles and joints, and an eruption over the body and is transmitted by the bite of a tick

fighting chair n **:** a chair attached to the deck of a boat from which a salt-water angler plays a hooked fish

figure–ground \'figyə(r),graund, esp Brit 'figə(r)-\ adj **:** relating to or being the relationships between the parts of a perceptual field which is perceived as divided into a part consisting of figures having form and standing out from a part comprising the background and being relatively formless ⟨an ambiguous diagram in which figure≈ground relationships are easily perceived as reversed⟩

fil·i·pin \'filəpən\ n [NL, fr. filipensis, species name + -in chemical compound] **:** an antifungal antibiotic $C_{35}H_{58}O_{11}$ produced by a bacterium of the genus Streptomyces (S. filipensis)

filler*n **:** an item of poor quality (as a worn coin) kept in a collection until a better specimen can be found to replace it

film·card \'film,kärd, 'füm-, -,kàd\ n **:** FICHE

film·og·ra·phy \fil'mägrəfē, fiü'm-\ n, pl **-phies** [film + connective -o- + -graphy writing, deriv. of Gk graphein to write] **:** a list of motion pictures featuring the work of a prominent film figure (as an actor or director) or relating to a particular film topic ⟨the present volumes each have a complete filmography of the stars —Henry Halpern⟩

film·script \'film,skript, 'fiüm-\ n **:** a script for a motion picture

film·set·ting \'film,sed·iŋ, 'füm-\ n **:** text composition done directly on film — **filmset** \-,set\ adj — **filmset** vt — **film·set·ter** \-,sed·ə(r)\ n

finance company*n **:** a company that specializes in making loans usu. to individuals

financial service n **:** an organization that studies the business situation and security market and makes investment recommendations usu. in a regularly issued publication

finder's fee n **:** a fee paid to a financial finder often in the form of a percentage of the sum involved

fine structure n **1 :** a multiplet occurring in an atomic spectrum as a result of electron interaction **2 :** microscopic structure of a biological entity or one of its parts esp. as studied in preparations for the electron microscope — **fine structural** adj

fine–tune \(')fīn't(y)ün\ vt **1 :** to adjust so to bring to the highest level of performance or effectiveness ⟨fine≈tune a TV set⟩ ⟨fine-tune the format⟩ **2 :** to stabilize (an economy) by small-scale fiscal and monetary manipulations

finger*n **:** BIRD 2 ⟨secretaries in Hartford, Connecticut, give the finger to ribald construction workers —Richard Woodley⟩

finger food *n* **:** a food (as a radish or carrot) that is meant to be picked up with the fingers and eaten

fin·ger–pop·ping \\'fiŋgə(r),päpiŋ\ *adj* **:** characterized by a pronounced beat ⟨*finger-popping,* toe-tapping music⟩

fingerprint*n **:** chromatographic, electrophoretic, or spectrographic evidence of the presence or identity of a substance; *esp* **:** the chromatogram or electrophoretogram obtained by cleaving a protein by enzymatic action and subjecting the resulting collection of peptides to two-dimensional chromatography or electrophoresis

fink*\\'fiŋk\ *n* **:** one who is disapproved of or is held in contempt ⟨I was the very model of a well-adjusted old *fink,* spending my working hours selling out and my leisure time up against the wall —Lou D'Angelo⟩

fink out *vi* **1 :** to fail miserably **2 :** to back out **:** cop out ⟨others from his roots as anxious to change the world have cracked under the pressure or *finked out* in the fat of middle age —Seymour Krim⟩

Fin·land·iza·tion \,finləndə'zāshən, -,dī'z-; (,)fin,landə'z-\ *n* [*Finland,* country in northern Europe + *-ization* action of treating in such a manner] **:** a foreign policy of neutrality which makes a non-Communist country susceptible to the influence of the Soviet Union; *also* **:** the conversion to such a policy

fire·base \\'fī(ə)r,bās, 'fīə,-\ *n* **:** a secured site from which field artillery can lay down interdicting fire

fire·fight \-,fīt\ *n* **:** a usu. brief intense exchange of fire between opposing infantry units

fire·flood \-,fləd\ *or* **fire·flood·ing** \-iŋ\ *n* **:** the process of injecting compressed air into a petroleum reservoir and burning some of the oil so as to drive the rest of the oil into producing wells

firm·ware \\'fərm,wa(ə)r, -,we(ə)r, 'fōm-, 'fəim-, -,waə, -,weə\ *n* **:** software functions (as a computer program) implemented through a small special-purpose computer memory unit (as a read-only memory)

first blood *n* **1 :** the first drawing of blood in a contest (as boxing) **2 :** an initial advantage over an opponent ⟨drew *first blood* when they won the pole and the third spot on the starting grid —Kim Chapin⟩

First World *n* **:** the Western industrialized non-Communist nations

fiscal court *n* **:** the executive agency of a county in some states of the U.S.

fish*vb — **fish in troubled waters :** to profit or attempt to profit from unsettled or troubled conditions ⟨with the major powers as willing as in the past to *fish in* such *troubled waters,* the main everyday peace-keeping job has changed —Arthur Larson⟩

fish–eye \\'fish,ī\ *adj* [fr. the resemblance of the lens to the protruding eye of a fish] **:** being, having, or produced by a wide-angle photographic lens that has a highly curved protruding front, that covers an angle of about 180 degrees, and that gives a circular image with barrel distortion ⟨a *fish-eye* view⟩ ⟨a *fish-eye* camera⟩

fish farm *n* **:** a commercial facility for raising aquatic animals (as fish) for human food — **fish–farm** *vt*

fishnet*n **:** a coarse open-mesh fabric

fish protein concentrate *n* **:** flour made of pulverized dried fish

five–o'clock shadow \,fīvə,kläk-\ *n* [fr. the resemblance of a dark beard's stubble to a shadow] **:** the growth of beard present late in the afternoon on the face of a man who has not shaved since morning

fixed–point \\'fiks(t),pȯint\ *adj* **:** involving or being a mathematical notation (as in a decimal system) in which the point separating whole numbers and fractions is fixed — compare FLOATING-POINT

flack \\'flak\ *vi* [*flack* press agent] **:** to provide publicity **:** engage in press-agentry ⟨the hard-working girl flew into New York to *flack* prettily for her film —*Time*⟩

flack·ery \\'flak(ə)rē, -ri\ *n* **:** publicity or promotion ⟨the . . . ineptness at press-agentry is rather refreshing to anyone who has been overexposed to *flackery* —John Fischer⟩

flag football *n* **:** a variation of football in which a player must remove a flag attached to a ballcarrier's clothing to stop the play

flagship*n **:** the finest, largest, or most important one of a series or group ⟨the company's *flagship* store⟩ ⟨the *flagships* of its computer line —*Newsweek*⟩ ⟨presenting the Boston Symphony Orchestra as the *flagship* of its cultural programs —Jonathan Price⟩

flak*\\'flak\ *n* **1 :** abusive criticism ⟨I've taken *flak* from newsmen who think I've sold out —Chet Huntley⟩ **2 :** heated discussion **:** opposition ⟨this modest proposal ran into *flak* —Charles MacDonald⟩

flake*n **1 :** one that is flaky **:** a screwball ⟨he is, in the snowfall of sports conformity, a self-designated refreshing *flake* —*Springfield* (*Mass.*) *Union*⟩ **2 :** cocaine

flake·board \\'flāk,bō(ə)rd, -,bȯ(ə)rd, -,bōəd, -,bȯəd\ *n* **:** a composition board made of flakes of wood bonded with synthetic resin

flaky*also **flak·ey** *adj* **flak·i·er; -est :** markedly odd or unconventional **:** crazy ⟨they used to call me *flaky* . . . but now that I'm a millionaire they'll be calling me an eccentric —Derek Sanderson⟩ ⟨in the last days of the election campaign, when we had all grown *flaky* from too little sleep —Ron Nessen⟩

flame–re·tar·dant \,flämrə'tärd²nt, -'tȧd-\ *adj* **:** made or treated so as to resist burning ⟨*flame-retardant* sleepware⟩

flame stitch *n* **:** a needlepoint stitch that produces a pattern resembling flames

flan·ken \\'flaŋkən, -äŋ-\ *n* [prob. fr. Yiddish *flanken;* akin to G *flanke* flank] **:** flank steak boiled in stock with spices and vegetables

flanker*or **flanker back** *n* **:** a football player stationed wide of the formation; *esp* **:** an offensive halfback who lines up on the flank slightly behind the line of scrimmage and serves chiefly as a pass receiver

flap·pa·ble \\'flapəbəl\ *adj* **:** lacking self-assurance and self-control **:** easily upset ⟨his resonant voice is friendly, yet decisive; constructive and reassuring to . . . the *flappable* chef —Doris Tobias⟩

flare*n **1 :** a short pass in football thrown to a back who is running toward the sideline **2 flares** *pl* **:** trousers that flare toward the bottoms

flash*vi **1 :** to expose one's genitals usu. suddenly and briefly in public **2 :** to have sudden insight — often used with *on* ⟨she just *flashed* on it: for once in her life, she ought to put her own needs right up front —Cyra McFadden⟩

flash*n **:** RUSH 1

flashback*n : a brief recurrence of an earlier psychedelic experience

flash-cube \'flash,kyüb\ n : a plastic cube containing four flashbulbs that fits into the top of a camera and revolves after each shot

flashed glass n : glass in which a very thin layer of colored glass or of a metallic oxide is flashed to clear glass

flasher*n : an exhibitionist who flashes

flash-for-ward \'flash'fôrwərd, -'fó(ə)wəd, sometimes -'fôrəd, South also -'färwərd, -'fawəd\ n [flash (as in flashback) + forward] : a literary or theatrical technique used esp. in motion pictures and television that involves interruption of the chronological sequence of events by interjection of events or scenes of future occurrence; also : an instance of a flash-forward

flash pho-tol-y-sis \-fō'täləsəs\ n : the process of decomposing a chemical with an intense flash of light and observing spectroscopically the transient molecular fragments produced

flavor*n : a property that distinguishes different types of quarks (as the up, down, strange, charmed, and bottom quarks) and different kinds of leptons (as the electron, muon, and tau)

flea collar n : a collar for animals that contains insecticide for killing fleas

fleur de coin \'flərdə'kwan, -lēd-\ adj [F à fleur de coin, lit., with the bloom of the die] : being in the preserved mint condition

flex-a-gon \'fleksə,gän, -əgon\ n [flex + -agon (as in hexagon)] : a folded paper figure that can be flexed along its folds to expose various arrangements of its faces

flex-or ret-in-ac-u-lum \'fleksə(r),ret'n'akyələm\ n [NL] : any of several bands of fascia that overlie and provide channels for tendons esp. of flexor muscles

flex-time \'fleks,tīm\ n [flexible + time] : a system that allows employees to choose their own times for starting and finishing work within a broad range of available hours

flick-knife \'flik,nīf\ n, Brit : a pocketknife with a spring-loaded blade that will fly open upon pressing a release catch : a switchblade knife

flight attendant n : a person who attends passengers (as by serving food) on an airplane

flight bag n 1 : a traveling bag usu. with zippered outside compartments for use esp. in air travel; esp : one that fits under an airplane seat 2 : a small thin lightweight canvas satchel decorated with the name of an airline

flight jacket n [so called fr. its similarity to aviators' jackets of World War II] : a zippered leather jacket with front pockets and knitted waistband and wristbands

flip*vi **flipped; flip-ping** 1 : to lose self-control ⟨when he flips it takes three men to hold him —Eddie Krell⟩ — often used with out ⟨mother was flipping out, drinking more each day —Wayne Ross⟩ 2 : to become extremely enthusiastic ⟨I flipped for that man's music —Melissa Hayden⟩

flip chart n [flip to turn over] : a series of hinged sheets (as of cardboard) that can be flipped over the top and out of view in presenting information sequentially

flip side n : the reverse and usu. less popular side of a phonograph record; broadly : the reverse or opposite side ⟨the flip side of a menu⟩ ⟨part of me is perfectly happy in jeans and sneakers; the flip side gets very involved in clothes —Romaine Maloney⟩

flit*n, slang : a male homosexual

float fishing n 1 : the practice of fishing from a boat or raft allowed to float down a river 2 chiefly Brit : the art or practice of fishing usu. with live bait at the end of a line buoyed by a float or bobber

floating decimal n : a system of decimal point placement in an electronic calculator in which the decimal point is free to move automatically across the display in order to allow the maximum number of decimal places in the readout

float-ing-point \'flōd-iŋ'pöint\ adj : involving or being a mathematical notation in which a quantity is denoted by one number multiplied by a power of the number base ⟨the fixed-point value 99.9 could be expressed in a floating-point system as .999 × 10²⟩ — compare FIXED-POINT

floating point n : a floating-point system or notation; also : a point used in such a system or notation

floc-cu-lo-nod-u-lar lobe \'fläkyə(,)lō'näjələr)-\ n [flocculus + connective -o- + nodular] : the posterior lobe of the cerebellum that consists of the nodulus and paired lateral flocculi and is concerned with equilibrium

flu-ka-ti \flō'kätē\ n, pl **-ti** or **-tes** \-ä,tes\ [NGk phlokutē, fr. phlokto strand of wool, prob. fr. G flocke flock of wool (fr. MHG vlocke)] : a hand-woven Greek rug with a thick shaggy pile

floor exercise n : an event in gymnastics competition consisting of various ballet and tumbling movements (as jumps, somersaults, and handstands) performed without apparatus

floor partner n : a member of a brokerage firm who owns a seat on an exchange and acts as floor broker for his firm

floor-through \'flō(ə)r'thrü, 'flō(ə)r-, 'flōə'-, 'flō(ə)'-\ n : an apartment that occupies an entire floor of a building

flop-py \'fläpe, -i\ n, pl **floppies** : FLOPPY DISK

floppy disk n : a small flexible plastic disk coated with magnetic material on which data for a computer can be stored

floss vt : to use dental floss on ⟨the correct way to floss your teeth⟩ ~ vi : to use dental floss ⟨everyone knows you should brush, but few know they should floss —Robert Brackett⟩

flour tortilla n : a tortilla made with wheat flour instead of cornmeal

flower bond n [prob. fr. the association of flowers with funerals; fr. the fact that these are frequently purchased for investors who are dying] : a U.S. Treasury bond that may be redeemed at face value before maturity if used in settling federal estate taxes

flower bug n : any of various small mostly black-and-white predaceous bugs (family Anthocoridae) that frequent flowers and feed on pest insects (as aphids and thrips)

flower child n : a hippie who advocates love, beauty, and peace by wearing or displaying flowers

flower people n pl : FLOWER CHILDREN ⟨smiling, mild-mannered flower people sang, chanted, tinkled bells, handed out flowers, blew bubbles and danced —D.A. Schmidt⟩

flu-er-ic \(')flü'erik\ adj [irreg. fr. L fluere to flow] : FLUIDIC

flu·er·ics \flü'eriks\ *n pl but usu sing in constr* **:** FLUIDICS

flu·id·ic* \flü'idik\ *adj* **:** of, relating to, or being a device (as an amplifier or control) that depends for operation on the pressures and flows of a fluid in precisely shaped channels — **fluidic** *n*

flu·id·ics \-iks\ *n pl but usu sing in constr* **:** the technology of fluidic devices

flu·id·on·ics \,flüə'däniks\ *n pl but usu sing in constr* [*fluid* + *-onics* (as in *electronics*)] **:** FLUIDICS

flu·o·cin·o·lone ac·e·to·nide \,flüə¦sin²l,ōn,asə'tō,nīd\ *n* [*fluorine* + *cinene*, a terpene (fr. *cineole* + *-ene* unsaturated carbon compound) + prednis*olone* + *acetone* + *-ide* derivative compound] **:** a glucocorticoid $C_{24}H_{30}F_2O_6$ used esp. as an anti-inflammatory agent in the treatment of skin diseases

flu·o·ri·diz·er \'flü(ə)rə,dīzə(r), -lōr-, -lòr-\ *n* **1 :** one that fluoridizes **2 :** a fluorine-containing water and oil repellent finish for textiles

flu·o·ro·poly·mer \-'päləmə(r)\ *n* **:** any of various homopolymers or copolymers that consist mainly of fluorine and carbon and that are characterized by chemical inertness, thermal stability, and a low coefficient of friction

flu·o·ro·ura·cil \-'yùrə,sil, -əsəl\ *n* **:** a fluorine-containing pyrimidine base $C_4H_3FN_2O_2$ used to treat some kinds of cancer; 5-fluorouracil

flur·az·e·pam \flü(ə)r'azə,pam\ *n* [*fluor-* containing fluorine + benzodi*azepine* + *-am* compound related to ammonia] **:** a benzodiazepine closely related structurally to diazepam that is used as a hypnotic in the form of its hydrochloride $C_{21}H_{23}ClFN_3O\cdot2HCl$ — see DALMANE

fly* *vi* **flew; flown; fly·ing** [*fly* to take flight] **1 :** to be high (as on drugs or alcohol) **2 :** to function successfully **:** win popular acceptance ⟨we knew from past campaigns that a pure human-rights approach would not *fly* —Charles Brydon⟩

fly* *n, pl* **flies :** a football pass pattern in which the receiver runs straight downfield

fly* *adj* [*fly* keen] **:** impressively good, attractive, or stylish ⟨would have to top myself and really come up with something *fly* —John Fuqua⟩

fly–cruise \'flī'krüz\ *n* **:** an excursion in which the price of air and ship travel are combined in a single fare

fly–off \'flī,òf\ *n* **:** an exhibition in which competing manufacturers attempt to win government contracts by demonstrating the superior performance of their aircraft

FMN \,ef(,)e'men\ *n* [*flavin mononucleotide*] **:** a yellow crystalline mono-phosphoric ester $C_{17}H_{21}N_4O_9P$ of riboflavin

FOBS *abbr* fractional orbital bombardment system

foil* *n* **:** a body similar to an airfoil but designed for action in or on water **:** a hydrofoil

fo·late \'fō,lāt\ *n* [*folic* (acid) + *-ate* derivative compound] **:** a crystalline pteroylglutamic acid $C_{19}H_{19}N_7O_6$ that is a vitamin of the B complex and is used in the treatment of nutritional anemias and sprue **:** folic acid; *also* **:** a salt or ester of folic acid

folk guitar *n* **:** a flat-topped acoustic guitar

¹folk·ie *also* **folky** \'fōkē, -ki\ *n, pl* **folkies** [*folk* + *-ie*, *-y* one having to do with] **1 :** a folk singer or musician ⟨a quiet-voiced English *folkie* —Stephen Holden⟩ **2 :** a fan of folk music ⟨his fans were the sincere, often politically committed . . . *folkies* of the Kennedy years —*Playboy*⟩

²folkie *or* **folky** *adj* **:** of or relating to folk music ⟨audiences are ready now for *folky* cabaret artists —John Rockwell⟩

folk·lor·is·tics \,fōk,lòr'istiks\ *n pl but sing or pl in constr* [*folkloristic* + *-s*, pl. suffix] **:** the study of folklore

folk mass *n* **:** a mass in which traditional liturgical music is replaced by folk music

folk–rock \'fōk,räk\ *n* **:** folk songs sung to a rock 'n' roll background — **folk–rock** *adj* — **folk–rock·er** \-,räkə(r)\ *n*

fon·due* \(')fän,d(y)ü\ *n* **1 :** a dish that consists of small pieces of food (as meat, fruit, or cake) cooked in or dipped into a hot liquid at the table ⟨beef *fondue*⟩ ⟨chocolate *fondue*⟩ **2 :** a chafing dish in which fondue is made

fondue fork *n* **:** a long slender usu. 2-tined fork used in cooking or eating fondue

fon·du·ta \fän'd(y)üd-ə, -ütə\ *n* [Piedmontese, fr. F *fondue*] **:** a preparation of melted cheese (as fontina) usu. with milk, butter, egg yolks, and sliced white truffles

food processor *n* **:** an electric appliance that performs many tasks of food preparation (as slicing, shredding, and chopping) with one of a set of interchangeable blades revolving inside a container

food pyramid *n* **:** an ecological hierarchy of food relationships esp. when expressed quantitatively (as in mass, numbers, or energy) in which a chief predator is at the top, each level preys on the next lower level, and usu. green plants are at the bottom

food stamp *n* **:** a government-issued coupon that is sold at little cost or given to low-income persons and is redeemable for food

foot·pad* \'fùt,pad\ *n* **:** a flattish foot on the leg of a spacecraft for distributing weight to minimize sinking into a surface

footwork* *n* **:** maneuvering, tactics ⟨a nice bit of political *footwork* —Tom Wicker⟩

for·mat \'fò(ə)r,mat, -ò(ə),m-\ *vt* **for·mat·ted; for·mat·ting** [*format*, n.] **:** to produce (as a book, printed matter, or data) in a specified form (as print) or style ⟨get complete reports of your experiment, *formatted* as you like them and prepared automatically during the experiment —*advt* ⟩ ⟨assigned to teach freshman composition from a trendily *formatted* collection of contemporary materials —Samuel McCracken⟩

for·mu·la \'fòrmyələ, -ò(ə)m-\ *adj* [*formula*, n.] *of a racing car* **:** conforming to prescribed specifications of size, weight, and engine displacement and usu. having a long narrow body, open wheels, a single-seat open cockpit, and an engine in the rear

formula investing *n* **:** investing according to a plan **(formula plan)** under which more funds are invested in equity securities when the market is low and more are put into fixed-income securities when the market advances

FOR·TRAN \'fò(ə)r,tran, 'fò(ə)-\ *n* [*formula translation*] **:** an algebraic and logical language for programming a computer

fortune cookie *n* **:** a thin folded cookie containing a slip of paper on which a fortune, proverb, or humorous statement is printed

forward contract *n* **:** an agreement between a buyer and a seller to conclude the sale of an item at a specified time and at a specified price

found object n [trans. of F objet trouvé] : a natural or discarded object (as a piece of driftwood or junk) found by chance and held to have aesthetic value esp. through the working of natural forces on it

found poem n : a poem consisting of words found in a nonpoetic context (as a product label) and usu. rearranged by the poet into poetic form

Fou·ri·er trans·form \ˈfu̇rēˌā'tran(t)s₁fȯrm, fu̇rˈyā-, -ˌfō(ə)m\ n [Baron Jean Baptiste Joseph Fourier †1830 Fr. geometrician and physicist] : a function (as $F(u)$) that under suitable conditions can be obtained from a given function (as $f(x)$) by multiplying by e^{iux} and integrating over all values of x

four·plex \ˈfō(ə)r₁pleks, ˈfō(ə)r₁-, ˈfȯəₐ-, ˈfȯ(ə)ₐ-\ n [four + -plex (as in duplex)] : a building that contains four separate apartments

fourth market n : the private market for the sale of securities by institutional investors — compare THIRD MARKET

fourth wall n : the opening of the proscenium seen as an imaginary wall between the stage set and the audience of a play

fourth world n, often cap F&W : a group of nations esp. in Africa and Asia characterized by extremely low per capita income and an absence of readily exportable natural resources — compare THIRD WORLD

four-wall·ing \ˈfō(ə)r₁wȯliṇ, ˈfȯ(ə)r₁-, ˈfȯə₁-, ˈfȯ(ə)₁-\ also four-walls—contract n [fr. the fact that the distributor takes over the entire theater] : an arrangement whereby a motion picture distributor rents a theater for the entire run of a film and keeps all the ticket receipts instead of splitting them with the theater owner

fox*n 1 slang : an attractive and stylish young woman 2 slang : an attractive young man

foxy*adj fox·i·er; -est : being good-looking : attractive, sexy ⟨looking incredibly foxy in a feathered boa —Cyra McFadden⟩

FPC*abbr fish protein concentrate

frab·jous \ˈfrabjəs\ adj [perh. alter. of fabulous] 1 : wonderful ⟨look forward to those frabjous days — Brendan Gill⟩ 2 : extraordinary — frab·jous·ly adv

fractional orbital bom·bard·ment system \-bäm'-bärdmənt-, -bəm'-\ n : a system for delivering a nuclear warhead from orbit by slowing it down by a retrorocket before completion of an orbit

frag \ˈfrag\ vt fragged; frag·ging [frag fragmentation grenade] : to deliberately injure or kill (one's military leader) by means of a fragmentation grenade ⟨officers and NCO's who insist on ordering troops into the field are commonly fragged — hit by a grenade rolled under their tent flaps —Fred Gardner⟩ — frag·ger \-ə(r)\ n — frag·ging \-iṇ, -ēṇ\ n

frame*n : a minimal unit of instruction or stimulus in a programmed instruction routine : a unit of programmed instruction calling for a response by the student

frame·shift \ˈfrām₁shift\ adj : relating to, being, or causing a mutation in which a number of nucleotides not divisible by three is inserted or deleted so that some triplet codons are read incorrectly during genetic translation — frameshift n

fran·chi·see \ˌfranchə₁zē, -ˌchī₁-, sometimes -ˌsē\ n [franchise + -ee one furnished with] : one who is granted a

franchise to operate a unit in a chain of business establishments

Fran·co–American \ˌfraŋ(ˌ)kōəˌmerəkən\ n [Franco-French (fr. ML, fr. Francus Frenchman) + American] : an American of French or esp. French-Canadian descent — Franco–American adj

fran·co·phone \ˈfraŋkə₁fōn\ adj, often cap [F, fr. franco-French + Gk phōnē voice, speech] : having or belonging to a French-speaking population esp. in a country where two or more languages are spoken

Francophone n : a French-speaking person esp. in a country where two or more languages are spoken

fran·glais \frän'glā, -äṇ'g-\ n, often cap [F, blend of français French and anglais English] : French marked by a considerable number of borrowings from English

freak*n 1 : one who uses illicit drugs ⟨a mescal freak⟩ ⟨a needle freak⟩ 2 : a highly individualistic critic or rebel; esp : a hippie ⟨how to raise a child who will not be a freak . . . or a man-in-the-gray-flannel-suit —Aline Willbur⟩ 3 : an ardent enthusiast ⟨a horror film we chiller freaks can recommend —Liz Smith⟩ ⟨fungus freaks have been flocking to the woods in record numbers — Newsweek⟩

freak vb [freak, n.] vi 1 : to withdraw from reality and society esp. by taking drugs — often used with out ⟨learns she enjoys freaking out on drugs —Hollis Alpert⟩ 2 : to experience nightmarish hallucinations as a result of taking drugs : have a bad trip — often used with out ⟨one or two participants freaked out and had a very hard time of it —W. J. Hinckle b1938⟩ 3 : to behave irrationally or unconventionally under or as if under the influence of drugs ⟨world is surely coming to an end. He begins to freak —Sol Yurick⟩ — often used with out ⟨she is freaking out as the birth of her child approaches —Sara Blackburn⟩ ~ vt 1 : to put under the influence of a psychedelic drug — often used with out 2 : to disturb the composure of : upset or anger ⟨freaked and outraged the whole psychoanalytic community —Catherine Breslin⟩ —often used with out ⟨what he saw freaked him out so much that he still gets shaken when he remembers it — Berkeley Barb⟩ — freaked or freaked–out \ˈfrēkˌdȧu̇t\ adj

freak·ery \ˈfrēk(ə)rē\ n, pl -er·ies [freak + -ery quality, condition] 1 : FREAKINESS 2 : something that is freaky

freak·i·ness \ˈfrēkēnəs, -kin-\ n : the quality or state of being freaky

freak·ing \ˈfrēkiṇ, -kən\ adj (or adv) [by folk etymology fr. frigging, pres. part. of frig copulate] : damned — used as an intensive ⟨it was too freaking much to believe — Chip Crossland⟩

freak–out \ˈfrē₁kȧu̇t\ n 1 : a withdrawal from reality esp. by means of drugs ⟨those who wanted a day-long or all-night freak-out could choose LSD —R.D. Lyons⟩ 2 a : a drug-induced state of mind characterized by terrifying hallucinations : a bad trip ⟨a murderer who is convinced he killed a girl while on a freak-out —advt⟩ b : an irrational act by one who freaks out 3 : a gathering of hippies ⟨the local hippies' social event of the season, the Easter Sunday freak-out in Elysian Park — Springfield (Mass.) Union⟩ 4 : one who freaks out ⟨unconvincing composite of guerrilla fighters, freak-outs, and Hottentots —W.J.J. Sheed⟩

free agent *n* **:** a professional athlete (as a football player) who is free to negotiate a contract with any team

free-as·so·ci·ate \,frēə'sos(h)ē,āt\ *vi* [back-formation fr. *free association*] **:** to engage in free association ⟨asked to *free-associate* about his dream —Maya Pines⟩

free base *n* **:** cocaine purchased on the street that is freed from impurities by treatment usu. with ether and heated to produce vapors for inhalation

free·bie *or* **free·bee** \'frēbē, -bi\ *n* [by alter. fr. earlier slang *freeby* gratis, irreg. fr. *free*] **:** something (as a theater ticket) given or received without charge ⟨a season *freebie* to the Giants —Frank Deford⟩

freedom ride *n, often cap F&R* **:** a ride made by civil rights workers through states of the southern U.S. to ascertain whether public facilities (as bus terminals) are desegregated — **freedom rider** *n, often cap F&R*

free-fire zone \'frē'fī(ə)r-\ *n* **:** a combat area where any moving thing is a legitimate target

free safety *n* **:** a safetyman in football who has no specific pass receiver to guard in a man-to-man defense and who usu. helps wherever needed on defense

free university *n* **:** an unaccredited autonomous free institution established within a university by students to present and discuss subjects not usu. dealt with in the academic curriculum

freeze-etch·ing \'frē,zechiŋ\ *n* **:** preparation of a specimen (as of tissue) for electron microscopic examination by freezing, fracturing along natural structural lines, and preparing a replica (as by simultaneous vapor deposition of carbon and platinum) — **freeze-etch** \'frē,zech\ *or* **freeze-etched** \-,zecht\ *adj*

freeze-frac·ture \'frēz,frakchə(r)\ *n* **:** FREEZE-ETCHING

freeze-frame \'frēz,frām\ *n* **:** a frame of a motion-picture film that is repeated so as to give the illusion of a static picture

fret* *vb* **fret·ted; fret·ting** *vt* **:** to depress (the strings of a musical instrument) against the frets ~ *vi* **:** to fret the strings of a musical instrument

Fried·man·ite \'frēdmə,nīt\ *n* [Milton *Friedman* b1912 Am. economist] **:** a monetarist who adheres to the theory of economist Milton Friedman that economic regulation should be through direct governmental manipulation of the money supply

friendly* *adj* **friendlier; -est :** easy esp. for a nonspecialist to use or understand ⟨the *friendliest* possible introduction to computers —Dan Watt⟩ ⟨programs are becoming more user *friendly* —Richard Berman⟩

fri·jo·les re·fri·tos \frē'hōlēz(,)rā'frē(,)tōz, -'hō,lās-, -'hò,lās-, -ōs\ *n pl* [Sp, lit., refried beans] **:** frijoles cooked with seasonings, fried, then mashed and fried again

frit·ta·ta \frē·'täd·ə\ *n* [It] **:** an unfolded omelet often containing chopped vegetables or meats

frit·to mis·to* \'frēd·ō'mistō, 'frētō-\ *n* [It, lit., mixed fried food] **:** small pieces of seafood, meat, or vegetables that are dipped in batter and fried

frog* *n* **:** a spiked or perforated holder used to keep flowers in position in a vase

front-end *adj* **:** relating to or required at the beginning of an undertaking ⟨take some time for the huge *front-end* investment to be paid off —*Wall Street Jour.*⟩

front-end load \'frənt,end-\ *n* **:** the part of the total load taken out of early payments under a contract plan for the periodic purchase of investment-company shares

fron·te·nis \'frən'tenəs, (')frän-\ *n* [AmerSp, blend of Sp *frontón* pelota court and *tenis* tennis, fr. E *tennis*] **:** a game of Mexican origin played with rackets and a rubber ball on a 3-walled court

front-lash \'frənt,lash\ *n* [*front* + -*lash* (as in *backlash*)] **:** a counterreaction to a political backlash

front money *n* **:** money that is paid in advance for a promised service or product

frosted* *adj* **:** having undergone frosting ⟨*frosted* hair⟩

frosting* *n* **:** the lightening (as by chemicals) of small strands of hair throughout the entire head to produce a two-tone effect — compare STREAKING 1

fruc·to·ki·nase \'frəktō'kī,nās, 'frúk-, 'frük-, -āz\ *n* [*fructose* + *kinase*] **:** a kinase that catalyzes the transfer of phosphate groups to fructose

fruit jar *n* **:** a mason jar

fruit leather *n* **:** a sheet of dried pureed fruit

fruit machine *n* [fr. the use of pictures of various fruits as symbols to be matched] *Brit* **:** a coin-operated machine for gambling **:** a slot machine

fru·se·mide \'früsə,mid\ *n* [by alter.] *chiefly Brit* **:** FUROSEMIDE

fry bread *n* **:** bread cooked (as by Navaho Indians) by deep frying

fry-up \'frī,əp\ *n, Brit* **:** a dish or meal of fried food

FSO \,ef(,)es'ō\ *n* **:** a foreign service officer

¹fuck \'fək\ *vb* [of Gmc origin; prob. fr. or akin to D *fokken* to breed (cattle), fr. MD, push, thrust, copulate; akin to Sw dial. *fock* penis] *vi* **1 :** to copulate — usu. considered obscene; sometimes used in the present participle as an intensive **2 :** to mess around — used with *with*; usu. considered vulgar ~ *vt* **1 :** to engage in coitus with — usu. considered obscene; sometimes used interjectionally with an object (as a pronoun) to express anger, contempt, or disgust **2 :** to deal with unfairly or harshly — usu. considered vulgar

²fuck *n* **1 :** an act of copulation — usu. considered obscene **2 :** a sexual partner — usu. considered obscene **3 a :** damn — usu. considered vulgar **b** — used esp. with *the* as a meaningless intensive; usu. considered vulgar

fucked-up \'fəkt'əp, 'fək'dəp\ *adj* **:** thoroughly confused or disordered — usu. considered vulgar

fuck·er \'fəkə(r)\ *n* **1 :** one that fucks — usu. considered obscene **2 :** an offensive or disagreeable person — usu. considered vulgar

fuck off *vi* **:** to leave forthwith **:** BUG OFF — usu. used as a command; usu. considered vulgar

fuck over *vt* **:** to take advantage of **:** exploit — usu. considered vulgar

fuck up *vt* **:** to ruin or spoil esp. through stupidity, ignorance, or carelessness **:** bungle — usu. considered vulgar ~ *vi* **:** to act foolishly or stupidly **:** blunder — usu. considered vulgar

fuck·up \'fək,əp\ *n* **1 :** one who fucks up — usu. considered vulgar **2 :** a botch or blunder — usu. considered vulgar

fuel cell *n* **:** a device that continuously converts the chemical energy of a fuel (as hydrogen) directly into electrical energy

fu·el·er \'fyü(ə)lə(r), -yù-\ *n* **:** a dragster that uses specially blended fuel rather than gasoline

full–service *adj* **:** providing comprehensive service of a particular kind ⟨a *full-service* bank⟩

ful·vic acid \ˌfülvik-, ˌfəl-\ *n* [fr. penicillium *fulv*um, a genus of fungi + *-ic* derived from] **:** a water-soluble substance of low molecular weight derived from humus that combines with lyophilic organic compounds and may serve to inactivate some toxic pollutants in aquatic environments

Fu Man·chu mustache \ˌfüˌmanˈchü-\ *n* [*Fu Manchu,* Chinese villain in stories by "Sax Rohmer" (A. S. Ward †1955)] **:** a heavy mustache with ends that turn down to the chin

fun and games *n pl but sing or pl in constr* **:** light amusement ⟨it is not *fun and games* but simply work —S. H. Schanberg⟩ ⟨a reputation for jet-set *fun and games* — *People*⟩

fund–rais·er \ˈfəndˌrāzə(r)\ *n*   **1 :** a person employed to raise funds (as for a political campaign)   **2 :** a social event (as a cocktail party) organized to raise funds

fun fur *n* **:** relatively inexpensive or synthetic fur for casual wear

funk*\ˈfəŋk\ *n*   **1 :** funky music   **2 :** the quality or state of being funky ⟨jeans . . . have lost much of their *funk* —Tom Wolfe⟩

funky*\ˈfəŋkē, -ki\ *adj* **funk·i·er; -est** [fr. *funky* musty, foul, fr. *funk* offensive smell]   **1 :** having an earthy unsophisticated style and feeling; *specif* **:** having the style and feeling of early blues ⟨*funky* piano playing⟩   **2 :** odd or quaint in appearance or style ⟨expected a *funky* . . . type, and instead I met this beautiful, gracious lady —Laura Cunningham⟩

funnel cake *n* [so called because the dough is poured through a funnel] **:** a small spiral-shaped cake fried in a skillet

funny car *n* **:** a specialized dragster that has a one-piece molded body resembling the body of a mass-produced car

funny farm *n, slang* **:** an insane asylum ⟨Edith, at least, sometimes appears to be in touch with reality; Amy seems like a candidate for the *funny farm* —Judy Klemesrud⟩

fu·ra·zol·i·done \ˌfyùrəˈzäləˌdōn, -zȯl-\ *n* [*fur-* related to furan + *azole* compound with a five-membered ring containing nitrogen + *-ide* derivative compound + *-one* ketone or analagous compound] **:** an antimicrobial drug $C_8H_7N_3O_5$ used against bacteria and some protozoa esp. in infections of the gastrointestinal tract

fu·ro·se·mide \f(y)əˈrōsəˌmīd\ *also* **fur·se·mide** \ˈfərsə-, ˈfȯsə-\ *n* [*fur-* + sulfur + *-emide,* prob. alter. of *amide*] **:** a powerful diuretic $C_{12}H_{11}ClN_2O_5S$ used esp. in the treatment of edema

fu·si·coc·cin \ˌfyüsəˈkäksən\ *n* [*Fusicoccum* (genus name) + *-in*] **:** a diterpenoid glucoside produced by a pathogenic fungus of the genus *Fusicoccum* (*F. amygdali*) that causes wilting of peach and almond leaves

future shock *n* **:** the physical and psychological distress suffered by one who is unable to cope with the rapidity of societal and technological changes

fu·tur·is·tics \ˌfyüchəˈristiks\ *n pl but sing in constr* [*futuristic* + *-s,* pl. suffix] **:** FUTUROLOGY

fu·tu·rol·o·gy \ˌfyüchəˈräləjē\ *n* [G *futurologie,* fr. *futur* future + connective *-o-* + *-logie* theory, science, deriv. of Gk *logos* word] **:** a study that deals with future possibilities based on current trends — **fu·tu·ro·log·i·cal** \ˌfyüchərəˈläjəkəl\ *adj* — **fu·tu·rol·o·gist** \ˌfyüchəˈräləjəst\ *n*

futz \ˈfəts\ *vi* [prob. fr. Yiddish; perh. akin to G *furzen,* E *fart*] *slang* **:** to spend time idly or aimlessly **:** fool — often used with *around* ⟨*futz* around without producing any worthwhile music —John Koegel⟩

fuzz tone *or* **fuzz box** *n* **:** an electronic device (as on an electric guitar) which by distorting the sound gives it a fuzzy quality

FWD**abbr, often not cap* front-wheel drive

G

G \'jē\ *adj* [general] *of a motion picture* **:** of such a nature that persons of all ages may be allowed admission — compare PG, R, X

G*abbr giga-

GABA *abbr* gamma-aminobutyric acid

ga·ga·ku \gä'gä(ˌ)kü\ *n, often cap* [Jp. fr. *ga* elegance + *gaku* music] **:** the ancient court music of Japan

gag order *n* **:** a court-imposed ruling barring public disclosure or discussion (as by the press) of evidence relating to an ongoing court case

ga·lac·to·kinase \gəˌlaktōˈkīˌnās, -āz\ *n* [*galactose* + *kinase*] **:** a kinase that catalyzes the transfer of phosphate groups to galactose

Gal·braith·ian \(ˌ)galˈbrāthēən, -thyən\ *adj* [John Kenneth *Galbraith b*1908 Am. economist] **:** of or relating to the economic theories or programs of John Kenneth Galbraith ⟨taking a *Galbraithian* attitude toward the gross national product —E.M. Harrington⟩

ga·le·ro \gəˈle(ə)r(ˌ)ō\ *n* [It, fr. L *galerus, galera* cap of skin worn by certain flamens] **:** the flat-crowned wide-brimmed tasseled red hat formerly worn by Roman Catholic cardinals — called also *cardinal's hat*

gal Friday *n* **:** a female assistant (as in an office) entrusted with a wide variety of tasks **:** girl Friday

gal·le·ria \ˌgaləˈrēə\ *n* [It, gallery, fr. ML *galeria*] **:** a roofed and usu. glass-enclosed promenade or court (as at a shopping mall)

gal·li·um ar·se·nide \'galēəmˈärsᵊnˌīd\ *n* **:** a synthetic compound GaAs used esp. as a semiconducting material

gallows humor *n* **:** humor that makes fun of very serious or terrifying situations ⟨the two last survivors in a dying world are whiling away their desolation with somber *gallows humor*—wit and sobriety yielding a combined swan song and hyena laughter —John Simon⟩

Ga·lois theory \(ˈ)galˈwä-\ *n* [Evariste *Galois* †1832 Fr. mathematician] **:** a part of the theory of mathematical groups concerned esp. with the conditions under which a solution to a polynomial equation with coefficents in a given mathematical field can be obtained in the field by the repetition of operations and the extraction of nth roots

gal·van·ic skin response \galˈvanik-\ *n* **:** a change in the electrical resistance of the skin that is a physiochemical response to a change in emotional state

ga·may \gaˈmā, 'gamˌā\ *n, often cap* [*Gamay,* village in France] **:** a light dry red table wine of California made from the purple grape that is also used for French Beaujolais

game ball*n **:** a ball (as a football) presented by the members of a team to a player or coach in recognition of his contribution to the team's victory

game plan *n* [fr. the use of a strategy or plan in a game like football] **:** a strategy for achieving an objective ⟨the unsettling impact of the fuzzy *game plan* for wage-and-price controls —C.J. Rolo⟩

gam·ma–ami·no·bu·ty·ric acid \ˌgamə-əˌmē(ˌ)nō-byüˌti(ə)rik-, -məˌaməˈ(-\ *also* γ**–aminobutyric acid** *n* [*gamma* + *amino-* containing the group NH_2 + *butyric acid*] **:** an amino acid $C_4H_9NO_2$ that is a neurotransmitter in the central nervous system — abbr. *GABA*

gamma decay *n* **1 :** a radioactive transformation of an atomic nucleus in which the nucleus loses energy by emitting a gamma ray without change of mass number or atomic number **2 :** the decay of an unstable elementary particle in which one or more photons are emitted

gamma ray*n **:** a high-energy photon

gam·ma–ray astronomy \ˌgaməˌrā-\ *n* **:** astronomy dealing with the properties of celestial bodies deduced from gamma rays they emit

gang bang *n* **:** copulation by several persons in succession with the same passive partner — **gang–bang** \'gaŋˌbaŋ\ *vb*

gang·bust·er \'gaŋˌbəstə(r)\ *n* **:** a person and esp. a law officer engaged in the aggressive breakup of organized criminal gangs — **like gangbusters :** with great vigor or enthusiasm ⟨knows how to just kind of play things cool — instead of coming on *like gangbusters* —Dave Brower⟩

gan·gle \'gaŋgəl\ *vi* **gan·gled; gan·gling** \-g(ə)liŋ\ [back-formation fr. *gangling*] **:** to walk or move with or as if with a loose-jointed gait **:** move like a gangling person ⟨the models came out and *gangled* down the catwalk — Germaine Greer⟩ ⟨there was no traffic; five minutes ago a couple tractors . . . *gangled* by —Elizabeth Enright⟩ — **gangle** *n*

gan·gli·o·si·do·sis \ˌgaŋglēōˌsīˈdōsəs, -ōsəˈdō-\ *n, pl* **-do·ses** \-ōˌsēz\ [*ganglioside* + *-osis* abnormal or diseased condition] **:** any of several inherited metabolic diseases (as Tay-Sachs disease) characterized by an enzyme deficiency which causes accumulation of gangliosides in the tissues

gang·sa \'gän(ˌ)sä\ *n* [Indonesian *gampang gangsa,* fr. *gampang* musical instrument consisting of bars struck by hammers + *gangsa* brass] **:** a Balinese metallophone with bamboo resonators

gang shag *n* **:** GANG BANG

gantry**n, pl* **gantries :** a movable scaffold with platforms at different levels for use in erecting and servicing rockets before launching

gap junction *n* **:** an area of contact between adjacent cells characterized by modification of the cell membranes for intercellular communication or transfer of low molecular-weight substances — **gap–junc·tion·al** \ˌgapˈjəŋ(k)shnəl, -shənᵊl\ *adj*

garage sale *n* **:** a sale of used household or personal articles (as furniture, tools, or clothing) held on the seller's own premises — called also *tag sale, yard sale*

ga·ra·gist \gə'räjəst, -äzhə-; Brit usu 'ga,räzhəst or -äj- or 'garij-\ n [garage + -ist specialist] chiefly Brit : a garage-man

garbage*n : inaccurate or useless data 〈no system is better than the information which it receives. In fact, data processing people refer to this common phenomenon as "GIGO" or "garbage in—garbage out" —Bob Donovan〉

gar·bol·o·gist \gär'bäləjəst, gȧ'b-\ n [garbage + -ologist (as in ecologist)] : a trash or garbage collector

gar·çon·nière \ˌgärsᵊnˌye(ə)r, -ˌ(ˌ)sȯn-\ n [F, fr. garçon boy, bachelor] : a bachelor apartment

garment bag n : a traveling bag that folds in half and has a center handle for easy carrying

Gar·vey·ism \'gärvēˌizəm, 'gȧv-\ n [Marcus Garvey †1940 Jamaican Black Nationalist] : a 20th century racial and political doctrine advocating black separation and the formation of self-governing black nations in Africa — Gar·vey·ite \-ēˌīt\ n

gas*n, slang : one that is very appealing or enjoyable 〈I could see it would be a gas to do something like that really well —Paul Newman〉 〈she is a trendy gas —Clive Barnes〉

GAS abbr general adaptation syndrome

gas chro·ma·to·graph \-krō'mad-ə,graf, -krə-\ n : an instrument used to separate a sample into components in gas chromatography

gas chro·ma·tog·ra·phy \-ˌkrōmə'tügrəfē, -fi\ n : chromatographic analysis in which the sample is moved in vapor form by a carrier gas (as nitrogen or helium) through a column of stationary phase comprised of a liquid or particulate solid and is separated in strata by absorption on the stationary phase according to the properties of its components — gas chro·mato·graph·ic \-krō,mad-ə-'grafik\ adj

gas·dy·nam·ics \ˌgas(ˌ)dī'namiks\ n pl but sing in constr : a branch of dynamics that deals with gaseous fluids including products of combustion and plasmas — gas·dy·nam·ic \-ik\ adj — gas·dy·nam·i·cist \-'nam-əsəst\ n

gas–guz·zler \ˌgasˌgəz(ə)lə(r)\ n : a usu. large automobile that gets relatively poor mileage — gas–guz·zling \-z(ə)liŋ\ adj

gas·ket·ed \'gaskəd·əd\ adj : furnished with a gasket 〈a gasketed screw-cap can〉

gas–liquid chromatography n : gas chromatography in which the stationary phase is a liquid — gas–liquid chromatographic adj

gas·o·hol \'gasə,hȯl, sometimes -ˌhäl\ n [blend of gasoline and alcohol] : a fuel consisting of a blend of 10% ethyl alcohol and 90% gasoline

gas·tro·co·lic reflex \ˌgastrə'kōlik-, -ˌkäl-\ n : the occurrence of peristalsis following the entrance of food into the empty stomach

gas·tro·duo·de·nos·to·my \ˌgastrō,d(y)üə,dē'nästəmē, -ˌd(y)ü,ädᵊn'äs-, -mi\ n, pl -mies [NL, fr. gastro- stomach and + duodeno- duodenum + -stomy surgical formation of an opening] : surgical formation of a passage between the stomach and the duodenum

gate*n : a device (as in a computer) that outputs a signal when specified input conditions are met 〈logic gate〉

gaudy iron·stone \-'ī(ə)rn,stōn, -'īən-\ n : a polychrome-decorated mid-19th century English ironstone ware

Gauss·ian integer \ˌgaùsēən-\ n [Karl Friedrich Gauss †1855 Ger. mathematician] : a complex number $a + bi$ where a and b are integers and $i = \sqrt{-1}$

gavel–to–gavel \'gavəltə'gavəl\ adj : running from start to finish 〈gavel-to-gavel coverage of a political convention〉

gay*n : a homosexual

gay·ola \gā'ōlə\ n [blend of gay homosexual and payola] : an undercover or indirect payment made (as to a crime syndicate) by establishments catering to homosexuals

ga·zump \gə'zəmp\ vt [origin unknown] Brit : to swindle or cheat; specif : to demand a higher price from (the buyer of a house) than that agreed on 〈the practice of raising the price of a house after an agreement with a buyer on what the price would be. The buyer would find he had been gazumped when he showed up for the closing —Norman Gelb〉

GB \(')jē'bē\ n [code name] : an extremely toxic chemical warfare agent $C_4H_{10}FO_2P$: sarin

GED abbr general educational development

gee–whiz \(')jē(h)wiz\ adj 1 : designed to arouse wonder or excitement or to amplify the merits or significance of something esp. by the use of clever or sensational language 〈gee whiz journalism〉 2 : marked by spectacular or astonishing qualities or achievement 〈the Andes are a gee-whiz mountain range. The highest, the longest, the driest —Jeanne A. Davis〉 3 : characterized by wide-eyed enthusiasm, excitement, and wonder 〈a gee-whiz approach to politics that wears a little thin —Business Week〉

gel filtration \'jel-\ n : chromatography in which the material to be fractionated separates primarily according to molecular size as it moves into a column of a gel and is washed with a solvent so that the fractions appear successively at the end of the column — called also gel chromatography

Gemini*n sing, pl Geminis : one born under the astrological sign Gemini

Gem·i·ni·an \ˌjemə'nīən\ n [gemini + E -ian one belonging to] : GEMINI

ge·müt·lich \gə'müetlik\ adj [G, fr. MHG gemüetlich, fr. gemüete spirit, heart (fr. ge-, perfective, associative, and collective prefix + muot mood, spirit, mind, fr. OHG) + -lich -ly, adj. suffix, fr. OHG lih] : agreeably pleasant : comfortable 〈easy, natural and gemütlich in her writing —Times Lit. Supp.〉 〈inside, the house is a gemütlich clutter, cosy as a cup of cocoa —Ellen Torgerson〉

ge·müt·lich·keit \gə'müetlik,kīt\ n [G, fr. gemütlich pleasant + -keit state, condition, fr. MHG, alter. of -heit, fr. OHG] : the quality or state of being gemütlich : cordiality, friendliness 〈a kind of imitation Bavarian village awash in prefabricated gemütlichkeit —Philip Shabecoff〉

gene conversion n : the production of gametes by a heterozygote esp. in fungi (as of the genera Saccharomyces, Neurospora, or Aspergillus) in unequal numbers and often in a 3:1 ratio that is thought to occur by selective copying during chromatid replication of one member of the gene pair in preference to the other

gene pool n : the collection of genes in an interbreeding population that includes each gene at a certain frequency in relation to its alleles **:** the genetic information of a population of interbreeding organisms

general adaptation syndrome *n* **:** the sequence of physiological reactions to prolonged stress that in the classification of the physician Hans Selye includes alarm, resistance, and exhaustion

general obligation bond *n* **:** a municipal bond of which payment of interest and principal is backed by the taxing power and credit of the issuing governmental unit

general term *n* **:** a mathematical expression composed of variables and constants that yields the successive terms of a sequence or series when integers are substituted for one of the variables often denoted by *k* $\langle x^k$ is the *general term* of the series $1 + x + x^2 + x^3 + \ldots \rangle$

gen·er·a·tive grammar \'jenə,rād·iv-, -n(ə)rəd·iv-\ *n* **1** **:** a description of a language in the form of an ordered set of rules for producing the grammatical sentences of that language **2 :** TRANSFORMATIONAL GRAMMAR

generative semantics *n pl but usu sing in constr* **:** a description of a language emphasizing a semantic deep structure that is logical in form, that provides syntactic structure, and that is related to surface structure by transformations

generator*n **:** a mathematical entity that when subjected to one or more operations yields another mathematical entity or its elements; *specif* **:** a point, line, or surface whose motion generates a line, surface, or solid **:** a generatrix

ge·ner·ic*\jə'nerik\ *n* **:** a generic drug 〈the consumer's desire to buy low-cost *generics* instead of more expensive brand name drugs —Barbara J. Culliton〉

gene–splic·ing \'jēn,splīsiŋ\ *n* **:** the techniques by which genes from several different species are introduced into and made to function in a single species — compare RECOMBINANT DNA

ge·net·ic code \jə'ned·ik-\ *n* **:** the biochemical basis of heredity consisting of codons in DNA and RNA that determine the specific amino acid sequence in proteins and that are essentially uniform for the forms of life studied so far — **genetic coding** *n*

genetic counseling *n* **:** medical education of affected individuals and the general public concerning inherited disorders that includes discussion of the probability of producing offspring with a disorder given that it has occurred in a family, techniques of diagnosis, and possibilities for treatment

genetic engineering *n* **:** alteration of hereditary defects by intervention in gene-controlled bodily processes and when practicable by directed changes in the genetic material — **genetic engineer** *n*

genetic map *n* **:** MAP 1

genetic marker *n* **:** a usu. dominant gene or trait that serves esp. to identify genes or traits linked with it

ge·noise \zhän'wäz\ *n* [F *génoise*, fem. of *génois* of or relating to Genoa, Italy] **:** a light cake of sugar, flour, and stiffly beaten eggs

gen·ta·mi·cin \jentə'mīsᵊn\ *n* [alter. of earlier *gentamycin*, fr. *genta-* (prob. irreg. fr. *gentian violet;* fr. the color of the organism from which it is produced) + *-mycin*, fr. *streptomycin*] **:** a broad-spectrum antibiotic mixture of two components that is derived from an actinomycete (*Micromonospora purpurea* or *M. echinospora*) and is ex-

tensively used in treating infections esp. of the urinary tract

gen·tle·per·son \'jentᵊl,pərsᵊn, -,pōs-, -,pəis-\ *n* **:** a gentleman or lady

gen·tri·fi·ca·tion \jen·trəfə'kāshən\ *n* [*gentry* + *-fication* process of making] **:** a reclaiming of older urban areas by the middle and upper classes — **gen·tri·fy** \'jen·trə,fī\ *vt*

geo·co·ro·na \jēəkə'rōnə, jēō-\ *n* [*geo-* earth, ground (deriv. of Gk *gē*) + *corona*] **:** the outermost part of the earth's atmosphere consisting primarily of hydrogen

geology*n **:** the study of the solid matter of a celestial body 〈lunar *geology*〉 〈the *geology* of Mars〉

geomagnetic storm *n* **:** a marked temporary disturbance of the earth's magnetic field that is held to be related to sunspots **:** a magnetic storm

geometric*or **geometrical****adj* **:** increasing in a geometric progression 〈*geometric* population growth〉

geo·pres·sured \jēō'preshərd\ *adj* **:** being under great pressure from geologic forces 〈*geopressured* methane〉 〈geothermal energy would come from superheated water in the Gulf Coast *geopressured* belt of brine —James R. Adams〉; *also* **:** of, relating to, or derived from geopressured natural deposits 〈*geopressured* energy〉 〈a 16,500≠ foot *geopressured* well —*Science News*〉

geo·probe \'jēə,prōb, 'jēō-\ *n* **:** a rocket designed for space exploration near the earth but at distances of more than 4000 miles

geo·sta·tion·ary \jē(,)ō'stāshə,nere, *sometimes* -'stāsh(ə)nərē\ *adj* **:** of, relating to, or being an artificial satellite that travels from west to east at an altitude of over 22,000 miles above the equator and at the same speed as that of the earth's rotation so that the satellite seems to remain in the same place

geo·syn·chro·nous \-'siŋkrənəs, -'sin-\ *adj* **:** GEOSTATIONARY — **geo·syn·chro·nous·ly** \-lē, -li\ *adv*

German wire·haired pointer \-'wi(ə)r,ha(ə)rd-, -,he(ə)rd-\ *n* **1 :** a German breed of liver or liver and white hunting dogs that have a flat-lying wiry coat composed of hairs one and one-half to two inches in length **2 :** a dog of the German wirehaired pointer breed

germ·free \'jərm,'frē, 'jəm-, 'jəim-\ *adj* **:** free of microorganisms **:** axenic

Ge·samt·kunst·werk \gə'zämt,kŭnst,verk\ *n* [G, fr. *gesamt* whole, entire + *kunst* art + *werk* work, production] **:** an art work produced by a synthesis of various art forms (as music and drama)

ges·to·sis \je'stōsəs\ *n, pl* **-to·ses** \-ō,sēz\ [NL, fr. *gestation* + *-osis* abnormal condition] **:** any disorder of pregnancy and esp. toxemia of pregnancy

get*vb — **get it on 1 :** to become enthusiastic, energetic, or excited 〈when they get with a rock group they just really *get it on* —John Von Ohlen〉 **2 :** to engage in sexual intercourse — **get it up :** to have an erection — **get one's back up :** to raise one's hackles **:** make one angry, irritated or annoyed 〈*getting our backs up* about foreign snobbery —J. L. Hess〉 — **get one's rocks off 1 :** to experience orgasm **2 :** to become pleasurably excited — **get on the stick :** to begin functioning energetically 〈worrying what might happen if we didn't *get on the stick* pretty fast —Tim Findley〉 get off* *vi* **1 :** to get high on a drug — usu. used with *on* ⟨*get off* on heroin⟩ **2 :** to experience orgasm **3 :** to become pleasurably excited — usu. used with *on* ⟨it was my first audience, and I really *got off* on it —Richard Lewis⟩ ~ *vt* **:** to cause to get off

ge·wurz·tra·mi·ner \gə¦vü(ə)rt¦stramənər, -¦vuert-, -räm-\ *n, often cap* [G, fr. *gewürz* spice + *traminer* of or relating to Tramin (Termeno, Italy)] **:** a light dry Alsatian white wine with a spicy bouquet; *also* **:** a similar wine made elsewhere

gi \'gē\ *n* [Jp] **:** a garment worn in practice or exhibition of oriental martial arts (as karate or judo) consisting of loose-fitting pants and a loose jacket held closed by a cloth belt

giga·bit \'jigə₁bit, 'gigə-\ *n* [*giga-* billion (deriv. of Gk *gigas* giant) + *bit*] **:** one billion bits

giga·cy·cle \-₁sīkəl\ *n* **:** a unit of frequency equal to one billion hertz

giga·watt \-₁wät\ *n* **:** a unit of power equal to one billion watts

giggle* *n* **:** someone or something amusing ⟨when we heard about it, we thought it was a bit of a *giggle* —*Daily Express*⟩

GI·GO \'gī₁gō, 'gē-\ *abbr* garbage in, garbage out

gimmickry* *n* **:** the use of gimmicks ⟨avoidance of *gimmickry* or pretentiousness in his very original experimental technique —*Times Lit. Supp.*⟩

gi·ro \'ji(ə)rō, 'zhi-; 'jē(₁)rō, 'zhē-; *esp Brit* 'jī₁rō\ *n* [It *giro* circulation (of currency)] **:** a system of money transfer in Britain and much of Europe that involves a simple transfer of credits from one account to another without money orders or checks

give·back \'giv₁bak\ *n* **:** a previous gain (as an increase in wages or benefits) given back to management by workers (as in a labor contract) ⟨union workers in the rubber, airline, meatpacking and steel industries agreed to *givebacks* to avoid layoffs —Lawrence Ingrassia⟩

give–up* *n* [fr. the giving up by the first broker of part of the commission to the second] **1 :** a security or commodity market order which one broker executes for a client of a second broker and the commission for which is shared by the two brokers **2 :** the part of a commission due a broker from a major client (as a mutual fund) that he is directed by the client to turn over to another broker who has provided special services (as research or sale of fund shares) to the client

glas·phalt \'gla₁sfôlt\ *n* [blend of *glass* and *asphalt*] **:** a mixture of asphalt and crushed glass used to surface roads

glasshouse* *n, Brit* **:** a military prison **:** guardhouse

gleam·er \'glēmə(r)\ *n* [*gleam* + *-er*, n. suffix] **:** a cosmetic applied to the face or lips to give the appearance of shine or to accent an area (as the cheekbones)

glitch \'glich\ *n* [prob. fr. G *glitschen* to slip, slide, fr. MHG, intensive of *glīten* to glide, fr. OHG *glītan*] **1 :** an unwanted brief surge of electric power **:** a false or spurious electronic signal **2 a :** a failure to function properly **:** a malfunction ⟨a *glitch* in the fuel cell of a spacecraft⟩ ⟨a *glitch* lurking in the scoreboard clock had shaved off the extra .21 —Craig Neff⟩ **b :** a minor problem that causes a temporary setback **:** a snag or hitch ⟨whether he was going to make it through each answer without a *glitch* —

Wall St. Jour.⟩ **3 :** a sudden change in the period of rotation of a neutron star

glit·te·ra·ti \₁glidə'räd·ē, -'rȧ-, -i, *also* -'rä₁tī\ *n pl* [fr. *glitter* + *-ati* (as in *literati*)] **:** BEAUTIFUL PEOPLE

glitter rock *n* **:** rock music performed by male musicians who are made up to look grotesquely feminine — **glitter rocker** *n*

glitz \'glits\ *n* [Yiddish, glitter; akin to G *glitzerig* sparkling] **:** extravagant showiness **:** glitter, ostentation ⟨from the looks of the grandiose worlds being conjured up by the press agents, this is going to be dance's year of ultimate *glitz* —Marcia B. Siegel⟩ — **glitzy** \-sē, -si\ *adj*

glo·mus tumor \'glōməs-\ *n* **:** a painful benign tumor that develops by hypertrophy of a glomus

¹glop \'gläp\ *n* [prob. imit.] **1 a :** a thick semiliquid food or mixture of foods that is usu. unappetizing in appearance ⟨got himself full of whatever *glop* it was the child was supposed to eat —James Thurber⟩ **b :** a thick sticky liquid ⟨freakishly shaving the top of their heads to demonstrate some new aerosol *glop* —Charles Hollander⟩ **2 :** tasteless or worthless stuff ⟨clothing its rhetoric with gooey slabs of prose *glop* —Pete Hamill⟩ — **glop·py** \-pē\ *adj*

²glop *vt* glopped; glop·ping **1 :** to put glop on — often used with *up* ⟨don't *glop* up my hamburger with catsup⟩ **2 :** to put (something gloppy) on food ⟨*glop* blue cheese dressing over the delicate leaves —James Villas⟩

glory hole* *n* **:** a hole made through the partition of adjoining toilet stalls to enable homosexuals to perform fellatio anonymously

gloss* *n* **:** a transparent cosmetic preparation for adding shine and usu. color to the lips

glu·can \'glü₁kan, -ükən\ *n* [*gluc-* glucose + *-an* polymer of a carbohydrate] **:** a polysaccharide (as glycogen or cellulose) that is a polymer of glucose

glu·ca·nase \'glükə₁nās, -āz\ *n* [*glucan* + *-ase* enzyme] **:** any of various enzymes that digest glucans

glu·co·cer·e·bro·si·dase \₁glükō₁serəbrō'sī₁dās, -āz\ *n* [*glucocerebroside* + *-ase*] **:** an enzyme of mammalian tissue that catalyzes the hydrolysis of the glucose part of a glucocerebroside and is deficient in patients affected with Gaucher's disease

glu·co·cer·e·bro·side \₁glükō¦serəbrō₁sīd\ *n* [*gluco-* glucose + *cerebroside*] **:** a lipid composed of a ceramide and glucose that accumulates in the tissues of patients affected with Gaucher's disease

glu·co·gen·ic \₁glükō¦jenik\ *adj* [*gluco-* + *genic* producing] **:** tending to produce a pyruvate residue in metabolism which undergoes conversion to a carbohydrate (as glucose) and is eventually stored as a complex carbohydrate (as glycogen) ⟨*glucogenic* amino acids⟩

glu·co·syl·trans·fer·ase \₁glükō₁sil¦tran(t)s(₁)fər₁ās, -₁āz\ *n* [*glucosyl* + *transferase*] **:** an enzyme that catalyzes the transfer of a glucosyl group; *esp* **:** one implicated in the formation of dental plaque that catalyzes the formation of glucans

glue–sniff·ing \'glü¦snifiŋ\ *n* **:** the deliberate inhalation of volatile organic solvents from plastic glues that may result in symptoms ranging from mild euphoria to disorientation and coma

glu·on \'glü₁än\ *n* [*glue* + *-on* elementary particle] **:** a hypothetical neutral massless particle thought to bind together quarks to form hadrons (as pions, protons, and neutrons)

glu·tar·al·de·hyde \ˌglüd·ə'raldə,hīd\ *n* [*glutar*yl + *aldehyde*] **:** a compound $C_5H_8O_2$ that contains two aldehyde groups and is used esp. in leather tanning, disinfection, and fixation of biological tissues

glu·teth·i·mide \glü'tethə,mīd, -əməd\ *n* [*glutar*yl + *eth*yl + *imide* compound derived from ammonia] **:** a sedative-hypnotic drug $C_{13}H_{15}NO_2$ that induces sleep with less depression of respiration than occurs with comparable doses of barbiturates

gly·co·ca·lyx \ˌglīkō'kāliks, *also* 'kal-\ *n* [*glyco-* + *calyx*] **:** a polysaccharide and glycoprotein covering on a cell surface esp. of bacteria

gly·co·ge·no·sis \ˌglīkōjə'nōsəs\ *n, pl* **-no·ses** \-ō,sēz\ [*glycogen* + *-osis* abnormal condition] **:** any of several metabolic disorders that are characterized esp. by hypoglycemia and abnormal deposits of glycogen and are caused by enzyme deficiencies in glycogen metabolism

gly·cos·ami·no·gly·can \ˌglīkōsə'mē(ˌ)nō'glī,kan, -kō'samə(ˌ)nō-\ *n* [*glycose* + *amino-* containing the group NH_2 + *glycan*] **:** any of a class of polysaccharides (as chondroitinsulfuric acid, mucoitinsulfuric acid, or heparin) **:** mucopolysaccharide

gly·co·sphin·go·lip·id \ˌglīkō'sfiŋ(ˌ)gō'lipəd\ *n* [*glyco-* + *sphingolipid*] **:** any of various lipids (as a cerebroside or a ganglioside) which are derivatives of ceramides, do not contain the phosphorus or the extra nitrogenous base of the sphingomyelins, and do contain a carbohydrate (as glucose), and some of which accumulate in disorders of lipid metabolism (as Tay-Sachs disease)

glyph*\'glif\ *n* [short for *hieroglyph*] **:** a symbol (as a curved arrow on a road sign) that carries information nonverbally ⟨*glyph* signs at airports, docks, and railroad stations could simplify foreign travel —*Nat'l Geographic School Bull.*⟩ ⟨touches a typewriter-like keyboard . . . and the notation *glyphs* appear on the screen —Earl Ubell⟩

gno·to·bi·ol·o·gy \ˌnōd·ə(ˌ)bī'äləjē\ *n* [Gk *gnōtos* known (fr. *gignōskein* to know) + E *biology*] **:** GNOTOBIOTICS — **gno·to·bi·ol·o·gist** \-əjəst\ *n*

gno·to·bi·ot·ic \ˌnōd·ə(ˌ)bī'äd·ik, *also* -bē'ä-\ *adj* [Gk *gnōtos* + E *biotic* relating to life] **:** of, relating to, living in, or being a controlled environment containing one or a few kinds of organisms; *also* **:** free from other living organisms **:** axenic ⟨*gnotobiotic* mice⟩ — **gno·to·bi·ote** \ˌnōd·ə'bī,ōt\ *n* — **gno·to·bi·ot·i·cal·ly** \ˌnōd·ə(ˌ)bī·'äd·ək(ə)lē, *also* -bē'ä-\ *adv*

gno·to·bi·ot·ics \ˌnōd·ə(ˌ)bī'äd·iks\ *n pl but sing in constr* **:** a biological science concerned with the raising and study of animals under gnotobiotic conditions

go*vt **1 :** to pitch (as a specified part of a game) in baseball ⟨he went $7^1/_3$ innings and gave up no runs —D.S. Looney⟩ **2 :** to say — used chiefly in oral narration of speech ⟨I'm the last person to admit I've achieved anything. . . . But now my friends say it to me, and I go "You're right" —Steve Martin⟩ — **go public 1** *of a close corporation* **:** to offer stock for sale to the general public **2 :** to disclose to a much wider audience something not generally known ⟨lying low for now . . . and *going public* at some gauzy future time with a definitive reply to all the charges —*Newsweek*⟩

go*n **:** permission to proceed **:** go-ahead ⟨gave the astronauts a *go* for another orbit⟩

go *adj* **:** functioning properly **:** being in good and ready condition ⟨declared all systems *go*⟩

goal·mouth \'gōl,maůth\ *n* **:** the area directly in front of the goal (as in soccer or hockey)

goal·tend·ing \-ˌtendiŋ\ *n* **1 :** the action of guarding a goal (as in hockey) **2 :** a violation of the rules that involves touching or deflecting a basketball which is on its downward path toward the basket or on or within the rim of the basket

go down*vi **:** to take place **:** happen ⟨I'll tell you everythin' that *went down* —V.E. Smith⟩ — **go down on :** to perform fellatio or cunnilingus on — usu. considered vulgar

go·fer *also* **go·pher** \'gōfə(r)\ *n* [alter. of *go for;* fr. his being required to go for or go after things] **:** an employee whose duties include running errands ⟨the office *gofer*, who is sent out to buy coffee, cigarettes, and the like — *Time*⟩

go–go \'gō(ˌ)gō\ *adj* [a-go-go] **1 :** being fashionable **:** chic ⟨will change the name . . . to something more go-go —Al Fleming⟩ **2 a :** of, relating to, or being a discotheque or the music or dances performed there **b :** employed as a featured dancer to entertain patrons esp. in a discotheque or bar ⟨a pretty teenage go-go girl dances on top of the pedestal —C.D.B. Bryan⟩ **3 :** marked by spirited or aggressive action ⟨playing go-go baseball⟩ ⟨the go-go U.S. businessman must change his style here, where meetings begin with endless cups of tea —Ray Vicker⟩ **4 a :** relating to, dealing in, or offering popular often speculative investment expected to yield high returns ⟨go-go mutual funds⟩ **b :** marked by ready and often speculative investment or fast-paced growth and modernization ⟨losses, then, of three hundred billion dollars . . . such were the bitter fruits of the go-go years —John Brooks⟩

go–go boot *n* [go-go] **:** a woman's knee-high boot made esp. of patent leather or shiny vinyl that has a moderate-to-high heel

gold*adj **:** qualifying for a gold record ⟨five . . . recordings are certified *gold* —Henry Edwards⟩

gold·en·ag·er \ˌgōldə'nājə(r)\ *n* [fr. *Golden Age clubs*, organizations for recreational activities of the elderly] **:** an elderly person; *esp* **:** one who has retired

golden old·ie \-'ōldē, -i\ *n* **:** one (as a song, recording, or television show) that was a hit in the past ⟨rock and roll is a field in which last month's No. 1 hit is today's *golden oldie* —*New Yorker*⟩

gold point*n **:** a fixed point on the international temperature scale equal to the melting point of gold or 1064.43°C

gold record *n* **:** a gold phonograph record awarded to a singer or group whose single record has sold at least one million copies or whose album has sold at least 500,000 copies

gold sodium thio·ma·late \-,thīō'mal,āt, -'mā,lāt\ *n* [*thio-* containing sulfur + *malate*] **:** a gold salt $C_4H_3AuNa_2O_4S·H_2O$ used in the treatment of rheumatoid arthritis

golf ball*n **:** a spherical printing element of an electric typewriter

golf cart *n* **1 :** a small cart for wheeling a golf bag around a golf course **2 :** a motorized cart for carrying a golfer and his equipment around a golf course

gondola*n* **:** an enclosed car suspended from a cable and used for transporting passengers; *esp* **:** one used as a ski lift

G₁ phase \(')jē¦wən-\ *n* [growth] **:** the period in the cell cycle from the end of cell division to the beginning of DNA replication — compare G₂ PHASE, M PHASE, S PHASE

gong*n*, *Brit* **:** a medal

go·ni·al angle \¦gōnēəl\ *n* **:** the angle formed by the junction of the ramus and the body of the human mandible **:** angle of the mandible

go·ni·ot·o·my \¸gōnē'äd·əmē, -ätə-\ *n*, *pl* **-mies** [gonio-corner, angle + -tomy incision] **:** surgical relief of glaucoma used in some congenital types and achieved by opening Schlemm's canal

gon·o·coc·ce·mia \¸gänə¸käk'sēmēə\ *n* [gonococcus + -emia blood condition] **:** the presence of gonococci in the blood — **gon·o·coc·ce·mic** \-mik\ *adj*

go–no–go \'gō'nō¸gō\ *adj* **1 :** being or relating to a required decision to continue or stop a course of action ⟨one of the toughest parts of a spaceman's job is making *go-no-go* decisions —Russell Baker⟩ **2 :** being or relating to a point at which a go-no-go decision must be made ⟨*go-no-go* decision points when ground controllers or the astronauts themselves can elect not to take the next step —*Science News*⟩

gon·zo \'gän(¸)zō\ *adj* [prob. fr. It *gonzo* simpleton, perh. fr. It *Borgonzone* Burgundian] **1 :** of or relating to a style of journalism that is a mixture of fact and fiction and is held to be produced under the effect of drugs **2 :** FAR OUT ⟨his music has a certain *gonzo* charm —John Rockwell⟩ **3 :** ZONKED

good old boy \'gủd(¸)ōl(d)¸bói, *South also* -(¸)ō¸bói\ *n* **:** a usu. rural white Southerner who conforms to the social behavior of his peers

goof–off \'gü¸fóf\ *n* **:** one who evades work or responsibility ⟨an all-round *goof-off* heavily in debt —John Simon⟩

goofy–foot \'güfē¸fủt\ *or* **goofy–foot·er** \-ủd·ə(r)\ *n*, *pl* **goofy–foots** *or* **goofy–footers** [fr. the fact that this is an unusual position] **:** a surfer who rides a surfboard with the right foot forward

goose*vt* **goosed; goos·ing :** to spur to action or accelerated growth **:** push, prod ⟨an effort to *goose* newsstand sales⟩ ⟨the one who *goosed* her into producing . . . my elder half-brother —Colin MacInnes⟩

gorp \'gó(ə)rp, 'góəp\ *n* [perh. fr. slang *gorp* to eat greedily] **:** a snack consisting usu. of high-energy food (as raisins and nuts)

gospel*adj* **:** of, relating to, or being religious songs of American origin associated with evangelism and popular devotion and marked by simple melody and harmony and elements of folk songs, spirituals, and occas. jazz ⟨*gospel* singer⟩

gox \'gäks\ *abbr* gaseous oxygen

GPA *abbr* grade-point average

grab*vt* **grabbed; grab·bing :** to seize the attention of **:** impress, strike ⟨the technique of *grabbing* an audience —Pauline Kael⟩

grade point *n* **:** a numerical value assigned to each letter grade (as F = 0, D = 1, C = 2, B = 3, A = 4) received in a school or college course that is multiplied by the number of credits for the course

grade–point average \¦grād¦póint-\ *n* **:** the average obtained by dividing the total number of grade points by the total number of credits earned

grammar*n* **:** a system of rules that defines the grammatical structure of a language

gram·mat·i·cal·i·ty \grə¸mad·ə'kaləd·ē\ *n* **:** the quality or state of being grammatical

Gram·my \'gramē, -mi\ *service mark* — used for the annual presentation of a statuette for notable achievement in the recording industry

grand touring car *n* **:** a usu. 2-passenger coupe

granny dress *n* **:** a long loose-fitting dress usu. with high neck and long sleeves

granny glasses *n pl* **:** spectacles with usu. small oval, round, or square lenses and metal frames

gra·no·la \grə'nōlə\ *n* [fr. *Granola*, a former trademark] **:** rolled oats mixed with other ingredients (as brown sugar, raisins, coconut, or nuts) and used esp. as a breakfast food and health food

grants·man·ship \'gran(t)smən¸ship\ *n* **:** the art of obtaining grants of money (as for research projects) ⟨the only kinds of *grantsmanship* that . . . officials concede are effective are the literary virtues of clarity and succinctness. The art is more usually understood to mean dressing up an idea —Nicholas Wade⟩ — **grants·man** \-mən\ *n*

gra·num \'gränəm\ *n*, *pl* **gra·na** \-nə\ [NL, fr. L, grain] **:** one of the lamellar stacks of chlorophyll-containing material in plant chloroplasts

graphic*n* **1 :** a graphic representation displayed by a computer (as on a cathode-ray tube) **2 graphics** *pl but sing or pl in constr* **:** the process whereby a computer displays graphics and an operator can manipulate them (as with a light pen)

GRAS *abbr* generally recognized as safe

grasp*— **grasp the nettle :** to take positive and decisive steps to deal with a problem **:** take the bull by the horns ⟨the majority of them . . . exude nothing but a rather dismal pessimism. Only scientists seem to have *grasped the nettle* —Francis Crick⟩

grass*n* **:** marijuana

grass carp *n* **:** an herbivorous fish (*Ctenopharyngodon idella*) of Russia and mainland China that has been introduced elsewhere to control aquatic weeds — called also *white amur*

grasshopper*n* **:** a cocktail made with crème de menthe, crème de cacao, and usu. light cream

gravi·sphere \'gravə¸sfi(ə)r, -iə\ *n* [gravity + sphere] **:** the sphere of space in which the gravitational influence of a particular celestial body is predominant

grav·i·ta·tion·al collapse \¸gravə'tāshnəl-, -shənᵊl-\ *n* **:** the tendency of matter to move rapidly toward a common center of gravity that results in the formation of stars, star clusters, and galaxies from the dilute gas of interstellar space

gravitational interaction *n* **:** a weak fundamental interaction that is hypothesized to occur between elementary particles but that has been observed only on a scale larger than that hypothesized — compare ELECTROMAGNETIC INTERACTION, STRONG INTERACTION, WEAK INTERACTION

gravitational wave *n* **:** a hypothetical wave held to travel at the speed of light and to propagate the gravitational field

grav·i·ton \'gravə̇ˌtän\ *n* [ISV *gravity* + *-on* elementary particle] **:** a hypothetical particle with zero charge and rest mass that is held to be the quantum of the gravitational field

gravity wave*n **:** GRAVITATIONAL WAVE

grav·lax \'gravˌlaks\ *or* **grav·laks** *n* [Norw *gravlaks,* fr. *grav* buried + *laks* salmon; so called fr. being packed in salt] **:** salmon usu. cured with salt, black pepper, dill, and aquavit

gray*vi **:** to comprise an increasing percentage of older people ⟨the *graying* of America⟩

Gray Panther *n* [*gray* + *Panther* (as in *Black Panther*); fr. the fact that many elderly people have gray hair] **:** a member of an organization of militant elderly people

greaser*n **:** an aggressive swaggering young white male usu. of working-class background

green*vt **:** to rejuvenate or revitalize

Green Beret *n* [fr. the green beret worn as part of his uniform] **:** a member of the U.S. Army Special Forces

green–card·er \'grēnˌkärdər, -ˌkȧdə(r\ *n* [fr. the color of the work permit issued] **:** a foreign national with permission to work in the U.S.

green–fin·gered \'grēnˌfiŋgə(r)d\ *adj, chiefly Brit* **:** adept at growing plants

green goddess dressing *n* [*The Green Goddess* (1921) play by William Archer †1924 Scot. dramatist and critic] **:** a green salad dressing consisting of mayonnaise, sour cream, anchovies, chives, parsley, tarragon vinegar, and seasonings

greenhouse effect *n* **:** a warming of the lower layers of the atmosphere that tends to increase with increasing atmospheric carbon dioxide and that is caused by conversion of solar radiation into heat in a process involving selective transmission of short wave solar radiation by the atmosphere, its absorption by the earth's surface, and reradiation as infrared which is absorbed and partly reradiated back to the surface by carbon dioxide and water vapor in the air; *also* **:** a comparable warming of the lower layers of the atmosphere of a planet (as Venus) other than the Earth

greening*n **:** a restoration of freshness or vigor **:** revitalization, rejuvenation ⟨despite the warnings of those professional doomsayers . . . the signs are all of a continued linguistic *greening* —John Algeo⟩

green paper *n, often cap G&P, Brit* **:** a government document that discusses proposed approaches to a problem

green revolution *n* **:** the great increase in production of food grains (as rice, wheat, and maize) due to the introduction of high-yielding varieties, to the use of pesticides, and to better management techniques

grem·mie *also* **grem·my** \'gremē, -mi\ *n, pl* **grem·mies** [*gremlin* + *-ie,* dim. suffix] **:** a young or inexperienced surfer; *esp* **:** one whose behavior is objectionable — called also *gremlin*

grid*n **1 :** a network of conductors for the distribution of electric power; *also* **:** a network of radio or television stations **2 :** the starting positions of cars on a racecourse **3 :** a device (as of glass) in a photocomposer on which are located the characters to be exposed as the text is composed

gri·ot \'grē(ˌ)ō\ *n* [perh. fr. F, fr. native name in Gambia] **:** any of a class of musician-entertainers of West Africa whose performances include tribal histories and genealogies

grok \'gräk\ *vt* **grokked; grok·king** [coined 1961 in science fiction novel *Stranger in a Strange Land* by Robert A. Heinlein *b*1907 Am. author] **:** to understand profoundly and intuitively **:** establish deep compassionate rapport with ⟨finally they came to *grok* each other in their fullness —Bob Singer⟩

groove*vb **grooved; groov·ing** [fr. the phrase *in the groove*] *vt* **1 :** to enjoy appreciatively ⟨some dopey gals in the Village who would have *grooved* this combination of paint shop, cookery, and baby crap —Alexander King⟩ **2 :** to excite pleasurably ⟨*grooving* their minds with cannabis —Stephen Nemo⟩ ∼ *vi* **1 :** to enjoy oneself intensely **:** experience keen pleasure ⟨self-perception that informs you how and when to *groove* in your own way —Al Calloway⟩ ⟨if you don't feel like reading it, you can *groove* at the pictures —*Punch*⟩ **2 :** to interact harmoniously ⟨contemporary minds and rock *groove* together —Benjamin De Mott⟩

groove*n **:** an enjoyable, pleasurable, or exciting experience ⟨I found the theater a *groove* and a gas —Lee Marvin⟩

gross out *vt* **:** to offend, disgust, or insult by something gross ⟨could you move your socks . . . Because they smell outrageous. I mean, they're really *grossing* me *out* —Cyra McFadden⟩ ⟨cards . . . guaranteed to *gross out* your friends, enemies or friendly politician —*advt*⟩ — **gross-out** \'grōˌsau̇t\ *n*

grot·ty \'grätē, -äd·ē, -i\ *adj* **grot·ti·er; -est** [alter. (influenced by *rotten*) of *grotesque*] *chiefly Brit* **:** wretchedly shabby **:** of poor quality ⟨but, to some, simply seeing their work in print, however *grotty,* is better than it not appearing at all —John Cotton⟩

ground*vt **:** to throw (a football) intentionally to the ground to avoid being tackled for a loss

ground–ef·fect machine \ˌgrau̇ndə̇ˌfekt-, -ēˌfekt-\ *n* [fr. the support provided by the cushion of air as if the vehicle rode on the ground] **:** an air-cushion vehicle for traveling over land or water

ground·out \'grau̇nˌdau̇t\ *n* [*grounder* + *out*] **:** a play in baseball in which a batter is put out after hitting a grounder to an infielder ⟨retired on a *groundout* to second base⟩

group*n **:** a mathematical set that is closed under a binary associative operation and that has an identity element and an inverse for every element

grouper*n **:** one of a group of unrelated people who share a rented house (as at the seashore) ⟨in bumper-to-bumper procession over clogged highways to a seaside shack often shared with as many as a dozen other *groupers* — *Newsweek*⟩

group grope *n, slang* **:** a sex orgy ⟨live out their sexual fantasies in either single encounters or *group gropes* — *Newsweek*⟩

group·ie \'grüpē, -pi\ *n* [*group* + *-ie,* n. suffix] **1 :** a fan of a rock group who usu. follows the group around on concert tours ⟨*groupies,* who follow rock stars not to get their autographs but to get them into bed —Fred Sparks⟩ **2 :** a fan of a celebrity who attends as many of his or her appearances as possible ⟨a celebrity *groupie* who learned quickly that his grandfather's name gave him instant social entrance —Joe Eszterhas⟩

group theory *n* **:** a branch of mathematics concerned with finding all mathematical groups and determining their properties

group·think \'grüp,thiŋk\ *n* [*group* + *think* (as in *doublethink*)] **:** conformity to group values and ethics ⟨a product of *groupthink* and the bureaucrat's instinct to keep programs running no matter what the cost — Robert Gillette⟩

growth* *n* **:** anticipated progressive growth in capital value and income ⟨some investors may prefer *growth* to immediate income⟩

growth company *n* **:** a company that grows at a greater rate than the economy as a whole

grun·gy \'grənjē, -ji\ *adj* **grun·gi·er; -est** [origin unknown] **:** shabby or dirty in character or condition ⟨*grungy* old boots⟩ ⟨*grungy* bars⟩ ⟨every little town was clean and electrified and civilized — nothing like the *grungy* outposts —P.D. Young⟩ ⟨sprawls his long frame in a *grungy* office in the Legislature Buildings and reflects —Paul St. Pierre⟩

grunt* *n* **1 :** a U.S. army or marine foot soldier esp. in the Vietnam war ⟨officers often relied upon artillery strikes to do the killing and the *grunts* to do the counting after death —John Larsen⟩ **2 :** one who does routine unglamorous work ⟨not moving . . . because the union *grunts* won't be available to unload their cargo —L. L. King⟩

GT \,jē'tē\ *n* [*grand touring (car)*] **:** GRAND TOURING CAR

GTP \,jē(,)tē'pē\ *n* [*guanosine triphosphate*] **:** an energy-rich nucleoside triphosphate analogous to ATP that is composed of guanine linked to ribose and three phosphate groups and is necessary for the formation of peptide bonds during protein synthesis — called also *guanosine triphosphate*

G₂ phase \(')jē'tü-\ *n* [*growth*] **:** the period in the cell cycle from the completion of DNA replication to the beginning of cell division — compare G₁ PHASE, M PHASE, S PHASE

gua·neth·i·dine \gwä'nethə,dēn, -ədən\ *n* [*guanidine* + *ethyl*] **:** a synthetic guanidine derivative $C_{10}H_{22}N_4$ used esp. as the sulfate in treating severe high blood pressure

gua·no·sine mono·phos·phate \,gwänə,sēn,mä(,)nō-'fäs,fat, -,mō(,)nō-\ *n* [*mono-* containing one atom, radical, or group + *phosphate*] **:** CYCLIC GMP

guanosine tri·phos·phate \-(,)trī'fäs,fāt\ *n* **:** GTP

gua·nyl·ate cy·clase \,gwän³l,āt;si,klās, -āz\ *n* [*guanyl* + *-ate* derivative compound] **:** an enzyme that catalyzes the formation of cyclic GMP from GTP

guerrilla theater *n* **:** STREET THEATER

gull wing door *n* **:** an automobile door that is hinged at the top and that resembles an airplane gull wing when open

gun* *n* **:** a heavy surfboard that is usu. longer than a Malibu board, has a round nose and a tapered tail, and is usu. used in surf over 15 feet in height

gunboat diplomacy *n* **:** diplomacy backed by the use or threat of military force ⟨the restraints of nuclear deterrence, and of world public opinion, seem to have ended the effectiveness of *gunboat diplomacy* —H.S. Ashmore⟩

gun lap *n* **:** the final lap of a race in track signaled by the firing of a gun as the leader begins the lap

Gunn effect \'gən-\ *n* [J. B. *Gunn* b1928 Brit. physicist] **:** the production of rapid fluctuations of current when the voltage applied to a semiconductor device exceeds a critical value with the result that microwave power is generated

gun patch *n* **:** a patch so placed on a shirt or jacket as to be able to cushion the shoulder from the recoil of a rifle

gun·ship \'gən,ship\ *n* **:** an armed helicopter used esp. for protecting troop transport helicopters against ground fire ⟨hovering . . . *gunships* laced the weeds with rockets and .50-cal. bullets —*time*⟩

gus·sy up \,gəsē'əp\ *vt* **gus·sied up; gus·sy·ing up** \,gəs(ē)iŋ-\ [origin unknown] **:** to dress up ⟨women were thought to be more provocative of sinful deliberation if *gussied up* in snaps, bows and frills —Russell Baker⟩ ⟨the emphasis is on visual effect, and in *gussying up* form many architects sacrifice function —W.H. Whyte⟩

gut *adj* **1 :** arising from one's inmost self **:** visceral ⟨a *gut* reaction to the misery he has seen —J.A. Lukas⟩ **2 :** having strong impact or immediate relevance ⟨ordinary voters are likely to be moved by *gut* issues —Anthony Lewis⟩

gut course *n* [prob. fr. its being likened in softness to the belly] **:** a course (as in college) that is easily passed ⟨had planned to major in English because it is usually an innocuous, gentlemanly major which is made up of *gut courses* —*Williams Alumni Rev.*⟩

gut·si·ness \'gətsēnəs, -sin-\ *n* **:** the quality or state of being gutsy

guy* *n* **:** a person — used in pl. to refer to the members of a group regardless of sex ⟨saw her and the rest of the *guys*⟩

gyp·lure \'jip,lü(ə)r, -lür\ *n* [*gypsy* (moth) + *lure*] **:** a synthetic sex attractant used in trapping male gypsy moths

gyp·py tummy \,jipē-, -pi-\ *n* [*gyppy* alter. of *Egyptian;* fr. association of the illness with eating in a foreign country] **:** diarrhea

gyp·sum board \'jipsəm-\ *n* **:** wallboard with a center of gypsum plaster **:** plasterboard

gypsy cab *n* **:** a taxicab licensed only to answer calls; *esp* **:** such a cab that cruises in search of passengers

gy·ro \'zhi(ə)r(,)ō, 'ji(-, 'yi(-\ *n, pl* **gyros** [perh. fr. NGk *gyrō* rounded] **:** a sandwich esp. of lamb, tomato, and onion on pita bread

gy·ro·cop·ter \'jīrə,käptə(r)\ *n* [*autogyro* + *helicopter*] **:** a usu. one-passenger rotary-wing aircraft that is driven forward by a conventional propeller

H

ha·bit·u·ate*\hə'bichə,wāt, ha-\ *vi* **-at·ed; -at·ing :** to cause habituation ⟨marijuana may be *habituating*⟩

hack·ing pocket \'hakiŋ-\ *n* [fr. its use on hacking coats] **:** a slanted coat pocket usu. with a flap

ha·dal \'hād°l\ *adj* [F, fr. *Hadès* Hades + -*al*, adj. suffix] **:** of, relating to, or being the parts of the ocean below 6000 meters

had·ron \'ha,drän\ *n* [ISV *hadr*- thick, heavy (fr. Gk *hadros*) + -*on* elementary particle] **:** any one of the fundamental particles that take part in the strong interaction — **ha·dron·ic** \ha'dränik, -ēk\ *adj*

haf·nia \'hafnēə\ *n* [NL, fr. *hafnium* + -*a* oxide] **:** a white refractory crystalline oxide HfO_2 of hafnium

hail·er*\'hālə(r)\ *n* [short for *loud-hailer*] **:** a hand-held combined microphone and loudspeaker **:** a bullhorn

hair spray *n* **:** a preparation that is sprayed on the hair to keep it in place

hair·weav·ing \'ha(ə)r,wēviŋ, 'he(ə)r-\ *n* **:** the process of covering a bald spot with human hair and nylon thread woven into the wearer's own hair — **hair·weave** \-,wēv\ *n* — **hair weaver** *n*

ha·la·la *also* **ha·la·lah** \hə'lälə\ *n, pl* **halala** *or* **hala·las** [Ar] **1 :** a monetary unit of Saudi Arabia equal to $^1/_{100}$ riyal **2 :** a coin representing one halala

halfway house*n **:** a center for formerly institutionalized individuals (as mental patients or drug addicts) that is designed to facilitate their readjustment to private life

hal·lu·ci·nate*\hə'lüs°n,āt\ *vt* **-nat·ed; -nat·ing :** to perceive or experience as an hallucination ⟨the child tends to objectify strong but insubstantial experiences, as when he *hallucinates* an imaginary companion —Joseph Church⟩ — **hal·lu·ci·na·tor** \-,ād·ə(r), -,ātə-\ *n*

halo·car·bon \'halə,kärbən, -,káb-\ *n* [*halogen* + *carbon*] **:** any of various compounds of carbon and one or more halogens and sometimes also hydrogen

halo·cline \'halə,klīn\ *n* [*halo*- salt (deriv. of Gk *hals*) + -*cline* slope, deriv. of Gk *klinein* to lean] **:** a usu. vertical gradient in salinity

halo·per·i·dol \,halō'perə,dȯl, -,dōl\ *n* [*halogen* + *piperi*·dine + -*ol* compound containing hydroxyl] **:** a depressant $C_{21}H_{23}ClFNO_2$ of the central nervous system used esp. as an antipsychotic

halo·thane \'halə,thān\ *n* [*halogen* + *ethane*] **:** a nonexplosive inhalational anesthetic $C_2HBrClF_3$

ha·mate \'hā,māt\ *n* [*hamate* shaped like a hook, fr. L *hamatus*, fr. *hamus* hook] **:** a bone on the inner side of the second row of the carpus in mammals

hamstring* *or* **hamstring muscle** *n* **:** any of three muscles at the back of the thigh that function to flex and rotate the leg and extend the thigh

hand·job \'han,jäb\ *n, slang* **:** an act of stimulating the genitals manually usu. to orgasm

hand·print \'han(d),print\ *n* **:** an impression of a hand on a surface

hands–on \'han(d),zȯn, -,zän\ *adj* [*hands*- (as in *hands≠ off*) + *on*] **:** including or devoted to individual involvement in practical occupational activities ⟨combines fast≠ paced academic work with *hands-on* training for real jobs — Peter Janssen⟩

hand–wring·ing \'han,driŋiŋ\ *n* **:** an overwrought expression of concern or guilt ⟨the memoirs are elegantly free of *hand-wringing* and sighs —Robert Sherrill⟩

hang*vb **hung; hang·ing** *vt* **:** to throw (a breaking pitch) so that it fails to break properly ⟨*hung* a curve out there like an apple on a tree, and Shannon picked it off. The drive was a mile high and hit against the beer sign above the scoreboard —Ray Fitzgerald⟩ ∼ *vi, of a thrown ball* **:** to fail to break or drop as intended ⟨the pass *hung*, as the football buffs say, and [a defender] intercepted —W. N. Wallace⟩ — **hang five :** to ride a surfboard with the weight of the body forward and the toes of one foot turned over the front edge of the board — **hang in there :** to persist in the face of adversity **:** persevere ⟨became the dogged competitor, *hanging in there*, taking the bad shots . . . with the good ones —Theodore Solotaroff⟩ — **hang loose :** to remain calm **:** relax — **hang ten :** to ride a surfboard with the weight of the body forward and the toes of both feet turned over the front edge of the board — **hang tough :** to persist in the face of adversity ⟨at last we have a bunch in power who know how to *hang tough* and make a cover-up stick —William Safire⟩

hang glider *n* **:** a kitelike glider from which a harnessed rider hangs while gliding down from a cliff or hill — **hang gliding** *n*

hang–loose \'haŋ,lüs\ *adj* [fr. the verb phrase *hang loose*] **:** being highly informal, relaxed, unstructured, or uninhibited ⟨adherence to the hedonistic *hang-loose* ethic—Geoffrey Semmon & Grafton Trout⟩ ⟨it's a *hang≠ loose* outfit. Totally disorganized. Nobody knows which end is up —Beatrice Berg⟩

Hang·town fry \'haŋ,taún-\ *n, often cap F* [fr. *Hang·town*, nickname for a California town (perh. San Francisco)] **:** a scrambled egg dish or omelet containing fried oysters

hang–up*\'haŋ,əp\ *n* **:** a source of mental or emotional difficulty; *broadly* **:** a problem ⟨people were honest about their fears . . ., their *hang-ups*, their panic, their prejudices —Kate Millett⟩

ha·ni·wa \'hänə,wä\ *n, pl* **haniwa** [Jp] **:** a large baked clay figure usu. in the form of a hollow cylinder or a crude human figure customarily placed on early Japanese grave mounds

hanky–pank \'haŋkē,paŋk\ *n* **:** any of various carnival games in which contestants may win small prizes for the exercise of simple skills (as dart throwing)

hao \'haů\ n, pl hao [native name in Vietnam]   1 : a monetary unit of Vietnam equal to ¹/₁₀₀ dong   2 : a coin representing one hao

happening*n   1 : an event or series of events designed to evoke a spontaneous audience reaction to sensory, emotional, or spiritual stimuli   2 : something (as an event) that is particularly interesting, entertaining, or important ⟨the hearing is a *happening*, one of those unique events . . . which will be talked about for years — Douglas Kiker⟩

happy hour n : a period of time during which the prices of drinks at a bar or lounge are reduced or hors d'oeuvres are served gratis

hap·to·glo·bin \'haptə₂glōbən\ n [Gk *haptein* to fasten, bind + E connective -o- + hemo*globin*] : any of several carbohydrate-containing serum alpha globulins that can combine with free hemoglobin in the plasma and thereby prevent the loss of iron into the urine

hard*adj   1 : being at once addictive and gravely detrimental to health ⟨such *hard* drugs as heroin⟩   2 : resistant to biodegradation ⟨*hard* detergents⟩ ⟨*hard* pesticides like DDT⟩   3 : being, schooled in, or using the methods of one or more branches of mathematics, the life sciences, or the physical sciences ⟨a *hard* scientist⟩

hardball*n : forceful uncompromising methods employed to gain an end ⟨has no right to threaten an entire city because its mayor won't fall into line. That's political *hardball* at its roughest —*Los Angeles Times*⟩

hard copy n : copy (as that produced in connection with a computer) that is readable without use of a special device

hard–core \'härd₂ko(ə)r, -₂kò(ə)r; ₂hàd₂koə(r, -₂kò(ə)(r\ adj   1 : of, relating to, or being persons whose economic position and educational background are substandard and who experience chronic unemployment ⟨the major ills of our nation—rampant crime, inadequate educational systems, *hard-core* unemployment —G.R. Ford⟩   2 *of pornography* : containing explicit descriptions of sex acts or scenes of actual sex acts — compare SOFT-CORE

hard–edge \'härd₂ej, 'hàd-\ adj : of or relating to abstract painting characterized by geometric forms with clearly defined boundaries

hardened*adj : protected from possible danger from blast or heat by means of concrete or earth or by being situated underground ⟨a *hardened* missile launching site⟩ ⟨a *hardened* missile⟩

hard–hat \'härd₂hat, 'hàd-\ n   1 [fr. the fact that construction workers wear protective hard hats] : a construction worker   2 [fr. the fact that some construction workers are outspokenly opposed to nonconformists] : a conservative who is strongly opposed to nonconformists ⟨a *hardhat* type, mouthing prejudices about the young and the blacks and the freeloaders on welfare —*New Yorker*⟩

hard–line \-'₂līn\ adj : advocating a persistently firm course of action ⟨a *hard-line* policy toward polluters⟩ ⟨ran on a *hard-line* segregationist platform —*Current Biog.*⟩

hard–lin·er \-'līnə(r)\ n : an advocate of a hard-line policy ⟨accused of being simplistic *hard-liners* against even the most moderate demands —Jack Rosenthal⟩

hard rock n : rock 'n' roll in its original style marked by loudness and a steady insistent beat

hard ticket n : a reserved seat ticket

hardware*n   1 : the physical components (as electronic and electrical devices) of a vehicle (as a spacecraft) or an apparatus (as a computer)   2 : devices (as tape recorders, phonographs, and closed-circuit television) used as instructional equipment — compare SOFTWARE

hard·wired \₂härd₂wī(ə)rd; ₂hàd₂wīəd\ adj : being in the form of permanent electronic circuits ⟨an instruction repertoire . . . implemented in 400 *hardwired* specifics — *Datamation*⟩

Har·dy–Wein·berg \₂härdē'wīn₂bərg\ adj : of, relating to, or governed by the Hardy-Weinberg law ⟨*Hardy=Weinberg* equilibrium⟩

Hardy–Weinberg law n [G.H. *Hardy* †1947 Eng. mathematician and W. *Weinberg*, 20th cent. Ger. scientist] : a fundamental principle of population genetics: population gene frequencies and population genotype frequencies remain constant from generation to generation if mating is random and if mutation, selection, immigration, and emigration do not occur — called also *Hardy-Weinberg principle*

Ha·re Krish·na \₂härē'krishnə\ n, pl Hare Krishnas [fr. Hindi *hare* invocation of God + *Krishna* eighth avatar of Vishnu, one of the principal Hindu gods] : a member of a religious group dedicated to the worship of the Hindu god Krishna

Har·vey Wall·bang·er \₂här ve'wòl₂baŋər, ₂have-'wòl₂baŋə(r, -vi-\ n, pl Harvey Wallbangers [origin unknown] : a screwdriver with an Italian liqueur floated on top

hash \'hash\ n [short for *hashish*] : the unadulterated resin from the flowering tops of the female hemp plant (*Cannabis sativa*) : hashish

Ha·shi·mo·to's disease \₂häshē₂mōd·(₂)ōz-, -shi₂-\ also Hashimoto's thyroiditis or Hashimoto's struma n [Hakaru *Hashimoto* †1934 Jp. surgeon] : chronic thyroiditis characterized by goiter, thyroid fibrosis, infiltration of thyroid tissue by lymphoid tissue, and the production of autoantibodies that attack the thyroid

hassle*vt has·sled; has·sling : to subject to persistent or acute annoyance : harass ⟨we're still being *hassled* by male officials, and we still have to fight twice as hard as the men do to get fair treatment —Billie Jean King⟩

hatch·back \'hach₂bak\ n   1 : a back on a closed passenger automobile (as a coupe) having an upward-opening hatch   2 : an automobile having a hatchback

haul*vb — haul ass slang : to move quickly

haute cuisine \₂(h)ōtkwə'zēn, -kwē-\ n [F, lit., high cuisine] : a refined style of cooking marked by artful or elaborate methods of preparation ⟨a hotel dining room doesn't expect to be judged in terms of *haute cuisine* — New York⟩ ; *also* : food prepared in this style ⟨an artful combination of the crudest country food plus whatever *haute cuisine* he could obtain by cajolery rather than a large outlay of money —J.A. Michener⟩

Havana Brown n [*havana* (cigar)] : any of a breed of short-haired domestic cats developed in England and having a mahogany-brown coat and chartreuse eyes

Ha·var·ti \hə'värtē, -'vàt-, -i\ n [fr. *Havarti*, place name in Denmark] : a semisoft Danish cheese with a mild to sharp flavor

Hawaiian shirt n : a usu. short-sleeved sport shirt with a colorful pattern

hawk*n **:** one who takes a militant attitude (as in a dispute) and advocates immediate vigorous action — compare DOVE — **hawk·ish** \'hókish\ *adj* — **hawk·ish·ly** \-lē, -li\ *adv* — **hawk·ish·ness** \-nəs\ *n*

Haw·thorne effect \'hò,thórn-\ *n* [fr. the *Hawthorne Works* of the Western Electric Co., Cicero, Ill., where its existence was established by experiment] **:** the stimulation to increase output or accomplishment (as in an industrial or educational methods study) that results from the mere fact of being under concerned observation; *also* **:** such an increase in output or accomplishment

hay·lage \'hālij\ *n* [*hay* + si*lage*] **:** stored forage that is essentially grass silage wilted to 35 to 50 percent moisture

HC*abbr hard copy

head*n [short for *pothead* or *acidhead*] **:** one who uses a drug (as LSD or marijuana); *also* **:** an enthusiast or devotee ⟨chili *heads*⟩

head·count·er \'hed,kauntə(r)\ *n* **:** a pollster

head dip *n* **:** a surfing feat in which a surfer squats on the board, leans forward, and dips his head into the wave

head·er*\'hedə(r)\ *n* **1 :** a mounting plate through which electrical terminals pass from a sealed device (as a transistor) **2 :** a fall or dive head foremost ⟨took a *header* down the stairs⟩ **3 :** a shot or pass in soccer made by heading the ball **4 :** a word or series of words often in larger letters placed at the beginning of a passage or at the top of a page in order to introduce or categorize

headhunter*n **:** a recruiter of senior personnel (as executives for a corporation)

head·rest*\'hed,rest\ *n* **:** a resilient pad at the top of the back of an automobile seat esp. for preventing whiplash injury

head restraint *n* **:** HEADREST

head shop *n* [*head* drug user] **:** a shop that specializes in articles (as hashish pipes, incense, posters, and beads) of interest to drug users

head–trip \'hed,trip\ *n* [*head* + *trip* exciting experience] **:** an experience that affects the mind usu. in a stimulating or exhilarating way ⟨feminism has been the biggest *head=trip* I've ever gone through —Susan Brownmiller⟩

health food *n* **:** a food promoted as highly conducive to health

health maintenance organization *n* **:** an organization that provides health care to voluntarily enrolled individuals and families in a particular geographic area by organization physicians with limited referral to outside specialists and that is financed by fixed periodic payments determined in advance

health spa \-,spä, -,spò, -,spá\ *n* **:** a commercial establishment with facilities for assisting its patrons to lose weight — called also *fat farm*

heat*n, *slang* **:** the police ⟨didn't even know that the *heat* had busted a friend of mine until I read about it —Robert Courtney⟩

heat island *n* **:** an urban area in which significantly more heat is absorbed and retained (as by buildings and streets) than in surrounding areas

heat pipe *n* **:** a closed container in which a continuing cycle of evaporation and condensation of a fluid takes place with the heat being given off at the condenser end and which is more effective in transferring heat than a metallic conductor

heat pol·lu·tion \-pə'lüshən\ *n* **:** THERMAL POLLUTION

heat sink *n* **:** a substance or device for the absorption or dissipation of unwanted heat (as from a process or an electronic device)

heavy*adj **1 :** esp. strong in or esp. well furnished with **:** long — usu. used with *on* ⟨*heavy* on creative ideas and light on financial plans —Susan Davis⟩ **2 :** being or playing hard rock **3 :** important, prominent ⟨a *heavy* star unable to escape his groupies —Garry Wills⟩

heavy*n, *pl* **heavies** **1 :** someone or something influential, serious, or important ⟨aren't bold enough to match wits with the pedagogical *heavies* —Nancy B. Evans & Susan D. Fernandez⟩ **2 :** a muscleman or thug

heavy chain *n* **:** either of the two larger of the four polypeptide chains that comprise antibodies — compare LIGHT CHAIN

heavy metal *n* **:** energetic and highly amplified electronic rock music having a hard beat and usu. an element of the fantastic

hedge fund *n* **:** an investing group usu. in the form of a limited partnership that employs speculative techniques (as short selling and leverage) in the hope of obtaining large capital gains

Heim·lich maneuver \'hīmlik-\ *n* [Henry J. *Heimlich* b1920 Am. surgeon] **:** the manual application of sudden upward pressure on the upper abdomen of a choking victim to force a foreign object from the windpipe

hei·she \'hēshē\ *n* [Navajo, lit., shell] **:** a necklace made usu. by No. American Indians composed of disk-shaped shell or tubular silver beads

HeLa cell \'helə-\ *n* [*Helen Lane*, cancer victim who donated such cells in 1951] **:** a cell of a continuously cultured strain isolated from a human uterine cervical carcinoma in 1951 and used in biomedical research esp. to culture viruses

heli·borne \'helə,bō(ə)rn, 'hēl-, -,bò(ə)rn\ *adj* [*helicopter* + *borne*] **:** transported by helicopter ⟨*heliborne* troops⟩

he·lic·i·ty \he'lisəd-ē, hə-\ *n*, *pl* **-ties** [*helic-* helix + *-ity* state, quality] **1 :** the motion of a particle about an axis parallel to its direction of motion **2 :** the component of the spin of a particle in its direction of motion measured in quantum units of spin **3 a :** the quality or state of being helical ⟨the degree of *helicity* in a protein⟩ **b :** the amount or degree of helical curve ⟨a prediction of *helicity* from amino acid sequence⟩

heli·lift \'helə,lift, 'hēl-\ *vt* [*helicopter* + *lift*] **:** to transport (troops) by helicopter

heli·pad \-,pad\ *n* **:** a landing and takeoff surface for helicopters

heli·spot \-,spät\ *n* **:** a temporary landing surface for helicopters

heli·stop \-,stäp\ *n* **:** a place to land helicopters **:** heliport

he·li·um–4 \,hēlēəm'fō(ə)r, -'fò(ə)r, -'fōə, -'fòə\ *n* **:** the most common isotope of helium having the mass number four

helium–3 \-'thrē\ *n* **:** the isotope of helium having the mass number three

hemi·cho·lin·ium \,hemēkō'linēəm, -mək-, -,mīk-\ *n* [*hemi-* half in respect to combining ratio + *choline* + *-ium* chemical radical] **:** any of several blockers of the parasympathetic nervous system that interfere with the synthesis of acetylcholine

Hem·ing·way·esque \,hemin,wā,esk\ *adj* [Ernest Miller *Hemingway* †1961 Am. writer] **:** of, relating to, or suggestive of Ernest Hemingway or his writings ⟨striving for a kind of *Hemingwayesque* elemental truth amid the sun‡drenched walls and deep interior shadows of an endlessly picturesque Spain —Roger Greenspun⟩ ⟨evolved what we thought was a *Hemingwayesque* fatalism—this mainly involved consuming a lot of beer, as I recall — R.R. Lingeman⟩

he·mo·di·al·y·sis \ˌhēmōdīˈaləsəs, ˌhemō-\ *n* [*hemo*-blood (deriv. of Gk *haima*) + *dialysis*] **:** the process of removing blood (as of a kidney patient) from an artery, purifying it by dialysis, adding vital substances, and re-turning it to a vein

hemoglobin S *n* [*sickle* cell] **:** a hemoglobin that occurs in the red blood cells in sickle-cell anemia and sickle-cell trait

he·pa·to·bil·i·ary \həˌpad·əˈbilēˌerē, ˈhepəd-ō-\ *adj* [*hepato*- liver and + *biliary*] **:** of, relating to, situated in or near, produced in, or affecting the liver and bile, bile ducts, and gallbladder ⟨*hepatobiliary* disease⟩

he·pa·to·cyte \həˈpad·əˌsit, ˈhepəd·ə-\ *n* [*hepato*- liver (deriv. of Gk *hēpat-, hēpar*) + *-cyte* cell, deriv. of Gk *kytos* hollow vessel] **:** an epithelial parenchymatous cell of the liver

hep·a·top·a·thy \ˌhepəˈtäpəthē\ *n, pl* **-thies** [*hepato*- + *-pathy* disease] **:** an abnormal or diseased state of the liver

hep·a·to·tox·ic·i·ty \ˌhepəd·ō‚täkˈsisəd·ē\ *n, pl* **-ties** **1** **:** a state of toxic damage to the liver **2** **:** capacity to cause hepatotoxicity

hep·a·to·tox·in \ˈhepəd·ōˈtäksən\ *n* [*hepato*- + *toxin*] **:** a substance toxic to the liver

her·ma·typ·ic \ˌhərməˈtipik\ *adj* [Gk *herma* prop, reef + E *typ*- (fr. Gk *typtein* to strike, coin) + *-ic* relating to] **:** building reefs ⟨*hermatypic* corals⟩

Her·mi·tian matrix \erˈmēshən-, (ˌ)hərˈmish-\ *n* [Charles Hermite †1901 Fr. mathematician] **:** a square matrix having the property that each pair of elements comprised of one in the *i*th row and *j*th column and the other in the *j*th row and *i*th column are conjugate com-plex numbers

her·pes·vi·rus \ˈhərˌpēzˈvīrəs\ *n* **:** any of a group of DNA-containing viruses that replicate in cell nuclei and produce herpes

¹het·ero \ˈhed·ə(ˌ)rō\ *adj* [short for *heterosexual*] **:** being heterosexual ⟨find that heterosexual marriages are as mis-erable as *hetero* ones —Rosalyn Regelson⟩

²hetero *n, pl* **-eros** **:** one who is heterosexual ⟨no more of a security risk than the *heteros* around him —Tom Wicker⟩

het·ero·at·om \ˈhed·ərōˈad·əm\ *n* [*hetero*- different (deriv. of Gk *heteros*) + *atom*] **:** an atom other than car-bon in the ring of a heterocyclic compound

het·ero·nym \ˈhed·ərəˌnim, -ə(ˌ)rōˌn-\ *n* [*heter*- other, different + *-onym* word] **:** one of two or more homo-graphs that differ in pronunciation and meaning (as a *bass* voice and *bass*, a fish)

het·ero·poly·sac·cha·ride \ˈhed·ərōˌpäleˈsakəˌrīd\ *n* [*hetero*- different, different kinds + *polysaccharide*] **:** a polysaccharide consisting of more than one type of monosaccharide

het·ero·sex \ˈhed·ərōˌseks\ *n* [short for *heterosexuality*] **:** the quality or state of being heterosexual **:** heterosexual-ity

het·ero·sex·ism \ˈhed·ərōˌsek‚sizəm\ *n* [*hetero*- + *sex-ism*] **:** discrimination or prejudice by heterosexuals against homosexuals — **het·ero·sex·ist** \-ˈseksəst\ *adj*

heu·ris·tic\hyüˈristik, -ēk\ *n* **:** a heuristic method or procedure

hexa·dec·i·mal \ˈheksəˈdes(ə)məl\ *adj* [alter. (influ-enced by *hexa*- six, fr. Gk *hex*) of *sexadecimal*] **:** of, relat-ing to, utilizing, or being a system of numbers having 16 as a base

hexa·meth·y·lene·tet·ra·mine \ˈheksəˌmethəˌlēnˈte-·trəˌmēn, -əmən\ *n* [ISV, fr. *hexa*- + *methylene* + *tetramine*] **:** a crystalline compound $C_6H_{12}N_4$ used esp. as an accelerator in vulcanizing rubber, as an absorbent for phosgene, and as a diuretic

hex·os·a·min·i·dase \ˌhekˌsäsəˈminəˌdās, -āz\ *n* [*hexos-amine* + *-ide* acetal derivative of a sugar + *-ase* enzyme] **:** either of two hydrolytic enzymes that catalyze the split-ting off of a hexose from a ganglioside and are deficient in some metabolic diseases (as a variant of Tay-Sachs dis-ease)

hick·ey\ˈhikē, -ki\ *n, pl* **hickeys** [*hickey* pimple, of unknown origin] **:** a temporary red mark produced in lovemaking by biting and sucking the skin

hidden tax *n* **:** a tax exacted from a person other than the one on whom the ultimate burden of the tax is expected to fall **:** an indirect tax

high–energy \ˈhīˈenə(r)jē, -ji\ *adj* **1 a :** having such speed and kinetic energy as to exhibit relativistic depar-ture from classical laws of motion — used esp. of elemen-tary particles whose velocity has been imparted by an accelerator **b :** of or relating to high-energy particles ⟨a *high-energy* reaction⟩ **2 :** yielding a relatively large amount of energy when undergoing hydrolysis ⟨*high-energy* phosphate bonds in ATP⟩ **3 :** dynamic ⟨*high-energy* music⟩ ⟨a *high-energy* barrage of tales —John Jus-tice⟩

high energy physics *n* **:** physics that deals with the constitution, properties, and interactions of elementary particles as revealed by experiments involving particle accelerators

highflier*n* **:** a stock whose price rises much more rap-idly than the market average

high hat*or **hi–hat** \ˈhīˌhat\ *n* **:** a pair of cymbals oper-ated by a foot pedal

high·light·er \ˈhīˌlīd·ə(r)\ *n* **:** a cosmetic for highlighting facial features

¹high–rise \ˈhīˈrīz\ *adj* **1 :** being multistory and equipped with elevators ⟨*high-rise* buildings⟩ **2 :** of, relating to, or characterized by high-rise buildings ⟨a *high-rise* district⟩ **3 a :** of, relating to, or being extra‡long bicycle handlebars **b :** being a bicycle equipped with high-rise handlebars

²high–rise *n* **:** a high-rise building

high–ris·er \-ə(r)\ *n* **1 :** HIGH-RISE **2 :** a high-rise bicycle

high tech \ˈhīˈtek\ *n* **1 :** a style of interior decoration in which industrial products, materials, or designs are ap-propriated or adapted for use in the home **2 :** HIGH TECHNOLOGY

high technology *n* **:** technology using or involving the use of sophisticated methods or devices

hi·jack \ˈhīˌjak\ *n* **:** an instance of hijacking

Hil·bert space \‚hilbə(r)t-\ *n* [David *Hilbert* †1943 Ger. mathematician] **:** a vector space for which a scalar product is defined and in which every Cauchy sequence composed of elements in the space converges to a limit in the space

Himalayan*n **:** any of a breed of domestic cats developed by crossing the Persian and the Siamese and having the stocky build and long thick coat of the former and the blue eyes and coat patterns of the latter

hip*n **:** HIPNESS ⟨a spiritual hustler, the Elmer Gantry of *hip* —Tim Cahill⟩

hip–hug·gers \'hip‚həgə(r)z\ *n pl* **:** low-slung usu. close‑fitting trousers that rest on the hips

hip·ness \'hipnəs\ *n* **:** the quality or state of being hip ⟨remarks intended to show his *hipness* —Jack Kerouac⟩

hip·pie *or* **hip·py** \'hipē, -pi\ *n, pl* **hippies** [*hip* + *-ie*, *n*. suffix] **:** a young person who rejects the mores of established society (as by dressing unconventionally or favoring communal living) and adheres to a nonviolent ethic; *broadly* **:** a long-haired unconventionally dressed young person

hip·pie·dom \'hipēdəm, -pid-\ *n* [*hippie* + *-dom* realm, area, group of people] **:** the world of hippies ⟨a tribal rock 'n' roll musical about *hippiedom* —Lewis Funke⟩

hip–pocket *adj* **:** of small size or scope ⟨range from large . . . companies to *hip-pocket* operations —Jo Thomas⟩

hip·ster·ism \'hipstə‚rizəm\ *n* **1 :** HIPNESS **2 :** the way of life characteristic of hipsters

His·pan·ic \(')hi‚spanik\ *n* **:** an American of Spanish or esp. Latin-American descent

his·to·com·pat·i·bil·i·ty \‚hi(‚)stōkəm‚pad-ə'biləd-ē\ *n* [*histo-* tissue (deriv. of Gk *histos* mast, loom, beam, web) + *compatibility*] **:** a state of mutual tolerance between tissues that permits one to be grafted effectively to the other — **his·to·com·pat·i·ble** \-kəm'pad-əbəl\ *adj*

his·to·phys·i·o·log·i·cal \-‚fizēə'läjəkəl\ *or* **his·to·phys·i·o·log·ic** \-'läjik\ *adj* **:** of or relating to histophysiology

hit**vb** —**hit the fan :** to have a major usu. undesirable impact ⟨eventually, of course, the facts . . . began *hitting the fan* through reports by the press —Robert Claiborne⟩

hit*n **1 :** a single dose of a narcotic drug ⟨the junkie is relatively cool between *hits* —Jonathan Black⟩ **2 :** a premeditated murder usu. committed by a member of a crime syndicate ⟨setting up *hits* . . . during the family wars of Prohibition —*Newsweek*⟩

Hitch·cock·ian \(')hich‚käkēən, -kyən\ *adj* [Alfred Joseph *Hitchcock* †1980 Am. (Eng.-born) motion-picture director] **:** of, relating to, or suggestive of the cinematic style or technique of Alfred Hitchcock ⟨production has just the right escalating *Hitchcockian* panic —Michael Billington⟩

hit list *n* **:** a list esp. of persons or programs to be opposed or eliminated ⟨put on their *hit list* for the next senatorial elections —L. H. Gelb⟩

hit man *n* [*hit* murder] **1 :** a professional assassin who works for a crime syndicate ⟨reported that the shootings were done by professional mob *hit men* —Buddy Nevins⟩ **2 :** a hatchet man

HMO \‚ā(‚)chem'ō\ *n* **:** HEALTH MAINTENANCE ORGANIZATION

hoa·gie *also* **hoa·gy** \'hōgē\ *n, pl* **hoagies** [origin unknown] **:** a large sandwich made from a long roll split and generously filled (as with cold cuts, cheese, onion, lettuce, and tomato)

ho·dad \'hō‚dad\ *n* [perh. alter. of *hodag*, a mythical animal noted for its ugliness] **:** a nonsurfer who frequents surfing beaches and pretends to be a surfer

hoi·sin sauce \‚hói‚s(h)in-\ *n* [Chin *hai shan* delicacy of the sea, fr. *hai*[3] sea + *shan*[4] provisions] **:** a thick reddish sauce of soybeans, spices, and garlic used in oriental cookery

hold*n **:** a delay in a countdown (as in launching a missile)

holding pattern *n* **1 :** a usu. oval course flown (as over an airport) by aircraft awaiting clearance to land ⟨New York is a multi-layered traffic tangle: in the air (a two‑hour *holding pattern*) —Robert Craft⟩ **2 :** a state of waiting or suspended activity

ho·lid·ic \hä'lidik, hō'-\ *adj* [*hol-* complete, total (deriv. of Gk *holos* whole) + *-idic* (as in *meridic*)] **:** having the active constituents chemically defined ⟨*holidic* diets⟩ — compare MERIDIC, OLIGIDIC

holism*n **:** a holistic study or method of treatment

ho·lis·tic* \hō'listik\ *adj* **:** relating to or concerned with wholes or with complete systems rather than with the analysis of, treatment of, or dissection into parts ⟨*holistic* medicine attempts to treat both the mind and the body⟩ ⟨*holistic* ecology views man and the environment as a single system⟩

Hol·ler·ith \'hälə‚rith\ *n* [Herman *Hollerith* †1929 Am. engineer] **:** code for representing alphanumeric information on punch cards — called also *Hollerith code*

Hollerith card *n* **:** a punch card for data processing

holocaust*n **1 :** a great slaughter; *specif, often cap* **:** the genocidal slaughter of European Jews by the Nazis during World War II **2 :** a disaster ⟨turn an ordinary matrimonial civil war into an explosive do-or-die end-of-the‑world *holocaust* —J. A. Ornstein⟩ — **ho·lo·caus·tal** \‚hälə‚kòst°l, ‚hōl- *also* ‚hòl- *or* -‚käst-\ *adj*

ho·lo·gram \'hälə‚gram, 'hōl-\ *n* [*holo-* complete, total (deriv. of Gk *holos* whole) + *-gram* drawing, writing, record, deriv. of Gk *gramma* letter, writing] **:** a three-dimensional picture produced in the form of an interference pattern on a photographic film or plate without use of a lens by two beams of coherent light (as from a laser) so that for reconstruction of the image the pattern is viewed by coherent light passing through the film or plate

ho·lo·graph \-‚graf\ *n* [*holo-* + *-graph* something written, deriv. of Gk *graphein* to write] **:** HOLOGRAM

ho·log·ra·phy \hə'lägrəfē, hō-, -fi\ *n* **:** the process of making or using a hologram — **holograph** *vt* — **ho·lo·graph·ic** \‚hälə'grafik, ‚hō-, -ēk\ *adj* — **ho·lo·graph·i·cal·ly** \-k(ə)lē, -li\ *adv*

home free \‚hōm'frē\ *adj* **:** being out of jeopardy **:** in a comfortable position with respect to some objective ⟨knew . . . that he had a hit and was *home free* —Martin Kasindorf⟩

home screen *n* **:** television

home stand *n* **:** a series of baseball games played at a team's home field

home·stay \'hōm‚stā\ *n* **:** a period during which a visiting foreign student lives in the home of a host family

hom·i·ni·za·tion \‚hämənə̇zāshən, -‚nī-\ *n* [*homin-* human (fr. L *homin-*, *homo* human being) + *-ization* making] **1 :** the evolutionary development of human charac‑

teristics that differentiate man from his primate ancestors **2 :** the process of altering the environment and adapting it to the uses of human beings

hom·i·nized \'hämə,nīzd\ *adj* **:** characterized by hominization

hommos *var of* HUMMUS

ho·moe·ol·og·ous \,hōmē'äləgəs, ,häm-\ *adj* [*homoe*-similar + hom*ologous*] **:** of similar genic constitution — used of chromosomes believed to have been completely homologous in an ancestral form — **ho·moeo·logue** *or* **ho·moeo·log** \'hōmēə,lóg, 'häm-, -,läg\ *n*

ho·mo·ge·ne·ity* \,hōməjə'nēəd·ē, ,hä-, -(,)mōj-, -'nāə-, ÷-'nīə-\ *n* **:** the state of having identical distribution functions or values ⟨a test for *homogeneity* of variances⟩ ⟨*homogeneity* of two statistical populations⟩

Ho·mo ha·bi·lis \,hō(,)mō'habələs\ *n* [NL, fr. L *homo* man + *habilis* skillful, handy] **:** an extinct primate that is known from eastern African fossil remains associated with crude tools, is believed to have flourished some two million years ago, and is variously interpreted as the earliest true man or an australopithecine

ho·mo·mor·phism* \,hōmə'mòr,fizəm, ,häm-\ *n* **:** a mapping of a mathematical group, ring, or vector space into or onto another set or itself in such a way that the result obtained by applying an operation to elements of the domain is mapped onto the result obtained by applying the same or a corresponding operation to their images in the range

¹ho·mo·phile \'hōmə,fīl\ *adj* [*homo*sexual + *-phile* loving, deriv. of Gk *philos* beloved, loving] **:** oriented toward and concerned with the rights or welfare of the homosexual; *also* **:** being homosexual

²homophile *n* **:** one who is homosexual

ho·mo·pho·bia \,hōmə'fōbēə\ *n* [*homo*sexual + *phobia*] **:** irrational fear of homosexuality or homosexuals — **ho·mo·pho·bic** \-bik, -bēk\ *adj*

ho·mo·sex \'hōmə,seks\ *n* [short for *homosexuality*] **:** the quality or state of being homosexual **:** homosexuality

hon·cho \'hän(,)chō\ *n, pl* **honchos** [Jp *hanchō* squad leader, fr. *han* squad + *chō* head, chief] **:** someone in charge **:** a boss or leader ⟨the Democrats' big *honchos* believe they need a woman on the ticket this year — Michael Kramer⟩; *also* **:** a showily skillful person **:** hotshot ⟨every other slick guitar *honcho* in the city was looking to jam with you —Tim Cahill⟩ ⟨the spotlight is on today's young *honcho* film makers —Richard Boeth⟩

honest broker *n* **:** a neutral mediator ⟨his role has been rather that of the *honest broker*, in conformity with the conception of positive neutrality —*Times Lit. Supp.*⟩

honey bucket *n* **:** a bucket for collecting human excrement

honey wagon *n* **1 :** a vehicle for transporting human excrement **2 :** a portable outdoor toilet

hon·ky *or* **hon·kie** *also* **hon·key** \'hòŋkē, 'hä-, -ki\ *n, pl* **honkies** [origin unknown] **:** a white man — usu. used disparagingly

hook* *n* **:** a distinctive catchy musical or literary device ⟨trick is to find some sonic *hook* that will galvanize dancers on the floor —*Newsweek*⟩

hook up* *vi* **:** to become associated esp. in a working or social relationship ⟨moved here and *hooked up* with three musicians from the city —Robert Palmer⟩

hootch *or* **hooch** \'hüch\ *n* [modif. of Jp *uchi* house] **:** a thatched hut esp. in Vietnam; *broadly* **:** a house, dwelling, or barracks

hopefully* *adv* **:** it is hoped **:** we hope ⟨procedures which would *hopefully* lead to the resolution of the more important substantive issue —*AAUP Bull.*⟩ ⟨to get good or (*hopefully*) rave reviews —H.C. Schonberg⟩ ⟨this mask might, *hopefully*, become indistinguishable from what one actually was —S.N. Behrman⟩ ⟨*hopefully* better coordinated and more effective programs may result — N.M. Pusey⟩

horse's ass *n* **:** a stupid or incompetent person **:** blockhead — often considered vulgar

HO scale \(')ā,chō-\ *n* [fr. its fitness for rails of HO gage] **:** a scale of 3.5 millimeters to one foot used esp. for model toys (as automobiles or trains)

hospice* *n* **:** a facility or program providing for the physical and emotional needs of the terminally ill and often of their families

hospitality suite *n* **:** a room or suite esp. in a hotel set aside as a place for socializing usu. in connection with a business meeting or convention

host plant *n* **:** a plant upon which an organism (as an insect or mildew) lodges and subsists

hot* *adj* **hot·ter; hot·test** **:** being full of detail and information and requiring little or no involvement of the listener, viewer, or reader ⟨distinguishes a *hot* medium like radio . . . from a cool one like TV —H.M. McLuhan⟩

hot comb \'hät,kōm\ *n* **:** a metal comb usu. electrically heated for straightening or styling the hair

hot damn \'hät'dam\ *interj* — usu. used to express pleasant surprise ⟨*hot damn*, that was a good audience out there —Steve Miller⟩

hot dog* *n* **:** one that hotdogs; *also* **:** a show-off

hot·dog \'hät,dòg, *sometimes* -,däg\ *vi* **-dogged; -dog·ging** [prob. fr. *hot dog*, exclamation of approval or gratification] **:** to perform in a conspicuous or often ostentatious manner; *esp* **:** to perform fancy stunts and maneuvers (as when surfing or skiing) — **hot·dog·ger** \-ə(r)\ *n* — **hotdogging** *n*

hotel china *n* [fr. its capacity to withstand the hard use typically met with in hotels] **:** a high-fired well-vitrified American ceramic ware approaching hard-paste porcelain in composition

hot line *n* **1 :** a direct telephone line in constant readiness to operate so as to facilitate immediate communication (as between heads of two governments) **2 :** a telephone service by which usu. unidentified callers can talk confidentially about personal problems to a sympathetic listener ⟨drug-counseling services, some with around-the-clock "crisis" *hot lines* —R.D. McFadden⟩

hot pants* *n pl* **:** very short shorts

hots \'häts\ *n pl* **:** strong sexual desire — used with *the* ⟨about a young girl . . . with the *hots* for gypsy-dark men —H.C. Veit⟩

hot shit *n* **:** a showily skillful person **:** hotshot; *also* **:** someone or something unusually good **:** hot stuff — usu. considered vulgar

hot shoe *n* **:** a receptacle on a camera that provides a point of attachment and electrical contact for an electronic flash lamp

hot tub \'hät,təb\ *n* **:** a large usu. wooden tub of hot water in which bathers soak and usu. socialize

hot–wire \'hät'wī(ə)r, -'wīə\ *vt* **:** to short-circuit the wires of (an automotive vehicle or its ignition system) in order to start the engine without using a key

house·hus·band \'haus'hȯzbənd\ *n* **:** a husband who does housekeeping usu. while his wife earns the family income

house nigger *n* **:** a Negro having a humble and submissive attitude or philosophy — used disparagingly

house sitter *n* **:** a person who occupies a dwelling to provide security and maintenance while the tenant is away — **house–sit** \'haus'sit\ *vi* — **house–sit·ting** \-'sid·iŋ\ *n*

Hub·ble constant \'həbəl-\ *n* [Edwin P. *Hubble* †1953 Am. astronomer] **:** a proportionality constant used in relating the apparent velocity of recession of a distant galaxy and its distance so that a greater rate of recession indicates a greater distance

Hu·go \'(h)yügō\ *n, pl* **Hugos** [*Hugo* Gernsback †1967 Am. (Luxembourg-born) author, inventor, and publisher] **:** any of several trophies awarded annually by a professional organization for notable achievement in science-fiction writing

hum·mus \'həməs\ *also* **hom·mos** \'həm-, 'häm-\ *n* [perh. fr. Ar *hummuṣ* chick-pea] **:** a paste of pureed chick- peas usu. mixed with sesame oil or sesame paste and eaten as a dip or sandwich spread

hu·mon·gous \(h)yü'məŋgəs, -'mäŋ-\ *or* **hu·mun·gous** \-'məŋ-\ *adj* [alter. of *huge* + *tremendous*] *slang* **:** extremely large **:** huge

hung \'həŋ\ *adj* **:** having a large penis

hunger*n* — **from hunger :** very bad **:** inferior, poor ⟨they were strictly patchwork and strictly *from hunger* — A.J. Daley⟩

hung up*adj* **1 :** having a hang-up **:** anxious ⟨don't know why women have to be so *hung up* about age — Pauline Kael⟩ **2 :** being much involved with: as **a :** infatuated ⟨they get *hung up* on some fellow here —Jeff Brown⟩ **b :** enthusiastic ⟨people who are *hung up* on French Provincial —Walter Goodman⟩ **c :** preoccupied ⟨*hung up* on winning⟩

hunting*n* **1 :** a periodic variation in speed of a synchronous electrical machine from that of the true synchronous speed **2 :** a self-induced and undesirable oscillation of a variable above and below the desired value in an automatic control system **3 :** a continuous attempt by an automatically controlled system to find a desired equilibrium condition

hutzpah *or* **hutzpa** *var of* CHUTZPAH

hwyl \'hüil\ *n* [W] *Brit* **:** fervor, excitement

hybrid computer *n* **:** a computer system consisting of a combination of analog and digital computer systems

hy·brid·oma \‚hī(‚)brid'ōmə\ *n* [*hybrid* + *-oma* tumor] **:** a hybrid cell produced by the fusion of an antibody- producing lymphocyte with a tumor cell and used to continously culture a specific antibody of a single molecular species

hy·dra·tase \'hīdrə‚tās, -‚drād-‚ās, -āz\ *n* [*hydrate* + *-ase* enzyme] **:** any of several lyases that catalyze the hydration or dehydration of a carbon-oxygen bond

hy·dro*\'hī(‚)drō\ *n, pl* **hydros** [short for *hydroplane*] **:** a speedboat with hydrofoils or a stepped bottom so that the hull will rise wholly or partly out of the water as the boat attains speed **:** a hydroplane

hy·dro·acous·tic \‚hī(‚)drōə'küstik\ *adj* [*hydro-* water (deriv. of Gk *hydōr*) + *acoustic*] **1 :** of or relating to the production of acoustic energy from the flow of fluids under pressure **2 :** of or relating to the transmission of sound in water

hy·dro·bi·ol·o·gist \-(‚)bī'äləjȯst\ *n* **:** a specialist in hydrobiology

hy·dro·chlo·ro·thi·a·zide \‚hīdrə‚klōrə'thīə‚zīd\ *n* [*hydrogen* + *chlor*ine + *thiazide*] **:** a diuretic and antihypertensive drug $C_7H_8ClN_3O_4S_2$

hy·dro·crack \'hī(‚)drō'krak\ *vt* [*hydrogen* + *crack*] **:** to crack (hydrocarbons) in the presence of hydrogen

hy·dro·crack·er \-ə(r)\ *n* **:** an apparatus for hydrocracking

hy·dro·dy·nam·i·cist \‚hīdrōdī'naməsȯst\ *n* **:** one who specializes in hydrodynamics

hy·dro·foil*\'hīdrə‚fȯil\ *n* **:** a motorboat that has metal plates or fins attached by struts fore and aft so that they act in water as airplane wings do in air and lift the hull a short distance above the water

hy·dro·gas·i·fi·ca·tion \‚hīdrō‚gasəfə'kāshən\ *n* [*hydrogen* + *gasification*] **:** the process of reacting hydrogen or a mixture of steam and hydrogen with coal at high temperature and high pressure so that the carbon in the coal reacts directly or indirectly to produce methane used for fuel — **hy·dro·gas·i·fi·er** \-'gasə‚fī(ə)r\ *n*

hy·dro·mag·net·ic \-(‚)mag'ned·ik\ *adj* [*hydro-* water, liquid + *magnetic*] **1 :** of or relating to phenomena arising from the motion of electrically conducting fluids in the presence of electric and magnetic fields **2 :** being a wave in an electrically conducting fluid immersed in a magnetic field

hy·dro·mag·net·ics \-iks\ *n pl but sing in constr* **:** a branch of physics that deals with hydromagnetic phenomena

hy·dro·naut \'hīdrə‚nȯt, -nät\ *n* [*hydro-* water + *-naut* (as in *astronaut*)] **:** a member of the crew of a deep-sea vehicle (as a bathyscaphe) other than a submarine

hy·dro·nau·tics \(‚)hīdrə'nȯd·iks, -‚näd-\ *n pl but sing in constr* [*hydro-* + *-nautics* (as in *aeronautics*)] **:** the science of constructing and operating marine craft and instruments designed to explore the ocean environment

hy·dron·ic \hī'dränik\ *adj* [*hydro-* + *-onic* (as in *electronic*)] **:** of, relating to, or being a system of heating or cooling that involves transfer of heat by a circulating fluid in a closed system of pipes — **hy·dron·i·cal·ly** \-nək(ə)lē\ *adv*

hy·dron·ics \-niks\ *n pl but usu sing in constr* **:** a hydronic system

hydroplane*vi, of a vehicle or tire* **:** to ride supported by a film of water on a wet surface when a critical speed is reached and when the lift between the tire and the pavement exceeds the weight riding on the tire with a resultant loss of directional stability and braking effectiveness

hy·dro·skim·mer \'hīdrō‚skimə(r)\ *n* **:** an air-cushion vehicle for use over water

hy·dro·space \-‚spās\ *n* **:** the regions beneath the surface of the ocean

hy·dro·treat \-‚trēt\ *vt* [*hydrogen* + *treat*] **:** to subject to hydrogenation ⟨*hydrotreat* lube oil⟩ — **hy·dro·treat·er** \-‚trēd-ə(r)\ *n*

hy·dro·trope \'hīdrə‚trōp\ *n* [back-formation fr. *hydrotropic*] **:** a hydrotropic substance

hy·droxo·co·bal·amin \hī¦dräksə(¸)kō'baləmən, -(¸)sō-\ *n* [*hydroxyl* + connective -*o*- + *cobalamin* member of the vitamin B₁₂ group] **:** a member C₆₂H₈₉CoN₁₃O₁₅P of the vitamin B₁₂ group used in treating and preventing B₁₂ deficiency

hy·droxy·ly·sine \hī¦dräksə¸lī¸sēn\ *n* [*hydroxy* containing *hydroxyl* + *lysine*] **:** an amino acid C₆H₁₄N₂O₃ that is found esp. in collagen

hy·droxy·urea \(¦)hī¸dräksēyù'rēə, -si-\ *n* [*hydroxyl* + *urea*] **:** an antineoplastic agent CH₄N₂O₂ used esp. to treat some forms of leukemia

hype*\'hīp\ *n* [*hype* hypodermic] **1 :** something intended to deceive **:** a deception ⟨had come upon some way I could work a *hype* on the penal authorities — Malcolm X⟩ **2 :** extravagant promotional advertising ⟨the premiere . . . ended weeks of calculated frenzy, hoopla and *hype* —Judy Klemesrud⟩ ⟨*hype* was artfully elevated by Barnum to the level of entertainment —James Childs⟩

hype *vt* **hyped; hyp·ing 1 :** to put on **:** mislead, deceive ⟨no hustler could have it known that he'd been *hyped* —Malcolm X⟩ **2 a :** to rouse or stimulate — usu. used with *up* ⟨his assignment is to *hype* up the crowd —J.S. Radosta⟩ **b :** to cause to increase ⟨there are no cut-rate subscriptions to *hype* the figures —James Brady⟩ **3 :** to promote or publicize extravagantly ⟨*hype* youth-oriented products to young people —Nancy McCarthy⟩ — **hyped–up** \'hīp¦dəp\ *adj*

hy·per \'hīpə(r)\ *adj* [by shortening fr. *hyperactive*] **:** high-strung, excitable ⟨a former producer who may have to work with *hyper* wheeler-dealers but doesn't act like one —Glenn Esterly⟩

hyper-*prefix* **:** that is or exists in a space of more than three dimensions ⟨*hyper*cube⟩ ⟨*hyper*space⟩

hy·per·al·do·ste·ron·ism \¸hīpə¸ral'dästə¸rō¸nizəm, -¸raldōstə'rō-\ *n* [*hyper*- above, beyond, excessive (deriv. of Gk *hyper* over) + *aldosteronism*] **:** ALDOSTERONISM

hy·per·baric*\¸hīpə(r)'barik\ *adj* **:** of, relating to, or utilizing greater than normal pressure esp. of oxygen ⟨*hyperbaric* medicine⟩ ⟨*hyperbaric* chamber⟩ — **hy·per·bar·i·cal·ly** \-rək(ə)lē\ *adv*

hy·per·bolic*\¸hīpə(r)'bälik\ *adj* **:** of, relating to, or being a space in which more than one line parallel to a given line passes through a point ⟨*hyperbolic* geometry⟩

hy·per·charge \'hīpər¸chärj, 'hīpə¸chàj\ *n* **:** a quantum characteristic of a closely related group of strongly interacting particles represented by a number equal to twice the average value of the electric charge of the group

hy·per·com·plex \¸hīpə(r)(¸)käm¦pleks, -ə(r)kəm¦pleks\ *adj* **:** of, relating to, or being a general form of number that can be expressed as a vector of *n* dimensions in the form $x_1e_1 + x_2e_2 + \ldots + x_ne_n$ where the coefficients x_1, $x_2, \ldots x_n$ range over a given number field and $e_1 = (e, 0, 0, \ldots 0)$, $e_2 = (0, e, 0, \ldots 0)$, $\ldots e_n = (0, 0, \ldots e)$ where e is the multiplicative identity of the field ⟨*hypercomplex* variable⟩

hy·per·dip·loid \-¦dip¸lòid\ *adj* **:** having slightly more than the diploid number of chromosomes — **hy·per·dip·loi·dy** \-¸lòidē\ *n*

hy·per·ex·cit·abil·i·ty \¸hīpərək¸sīd·ə'biləd·ē, -i\ *n* **:** the state or condition of being unusually or excessively excitable — **hy·per·ex·cit·able** \-¸sīd·əbəl\ *adj*

hy·per·fine structure \¸hīpə(r)¸fīn-\ *n* **:** a fine structure multiplet occurring in an atomic spectrum that is due to interaction between electrons and nuclear spin

hy·per·geo·met·ric distribution \¸hīpə(r)¸jēə¸me·trik-\ *n* **:** a probability function of the form

$$f(x) = \frac{\binom{M}{x}\binom{N-M}{n-x}}{\binom{N}{n}} \text{ where } \binom{M}{x} = \frac{M!}{x!(m-x)!}$$

that gives the probability of obtaining exactly x elements of one kind and $n - x$ elements of another if n elements are chosen at random without replacement from a finite population containing N elements of which M are of the first kind and $N - M$ are of the second kind

hy·per·in·fla·tion \¸hīpərin¦flāshən\ *n* **:** extreme inflation

hy·per·ka·le·mia \¸hīpə(r)¸kā'lēmēə\ *n* [NL, fr. *hyper*- + E *kalium* + NL -*emia* blood condition] **:** the presence of an abnormally high concentration of potassium in the blood

hy·per·lip·id·emia \¸hīpə(r)¸lipə'dēmēə\ *n* [NL, fr. ISV *hyper*- + *lipid* + -*emia*] **:** the presence of excess fats or lipids in the blood — **hy·per·lip·id·emic** \-mik\ *adj*

hy·per·li·po·pro·tein·emia \-¸lipə¸prō¸tē'nēmēə, -¸lip-also-¦prōd·ēə'n-\ *n* [NL, fr. *hyper*- + E *lipoprotein* + NL -*emia*] **:** the presence of excess lipoprotein in the blood

hy·per·mar·ket \'hīpər¸märkət, 'hīpə¸màkət\ *n, Brit* **:** a very large department store that includes a supermarket

hy·per·pha·gic \¸hīpə(r)'fājik\ *adj* **:** relating to or affected with hyperphagia ⟨*hyperphagic* rats⟩

hy·per·po·lar·ize \¸hīpə(r)'pōlə¸rīz\ *vt* **:** to produce an increase in potential difference across (a biological membrane) or across the membrane of (a nerve cell) — **hy·per·po·lar·iza·tion** \-¸pōlərə'zāshən, -¸rī'z-\ *n*

hy·per·sex·u·al \-¦seksh(ə)wəl, -¦sekshəl\ *adj* **:** characterized by excessive sexual arousal or overindulgence in sexual activity — **hy·per·sex·u·al·i·ty** \¸hīpə(r)¸sekshə'waləd·ē\ *n*

hy·per·tri·glyc·er·i·de·mia \¸hīpə(r)¸trī¦glisə¸rī'dēmēə\ *n* [NL, fr. *hyper*- + E *triglyceride* + NL -*emia*] **:** the presence of an excess of triglycerides in the blood

hy·per·ve·loc·i·ty \-və'läsəd·ē, -'lästē\ *n* **:** a high or relatively high velocity; *esp* **:** one greater than 10,000 feet per second

hy·po·cen·ter \'hīpə¸sentə(r)\ *n* [*hypo*- under + *center*] **:** the focus of an earthquake

hy·po·der·mis*\¸hīpə'dərməs, -'dōm-, -'dòim-\ *n* **:** the thin layer of loose fatty connective tissue underlying the skin and binding it to the parts beneath

hy·po·dip·loid \¸hīpō¦dip¸lòid\ *adj* [*hypo*- under, down, less than normal (deriv. of Gk *hypo* under) + *diploid*] **:** having slightly fewer than the diploid number of chromosomes — **hy·po·dip·loi·dy** \-¸lòidē\ *n*

hy·po·gam·ma·glob·u·li·ne·mia \¸hīpə¸gamə'gläbyələ'nēmēə, -pō-\ *n* [NL, fr. *hypo*- + E *gamma globulin* + NL -*emia*] **:** deficiency of gamma globulins and esp. immunoglobulins in the blood; *also* **:** a state of immunological deficiency characterized by this

hy·po·ther·mic \ˌhīpəˈthərmik, -ˈthēm-, -ˈthəim-\ *adj*
꞉ relating to, utilizing, or characterized by hypothermia
⟨*hypothermic* cardiovascular surgery⟩ ⟨*hypothermic* dogs⟩

hy·pox·emic \ˌhīˌpäkˈsēmik\ *adj* ꞉ relating to, characterized by, or affected with hypoxemia

I

ibu·pro·fen \ˌībyü'prōfən, -ˌfen, -ˌfēn\ *n* [*isobutyl* + *propionic* acid + *fen* (alter. of *phenyl*)] **:** an anti-inflammatory drug $C_{13}H_{18}O_2$ used esp. to relieve the symptoms of rheumatoid arthritis and degenerative arthritis

IC \ˌī'sē\ *n* **:** INTEGRATED CIRCUIT

ice***n* **:** an undercover premium paid to a theater employee for choice theater tickets

ice***vt* **1 :** to shoot (an ice hockey puck) the length of the rink and beyond the opponents' goal line **2** *slang* **:** to kill

ice–cream chair \ˈīˌskrēm-\ *n* [fr. its use in ice-cream parlors] **:** a small armless chair with a circular seat for use at a table

ice·kha·na \ˈīsˌkänə, -kan-, -kán-, ˌīsˈk-\ *n* [*ice* + *gymkhana*] **:** an automobile gymkhana held on a frozen lake or river

ice lolly *n, Brit* **:** a confection made of flavored and colored water frozen on a stick

ice–out \ˈīsˌaút\ *n* **:** the melting of ice from the surface of a body of water (as a lake) in the spring

icing***n* **:** an addition that is not essential but adds to the interest or appeal of the main item or event ⟨the few clothes carried by the . . . shops have been merely *icing* to tempt the customer —Angela Taylor⟩ — often used in the phrase *icing on the cake*

ICU *abbr* intensive care unit

ID \ˌī'dē\ *n* [*identification*] **:** a pause in a radio or television broadcast for announcement of the identity of the station or network

IDDD *abbr* international direct distance dialing

idem·po·tent \ˈī'dempəd·ənt, ə'dem-; ˈīdəmˌpōtᵊnt, ˌīˌdem-\ *adj* [ISV *idem-* same (fr. L *idem*) + L *potent-, potens* having power] **:** relating to or being a mathematical quantity which is not zero and which when applied to itself under a given binary operation (as multiplication) equals itself; *also* **:** relating to or being an operation under which a mathematical quantity is idempotent — **idem·po·ten·cy** \-ən(t)sē, -ᵊn(t)sē\ *n* — **idempotent** *n*

identification parade *n, Brit* **:** a line of persons arranged by the police esp. for the identification of a suspected criminal by a victim or an eyewitness **:** a lineup

identity crisis *n* **:** psychosocial conflict or confusion in an individual concerning his social role that may be accompanied by loss of feelings of sameness and continuity of the personality and that occurs esp. during adolescence in response to changes in internal drives and to external pressures to adopt new roles; *broadly* **:** a similar state of confusion in an institution or organization ⟨both weeklies now seem involved in a sort of middle-aged, corporate *identity crisis* —Dan Wakefield⟩

identity ma·trix \-'mā·triks\ *n* **:** a square matrix with numeral 1's along the principal diagonal and 0's elsewhere

idiot box *n* **:** BOOB TUBE

idiot light *n* **:** a colored light on an automobile instrument panel designed to give a warning (as of an overheated engine or a low fuel tank)

id·io·type \'idēəˌtip\ *n* [*idio-* distinct + *type*] **:** the molecular structure and conformation of an immunoglobulin that confers its specificity

IDP *abbr* **1** inosine diphosphate **2** integrated data processing **3** international driving permit

ig·nim·brite \'ignəmˌbrīt\ *n* [G *ignimbrit*, fr. L *ignis* + *imbr-* (fr. *imber* rain, rain shower) + G *-it* -ite (mineral)] **:** a hard rock formed by solidification of chiefly fine deposits of volcanic ash

ike·ba·na \ˌikə'bänə, ˌēk-, -kē'-\ *n* [Jp, fr. *ikeru* to keep alive, arrange + *hana* flower] **:** the Japanese art of flower arranging that emphasizes form and balance

il·legal \(')il'(l)ēgəl, ə'lē-\ *n* **:** an illegal immigrant

il·lo·cu·tion·ary \ˌil(l)ō'kyüish(ə)ˌnerē, -i\ *adj* [*in-* within + *locutionary*] **:** of, relating to, or being an act (as informing, warning, or predicting) performed by a speaker in the course of making an utterance — compare LOCUTIONARY, PERLOCUTIONARY — **il·lo·cu·tion** \-'kyüshən\ *n*

illuminate***vt* **-nat·ed; -nat·ing :** to subject to radiation ⟨warning system . . . would alert the pilot when his plane was being *illuminated* by hostile radar —*Technical Survey*⟩

IM***abbr* **1** intermodulation distortion **2** individual medley

image***n* **1 :** a set of values of a mathematical function (as a homomorphism) that corresponds to a particular subset of the domain **2 :** a popular conception (as of a person, institution, or nation) projected esp. through the mass media ⟨promoting a corporate *image* of brotherly love and concern —R.C. Buck⟩

im·bal·anced \(')im'balən(t)st\ *adj* **:** not balanced; *esp* **:** having a disproportionately large number of members of one racial or ethnic group ⟨*imbalanced* schools⟩

imip·ra·mine \ə'miprəˌmēn, 'im-, -əmən, ˌimə'pra-\ *n* [*imide* + *propyl* + *amine*] **:** a tricyclic antidepressant drug $C_{19}H_{24}N_2$

imitation milk *n* **:** a dietary whole-milk substitute: as **a :** milk with the natural fat replaced by a vegetable oil **b :** a wholly artifical product made with carbohydrate, fat, and protein of plant or synthetic origin

im·mit·tance \i'mitᵊn(t)s\ *n* [*impedance* + ad*mittance*] **:** electrical admittance or impedance — used of transmission lines, networks, and measuring instruments

immune***adj* **:** concerned with or involving immunity ⟨*immune* globulins⟩ ⟨an *immune* response⟩

immuno-***comb form* **:** immunologic ⟨*immuno*-hematology⟩

im·mu·no·ad·sor·bent \ˌimyənōˌad'sörbənt, ə'myünō-, -adˌ-, -ˌsó(ə)b-\ *n* **:** a preparation of a specific antibody chemically combined with an insoluble substance (as cellulose) that is used to selectively remove its specific antigen from solution; *also* **:** a similar preparation of an antigen used to remove its specific antibody from solution

im·mu·no·as·say \-'as,ā, -(,)a'sā\ *n* **:** the determination of the presence, absence, or quantity of a substance (as a protein) through its capacity to act as an antigen — **immunoassay** *vt* — **im·mu·no·as·say·able** \-a;säəbəl\ *adj*

im·mu·no·com·pe·tence \-'kämpəd-ən(t)s\ *n* **:** the capacity for a normal immune response ⟨altered the *immunocompetence* of the lymphocytes⟩ — **im·mu·no·com·pe·tent** \-pəd-ənt\ *adj*

im·mu·no·cy·to·chem·is·try \-,sīd-ō'kemóstrē\ *n* **:** the biochemistry of cellular immunology — **im·mu·no·cy·to·chem·i·cal** \-'kemókəl\ *adj* — **im·mu·no·cy·to·chem·i·cal·ly** \-ók(ə)lē\ *adv*

im·mu·no·de·fi·cien·cy \-dó'fishənsē\ *n* **:** inability to produce a normal complement of antibodies or immunologically sensitized T cells esp. in response to specific antigens

im·mu·no·de·pres·sion \-dó'preshən, -dē'-\ *n* **:** IMMUNOSUPPRESSION — **im·mu·no·de·pres·sant** \-'presᵊnt\ *n* — **im·mu·no·de·pres·sive** \-'presiv\ *adj*

im·mu·no·di·ag·no·sis \-,diôg'nōsós\ *n* **:** diagnosis (as of cancer) by immunological methods — **im·mu·no·di·ag·nos·tic** \-'nästik\ *adj*

im·mu·no·dif·fu·sion \-dó'fyüzhən\ *n* **:** any of several techniques for obtaining a precipitate between an antibody and its specific antigen by suspending one in a gel and letting the other migrate through it from a well or by letting both antibody and antigen migrate through the gel from separate wells to form an area of precipitation

im·mu·no·elec·tro·pho·re·sis \,imyənōó,lektrəfó'rē-sós, ó;myünō-\ *n, pl* **-re·ses** \-'rē,sēz\ *:* electrophoretic separation of proteins followed by identification by the formation of precipitates through specific immunologic reactions — **im·mu·no·elec·tro·pho·ret·ic** \-'red·ik\ *adj* — **im·mu·no·elec·tro·pho·ret·i·cal·ly** \-ók(ə)lē\ *adv*

im·mu·no·flu·o·res·cence \-(,)flú(ə)r'esᵊn(t)s, -flōr-, -flór-\ *n* **:** a labeling of antigen or antibody with fluorochrome dyes esp. for the purpose of demonstrating the presence of corresponding antibodies or antigens in a tissue preparation or a smear

im·mu·no·glob·u·lin \-'gläbyələn\ *n* **:** any of the vertebrate serum proteins that are made up of light chains and heavy chains usu. linked by disulfide bonds and that include all known antibodies

im·mu·no·he·ma·tol·o·gy \-,hēmə'tälэjē\ *n* **:** a branch of immunology that deals with the immunologic properties of blood — **im·mu·no·he·ma·to·log·ic** \-,hē-mэd-ᵊl'äjik\ *adj* — **im·mu·no·he·ma·to·log·i·cal** \-jókэl\ *adj* — **im·mu·no·he·ma·tol·o·gist** \-,hēmó'tälэjóst\ *n*

im·mu·no·his·to·chem·i·cal \-,histō'kemókэl\ *adj* **:** of or relating to the application of histochemical and immunologic methods to chemical analysis of living cells and tissues — **im·mu·no·his·to·chem·i·cal·ly** \-ók(ə)lē, -li\ *adv* — **im·mu·no·his·to·chem·is·try** \-'kemóstrē, -ri\ *n*

im·mu·no·his·tol·o·gy \,imyэnō(,)his'tälэjē, ó;myünō-\ *n* **:** a branch of immunology that deals with the application of immunologic methods to histology — **im·mu·no·his·to·log·ic** \-,histɘ'läjik\ *adj* — **im·mu·no·his-**

to·log·i·cal \-'läjókэl\ *adj* — **im·mu·no·his·to·log·i·cal·ly** \-ók(ə)lē\ *adv*

im·mu·no·pa·thol·o·gy \-pə'thälэjē, -pa'-\ *n* **:** a branch of medicine that deals with immune responses associated with disease — **im·mu·no·path·o·log·ic** \-,pathɘ'läjik, -ēk\ *adj* — **im·mu·no·path·o·log·i·cal** \-jókэl\ *adj* — **im·mu·no·pa·thol·o·gist** \-pə'thälэjóst, -pa'-\ *n*

im·mu·no·phar·ma·col·o·gy \-,färmə'kälэjē, -ji\ *n* **1** **:** a branch of pharmacology concerned with the application of immunological techniques and theory to the study of the effects of drugs esp. on the immune system **2 :** the immunological effects and significance of a particular drug (as morphine) — **im·mu·no·phar·ma·col·o·gist** \-jóst\ *n*

im·mu·no·pre·cip·i·ta·tion \-prэ,sipó'tāshən, -(,)prē-\ *n* **:** precipitation of a complex of an antibody and its specific antigen — **im·mu·no·pre·cip·i·tate** \-'sipэd-ót, -'sipэ,tāt\ *n* — **im·mu·no·pre·cip·i·tate** \-'sipэ,tāt\ *vt*

im·mu·no·re·ac·tive \-rē'aktiv\ *adj* **:** reacting to particular antigens or haptens ⟨serum *immunoreactive* insulin⟩ — **im·mu·no·re·ac·tiv·i·ty** \-(,)rē,ak'tivód-ē, -i\ *n*

im·mu·no·sor·bent \-;sórbənt, -;só(ə)b-\ *n* **:** IMMUNOADSORBENT — **immunosorbent** *adj*

im·mu·no·sup·pres·sion \-sэ'preshən\ *n* **:** suppression (as by drugs) of natural immune responses — **im·mu·no·sup·pres·sant** \-sэ'presᵊnt\ *n* — **im·mu·no·sup·pres·sive** \-sэ'presiv\ *adj*

im·mu·no·ther·a·peu·tic \-,therэ'pyüd·ik, -ēk\ *adj* **:** of, relating to, or characterized by immunotherapy ⟨*immunotherapeutic* strategies for treating cancer —Jean L. Marx⟩

impact*vt* **:** to have an adverse effect on ⟨imports of stainless steel products continued to *impact* . . . profits — *Annual Report Armco Steel Corp.*⟩ ~ *vi* **:** to have an adverse effect ⟨limit individual risks to proportions that cannot seriously *impact* on the financial stature of our institution —R.H. Mulford & E.D. Dodd⟩

impacted*adj* **:** wedged or packed in ⟨the ponderous *impacted* irony that marred many of his earlier books — Richard Locke⟩

impacted area *n* **:** an area in which a large number of public school students are from families living or working on nontaxable federal property

implicit differentiation *n* **:** the process of finding the derivative of a dependent variable in an implicit function by differentiating each term separately, by expressing the derivative of the dependent variable as a symbol, and by solving the resulting expression for the symbol

im·plode*\əm'plōd\ *vi* **im·plod·ed; im·plod·ing** **1 :** to undergo violent compression ⟨massive stars which *implode*⟩ **2 :** to collapse inward as if from external pressure ⟨the nation's banking system . . . *imploded* —*Time*⟩ ⟨the devastations of a civilization collapsing in on itself. *Imploding* —David Black⟩; *also* **:** to become greatly reduced as if from collapsing ⟨our dream isn't dead. It has *imploded* —Vincent Canby⟩ ~ *vt* **:** to cause to implode ⟨is *imploded* by means of a number of external detonators —G.T. Seaborg⟩

implosion*n* **:** an inward collapse ⟨some sort of *implosion* of outworn ideas seemed to be taking place —Patricia Hutchins⟩ ⟨some cataclysmic *implosion* of time — Marshall Frady⟩; *also* **:** a reduction or compaction as if from external pressure ⟨the population *implosion*. The number of children born has been decreasing —E.C. Harwood⟩ ⟨this *implosion* of cultures makes realistic for the first time the age-old vision of a world culture — Kenneth Kenniston⟩

imported fire ant *n* : either of two fire ants (*Solenopsis richteri* and *S. invicta*) that have been introduced into the southern U.S. where they are destructive pests

im·pres·sion·ist**əm'presh(ə)nəst\ *n* : an entertainer who does impressions of noted personalities

imu \'ē(ˌ)mü\ *n* [Hawaiian] : a Hawaiian cooking pit in which hot stones bake the food

in*adj* **1** : keenly aware of and responsive to what is new and smart ⟨the *in* crowd⟩ **2** : highly approved by those who are au courant ⟨became an *in* place for fashionable people —N.T. Kenney⟩ — **in·ness** \'innəs\ *n*

-in \ˌin\ *n comb form* [*in* (as in *sit-in*)] **1** : organized public protest by means of or in favor of : demonstration ⟨teach-*in*⟩ ⟨love-*in*⟩ **2** : public group activity ⟨swim*in*⟩

in–and–out*\ˌinəˌnaút\ *adj* : involving purchase and sale of the same security within a short period ⟨*in-and-out* trading⟩

in·bounds \'inˌbaún(d)z\ *adj* : of or relating to putting a basketball in play by passing it onto the court from out of bounds ⟨an *inbounds* pass⟩

inc*abbr* incomplete

in·ca·pac·i·tant \ˌinkə'pasətənt, -səd-ə-\ *n* : an incapacitating agent ⟨a chemical *incapacitant*⟩

in·ca·pac·i·ta·tor \-ə,tād-ə(r)\ *n* : INCAPACITANT

in·cen·dive \ən'sendiv\ *adj* [L *incendere* to set fire to + E -*ive*, adj. suffix] : capable of starting a fire ⟨sparks of high *incendive* power⟩

inconsistent*adj* : not satisfiable by the same set of values for the unknowns ⟨*inconsistent* equations⟩ ⟨*inconsistent* inequalities⟩

in·cre·men·tal·ism \ˌiŋkrə'mentˀl,izəm, ˌink-\ *n* : a policy or advocacy of a policy of political or social change in small increments — **in·cre·men·tal·ist** \-ˀləst\ *n*

independent*adj* **1** : having linear independence ⟨an *independent* set of vectors⟩ **2** : having the property that the joint probability (as of events or samples) or the joint probability density function (as of random variables) equals the product of the probabilities or probability density functions of separate occurrence

independent assortment *n* : formation of combinations of chromosomes in meiosis with one of each diploid pair of homologous chromosomes passing at random into each gamete independently of each other pair; *also* : the similar process when genes on different pairs of homologous chromosomes are considered

in–depth \'inˌdepth\ *adj* : comprehensive, thorough ⟨an *in-depth* study⟩ ⟨with a small number of *in-depth* conversations, rather than with large numbers of brief interviews —Richard Reeves⟩

in·dex·ation \ˌin,dek'sāshən\ *n* : a system of economic control in which certain variables (as wages and interest) are tied to a cost-of-living index so that both rise or fall at the same rate and the detrimental effect of inflation is theoretically eliminated — called also *indexing*

indicator*n* : any of a group of statistical values (as level of employment and change in the price of industrial raw materials) that taken together give an indication of the

health of the economy — compare COINCIDENT, LAGGER, LEADER

individual retirement account *n* : a savings account in which a person may deposit up to a stipulated amount each year with the deposits deductible from income tax and the interest not taxable until the person's retirement

in·do·cy·a·nine green \ˌində'sīə,nēn-, -'sīənən-\ *n* [*indo-* indigo + *cyanine*] : a green tricarbocyanine dye $C_{43}H_{47}N_2NaO_6S_2$ used esp. in testing liver blood flow and cardiac output

in·dole·amine \ˌin,dōˀlam(ˌ)ēn, -ˌdōlə'mēn\ *n* : any of various indole derivatives (as serotonin or tryptamine) that contain an amine group

in·do·meth·a·cin \ˌindōˀmethəsən\ *n* [*indole* + *methyl* + *acetic acid* + *-in* chemical compound] : a nonsteroid anti-inflammatory antipyretic analgesic drug $C_{19}H_{16}ClNO_4$ used esp. in the treatment of arthritis

in·duc·er*\in'd(y)üsə(r)\ *n* : a substance capable of activating a structural gene by combining with and inactivating a genetic repressor

industrial action *n, Brit* : JOB ACTION

industrial archaeology *n* : the study of the buildings, machinery, and equipment of the industrial revolution — **industrial archaeologist** *n*

in·dus·tri·al–rev·e·nue bond \ən,dəstrēəlˌrevən(y)ü-\ *n* : a revenue bond issued to provide industrial facilities for lease and dependent on the lease revenue for amortization and interest payments

inertial platform *n* : an assemblage of devices used in inertial guidance together with the mounting

inertial space *n* : a part of space away from the earth assumed to have fixed coordinates so that the trajectory of an object (as a spacecraft or missile) may be calculated in relation to it

in·fan·ti·lize \'infantˀl,īz, *sometimes* in'fantˀl-\ *vt* **-lized**; **-liz·ing** **1** : to make or keep infantile ⟨this institutional method of raising youngsters ... *infantilizes* them — Helen Steele⟩ **2** : to treat as if infantile ⟨how easy it is to *infantalize* a group of people —R.D. Rosen⟩ — **in·fan·ti·li·za·tion** \ˌinfantˀlə'zāshən, -ˀl,i'z-, *sometimes* in,fantˀl-\ *n*

in·fau·na \'in,fónə, -,fän-\ *n* [NL, fr. *in-* within + *fauna*] : benthic fauna living in the substrate and esp. in a soft sea bottom — compare EPIFAUNA — **in·fau·nal** \-nˀl\ *adj*

infectious bovine rhi·no·tra·che·i·tis \-ˌrī(ˌ)nō-,trākēˌid-əs\ *n* [NL *rhinotracheitis*, fr. *rhino-* nose, nasal + *tracheitis*] : a disease of cattle caused by a virus serologically related to human herpesvirus and characterized by inflammation and ulceration of the nasal cavities and trachea

in–flight \(ˌ)in,flīt\ *adj* **1** : made or carried out while in flight ⟨*in-flight* calculations⟩ **2** : provided for use or enjoyment while in flight ⟨*in-flight* movies⟩

in·flu·en·tial \ˌin,flü'enchəl\ *n* : one that has great influence

in·for·mat·ics \ˌinfə(r)'mad·iks\ *n pl but sing in constr* [ISV *information* + *-ics* study, knowledge] *chiefly Brit* : INFORMATION SCIENCE

information retrieval *n* : the techniques of storing and recovering and often disseminating recorded data esp. through the use of a computerized system

information science *n* **:** the collection, classification, storage, retrieval, and dissemination of recorded knowledge treated both as a pure and as an applied science — **information scientist** *n*

in·fra·sound \'infrə,saùnd\ *n* [*infra-* below (fr. L *infra*) + *sound*] **:** a wave phenomenon of the same physical nature as sound but with frequencies below the range of human hearing

in–house \'in,haùs\ *adj* **:** existing, originating, or carried on within a group or organization or its facilities **:** not outside (reform of the judicial system must be *in-house* — Tim Murphy) (*in-house* industrial psychologists employed by some large companies —Caroline Donnelley)

ini·tial·ism \ə'nishə,lizəm\ *n* **:** an acronym formed from initial letters

ini·tial·ize \-,līz\ *vt* **-ized; -iz·ing :** to set (as a computer program counter) to a starting position or value — **ini·tial·iza·tion** \ə,nish(ə)lə'zāshən\ *n*

initial teaching alphabet *n* [fr. the fact that it is used only in the initial stages of teaching reading] **:** a 44-symbol alphabet designed esp. for children who are learning to read English

in·jec·tant \in'jektənt\ *n* **:** a substance that is injected into something

injection*n **1 a :** the placing of an artificial satellite or a spacecraft into an orbit or on a trajectory—called also *insertion* **b :** the time or place at which injection occurs **2 :** a mathematical function that is a one-to-one mapping — compare BIJECTION, SURJECTION

in·jec·tive \in'jektiv\ *adj* [*inject* + *-ive*, adj. suffix] **:** being a one-to-one mathematical function

in·ject·or razor \ən'jektə(r)-\ *n* **:** a safety razor with a narrow single-edged blade that is forced into place by a blade dispenser

in–joke \'in-,jōk\ *n* **:** a joke for or about a select group of people (a dramatic inversion of the American mystery, laden with literary *in-jokes* —Peter Winn)

in–line \(')in,līn\ *adj or adv* **:** having the parts or units arranged in a straight line; *also* **:** being so arranged

inner city *n* **:** the usu. oldest and most densely populated central section of a city (decided to keep its plant in the *inner city* instead of fleeing to the suburbs —Carol G. Kleiman) — **in·ner–city** \,inə(r),'sid-ē, -i\ *adj*

inner space *n* **1 :** space at or near the earth's surface and esp. under the sea **2 :** one's inner self

in·nu·mer·a·cy \(')in,'n(y)üm(ə)rəsē, -si\ *n* [*in-* not + *numeracy*] *Brit* **:** ignorance of mathematics

¹in·nu·mer·ate \-,'n(y)üm(ə)rət\ *adj* [fr. *innumeracy;* after such pairs as E *illiteracy: illiterate*] *Brit* **:** marked by innumeracy

²innumerate *n, Brit* **:** one who is innumerate

in·put \'in,pùt\ *vt* **in·put·ted** *or* **input; in·put·ting** [*input*, n.] **:** to enter (as data) into a computer or data processing system (a large volume of data . . . will be *input* to the file —R.L. Venezky) (could employ a typewriter keyboard to *input* questions to a computer —Harrison Bryan)

insertion*n **:** INJECTION 1

in–service*adj **:** of, relating to, or being one that is fully employed (*in-service* teachers) (*in-service* police officers)

inside*adv **:** in prison

instant*adj **:** produced or occurring with or as if with astonishing rapidity and ease (this 15,000-pound concus-

sion weapon clears an area the size of a football field to make an *instant* landing zone for helicopters —P.R. Ehrlich & J.P. Holdren) (what the technology of communications now offers us—*instant* knowledge on the one hand, and *instant* boredom . . . on the other —Arlene Croce) (became an *instant* celebrity) (does not offer the *instant* answers of closed ideologies —Warren Taylor)

instant re·play \-'rē,plā\ *n* **:** a videotape recording of an action (as a play in football) that can be played back (as in slow motion) immediately after the action has been completed

instruction*n **:** a code that tells a computer to perform a particular operation

instrumental*adj **:** based on or involving reward or avoidance of distress (*instrumental* learning) (*instrumental* conditioning)

insurance *adj* **:** being a score that adds to a team's lead so that the opponents cannot tie the game with their next score (an *insurance* run) (grabbed the next rebound and, after a foul, sank two *insurance* free throws with one second left —*N.Y. Times*)

integral domain *n* **:** a mathematical ring in which multiplication is commutative, which has a multiplicative identity element, and which contains no pair of nonzero elements whose product is zero (the integers under the operations of addition and multiplication form an *integral domain*)

integrated circuit *n* **:** a tiny complex of electronic components (as transistors, resistors, and capacitors) and their interconnections produced in or on a single small slice of material (as silicon) — called also *chip* — **integrated circuitry** *n*

in·te·gro·dif·fer·en·tial \,intə(,)grō,difə'renchəl, in,te-, in,tē-\ *adj* [*integral* + connective *-o-* + *differential*] **:** involving both mathematical integration and differentiation (*integrodifferential* equations)

intelligent*adj **:** able to perform some of the functions of a computer (an *intelligent* terminal)

intensive care *adj* **:** having special medical facilities, services, and monitoring devices to meet the needs of gravely ill patients (an *intensive care* unit) — **intensive care** *n*

interactive*adj **:** of, relating to, or being a two-way electronic communication system (as a telephone, cable television, or a computer) that involves a user's orders (as for information or merchandise) or responses (as to a poll) — **in·ter·ac·tive·ly** *adv*

in·ter·cep·tion*,intə(r)'sepshən\ *n* **:** an intercepted forward pass (threw three *interceptions* in one game)

in·ter·cru·ral \,intə(r),krü(ə)rəl\ *adj* [*inter-* between (deriv. of L *inter*) + *crural*] **:** situated or taking place between two crura and esp. in the region of the groin (*intercrural* intercourse)

in·ter·eth·nic \,intə,rethnik\ *adj* [*inter-* between + *ethnic*] **:** existing or occurring between ethnic groups (the more subtle manifestations of *interethnic* conflicts —K.B. Clark)

in·ter·face*\'intə(r),fās\ *n* **1 :** the place at which two independent systems meet and act upon or communicate with each other (the *interface* between engineering and science) (the man-machine *interface*); *broadly* **:** an area in which diverse things interact on each other (*interface* between the known and unknown) (the high school-college *interface*⟩ **2 :** the means by which interaction or communication is effected at an interface ⟨an *interface* between a computer and a typesetting machine⟩

interface *vb* **-faced; -fac·ing** *vt* **1 :** to connect by means of an interface ⟨*interface* a machine with a computer⟩ **2 :** to serve as an interface for ~ *vi* **1 :** to become interfaced ⟨a system that *interfaces* with a computer⟩ **2 :** to interact or coordinate harmoniously ⟨the computer technicians ... *interface* with the flight controllers —H.S.F. Cooper, Jr.⟩

in·ter·fer·on \ˌintə(r)ˈfi(ə)ˌrän\ *n* [*interfer*ence + *-on* chemical compound] **:** a heat-stable soluble basic antiviral glycoprotein of low molecular weight produced usu. by cells exposed to the action of a virus, sometimes to that of another intracellular parasite (as a brucella), or experimentally to that of some chemicals

in·ter·gen·er·a·tion·al \ˌintə(r)ˌjenəˈrāshnəl, -shənᵊl\ *adj* **:** existing or occurring between generations ⟨*intergenerational* conflicts⟩

in·ter·in·di·vid·u·al \ˌintə(r)ˌindəˈvij(ə)wəl, -jəl\ *adj* **:** involving or taking place between individuals ⟨*interindividual* cooperation⟩

in·ter·lab·o·ra·to·ry \-ˈlab(ə)rəˌtōrē, -ˌtȯr-, *Brit usu* ləˈbärət(ə)rē, -i\ *adj* **:** of, relating to, or engaged in by more than one laboratory ⟨*interlaboratory* measurements⟩ ⟨*interlaboratory* study⟩

in·ter·leave \-ˈlēv\ *vt* **-leaved; -leav·ing :** to arrange in or as if in alternate layers

interlock *n* **1 :** a stretchable fabric made on a circular knitting machine and consisting of two ribbed fabrics joined by interlocking **2 :** a garment made of interlock

¹in·ter·me·dia \ˌintə(r)ˈmēdēə\ *adj* [*inter-* between + *media*] **:** of, relating to, or involving the use or effect of several media and esp. several electronic media ⟨the *intermedia* show, with slides and movies and dancers and electronic music —R.R. Lingeman⟩

²intermedia *n* **:** an art form involving the simultaneous use of several media ⟨the mixing of genres in *intermedia* that makes use of dance, films, painting, electronics — Roger Shattuck⟩

intermediate *n* **:** an automobile larger than a compact but smaller than a full-sized automobile

in·ter·mod·al \ˌintə(r)ˈmōdᵊl\ *adj* [*inter-* between + *mode* + *-al*, adj. suffix] **1 :** being or involving transportation by more than one form of carrier during a single journey **2 :** used for intermodal transportation

interpreter *n* **:** a computer program that translates an instruction into machine language and executes it before going to the next instruction

in·ter·ro·bang *also* **in·tera·bang** \inˈterəˌbaŋ\ *n* [*interro*gation (point) + *bang* printers' slang for *exclamation point*] **:** a punctuation ‽ designed for use esp. at the end of an exclamatory rhetorical question

interrogate *vt* **-gat·ed; -gat·ing :** to give or send out a signal to (as a transponder or computer) for triggering an appropriate response

interrupt *n* **:** a feature of a computer that permits the execution of one program to be interrupted in order to execute another; *also* **:** the interruption itself

in·ter·sen·so·ry \ˌintə(r)ˈsen(t)s(ə)rē, -ri\ *adj* **:** involving two or more sensory systems ⟨*intersensory* factors in memory loss⟩

in·ter·state \ˈintə(r)ˌstāt\ *n, often cap* **:** any of a system of highways connecting most major U.S. cities

in·ter·stock \ˈintə(r)ˌstäk\ *n* **:** a piece inserted between scion and stock in grafting (as to allow union of incompatible varieties or to induce dwarfing)

in·ter·term \ˈintərˌtərm; ˈintəˌtŏm, -ˌtȯim\ *n* **:** a period between two academic sessions or terms sometimes utilized for brief concentrated courses **:** intersession

interview *n* **:** a person who is interviewed ⟨he was our *interview* that morning —Sally Quinn⟩

interview *vi* **:** to have an interview (as with a prospective employer) ⟨one of my law school classmates *interviewed* with a ... law firm —Lana Borsook⟩

into *prep* **:** strongly involved with or deeply interested in ⟨her two children ... are both *into* art —*New York*⟩ ⟨is *into* carved ivory rings and pale-green jade bracelets — *McCall's*⟩ ⟨the perfect book for anyone who's deeply *into* plants —C.H. Simonds⟩

in·tra·ar·te·ri·al \ˌin-trə(ˌ)ärˈtirēəl, ˌin-(ˌ)trä-\ *adj* [*intra*-within (deriv. of L *intra*) + *arterial*] **:** situated or occurring within, administered into, or involving entry by way of an artery ⟨*intra-arterial* chemotherapy⟩ ⟨an *intra-arterial* catheter⟩ — **in·tra·ar·te·ri·al·ly** \-ēəlē\ *adv*

in·tra·car·di·ac \-ˈkärdēˌak, -ˌkäd-\ *also* **in·tra·car·di·al** \-dēəl\ *adj* **:** situated or occurring within, introduced into, or involving entry into the heart ⟨*intracardiac* surgery⟩ ⟨an *intracardiac* catheter⟩ — **in·tra·car·di·al·ly** \-dēəlē\ *adv*

in·tra·day \ˌin-trəˌdā\ *adj* **:** occurring in the course of a single day ⟨the market showed wide *intraday* fluctuations⟩

in·tra·der·mal test \ˌin-trəˌdərməl-, -(ˌ)trä-, -ˌdŏm-, -ˌdȯim-\ *n* **:** a test for immunity or hypersensitivity made by injecting a minute amount of diluted antigen into the skin

in·tra·ga·lac·tic \-gəˈlaktik\ *adj* **:** situated or occurring within the confines of a single galaxy ⟨if radio engineers on a planet with a technology more advanced than ours wanted to establish an *intragalactic* communication network —*Scientific American*⟩

in·tra·gov·ern·men·tal \-ˌgəvə(r)nˈmentᵊl, -və(r)ˌme-, -vᵊmˌe-, -ˌgəbᵊmˌe-\ *adj* **:** occurring or existing between different branches or departments of government ⟨*intragovernmental* cooperation⟩ ⟨*intragovernmental* competition⟩

in·tra·op·er·a·tive \-ˈäp(ə)rədiv, -ˌäpəˌrādiv\ *adj* **:** occurring, carried out, or encountered in the course of surgery ⟨*intraoperative* radiation⟩ ⟨*intraoperative* infarction⟩ — **in·tra·op·er·a·tive·ly** \-lē, -li\ *adv*

in·tra·per·son·al \-ˈpərs(ᵊ)nəl, -ˌpās-, -ˌpais-\ *adj* **:** occurring within the individual mind or self ⟨*intrapersonal* concerns of the aged⟩

in·tra·pop·u·la·tion \-ˌpäpyəˈlāshən\ *adj* **:** occurring within or taking place between members of a population ⟨*intrapopulation* allografts⟩

in·tra·uter·ine device \-ˈyüdərən-, -ˌrīn-\ *n* **:** a device (as a spiral of plastic or a ring of stainless steel) inserted and left in the uterus to prevent effective conception — called also *intrauterine contraceptive device*, *IUD*

in·tra·vas·cu·lar \-ˈvaskyələ(r)\ *adj* **:** situated, occurring, or performed within or administered into a blood vessel ⟨*intravascular* radionuclide therapy⟩ ⟨an *intravascular* injection⟩ — **in·tra·vas·cu·lar·ly** *adv*

in·tro·gres·sant \,in·trə'gres°nt, -trō-\ *n* **:** an individual resulting from and exhibiting evidence of introgression — **introgressant** *adj*

in·tron \'in,trän\ *n* [*intervening* sequence + *-on* basic hereditary component or region] **:** a polynucleotide sequence in a nucleic acid that does not code information for protein synthesis and is removed before translation of messenger RNA — compare EXON

inverse*n **:** a set element that is related to another element in such a way that the result of applying a given binary operation to them is an identity element of the set — see ADDITIVE INVERSE, MULTIPLICATIVE INVERSE

inverse variation *n* **:** a relationship between variables in which one variable is equal to a nonzero constant divided by the other variable — compare DIRECT VARIATION

investment letter stock *n* **:** LETTER STOCK

I/O *abbr* input/output

ion–exchange chromatography *n* **:** chromatography in which the separation and deposition of components in the liquid phase is achieved by differences in their rate of migration through a column, layer, or impregnated paper containing an ion-exchange material and by the exchange of ions in solution for those of like charge in the ion-exchange material

ion·ic propulsion \i'änik-\ *n* **:** ION PROPULSION

ion·o·mer \i'änəmə(r)\ *n* [*ion* + connective *-o-* + *polymer*] **:** any of a class of tough synthetic ethylene-based thermoplastic resins consisting of a long-chain polymer

ion·ophore \i'änə,fō(ə)r, -,fö(ə)r, -,fōə, -,fö(ə)\ *n* [*ion* + connective *-o-* + *-phore* carrier] **:** a compound that facilitates transmission of an ion (as of calcium) across a lipid barrier (as in a cell membrane) by combining with the ion or by increasing the permeability of the barrier to it

ion·o·sonde \i'änə,sänd\ *n* [ISV *iono*sphere + *sonde*] **:** a device for determining and recording the heights of ionized layers in the ionosphere by shortwaves reflected from them

ion propulsion *n* **:** propulsion of a body by the forces resulting from the rearward discharge of a stream of ionized particles

ion rocket *n* **:** a reaction engine deriving thrust from the ejection of a stream of ionized particles **:** an ion engine

IRA \,i(,)är'ā\ *n* **:** INDIVIDUAL RETIREMENT ACCOUNT

ir·i·dol·o·gy \,i(ə)rə'däləjē, -ji\ *n* [*irido-* iris of the eye + *-logy* study] **:** the study of the iris of the eye for indications of the state of bodily health and of the presence of disease — **ir·i·dol·o·gist** \-əjəst\ *n*

iron maiden *n* **:** a supposed medieval instrument of torture consisting of an iron frame in human form hinged to admit a victim who was impaled on the spiked interior as the frame closed

irreducible*adj **:** incapable of being factored into polynomials of lower degree with coefficients in some given field (as the rational numbers) or integral domain (as the integers) 〈*irreducible* polynomials〉

ISBN *abbr* International Standard Book Number

iso·an·dros·ter·one \,i(,)sō,an,drästə,rōn, *also* ,i(,)zō-\ *n* [*iso-* equal, uniform (deriv. of Gk *isos* equal) + *androsterone*] **:** EPIANDROSTERONE

iso·en·zyme \,isō'en,zīm, *also* ,izō-\ *n* [*iso-* + *enzyme*] **:** any of two or more chemically distinct but functionally similar enzymes — **iso·en·zy·mat·ic** \-,enzə'mad·ik, -zi'-\ *or* **iso·en·zy·mic** \-(,)en'zimik\ *adj*

iso·ge·ne·ic \,isōjə'nēik, *also* ,izō-\ *adj* [*iso-* + *-geneic* (as in *syngeneic*)] **:** SYNGENEIC 〈an *isogeneic* graft〉

isolated camera *n* [fr. its focusing on isolated activities] **:** a television camera used to videotape something (as the play of an individual player during a play in football) for an instant replay

iso·la·to \,isə'läd·ō, *also* ,izə-\ *n, pl* **-toes** [It, adj., iso-lated] **:** one who is physically or spiritually isolated from his fellowman

iso·met·rics \,isə'me·triks, *also* ,izə-\ *n pl but sing or pl in constr* [*isometric* + *-s*, pl. suffix] **:** exercise or a system of exercises involving isometric contraction of muscles

isom·e·try \i'sämə,trē\ *n, pl* **-tries** [*iso-* + *-metry* measuring, deriv. of Gk *metron* measure] **:** a mapping of a metric space onto another or onto itself so that the distance between any two points in the original space is the same as the distance between their images in the second space 〈rotation and translation are *isometries* of the plane〉

iso·mor·phic*\,isə'mö(r)fik, *also* ,izə-\ *adj* **:** related by an isomorphism 〈*isomorphic* mathematical rings〉 — **iso·mor·phi·cal·ly** \-fək(ə)lē\ *adv*

iso·mor·phism*\-'mö(r),fizəm\ *n* **:** a one-to-one correspondence between two mathematical sets; *esp* **:** a homomorphism that is one-to-one — compare ENDOMORPHISM

iso·spin \'isə,spin, *also* 'izə-\ *n* [*isotopic spin*] **:** a quantum characteristic of a group of closely related elementary particles (as a proton and a neutron) handled mathematically like ordinary spin with the possible orientations in a hypothetical space specifying the number of particles of differing electric charge comprising the group

iso·to·pic spin \,isə'täpik-, -'tōp-, *also* ,izə-\ *n* **:** ISOSPIN

iso·zyme \'isə,zīm, *also* 'izə-\ *n* [*iso-* + *-zyme* enzyme, fr. Gk *zymē* leaven] **:** ISOENZYME — **iso·zy·mic** \,isə,zīmik, *also* ,izə-\ *adj*

ITA *abbr* initial teaching alphabet

Italian sandwich *n* **:** HOAGIE

it·er·a·tive*\'id·ə,rād·iv, -ərəd·-\ *adj* **:** relating to or being a computational procedure in which replication of a cycle of operations produces results which approximate the desired result more and more closely 〈an *iterative* procedure in computer programming〉

IUD \,īyü'dē, ,ī,yü-\ *n* **:** INTRAUTERINE DEVICE

J

jackboot*n : the spirit or policy of militarism or totalitarianism ⟨hurried to completion under threat of Hitler's jackboot —Commonweal⟩
jackbooted*adj : ruthlessly and violently oppressive ⟨jackbooted militarism⟩
Ja·cuz·zi \jə'küzē, ja-, -zi\ trademark — used for a whirlpool bath and a recreational bathing tub or pool
jam*n : a round in roller derby in which a jammer from each team attempts to circle the course and pass members of the opposing team in order to score points
jam·mer*\'jamə(r)\ n : a player on a roller derby team who attempts to score during a jam
jams \'jamz\ n pl [prob. short for pajamas] : knee-length loose-fitting swim trunks usu. having a drawstring waist and large brightly colored patterns
Japanese Bobtail n 1 : a breed of short-haired domestic cat that originated in Japan and has a short stumpy tail resembling a pompom and a coat often marked with solid patches of black, white, and red 2 : a cat of the Japanese Bobtail breed
Japanese quail n : any of a subspecies (Coturnix coturnix japonica) of Old World quail from China and Japan used extensively in laboratory research
Ja·pa·nol·o·gist \japə'näləjəst, jə,pa'n-\ n [Japan + connective -o- + -logy + -ist specialist] : a specialist in the study of Japan and the Japanese
Jap·lish \'japlish\ n [Japanese + English] : Japanese marked by a considerable number of borrowings from English
ja·po·nais·erie \zhá,pónez(ə)'rē\ n [F, fr. japonais Japanese + -erie -ery (quality, character)] : a style of art reflecting Japanese qualities or motifs; also : a work of art in this style
jaw·bone \'jô,bōn\ vt -boned; -bon·ing [jawbone, n.] : to attempt to influence by jawboning ⟨use the presidential power to jawbone prices and profits into line — Nicholas Von Hoffman⟩
jawboning n : the use of public appeals (as by a president) to influence the actions of business and labor leaders ⟨guidelines and presidential jawboning were used to deter wage and price leapfrogging —J.R. Walsh⟩
jay*n [jay the letter j] : a marijuana cigarette : a joint
jazz*n : similar but unspecified things : stuff ⟨I love sailing ... all that wind, and the waves, and all that jazz — John Updike⟩
jazz–rock \'jaz,räk\ n : a blend of jazz and rock music
Jesus freak n, often cap F [Jesus Christ] : a member of a fundamentalist youth group whose life-style includes communal living, Bible study, street preaching, and abstinence from illicit drugs
jet·a·va·tor \'jed·ə,vād·ə(r)\ n [irreg. fr. jet + elevator] : a control surface for deflecting a rocket's exhaust stream so as to change the direction of thrust
jet boat n : a boat propelled by an engine which expels a powerful jet of water

jet lag n : a group of mental and physical symptoms (as fatigue and irritability) following rapid travel through several time zones that prob. result from disruption of circadian rhythms in the human body
jet set n [fr. the fact that jet-setters frequently travel by jet] : an international social group of wealthy individuals who frequent fashionable resorts ⟨she glides easily from Washington society to the international jet set —Susanna McBee⟩ — jet–set·ter \'jet,sed·ə(r)\ n
Jet·way \'jet,wā\ trademark — used for a telescoping bridge ramp for loading and unloading passengers between an aircraft and a terminal building
jim·mies \'jimēz, -iz\ n pl [origin unknown] : tiny rod-shaped bits of variously flavored candy often sprinkled on ice cream and pastry
jive \'jīv\ adj [jive deceptive or foolish talk] slang : being misleading, deceitful, or phony ⟨if you are late getting to heaven, you will give Saint Peter some jive excuse — Langston Hughes⟩ ⟨you could tell that these cats were jive by the way they went around saying, "Yeah, man, do you shoot stuff?" and all this sort of nonsense —Claude Brown⟩
job action n : a temporary action (as a slowdown) by workers as a protest and means toward forcing compliance with demands ⟨massive sick calls, mass rallies, demonstrations and other job actions —Boston Sunday Advertiser⟩
job bank n : a usu. computerized job listing or placement service for the unemployed
job–hop·ping \'jäb,häpin\ n : the practice of moving (as for immediate financial gain) from job to job — job–hop·per \-pə(r)\ n
jock*n [fr. the wearing of jockstraps by male athletes] : an athlete and esp. a school or college athlete ⟨old scrapbooks that testify to his glory as a high school jock — Chris Chase⟩ ⟨longstanding lack of opportunities for women jocks —Grace Lichtenstein⟩
Jock·ey \'jäkē, -ki\ trademark — used for briefs for men
jogging n : running at a slow even pace; also : exercise consisting of walking and jogging
John Birch·er \'jän'bərchər, -bāchə(r, -bəichə(r\ n : BIRCHER
join*n : UNION 1
joint*n 1 slang : prison 2 : penis — usu. considered vulgar
joint*adj : being a function of or involving two or more variables and esp. random variables ⟨a joint probability density function⟩
jo·mon \'jō,män\ adj, often cap [Jp jōmon straw rope pattern; fr. the characteristic method of forming designs on pottery of the period] : of, relating to, or typical of a Japanese neolithic cultural period extending from about 3000 B.C. or earlier to about 200 B.C. and characterized esp. by

elaborately ornamented hand-formed unglazed pottery (Jomon ware)

jones \'jōnz\ *n, pl* **jones·es** [prob. fr. the name *Jones*] **1** *slang* **:** habit, addiction; *esp* **:** addiction to heroin 〈all of a sudden his *jones* comes on him so bad he starts to lose his cool —V.E. Smith〉 **2** *slang* **:** heroin

Jor·dan curve the·o·rem \'jòrdᵊn'kərv'thēərəm, -'thi(ə)rəm\ *n* [*Jordan curve* simple closed curve, after Camille *Jordan* †1922 Fr. mathematician] **:** a fundamental theorem of topology: every simple closed curve divides the plane into two regions and is the common boundary between them

Jo·seph·son effect \'jōzəfsən-, *also* -ōsə-\ *n* [B.D. *Josephson*, 20th cent. Eng. physicist] **:** the passage of electrons at superconductivity temperatures through a thin insulator separating two superconductors so that when the electrons are accelerated through the barrier by application of a voltage the energy they gain is emitted as electromagnetic radiation

Josephson junction *n* **:** a thin layer of insulation exhibiting the Josephson effect

jou·al \zhü'ál, -'al, -'äl\ *n, often cap* [CanF, fr. Joual *joual* horse, fr. F *cheval*] **:** a French patois spoken esp. by uneducated French Canadians

joy·stick*\'jòi,stik\ *n* **:** a manual control for any of various devices (as a computer display) that resembles an airplane's joystick esp. in being capable of motion in two or more directions

J particle *n* **:** an unstable neutral fundamental particle of the meson group that has a mass about 6000 times the mass of an electron — called also *J/psi particle, psi particle*

Jpn *abbr* Japan; Japanese

ju·do·ist \'jü(ˌ)dō̇əst, 'jüdəwə̇st\ *n* **:** one who is trained or skilled in judo

jug band *n* **:** a band that uses usu. crude improvised instruments (as jugs, washboards, and kazoos) to play blues, jazz, and folk music

juice*n **1** *slang* **:** alcoholic liquor 〈I was never a speed freak or a coke head. My main problem was the *juice* —Kris Kristofferson〉 **2** *slang* **:** exorbitant interest exacted of a borrower under the threat of violence **3** *slang* **:** influence, pull, or clout 〈a cop may go out of his way to prove that your *juice* doesn't influence him —George Frazier〉 **4** **:** a motivating, inspiring, or enabling force or factor 〈when the creative *juices* were running high and there was a heady current of daring in the air —Eudora Welty〉

juice·head \'jüs,hed\ *n* [*juice* + *head* (as in *acidhead*)] *slang* **:** JUICER

juice man *n, slang* **:** a loan shark

juicer*n, *slang* **:** a heavy or habitual drinker of alcoholic beverages

juke \'jük\ *vt* **juked; juk·ing** [prob. alter. of E dial. *jouk* to cheat, deceive] **:** to fake out of position (as in football) 〈I beat my man, every time. Sometimes I *juke* him right

out of his shoes and he's lying on the ground in his socks —Gail Cogdill〉

jump*vi **:** to go from one sequence of instructions in a computer program to another 〈*jump* to a subroutine〉

jump*n **:** a transfer from one sequence of instructions in a computer program to a different sequence 〈a conditional *jump*〉

jump cut *n* **:** a discontinuity or acceleration in the action of a filmed scene brought about by removal of medial portions of the shot — **jump–cut** \'jəmp'kət\ *vb*

jumper*n **:** a shot in basketball made while jumping 〈hit a *jumper* from the top of the key〉

jump·ing jack \'jəmpiŋ'jak\ *n* **:** a conditioning exercise performed while standing by jumping from a position with the feet together and arms at the sides to a position with legs spread and hands touching overhead and then to the original position — called also *side-straddle hop*

jump·suit \'jəmp,süt\ *n* **:** a one-piece garment consisting of a blouse or shirt with attached trousers or shorts

jun \'jün\ *n, pl* **jun** [Korean] **1** **:** a monetary unit of North Korea equal to $1/100$ won **2** **:** a coin or note representing one jun

junk art *n* **:** three-dimensional art made from discarded material (as of metal, mortar, glass, or wood) — **junk artist** *n*

junk food *n* **1** **:** food high in calories but low in nutritional value 〈*junk foods* seem to be a prime fuel for marathon runners —S. L. Jacobs〉 **2** **:** something that is appealing or enjoyable but of little or no real value 〈the ultimate in *junk food* for young minds —Cleveland Amory〉

junkie*or **junky** *n, pl* **junkies** **:** one that derives inordinate pleasure from or that is dependent on something 〈this is a network for sports *junkies*. It's not for soft-core fans who like to watch an NFL game, then switch to the news —Scott Rasmussen〉

ju·ri·me·tri·cian \ˌjùrəmə-'trishən\ *n* **:** a specialist in jurimetrics

ju·ri·met·rics \ˌjùrə'me·triks\ *n pl but usu sing in constr* [L *juri-, jus* law + E -*metrics* (as in *econometrics*)] **:** the application of scientific methods to legal problems

Ju·ris Doctor \'jürəs-\ *n* [NL, fr. L, doctor of law] **:** a degree equivalent to bachelor of laws

jury–rig \'jürē,rig, -ri,-\ *vt* [*jury* improvised] **:** to erect, construct, or arrange in a makeshift fashion

juvenile hor·mone \-'hō(ə)r,mōn, -'hȯ(ə)r,-, -'hōä,-, -'hȯä,-\ *n* **:** an insect hormone that is secreted by the corpora allata, inhibits maturation to the imago, controls maturation of eggs and yolk deposition in the imago, and has been used experimentally to control pest insects by disrupting their life cycles

ju·ve·nil·ize \'jüvənᵊl,īz, -vnəl-\ *vt* **-ized; -iz·ing** [*juvenile* + -*ize*, vb. suffix] **:** to restrain from normal development and maturation **:** prolong the immaturity of 〈chemicals that *juvenilize* insect larvae〉 — **ju·ve·nil·iza·tion** \ˌjüvənᵊlə'zāshən, -vnəl-, -ˌlˌiᵊz-\ *n*

jux·ta·glo·mer·u·lar \ˌjəkstəglə'mer(y)ələr, -glō-\ *adj* [*juxta*- situated near + *glomerular*] **:** situated near a kidney glomerulus 〈*juxtaglomerular* cells〉

K

k*n, *often cap* [kilo- thousand, deriv. of Gk *chilioi*] **1** : thousand ⟨a salary of $24K⟩ **2** [fr. the fact that 1024 (2^{10}) is the power of 2 closest to 1000] : a unit of computer storage capacity equal to 1024 bytes ⟨a computer memory of 64K ⟩

k*abbr* kindergarten

K *n* [struck] : a strikeout

Kaf·ka·esque \ˌkäfkəˈesk, ˈkaf-\ *adj* [Franz *Kafka* †1924 Austrian writer] : of, relating to, or suggestive of Franz Kafka or his writings ⟨pathetically reveal her gradual disintegration . . . to a pale wreck trapped in a *Kafka-esque* nightmare —John Ardagh⟩

kai·nic acid \ˌkīnik-, ˌkān-\ *n* [Gk *kainos* new + E -ic derived from] : the neurotoxic active principle $C_{10}H_{15}NO_4$ from a dried red alga (*Digenia simplex*) used as an ascaricide

ka·lim·ba \kəˈlimbə, ka-\ *n* [of African origin, akin to Bemba *akalimba* zanza, Kimbundu *marimba* xylophone] : an African thumb piano that is derived from the zanza or mbira

kal·li·din \ˈkalədən\ *n* [G, fr. *kalli*krein + -d- (prob. fr. *deka*peptid peptide having 10 amino acids, fr. *deka*- ten + *peptid* peptide) + -*in* chemical compound] : either of two vasodilator kinins formed from blood plasma globulin by the action of kallikrein: **a** : BRADYKININ **b** : one that has the same amino acid sequence as bradykinin with a terminal lysine added

kal·li·kre·in \ˌkaləˈkrēən, kəˈlik-\ *n* [G, fr. *kalli*- beautiful, white (deriv. of Gk *kallos* beauty) + pan*kreas* pancreas (fr. Gk) + -*in* chemical compound; prob. fr. its therapeutic use in pancreatic disorders] : a hypotensive proteinase that liberates kinins from blood plasma proteins and is used therapeutically for vasodilatation

ka·na·my·cin \ˌkanəˈmīsᵊn, ˌkän-\ *n* [NL *kanamyceticus* (specific epithet of *Streptomyces kanamyceticus*) + E -*in* chemical compound] : a broad-spectrum antibiotic from a Japanese soil actinomycete (*Streptomyces kanamyceticus*)

kangaroo pocket *n* : a large front pocket (as in a winter jacket)

ka·on \ˈkäˌän\ *n* [ISV *ka* (fr. *K-meson*) + -*on* elementary particle] : an unstable meson of cosmic radiation or produced in high-energy particle collisions with its charged forms 966.3 times more massive than the electron and its neutral form 974.6 times more massive than the electron

Ka·po·si's sarcoma \kaˈpōs(h)ēz-, ˈkapəs(h)ēz-\ *n* [Moritz *Kaposi* †1902 Hungarian dermatologist] : a disease prob. of viral origin affecting esp. the skin and mucous membranes, characterized esp. by the formation of reddish-brown or bluish tumorous plaques on the lower extremities, and formerly limited primarily to elderly men in whom it followed a benign course but now being a major and sometimes fatal disease associated with im-

munodeficient individuals (as young homosexual males) with AIDS

ka·rass \kəˈras, ka-\ *n* [coined 1963 by Kurt Vonnegut *b*1922 Am. writer] : a group of people sharing a central common interest and usu. a personal relationship

Ka·ra·tsu ware \kəˈrät(ˌ)sü-\ *n* [*Karatsu*, city in Japan] : a Japanese ceramic ware traditionally made from the 7th century at Karatsu on Kyushu island that is probably the earliest glazed Japanese ceramic ware, includes both earthenware and stoneware, and comprises chiefly vessels for chanoyu

kar·ma*\ˈkärmə, ˈkämə, *also* ˈkərmə\ *n* : a characteristic emanation, aura, spirit, or atmosphere that can be sensed : vibrations ⟨enthusiastic ease was the predominating *karma* at Rainbow Party headquarters —Stu Werbin⟩

kart \ˈkärt\ *n* [prob. fr. *GoKart*, a trademark] : a miniature motorcar used esp. for racing

kart·ing \ˈkärd·iŋ\ *n* : the sport of racing miniature motorcars

kbar *abbr* kilobar

keeper*n : an offensive football play in which the quarterback runs with the ball

kel·vin \ˈkelvən\ *n* : a unit of temperature equal to $1/273.16$ of the Kelvin scale temperature of the triple point of water

Ken·ya·pi·the·cus \ˌkenyəpəˈthēkəs, ˌkenyə-, -ˈpithək-\ *n* [NL, genus name, fr. *Kenya*, country in Africa + -*pithecus* ape, deriv. of Gk *pithēkos*] **1** : a genus of ancient prehuman African primates that is held to belong to the human ancestral line and is sometimes included in the genus *Ramapithecus* **2** : a primate of the genus *Kenyapithecus*

Keogh plan \ˈkē(ˌ)ō-\ *n* [Eugene James *Keogh* *b* 1907 Am. politician] : an individual retirement account for the self-employed

ke·rat·in·o·cyte \kəˈrat⟨ᵊ⟩nəˌsīt\ *n* [NL, fr. *keratin* + connective -*o*- + -*cyte* cell] : an epidermal cell that produces keratin

keratosis fol·li·cu·lar·is \-ˌfäləkyəˈlerəs, -fəˌlik-\ *n* [NL *follicularis*, fr. L *folliculus* small sac (dim. of *follis* bag) + L -*aris* -ar (of, resembling)] : DARIER'S DISEASE

kernel*n **1** : a subset of the elements of one set (as a group) that a function (as a homomorphism) maps onto an identity element of another set **2** : KERNEL SENTENCE

kernel sentence *n* : a sentence (as "John is big" or "John is a man") exemplifying in a language one of a very small group of grammatically simple sentence types or patterns (as noun phrase + be + adjective phrase or noun phrase + be + noun phrase) cannot be broken down into simpler sentence types and which in transformational grammar are the basic stock or source from or according to which all sentences in that language are formed or derived and in terms of which all sentences of the language can ultimately be described — called also *kernel*

ke·to·glu·ta·rate \ˌkēd-ō(ˌ)glü'tä·rāt\ n [*ketoglutaric* (acid) + *-ate* salt or ester of an acid] **:** a salt or ester of ketoglutaric acid

key* vi **keyed; key·ing :** to observe the position or movement of an opposing player in football in order to anticipate the play — usu. used with *on* ⟨the middle linebacker was *keying* on the halfback⟩

key \'kē\ n, pl **keys** [by shortening and alter. fr. *kilo* kilogram] *slang* **:** a kilogram esp. of marijuana or heroin

key club n [fr. the fact that each member is provided with a key to the premises] **:** an informal private club serving liquor and providing entertainment

key·pad \'kē,pad\ n **:** a small often hand-held keyboard

key·set \'kē,set\ n **:** a set of systematically arranged keys for operating a machine (as a typewriter) **:** a keyboard

key·stroke \'kē,strōk\ n **:** the act or an instance of depressing a key on a keyboard — **keystroke** vb

khoum \'küm, 'küm\ n [native name in Mauritania] **1 :** a monetary unit of Mauritania equal to ⅕ ouguiya **2 :** a coin representing one khoum

kick* vb — **kick ass :** to use bluntly forceful or coercive measures in order to achieve a desired end

kick out* vi **:** to turn a surfboard around and drive it over the top of a wave by pushing down on the rear of the board with the foot

kicky* \'kikē\ adj **kick·i·er; -est :** providing a kick or thrill ⟨*kicky* violent scenes, carefully estranging you from the victims so that you can enjoy the rapes and beatings —Pauline Kael⟩ — often used as a generalized term of approval ⟨*kicky* clothes⟩

kid·nap·ee \ˌkid,na'pē\ n **:** a person who has been kidnapped

kid·vid \'kid,vid\ n [*kid* + *vid*eo] **:** television programs for children

kill ratio n **:** the ratio of combatants killed on each side in an engagement or conflict

ki·lo·bar \'kēlə,bär, 'kilə-, -,bá(r\ n [ISV *kilo-* thousand (deriv. of Gk *chilioi*) + *bar*] **:** a unit of pressure equal to 1000 bars — abbr. *kbar*

ki·lo·baud \-,bȯd, -,bōd\ n **:** 1000 baud

ki·lo·bit \-,bit\ n **:** 1024 bits

kilo·byte \-,bīt\ n **:** 1024 bytes

kilo·mega·cy·cle \'kēlə¦megə,sīkəl, 'kilə-\ n **:** 1000 megacycles **:** one billion cycles

ki·lo·oer·sted \'kēlō'ərstəd, 'kilō-, -'ȯr-\ n **:** 1000 oersteds

ki·lo·rad \'kēlō,rad, 'kilō-\ n **:** 1000 rads

ki·na \'kēnə\ n, pl **kina** also **kinas** [native name in Papua New Guinea] **1 :** the basic monetary unit of Papua New Guinea **2 :** a coin or note representing one kina

ki·net·ic art \kə'ned·ik-, kī'-\ n **:** art in which movement (as of a motor-driven part or a changing electronic image) is a basic element — **kinetic artist** n

ki·net·i·cism \kə'ned·ə,sizəm, kī'-\ n **:** KINETIC ART

ki·net·i·cist \-əsəst\ n **1 :** a specialist in kinetics **2 :** KINETIC ARTIST

ki·ne·tin \'kīnətən\ n [*kinet-* motion (fr. Gk *kinētos* moving) + *-in* chemical compound] **:** a cytokinin $C_{10}H_9N_5O$ that increases mitosis and callus formation

ki·neto·some \kə'ned·ə,sōm, kī'-\ n [*kineto-* + *-some* body, deriv. of Gk *sōma*] **:** a minute distinctively

staining granule typically found at the base of every flagellum or cilium

king·side \'kiŋ,sīd\ n **:** the side of a chessboard containing the file on which both kings sit at the beginning of the game

ki·nin \'kīnən\ n [Gk *kinein* to move, stimulate + E *-in* chemical compound] **1 :** any of various polypeptide hormones that are formed locally in the tissues and have their chief effect on smooth muscle **2 :** CYTOKININ

ki·ni·nase \'kīnə,nās, -āz\ n [*kinin* + *-ase* enzyme] **:** an enzyme in blood that destroys a kinin

ki·nin·o·gen \kī'ninəjən\ n [*kinin* + connective *-o-* + *-gen* producer, deriv. of Gk *-genēs* born] **:** an inactive precursor of a kinin — **ki·nin·o·gen·ic** \(¦)kī¦ninə¦jenik\ adj

kinky* \'kiŋkē, -ki\ adj **kink·i·er; -est 1 :** relating to, having, or appealing to bizarre or unconventional tastes esp. in sex ⟨an egregious attempt to exploit both sentimental and *kinky* appetites —Mark Goodman⟩ ⟨every *kinky* weirdo thing you want to do —Philip Roth⟩ ⟨delicious tangles may ensue, a bit of *kinky* sex, a jolly murder —Mary E. Barrett⟩; *also* **:** being sexually deviant ⟨a *kinky* baron in leg irons, begging for another spanking —Diana Davenport⟩ **2 :** outlandish, strange, odd, far₌ out ⟨likes to dress in ... *kinky* clothes, and he does appear to be flamboyant —Rosemary Brown⟩ ⟨one of the *kinkiest* divisions in the army of culinary skeptics, the health-food addicts —*Time*⟩ — **kink·i·ness** \-nəs\ n

Kir·li·an photography \ˌki(ə)rlēən-\ n [Semyon D. *Kirlian* and Valentina K. *Kirlian* fl 1939 Soviet inventors] **:** a process in which an image is obtained by application of a high-frequency electrical field to an object (as a leaf or metal coin) so that it radiates a characteristic pattern of luminescence that is recorded on photographic film

Ki·run·di \kə'ründē, -di\ n **:** the Bantu language of the central African republic of Burundi

kissing disease n [fr. the belief that it is frequently transmitted by kissing] **:** the disease infectious mononucleosis

kiss of life 1 *Brit* **:** artificial respiration by the mouth-to-mouth method **2** *Brit* **:** something that restores vitality ⟨manages some trick of timing that gives clichés the *kiss of life* —Irving Wardle⟩

Kis·wa·hi·li \(ˌ)ki,swä'hēlē, -li\ n **:** the Swahili language

kitchen-sink \ˌkichən,siŋk\ adj, chiefly Brit **:** portraying or emphasizing the squalid aspects of modern life ⟨the *kitchen-sink* realism of contemporary British drama — *Current Biog.*⟩

ki·wi·fruit \'kē-(ˌ)wē-\ n [*kiwi*, nickname for New Zealanders, fr. the fact that it was first established as a commercial crop in New Zealand] **:** the fruit of the Chinese gooseberry — called also *kiwi*.] *slang* **:** kilometer

klick \'klik\ n [by shortening & alter.] *slang* **:** kilometer

Kline·fel·ter's syndrome \'klīn,feltə(r)'sin,drōm, also -'sindrəm\ n [Harry F. *Klinefelter* b1912 Am. physician] **:** an abnormal condition characterized by two X and one Y chromosomes and an infertile male phenotype with small testicles

kludge or **kluge** \'klüj\ n [origin unknown] **:** a system and esp. a computer system made up of components that are poorly matched or were orig. intended for some other use

klutz \'kləts\ n [Yiddish *klotz, klutz*, fr. G *klotz*, lit., wooden block, fr. MHG *kloz* lumpy mass] **:** a clumsy and awkward person ⟨is such a *klutz* you have to laugh as he slinks across a sumptuous Texas lawn accidentally turning on the sprinklers —Liz Smith⟩ — **klutzy** \'klətsē, -si\ *adj*

K–me·son \'kā¦mez¸än, -¦mes¸än, -¦mā-, -¦mē-\ *n* : KAON

knee–jerk \¦nē¸jərk, -¸jək, -¸jəik\ *adj* : readily predictable : automatic ⟨the latest response of public officials to mounting crime in the streets amounts to nothing more than another *knee-jerk* reaction —J.F. Ahern⟩; *also* : reacting in a readily predictable way ⟨*knee-jerk* liberals⟩ ⟨seeming to be your own man, rather than a *knee-jerk* reactor to events —Benjamin DeMott⟩

knock off*\(')näk¸óf\ *vt* **1** : to make a knockoff of ⟨*knocks off* popular dress designs⟩ **2** : to undersell by means of knockoffs

knock·off \'näk¸óf\ *n* : a copy (as of a dress design) that sells for less than the original

knuckle sandwich *n, slang* : a punch in the mouth

ko·bo \'kò¸bò\ *n, pl* **kobo** [alter. of *copper*] **1** : a monetary unit of Nigeria equal to ¹/₁₀₀ naira **2** : a coin representing one kobo

kook \'kük\ *n* [by shortening and alter. fr. *cuckoo*] : one whose ideas or actions are eccentric, fantastic, or insane ⟨must listen to the deviants of our society before pronouncing them all *kooks* —H.G. Cox⟩

kooky *also* **kook·ie** \'kükē, -ki\ *adj* **kook·i·er; -est** : having the characteristics or being characteristic of a kook : crazy, offbeat ⟨*kooky*, lovable characters who look like everyone's zany brother —Rex Reed⟩ ⟨*kooky*... adventure of a couple of romantic iconoclasts —William Fadiman⟩ — **kook·i·ly** \'kükəlē, -li\ *adv* — **kook·i·ness** \'kükēnəs, -kin-\ *n*

ko·ra \'kōr(¸)ä, 'kòr-, -rə\ *n* [native name in Senegal] : a 21-string musical instrument of African origin that resembles a lute

Ko·rat \kō'rät\ *n* [*Khorat* plateau, Thailand, where the breed originated] **1** : a breed of short-haired domestic cat that originated in Thailand and is characterized by a heart-shaped face, a silver-blue coat, and green eyes **2** : a cat of the Korat breed

kovsh \'kòvsh\ *n, pl* **kov·shi** \-shē\ [Russ, scoop, ladle] : a low boat-shaped drinking vessel with a long handle at one end

K particle *n* : KAON

krad \'kā¸rad\ *n, pl* **krad** *also* **krads** [*kilorad*] : KILO-RAD

Krem·lin·ol·o·gy \¸kremlə'näləjē\ *n* [*Kremlin* + connective *-o-* + *-logy* study, science, deriv. of Gk *logos* word] : the study of the policies and practices of the Soviet Russian government ⟨prognostications here are subject to all the usual pitfalls of *Kremlinology* —Robert Gillette⟩ —

Krem·lin·olog·i·cal \¦kremlən³l¦äjəkəl\ *adj* — **Kremlin·ol·o·gist** \¸kremlə'nälojəst\ *n*

krewe \'krü\ *n* [alter. of *crew*] : a private organization staging festivities (as parades and balls) during Mardi Gras in New Orleans

Kro·neck·er delta \¦krō¸nekə(r)-\ *n* [Leopold *Kronecker* †1891 Ger. mathematician] : a function of two variables that is 1 when the variables have the same value and is 0 when they have different values

Kru·ger·rand \'krügə¸rand, *in So. Afr. usu* -¸ránd *or* -¸ránt *or* -¸ränt\ *n* [S.J.P. *Kruger* †1904 So. African statesman + *rand* monetary unit] : a one-ounce gold coin of the Republic of So. Africa

ku·do \'k(y)üd(¸)ō\ *n, pl* **kudos** [back-formation fr. *kudos* (taken as a pl.)] **1** : an award or honor ⟨a score of honorary degrees and . . . other *kudos* —*Time*⟩ **2** : a compliment or tribute ⟨to all three should go some kind of special *kudo* for refusing to succumb —Al Hine⟩

kun·da·li·ni \¸kùnd³l'ēnē, -dä'lē-\ *n, often cap* [Skt *kuṇḍalinī*, fr. fem. of *kuṇḍalin* circular, coiled, fr. *kuṇḍala* ring] : the yogic life-force that is held to lie coiled at the base of the spine until it is aroused and sent to the head to trigger enlightenment

kung fu \¸kəŋ'fü, ¸kúŋ-\ *n* [Chin dial.; akin to Chin (Pek) *ch'üan²* *fa*³, lit., boxing principles] : a Chinese art of self-defense resembling karate

ku·ru \'kü(¸)rü\ *n* [native name in New Guinea, lit., trembling] : a fatal disease of the nervous system that is caused by a slow virus, resembles scrapie in sheep, and occurs among tribesmen of eastern New Guinea

Ku·ta·ni \kù'tänē\ *or* **Kutani ware** *n* [*Kutani*, village in Japan] : a Japanese porcelain produced in and about the village of Kutani on Honshu island since the mid-17th century and esteemed for originality of design and coloring

¹kvetch \kə'vech, 'kve-, 'kfe-\ *vi* [Yiddish *kvetshn*, lit., to squeeze, pinch, akin to G *quetschen* to pinch, to bruise] : to complain habitually ⟨*kvetches* constantly about being 33 years old —H.F. Waters⟩

²kvetch *n* [Yiddish, complainer, fr. *kvetch* pinch] **1** : an habitual complainer ⟨enormous *kvetches* with . . . mean little faces —Maurice Sendak⟩ **2** : a complaint

kwa·cha \'kwächə\ *n, pl* **kwacha** [native name in Zambia, lit., dawn] **1** : the basic monetary unit of Malawi and Zambia **2** : a note representing one kwacha

kwan·za \'kwänzə\ *n, pl* **kwanza** *or* **kwanzas** [perh. fr. Swahili *kwanza* first] **1** : the basic monetary unit of Angola **2** : a coin or note representing one kwanza

KWIC \'kwik\ *n* [keyword *in* context] : a computer-generated index alphabetized on a keyword that appears within a portion of its context

KWOC \'kwäk\ *n* [keyword *out* of context] : a computer-generated index in which the keyword is followed by its context

L

La·ba·no·ta·tion \ˌläbənōˈtäshən\ *n* [Rudolf von *Laban* †1958 Czech dance theorist + *notation*] **:** a method of recording bodily movement (as in a dance) on a staff **:** laban system

labor–intensive *adj* **:** having high labor costs per unit of output; *esp* **:** requiring greater expenditure on labor than in capital

La·combe \ləˈkōm\ *n* [*Lacombe* Experiment Station, Lacombe, Alberta, Canada, where the breed was developed] **1 :** a breed of white bacon-type swine developed in Canada from Landrace, Chester White, and Berkshire stock **2** *often not cap* **:** an animal of the Lacombe breed

lac·tate de·hy·dro·ge·nase \ˈlak͟ˌtātˌdēˈ(ˌ)hiˈdräjəˌnās, -(ˌ)dēˈhidrəjə-, -ˌāz\ *n* **:** any of a group of isoenzymes that catalyze reversibly the conversion of pyruvic acid to lactic acid

lac·tic dehydrogenase \ˈlaktik-\ *n* **:** LACTATE DEHYDROGENASE

lac·to·per·ox·i·dase \ˈlak(ˌ)tōpəˈräksəˌdās, -ˌāz\ *n* [*lacto-* milk + *peroxidase*] **:** a peroxidase that is found in milk and saliva and is used to catalyze the iodination of tyrosine-containing proteins (as thyroglobulin)

la·e·trile \ˈlāəˌtril, -əˈtrōl\ *n, often cap* [*laevorotarynitrile* (fr. *laevo-* left + *rotary* + *nitrile*)] **:** a drug derived from apricot pits that contains amygdalin and has been used in the treatment of cancer although of unproved effectiveness

laggard*n **:** a security whose price has lagged for no obvious reason behind the average of its group or of the market

lag·ger\ˈlagə(r)\ *n* **:** an economic indicator (as spending on new plants and equipment) that more often than not maintains an existent trend for some time after the state of the economy has turned onto an opposite trend — called also *lagging index*

laid–back \ˈlādˈbak\ *adj* **:** being relaxed in style, character, or manner **:** easygoing, unhurried ⟨an insinuating kind of country rock, so *laid-back* that it almost falls asleep —John Rockwell⟩ ⟨concentrated on her mantra until she was feeling *laid-back* again —Cyra McFadden⟩ ⟨looking like a *laid-back* collegian in sweater, slacks and jogging shoes —Robert Berkvist⟩ ⟨images of golden youth in *laid-back* academia —F. J. Prial⟩

La·maze \ləˈmäz\ *adj* [Fernand *Lamaze* †1957 Fr. obstetrician] **:** relating to or being a method of childbirth that involves psychological and physical preparation by the mother in order to suppress pain and facilitate delivery without drugs

lamb·da\ˈlamdə\ *or* **lambda particle** *n* **:** an uncharged elementary particle that has a mass 2183 times that of an electron, is an unstable baryon, and decays typically into a nucleon and a pion with an average lifetime of 2.6×10^{-10} second

lame**adj, slang* **:** not being in the know **:** square

lame \ˈlām\ *n, slang* **:** a person who is not in the know **:** a square ⟨one either knows what's happening on the street, or he is a *lame* —John Horton⟩

land·er\ˈlandə(r)\ *n* **:** one that lands; *esp* **:** a space vehicle that is designed to land on a celestial body (as the moon or a planet)

landmark*n **:** a structure (as a building) of unusual historical and usu. aesthetic interest; *esp* **:** one that is officially designated and set aside for preservation

lane cake *n* [origin unknown] **:** a white layer cake with a rich filling usu. containing whiskey or wine, pecans, coconut, raisins, and candied fruit

language*n **:** MACHINE LANGUAGE

Lan·tian man \ˈlanˌtyan-\ *or* **Lan·t'ien man** \-ˌtyen-\ *n* [*Lan-t'ien*, district in Shensi province, China] **:** an extinct man known from parts of a skull excavated in China and held to be an extremely primitive example of modern man

lap·a·ro·scope \ˈlap(ə)rəˌskōp\ *n* [ISV *laparo-* (fr. Gk. *lapara* flank, fr. *laparos* slack, loose) + *-scope* viewing instrument] **:** a long slender instrument for insertion through the abdominal wall that is used to visualize the interior of the peritoneal cavity

lap·a·ros·co·py \ˌlapəˈräskəpē, -pi\ *n, pl* **-pies** [ISV *laparo-* + *-scopy* examination] **1 :** visual examination of the interior of the abdomen by means of a laparoscope **2 :** an operation involving laparoscopy; *esp* **:** one for sterilization of the female (as by electrocoagulation of the fallopian tubes) or for removal of ova that involves use of a laparoscope to guide surgical procedures within the abdomen — **lap·a·ro·scop·ic** \-ərəˈskäpik\ *adj* — **lap·a·ros·co·pist** \-əˈräskəpəst\ *n*

lap belt *n* **:** a seat belt that fastens across the lap

La·place trans·form \ləˈpläsˌtran(t)sˌfȯrm, -ˈplas-\ *n* [Pierre Simon de *Laplace* †1827 Fr. astronomer and mathematician] **:** a transformation of a function $f(x)$ into the function $g(t) = \int_0^\infty e^{xt} f(x) dx$ that is useful esp. in reducing the solution of an ordinary linear differential equation with constant coefficients to the solution of a polynomial equation

lase \ˈlāz\ *vi* **lased; las·ing** [back-formation fr. *laser*] **:** to emit coherent light

L–as·par·a·gi·nase \ˌela'sparəjəˌnās, -ˌāz\ *n* [L- levorotatory + *asparagine* + *-ase* enzyme] **:** an enzyme that breaks down the physiologically commoner form of asparagine, is obtained esp. from bacteria, and is used esp. to treat leukemia

Las·sa fever \ˌlasə-\ *n* [*Lassa*, village in Nigeria] **:** a virus disease esp. of Africa that is characterized by a high fever, headaches, mouth ulcers, muscle aches, small hemorrhages under the skin, heart and kidney failure, and a high mortality rate

last hurrah *n* [*The Last Hurrah* (1956) by Edwin O'Connor †1968 Am. novelist] **:** a last effort or attempt ⟨his unsuccessful Senate run was his *last hurrah* —R.W. Daly⟩

latchkey child *n* **:** a young child of working parents who must spend part of the day at home unsupervised

latent root *n* **:** a characteristic root of a matrix

lateral condyle *n* **:** a condyle on the outer side of the lower extremity of the femur; *also* **:** a corresponding eminence on the upper part of the tibia that articulates with the lateral condyle of the femur — compare MEDIAL CONDYLE

lateral thinking *n* **:** thinking that is not deductive

lath·y·rit·ic \,lathə'rid·ik\ *adj* **:** of, relating to, affected with, or characteristic of lathyrism ⟨*lathyritic* rats⟩ ⟨*lathyritic* cartilage⟩ ⟨*lathyritic* collagen⟩

la·tic·i·fer \lə'tisəfə(r)\ *n* [ISV latici- (fr. NL latic-, latex) + -fer bearing, one that bears, deriv. of L ferre to carry] **:** a plant cell or vessel that contains latex

Latin Americanist *n* **:** a specialist in Latin-American civilization

launder* *vt* **:** to cause (illegally obtained money) to appear legitimate by channelization through a third party so as to conceal the true source ⟨banks were used to *launder* money illegally skimmed from casinos —*Private Eye*⟩ ⟨involved in bugging, surveillance, collecting and *laundering* campaign funds B.J. Wattenberg⟩

laundry list *n* [fr. the listing of articles of clothing sent to a laundry] **:** a usu. long list of items ⟨the *laundry list* of new consumer-protection bills —N.C. Miller⟩

law of par·si·mo·ny \-'pärsə,mōnē, -'pås-\ **:** a scientific and philosophic rule that entities should not be multiplied unnecessarily which is interpreted as requiring that the simplest of competing theories be preferred to the more complex and that explanations of unknown phenomena be sought first in terms of known quantities

law·ren·cium \lȯ'ren(t)sēəm, lə'-, -nch(e)əm\ *n* [NL, fr. Ernest O. *Lawrence* †1958 Am. physicist + NL -ium chemical element] **:** a short-lived radioactive element of atomic number 103 that is produced artificially from californium — symbol Lr

lay·about \'lāə,baȯt\ *n* [fr. the phrase *lay about*, nonstandard alter. of *lie about*] *chiefly Brit* **:** one who spends his time in idleness **:** idler, loafer ⟨equating all those in need of relief with the hard core of professional beggars, spongers and *layabouts* —*Times Lit. Supp.*⟩

lay–by* \'lā,bī\ *n* **:** the final operation (as a last cultivating) in the growing of a field crop

layer* *vt* **:** to wear (clothes) in layers ~ *vi* **:** to form out of superimposed layers

lay·per·son \'lā,pərs³n, -,pōs- , -,pȯis-\ *n* **1 :** a person who is not a member of the clergy **2 :** a person who is not a member of a particular profession or who is not an expert in some field

lazy eye *n* [fr. the fact that a person suffering from this condition uses only one eye] **:** dimness of sight without apparent change in the eye structures that is associated esp. with toxic effects or dietary deficiencies — called also *lazy eye blindness*

LCD \,el(,)sē'dē\ *n* [liquid crystal display] **:** a constantly operating display (as of the time in a digital watch) that consists of segments of a liquid crystal whose reflectivity varies according to the voltage applied to them

L cell *n* **:** a fibroblast cell of a strain isolated from mice and used esp. in virus research

LDC \,el(,)dē'sē\ *n* **:** a less developed country

LDH *abbr* **1** lactate dehydrogenase **2** lactic dehydrogenase

L–do·pa \(')el'dōpə\ *n* [l- levorotatory + *dopa*] **:** the levorotatory form of dopa found esp. in broad beans or prepared synthetically and used in treating Parkinson's disease

leader* *n* **:** an economic indicator (as the level of corporate profits or of stock prices) that more often than not shows a change in direction before a corresponding change in the state of the economy — called also *leading indicator*

leaf·let \'lēflət\ *vb* **leaf·let·ed** *or* **leaf·let·ted; leaf·let·ing** *or* **leaf·let·ting** *vi* **:** to pass out leaflets ~ *vt* **:** to pass out leaflets to

lean* *vb* — **lean on :** to apply pressure to ⟨they kept *leaning on* him and the kid still wouldn't crack —Joe Eszterhas⟩ ⟨it may soon be time . . . for Washington to *lean* hard *on* Israel —Ned Temko⟩

leash law *n* **:** a usu. municipal ordinance requiring dogs to be restrained when not confined to their owners' property

¹lech \'lech\ *n* [alter. of *letch* sexual craving] **1 :** sexual craving **2 :** a lecher

²lech *vi* **:** to experience sexual desire

LED *n* [light-emitting diode] **:** a semiconductor diode that emits light when subjected to an applied voltage and that is usu. used in an electronic display (as for a pocket calculator or a digital watch)

left field* *n* **:** a position far from the mainstream (as of prevailing opinion) ⟨they're way out in *left field*. . . . They see themselves possessed by Satan —Louis Schlan⟩

legal pad *n* **:** a writing tablet of usu. 8½ by 14 inch ruled yellow paper

Legionnaires' disease *n* [so called fr. its first recognized occurrence during the 1976 American Legion convention] **:** a lobar pneumonia caused by a bacterium (*Legionella pneumophila*)

Leish·man–Don·o·van body \'līshmən'dänəvən-, -'dən-\ *n* [Sir William B. *Leishman* †1926 Eng. army surgeon & Charles *Donovan* †1951 Irish physician] **:** a protozoan of the genus *Leishmania* (esp. *L. donovani*) in its nonmotile stage that is found esp. in cells of the skin, spleen, and liver of individuals affected with leishmaniasis and esp. kala-azar

leisure suit *n* **:** a suit consisting of a shirt jacket and matching trousers for informal wear

lek·var \'lek,vär, -,vå(r\ *n* [Hung] **:** a prune butter used as a pastry filling

LEM \'lem\ *n* **:** LUNAR EXCURSION MODULE

lem·ma·tize \'lemə-,tīz, -əd-,īz\ *vt* **-tized; -tiz·ing** [*lemmata,* pl. of *lemma* + -ize, vb. suffix] **:** to sort (words in a corpus) in order to group with a lemma all its variant and inflected forms — **lem·ma·ti·za·tion** \,leməd-ə'zāshən, -ə-,tī'z-\ *n*

Leo* *n* **:** one born under the astrological sign Leo

le·one \lē'ōn\ *n* [Sierra *Leone,* Africa] **1 :** the basic monetary unit of Sierra Leone **2 :** a note representing one leone

Le·oni·an \lē'ōnēən\ *n* [fr. leon-, alter. (perh. influenced by *leonine*) of Leo + -ian one belonging to] **:** LEO

Leo·nid \'lēənəd\ *n, pl* **Leonids** *or* **Le·on·i·des** \lē'änə,dēz\ [L Leon-, Leo, a constellation, lit., lion + E

-id meteor; fr. their appearing to radiate from a point in the constellation Leo] **:** one of the shooting stars constituting the meteor shower that recurs near the 14th of November

lep·ton·ic \(')lep¦tänik\ *adj* **:** of, relating to, or producing a lepton ⟨*leptonic* decay of a hyperon⟩

lepton number \'lep͵tän-\ *n* **:** a number equal to the number of leptons minus that of antileptons in a system of elementary particles

lep·to·spire \'lepta͵spī(a)r, -īa(r\ *n* **:** a spirochete of the genus *Leptospira*

lesion *vt* **:** to produce lesions in

let*vb* — **let it all hang out** **:** to reveal one's true feelings **:** act without dissimulation ⟨*lets it all hang out* in an emotionally charged autobiography —*Publishers Weekly*⟩ — **let the chips fall where they may** **:** to act knowing that the consequences may prove to be undesirable or disadvantageous ⟨clever and well-informed at cross-examining his subjects, and he *lets the chips fall where they may* —Deborah Shapley⟩

letter bomb *n* **:** an explosive device concealed in an envelope and mailed to the intended victim

let·ter·form \'led-ər͵fórm, -ə͵fó(ə)m\ *n* **:** the shape of a letter of an alphabet esp. from the standpoint of design or development ⟨squared *letterforms* came into use for Greek inscriptions long before Roman engravers adopted them —Richard Olson⟩

let·ter·set \-͵set\ *n* [*letter*press + off*set*] **:** offset printing in which an image on a letterpress plate is transferred to a rubber roller and offset onto the paper

letter stock *n* [fr. the letter signed by the purchaser stating that the stock is acquired for investment and not for public sale] **:** restricted and unregistered stock that may not be sold to the general public without undergoing registration

leu·ke·mic \lü'kēmik\ *n* **:** a person suffering from leukemia

leu·ko·dys·tro·phy \͵lükō'distrəfē\ *n* [*leuko-* white (deriv. of Gk *leukos*) + *dystrophy*] **:** any of several genetically determined diseases characterized by progressive degeneration of the white matter of the brain

lev·al·lor·phan \͵levə'lór͵fan, -fən\ *n* [*lev-* levorotatory + *all*yl + *morph*ine + *-an* unsaturated carbon compound] **:** a drug $C_{19}H_{25}NO$ related to morphine that is used to counteract morphine poisoning

level of significance **:** the probability of rejecting the null hypothesis in a statistical test when it is true — called also *significance level*

le·ver·age*\'lev(ə)rij, 'lēv-, -rēj\ *n* **:** the use of credit to enhance one's speculative capacity ⟨buying stocks on margin is a simple example of *leverage*⟩

leverage *vt* **-aged; -ag·ing** **:** to provide (as a corporation) or supplement (as money) with leverage ⟨mismanaged, unwisely *leveraged*, and highly illiquid corporations . . . reap the whirlwind of bankruptcy —N.A. Bailey⟩ ⟨margin may *leverage* the speculator too much —D.W. Kelly⟩

lex·is \'leksəs\ *n, pl* **lex·es** \-k͵sēz\ [Gk, speech, word] **:** the words of a language **:** vocabulary

lib \'lib\ *n* [by shortening] **:** LIBERATION

lib·ber \'libə(r)\ *n* **:** one who advocates liberation ⟨a women's *libber*⟩

lib·er·a·tion*\͵libə'rāshən\ *n* **:** a movement seeking equal rights and status for a group ⟨women's *liberation*⟩ ⟨gay *liberation*⟩

Libra*n* **:** one born under the astrological sign Libra

Li·bran \'lēbrən, 'līb-\ *n* [*libra* + E *-an* one belonging to] **:** LIBRA

Lib·ri·um \'librēəm\ *trademark* — used for a preparation of chlordiazepoxide

licensed practical nurse *n* **:** a trained person authorized by license (as from a state) to provide routine care for the sick

licensed vocational nurse *n* **:** a licensed practical nurse authorized by license to practice in the states of California or Texas

lid*n* **:** an ounce of marijuana

li·dar \'lī͵där\ *n* [*light* + ra*dar*] **:** a device or system for locating an object that is similar in operation to radar but emits pulsed laser light instead of microwaves

life·line \'līf͵līn\ *adj* **:** of, relating to, or being a utility rate structure under which a specified minimum consumption is billed at the lowest rate

life list *n* **:** a record kept of all birds sighted and identified by a birder

lif·er*\'līfə(r)\ *n* **1** **:** a career member of the armed forces ⟨professional soldiers, *lifers* who believe in the military and its mission —S.V. Roberts⟩ **2** **:** a person who has made a life-long commitment (as to a way of life) ⟨a baseball *lifer*, a man who subscribes to all the Biblical tenets of the grand old game —Mark Kram⟩ ⟨hated the city enough to become country *lifers* —Richard Ellmann⟩

life science *n* **:** a branch of science (as biology, medicine, anthropology, or sociology) that deals with living organisms and life processes — usu. used in pl. — **life scientist** *n*

life–sup·port system \'līfsə͵pō(ə)rt-, -͵pó(ə)rt-, -͵pōət-, -͵pō(ə)t-\ *n* **:** a system that provides all or some of the items (as oxygen, food, water, control of temperature and pressure, disposition of carbon dioxide and body wastes) necessary for maintaining life or health: as **a** **:** one used to maintain the health of a person or animal in outer space, underwater, or in a mine **b** **:** one used to maintain the life of an injured or ill person unable to maintain certain physiological processes without artificial support **c** **:** the part of the world in which life can exist **:** biosphere

lifting body *n* **:** a maneuverable rocket-propelled wingless vehicle that is capable of travel in aerospace or in the earth's atmosphere where its lift is derived from its shape and that can be landed on the ground

li·gase \'lī͵gās, -͵gāz\ *n* [ISV *lig-* (fr. L *ligare* to bind, tie) + *-ase* enzyme] **:** an enzyme that catalyzes the linking together of two molecules usu. with concurrent splitting off of a pyrophosphate group from ATP

light–adapt·ed \'līd-ə͵daptəd, 'līt-\ *adj* **:** adjusted for vision in bright light **:** having undergone light adaptation

light chain *n* **:** either of the two smaller of the four polypeptide chains that comprise antibodies — compare HEAVY CHAIN

light–day \'līt¦dā\ *n* **:** a unit of length in astronomy equal to the distance that light travels in one day in a vacuum

light guide *n* **:** fiber optics used esp. for telecommunication with light waves

light–hour \\'līd-ˌaū̇(ə)r, -ˌaū̇ə(r\\ *n* **:** a unit of length in astronomy equal to the distance that light travels in one hour in a vacuum

light pen *n* **:** a pen-shaped device for direct interaction with a computer through a cathode-ray tube display

light pollution *n* **:** artificial skylight (as from city lights) that interferes with astronomical observations

light show *n* **:** a kaleidoscopic display of colored lights, slides, and films suggestive of the hallucinogenic effects of psychedelic drugs

light water *n* **:** ordinary water as distinguished from heavy water

lig·no·caine \\'lignə.kān\\ *n* [*ligno-* lignin (deriv. of L *lignum* wood) + *-caine* synthetic alkaloid anesthetic, deriv. of G *kokain* cocaine] **:** a crystalline compound that is used in the form of its hydrochloride as a local anesthetic

like \\(ˌ)līk\\ *interj* [*like*, adv.] — used chiefly in informal speech to preface a statement or to express hesitation ⟨*like*, man, the self is, *like*, an individuality, dependent on consciousness —Benjamin DeMott⟩

li·ku·ta \\lə'kütə, (ˌ)lēˌk-\\ *n*, *pl* **ma·ku·ta** \\(')mäˌküta\\ [of Niger-Congo origin; prob. akin to obs. Nupe *kuta* stone] **1 :** a monetary unit of Zaire equal to $^1/_{100}$ zaire **2 :** a coin representing one likuta

li·lan·geni \\ˌlē(ˌ)län'(g)enē\\ *n*, *pl* **ema·lan·geni** \\ˌemə(ˌ)län'(g)enē\\ [native name in Swaziland] **1 :** the basic monetary unit of Swaziland **2 :** a coin or note representing one lilangeni

lim·bic\\'limbik\\ *adj* **:** of, relating to, or being the limbic system of the brain

limbic system *n* **:** a group of subcortical structures (as the hypothalamus, the hippocampus, and the amygdala) of the brain that are concerned esp. with emotion and motivation

lim·bo \\'lim(ˌ)bō\\ *n*, *pl* **limbos** [native name in West Indies] **:** a West Indian acrobatic dance orig. for men that involves bending over backward and passing under a horizontal pole which is lowered slightly for each successive pass

limit point *n* **:** a point that is related to a set of points in such a way that every neighborhood of the point no matter how small contains another point belonging to the set — called also *point of accumulation*

limo \\'lim(ˌ)ō\\ *n*, *pl* **limos** [short for *limousine*] **:** a limousine ⟨they rode *limos* to the airport with groupies in the glove compartment and a tax man riding shotgun — Richard Boeth⟩

Lim·ou·sin \\'liməˌzēn, ˌlimə'-, *F* lēmüzaⁿ\\ *n* [F, of or relating to Limoges, France] **1 :** a French breed of medium-sized yellow-red cattle bred esp. for meat **2 :** an animal of the Limousin breed

limousine liberal *n* **:** a wealthy political liberal

limp·en \\'limpən\\ *vi* **:** to become limp ⟨few heard the blow, but Grown Boy *limpened* instantly and fell — Carson McCullers⟩

limp–wrist·ed \\'limˌpristəd\\ *adj* **1 :** effeminate **2 :** weak or flabby ⟨a balance has to be drawn in the US response so that it is neither overly provocative nor overly *limp-wristed* —David Obey⟩

lin·ac \\'linˌak\\ *n* [*linear accelerator*] **:** a device in which charged particles are accelerated in a straight line by successive impulses from a series of electrical fields **:** linear accelerator

lin·co·my·cin \\ˌliŋkə'mīsᵊn\\ *n* [*linco-* (fr. *Streptomyces lincolnensis*, an actinomycete) + *-mycin* substance obtained from a fungus, fr. *streptomycin*] **:** an antibiotic $C_{18}H_{34}N_2O_6S$ obtained from an actinomycete (*Streptomyces lincolnensis*) and found effective esp. against cocci

line*n — **on line :** in or into operation ⟨the lead time necessary to bring a nuclear plant *on line* is at least ten years —*Newsweek*⟩

linear*adj **1 :** composed of simply drawn lines with little attempt at pictorial representation ⟨*linear* script⟩ **2 :** relating to, concerned with, or psychologically influenced by the sequential structure of the printed line ⟨*linear*, word-oriented people who feel restive at being cut off from the great, younger majority of visual, media= message unthinkers —Roy Bongartz⟩

Linear A *n* **:** a linear form of writing used in Crete from the 18th to the 15th centuries B.C.

linear algebra *n* **1 :** a branch of mathematics that is concerned with mathematical structures closed under the operation of addition and scalar multiplication and with their applications and that includes the theory of systems of linear equations, matrices, determinants, vector spaces, and linear transformations **2 :** a mathematical ring which is also a vector space with scalars from an associated field and whose multiplicative operation is such that $(aA)(bB) = (ab)(AB)$ where a and b are scalars and A and B are vectors — called also *algebra*

linear al·ky·late sul·fo·nate \\-ˌalkəˌlātˌsəlfəˌnāt\\ *n* **:** a biodegradable salt of sulfonic acid used in detergents as a surface-active agent

Linear B *n* **:** a linear form of writing employing syllabic characters used at Knossos on Crete and on the Greek mainland from the 15th to the 12th centuries B.C. for documents in the Mycenaean language

linear combination *n* **:** a mathematical entity (as $4x + 5y + 6z$) which is composed of sums and differences of elements (as variables, matrices, or equations) whose coefficients are not all zero

linear dependence *n* **:** the property of one set (as of matrices or vectors) of having at least one linear combination equal to zero when the coefficients are taken from another given set and at least one of the coefficients is not equal to zero — **lin·ear·ly dependent** \\'linēə(r)lē-, 'linyə(r)lē-\\ *adj*

linear independence *n* **:** the property of a set (as of matrices or vectors) of having no linear combination of the elements equal to zero when coefficients are taken from a given set unless the coefficient of each element is zero — **lin·ear·ly independent** \\'linēə(r)lē-, 'linyə(r)lē-\\ *adj*

linear motor *n* **:** a motor that produces thrust in a straight line by direct induction rather than with the use of gears

linear transformation *n* **1 :** a transformation in which the new variables are linear functions of the old variables **2 :** a function that maps the vectors of one vector space onto the vectors of the same or another vector space with the same field of scalars in such a way that the image of the sum of two vectors equals the sum of their images and the image of a scalar product equals the product of the scalar and the image of the vector

line judge *n* **:** a football linesman whose duties include keeping track of the official time for the game

line printer *n* **:** a high-speed printing device (as for a computer) that prints each line as a unit rather than character by character — **line printing** *n*

line score *n* **:** a printed score of a baseball game giving the runs, hits, and errors made by each team

line-up*n **:** a television programming schedule

lin·gui·ne \liŋ'gwēnē, -(ˌ)nä\ *also* **lin·gui·ni** \-nē, -ni\ *n* [It, pl. of *linguina*, dim. of *lingua* tongue, fr. L] **:** pasta in flat narrow strips

link*n **:** an identifier attached to an element (as an index term) in a system in order to indicate or permit connection with other similarly identified elements

linked*adj **:** having or provided with links

lin·u·ron \'linyəˌrän\ *n* [prob. fr. *lin*dane, an insecticide + *urea* + *-on* chemical compound] **:** a selective herbicide $C_9H_{10}O_2Cl_2N_2$ used esp. to control weeds in crops of soybeans or carrots

lip cell *n* **:** one of the narrow thin-walled cells of the sporangia in some ferns that mark the point at which dehiscence begins

li·pid·ic \lə'pidik\ *adj* **:** of or relating to lipids ⟨*lipidic* antigens⟩ ⟨*lipidic* inclusions⟩

li·po·poly·sac·cha·ride \ˌlīpō,päli'sakəˌrīd, ˌlipō-\ *n* [ISV *lipo-* fat, lipid (deriv. of Gk *lipos* fat) + *polysaccharide*] **:** a large molecule consisting of lipids and sugars joined by chemical bonds

li·po·tro·pin \ˌlipə'trōpən, ˌlī-\ *n* [*lipotrop*ic promoting the utilization of fat + *-in* chemical compound] **:** either of two protein hormones of the anterior pituitary held to function in the mobilization of fatty reserves; *esp* **:** BETA⁼ LIPOTROPIN

Lip·pes loop \ˌlipəs-, *also* 'lips-\ *n* [Jack *Lippes*, 20th cent. Am. physician] **:** an S-shaped plastic intrauterine contraceptive device

Lip·tau·er \'lipˌtaú(ə)r, -aúə(r\ *n* [G, fr. *Liptau* Liptow, Hungary] **1 :** a soft Hungarian cheese **2 :** a cheese spread of Liptauer and seasonings (as paprika); *also* **:** an imitation of this made with cream cheese or cottage cheese

lit–crit \ˌlit'krit\ *n* [*literary crit*icism] **:** literary criticism ⟨responsiveness, in a fist-rate patch of *lit-crit*, to a great writer —Benjamin DeMott⟩ ⟨knows every *lit-crit* cliché in the book —R.A. Sokolov⟩

litmus test *n* **:** a test in which a single indicator (as an attitude, event, or fact) is decisive ⟨in Soviet intellectual circles the name Osip Mandelstam . . . could be used as a *litmus test* to determine people's loyalties —*Times Lit. Supp.*⟩

lit·ter·bag \'lidˌə(r)ˌbag\ *n* **:** a bag used (as in an automobile) for disposal of refuse

little man *n* **:** the ordinary individual **:** the common man

live \'līv\ *adv* **:** at the actual time of occurrence **:** during or at a live performance ⟨the sessions were carried *live* in their entirety by the public television station —Peter Binzen⟩

lived–in \ˌliv,din\ *adj* **:** of or suggesting long-term human habitation or use **:** comfortable ⟨the *lived-in* look of lower-class, garden-apartment suburbs —D.K. Shipler⟩ ⟨the trend to manufacture new clothes that have a *lived-in* appearance —R.A. Kagan⟩

live–in \ˌliv,in\ *adj* **1 :** living in one's place of employment ⟨a *live-in* maid⟩ **2 :** involving or involved with cohabitation ⟨a *live-in* relationship⟩ ⟨a *live-in* partner⟩

living will *n* **:** a document in which the signer requests to be allowed to die rather than be kept alive by artificial means in the event of becoming disabled beyond a reasonable expectation of recovery

LM *n* **:** LUNAR MODULE

LNG *abbr* liquefied natural gas

load*n **:** the decrease in capacity for survival of the average individual in a population due to the presence of deleterious genes in the gene pool ⟨the mutational *load* is the genetic *load* caused by mutation⟩

load·mas·ter \'lōdˌmastə(r)\ *n* **:** a crew member of a transport aircraft who is in charge of the cargo

locked–in\'läk,din\ *adj* **:** unable or unwilling to shift invested funds because of the tax effect of realizing capital gains

lo·cu·tion·ary \lō'kyüsh(ə)ˌnerē\ *adj* [*locution* + *-ary*, adj. suffix] **:** of or relating to the physical act of saying something considered apart from the statement's effect or intention — compare ILLOCUTIONARY, PERLOCUTIONARY

logic*n **:** the fundamental principles and applications of truth tables and of the interconnection of circuit elements and gates necessary for computation in a computer; *also* **:** the circuits themselves

log·nor·mal \(')lȯg'nȯrməl, (')läg-\ *adj* **:** of, relating to, or being a normal distribution of the logarithm of a random variable; *also* **:** relating to or being such a random variable — **log·nor·mal·i·ty** \ˌlȯgnȯr'maləd-ē, ˌläg-\ *n* — **log·nor·mal·ly** \(')lȯg'nȯrməlē, (')läg-\ *adv*

Lo·go \'lō(ˌ)gō\ *n* [Gk *logos* word] **:** an interactive simplified computer programming language with an emphasis on graphics as a means to learning

loll·er \'lälə(r)\ *n* **:** one that lolls around

lonely hearts *adj* **:** of or relating to lonely people who are seeking companions or spouses ⟨*lonely hearts* club⟩

long–term\'lȯŋˌtərm, -ˌtōm, -ˌtəim\ *adj* **:** generated by assets held for longer than six months ⟨*long-term* capital gains⟩

look–alike \'lükəˌlīk\ *n* **:** one that looks like another ⟨twins we were . . . *look-alikes* and inner opposites — John Barth⟩ ⟨there are many *look-alikes* in genetic diseases —Victor McKusick⟩ ⟨most of the shopping centers are suburban *look-alikes* —Ada L. Huxtable⟩ — **look-alike** *adj*

look–in\'lük,in\ *n* **:** a quick pass in football to a receiver running diagonally toward the center of the field

look·up \'lùk,əp\ *n* **:** the process or an instance of looking something up; *esp* **:** the process of matching by computer the words of a text with material stored in memory ⟨an automatic hyphenation system using logic and dictionary *lookup*⟩

loop*n **1 :** a series of instructions (as for a computer) that is repeated until a terminating condition is reached **2 :** INTRAUTERINE DEVICE; *esp* **:** LIPPES LOOP

Lo·rentz force \'lȯr,en(t)s-, ,lȯr-\ *n* [Hendrik A. *Lorentz* †1928 Du. physicist] **:** the force exerted on a moving charged particle in electric and magnetic fields

LOS *abbr* **1** line of scrimmage **2** line of sight

loser*n **:** one who is incompetent or unable to succeed ⟨believes that any woman unmarried after the age of twenty-two is a *loser* —Lyn Tornabene⟩; *also* **:** something doomed to fail or disappoint ⟨the breaded and fried veal cutlet Milanese . . . had to be a *loser* —Mimi Sheraton⟩

Lou Geh·rig's disease \ˌlü,ge(ə)rigz-, -,ga(ə)r-\ *n* [*Lou Gehrig* †1941 Am. baseball player who died of this disease] **:** AMYOTROPHIC LATERAL SCLEROSIS

love beads *n pl* **:** a necklace of beads; *esp* **:** beads worn as a symbol of love and peace

love·bug \'ləv,bəg\ *n* [fr. the fact that it is usually seen copulating] **:** a small black bibionid fly (*Plecia nearctica*) with a red thorax that is often a nuisance esp. while copulating along highways in states of the U.S. bordering the Gulf of Mexico

love–in \'ləv,in\ *n* **:** a gathering of people for the expression of mutual love

low·ball \'lō,bol\ *vt* **:** to give (a customer) a deceptively low cost estimate that one has no intention of honoring ⟨request that the statement be signed by an official of the firm. That way, a salesman won't be able to *lowball* you —*Consumer Reports*⟩ — **lowball** *n*

low blow* *n* **:** an unprincipled attack ⟨gossip column that landed one *low blow* after another —James Fallows⟩

lowest terms *n pl* **:** the numerator and denominator of a fraction that have no factor in common ⟨reduce a fraction to *lowest terms*⟩

low–rise \'lō,rīz\ *adj* **1 :** being one or two stories and not equipped with elevators ⟨a *low-rise* classroom building⟩ **2** *of trousers* **:** low-slung and usu. close-fitting

LPM *abbr, often not cap* lines per minute

LPN \ˌel(,)pē'en\ *n* **:** LICENSED PRACTICAL NURSE

Lr *symbol* lawrencium

LSM* *abbr* letter-sorting machine

Lu·ba·vitch·er \'lübə,vichə(r), lü'bä,v-\ *n* [Yiddish, fr. *Lubavitch*, lit., city of love, Jewish town in Russia + -*er* -er] **:** a member of a Hasidic sect founded by Schncour Zalman of Lyady in the late 18th century — **Luba·vitcher** *adj*

Luddite* \'ləd,īt\ *n* **:** one who is opposed to change and esp. to technological change ⟨literary *Luddites* would take arms against the computers —V.S. Navasky⟩

lu·mi·nar·ia \ˌlümə'nerēə\ *n, pl* -**nar·ias** [Sp, decorative light, fr. L *lumenarium* light, torch, fr. *lumen* light + -*arius* -ary] **:** a traditional Mexican Christmas lantern consisting of a brown paper bag with a lighted candle inside

lump* *n, Brit* **:** nonunion construction workers who work as self-employed subcontractors ⟨*lump* labour⟩

lump·ec·to·my \ˌləm'pektəmē, -i\ *n, pl* -**mies** [*lump* + -*ectomy* cutting out] **:** excision of a breast tumor with a limited amount of associated tissue

lum·pen \'lümpən, 'ləm-\ *n, pl* **lumpen** *or* **lumpens** **:** a member of the ignorant and underprivileged lower classes

lunar excursion mod·ule \-ˌmäj(,)ü(ə)l\ *or* **lunar module** *n* **:** a space vehicle module designed to carry astronauts from the command module to the surface of the moon and back

lu·nar·naut \'lünə(r),not, -ˌnät\ *n* [*lunar* + astro*naut*] **:** an astronaut who explores the moon

lunch* *n* — **out to lunch :** out of touch with reality **:** crazy

lu·te·in·iz·ing hormone–releasing hormone \ˌlüd·ēə,nīziŋ-\ *n* **:** a hormone secreted by the hypothala-

mus that stimulates the pituitary gland to release luteinizing hormone — called also *luteinizing hormone-releasing factor*

LVN \ˌel(,)vē'en\ *n* **:** LICENSED VOCATIONAL NURSE

lwei \lə'wā\ *n, pl* **lwei** *also* **lweis** [native name in Angola] **1 :** a monetary unit of Angola equal to $^1/_{100}$ kwanza **2 :** a coin representing one lwei

ly·ase \'lī,ās, -,āz\ *n* [Gk *lyein* to loosen, release + E -*ase* enzyme] **:** an enzyme (as a decarboxylase) that forms double bonds by removing groups from a substrate other than by hydrolysis or that adds groups to double bonds

lym·phan·gi·og·ra·phy \ˌlim,fanjē'ägrəfē\ *n* [*lymphangio*- lymph vessels (fr. NL *lymphangion* lymph vessel, fr. *lympha* lymph + Gk *angeion* vessel, blood vessel) + -*graphy* writing, recording, deriv. of Gk *graphein* to write] **:** X-ray depiction of lymph vessels and nodes after use of a radiopaque material — **lym·phan·gio·gram** \lim'fanjēə,gram\ *n* — **lym·phan·gio·graph·ic** \(,)lim,fanjēə'grafik\ *adj*

lym·pho·gran·u·lo·ma·tous \ˌlim(p)fə,granyə-'lōməd·əs\ *adj* [NL *lymphogranulomat*-, *lymphogranuloma* + E -*ous*, adj. suffix] **:** of, relating to, or characterized by lymphogranulomas ⟨*lymphogranulomatous* skin diseases⟩

lym·phog·ra·phy \lim'fägrəfē\ *n* [*lympho*- lymph + -*graphy* writing, recording] **:** LYMPHANGIOGRAPHY — **lym·pho·gram** \'lim(p)fə,gram\ *n* — **lym·pho·graph·ic** \ˌlim(p)fə'grafik\ *adj*

lym·pho·kine \'lim(p)fə,kīn\ *n* [NL, fr. *lympho*- lymph, lymphocyte, + Gk *kinein* to move, arouse] **:** any of various substances (as interferon) of low molecular weight that are not immunoglobulins, are secreted by T cells in response to stimulation by antigens, and have a role (as the activation of macrophages or the enhancement or inhibition of antibody production) in cell-mediated immunological reactions

lym·pho·sar·co·ma·tous \ˌlim(p)fəsär'kōməd·əs\ *adj* [NL *lymphosarcomat*-, *lymphosarcoma* + E -*ous*, adj. suffix] **:** being, affected with, or characterized by lymphosarcomas ⟨large *lymphosarcomatous* masses⟩ ⟨human *lymphosarcomatous* disease⟩

ly·oph·i·liz·er \(,)lī'afə,līzə(r)\ *n* [*lyophilize* to freeze-dry + -*er*, agent suffix] **:** a device used to carry out the process of freeze-drying

ly·si·me·tric \ˌlīsə'me·trik\ *adj* **:** relating to or involving the use of a lysimeter ⟨*lysimetric* observations⟩

ly·so·gen* \'līsəgən\ *n* **:** a lysogenic bacterium or bacterial strain

ly·so·gen·ic* \ˌlīsə'jenik\ *adj* **:** not virulent **:** temperate ⟨*lysogenic* viruses⟩

ly·sog·e·nize \lī'säjə,nīz\ *vt* -**nized; -niz·ing :** to make lysogenic — **ly·sog·e·ni·za·tion** \-,säjənə'zāshən, -,nī'-\ *n*

ly·sog·e·ny \lī'säjənē\ *n* **:** the state of being lysogenic

ly·so·some \'līsə,sōm\ *n* [ISV *lyso*- lysis + -*some* body, deriv. of Gk *sōma;* orig. formed in F] **:** a saclike cellular organelle that contains various hydrolytic enzymes — **ly·so·som·al** \ˌlīsə'sōməl\ *adj* — **ly·so·som·al·ly** \-məlē\ *adv*

ly·so·staph·in \ˌlīsə'stafən\ *n* [*lyso*- lysis + *staph* staphylococcus + -*in* chemical compound] **:** an antimicrobial enzyme that is obtained from a strain of staphylococcus and is effective against other staphylococci

M

MABE *abbr* master of agricultural business and economics

mac·chi·net·ta \ˌmäkə'netə, -ed·ə\ *n* [It *macchinetta* (*da caffè*) coffee machine, fr. dim. of *macchina* machine, fr. L *machina*] **:** a drip-coffee maker in which water is heated in the upper part which is then inverted to allow the water to run through the coffee into the lower part

mace \'mās\ *vt* **maced; mac·ing :** to spray with the liquid Mace ⟨grabbed a policeman's whistle and got *maced* in the face —*Rolling Stone*⟩

Mace \'mās\ *trademark* — used for a temporarily disabling liquid that when sprayed in the face of a person (as a rioter) causes tears, dizziness, immobilization, and sometimes nausea

machine language *n* **1 :** a code closely corresponding to a computer's internal representation of information ⟨a program written in *machine language*⟩ **2 :** a physical form of information that can be used by a computer **:** machine-readable form ⟨a list of literary works already converted to *machine language* —Gary Carlson⟩

ma·chine–read·able \mə'shēnˌrēdəbəl\ *adj* **:** directly usable by a computer ⟨*machine-readable* text⟩

machine translation *n* **:** automatic translation from one language to another

ma·chis·mo \mä'chēz(ˌ)mō, mə-, -'kē-, -'ki-, -'chi-, -s(ˌ)mō\ *n* [MexSp, fr. Sp *macho* male + *-ismo* characteristic behavior] **1 :** a strong sense of masculine pride**:** an exaggerated awareness and assertion of masculinity ⟨in its origins *machismo* is the sexual and familial ideology or value-system of the Mediterranean world — Frederic Hunter⟩ **2 :** an exaggerated or exhilarating sense of power or strength ⟨museums which flaunt their directional *machismo* —*Time*⟩

¹ma·cho \'mä(ˌ)chō, *chiefly Brit also* 'ma- *or* -(ˌ)kō\ *adj* [Sp, male, fr. L *masculus*] **:** aggressively virile ⟨all their *macho* swagger and bravado —Burr Snider⟩ ⟨the kind of *macho* humor football players find so appealing —Gary Cartwright⟩ ⟨his skintight stage armor of *macho* black leather —Ed McCormack⟩

²macho *n, pl* **machos 1 :** MACHISMO ⟨a compulsion to prove the collective *macho* by consenting to another bloody misadventure —L.L. King⟩ **2 :** one who exhibits machismo ⟨pride leads *machos* into betting sums they cannot afford —Evelyn P. Stevens⟩

mack·man \'makˌman, 'makmən\ *n* [*mack* pimp + *man*] *slang* **:** a pimp

Mac·lau·rin's series \mə'klȯrən(z)-\ *n* [Colin *Maclaurin* †1746 Scot. physician] **:** a Taylor's series of the form

$$f(x) = f(0) + \frac{f'(0)}{1!}x + \frac{f''(0)}{2!}x_2 + \ldots + \frac{f^{[n]}(0)}{n!}x^n + \ldots$$

in which the expansion is about the reference point zero — called also *Maclaurin series*

Mc·Lu·han·esque \mə'klüəˌnesk\ *adj* [Herbert Marshall *McLuhan* †1980 Canad. educator] **:** of, relating to, or suggestive of Marshall McLuhan or his theories ⟨the *McLuhanesque* mosaic of the TV screen —E. A. Kosner⟩

mac·ro \'mak(ˌ)rō\ *n, pl* **macros** [short for *macroinstruction*] **:** a single computer instruction that stands for a sequence of operations

mac·ro·ag·gre·gate \ˌmakrō'agrəgət\ *n* [*macro-* long, large (deriv. of Gk *makros* long) + *aggregate*] **:** a relatively large particle (as of soil or a protein) — **mac·ro·ag·gre·gat·ed** \-ˌagrəˌgādˌəd\ *adj*

mac·ro·ben·thos \-'benˌthäs\ *n* [*macro-* + *benthos*] **:** the relatively large organisms living on or in the bottom of bodies of water — **mac·ro·ben·thic** \-'ben(t)thik\ *adj*

mac·ro·bi·ot·ic*\-bī'ädˌik, -bē-\ *adj* **:** of, relating to, or being an extremely restricted diet (as one containing chiefly whole grains) that is usu. undertaken by its advocates to promote health and well-being although it may actually be deficient in essential nutrients (as fats)

ma·cro·bi·ot·ics*\-iks\ *n pl but sing in constr* **:** a macrobiotic dietary system

mac·ro·glob·u·lin \ˌmakrō'gläbyələn\ *n* [ISV] **:** a highly polymerized globulin of high molecular weight

mac·ro·glob·u·lin·emia \ˌmakrōˌgläbyələ'nēmēə\ *n* [NL, fr. ISV *macroglobulin* + NL *-emia* blood condition, deriv. of Gk *haima* blood] **:** a disorder characterized by increased blood serum viscosity and by macroglobulins in the serum — **mac·ro·glob·u·lin·emic** \-'nēmik\ *adj*

mac·ro·in·struc·tion \ˌmakrōin'strəkshən\ *n* **:** MACRO

mac·ro·in·ver·te·brate \-in'vərdˌəbrət, -ˌbrāt\ *n* **:** any of various invertebrate macroorganisms (as a crayfish or stonefly)

mac·ro·lide \'makrəˌlīd\ *n* [*macrocyclic* + *lactone* + *-ide* derivative compound] **:** any of several antibiotics that contain a macrocyclic lactone ring and are produced by actinomycetes of the genus *Streptomyces*

mac·ro·or·gan·ism \ˌmakrō'ȯrgəˌnizəm, -'ȯ(ə)g-\ *n* **:** an organism large enough to be seen by the normal unaided human eye

ma·fia*\'mäfēə, 'maf-\ *n, often cap* **:** a group of people of similar interests or backgrounds prominent in a particular field or enterprise **:** clique ⟨protesting the presumptions of the mental-health *mafia* —R.J. Neuhaus⟩ ⟨the most churlish of his detractors — which is to say most of the contemporary literary *Mafia* —Richard Boeth⟩

ma·fi·o·so \ˌmäfē'ō(ˌ)sō, ˌmaf-, -'ō(ˌ)zō\ *n, pl* **-si** \-sē, -zē\ *also* **-sos** *often cap* [It, fr. *mafioso*, adj., belonging to the Mafia, fr. *Mafia* + *-oso*, adj. suffix] **:** a member of the Mafia or a mafia ⟨key witness against alleged *Mafioso* is feared slain —*N.Y. Times*⟩ ⟨among . . . literary *mafiosi*, even violence has to be sandwiched between drinks — Lois B. Gould⟩

magazine*n **:** a radio or television program presenting usu. several short segments on a variety of topics

magic number *n* **1 :** one of a set of numbers for which an atomic nucleus exhibits a high degree of stability when either the proton or neutron count is equal to the number 2 : a number that represents a combination of wins for a leader (as in a baseball pennant race) and losses for a contender which mathematically guarantees the leader's winning the championship

mag·i·cube \'majə,kyüb\ *n* [blend of *magic* and *cube*] : a flashcube that for its firing depends only on the mechanical ignition of a primer within the device

magnetic* *n* : a magnetic substance

magnetic bottle *n* : a magnetic field for confining plasma for experiments in nuclear fusion

magnetic bubble *n* : a tiny magnetized cylindrical volume that is formed in a thin amorphous or crystalline magnetic material, that can be moved by a magnetic field, and that along with other like volumes can be used to represent a bit of information (as in a computer)

magnetic core *n* **1** : a mass of iron (as in an electromagnet or transformer) that serves to intensify the magnetic field resulting from current carried in a surrounding coil **2** : CORE 1

magnetic disk *n* : DISK 1

mag·ne·to·car·dio·gram \mag¦nēd·ō'kärdēə,gram, -¦ned--\ *n* [*magneto-* magnetic field, magnetism + *cardiogram*] : a recording of a magnetocardiograph

mag·ne·to·car·dio·graph \-'kärdēə,graf\ *n* : an instrument for recording the changes in the magnetic field around the heart that is used to supplement information given by an electrocardiograph — **mag·ne·to·car·dio·graph·ic** \-¦kärdēə¦grafik\ *adj* — **mag·ne·to·car·di·og·ra·phy** \-¦kärdē'ägrəfē\ *n*

mag·ne·to·flu·id·dy·nam·ic \-,flüə(d)dī¦namik\ *adj* : HYDROMAGNETIC 1 — **mag·ne·to·flu·id·dy·nam·ics** \-iks\ *n pl but sing or pl in constr*

mag·ne·to·flu·id·me·chan·ic \-,flüədmə¦kanik\ : HY-DROMAGNETIC 1 — **mag·ne·to·flu·id·me·chan·ics** \-iks\ *n pl but sing or pl in constr*

mag·ne·to·gas·dy·nam·ics \-,gasdī¦namiks\ *n pl but sing in constr* : HYDROMAGNETICS — **mag·ne·to·gas·dy·nam·ic** \-,gasdī¦namik\ *adj*

mag·ne·to·pause \mag'nēd·ə,póz, -'ned--\ *n* [*magnetosphere* + *pause*] : the outer boundary of a magnetosphere

mag·ne·to·plas·ma·dy·nam·ic \mag¦nēd·ō,plazmədī¦namik, -¦ned--\ *adj* : HYDROMAGNETIC 1 — **mag·ne·to·plas·ma·dy·nam·ics** \-iks\ *n pl but sing or pl in constr*

mag·ne·to·sphere \mag'nēd·ə,sfi(ə)r, -'ned--, -,sfiə\ *n* : a region of the upper atmosphere that surrounds the earth, extends out for thousands of miles, and is dominated by the earth's magnetic field so that charged particles are trapped in it **2** : a region that surrounds a celestial body (as a planet) and is comparable to the earth's magnetosphere in trapping charged particles — **mag·ne·to·spher·ic** \-,nēd·ə,sfi(ə)rik, -,ned--, -,sferik\ *adj*

mag·ne·to·tail \-,tā(ə)l\ *n* [*magneto-* + *tail*] : the region of the magnetosphere that is swept back by the solar wind so that it extends from a planet (as the earth) in the direction away from the sun

magnet school *n* : a school with superior facilities and staff designed to attract pupils from all segments of the community

mag·non \'mag,nän\ *n* [*magnetic* + *-on* elementary particle, quantum] : one of the quanta into which a spin wave is divided

Mah·ler·ian \mä'lerēən, -'lir-\ *adj* [Gustav *Mahler* †1911 Austrian composer] : of, relating to, or suggestive of Gustav Mahler or his music ⟨a symphony only in the *Mahlerian* sense of a song cycle with orchestra —Irving Kolodin⟩

mail cover *n* : a postal monitoring and recording of information (as return address and postmark) on all mail going to a designated addressee

Mail·gram \'mā(ə)l,gram\ *trademark* — used for a message that is transmitted by wire to a post office which delivers it to the addressee

main·frame \'mān¦frām\ *n* : a computer with its cabinet and internal circuits; *also* : a large computer

main·line* \'mān,līn\ *vt* : to take by or as if by mainlining ⟨nearly half had *mainlined* speed —Richard Blum⟩ ⟨while most of us are *mainlining* our morning caffeine — P.R. Range⟩ ⟨Americans have been *mainlining* Presidential power for so long —T.J. Lowi⟩

mainline *adj* [*main line,* n.] **1** : being part of an established group ⟨the homosexual issue — which catches all *mainline* churches in varying states of theological and emotional unpreparedness —John Deedy⟩ **2** : MAIN-STREAM ⟨there is just one position and it is very *mainline* in its elements —Carl Oglesby⟩

¹main·stream \'mān,strēm\ *adj* [*mainstream,* n.] : having, reflecting, or being compatible with the prevailing attitudes and values of a society or group ⟨a strictly *mainstream* Christian, Victorian approach toward marriage and morality —Gerda Lerner⟩

²mainstream *vt* : to place (as a handicapped child) in conventional school classes ⟨then, as the language takes hold, the children are *mainstreamed* into the regular system —Deborah Churchman⟩

mai tai \'mī,tī\ *n, pl* **mai tais** [Tahitian *maitai* good] : a cocktail made with rum, curaçao, orgeat, lime, and fruit juices, shaken with shaved ice, and often garnished with fruit (as pineapple and a maraschino cherry)

ma·jol·i·ca* \mə'jäləkə, *sometimes* -'yäl-\ *n* : a 19th century earthenware modeled in naturalistic shapes and glazed in bright colors

major–medical \¦mäjə(r)¦medəkəl\ *adj* : of, relating to, or being a form of insurance designed to pay all or part of the medical bills of major illnesses usu. after deduction of a fixed initial sum

make* *vb* — **make it** **1** : to be successful ⟨trying to *make it* as writer-in-residence at the university —Gershon Legman⟩ **2** : to have sexual intercourse ⟨one young couple who would . . . *make it* in a rear seat —Thomas Pynchon⟩ **3** : to be satisfactory or pleasing : make the grade ⟨southern cities, with their . . . climates, don't *make it* for me —Bill AuCoin⟩ — **make waves** : to disturb the status quo ⟨unimaginative, traditional career man who does not *make waves* —Henry Trewhitt⟩

make out* *vi* **1** : to engage in sexual intercourse ⟨I didn't know that I could *make out* with a true sack artist —Saul Bellow⟩ **2** : to engage in amorous kissing and caressing : neck ⟨he started *making out* with Kathy . . . kissing her, putting his hands all over her —John Reid⟩

makuta *pl of* LIKUTA

mal·ap·por·tioned \ˌmaləˈpȯrshənd, -ˌpȯ(ə)sh-\ *adj* [*mal-* poorly, irregularly + *apportioned,* past part. of *apportion*] **:** characterized by an inequitable or unsuitable apportioning of representatives to a legislative body ⟨one of the country's most *malapportioned* legislatures. Eight percent of the population controlled a majority of the Senate seats —*N.Y. Times*⟩

mal·ap·por·tion·ment \-shənmənt\ *n* **:** the state of being malapportioned

Mal·i·bu board \ˌmaləˌbü-\ *n* [*Malibu,* California] **:** a lightweight surfboard 9 to 10 feet long with a round nose, square tail, and slightly convex bottom

ma·lic \ˈmalək, ˈmāl-\ *adj* **:** involved in and esp. catalyzing a reaction in which malate participates ⟨*malic* dehydrogenase⟩

mall*n **1 :** an urban shopping area featuring a variety of shops surrounding a usu. open-air concourse reserved for pedestrian traffic **2 :** a large usu. suburban building or group of buildings containing various shops with associated passageways

ma·lo·lac·tic \ˌmalōˈlaktik, ˌmālō-\ *adj* [*malo-* malic acid + *lactic*] **:** relating to or involved in the bacterial conversion of malic acid to lactic acid in wine ⟨*malolactic* fermentation⟩

MALS *abbr* master of arts in library science

mam·mo·gram \ˈmaməˌgram\ *n* [*mamma* breast + connective -*o-* + -*gram* drawing, writing, record, deriv. of Gk *gramma* letter, writing] **:** a photograph of the breasts made by X rays

mam·mog·ra·phy \maˈmägrəfē\ *n* [*mamma* + connective -*o-* + -*graphy* writing, deriv. of Gk *graphein* to write] **:** X-ray examination of the breasts (as for early detection of cancer) — **mam·mo·graph·ic** \ˌmaməˈgrafik\ *adj*

Man*n **1 :** the police ⟨when I heard the siren, I knew it was the *Man* —*Amer. Speech*⟩ **2 :** the white establishment **:** white society ⟨surprise that any black man . . . should take on so about the *Man* —Peter Goldman⟩

mandate*vt **man·dat·ed; man·dat·ing :** to make mandatory **:** order ⟨this . . . verdict *mandating* school desegregation —M.L. Abramson⟩; *also* **:** to direct or require ⟨people are not *mandated* to wreck their own economic system —Norman Cousins⟩

man·eb \ˈmaˌneb\ *n* [*manganese* + *ethylene* + *bis-* twice, fr. L *bis*] **:** a carbamate agricultural fungicide $C_4H_6MnN_2S_4$

Man·hat·tan·iza·tion \ˌmanˌhat(ə)nəˈzāshən, -nˌiˈzā-\ *n* [*Manhattan,* borough of New York + -*ization* action of causing to resemble] **:** congestion of an urban area by tall buildings

ma·ni·cot·ti \ˌmanəˈkäd-ē\ *n, pl* **manicotti** [It., lit., muff, fr. *manica* sleeve, fr. L] **:** tubular pasta shells stuffed esp. with ricotta

manifold*n **1 :** a mathematical set **2 :** a topological space such that every point has a neighborhood which is homeomorphic to the interior of a sphere in euclidean space of the same number of dimensions

-man·ship \mənˌship\ *n suffix* [sports*manship*] **:** art or practice of maneuvering to gain a tactical advantage ⟨games*manship*⟩ ⟨one-up*manship*⟩ ⟨grants*manship*⟩

many-val·ued \ˌmenēˈval(ˌ)yüd, -ni-, -ˌvalyəd\ *adj* **:** MULTIPLE-VALUED

Mao \ˈmau̇\ *adj* [*Mao* Tse-tung †1976 Chin. communist leader] **:** having a long narrow cut and a mandarin collar ⟨*Mao* jacket⟩ ⟨designers are showing mandarin collars, kimono sleeves, *Mao* suits —*McCall's*⟩

MAO *abbr* monoamine oxidase

Mao·ism \ˈmau̇ˌizəm\ *n* **:** the theory and practice of Marxism-Leninism developed in China chiefly by Mao Tse-tung — **Mao·ist** \ˈmau̇əst\ *n or adj*

mao–tai \ˈmau̇ˈdī, -ˈti\ *n* [*Mao-Tai,* town in China] **:** a strong Chinese liquor made from sorghum

map*n **1 :** the arrangement of genes on a chromosome — called also *genetic map* **2 :** MAPPING

map*vt **mapped; map·ping :** to locate (a gene) on a chromosome ⟨mutants which have been genetically *mapped*⟩ ~ *vi, of a gene* **:** to be located ⟨a repressor *maps* near the corresponding structural gene⟩

MAP*abbr modified American plan

map·ping \ˈmapiŋ\ *n* **:** a mathematical correspondence that assigns exactly one element of one set to each element of the same or another set ⟨a one-to-one continuous *mapping*⟩

mar·ag·ing steel \ˌmärˌājiŋ-\ *n* [*martensite* + *aging*] **:** a strong tough low-carbon martensitic steel which contains up to 25 percent nickel and in which hardening precipitates are formed by aging

Mar·ek's disease \ˈmarəks-, ˈmer-\ *n* [J. *Marek* †1952 Ger. veterinarian] **:** a cancerous disease of poultry that is characterized esp. by proliferation of lymphoid cells and is caused by a virus resembling a herpesvirus

Mar·fan's syndrome *or* **Mar·fan syndrome** \ˌmärˌfanˌsinˌdrōm, -ˌsindrəm\ *n* [Antonin Bernard Jean *Marfan* †1942 Fr. pediatrician] **:** a hereditary disorder characterized by abnormal elongation of the long bones and often by ocular and circulatory defects

mar·ga·ri·ta \ˌmärgəˈrēd-ə\ *n* [MexSp, prob. fr. the name *Margarita* Margaret] **:** a cocktail consisting of tequila, lime or lemon juice, and an orange-flavored liqueur

mar·gin·al*\\ˈmärjnəl, -jənᵊl\ *adj* **:** relating to or being a function of a random variable that is obtained from a function of several random variables by integrating or summing over all possible values of the other variables ⟨a *marginal* probability function⟩

mari·cul·ture \ˈmarəˌkəlchə(r)\ *n* [*mari-* sea (fr. L *mare*) + *culture*] **:** the cultivation of marine organisms by exploiting their natural environment — **mari·cul·tur·ist** \ˌmarəˈkələst\ *n*

mar·i·na·ra \ˌmarəˈnara, ˌmerəˈnera, -när-\ *adj* [It (*alla*) *marinara* in sailor style, fr. *marinara,* fem. of *marinaro* of sailors, fr. *marino* marine] **:** made with tomatoes, onion, garlic, and spices ⟨*marinara* sauce⟩; *also* **:** served with marinara sauce ⟨spaghetti *marinara*⟩

mark*n [G] **:** the basic monetary unit of East Germany

marker*or **marker gene** *n* **:** GENETIC MARKER

market*n **1 :** the available supply of or potential demand for specified goods or services ⟨the labor *market*⟩ ⟨has captured more than two-thirds of the cleaning-agent *market* —Barry Commoner⟩ **2 :** a specified category of potential buyers ⟨youth *market*⟩

Mar·ko·vi·an \märˈkōvēən, -kȯ-, -fēən\ *or* **Mar·kov** \ˈmärˌkȯf, -ȯv\ *also* **Mar·koff** \-ȯf\ *adj* **:** of, relating to, or resembling a Markov process or Markov chain esp. by having probabilities defined in terms of transition from the possible existing states to other states ⟨*Markovian* models⟩ ⟨*Markovian* properties⟩

Markov process *also* **Markoff process** *n* [Andrei Andreevich *Markov* †1922 Russ. mathematician] **:** a stochastic process (as Brownian movement) that resembles a Markov chain except that the states are continuous; *also* **:** a Markov chain with discrete states

markup*n **:** the putting of a bill into final form by a U.S. congressional committee; *also* **:** the session at which this is done

martial art *n* **:** one of several arts of combat (as karate, judo, or kung fu) of oriental origin that are widely practiced as sport

Mar·tin Lu·ther King Day \ˌmärtˀnˌlüthərˈkiŋ-, ˌmàtˀnˌlüthəˈkiŋ-\ *n* [*Martin Luther King* †1968, Am. civil rights leader] **:** January 15 observed as a legal holiday in some states of the U.S.

Mary Gre·go·ry \ˌmerēˈgreg(ə)rē, ˌmär-, ˌmar-, -rēˈ-, -ˈgräg-, -rē\ *n* [*Mary Gregory*, thought to have been a late 19th cent. Am. glass painter] **:** colored glassware of a popular 19th century style marked by white enamel decoration usu. including figures of children

Mary Jane *n* [by folk etymology (influenced by Sp *Juana* Jane)] *slang* **:** marijuana

mas·con \ˈmasˌkän\ *n* [*mass* + *con*centration] **:** one of the concentrations of large mass under the surface of the moon's maria whose gravitational effect is held to cause perturbations of the paths of spacecraft orbiting the moon

mas·cu·lin·ist \ˈmaskyələnəst, -ˌlin-\ *n* **:** an advocate of male superiority or dominance **:** male chauvinist

mash*n, *Brit* **:** mashed potatoes ⟨bangers and *mash*⟩

massage*vt **1 :** to treat flatteringly **:** blandish ⟨regularly *massaging* party leaders —Ken Bode⟩ ⟨be attentive, *massage* my ego, advise me —Sally Quinn⟩ **2 :** to alter to suit one's purpose **:** doctor, manipulate ⟨researchers *massaged* the data to support their thesis⟩

mass·cult \ˈmasˌkəlt, *sometimes* ˈmàs-\ *n* [*mass* cul*ture*] **:** the artistic and intellectual culture associated with and disseminated through the mass media **:** mass culture

mass·less \ˈmaslàs, *sometimes* ˈmàs-\ *adj* **:** having no mass ⟨*massless* particles⟩ — **mass·less·ness** *n*

Mass of the Resurrection : a mass for the dead in which the celebrant wears white vestments to symbolize the joyous resurrection of the dead

mass spectrometry *or* **mass spectroscopy** *n* **:** the use of the mass spectrometer

master*vt **:** to produce a master phonograph record or magnetic tape of

master class *n* **:** a seminar for advanced students conducted by a master musician or dancer

mas·to·cy·to·ma \ˌmastəˌsīˈtōmə\ *n*, *pl* **-mas** *or* **-ma·ta** \-ōməd·ə, -ətə\ [*mastocyte* + *-oma* tumor] **:** a tumorous mass produced by proliferation of mast cells

MAT*abbr master of arts in teaching

matching *adj* **:** of, relating to, or being funds provided to match those raised or provided by the recipient ⟨federal *matching* funds⟩ ⟨a *matching* grant⟩

match·up \ˈmachˌəp\ *n* **:** a match: as **a :** a contest between two or more parties **b :** a partnership

ma·ter·ni·ty \məˈtərnàd·ē, -ˈtän-, -ˈtoin-, -ē\ *adj* **1 :** designed for wear during pregnancy ⟨a *maternity* dress⟩ **2**

: effective for the period close to and including childbirth ⟨*maternity* leave⟩

mathematical biology *n* **:** a branch of biology concerned with the construction of mathematical models to describe and solve biological problems — **mathematical biologist** *n*

ma·tri·fo·cal \ˌmaˈtrəˌfōkəl, ˌmä-\ *adj* [*matri-* mother (deriv. of L *mater*) + *focal*] **:** gravitating toward or centered on the mother **:** matricentric ⟨a *matrifocal* family structure⟩

ma·trix al·ge·bra \ˌmäˈtrikˌsaljəbrə\ *n* **:** generalized algebra that deals with the operations and relations among matrices

ma·trix sentence \ˌmäˈtrik(s)-\ *n* **:** that one of a pair of sentences joined by means of a transformation that keeps its essential external structure and syntactic status (in "the book that I want is gone," "the book is gone" is the *matrix sentence*⟩

ma·ven *also* **ma·vin** *or* **may·vin** \ˈmävən\ *n* [Yiddish *meyvn*, fr. LHeb *mēbhīn*, perh. fr. Heb *mēbhī* one who has brought in] **:** one who is experienced or knowledgeable **:** an expert ⟨committed enough malapropian misdemeanors to keep the *mavens* at Oxford busy for a generation —Leo Rosten⟩

maxi \ˈmaksē, -si\ *n* [fr. *maxi-*] **:** a long skirt or coat that usu. extends to the ankle — called *also* respectively *maxiskirt*, *maxicoat*

maxi- \ˈmaksē, -si\ *comb form* [fr. *maximum*, after E *minimum*: *mini-*] **1 :** extra long ⟨*maxi*-dress⟩ ⟨*maxi*-kilt⟩ **2 :** extra large ⟨*maxi*-sculpture⟩ ⟨*maxi*-problems⟩

max·il·lo·fa·cial \makˌsi(ˌ)lōˈfāshəl\ *adj* [*maxillo-* maxilla + *facial*] **:** of, relating to, or affecting the maxilla and the face ⟨*maxillofacial* lesions⟩

maxi-min \ˈmaksəˌmin\ *n* [*maxi*mum + *min*imum] **:** the maximum of a set of minima; *esp* **:** the largest of a set of minimum possible gains each of which occurs in the least advantageous outcome of a strategy followed by a participant in a situation governed by the theory of games — compare MINIMAX — **maximin** *adj*

maximum likelihood *n* **:** a statistical method for estimating population parameters (as the mean and variance) from sample data that selects as estimates those parameter values maximizing the probability of obtaining the observed data

ma·yo \ˈmā(ˌ)ō\ *n* [by shortening] **:** mayonnaise ⟨hold the *mayo* and lettuce but lay on the mustard —Don Imus⟩

mbi·ra \emˈbirə, əm-, -bēr-\ *n* [native word in southern Africa; of Bantu origin] **:** an African musical instrument that consists of a gourd resonator, a wooden box, and a varying number of tuned metal or wooden strips that vibrate when plucked with the thumb or fingers

MCS *abbr* **1** master of commercial science **2** master of computer science **3** missile control system

mean value theorem *n* **1 :** a theorem in differential calculus: if a function of one variable is continuous on a closed interval and differentiable on the interval minus its endpoints there is at least one point where the derivative of the function is equal to the slope of the line joining the endpoints of the curve representing the function on the interval **2 :** a theorem in integral calculus: if a function of one variable is continuous on a closed interval and differentiable on the interval minus its endpoints, there is at least one point in the interval where the product of the value of the function and the length of the interval is equal to the integral of the function over the interval

meat*n **:** penis — usu. considered vulgar

meat–and–po·ta·toes \ˌmētᵊnpəˈtād-(ˌ)ōz, -ᵊnbəˈ-, -ēd·ᵊn-, -ˌtād·əz\ adj **1 :** of fundamental importance **:** basic ⟨the meat-and-potatoes problems of everyday living and loving —D.J. Heckman⟩ **2 :** being practical and straightforward **:** down-to-earth ⟨a meat-and-potatoes town . . . where most people used to think of art as being for the rich, if not for the birds —William Marlin⟩

meat and potatoes n pl but sing or pl in constr **:** a main object of interest ⟨the real meat and potatoes are serious films —Woody Allen⟩

mec·a·myl·amine \ˌmekə'milə,mēn, -əmən\ n [methyl + camphane, a crystalline terpene + amine] **:** a drug that in the hydrochloride $C_{11}H_{21}N\cdot HCl$ is used orally as a ganglionic blocking agent to effect a rapid lowering of severely elevated blood pressure

mechanical bank also **mechanical*** n **:** a toy bank in which operation of a lever activates a mechanism that goes through some amusing or absurd routine and deposits a coin

mech·a·no·chem·i·cal \ˌmekənōˈkeməkəl\ adj [mechano- mechanical + chemical] **:** relating to or being chemistry that deals with the conversion of chemical energy into mechanical work (as in the contraction of a muscle) — **mech·a·no·chem·i·cal·ly** \-k(ə)lē\ adv — **mech·a·no·chem·is·try** \-ˈkemə̇strē\ n

mech·a·no·re·cep·tor \ˌmekə(ˌ)nōrə̇'septə(r)\ n **:** a neural end organ (as a tactile receptor) that responds to a mechanical stimulus (as a change in pressure) — **mech·a·no·re·cep·tion** \-rə̇'sepshən\ n — **mech·a·no·re·cep·tive** \-rə̇'septiv\ adj

mech·lor·eth·amine \ˌme,klȯr'etha,mēn, -lȯr-, -əmən\ n [methyl + chloroethyl + amine] **:** a nitrogen mustard $C_5H_{11}Cl_2N$ used as an insect chemosterilant, as a war gas, and in palliative treatment of some neoplastic diseases

media event n **:** a publicity event staged for coverage by the news media

me·dia·gen·ic \ˌmēdēə'jenik, -jēn-\ adj [media, pl. of medium + -genic (as in photogenic)] **:** likely to appeal to the audiences of the mass media and esp. television ⟨mediagenic politicians⟩

medial condyle n **:** a condyle on the inner side of the lower extremity of the femur; also **:** a corresponding eminence on the upper part of the tibia that articulates with the medial condyle of the femur — compare LATERAL CONDYLE

media mix n **:** a presentation (as in a theater) in which several media (as films, tapes, and slides) are employed simultaneously

me·di·an*\ˈmēdēən\ n **1 :** a vertical line that divides the histogram of a frequency distribution into two parts of equal area **2 :** a value of a random variable for which all greater values make the distribution function greater than one half and all lesser values make it less than one half

median eminence n **:** a raised area in the floor of the third ventricle of the brain produced by the infundibulum of the hypothalamus

med·ic·aid \ˈmedə̇,kād, -dē-\ n, often cap [medical + aid] **:** a program of medical aid designed for those unable to afford regular medical service and financed by the state and federal governments

medi·care \ˈmedə̇,ke(ə)r, -,ka(ə)r, -,keə, -,kaə\ n, often cap [blend of medical and care] **:** a government program of medical care esp. for the aged

me·di·og·ra·phy \ˌmēdē'ägrəfē, -fi\ n [medium + connective -o- + -graphy writing, deriv. of Gk graphein to write] **:** a list of multimedia materials relating to a particular subject

me·droxy·pro·ges·ter·one acetate \meˈdräksēprō-ˌjestə,rōn-\ n [methyl + hydroxy- containing a hydroxyl group + progesterone] **:** a synthetic steroid progestational hormone $C_{24}H_{34}O_4$ that is a derivative of progesterone and is used in oral and parenteral contraceptives

me·dul·lin \mə'dələn, me-; 'medᵊlən, 'mejəl-\ n [NL medulla + E -in chemical compound; fr. its isolation from the medulla of the kidney] **:** a renal prostaglandin effective in reducing blood pressure

mef·e·nam·ic acid \ˌmefə,namik-\ n [dimethyl + fen- (by shortening and alter. fr. phenyl) + aminobenzoic acid] **:** a crystalline compound $C_{15}H_{15}NO_2$ used esp. to relieve pain or inflammation

mega·bar \ˈmegə,bär, -,bá(r\ n [ISV mega- large, million (deriv. of Gk megas large) + bar] **:** a unit of pressure equal to one million bars

mega·bit \-,bit\ n **:** one million bits

mega·buck \-,bək\ n **:** one million dollars ⟨beyond the foundations . . . stood the feds and the megabucks from Washington —Peter Schrag⟩

mega·byte \-,bīt\ n **:** one million bytes

mega·death \-,deth\ n **:** one million deaths — used as a unit in reference to atomic warfare ⟨the estimate that the Kremlin can now destroy 40 per cent of our industry and take a toll of 13 megadeaths —Joseph Alsop⟩

mega·ma·chine \-mə,shēn\ n **:** a social system that functions impersonally like a gigantic machine ⟨through the army, in fact, the standard model of the megamachine was transmitted from culture to culture —Lewis Mumford⟩

mega·rad \-,rad\ n **:** one million rads

mega·struc·ture \-,strəkchə(r), -ksh-\ n **:** a very large multistory building ⟨a seven-block megastructure . . . of shops, parking garages, offices, and hotels, connected by plazas, walkways, and glass-enclosed arcades —Anthony Bailey⟩

mega·unit \-,yünə̇t\ n **:** one million units

mega·vi·ta·min \ˈmegə,vīd·əmən, Brit also -ˈvitəmən\ adj **:** relating to or consisting of very large doses of vitamins ⟨megavitamin therapy⟩

mega·vi·ta·mins \ˈmegə,vīd·əmənz, Brit also -,vitəmənz\ n pl **:** a large quantity of vitamins ⟨the role of megavitamins and nutrition in health and disease — Interface⟩

me·gil·lah also **me·gil·la** \mə'gilə\ n [Yiddish megillah, fr. Heb. mĕgillāh scroll, volume (used esp. of the Book of Esther, read aloud in its entirety at the Purim celebration)] slang **:** a long involved story or account ⟨the whole megillah ⟩ ⟨he'd had a lot of stuff patented over the years, but people had robbed him or swiped his ideas; the usual inventor's megillah —Alexander King⟩

me·la·no·cyte–stim·u·lat·ing hor·mone \mə'lanə-,sīt'stimyə,lād·iŋ'hȯr,mōn, 'melənō,sīt- \ n : a vertebrate hormone of the pituitary gland that darkens the skin by stimulating melanin dispersion in pigment-containing cells — called also MSH

mel·a·no·some \'melənō,sōm\ n [melano- melanin + -some body] : a melanin-producing granule in a melanocyte

mel·a·to·nin \,melə'tōnən\ n [prob. fr. melanocyte + serotonin; fr. its power to lighten melanocytes] : a vertebrate hormone of the pineal gland that produces lightening of the skin by causing contraction of melanin-containing cells and that plays a role in sexual development and maturation

Mel·lo·tron \'melə,trän\ trademark — used for an electronic keyboard instrument programmed to produce the tape-recorded sounds usu. of orchestral instruments

mellow*adj 1 slang : excellent, appealing, fine ⟨at first the gig looked mellow: $300 for two shows and a supposedly hip crowd —Mark Jacobson⟩ 2 : feeling relaxed and good from smoking marijuana

mel·pha·lan \'melfə,lan\ n [prob. fr. methanol + phenylalanine] : an antineoplastic drug $C_{13}H_{18}Cl_2N_2O_2$

meltdown*n : the melting of the core of a nuclear reactor

mcm·bran·al \,mcm'brän'l\ adj : relating to or characteristic of cellular membranes

memory*n : capacity for storing information ⟨a computer with 16K words of memory⟩

memory trace n : an alteration that is held to take place within the central nervous system and to constitute the physical basis of learning

men·a·zon \'menə,zän\ n [perh. fr. dimethyl + diamino- containing two amino groups + triazine + thionate] : an organophosphate insecticide $C_6H_{12}N_5O_2PS_2$ used esp. against parasitic insects of warm-blooded animals

me·nin·go·en·ceph·a·lit·ic \mə'niŋ(,)gȯən,sefə'lid·ik, -in(,)jo-\ adj : relating to or characteristic of meningoencephalitis ⟨meningoencephalitic lesions⟩

meno·tax·is \,menə'taksəs\ n [NL, fr. meno- remaining, persisting (deriv. of Gk menein to remain) + taxis] : a taxis involving a constant reaction (as movement at a constant angle to a light source) but not a simple movement toward or away from the directing stimulus

mensch \'mench, 'mensh\ n [Yiddish, fr. G. man, human being] : a person of integrity and honor ⟨was competent, and maybe even a mensch, but without much in the way of allure —John Corry⟩

mer·cap·to·eth·a·nol \(,)mər'kaptō,ethə,nȯl, -ōl\ n [mercapto- relating to a mercaptan + ethanol] : a reducing agent $HSCH_2CH_2OH$ used to break disulfide bonds in proteins (as for the destruction of their physiological activity)

mercy killing n : the act or practice of killing individuals (as persons or domestic animals) that are hopelessly sick or injured for reasons of mercy : euthanasia

me·rid·ic \mə'ridik\ adj [Gk merid-, meris part + E -ic, adj. suffix] : having some but not all active constituents chemically defined ⟨insects reared on a meridic diet⟩ — compare HOLIDIC, OLIGIDIC

mer·i·toc·ra·cy \,merə'täkrəsē\ n, pl -cies [merit + connective -o- + -cracy government, dominant class, deriv. of Gk kratos strength, power] 1 : a system (as an educational system) whereby the talented are chosen and moved ahead on the basis of their achievement 2 : leadership by the talented — mer·it·o·crat·ic \,merəd·ə-'krad·ik\ adj

mer·it·o·crat \'merəd·ō,krat\ n [merit + -crat member of a dominant class, deriv. of Gk kratos strength, power] : one who advances through a meritocratic system

mero·my·o·sin \,merə'mīəsən\ n [mero- part, partial (deriv. of Gk meros part) + myosin] : either of two structural subunits of myosin that are obtained esp. by tryptic digestion

me·son*\'mez,än, 'mes,än, 'mā-, 'mē-\ n : any of a group of fundamental particles (as the pion, kaon, and eta) that are strongly interacting and have zero or an integral number of quantum units of spin

me·so·pe·lag·ic \,mezōpə'lajik, ,mesō-, ,mē-\ adj [meso-mid, middle (deriv. of Gk mesos) + pelagic] : of, relating to, or inhabiting oceanic depths from about 600 feet to 3000 feet ⟨mesopelagic fish⟩

me·so·scale \'mezə,skāl, 'mes-, 'mē-\ adj : of or relating to a meteorological phenomenon approximately 1 to 100 kilometers in horizontal extent ⟨mesoscale cloud pattern⟩ ⟨mesoscale wind circulation⟩

me·so·some*\-,sōm\ n : an organelle of bacteria that appears in electron micrographs as an invagination of the plasma membrane and is a site of localization of respiratory enzymes

messenger RNA n : an RNA that carries the code for a particular protein from the nuclear DNA to the ribosome and acts as a template for the formation of that protein — compare TRANSFER RNA

mess over vt, slang : to treat harshly or unfairly : abuse ⟨the Syndicate and the government always mess over the people —Berkeley Barb⟩

mes·tra·nol \'mestrə,nȯl, -,nōl\ n [methyl + estrogen + pregnane, a crystalline steroid hormone + -ol chemical compound] : a synthetic estrogen $C_{21}H_{26}O_2$ used in oral contraceptives

meta·cen·tric \,med·ə'sen·trik\ n : a metacentric chromosome

me·tal·lic \mə'talik\ n : a fiber or yarn made of or coated with metal; also : a fabric made of this

met·al·lide \'med·'l,īd\ vt -lid·ed; -lid·ing [obs. metallide, n., a binary compound of metals, fr. metall- metal + -ide derivative compound] : to diffuse (atoms of a metal or metalloid) into the surface of a metal by electrolysis in order to impart a desired surface property (as hardness) to the bulk metal

me·tal·lo·en·zyme \mə'talō'en,zīm\ n [metallo- metal + enzyme] : an enzyme consisting of a protein linked with a specific metal

metal–oxide semiconductor n : a semiconductor device (as a diode or a capacitor) in which a metallic oxide (as silicon dioxide) serves as an insulating layer

meta·mer·ic*\,med·ə'merik, -'mi(ə)r-\ adj : of, relating to, or being color metamers ⟨a metameric pair⟩ — me·tam·er·ism*\mə'tamə,rizəm\ n

meta·ram·i·nol \,med·ə'ramə,nȯl, -,nōl\ n [perh. fr. meta- after, change, isomeric, deriv. of Gk meta with, among, after) + hydroxyl + amine + -ol chemical compound] : a sympathomimetic drug $C_9H_{13}NO_2$ used esp. as a vasoconstrictor

meta·rho·dop·sin \ˌmed-ərō'däpsən\ *n* **:** either of two intermediate compounds formed in the bleaching of rhodopsin by light

me·te·or·oi·dal \ˌmēd-ēəˌróid³l\ *adj* **:** of or relating to meteoroids

me·te·pa \mə'tēpə, me'-\ *n* [*methyl* + *tepa*] **:** an insect chemosterilant $C_9H_{18}N_3OP$ that is a methyl derivative of tepa

meter maid *n* **:** a female member of a police force who is assigned to write tickets for parking violations

metha·qua·lone \ˌmethə'kwāˌlōn\ *n* [*methyl* + *-a-* (arbitrary infix) + *quina*zoline + *-one* ketone or analogous compound] **:** a sedative and hypnotic drug $C_{16}H_{14}N_2O$ that is not a barbiturate but is habit-forming and subject to abuse — see QUAALUDE

Meth·e·drine \'methəˌdrēn, -ədrən\ *trademark* — used for methamphetamine

meth·i·cil·lin \ˌmethə'silən\ *n* [*methyl* + pen*icillin*] **:** a semisynthetic penicillin esp. effective against penicillinase-producing staphylococci

me·thi·ma·zole \me'thīməˌzōl, mə'-\ *n* [*methyl* + *imid*azole] **:** a drug $C_4H_6N_2S$ used to inhibit activity of the thyroid gland

Method*n* **:** a dramatic technique by which an actor seeks to gain complete identification with the inner personality of the character being portrayed

meth·o·trex·ate \ˌmethə'trekˌsāt, -ksət\ *n* [*methyl* + connective *-o-* + *-trex-* (arbitrary infix) + *-ate* derivative compound] **:** a toxic anticancer drug $C_{20}H_{22}N_8O_5$ that is an analogue of folic acid and an antimetabolite

me·thox·amine \me'thäksəˌmēn, -əmən\ *n* [*methyl* + *ox-* containing oxygen + *amine*] **:** a sympathomimetic amine $C_{11}H_{17}NO_3$ used as the hydrochloride esp. for its vasoconstrictor effects to increase blood pressure

me·thoxy·flu·rane \meˌthäksē'flu(ə)rˌān\ *n* [*methyl* + *oxy-* containing oxygen + *fluor-* containing fluorine + eth*ane*] **:** potent nonexplosive inhalational general anesthetic $C_3H_4Cl_2F_2O$ administered as a vapor

meths \'meths\ *n pl but sing in constr* [contr. of *methylated spirits*] *Brit* **:** ethyl alcohol denatured with methanol

meth·yl·ase \'methəˌlās, -āz\ *n* [*methyl* + *-ase* enzyme] **:** an enzyme that catalyzes methylation (as of RNA or DNA)

meth·yl·do·pa \ˌmethəl'dōpə\ *n* [*methyl* + *dopa*, an amino acid] **:** a drug $C_{10}H_{13}NO_4$ used to lower blood pressure

meth·yl·mer·cu·ry \-ˌmərkyərē, -'māk-, -'maik-, -k(ə)rē, -ri\ *n* **:** any of various toxic compounds of mercury containing the complex CH_3Hg- that tend to accumulate in the environment as pollutants formed as industrial by= products or pesticide residues, are rapidly and easily absorbed through the human intestinal wall, and cause neurological dysfunction in man

meth·yl para·thi·on \ˌmethəlˌparə'thīən, -'thīˌän\ *n* **:** a potent synthetic organophosphate insecticide $C_8H_{10}NO_5PS$ that is more toxic than parathion

meth·yl·phe·ni·date \ˌmethəl'fenəˌdāt, -'fēn-\ *n* [*methyl* + *phenyl* + piperi*d*ine + *acet*ate] **:** a mild stimulant $C_{14}H_{19}NO_2$ of the central nervous system that is an analogue of amphetamine and is used in the form of the hydrochloride to treat narcolepsy and hyperkinetic behavior disorders in children — see RITALIN

meth·yl·pred·nis·o·lone \ˌmethəlpred'nisəˌlōn\ *n* [*methyl* + *prednisolone*] **:** a glucocorticoid $C_{22}H_{30}O_5$ that is a derivative of prednisolone and is used as an anti-inflammatory agent; *also* **:** any of several of its salts (as an acetate) used similarly

meth·yl·trans·fer·ase \-ˌtranzfəˌrās, -n(t)sf-, -āz\ *n* **:** any of several transferases that promote transfer of a methyl group from one compound to another

meth·y·ser·gide \ˌmethə'sərˌjīd\ *n* [*methyl* + *lysergic* acid + am*ide*] **:** a serotonin antagonist $C_{21}H_{27}N_3O_2$ used in the form of its maleate esp. in the treatment and prevention of migraine headaches

met·o·clo·pra·mide \ˌmed-ə'klōprəˌmīd\ *n* [*methoxy* + *chlor*- chlorine, containing chlorine + *-pr-* (perh. arbitrary infix) + *amide*] **:** an antiemetic drug $C_{14}H_{22}ClN_3O_2$ administered as the hydrochloride

metric*n* **:** a mathematical function that associates with each pair of elements of a set a real nonnegative number constituting their distance and satisfying the conditions that the number is zero only if the two elements are identical, the number is the same regardless of the order in which the two elements are taken, and the number associated with one pair of elements plus that associated with one member of the pair and a third element is equal to or greater than the number associated with the other member of the pair and the third element

met·ri·cate \'me·trəˌkāt\ *vt* **-cat·ed; -cat·ing** *Brit* **:** METRICIZE

met·ri·ca·tion \ˌme·trə'kāshən\ *n* **:** the act or process of metricizing

met·ri·cize*\'me·trəˌsīz\ *vt* **-cized; -ciz·ing :** to change into or express in the metric system

metric space *n* **:** a mathematical set for which a metric is defined for any pair of elements

¹met·ro \'me-(ˌ)trō\ *n, pl* **met·ros** [fr. the phrase *metropolitan government*] **:** metropolitan regional government

²metro *adj* **:** of, relating to, or constituting a region including a city and the surrounding suburban areas that are socially and economically integrated with it **:** metropolitan ⟨*metro* government⟩ ⟨major *metro* markets⟩ ⟨branch libraries in *metro* Atlanta —*Library Jour.*⟩

met·ro·ni·da·zole \ˌme·trə'nīdəˌzōl\ *n* [*methyl* + *-tron-* (prob. fr. *nitro*) + im*ide* + *azole*] **:** a drug $C_6H_9N_3O_3$ used in treating vaginal trichomoniasis

me·tyr·a·pone \mə'tirəˌpōn\ *n* [perh. fr. *methyl* + *-rapone* (perh. alter. of *propanone*)] **:** a metabolic hormone $C_{14}H_{14}N_2O$ that inhibits biosynthesis of cortisol and corticosterone and is used to test for normal functioning of the pituitary gland

me·val·o·nate \mə'valəˌnāt\ *n* [*mevalonic* acid + *-ate* derivative compound] **:** a salt of mevalonic acid

MIA \ˌe(ˌ)mī'ā\ *n* [*missing in action*] **:** a member of the armed forces whose whereabouts following a combat mission are unknown and whose death cannot be established beyond reasonable doubt

Mi·chae·lis constant \miˌkäləs-, mə-\ *n* [Leonor *Michaelis* †1949 Am. biochemist] **:** a constant that is a measure of the kinetics of an enzyme reaction and that is equivalent to the concentration of substrate at which the reaction takes place at one half its maximum velocity

mick·ey–mouse \ˌmikē'maùs, -ki-\ *vt* [fr. *Mickey Mouse*, a trademark] **:** to provide (a film) with accompanying music that closely describes or mimics the action

¹**Mick·ey Mouse** \ˌmikēˈmaüs, -ki-\ *adj* [fr. *Mickey Mouse,* a trademark used for a cartoon character] **:** petty: as **a :** lacking importance **:** trivial, insignificant ⟨switch to *Mickey Mouse* courses, where you don't work too hard —Willie Cager⟩ **b :** annoyingly petty **:** small-minded ⟨directives did away with *Mickey Mouse* Navy regs —*Newsweek*⟩ **c :** small-time, second-rate, bush-league ⟨running a race in two stages ... is bad enough; two days for a 226-mile race is *Mickey Mouse* —J.S. Radosta⟩

²**Mickey Mouse** *n* **:** something that is Mickey Mouse ⟨eliminating the *Mickey Mouse* from the soldier's routine —L.J. Binder⟩

MICR *abbr* magnetic ink character recognition

micro*n, pl* **micros** **1 :** MICROCOMPUTER **2 :** MICROPROCESSOR

mi·cro·al·gae \ˌmīkrōˈal(ˌ)jē\ *n pl* [*micro-* microscopic + *algae*] **:** algae (as diatoms or chlorellas) not visible to the unaided eye — **mi·cro·al·gal** \-ˈalgəl\ *adj*

mi·cro·an·a·tom·i·cal \ˌmī(ˌ)krōˌanəˈtäməkəl\ *adj* [*microanatomy* + *-ical*, adj. suffix] **:** of or relating to the microscopic structure of the tissues of organisms **:** histological

mi·cro·an·gi·op·a·thy \-ˌanjēˈäpəthē, -thi\ *n* [*micro-* + *angio-* blood vessel + *-pathy* disease] **:** a disease of very fine blood vessels — **mi·cro·an·gio·path·ic** \-jēə-ˈpathik\ *adj*

mi·cro·beam \ˈmīkrōˌbēm\ *n* [*micro-* small, one millionth (deriv. of Gk *mikros* small) + *beam*] **:** a beam of radiation of small cross section ⟨a focused laser *microbeam*⟩ ⟨a *microbeam* of electrons⟩

mi·cro·body \-ˌbädē, -di\ *n* **:** PEROXISOME

mi·cro·cap·sule \-ˌkapsəl, -(ˌ)sül, *also* -ps(ˌ)yül *or* -psyəl\ *n* **:** a tiny capsule containing material (as an adhesive or a medicine) that is released when the capsule is broken, melted, or dissolved

mi·cro·chip \-ˌchip\ *n* **:** INTEGRATED CIRCUIT

mi·cro·cir·cuit \-ˌsərkət, -ˌsȯk-, -ˌsəik-\ *n* **:** INTEGRATED CIRCUIT — **mi·cro·cir·cuit·ry** \-kə-trē\ *n*

mi·cro·cir·cu·la·tion \ˌmīkrōˌsərkyəˈlāshən\ *n* **1 :** the part of the circulatory system made up of very fine channels (as capillaries or venules) **2 :** circulation through very fine channels — **mi·cro·cir·cu·la·to·ry** \-ˈsərkyələˌtōrē, -ˌtȯrē\ *adj*

mic·ro·coc·cal \-ˈkäkəl\ *adj* **:** relating to or characteristic of micrococci ⟨*micrococcal* enzymes⟩

mi·cro·code \ˈmīkrəˌkōd\ *n* **:** the microinstructions esp. of a microprocessor

mi·cro·com·put·er \ˌmī(ˌ)krōkəmˈpyüd-ə(r)\ *n* **:** a very small computer; *also* **:** MICROPROCESSOR

mi·cro·cul·ture \ˈmīkrōˌkəlchə(r)\ *n* **1 :** the culture of a small group of human beings with limited perspective ⟨those who have been educated by experience or by learning to a broader view may escape the *microculture* of the specific group with which they are identified —H.L. Shapiro⟩ **2 :** a microscopic culture of cells or organisms — **mi·cro·cul·tur·al** \ˌmīkrōˈkəlch(ə)rəl\ *adj*

mi·cro·dis·tri·bu·tion \ˌmīkrōˌdistrəˈbyüshən\ *n* **:** the precise distribution of one or more kinds of organisms in a microhabitat or in part of an ecosystem ⟨*microdistribution* of soil mites⟩

mi·cro·dot \ˈmīkrōˌdät\ *n* **1 :** a photographic reproduction of printed matter reduced to the size of a dot for ease or security of transmittal **2 :** a very small pill or capsule of LSD

mi·cro·earth·quake \ˌmīkrōˈərthˌkwāk, -ˈȧth-, -ˈȧith-\ *n* [*micro-* extremely small + *earthquake*] **:** an earthquake of low intensity; *esp* **:** one of magnitude of less than 3 on the Richter scale

mi·cro·ecol·o·gy \ˌmīkrōēˈkäləjē, -eˈkäl-, -ēˈkäl-\ *n* **:** ecology of all or part of a small community (as a microhabitat or a housing development) — **mi·cro·ec·o·log·i·cal** \-ˌēkəˈläjəkəl, -ˌekəˈläj-\ *adj*

mi·cro·eco·nom·ic \-ˌekəˈnämik, -ˌēk-\ *adj* **:** of or relating to microeconomics ⟨*microeconomic* theory⟩

mi·cro·elec·trode*\ˌmīkrōēˈlekˌtrōd\ *n* **:** a minute electrode; *esp* **:** one that is inserted in a living biological cell or tissue to study its electrical characteristics

mi·cro·elec·tron·ics \ˌmīkrōēˌlekˈträniks\ *n pl but sing in constr* **:** a branch of electronics that deals with the miniaturization of electronic circuits and components — **mi·cro·elec·tron·ic** \-ik\ *adj*

mi·cro·en·cap·su·late \-ən'kapsəˌlāt\ *vt* **:** to enclose in a microcapsule ⟨*microencapsulated* aspirin⟩ — **mi·cro·en·cap·su·la·tion** \-ˌən,kapsəˈlāshən\ *n*

mi·cro·fil·a·ment \-ˈfiləmənt\ *n* **:** any of the minute protein filaments that are widely distributed in the cytoplasm of eukaryotic cells, help maintain their structural framework, and play a role in the movement of cell components

mi·cro·flu·o·rom·e·try \-ˌflu(ə)ˈrämə-trē, -flō-, -flȯ-, -i\ *n* **:** the detection and measurement of the fluorescence produced by minute quantities of materials (as in cells) — **mi·cro·flu·o·rom·e·ter** \-ˈräməd-ə(r)\ *n* — **mi·cro·flu·o·ro·met·ric** \-ˌflu(ə)rəˌmeˈtrik, -ˌflȯrə-, -ˌflȯrə-\ *adj*

mi·cro·form*\ˈmīkrəˌfȯrm, -ˌfȯ(ə)m\ *n* **1 :** a process or medium for reproducing printed matter in a much reduced size ⟨store information in *microform*⟩ ⟨microfilm, microfiche, and other *microforms*⟩ **2 :** matter reproduced by microform or a copy of such matter ⟨companies now producing *microforms*⟩

mi·cro·fun·gus \ˌmīkrōˈfəngəs\ *n* **:** a fungus (as a mold) with a microscopic fruiting body — **mi·cro·fun·gal** \-gəl\ *adj*

mi·cro·gauss \ˈmīkrōˌgaùs\ *n* **:** one millionth of a gauss

mi·cro·graph·ics \ˌmīkrəˈgrafiks\ *n pl but sing in constr* **:** the industry concerned with the manufacture and sale of graphic material in microform; *also* **:** the production of graphic material in microform — **mi·cro·graph·ic** \-ik\ *adj*

mi·cro·im·age \ˈmīkrōˌimij, -ˌimēj\ *n* **:** an image (as on a microfilm) that is of greatly reduced size

mi·cro·in·struc·tion \ˌmīkrōənˈstrəkshən\ *n* **:** a computer instruction corresponding to a single machine operation

mi·cro·ma·chin·ing \ˈmīkrōməˌshēniŋ\ *n* **:** the removing (as in drilling, planing, or shaping) of small amounts of metal by action other than that of a sharp-edged tool ⟨*micromachining* done with an electron beam⟩

mi·cro·me·te·or·ite*\ˌmīkrōˈmēd-ēəˌrīt\ *n* **:** a meteoritic particle of very small size — **mi·cro·me·te·or·it·ic** \ˌmīkrōˌmēd-ēəˈrid-ik\ *adj*

mi·cro·me·te·or·oid \ˌmīkrōˈmēd-ēəˌröid\ *n* **:** MICROMETEORITE

mi·cro·min·ia·ture \-ˈminēəˌchü(ə)r, -ˈminəˌchü(ə)r, -ˈminyə-, -əchər, -ˌt(y)ü(ə)r\ *adj* **1 :** MICROMINIATUR-IZED **2 :** suitable for use with microminiaturized parts

mi·cro·min·ia·tur·iza·tion \-ˌminēəˌchürəˈzāshən, -ˌminəˌ-, -ˌminyə-, -əchər-, -ˌt(y)ür-\ *n* **:** the process of producing microminiaturized things

mi·cro·min·ia·tur·ized \-ˈminēəchəˌrīzd, -ˈminəchə-, -nyəchə-, -ˌtyüˌrīzd\ *adj* **:** reduced to or produced in a very small size and esp. in a size smaller than one considered miniature ⟨*microminiaturized* electronic circuit⟩

mi·cro·mod·ule \ˈmīkrōˌmäj(ˌ)ü(ə)l\ *n* **:** a microminiaturized module

mi·cro·mor·phol·o·gy \-mȯrˈfäləjē, -mȯ(ə)ˈf-\ *n* **1 :** the microscopic structure of a material — used esp. with reference to soils **2 :** minute morphological detail esp. as determined by electron microscopy; *also* **:** the study of such detail — **mi·cro·mor·pho·log·ic** \-ˌmȯrfəˈläjik\ *adj* — **mi·cro·mor·pho·log·i·cal** \-jəkəl\ *adj* — **mi·cro·mor·pho·log·i·cal·ly** \-jək(ə)lē\ *adv*

mi·cro·pop·u·la·tion \-ˌpäpyəˈläshən\ *n* **1 :** a population of microorganisms **2 :** the population of organisms within a small area

mi·cro·probe \ˈmīkrəˌprōb\ *n* **:** a device for microanalysis that operates by exciting radiation by means of a beam of electrons in a minute area or volume of material so that the composition may be determined by means of the emission spectrum

mi·cro·pro·ces·sor \ˈmīkrōˌpräsˌesə(r), -prōs-\ *n* **:** a computer processor contained on an integrated-circuit chip; *also* **:** such a processor with memory and associated circuits

mi·cro·pro·gram·ming \-ˈprōˌgramiŋ, -ˈprōgrəmiŋ\ *n* **:** the use of routines stored in memory rather than specialized circuits for controlling a device (as a computer) — **mi·cro·pro·gram** \-ˈprōˌgram, -ˈprōgrəm\ *n or vt*

mi·cro·pub·li·ca·tion \-ˌpəbləˈkāshən\ *n* **1 :** MICROPUBLISHING **2 :** something published in microform

mi·cro·pub·lish·ing \-ˈpəbləshiŋ\ *n* **:** the publishing of new or previously published material in microform — **mi·cro·pub·lish** \-ˈpəblish, -ēsh\ *vt* — **mi·cro·pub·lish·er** \-shə(r)\ *n*

mi·cro·punc·ture \-ˈpəŋ(k)chə(r)\ *n* **:** an extremely small puncture ⟨a *micropuncture* of the nephron⟩

mi·cro·quake \ˈmīkrōˌkwāk\ *n* **:** MICROEARTHQUAKE

mi·cro·spo·ran·gi·ate \ˌmī(ˌ)krōspəˈranjēət\ *adj* **:** bearing or being microsporangia

mi·cro·state \ˈmīkrōˌstāt\ *n* **:** an independent nation that is extremely small in area and population ⟨visiting statesmen get equal treatment, whether they represent a superpower or a *microstate* —*Christian Science Monitor*⟩

mi·cro·sur·gery \ˈmīkrōˌsərj(ə)rē, -ˈsəj-, -ˌsəij-\ *n* **:** minute dissection or manipulation (as by a micromanipulator or laser beam) of living structures (as cells) for surgical or experimental purposes — **mi·cro·sur·gi·cal** \-jəkəl\ *adj* — **mi·cro·sur·gi·cal·ly** \-k(ə)lē, -i\ *adv*

mi·cro·teach·ing \ˈmīkrōˌtēchiŋ\ *n* **:** practice teaching in which a student teacher's teaching of a small class for a short time is videotaped for subsequent evaluation

mi·cro·tek·tite \ˌmīkrōˈtekˌtīt\ *n* **:** a minute tektite one millimeter or less in diameter found esp. in sediments on the ocean floor

mi·cro·text \-ˌtekst\ *n* **:** text in microform

mi·cro·tu·bule \ˌmīkrōˈt(y)ü(ˌ)byü(ə)l\ *n* **:** any of the minute cylindrical structures that are widely distributed in protoplasm and are made up of longitudinal fibrils — **mi·cro·tu·bu·lar** \-ˈt(y)übyələ(r)\ *adj*

mi·cro·vas·cu·lar \-ˈvaskyələ(r)\ *adj* **:** of, relating to, or constituting the part of the circulatory system made up of minute vessels (as venules or capillaries) that average less than 0.3 millimeter in diameter — **mi·cro·vas·cu·la·ture** \-ˈvaskyələˌchü(ə)r, -ˌt(y)ü(ə)r\ *n*

mi·cro·ves·sel \-ˈvesəl\ *n* **:** a blood vessel (as a capillary, arteriole, or venule) of the microcirculatory system

mi·cro·vil·lus \-ˈviləs\ *n* **:** a microscopic projection of a tissue, a cell, or a cell organelle; *esp* **:** one of the fingerlike outward projections of some cell surfaces — **mi·cro·vil·lar** \-ˈvilər\ *adj* — **mi·cro·vil·lous** \-ləs\ *adj*

microwave oven \ˈmīkrəˌwāv-\ *n* **:** an oven in which food is cooked by the heat produced as a result of microwave penetration of the food

mid·course \ˈmidˌkō(ə)rs, -ˌkȯ(ə)rs, -ˌkōəs, -ˌkȯ(ə)s\ *adj* **:** being or relating to the part of a course (as of spacecraft) that is between the initial and final phases ⟨a *midcourse* correction⟩ — **mid·course** \ˈmidˌk-\ *n*

mid·cult \ˈmidˌkəlt\ *n* [*mid*dlebrow *cult*ure] **:** the artistic and intellectual culture that is neither highbrow culture nor lowbrow culture **:** middlebrow culture ⟨fastidious literary people disdainful even of *midcult* —H.J. Muller⟩

middle America *n, often cap M* **:** the middle-class segment of the U.S. population ⟨persuade *Middle America* to reduce its level of energy consumption —A.F. Buchan⟩; *esp* **:** the traditional or conservative element of the middle class ⟨appealed to *Middle America* with his emphasis on such traditional middle-class values as patriotism, social stability, and individual initiative — *Current Biog.*⟩ — **middle American** *n, often cap M*

mid·dle–of–the–road·ism \-ˈrōdˌizəm\ *n* [*middle-of-the-road* + *-ism*] **:** a policy or attitude for action that is midway between extremes

midi \ˈmidē, -di\ *n* [*mid* + *-i* (as in *mini*)] **:** a dress, skirt, or coat that usu. extends to the mid-calf — called also respectively *midi dress, midi skirt, midi coat*

mid·size \ˈmidˌsīz\ *adj* **:** of intermediate size ⟨a *midsize* car⟩

mike*vt **miked; mik·ing :** to supply with a microphone ⟨an acoustic bass properly *miked* would have been more appropriate —Doug Ramsey⟩

mil*\ˈmil\ *n* **:** thousand ⟨found a salinity of 38.4 per *mil* ⟩

Milanese*adj **:** coated with flour or bread crumbs, often seasoned with cheese, and sautéed ⟨veal cutlet *Milanese*⟩

mil·i·tar·ia \ˌmiləˈterēə\ *n pl* [*military* + *-ia* related things] **:** military objects (as firearms and uniforms) of historical value or interest

military collar *n* **:** a wide double-pointed collar that lies flat and open esp. on a double-breasted coat

millimicro- *comb form* [*milli-* thousandth (deriv. of L *mille* thousand) + *micro-* millionth, deriv. of Gk *mikros* small] **:** billionth ⟨*millimicro*second⟩

mil·li·ra·di·an \ˌmiləˈrādēən\ *n* **:** one thousandth of a radian

mil·li·rem \ˈmiləˌrem\ *n* **:** one thousandth of a rem

mim·eo \ˈmimē(ˌ)ō\ *n* [short for *mimeographed*] **:** a mimeographed publication

mim–mem \ˈmimˈmem\ *adj* [*mim*icry + *mem*orization] **:** of, relating to, or being a drill pattern in which students repeat usu. in chorus a foreign language phrase supplied by their instructor

mi·nau·diè·re \mēnōdyeer\ *n* [F, affected, coquettish, fr. *minauder* to simper, smirk, fr. OF *mine* appearance] **:** a small decorative case for cosmetics or jewelry often designed as a woman's fashion accessory

mind–blow·ing \'mīn(d)ˌbloiŋ\ *adj* **1 :** PSYCHEDELIC 1b ⟨some 400 *mind-blowing* experiences . . . initiated by sacred mushrooms, psilocybin, LSD or DMT —Howard Junker⟩ **2 :** mentally or emotionally exciting **:** overwhelming ⟨on the third martini, a *mind-blowing* and terrible idea comes straight out of the glass into your head —James Dickey⟩ — **mind·blow·er** \-ˌblō(ə)r, -ˌbloə\ *n*

mind–ex·pand·ing \'mīndək,spandiŋ\ *adj* **:** PSYCHEDELIC 1a ⟨*mind-expanding* drugs⟩

¹mini \'minē, -ni\ *n* [*mini-*] **:** one that is small of its kind: as **a : a** very small automobile **:** minicar **b :** MINISKIRT **c :** MINICOMPUTER

²mini *adj* **:** very small **:** miniature

mini- *comb form* [*mini*ature] **:** very small **:** miniature

miniature pin·scher \-'pinchə(r)\ *n* **1 :** a breed of toy dog that suggests a small Doberman pinscher and measures 10 to 12½ inches in height at the withers **2 :** a toy dog of the miniature pinscher breed

miniature schnau·zer \-'s(h)naûzə(r), -'shnaûtsə(r)\ *n* **1 :** a breed of schnauzer that is 12 to 14 inches in height and is classified as a terrier **2 :** a dog of the miniature schnauzer breed

mini·bike \'minē,bīk, -nə-\ *n* **:** a small one-passenger motorcycle having a low frame and elevated handlebars — **mini·bik·er** \-ˌbīkə(r)\ *n*

mini·bus \-ˌbəs\ *n* **:** a small bus

mini·cab \-ˌkab\ *n* **:** a small car used as a taxicab

mini·com·put·er \'minēkəm,pyüd-ə(r), -nək-\ *n* **:** a small comparatively inexpensive computer

min·i·mal* \'minəməl\ *adj, often cap* **:** of, relating to, or being minimal art ⟨*minimal* aluminum pieces —Grace H. Glueck⟩

minimal art *n* **:** abstract art (as painting or sculpture) consisting primarily of simple geometric forms executed in an impersonal style — **minimal artist** *n*

min·i·mal·ism \'minəmə,lizəm\ *n* **:** MINIMAL ART

min·i·mal·ist* \'minəmələst\ *n* **:** MINIMAL ARTIST

minimalist *adj* **:** MINIMAL

min·i·mal·ity \ˌminə'maləd-ē, -ˌtē, -i\ *n, pl* **-it·ies** [*minimal* + *-ity* quality, state] **:** the state or quality of being minimal

¹mini·max \'minəˌmaks, -nēˌm-\ *n* [*mini*mum + *maxi*mum] **:** the minimum of a set of maxima; *esp* **:** the smallest of a set of maximum possible losses each of which occurs in the most unfavorable outcome of a strategy followed by a participant in a situation governed by the theory of games — compare MAXIMIN

²minimax *adj* **:** of, relating to, or based on a minimax, the minimax principle, or the minimax theorem

minimax principle *n* **:** a principle of choice for a decision problem: one should choose the action which minimizes the loss that he stands to suffer even under the worst circumstances

minimax the·o·rem \-ˌthēərəm, -ˌthi(ə)rəm\ *n* **:** a theorem in the theory of games: the lowest maximum expected loss equals the highest minimum expected gain

minimum* *n* **:** the lowest speed allowed on a highway

mini·park \ˈminēˌpärk, -niˌ-, -ˌpák\ *n* **:** a small city park

mini·re·ces·sion \ˈminērəˌseshən, -ni-, -rē-\ *n* **:** a brief economic downturn of minor proportions

mini·se·ries \-ˌsi(ə)r,ēz, -ˌsē,rēz, -ˌsi(ə)rəz, -ˌsērəz\ *n* **:** a television production of a story presented in sequential episodes

mini·ski \'minē,skē, -ni-\ *n* **1 :** a short ski worn esp. by beginners **2 :** a miniature ski worn by a skibobber

mini·skirt \'minē,skərt, -ni-, -ˌskāt, -ˌskəit\ *n* **:** a short skirt or dress that usu. extends to the mid-thigh — called also minidress \-ˌdres\

mini·state \-ˌstāt\ *n* **:** MICROSTATE

mini·sub \-ˌsəb\ *n* **:** a very small submarine used esp. in research (as on the ocean bottom)

Min·ne·so·ta Mul·ti·pha·sic Personality Inventory \ˌminə'sōd-əˌmaltə'fāzik-, -tē-, -ˌtī-\ *n* [fr. the University of *Minnesota*, where it was developed] **:** a test of personal and social adjustment based on a complex scaling of the answers to an elaborate true or false test

minority* *n* **:** a member of a minority group

miracle fruit *n* [fr. the fact that its fruit causes foods eaten after it to taste sweet] **:** a small shrubby tree (*Synsepalum dulcificum*) of the family Sapotaceae having a fruit that is a fleshy single-seeded berry; *also* **:** its fruit

mi·rex \'mī,reks\ *n* [prob. fr. pis*mire* + *exterminator*] **:** an organochlorine insecticide $C_{10}Cl_{12}$ that is used esp. against ants and is a suspected carcinogen

¹MIRV \'mərv\ *n* [*multiple independently targeted reentry vehicle*] **:** a missile with two or more warheads that are designed to reenter the atmosphere on the way to separate enemy targets; *also* **:** any of the warheads of such a missile

²MIRV *vb* **MIRVed; MIRV·ing** *vt* **:** to equip with MIRV warheads ⟨both sides would *MIRV* their submarine-borne missiles —Stewart Alsop⟩ ~ *vi* **:** to arm one's forces with MIRVs

mis·al·lo·ca·tion \ˈmis,alə'kāshən, -lō-\ *n* [*mis* bad, wrongly, lack of + *allocation*] **:** faulty or improper allocation

mis·com·mu·ni·ca·tion \(')miskə,myünə'kāshən\ *n* **:** failure to communicate clearly

mis·di·ag·nose \-'dīəg,nōs, -ˌnōz\ *vt* **:** to diagnose incorrectly — **mis·di·ag·no·sis** \-ˌdīəg'nōsəs\ *n*

mis·ori·ent \-'ōrē,ent, -'ôr-\ *vt* **:** to orient improperly or incorrectly — **mis·ori·en·ta·tion** \-ˌōrēən'tāshən, -ˌôr-, -ē,en-\ *n*

mis·sense \'mis,sen(t)s\ *n* [*mis-* + *-sense* (as in *nonsense*)] **:** genetic mutation involving alteration of one or more codons so that different amino acids are determined — compare NONSENSE

missionary position *n* [perh. so called fr. the insistence of some missionaries that the traditional Western coital position is the only acceptable one] **:** a coital position in which the female lies on her back with the male on top of her

mist* *n* **:** a drink of alcoholic liquor (as Scotch) served over cracked ice and garnished with a twist of lemon peel

Mister Charlie *n* **:** MR. CHARLIE — usu. used disparagingly

mi·to·gen \'mīd·əjən\ *n* [*mito-* mitosis + *-gen* producer] **:** a substance that induces mitosis

mi·to·gen·ic \ˌmīd·əˈjenik\ adj : producing mitosis — **mi·to·ge·nic·i·ty** \ˌmīd·əjəˈnisəd·ē\ n

mi·to·my·cin \ˌmīd·əˈmīsᵊn\ n [prob. fr. ISV mito- + -mycin substance obtained from a fungus, fr. streptomycin] : a complex of antibiotic substances which is produced by a Japanese streptomyces (Streptomyces caespitosus) and one form of which acts directly on DNA and is an effective antineoplastic agent

mi·to·spore \ˈmīd·ə,spō(ə)r, -,spó(ə)r, -,spōə, -,spó(ə)\ n : a haploid or diploid spore produced by mitosis

Mit·tel·eu·ro·pa \ˌmid·ᵊlyüˈrōpə, G ,mitəlöiˈrōpə\ adj [G, central Europe, fr. mittel middle + Europa Europe] : of or from central Europe : of the kind or style prevalent in central Europe

mix* n 1 : a commercially prepared nonalcoholic mixture of ingredients for a mixed drink ⟨mai tai mix⟩ 2 : a phonograph record or tape produced by combining or adjusting sounds ⟨somewhere in the mix there's an organ —Stephen Davis⟩

mixed–me·dia \ˈmikst¦mēdēə\ adj : MULTIMEDIA

mixed media n : MULTIMEDIA

MLD abbr median lethal dose

MMPI abbr Minnesota Multiphasic Personality Inventory

MMT \ˌem(ˌ)emˈtē\ n [methylcyclopentadienyl manganese tricarbonyl] : an organometallic compound $CH_3C_5H_4Mn(CO)_3$ added to a motor fuel to increase the octane number

MNC \ˌem(ˌ)enˈsē\ n [multinational corporation] : MULTINATIONAL

¹mod \ˈmäd\ adj, often cap [short for modern] : modern, up-to-date; esp : bold, free, and unconventional in style, behavior, or dress ⟨mod suits⟩ ⟨the mod look in clothes⟩ ⟨the world's most mod Prime Minister —Forbes⟩

²mod n, often cap : one who wears mod clothes ⟨dresses of white organza with skirts that miss the floor by six or eight inches await the Mods among us; the faint at heart may have them full length —New Yorker⟩

³mod prep [short for modulo] : with respect to a modulus of

⁴mod n [short for module] : a class period in a modular schedule

model* n 1 : a system of postulates, data, and inferences presented as a mathematical description of an entity or state of affairs ⟨a mathematical model of the physical world⟩ 2 : a version or equivalent of something ⟨they departed sharply from the British model by denying to the President almost all features of the federative power —F. D. Wormuth⟩

model* vt : to produce a representation or simulation of ⟨using a computer to model a problem⟩

mo·dem \ˈmō,dem\ n [modulator + demodulator] : a device that converts signals from one form to a form compatible with another kind of equipment ⟨a modem for transmitting computer data over telephone lines⟩

modesty panel n : a panel designed to conceal the legs of a person sitting esp. at a desk or table

modified American plan n : a hotel rate whereby guests are charged a fixed sum (as by the day or week) for room, breakfast, and lunch or dinner

mod·u·lar* \ˈmäjələ(r)\ adj : of or relating to a school schedule in which subjects pertinent to more than one course are covered in common class sessions

modular arithmetic n : arithmetic that deals with whole numbers where the numbers are replaced by their remainders after division by a fixed number ⟨5 hours after 10 o'clock is 3 o'clock because clocks follow a modular arithmetic with modulus 12⟩

mod·u·lar·i·ty \ˌmäjəˈlarəd·ē, -ler-\ n : the use of discrete functional units in building an electronic or mechanical system

mod·u·lar·ized \ˈmäjələ,rīzd\ adj : constructed of modules ⟨modularized electronic equipment⟩

mod·ule* \ˈmäj(ˌ)ü(ə)l\ n 1 : any in a series of standardized units for use together: as a : a unit of furniture or architecture b : an educational or instructional unit which covers a single subject or a discrete part of a broad subject 2 : an assembly of components that are packaged or mounted together and constitute a functional unit for an electronic or mechanical system ⟨a module for a computer⟩ 3 : an independent unit that constitutes a part of the total structure of a space vehicle ⟨a propulsion module⟩ 4 a : a subset of an additive group that is also a group under addition b : a mathematical set that is a commutative group under addition and that is closed under multiplication which is distributive from the left or right or both by elements of a ring and for which $a(bx) = (ab)x$ or $(xb)a = x(ba)$ or both where a and b are elements of the ring and x belongs to the set

mod·u·lus* \ˈmäjələs\ n 1 : the factor by which a logarithm of a number to one base is multiplied to obtain the logarithm of the number to a new base 2 : the length of the radius·vector from the origin to the point representing the number in the complex plane 3 : the number of different numbers used in a system of modular arithmetic

mo·gul \ˈmōgəl\ n [prob. of Scand origin; akin to Norw dial. muge heap, pile, fr. ON mūgi] : a bump in a ski run

mois·tur·ize \ˈmóischə,rīz\ vt -ized; -iz·ing : to add moisture to ⟨moisturize the air⟩ — **mois·tur·iz·er** \-ə(r)\ n

moldy fig n 1 : a devotee of traditional jazz 2 : one that is old-fashioned

mole* n : a spy (as a double agent) who establishes a cover long before beginning espionage

mom–and–pop \ˌmämən(d)¦päp\ adj : being a small owner-operated business ⟨a mom-and-pop candy store⟩

moment of truth 1 : the final sword thrust in a bullfight 2 : a moment of crisis on whose outcome much or everything depends ⟨the lift-off of a . . . space vehicle with three men aboard is an awesome moment of truth —R.A. Petrone⟩

mon·e·ta·rism \ˈmänətə,rizəm, ˈmon-, also ˈmōn-\ n [monetary + -ism, n. suffix] : a theory in economics: stable economic growth can be assured only by control of the rate of money supply increase to match the capacity for growth of real productivity — **mon·e·ta·rist** \-tərəst\ n or adj

money* n — **on the money** : exactly right or accurate ⟨the author has done his homework. The material is right on the money —L.J. Nebel⟩

mon·go \ˈmäŋ(ˌ)gō\ n, pl mongo [Mongolian] 1 : a monetary unit of Outer Mongolia equal to $1/100$ tugrik 2 : a coin representing one mongo

monitor* n : software or hardware that monitors the operation of a system and esp. a computer system

monkey bars *n pl* **:** a three-dimensional framework of horizontal and vertical bars from which children can hang and swing

¹mono \\'män(ˌ)ō\\ *adj* [short for *monophonic*] **:** of or relating to sound transmission, recording, or reproduction involving a single transmission path **:** monophonic ⟨a *mono* phonograph record⟩

²mono *n, pl* **monos** **1 :** a mono phonograph record **2 :** mono reproduction ⟨recorded in both *mono* and stereo⟩

³mono \\'män(ˌ)ō, *also* 'mōn-\\ *n* [short for *mononucleosis*] **:** the disease mononucleosis

mono·amine* \\ˌmänōə'mēn, *also* ˌmōnō-\\ *n* **:** an amine RNH_2 having one organic substituent attached to the nitrogen atom; *esp* **:** one (as serotonin or norepinephrine) that is functionally important in neural transmission

monoamine ox·i·dase \\-'äksəˌdās, -ˌdāz\\ *n* **:** an enzyme that deaminates monoamines and that functions in the nervous system by breaking down monoamine neurotransmitters oxidatively

mono·am·i·ner·gic \\ˌmänōˌamə'nərjik, *also* ˌmōn-\\ *adj* [*monoamine* + *erg-* work (fr. Gk *ergon*) + *-ic*, adj. suffix] **:** liberating or involving monoamines (as serotonin or norepinephrine) in neural transmission ⟨*monoaminergic* neurons⟩

mono·cha·sial \\ˌmänə'käzh(ē)əl, ˌmōn-, -zeəl\\ *adj* **:** of, relating to, or being a monochasium

mono·chrome* \\'mänəˌkrōm, *also* 'mōn-\\ *adj* **:** characterized by reproduction or transmission of visual images in tones of gray rather than in colors **:** black-and-white ⟨*monochrome* motion pictures⟩

mono·clo·nal \\ˌmänə'klōnᵊl, *also* ˌmōn-\\ *adj* [*mono* containing one atom, radical, or group + *clone* + *-al*, adj. suffix] **:** produced by or being cells derived from a single cell ⟨*monoclonal* antibodies⟩ ⟨a *monoclonal* tumor⟩

mono·con·tam·i·nate \\ˌmän(ˌ)ōkən'taməˌnāt, *also* ˌmän(ˌ)ō- *or* -nə-\\ *vt* [*mono-* one, single (deriv. of Gk *monos* single, alone) + *contaminate*] **:** to infect (a germ-free organism) with one kind of pathogen — **mono·con·tam·i·na·tion** \\-kənˌtamə'nāshən\\ *n*

mono·crys·tal \\ˌmänō'kristᵊl, *also* ˌmōn-\\ *n* **:** a single crystal

mono·func·tion·al \\-'fəŋ(k)shnəl, -shənᵊl\\ *adj* **:** of, relating to, or being a compound with one highly reactive site in the molecule (as in polymerization) ⟨formaldehyde is a *monofunctional* reagent⟩

mono·germ \\-ˌjərm, -ˌjōm, -ˌjəim\\ *adj* [prob. fr. *mono-* + *germ*inate] **:** producing or being a fruit that gives rise to a single plant ⟨a *monogerm* variety of sugar beet⟩ — compare MULTIGERM

mono·ki·ni \\ˌmänə'kēnē, -ni\\ *n* [*mono-* + *-kini* (as in *bikini*)] **1 :** a topless bikini **2 :** extremely brief shorts for men — **mono·ki·nied** \\-nēd, -nid\\ *adj*

mono·lith·ic* \\ˌmänᵊl'ithik, *also* ˌmōn-\\ *adj* **1 :** formed from a single crystal ⟨a *monolithic* silicon chip⟩ **2 :** produced in or on a monolithic chip ⟨a *monolithic* circuit⟩ **3 :** consisting of or utilizing a monolithic circuit or circuits

mono·ox·y·gen·ase \\ˌmänō'äksəjəˌnās, ˌmōn-, -āz\\ *n* **:** any of several oxygenases that bring about the incorporation of one atom of molecular oxygen into a substrate

mono·ploid* \\'mänəˌplöid, 'mōn-\\ *adj* **:** having or being the basic haploid number of chromosomes in a polyploid series of organisms

mono·pole \\-ˌpōl\\ *n* **1 :** a single positive or negative electrical charge; *also* **:** a hypothetical north or south magnetic pole existing alone **2 :** a radio antenna in the form of a single often straight radiating element

mono·sex·u·al \\ˌmän(ˌ)ō'seksh(ə)wəl, -shəl, *also* ˌmōn- *or* -nə-\\ *adj* **1 :** being a male or a female rather than a bisexual **2 :** composed of or intended for individuals of one sex ⟨*monosexual* schools⟩ — **mono·sex·u·al·i·ty** \\-ˌsekshə'walədˌē, -i\\ *n*

mono·some* \\'mänəˌsōm, 'mōn-\\ *n* **:** a single ribosome

monster* *n* **:** a roving football linebacker who plays in no set position — called also *monster back, monster man*

mon·ta·gnard* \\ˌmōnᵊ'tän'yär(d), -ˌtan-; ˌmäntᵊn'yärd, -tən-\\ *n, often cap* **:** a member of a people inhabiting a highland region in southern Vietnam bordering on Cambodia — **montagnard** *adj, often cap*

Mon·te Car·lo \\ˌmäntē'kär(ˌ)lō-, -tə'k-\\ *adj* [*Monte Carlo*, Monaco, city noted for its gambling casino] **:** of, relating to, or involving the use of random sampling techniques and often the use of computer simulation to obtain approximate solutions to mathematical or physical problems esp. in terms of a range of values each of which has a calculated probability of being the solution ⟨*Monte Carlo* methods⟩ ⟨*Monte Carlo* calculations⟩

Mon·te·zu·ma's revenge \\ˌmäntəˈzüməz-\\ *n* [*Montezuma* II †1520 last Aztec ruler of Mexico] **:** diarrhea contracted in Mexico esp. by tourists

mon·uron \\'mänyəˌrän, 'mōn-\\ *n* [*mono-* + *urea* + *-on* chemical compound] **:** a persistent herbicide $C_9H_{11}ClN_2O$ used esp. to control mixed broad-leaved weeds

mood ring *n* **:** a ring with a stone made of crystals capable of changing color in response to minute variations in body temperature

Moog \\'mōg, 'müg\\ *trademark* — used for a music synthesizer

moon* *n, slang* **:** the naked buttocks

moon·craft \\'münˌkraft\\ *n* **:** MOONSHIP

moon·fall \\-ˌfôl\\ *n* [*moon* + *-fall* (as in *landfall*)] **:** a landing on the moon

moon·flight \\-ˌflīt\\ *n* **:** a flight to the moon

Moon·ie \\'münē, -i\\ *n* [Sun Myung *Moon* + E *-ie* one having to do with] **:** a member of the Unification Church founded by Sun Myung Moon

moon·ing \\'müniŋ\\ *n* **:** the practice of exposing one's buttocks (as through the window of a moving vehicle) as a prank

moon·port \\'münˌpō(ə)rt, -pȯ(ə)rt, -ˌpōət, -pȯ(ə)t\\ *n* **:** a facility for launching spacecraft to the moon

moon·ship \\-ˌship\\ *n* **:** spacecraft for travel to the moon

moonshot \\-ˌshät\\ *or* **moon shoot** *n* **:** the act or an instance of launching a spacecraft on a course to the moon

moon·walk \\-ˌwôk\\ *n* **:** an instance of walking on the moon — **moon·walk·er** \\-ˌwôkə(r)\\ *n*

mo·ped \\'mōˌped\\ *n* [Sw, fr. *motor* motor + *pedal* pedal] **:** a lightweight low-powered motorbike that can be pedaled

MOR *abbr* middle of the road

morn·ing-af·ter pill \\ˌmȯrniŋˈaftər-, ˌmȯ(ə)niŋˈaftə-\\ *n* [fr. its being taken after rather than before intercourse] **:** an oral drug (as diethylstilbestrol) that interferes with pregnancy by blocking implantation of a fertilized egg in the human uterus

morph \\'mȯ(ə)rf, 'mȯ(ə)f\\ n [Gk morphē form] **1 :** a local population of a species that consists of interbreeding organisms and is distinguishable from other populations by morphology or behavior though capable of interbreeding with them **2 :** a phenotypic variant of a species

morph- or **morpho-*** comb form **:** relating to form and ⟨morphofunctional⟩

mor·phac·tin \\mȯr'faktən\\ n [prob. fr. morph- form (deriv. of Gk morphē) + act- (fr. L actus motion) + -in chemical compound] **:** any of several synthetic fluorine‑containing compounds that tend to produce morphological changes and suppress growth in plants

mor·pho·phys·i·ol·o·gy \\ˌmȯr(ˌ)fō‚fizē'äləjē\\ n [ISV morpho- form (deriv. of Gk morphē) + physiology] **:** a branch of biology that deals with the interrelationships of structure and function — **mor·pho·phys·i·o·log·i·cal** \\-ˌfizēə'läjəkəl\\ adj

MOS abbr metal-oxide semiconductor

Mos·ley·ite \\'mōzlē‚īt\\ n [Sir Oswald Ernald Mosley †1980 Brit. politician] **:** an adherent of the fascist political views of Sir Oswald Mosley

Möss·bau·er effect \\ˈma(r)s‚baú(ə)r-, ˈmȯs-, ˈmœs-, ˈmes-\\ n [Rudolph L. Mössbauer b1929 Ger. physicist] **:** the emission and absorption of gamma rays without recoil by various radioactive nuclei embedded in solids — compare NUCLEAR RESONANCE

Mössbauer spectroscopy n **:** spectroscopy that utilizes the Mössbauer effect

mos·tac·cio·li \\ˌmȯstä(t)'chōlē\\ n [It, lit., moustaches, fr. It mostaccio moustache] **:** pasta in the form of a short tube with oblique ends

mother*n [by shortening] **:** MOTHERFUCKER — usu. used as a generalized term of abuse

moth·er·fuck·er \\'məthə(r)‚fəkə(r)\\ n **:** one that is formidable, contemptible, or offensive — usu. considered obscene; usu. used as a generalized term of abuse — **moth·er·fuck·ing** \\ˌməthə(r)‚fəkiŋ, -kən\\ adj

mo·to·cross \\'mōd-ō‚krȯs\\ n [motor + cross-country] **:** a motorcycle race on a tight closed course over natural terrain that includes steep hills, sharp turns, and often mud

motor home n **:** an automotive vehicle built on a truck or bus chassis and equipped as a self-contained traveling home

motor inn or **motor hotel** n **:** a usu. multistory urban motel

mouse*n **:** a small mobile manual device that controls movement of the cursor on a computer display and facilitates other tasks

mous·sa·ka \\mü'säkə, 'mü‚s-, ‚müsä'kä\\ n [NGk mousakas] **:** a dish of ground meat (as lamb) and sliced eggplant often topped with a seasoned sauce

mouth hook n **:** one of a pair of hooked larval mouthparts of some two-winged flies that function as jaws

mox·i·bus·tion \\ˌmäksə‚bəschən\\ n [moxa + connective -i- + -bustion (as in combustion)] **:** medical use of a moxa

MPA abbr master of public administration

MPH*abbr master of public health

M phase n [mitosis] **:** the period in the cell cycle during which cell division takes place — called also D phase; compare G₁ PHASE, G₂ PHASE, S PHASE

Mr. Charlie \\-'chärlē, -äl-, - i\\ n [Charlie, fr. Charles, proper name] **:** a white man **:** white people — usu. used disparagingly

mri·dan·ga \\mrē'däŋgə, ‚mərē-\\ or **mri·dan·gam** \\-gəm\\ n [Skt mṛdaṅga, prob. of imit. origin] **:** a drum of India that is shaped like an elongated barrel and has tuned heads of different diameters

mRNA \\ˌe‚mär(ˌ)e'nä\\ n **:** MESSENGER RNA

Mr. Right n **:** a man who would make the perfect husband ⟨the romantic notion so many women have been brought up on that there is only one ... Mr. Right — Leslie A. Westoff⟩

Ms. \\(')miz, sometimes (')mis\\ n [prob. blend of miss and Mrs.] — used instead of Miss or Mrs. (as when the marital status of a woman is unknown or irrelevant) ⟨Ms. Mary Smith⟩

MSG*abbr master sergeant

MSH \\ˌem(ˌ)e'säch\\ n **:** MELANOCYTE-STIMULATING HORMONE

M 16 \\ˈemsik'stēn\\ n **:** a .223 caliber (5.56 mm.) gas-operated magazine-fed automatic or semiautomatic rifle used by U.S. troops since the mid 1960s

MSLS abbr master of science in library science

MSW abbr **1** master of social welfare **2** master of social work

mu·co·cil·i·ary \\ˌmyükō'silē‚erē, -rē\\ adj [muco- mucus + ciliary] **:** of, relating to, or involving cilia of the mucous membranes of the mammalian respiratory system

MUF abbr material unaccounted for

mug·gee \\ˌməg'ē\\ n [mug to assault and rob + -ee one who receives or is affected] **:** a person who is mugged

mule*n, slang **:** an individual who smuggles or delivers illicit drugs

mul·ti·band \\ˈməl‚ti‚band, -ltē-, -ltə-\\ adj [multi- many, two or more (deriv. of L multus much, many) + band] **:** of, relating to, or operable on two or more bands (as of frequencies or wavelengths) ⟨a multiband radio⟩

mul·ti·cen·tric \\-'sen‚trik\\ adj [multi- + -centric centered] **:** having multiple centers of origin ⟨a multicentric tumor⟩ — **mul·ti·cen·tri·cal·ly** \\-trik(ə)lē\\ adv — **mul·ti·cen·tric·i·ty** \\-sen'trisəd-ē\\ n

mul·ti·com·pa·ny \\-'kəmp(ə)nē, -ni\\ n **:** a large corporate enterprise with interests in two or more separate industries

mul·ti·fac·to·ri·al*\\-fak'tōrēal, -'tȯr-\\ or **mul·ti·fac·tor** \\-'faktə(r)\\ adj **:** having or involving a variety of elements or causes ⟨a multifactorial study⟩ ⟨a disease with multifactorial etiology⟩

mul·ti·germ \\-'jərm, -‚jəm, -‚jəim\\ adj [prob. fr. multi- + germinate] **:** producing or being a fruit cluster capable of giving rise to several plants ⟨a multigerm variety of sugar beet⟩ — compare MONOGERM

mul·ti·grade \\-'grād\\ adj, of motor oil **:** characterized by a range of viscosities that permits use in either high or low temperatures

mul·ti·hull \\-'həl\\ adj **:** having more than one hull ⟨a multihull boat⟩; also **:** of or relating to multihull boats

mul·ti–in·dus·try \\-'indəstrē, -rē\\ adj **:** active in or concerned with two or more separate industries ⟨multi-industry companies⟩

mul·ti·lay·ered \-'lāə(r)d, -'le(ə)rd, -'leəd\ *or* **mul·ti·lay·er** \-'lāə(r), -'le(ə)r, -'leə\ *adj* **:** having or involving several distinct layers, strata, or levels ⟨*multilayered* epidermis⟩ ⟨*multilayered* tropical rain forest⟩ ⟨*multilayered* insights⟩

mul·ti·mar·ket \'məl,tī'märkət, -ltē-, -ltə-, -'māk-\ *adj* **:** MULTI-INDUSTRY

¹**mul·ti·me·dia** \-'mēdēə\ *adj* **:** using, involving, or encompassing several media ⟨*multimedia* kits for teachers⟩ ⟨a *multimedia* presentation⟩ ⟨just sat there — through movies on a triptych of screens, voices over microphones, and other *multimedia* distractions —Edith Oliver⟩

²**multimedia** *n pl but sing or pl in constr* **:** communication, entertainment, or art in which several media are employed

mul·ti·na·tion \-'nāshən\ *adj* **:** MULTINATIONAL 1

¹**mul·ti·na·tion·al** \-'nashnəl, -shənᵊl\ *adj* **1 a :** of, relating to, or involving more than two nations ⟨a *multinational* nuclear force⟩ **b :** having divisions in more than two countries ⟨a *multinational* corporation⟩ **2 :** of or relating to more than two nationalities ⟨the attractive young Americans in the Islands are all proud of their *multinational* ancestry and mixed blood —*Amer. Labor*⟩

²**multinational** *n* **:** a multinational corporation

mul·ti·na·tion·al·ism \-'nashnə,lizəm, -shənᵊl,izəm\ *n* **:** the establishment or operation of multinational corporations

mul·ti·par·ty \-'pärd·ē, -'pád·ē, -i\ *adj* **:** of, relating to, or involving more than two political parties

multiple re·gres·sion \-rə'greshən, -re-\ *n* **:** regression in which one variable is estimated by the use of more than one other variable

multiple store *n, chiefly Brit* **:** a chain store

mul·ti·plet*\'məltəplət\ *n* **1 :** any of two or more atomic, molecular, or nuclear quantum states that are usu. close together in energy and that arise from different relative orientations of angular momenta **2 :** a group of spectral frequencies arising from transitions to or from a multiplet quantum state **3 :** a group of elementary particles that are different in charge but similar in other properties (as mass)

mul·ti·ple-val·ued \'məltəpəl'val(,)yüd, -lyəd\ *adj* **:** having at least one and sometimes more of the values of the range associated with each value of the domain ⟨a *multiple-valued* function⟩

multiplication sign *n* **:** a symbol (as a times sign or a dot) used to indicate multiplication

mul·ti·pli·ca·tive identity \,məltə'plikəd·iv-, 'məltəplə-'kād·iv-\ *n* **:** an identity element (as 1 in the group of rational numbers without 0 under the operation of multiplication) that in a given mathematical system leaves unchanged any element by which it is multiplied

multiplicative inverse *n* **:** an element of a mathematical set that when multiplied by a given element yields the identity element — called also *reciprocal*

multiplier effect *n* **:** the effect of a relatively minor factor in precipitating a great change; *esp* **:** the effect of a relatively small change in one economic factor (as rate of saving or level of consumer credit) in inducing a disproportionate increase or decrease in another (as gross national product)

mul·ti·ply \'məltə,plī\ *n, pl* **-plies :** an instance of multiplication performed by a computer; *also* **:** the means for performing multiplication

multipolar*adj **:** characterized by more than two centers of power or interest ⟨a *multipolar* world has replaced the uncomplicated certainties of two superpowers —Drew Middleton⟩ — **mul·ti·po·lar·i·ty** \'məl,tīpō'larəd·ē, -ltē-, -ltə-\ *n*

mul·ti·pro·cess·ing \'məl,tī'präs,esiŋ, -ltē-, -ltə-, -'präsəs-, -'prōs-\ *n* **:** the processing of several computer programs at the same time esp. by a computer system with several processors sharing a single memory — **mul·ti·pro·ces·sor** \-s,esə(r), -səs-\ *n*

mul·ti·pro·gram·ming \-'prō,gramiŋ, -'prōgrəm-\ *n* **:** the technique of utilizing several interleaved programs concurrently in a single computer system — **mul·ti·pro·grammed** \-'prō,gramd, -'prōgrəmd\ *adj*

mul·ti·pronged \-'prónd\ *adj* **1 :** having several prongs ⟨*multipronged* fishing spears⟩ **2 :** having several distinct aspects or elements ⟨a *multipronged* attack on the problem⟩

mul·ti·re·sis·tant \-rə'zistənt, -re-\ *adj* **:** biologically resistant to several toxic agents ⟨*multiresistant* falciparum malaria⟩ — **mul·ti·re·sis·tance** \-tən(t)s\ *n*

mul·ti·sen·so·ry \-'sen(t)s(ə)rē, -ri\ *adj* **:** relating to or involving perception by several physiological senses ⟨*multisensory* teaching methods⟩

mul·ti·ver·si·ty \'məltə'vərsəd·ē, -tē,v-, -stē-\ *n, pl* **-ties** [*multi-* + *-versity* (as in *university*)] **:** a very large university with many component schools, colleges, or divisions, with widely diverse functions (as the teaching of freshmen and the carrying on of advanced research), and with a large staff engaged in activities other than instruction and esp. in administration

mu-me·son*\'m(y)ü,mez,än, -'mes,än, -'mā-, -'mē-\ *n* **:** MUON

mun·chies \'mənchez, -iz\ *n pl* [*munch* + *-ie*, dim. suffix + *-s*, plural suffix] **1 :** light snack foods ⟨a free bar, free cigarettes, free *munchies* —Timothy Crouse⟩ **2 :** hunger pangs; *esp* **:** hunger pangs induced by the use of marijuana ⟨a supply of peanut butter, tangerine juice, and sunflower seeds for those who succumb to the screaming *munchies* —R. A. Sokolov⟩

mu·on*\'myü,än\ *n* **:** an unstable lepton that is common in the cosmic radiation near the earth's surface, has a mass 206.77 times the mass of the electron and an average lifetime of 2.20×10^{-6} second, and exists in negative and positive forms related as particle and antiparticle — **mu·on·ic** \myü'änik\ *adj*

mu·on·ium \m(y)ü'ōnēəm, -'än-\ *n* [*muon* + *-ium* chemical element] **:** a short-lived quasi-atom consisting of an electron and a positive muon

mu·ram·ic acid \myù,ramək-\ *n* [*mur-* (fr. L *murus* wall) + glucos*amide* + *-ic*, adj. suffix] **:** an amino sugar $C_9H_{17}NO_7$ that is a lactic acid derivative of glucosamine and is found esp. in bacterial cell walls and in blue-green algae

mu·rein \'myùrēən, 'myü(ə)r,ēn\ *n* [*mur*amic acid + *-ein* chemical compound] **:** PEPTIDOGLYCAN

Mur·phy \'mərfē, 'məfē, 'məifē, -i\ *n* [fr. the name *Murphy*] **:** a confidence game and esp. one in which the victim believes he is paying for sex

Murphy's Law \ˌmərfēz-, ˌmōf-, ˌmɔif-\ *n* [fr. the name *Murphy*] **:** an observation: anything that can go wrong will go wrong ⟨it has been established that computers are followers of *Murphy's Law* —P.H. Dorn⟩ ⟨the plethora of defects simply validates *Murphy's Law* —*Time*⟩

mus·ca·det \ˌməskə'dā, *F* mūēskȧde\ *n, often cap* [F, fr. Prov, muscadet grape, fr. *musc* musk scent] **:** a dry white wine from the Loire valley of France

muscle car *n* **:** any of a group of American-made 2-door sports coupes of various makes with powerful engines that are designed for high-performance driving

Muslim*n **:** BLACK MUSLIM

mu·ta·ge·nic·ity \ˌmyüd·əjə'nisəd·ē\ *n* [*mutagenic* + *-ity*, n. suffix] **:** the capacity to induce mutations

mu·ta·ro·tase \ˌmyüd·ə'rō‚tās, -āz\ *n* [*mutarotation* + *-ase* enzyme] **:** an isomerase found esp. in mammalian tissues that catalyzes the interconversion of anomeric forms of certain sugars

mu·ta·tor gene \ˈmyüˈtād·ə(r)-\ *also* **mutator** \ˈmyüˌtād·ə(r), myüˈtād·ə(r)\ *n* [L *mutator* one that changes, fr. *mutatus*, past part. of *mutare* to change] **:** a gene that increases the rate of mutation of one or more other genes

Mu·zak \ˈmyüˌzak\ *trademark* — used for recorded background music that is transmitted by wire to the loudspeaker of a subscriber (as an office or restaurant)

MV*abbr main verb

MVP *abbr* most valuable player

MY *abbr, often not cap* million years

my·co·plas·ma \ˌmīkō'plazmə\ *n, pl* **-mas** *or* **-ma·ta** \-mәd·ә\ **:** a microorganism of the genus *Mycoplasma* — **my·co·plas·mal** \-məl\ *adj*

my·co·tox·in \-'täksən\ *n* [*myco-* fungus (deriv. of Gk *mykēs*) + *toxin*] **:** a poisonous substance produced by a fungus and esp. a mold — compare AFLATOXIN — **my·co·tox·ic** \-'täksik\ *adj* — **my·co·tox·ic·i·ty** \-‚täk-'sisәd·ē\ *n* — **my·co·tox·i·co·sis** \-‚täksə'kōsәs\ *n*

my·elo·cyt·ic leukemia \ˌmīәlō'sid·ik-\ *n* **:** leukemia characterized by proliferation of myeloid tissue and an abnormal increase in the number of granulocytes, myelocytes, and myeloblasts in the circulating blood **:** myelogenous leukemia

my·elo·fi·bro·sis \ˌmīәlōfī'brōsәs\ *n* [NL, fr. *myelo-* marrow, spinal cord (fr. NL, fr. Gk *myelos* marrow, fr. *mys* mouse, muscle) + *fibrosis*] **:** an anemic condition in which bone marrow becomes fibrotic and the liver and spleen usu. exhibit development of blood cell precursors — **my·elo·fi·bro·tic** \-'bräd·ik\ *adj*

my·elo·per·ox·i·dase \-pә'räksә‚dās, -āz\ *n* [*myelo-* marrow + *peroxidase*] **:** a peroxidase of phagocytic cells (as polymorphonuclear leukocytes) that is held to assist in bactericidal activity by catalyzing the oxidation of ionic halogen to free halogen

my·e·lo·pro·lif·er·a·tive \-prә'lifә‚rād·iv, -'lif(ә)rәd·-\ *adj* **:** of, relating to, or being a disorder (as leukemia) marked by excessive proliferation of bone marrow elements and esp. blood cell precursors

My·lar \ˈmīˌlär\ *trademark* — used for a polyester film

myo·elec·tric \ˌmīōә'lek·trik, -ē'l-\ *also* **myo·elec·tri·cal** \-kәl\ *adj* [*myo-* muscle (deriv. of Gk *mys* mouse, muscle) + *electric*] **:** of, relating to, or utilizing electricity generated by muscle — **myo·elec·tri·cal·ly** \-k(ә)lē, -li\ *adv*

myo·fil·a·ment \-'filәmәnt\ *n* **:** one of the individual filaments of actin or myosin that make up a myofibril

myo·tube \ˈmīōˌt(y)üb\ *n* [*myo-* + *tube*] **:** a developmental stage of a muscle fiber composed of a syncytium formed by fusion of myoblasts

mys·te·ri·um \mә'stirēәm, -tēr-\ *n* [NL, fr. E *mystery* + NL *-ium* chemical radical] **:** a source of fluctuating radio emissions in the Milky Way galaxy held to be excited hydroxyl radicals

myxo·vi·rus \ˈmiksәˌvīrәs\ *n* [NL, fr. *myxo-* mucus, slime (deriv. of Gk *myxa* lampwick, nasal slime) + *virus*; fr. its affinity for certain mucins] **:** any of a group of rather large RNA-containing viruses that includes influenza viruses — **myxo·vi·ral** \ˌmiksә'vīrәl\ *adj*

N

n*abbr nano-

NA*abbr not available

Nab·o·kov·ian \‚nabə'kōvēən, -'kóv-, -'kófēən\ adj [Vladimir Vladimirovich *Nabokov* †1977 Am. (Russ.-born) novelist & poet] **:** of, relating to, or suggestive of Vladimir Nabokov or his writings 〈*Nabokovian* marginal people inhabiting interims and delusions —Guy Davenport〉

na·cho \'näch(‚)ō\ n, pl **nachos** [perh. fr. Sp *nacho* flat-nosed] **:** a tortilla chip topped with cheese and a savory substance (as chili peppers or refried beans) and broiled

NAD \‚e(‚)nä'dē\ n **:** NICOTINAMIDE ADENINE DINUCLE-OTIDE

NADH \‚e‚nä(‚)dē'āch\ n **:** the reduced form of NAD

NADP \‚e‚nä(‚)dē'pē\ n **:** NICOTINAMIDE ADENINE DINU-CLEOTIDE PHOSPHATE

NADPH \‚e‚nä‚dē(‚)pē'āch\ n **:** the reduced form of NADP

nai·ra \'nī(ə)rə\ n [alter. of *Nigeria*, country in West Africa] **1 :** the basic monetary unit of Nigeria **2 :** a coin or note representing one naira

naive*adj **1 :** not previously subjected to experimentation or to a particular experimental situation 〈experimentally *naive* rats〉; *also* **:** not having previously used a particular drug (as marijuana) 〈comparison between *naive* and chronic users —Lucien Joubert〉 **2 :** primitive 〈*naive* artists〉 〈an ardent admirer of *naive* American folk art —Katharine Kuh〉

naked*adj **:** not backed by the writer's ownership of the commodity contract or security 〈selling *naked* options〉

na·led \'nā‚led\ n [origin unknown] **:** a short-lived insecticide $C_4H_7O_4PBr_2Cl_2$ of relatively low toxicity to warm-blooded animals that is used esp. to control crop pests and mosquitoes

na·li·dix·ic acid \‚nälə‚diksik-\ n [perh. fr. *naphthyri-dine*, $C_8H_6N_2$ (fr. *naphth*alene + *pyr*idine) + carboxyl*ic acid*] **:** an antibacterial agent $C_{12}H_{12}N_2O_3$ that is used esp. in the treatment of genitourinary infections

nal·ox·one \'nalək‚sōn\ n [N-*allyl* + *hydrox*yl + -*one* oxygen compound] **:** a potent antagonist $C_{19}H_{21}NO_4$ of narcotic drugs and esp. morphine that is administered esp. as the hydrochloride

nal·trex·one \nal'trek‚sōn\ n [N-*allyl* + -*trex*- (as in *methotrexate*) + -*one* ketone or analogous compound] **:** a narcotic antagonist $C_{20}H_{23}NO_4$

name of the game : the essential or intrinsic quality or nature of a situation **:** the fundamental goal of an activity 〈the American businessman is taught early that profits are the *name of the game* —Frank Gibney〉

¹Na·mib·i·an \nə'mibēən\ adj [*Namibia* (formerly South-West Africa), country in southwest Africa, fr. *Namib*, desert on the southwest coast of Africa + E -*an*, adj. suffix] **:** of or relating to Namibia or its inhabitants

²Namibian n **:** a native or inhabitant of Namibia

NAND \'nand\ n [*not AND*] **:** a computer logic circuit that produces an output which is the inverse of that of an AND circuit

nan·no·fos·sil \‚nanō'fäsəl\ n [*nanno*- dwarf (deriv. of Gk *nannos, nanos*) + *fossil*] **:** a fossil of nannoplankton

nano·me·ter \'nanə‚mēd-ə(r)\ n [ISV *nano*- billionth (fr. L *nanus* dwarf, fr. Gk *nannos, nanos*) + *meter*] **:** one billionth of a meter

nano·sec·ond \-‚sekənd, -ənt\ n **:** one billionth of a second — abbr. *nanosec, nsec*

Nan·tua sauce \näⁿ(n)'twä-\ n [*Nantua*, France] **:** a cream sauce flavored with shellfish (as crayfish or lobster)

nap*n [*nap* napoleon (a card game)] *Brit* **:** a pick or recommendation as a good bet to win a contest (as a horse race); *also* **:** one named in a nap

¹nap \'nap\ vt **napped; nap·ping** *Brit* **:** to pick or single out (as a race horse) in a nap

²nap vt **napped; nap·ping** [by shortening fr. F *napper* to cover meat in a sauce] **:** to pour or spread a sauce over (a prepared dish) 〈*nap* the fish with the hollandaise sauce —Joseph Wechsburg〉

na·prox·en \nə'präksən\ n [*naph*tha + *pro*pionic acid + *ox*- containing oxygen + -*en* (arbitrary suffix)] **:** an anti-inflammatory analgesic antipyretic drug $C_{14}H_{14}O_3$ used esp. to treat arthritis

narc or **nark** \'närk, 'nák\ n [short for *narcotics agent*] **:** one (as a government agent) who investigates narcotics violations

narcotic*n **:** a drug (as marijuana or LSD) that is subject to restriction similar to that of addictive narcotics whether in fact it is physiologically narcotic and addictive or not

nar·row·cast \'narō‚kast, *also* 'ner-\ vi -**cast; -cast·ing** [*narrow* + -*cast* (as in *broadcast*)] **:** to aim a broadcast at a narrowly defined area or audience

na·ta·lism \'nāt²l‚izəm\ n [*natalist*, after such pairs as *Communist: Communism*] **:** an attitude or policy favoring or encouraging population growth

na·ta·list \-²ləst\ n [F *nataliste*] **:** one who advocates or encourages an unchecked population growth — often used in combination with *pro*- or *anti*-

natch \'nach\ adv [by shortening & alter.] *slang* **:** of course **:** naturally

national seashore n **:** an area of seacoast maintained by the federal government as a preserve for the natural environment and wildlife and as a public recreation area

Native American*adj **1 :** of or relating to Native Americans 〈*Native American* languages〉 **2 :** of American Indian descent 〈*Native American* students〉

Native American*n **:** an American Indian

na·tri·ure·sis \‚nä‚trē(y)ə‚rēsəs, ‚na-\ *also* **na·tru·re·sis** \-trə‚rē-\ n [NL, fr. *natri*um sodium + *uresis* urination] **:** excessive loss of cations and esp. sodium in the urine — **na·tri·uret·ic** \-trē(y)ə‚red·ik\ adj or n

natural*adj **:** AFRO

natural*n : AFRO

natural food n : food that contains no additives (as preservatives and artificial flavorings)

natural language*n : the language of ordinary speaking and writing — distinguished from *machine language*

natural scientist n : a specialist in natural science

nature trail n : a trail (as through a woods) usu. with natural features identified for facilitating the enjoyment or study of nature

Nau·ga·hyde \'nôgə,hīd, 'näg-\ *trademark* — used for vinyl-coated fabrics

NEB *abbr* New English Bible

neb·bish \'nebish\ n [Yiddish *nebach, nebech* poor thing (used interjectionally), of Slav origin; akin to Czech *nebohy* wretched, Pol *niebożę* poor creature] : a timid, meek, or ineffectual person ⟨always plays *nebbishes* named Claude — in fantasies, Claude is a tiger; in life, old ladies have to help him across the street —Chris Chase⟩ — neb·bishy \-ē, -i\ *adj*

negative income tax n : a system of federal subsidy payments to families with incomes below a stipulated level proposed as a substitute for or supplement to welfare payments

negative option n : a provision in a mail-order contract (as of a book club) that requires the customer either to return a refusal card within a specified time or to accept the current selection

negative transfer n : the impeding of learning or performance in a situation by the carry-over of learned responses from another situation — called also *negative transfer effect*

ne·gri·tude \'nēgrə,tüd, 'neg-, -,tyüd\ n [F *négritude*, fr. *nègre* Negro + connective -*i*- + -*tude*, n. suffix] 1 : a consciousness of and pride in the cultural and physical aspects of the African heritage 2 : the state of being a Negro

Ne·gro·ness \'nē(,)grōnəs; *esp South* 'ni(,)-, 'nigrə-, 'nēgrə-\ n : the quality or state of being Negro : NEGRITUDE

ne·gro·ni \nə'grōnē, -ni\ n, *often cap* [prob. fr. the name *Negroni*] : a cocktail consisting of sweet vermouth, bitters, and gin

Neh·ru \'ne(ə)r(,)ü, 'nā(,)rü\ *adj* [Jawaharlal *Nehru* †1964 Indian nationalist] : MAO ⟨a *Nehru* jacket⟩

¹nelly*or nel·lie \'nelē\ n, *pl* nellies : an effeminate homosexual — not on your nelly [perh. fr. the phrase *not on your Nelly Duff*, rhyming slang for Brit slang *puff* breath, life] *Brit* : certainly not

²nelly *or* nellie *adj* : conspicuously effeminate

neo·co·lo·nial·ism \,nē(,)ōkə'lōnyə,lizəm, -nēə-\ n [*neo*- new (fr. Gk *neos*) + *colonialism*] : the economic and political policies by which a Great Power indirectly maintains or extends its influence over other areas or peoples — neo·co·lo·nial·ist \-nyəlȯst, -nēə-\ n *or adj*

neo·cor·ti·cal \,nēō'kȯrtəkəl, -'kȯ(ə)d--\ *adj* : of or relating to the neocortex

neo–Da·da \,nēō'dä(,)dä, -'dá(,)dä\ n : an anti-art movement esp. of the late 1950s and the 1960s based on tenets similar to those of Dada but having more interest in the object than Dada claimed to have; *broadly* : JUNK ART — neo–Da·da·ism \-,izəm; -'dä,dizəm,

-'dá,dizəm\ n — neo–Da·da·ist \-,ist; -'dä,dääst, -'dá,dáȯst, -,dȯst\ *adj or n*

neo·phil·ia \,nēō'filēə\ n [*neo*- + -*philia* liking for or love of something] : love of or enthusiasm for what is new or novel

neo·phil·i·ac \-'filē,ak\ n [*neophilia*, after such pairs as *necrophilia: necrophiliac*] : one who has or expresses neophilia

Neo·ri·can \,nēō'rēkən\ n [*neo*- + Puerto *Rican*] : a Puerto Rican who lives on the U.S. mainland or who has lived there but has returned to Puerto Rico

neo·vas·cu·lar·iza·tion \,nē(,)ō,vaskyələrə',zāshən, -(,)rī,-\ n : vascularization esp. in abnormal quantity (as in some conditions of the retina) or in abnormal tissue (as a tumor)

ne·phros·to·my \nə'frästəmē, ne-, -mi\ n [NL, fr. *nephro*- kidney + -*stomy* surgical formation of an opening] : the surgical formation of an opening between a kidney pelvis and the outside of the body

nerd \'nərd, 'nȯd, 'nȯid\ n [perh. alter. of *nut*] *slang* : an unpleasant, unattractive, or insignificant person

nerf \'nərf, 'nȯf, 'nȯif\ *vt* [origin unknown] : to bump (another car) in an automobile race

nerf bar *or* nerf·ing bar \'nərfiŋ-, 'nȯf-, 'nȯif-\ n : a usu. tubular steel bumper on some racing cars to keep wheels from touching when cars bump during a race

network*n : a system of computers, terminals, and data bases connected by communication lines

net·work·ing \'net,wȯrkiŋ, -,wȯk-, -,wȯik-\ n 1 : the exchange of information or services among individuals, groups, or institutions 2 : the establishment or use of a computer network

neur·amin·i·dase \,n(y)ürə'minə,dās, -ú-, -āz\ n [*neuraminic* acid + -*idase* (as in *glucosidase*)] : a glycosidase that splits mucoproteins by breaking a glucoside link and occurs esp. in influenza viruses as an antigen

neu·ris·tor \n(y)ú'ristə(r)\ n [*neuron* + trans*istor*; fr. its functioning like a neuron and not requiring the use of transistors] : a usu. electronic device along which a signal propagates with uniform velocity and without attenuation

neu·ro·ac·tive \,n(y)ürō'aktiv, -ú-\ *adj* [*neuro*- nerve, neural (deriv. of Gk *neuron* nerve, sinew) + *active*] : stimulating neural tissue ⟨*neuroactive* substances⟩

neu·ro·bi·ol·o·gy \-bī'äləjē\ n : a branch of the life sciences that deals with the anatomy, physiology, and pathology of the nervous system — neu·ro·bio·log·i·cal \-,bīə'läjəkəl\ *adj* — neu·ro·bio·log·i·cal·ly \-k(ə)lē\ *adv* — neu·ro·bi·ol·o·gist \-bī'äləjȯst\ n

neu·ro·chem·is·try \-'keməstrē\ n 1 : the study of the chemical makeup and activities of nervous tissue 2 : chemical processes and phenomena related to the nervous system — neu·ro·chem·i·cal \-'keməkəl\ *adj* — neu·ro·chem·ist \-'keməst\ n

neu·ro·en·do·crine*\-,'endəkrən, -,krīn, -,krēn\ *adj* : of, relating to, or functioning in neurosecretion

neu·ro·en·do·crin·ol·o·gy \-,endəkrə'näləjē\ n : a branch of the life sciences dealing with neurosecretion and the physiological interaction between the central nervous system and the endocrine system — neu·ro·en·do·crin·o·log·i·cal \-,endəkrȯn°l'äjəkəl\ *adj* — neu·ro·en·do·crin·ol·o·gist \-krə'näləjȯst\ n

neu·ro·gen·e·sis \-'jenəsəs\ n [neuro- + genesis] : development of nerves, nervous tissue, or the nervous system

neu·ro·he·mal organ also **neu·ro·hae·mal organ** \,n(y)ürō,hēməl-, -ù-\ n [neuro- + hem- blood (deriv. of Gk haima) + -al, adj. suffix] : an organ (as a corpus cardiacum of an insect) that releases stored neurosecretory substances into the blood

neu·ro·hy·po·phy·se·al or **neu·ro·hy·po·phy·si·al** \,n(y)ürō(,)hi,päfə',sēəl, -ù-, -,hīpə-, -,zē-, -,hīpə,fiz-\ adj : of, relating to, or secreted by the neurohypophysis ⟨neurohypophyseal hormones⟩

neu·ro·ki·nin \-'kīnən\ n : a vasodilator kinin that may be a cause of migraine headaches

neu·ro·lept·an·al·ge·sia \,n(y)ürō,lep,tanəl'jēzhə, -ù-, -z(h)ēə\ or **neu·ro·lep·to·an·al·ge·sia** \,n(y)ürō,leptō,an-, -ù-\ n [NL, fr. ISV neurolept- or neurolepto- (fr. neuroleptic) + analgesic + NL -ia (as in analgesia)] : joint administration of a tranquilizing drug and an analgesic esp. for relief of surgical pain — **neu·ro·lept·an·al·ge·sic** \,n(y)ürō,lep,tanəl'jēzik\ adj

neu·ro·lep·tic \,n(y)ürō'leptik, -ù-\ n [ISV neuro- + psycholeptic; orig. formed as F neuroleptique] : a drug used to reduce mental disturbance (as anxiety and tension) in people and animals : tranquilizer — **neuroleptic** adj

neu·ro·phar·ma·col·o·gy \'n(y)üro,färmə'käləjē, -ù-\ n 1 : a branch of medical science dealing with the action of drugs on and in the nervous system 2 : the properties and reactions of a drug on and in the nervous system ⟨the neuropharmacology of lithium⟩ — **neu·ro·phar·ma·co·log·i·cal** \-,färməkə'läjəkəl\ also **neu·ro·phar·ma·co·log·ic** \-'läjək\ adj — **neu·ro·phar·ma·col·o·gist** \-'käləjəst\ n

neu·ro·phys·in \,n(y)ürō'fiz,ēn, -ù-, -zən\ n [neuro- + physin (fr. Gk physis natural constitution + E -in chemical compound)] : any of several brain hormones that bind with and carry either oxytocin or vasopressin

neu·ro·psy·chic \-'sīkik\ also **neu·ro·psy·chi·cal** \-'sīkəkəl\ adj : of or relating to both the mind and the nervous system as affecting mental processes

neu·ro·ra·di·ol·o·gy \-,rādē'äləjē, -i\ n [neuro- + radiology] : radiology of the nervous system — **neu·ro·ra·dio·log·i·cal** \-ēə'läjəkəl\ also **neu·ro·ra·dio·log·ic** \-ēə'läjək\ adj — **neu·ro·ra·di·ol·o·gist** \-ē'äləjəst\ n

neu·ro·sci·ence \-'sīən(t)s\ n : a branch (as neurology or neurophysiology) of the life sciences that deals with the anatomy, physiology, biochemistry, or molecular biology of nerves and nervous tissue and esp. with their relation to behavior and learning — **neu·ro·sci·en·tist** \-əntəst\ n

neu·ro·sen·so·ry \-'sen(t)s(ə)rē\ adj : of or relating to afferent nerves ⟨neurosensory control of feeding behavior⟩

neu·ros·po·ra \n(y)ù'räspərə\ n : a fungus of the genus Neurospora

neu·ro·trans·mis·sion \'n(y)ürō·tran(t)'smishən, -ù-, -tranz'm-\ n [neuro- + transmission] : the transmission of nerve impulses across a synapse

neu·ro·trans·mit·ter \'n(y)ürō'tran(t)smid·ə(r), -ù-, -tranz-\ n : a chemical substance (as norepinephrine or acetylcholine) that transmits nerve impulses across a synapse

neu·ter·cane \'n(y)üd·ə(r),kān\ n [L neuter neither + E -cane (as in hurricane); fr. the difficulty of classifying it as either hurricane or frontal storm] : a subtropical cyclone that is usu. less than 100 miles in diameter and that draws energy from sources common to both the hurricane and the frontal cyclone

neutral current n : an interaction between a lepton (as a neutrino) and a hadron (as a neutron) that yields another lepton of the same charge and another hadron of the same charge

neutron bomb n : a nuclear bomb that produces lethal neutrons but less blast and fire damage than other nuclear bombs

neutron star n [fr. the hypothesis that the cores of such stars are composed entirely of neutrons] : any of various hypothetical very dense celestial objects that consist of closely packed neutrons resulting from the collapse of a much larger stellar body and that may be detectable through their emission of X rays

new drug n : a drug that has not been declared safe and effective by qualified experts under the conditions prescribed, recommended, or suggested on the label and that may be a new chemical formula or an established drug prescribed for use in a new way

new economics n pl but usu sing in constr : an economic concept that is a logical extension of Keynesianism and that holds that appropriate fiscal and monetary maneuvering can maintain healthy economic growth and prosperity indefinitely

new guard n : a group of persons who have recently gained prominence or power in a particular field (as politics or business); also : a group of persons united in an effort to change the status quo

new issue n : a new security or an additional amount of a security made available for the first time to the general public

New Journalism n : journalism which features the author's subjective responses to people and events and which often includes fictional elements meant to illuminate and dramatize those responses — **New Journalist** n

New Left n : a political movement originating in the U.S. in the 1960s that is composed chiefly of students and various militant groups and that actively advocates (as by demonstrations) radical changes in prevailing political, social, and educational practices — **new leftist** n, often cap N&L

new math or **new mathematics** n : mathematics that is based on set theory esp. as taught in elementary and secondary schools

new·speak \'n(y)ü,spēk\ n, often cap [Newspeak, a language "designed to diminish the range of thought" in the novel Nineteen Eighty-Four (1949) by George Orwell †1950 Eng. author] : propagandistic language characterized by euphemism, circumlocution, and the inversion of customary meanings ⟨specializes in "outplacement"; that is, helping a company get rid of people it doesn't want and finding new jobs for them . . . the "terminating executive" or "candidate," as he is called in the newspeak of the trade —Jeremy Main⟩

news·per·son \'n(y)üz,pərs°n, -,pās-, -,pəis-\ n : one who gathers or reports news for a magazine, newspaper, or radio or television program : reporter

new town *n : an urban development comprising a small to medium-size city with a broad range of housing and planned industrial, commercial, and recreational facilities

new wave n, often cap N&W [trans. of F nouvelle vague] **1 :** a cinematic movement that is characterized by improvisation, abstraction, and subjective symbolism and that often makes use of experimental photographic techniques **2 :** a new movement in a particular field (as art or cooking) ⟨young chefs who call themselves the New Wave — R.A. Sokolov⟩ **3 :** rock music characterized by cohesive ensemble playing rather than extended solos and usu. lyrics which express anger and social discontent

N–galaxy n [nuclear] **:** a galaxy that has a brilliant starlike nucleus surrounded by a much fainter halo or extension

ngul·trum \en'gŭltrəm, eŋ'-\ n, pl **ngultrums** also **ngultrum** [native name in Bhutan] **1 :** the basic monetary unit of Bhutan **2 :** a coin or note representing one ngultrum

ngwee \eŋ'gwē, en-\ n, pl **ngwee** [native name in Zambia, lit., bright] **1 :** a monetary unit of Zambia equal to $^1/_{100}$ kwacha **2 :** a coin representing one ngwee

ni·al·amide \nī'alə,mīd, -əmə̇d\ n [nicotinic acid + amyl + amide] **:** an antidepressant drug $C_{16}H_{18}N_4O_2$ that is an inhibitor of monoamine oxidase

nick*vt **:** to produce a nick in (DNA or RNA) ⟨circular DNA that has been nicked and closed⟩

nick*n **1** slang Brit **:** jail; also **:** a police station **2 :** a break in a strand of DNA or RNA

nickel*n **1** slang **:** five dollars **2** slang **:** a packet containing five dollars worth of an illicit drug (as marijuana) — called also nickel bag

nickel–and–dime adj **1 :** involving or offering only a small amount of money ⟨nickel-and-dime insurance claims⟩ ⟨nickel-and-dime jobs⟩ **2 :** insignificant in performance and standing **:** small-time ⟨nickel-and-dime dealers⟩

nickel and dime vt **nick·eled and dimed** also **nickel and dimed; nick·el·ing and dim·ing** also **nickel and dim·ing :** to impair, weaken, or defeat gradually (as through a series of small incursions or excessive attention to minor details) ⟨to keep from being nickeled and dimed to poverty by the piling on of one piece of special-interest legislation after another —Milton Friedman⟩

nic·o·tin·amide ad·e·nine di·nu·cle·o·tide \,nikə,tē-nə,mīd,'adᵊn,ēn,dī,n(y)üklēə-,tīd, -,tin-, -əmə̇d-, -ᵊnən-\ n **:** a coenzyme $C_{21}H_{27}N_7O_{14}P_2$ of numerous dehydrogenases that occurs in most cells and plays an important role in all phases of intermediary metabolism as an oxidizing agent or when in the reduced form as a reducing agent for various metabolites

nicotinamide adenine dinucleotide phos·phate \-,fäs,fāt\ n **:** a coenzyme $C_{21}H_{28}N_7O_{17}P_3$ of numerous dehydrogenases (as that acting on glucose-6-phosphate) that occurs esp. in red blood cells and plays a role in intermediary metabolism similar to nicotinamide adenine dinucleotide but acting often on different metabolites

nig·ger*\'nigə(r)\ n **:** a member of a socially disadvantaged class of persons ⟨it's time for somebody to lead all of America's niggers.... And by this I mean the Young, the Black, the Brown, the Women, the Poor—all the people who feel left out of the political process —Ron Dellums⟩

night·glow \'nīt,glō\ n [night + airglow] **:** airglow seen during the night

nig–nog \'nig'nȯg, -'näg\ n [redupl. of nig] Brit **:** a Negro — usu. used disparagingly

ni·gro·stri·a·tal \,nigrō(')strī,ād·ᵊl, ,nig-, -,ätᵊl\ adj [fr. substantia nigra + connective -o- + striatal] **:** of, relating to, or joining the corpus striatum and the substantia nigra ⟨the nigrostriatal dopamine pathway degenerates in Parkinson's disease —S.H. Snyder et al⟩

-nik \(,)nik\ n suffix [Yiddish, fr. Pol & Russ] **:** one connected with or characterized by being ⟨peacenik⟩ ⟨neatnik⟩

nil·po·tent \'nil,pōtᵊnt\ adj [L nil nothing + potent-, potens having power] **:** equal to zero when raised to some power ⟨nilpotent matrices⟩ — **nil·po·ten·cy** \(')nil,-pōtᵊn(t)sē, -i\ n — **nil·po·tent** \'nil,pōtᵊnt\ n

nine–to–fiv·er \,nīntə,'fīvə(r), ,nīndə-\ n [nine-to-five + -er, agent suffix] **:** a person who works at a job with regular daytime hours

nit \'nit\ n [ISV, fr. L nitēre to shine] **:** a unit of brightness equal to one candle per square meter of cross section perpendicular to the rays

ni·ti·nol \'nītᵊn,ȯl, -ōl\ n [Ni symbol for nickel + Ti symbol for titanium + -nol (fr. Naval Ordinance Laboratory, where the alloy was created)] **:** a nonmagnetic alloy of titanium and nickel that after being deformed returns to its original shape upon being reheated

nit·pick \'nit,pik\ vb [back-formation fr. nit-picking] vi **:** to engage in nit-picking ⟨the program was so unusual and adventurous ... that nobody was inclined to nitpick —H.C. Schonberg⟩ ~ vt **:** to criticize by nitpicking ⟨was merely saying that scientists could nitpick a popular book like mine to death —Lowell Ponte⟩ — **nit·pick·er** \-ə(r)\ n

nit–pick·ing \-iŋ\ n [nit louse egg, young louse] **:** minute and usu. petty criticism ⟨an impish parody of the pretensions and nit-picking of academic scholarship —Current Biog.⟩

ni·tro·fu·ran·to·in \,nī-(,)trōfyə'rantəwə̇n\ n [nitrofuran + hydantoin a crystalline compound $C_3H_4N_2O_2$] **:** a nitrofuran derivative $C_8H_6N_4O_5$ that is a broad-spectrum antimicrobial agent esp. valuable in urinary tract infections

ni·tro·ge·nase \,nī·'träjə,nās, 'nī·trəj-, -āz\ n [nitrogen + -ase enzyme] **:** an iron- and molybdenum-containing enzyme of various nitrogen-fixing microorganisms (as some bacteria and blue-green algae) that catalyzes the reduction of molecular nitrogen to ammonia

nitrogen nar·co·sis \-när,kōsə̇s, -nä,k-\ n **:** a state of euphoria and exhilaration that occurs when nitrogen in normal air enters the bloodstream at approximately seven times atmospheric pressure (as in deep-water diving) — called also rapture of the deep

ni·tro·so·di·meth·yl·amine \nī-,trō(,)sō,dī,methə,lam-,ēn, -ələ,mēn\ n [nitroso- containing the univalent group –NO + dimethylamine] **:** DIMETHYLNITROSAMINE

ni·tro·so·gua·ni·dine \-,gwänə̇,dēn, -ə̇də̇n\ n **:** an explosive compound CH_4N_4O often used as a mutagen in biological research

ni·tro·so·urea \-yü,rēə, sometimes -,yúrēə\ n **:** any of a group of lipid-soluble drugs that function as alkylating agents, have the ability to enter the central nervous system, and are effective in the treatment of some brain tumors and meningeal leukemias

nit·ty–grit·ty \ˌnid·ēˈgrid·ē\ *n* [origin unknown] **:** what is essential or basic **:** specific practical details ⟨getting down to the *nitty-gritty*⟩ ⟨has kept the *nitty-gritty* of politics as background for what is essentially a novel of character — Patrick Anderson⟩ — **nitty–gritty** *adj*

Nix·ie \ˈniksē, -si\ *trademark* — used for an electronic indicator tube

nob·ble* \ˈnäbəl\ *vt* **nob·bled; nob·bling** \-b(ə)liŋ\ *Brit* **:** to get hold of **:** catch, nab ⟨say the lion had caught the Admiral, and the General was trying to rescue his brother and got *nobbled,* too —Peter Dickinson⟩

nod* *n* **:** a drowsy stupefied state caused by the use of narcotic drugs — used esp. in the phrase *on the nod*

node* *n* **:** the termination or intersection of lines or curves **:** vertex

nod out *vi* **:** to pass out ⟨parks lined with winos and junkies *nodding out* —Tony Kornheiser⟩

no–fault \ˈnōˈfȯlt\ *adj* **1 :** of, relating to, or being a motor vehicle insurance plan under which an accident victim is compensated usu. up to a stipulated limit for actual losses (as medical bills and lost wages) but not for nuisance claims (as of pain or suffering) by his own insurance company regardless of who is responsible for the accident **2 :** of, relating to, or being a divorce law according to which neither party is held responsible for the breakdown of the marriage **3 :** being such that individuals are not held responsible for harmful acts or for personal shortcomings ⟨we established a *no-fault* society, a guilt-free age —Eugene Kennedy⟩

noise* *n* **1 :** electromagnetic radiation (as light or radio waves) that is composed of several frequencies and that involves random changes in frequency or amplitude **2 :** something that attracts attention ⟨Utah makes big *noise* this year —*Ski*⟩ ⟨the play . . . will make little *noise* in the world —Brendan Gill⟩ **3 :** something spoken or uttered ⟨when he responded, gave him some supportive *noises:* "Outasight" —Judson Jerome⟩ ⟨made some encouraging *noises* about Britain's good standing in Arab eyes —William Hardcastle⟩ **4 :** irrelevant or meaningless bits or words occurring along with desired information (as in a documentary search or a computer output) ⟨retrieving a small subset of high-relevance documents with very little *noise* —*Amer. Documentation*⟩

noise pol·lu·tion \-pəˈlüshən\ *n* **:** environmental pollution consisting of annoying or harmful noise (as of automobiles or jet airplanes) — called also *sound pollution*

no–knock \ˈnōˈnäk\ *adj* **:** of, relating to, or being the entry by police into private premises without knocking and without identifying themselves (as to make an arrest) ⟨suggests that the name of the *no-knock* law be changed to something more felicitous, like "quick-entry" — Elizabeth B. Drew⟩ — **no–knock** *n*

no–load \ˈnōˈlōd\ *adj* **:** charging no sales commission ⟨*no-load* mutual funds⟩ — **no–load** *n*

nominal* *adj* **:** being according to plan **:** falling within a range of acceptable planned limits **:** satisfactory ⟨everything was *nominal* during the spacecraft launch⟩ ⟨the satellite had a *nominal* orbit⟩

nominal* *n* **1 :** a linguistic form (as English *boy* or *he*) that inflects for number or case or for both **2 :** a word or word group functioning as a noun normally functions

non·ad·di·tive \ˈ(ˈ)nänˈadəd·iv, -tiv\ *adj* [*non-* not (deriv. of L *non*) + *additive*] **1 :** not having a numerical value equal to the sum of values for the component parts **2 :** of, relating to, or being a genic effect that is not additive — **non·ad·di·tiv·i·ty** \-ˌadəˈtivəd·ē\ *n*

non·aligned \ˌnänəlˈīnd\ *adj* **:** not allied with other nations and esp. with either the Communist or the non≠ Communist blocs ⟨*nonaligned* countries⟩

non·align·ment \ˌnänəlˈīnmənt\ *n* **:** the condition of a state or government that is nonaligned

non·book \ˈnänˌbūk, *sometimes* ˈnən-\ *n* **:** a book which has little literary merit or factual information and which is often a compilation (as of pictures or press clippings) ⟨a new *nonbook* (transcribed from a series of TV interviews) —William Brandon⟩

non·can·di·date \ˈ(ˈ)nänˈkan(d)əˌdāt, -ədət\ *n* **:** one who is not a candidate; *esp* **:** one who has declared himself not a candidate for a particular political office ⟨the Republican Party's most insistent *noncandidate* for the presidential nomination —David Holstrom⟩ — **non·can·di·da·cy** \-ˈkan(d)ədəsē, -si\ *n*

non·chro·mo·so·mal \ˌnänˌkrōməˈsōməl, *sometimes* ˌnən-\ *adj* **1 :** not situated on a chromosome **2 :** not involving chromosomes

non·cross·over \ˈ(ˈ)nänˈkrȯˌsōvə(r)\ *adj* **:** having or being chromosomes that have not participated in genetic crossing-over ⟨*noncrossover* offspring⟩

non·dairy \ˈnänˌde(ə)rē, -ˈda(ə)rē, *sometimes* ˈnən-\ *adj* **:** containing no milk or milk products ⟨*nondairy* coffee lightener⟩

non·de·gree \-dōˈgrē\ *adj* **:** not being, leading to, or required for an academic degree ⟨*nondegree* award⟩ ⟨*nondegree* program⟩ ⟨*nondegree* courses⟩

non·de·struc·tive \-dəˈstrəktiv\ *adj* **:** not destructive; *specif* **:** not causing destruction of material being investigated or treated ⟨*nondestructive* testing of metal⟩ — **non·de·struc·tive·ly** \-lē, -li\ *adv*

non·di·a·bet·ic \-ˌdīəˈbed·ik\ *adj* **:** not affected with diabetes — **nondiabetic** *n*

non·dia·paus·ing \-ˌdīəˈpȯziŋ\ *adj* **1 :** not having a diapause **2 :** not being in a state of diapause

non·dis·crim·i·na·tion \-dəˌskriməˈnāshən\ *n* **:** the absence or avoidance of discrimination ⟨*nondiscrimination* in employment⟩ — **non·dis·crim·i·na·to·ry** \-dəˌskrimənəˌtōrē, -ˌtȯrē\ *adj*

non·di·vid·ing \-dəˈvīdiŋ\ *adj* **:** not undergoing cell division

non·drink·er \ˈ(ˈ)nänˈdriŋkə(r)\ *n* **:** one who abstains from alcoholic beverages

non·drink·ing \-ˈdriŋkiŋ\ *adj* **:** abstaining from alcoholic beverages ⟨a *nondrinking* family⟩

non·emp·ty \ˈnänˈem(p)tē, *sometimes* ˈnən-\ *adj* **:** not empty; *specif* **:** containing at least one element ⟨*nonempty* sets⟩

non·en·zy·mat·ic \-ˌenzəˈmad·ik\ *or* **non·en·zy·mic** \-(ˌ)enˈzīmik\ *also* **non·en·zyme** \-ˈenˌzīm\ *adj* **:** not involving the action of enzymes ⟨*nonenzymatic* cleavage of protein⟩ — **non·en·zy·mat·i·cal·ly** \-ˌenzəˈmad·ə·k(ə)lē\ *adv*

non·event \ˈnänəˌvent, -ēˌv-\ *n* **1 :** a highly publicized event of little intrinsic interest ⟨the . . . press giggled and yawned as it went through the motions of covering that dreaded occupational bane, the *nonevent* —Burr Snider⟩

2 : an occurrence that is officially ignored ⟨this week's anniversary of his death is a Soviet *nonevent* —*Newsweek*⟩

non·flu·en·cy \(ˌ)nänˈflüən(t)sē\ *n* **1 :** lack of fluency **2 :** an instance of nonfluency — **non·flu·ent** \-ˈflüənt\ *adj*

non·gon·o·coc·cal \ˌnän͵gänəˈkäkəl, *sometimes* ͵nən-\ *adj* **:** not caused by the gonococcus ⟨*nongonococcal* urethritis⟩

non·grad·ed \-ˈgrādəd\ *adj* **:** having no grade levels ⟨*nongraded* schools⟩

non·green \-ˈgrēn\ *adj* **:** not green; *specif* **:** containing no chlorophyll ⟨fungi and other *nongreen* saprophytes⟩

non·he·ro \ˈnän͵hē(ˌ)rō, -ˌhi(ə)r(ˌ)ō\ *n* **:** ANTIHERO

non·hi·ber·nat·ing \(ˈ)nänˈhībə(r)ˌnäd·iŋ\ *adj* **1 :** not being in hibernation **2 :** not capable of hibernation ⟨a *nonhibernating* strain of hamster⟩

non·his·tone \-ˈhistˌōn\ *adj* **:** rich in aromatic amino acids and esp. tryptophan ⟨*nonhistone* proteins⟩

non·host \ˈnänˈhōst\ *n* **:** a plant that is not attacked or parasitized by a particular organism

non·iden·ti·cal \ˌnän(ˌ)īˌdentəkəl, ͵nänəˈd-, *sometimes* ͵nən-\ *adj* **:** not identical: **a :** different ⟨*nonidentical* terms⟩ **b :** derived from two ova **:** fraternal ⟨*nonidentical* twins⟩

non·in·sec·ti·ci·dal \-(ˌ)inˌsektəˈsīdʳl\ *adj* **1 :** lacking an insecticidal action **2 :** not involving the use of an insecticide

non·in·va·sive \-ənˈvāsiv, -ziv\ *adj* **1 :** not tending to spread; *specif* **:** not tending to infiltrate and destroy healthy tissue ⟨*noninvasive* cancer of the bladder⟩ **2 :** not involving penetration (as by surgery or hypodermic needle) of the skin of the intact organism ⟨*noninvasive* diagnostic techniques⟩

non·judg·men·tal \-ˌjəjˈmentʳl\ *adj* **:** avoiding judgments based on one's personal and esp. moral standards ⟨*nonjudgmental* counseling on birth control and abortion —*N.Y. Times*⟩ ⟨the facts are marshaled in a clear, *nonjudgmental* presentation —A.H. Johnston⟩

non·neg·a·tive \-ˈnegəd·iv\ *adj* **:** not negative: **a :** being either positive or zero ⟨a *nonnegative* integer⟩ **b :** taking on nonnegative values ⟨a *nonnegative* function⟩

non·neo·plas·tic \-ˌnēəˈplastik, -ˌnēō-\ *adj* **:** not being or not caused by neoplasms ⟨*nonneoplastic* diseases⟩

non·nu·cle·ar \-ˈn(y)üklēə(r), ÷ -kyələ(r)\ *adj* **1 :** not producing or involving a nuclear explosion ⟨a *nonnuclear* bomb⟩ ⟨a *nonnuclear* mining blast⟩ **2 :** not operating by or involving atomic energy ⟨a *nonnuclear* propulsion system⟩ **3 :** not having developed or not having the atom bomb ⟨a *nonnuclear* country⟩ **4 :** not involving the use of atom bombs ⟨*nonnuclear* war⟩

no–no \ˈnōˌnō\ *n, pl* **no–no's** *or* **no–nos :** something that is unacceptable or forbidden ⟨raising taxes. That's considered a political *no-no* —Marjorie Hunter⟩ ⟨a list of *no-no's* about language usage —C.C. Revard⟩

non–oil \(ˈ)nänˈȯi(ə)l, *sometimes* (ˈ)nən-\ *adj* **:** being a net importer of petroleum or petroleum products ⟨*non-oil* nations⟩

non·per·sis·tent \ˌnänpə(r)ˈsistənt, *sometimes* ͵nən-\ *adj* **:** not persistent: as **a :** decomposed rapidly by environmental action ⟨*nonpersistent* insecticides⟩ **b :** capable of being transmitted by a vector for only a relatively short time ⟨*nonpersistent* viruses⟩

non·per·son \ˈnän͵pərsᵊn, -ˌpäsᵊn, -ˌpəisᵊn, *sometimes* ˈnən-\ *n* **:** a person regarded as nonexistent: as **a :** one

regarded as never having existed **:** UNPERSON ⟨became a *nonperson* in the bureaucracy, a ghost —Robert Sherrill⟩ **b :** one having no social or legal status ⟨the majority, who are here illegally, exist virtually as civic *nonpersons* — Gary Hoenig⟩ ⟨how psychiatric patients are treated as *nonpersons* —*Publishers Weekly*⟩

non·pol·lut·ing \ˌnänpəˈlüd·iŋ, *sometimes* ͵nən-\ *adj* **:** causing little or no pollution ⟨a freely available, *nonpolluting*, renewable source of energy — sunlight —Barry Commoner⟩

non·pro·lif·er·a·tion \-prəˌlifəˈrāshən\ *adj* **:** providing for the stoppage of proliferation esp. of nuclear weapons ⟨*nonproliferation* treaty⟩ — **nonproliferation** *n*

non·re·com·bi·nant \-(ˌ)rēˈkämbənənt\ *adj* **:** not exhibiting the results of genetic recombination ⟨*nonrecombinant* progeny⟩ — **nonrecombinant** *n*

non·re·pro·duc·tive \-ˌrēprəˈdəktiv\ *adj* **:** not reproducing; *esp* **:** not capable of reproducing ⟨a *nonreproductive* caste of colonial insects⟩ — **nonreproductive** *n*

non·sed·i·ment·able \-ˌsedəˈmen(t)əbəl\ *adj* **:** not capable of being sedimented under specified conditions (as of centrifugation)

nonsense*n **:** genetic mutation involving formation of one or more codons that do not code for any amino acid and usu. cause termination of the molecular chain in protein synthesis — compare MISSENSE

nonsense*adj **:** consisting of one or more codons that are genetic nonsense

non·sexist \(ˈ)nänˈseksəst, *sometimes* (ˈ)nən-\ *adj* **:** not biased or discriminating against persons on the basis of sex ⟨insofar as possible, job titles should be *nonsexist* — *N.Y. Times Mag.*⟩; *esp* **:** not biased or discriminating against women ⟨inspiring, *nonsexist* models for a generation of little girls —Grace Lichtenstein⟩

non·sig·nif·i·cant\ˌnän(ˌ)sigˈnifəkənt, *sometimes* ͵nən-\ *adj* **:** having or yielding a value lying within limits between which variation is attributed to chance ⟨a *nonsignificant* statistical test⟩ — **non·sig·nif·i·cant·ly** \-lē, -li\ *adv*

non·start·er \(ˈ)nänˈstärd·ər, -ˌståd·ə(r, *sometimes* (ˈ)nən-\ *n* **1 :** one that does not start ⟨if a boat is not off her moorings at the preparatory signal, she is a *nonstarter* —Guy Pennant⟩ **2 :** someone or something that is not productive or effective ⟨his son has been in politics a *nonstarter* —Anthony Lejeune⟩ ⟨it was my opinion that this effort was a *nonstarter* —Chester Bowles⟩

non·ste·roid \-ˈsti(ə)r͵ȯid, *also* -ˈste(ə)r-\ *or* **non·ste·roi·dal** \-stəˈrȯidʳl\ *adj* **:** of, relating to, or being a compound esp. a drug that is not a steroid — **nonsteroid** *n*

non·stick \-ˈstik\ *adj* **:** allowing of easy removal of cooked food particles ⟨a *nonstick* coating on a frying pan⟩

non·sys·tem \-ˈsistəm\ *n* **:** a system that lacks effective organization

non·tar·get \-ˈtärgət, -ˈtåg-\ *adj* **:** not being the intended object of action by a particular agent ⟨effect of insecticides on *nontarget* organisms⟩

non·ti·tle \-ˈtīd·ʳl\ *adj* **:** of, relating to, or being an athletic contest in which a title is not at stake ⟨a *nontitle* bout⟩

non·triv·i·al \(ˈ)nänˈtrivēəl\ *adj* **1 :** not trivial ⟨stress the importance of an extremely large file in the construction of *nontrivial* inferences —Christine A. Montgomery⟩

2 : having the value of at least one variable not equal to zero ⟨*nontrivial* solutions to linear equations⟩

non–U \'∤nän∤yü\ *adj* **:** not upper-class **:** of, relating to, or typical of the lower classes ⟨a thoughtful, *non-U* escapee from a technical college —Timothy Foote⟩ ⟨obscenities are *non-U* signals —D.B. Sands⟩

non·vec·tor \(')nän∤vektə(r), *sometimes* (')nən-\ *n* **:** an organism (as an insect) that does not transmit a particular pathogen (as a virus)

non·vo·coid \-∤vō̜kȯid\ *n* **:** CONTOID

non·vot·er \-∤vōd-ə(r)\ *n* **:** one that does not vote

noo·sphere \'nōə₁sfi(ə)r, -₁sfiə\ *n* [ISV *noo-* mind (fr. Gk *noos, nous*) + *sphere*; prob. orig. formed as Russ *noosfera*] **:** the sphere of human consciousness and mental activity esp. in regard to its influence on the biosphere and in relation to evolution

NOR \'nȯ(ə)r\ *n* [*not OR*] **:** a computer logic circuit that produces an output that is the inverse of that of an OR circuit

nor·ad·ren·er·gic \'∤nȯ(ə)r₁adrə'nərjik, -'näj-, -'∤nȯij-\ *adj* [*noradrenaline* + *-ergic* (as in *adrenergic*)] **:** liberating, activated by, or involving norepinephrine in the transmission of nerve impulses ⟨a progressive deterioration of central *noradrenergic* pathways —C.D. Wise & Larry Stein⟩ ⟨*noradrenergic* synapses⟩

Nor·dic*\'nȯrdik, -ēk\ *adj* **:** of or relating to competitive ski events consisting of ski jumping and cross-country racing — compare ALPINE

nor·eth·in·drone \nȯ'rethən₁drōn\ *n* [*nor-* homologue lower by one methylene group + *ethinyl* (var. of *ethynyl*) + *-dr-* (perh. fr. *androgen*) + *testosterone*] **:** a synthetic progestational hormone C₂₀H₂₆O₂ used in oral contraceptives often in the form of its acetate

nor·ethis·te·rone \₁nȯ(ə)rə'thistə₁rōn\ *n* [*nor-* + *ethisterone*] *chiefly Brit* **:** NORETHINDRONE

nor·ethyn·o·drel \₁nȯrə'thinə₁drel\ *n* [*nor-* + *ethynyl* + connective *-o-* + *-dr-* (perh. fr. *androgen*) + *-el* (perh. alter. of *-al* pharmaceutical product)] **:** a progesterone derivative C₂₀H₂₆O₂ used in oral contraceptives and clinically in the treatment of abnormal uterine bleeding and the control of menstruation

norm*n **1 :** a real-valued nonnegative function defined on a vector space and satisfying the conditions that the function is zero if and only if the vector is zero, that the function of the product of a scalar and a vector is equal to the product of the absolute value of the scalar and the function of the vector, and that the function of the sum of two vectors is less than or equal to the sum of the functions of the two vectors; *specif* **:** the square root of the sum of the squares of the absolute values of the elements of a matrix or of the components of a vector **2 :** the greatest distance between two successive points of a set of points that partition an interval into smaller intervals

normal*adj **1** *of a subgroup* **:** having the property that every coset produced by operating on the left with a given element is equal to the coset produced by operating on the right with the same element **2 :** relating to, involving, or being a normal curve or normal distribution ⟨*normal* approximation to the binomial distribution⟩ **3** *of a matrix* **:** having the property of commutativity under multiplication by the transpose of a matrix each of whose elements is a conjugate complex number with respect to the corresponding element of the given matrix

normal divisor *n* **:** a normal subgroup

nor·mal·ize*\'nȯrmə₁līz, 'nȯ(ə)m-\ *vt* **-ized; -iz·ing 1** **:** to make mathematically or statistically normal (as by a transformation of variables) **2 :** to bring or restore (as relations between countries) to a normal condition — **nor·mal·iz·able** \-₁lī-zə-bəl\ *adj*

nor·mal·iz·er*\-₁līzə(r)\ *n* **1 :** a subgroup consisting of those elements of a group for which the group operation with regard to a given element is commutative **2 :** the set of elements of a group for which the group operation with regard to every element of a given subgroup is commutative

normal or·thog·o·nal \-ȯr'thägənᵊl, -ȯ(ə)'th-\ *adj* **:** OR-THONORMAL

normed \'nȯ(ə)rmd, 'nȯ(ə)md\ *adj* **:** being a mathematical entity upon which a norm is defined ⟨a *normed* vector space⟩

nor·mo·ther·mia \₁nȯrmə'thərmēə\ *n* [NL, fr. *normo-* normal + *-thermia* state of heat, deriv. of Gk *thermē* heat] **:** normal body temperature — **nor·mo·ther·mic** \-∤thərmik\ *adj*

northern corn root·worm \-'rüt₁wȯrm, -'rüt-, -₁wȯm, -₁wȯim\ *n* **:** a corn rootworm (*Diabrotica longicornis*) often destructive to maize in the northern parts of the central and eastern U.S.

nor·trip·ty·line \nȯr'triptə₁lēn\ *n* [*normal* + *tript-* (alter. of *trypt-* — as in *tryptophan*) + *-yl* chemical radical + *-ine* chemical substance] **:** a tricyclic antidepressant C₁₉H₂₁N often used in the form of its hydrochloride

nose job *n, slang* **:** plastic surgery on the nose usu. for cosmetic purposes

nose-ride \'nōz₁rīd\ *vi* **:** to ride or perform stunts on the nose of a surfboard — **nose-rid·er** \-ə(r)\ *n*

¹nosh \'näsh\ *vb* [Yiddish *nashn*, fr. MHG *naschen* to eat on the sly] *vi* **:** to eat between meals **:** snack ⟨*noshing* on a chili dog and coke —Lyn Tornabene⟩ ~ *vt* **:** to snack on **:** eat ⟨the cost of food *noshed* by the assembled multitude —Beatrice Berg⟩ — **nosh·er** \-shə(r)\ *n*

²nosh *n* **1 :** a light snack ⟨bring her something to eat, just a little *nosh*, anything at all —Ed McCormack⟩ **2** *chiefly Brit* **a :** a meal ⟨a slap-up Christmas *nosh* for 100 stray cats and dogs —*Sunday Mirror (London)*⟩ **b** **:** food ⟨recipes for some of the world's niftiest *nosh* — *Daily Mirror (London)*⟩

no-show*n* **:** a person who buys a ticket (as to a sporting event) but does not attend ⟨some 50,000 *no-shows* at the... stadiums —*Richmond (Va.) Times-Dispatch*⟩; *broadly* **:** a person who is expected but does not show up ⟨unexpected guests arrive while others are *no-shows* — Mimi Sheraton⟩

nosh-up \-₁əp\ *n, chiefly Brit* **:** a meal and esp. a large or elaborate meal ⟨a demo outside the Town Hall protested against a *nosh-up* for 250 inside —*Wolverhampton Express & Star*⟩

nos·tal·gist \nä'staljəst, nə-, *also* nȯ-, nō-; nə'stäl-\ *n* [*nostalgia* + *-ist* one who is interested in, specialist] **:** a person fond of the objects and style of the past ⟨the *nostalgists* who go around lamenting the loss of labor's old crusading zeal —J.D. Hodgson⟩

NOT \'nät\ *n* [*not*] **:** a logical operator that produces a statement that is the inverse of an input statement

notch·back \'näch‚bak\ n **1 :** a back on a closed passenger automobile having a distinct deck — compare FASTBACK **2 :** an automobile having a notchback
not·geld \'nȯt‚gelt, 'nät-, -ld\ n [G, emergency money, fr. *not* necessity + *geld* money] **:** necessity money used in Germany and some eastern European states esp. after World War I
no–till \(')nō'til\ n **:** NO-TILLAGE
no–till·age \-ij, -ēj\ n **:** a system of farming that consists of planting a narrow slit trench without tillage and with the use of herbicides to suppress weeds
nou·velle cuisine \nü'vel-\ n [F, lit., new cooking] **:** a form of French cuisine that uses little flour or fat and stresses light sauces and the use of fresh seasonal produce
nou·velle vague \(‚)nü‚vel'väg, -'vȧg\ n [F, lit., new wave, fr. *nouvelle* (fem. of *nouveau* new, fr. L *novellus*) + *vague* wave, fr. OF *wage*, fr. ON *vāgr*; akin to OE *wǣg* wave, *wegan* to move] **:** NEW WAVE 1
NOW account \'naû-\ n [*negotiable order of withdrawal*] **:** a savings account on which checks may be drawn
no way \'nō'wā\ adv — used interjectionally to express emphatic negation
no–win \(')nō‚win\ adj **:** not likely to give victory, success, or satisfaction **:** that cannot be won ⟨a *no-win* situation⟩ ⟨a *no-win* war⟩
nsec abbr nanosecond
nuclear force n **1 :** the powerful force between nucleons that holds atomic nuclei together **2 :** STRONG INTERACTION
nuclear magnetic resonance n **:** the magnetic resonance of an atomic nucleus
nuclear resonance n **:** the resonance absorption of a gamma ray by a nucleus identical to the nucleus that emitted the gamma ray — compare MÖSSBAUER EFFECT
nu·cleo·cap·sid \‚n(y)üklēō'kapsəd\ n [*nucleo-* nucleus, nucleic acid + *capsid*] **:** the nucleic acid and surrounding protein coat in a virus
nu·cleo·gen·e·sis \-'jenəsəs\ n **:** NUCLEOSYNTHESIS
nu·cle·o·lo·ne·ma \(‚)n(y)ü‚klēələ'nēmə\ *also* **nu·cle·o·lo-neme** \-'klēələ‚nēm\ n [NL *nucleolonema* fr. *nucleolus* + connective *-o-* + Gk *nēma* thread] **:** a filamentous network consisting of small granules in some nucleoli
nu·cle·on*\'n(y)üklē‚än\ n **:** a hypothetical single entity with one-half unit of isospin capable of manifesting itself as either a proton or a neutron and of making transitions between these two states
nu·cleo·phile \'n(y)üklēō‚fil\ n [*nucleo-* nucleus, nucleic acid + *-phile* lover, deriv. of Gk *philos* beloved, loving] **:** a nucleophilic substance (as an electron-donating reagent)
nu·cleo·some \'n(y)üklēə‚sōm\ n [ISV *nucleo-* + *-some* body] **:** any of the repeating globular subunits of chromatin consisting of a complex of DNA and histone and thought to be present only in interphase — **nu·cleo·so·mal** \‚n(y)üklēə‚sōməl\ adj
nu·cleo·syn·the·sis \‚n(y)üklēō'sin(t)thəsəs\ n **:** the production of a chemical element in nature from hydrogen nuclei or protons (as in stellar evolution) — **nu·cleo·syn·thet·ic** \-sən‚thed·ik\ adj
nu·cleo·ti·dyl·trans·fe·rase \‚n(y)üklēō‚tid°l‚tran(t)s-fə‚rās, -anzf-, -āz\ n [*nucleotide* + *-yl* chemical radical +

transferase] **:** any of several enzymes that catalyze the transfer of a nucleotide residue from one compound to another
¹nud·ie \'n(y)üdē, -di\ n **1 :** SKIN FLICK **2 :** a publication that features photographs of nudes
²nudie adj **:** featuring nudes ⟨*nudie* films⟩ ⟨*nudie* magazines⟩
¹nuke \'n(y)ük\ n [by shortening & alter.] **1 :** a nuclear bomb **2 :** a nuclear-powered electric generating station
²nuke vt **nuked; nuk·ing :** to destroy with nuclear bombs ⟨not thinking of *nuking* anybody back to Stone Ages —William Safire⟩
null*adj 1 : having zero as a limit ⟨*null* sequence⟩ **2** *of a matrix* **:** having all elements equal to zero
nullity*n : the number of elements in a basis of a null= space
null–space \'nəl‚spās\ n **:** a subspace of a vector space consisting of vectors that under a given linear transformation are equal to zero
number line n **:** a line of infinite extent whose points correspond to the real numbers according to their distance in a positive or negative direction from a point arbitrarily taken as zero
nu·mer·a·cy \'n(y)üm(ə)rəsē\ n [L *numerus* number + E *-acy* (as in *literacy*)] **:** the capacity for quantitative thought and expression
nu·mer·ate \-rət\ adj [L *numerus* number + E *-ate* (as in *literate*)] **:** marked by numeracy **:** having or showing the ability to think quantitatively ⟨designers in this country tend to be more literate than *numerate* —Paul Reilly⟩
nu·mer·ic \n(y)u'merik\ n [*numeric*, adj.] **:** a number or numeral
numerical analysis n **:** the study of quantitative approximations to the solutions of mathematical problems including consideration of the errors and bounds to the errors involved
numerical control n **:** automatic control (as of a machine tool) by a digital computer — **nu·mer·i·cal·ly controlled** \n(y)u‚mer‚k(ə)lē-\ adj
numerical taxonomy n **:** taxonomy that applies the quantitative measurement of many characters to the determination of taxa and to the construction of diagrams indicating systematic relationships — **numerical tax·o·nom·ic** \-‚taksə'nämik\ adj — **numerical tax·on·o·mist** \-tak'sänəməst\ n
¹nu·me·ro uno \‚n(y)ümə(‚)rō'ü(‚)nō\ n [Sp] **:** oneself or one's own interests ⟨she'd earned the right to just look after *Numero Uno* —Cyra McFadden⟩
²numero uno adj [It] **:** of first rank or importance ⟨rum is *numero uno* on the tropical juice charts —Emanuel Greenberg⟩
nun·cha·ku \nün'chäk(‚)ü\ n [Jp] **:** a Japanese weapon which consists of two hardwood sticks joined end to end by a short length of rawhide, cord, or chain
nurd var of NERD
nur·tur·ance \'nərchərən(t)s\ n **:** affectionate care and attention — **nur·tur·ant** \-rənt\ adj
nut*n 1 : a large sum of money **2** *slang* **:** a bribe given to a police officer
nuts–and–bolts \‚nətsᵊn(d)'bōlts\ adj **:** of, relating to, or dealing with specific practical details ⟨she does the actual *nuts-and-bolts* planning of a building after an architect has designed it —Sam Merrill⟩ ⟨this *nuts-and≠*

bolts book of basic advice to the aspiring screenwriter — Barbara A. Bannon⟩

nuts and bolts *n pl* **1 :** the working parts or elements **2 :** the practical workings of a machine or enterprise as opposed to theoretical considerations or speculative pos-

sibilities ⟨the *nuts and bolts* of municipal government⟩

Ny·norsk \'n(y)ü'nò(ə)rsk, 'nū̇'-\ *n* [Norw, lit., new Norwegian, fr. *ny* new (fr. ON *nȳr*) + *norsk* Norwegian] **:** a literary form of Norwegian based on the spoken dialects of Norway **:** Landsmål —compare BOKMÅL

O

Obie \'ōbē\ n [O.B., abbr. for off-Broadway] **:** any of several prizes awarded annually by a newspaper for excellence in off-Broadway theater

object language n **:** TARGET LANGUAGE

ob·jet trou·vé \,ȯb,zhā(,)trü'vā\ n, pl **objets trouvés** \same\ [F, lit., found object] **:** FOUND OBJECT

ocea·naut \'ōshə,nȯt, -,nät\ n [blend of ocean and -naut (as in aquanaut)] **:** AQUANAUT

ocean engineering n **:** engineering that deals with the application of design, construction, and maintenance principles and techniques to the ocean environment

oce·an·ics \,ōshē'aniks\ n pl but usu sing in constr **:** a group of sciences that deal with the ocean

ocean·o·log·ic \,ōshənə'läjik\ or **ocean·o·log·i·cal** \-jəkəl\ adj **:** of or relating to oceanology **:** oceanographic — **ocean·o·log·i·cal·ly** \-nə'läjək(ə)lē\ adv

ocean·ol·o·gist \,ōshə'näləjəst\ n **:** a specialist in oceanology **:** oceanographer

och·ra·tox·in \,ōkrə'täksən\ n [NL ochraceus (specific epithet of Aspergillus ochraceus) + E toxin] **:** a mycotoxin produced by an aspergillus (Aspergillus ochraceus)

OCR abbr optical character reader; optical character recognition

oc·ta·pep·tide \,äktə'pep,tīd\ n [octa- eight (fr. Gk oktō & L octo) + peptide] **:** a protein fragment or molecule (as oxytocin or vasopressin) that consists of eight amino acids linked in a polypeptide chain

oc·to·pa·mine \äk'tōpə,mēn, -əmən\ n [NL, fr. octopus + amine] **:** an adrenergic biogenic amine $C_8H_{11}NO_2$ that has been implicated as a neurotransmitter

¹OD \,ō'dē\ n [overdose] **1 :** an overdose of a narcotic ⟨some junkie croaks in the Bronx, right? He takes an OD —Richard Woodley⟩ **2 :** one who has taken an overdose of a narcotic ⟨died at his home . . . an apparent smack OD —Rolling Stone⟩

²OD vi **OD'd** or **ODed** \,ō'dēd\ **OD'ing** \,ō'dē(i)ŋ\ **1 :** to become ill or die from an OD ⟨ragged girls would stumble across the room, OD'd on pills — Lair Mitchell⟩ ⟨twenty-three kids . . . had been killed in drug- or pimp⁼ related murders, and this doesn't include the minors who OD'd —Larry Zicht⟩ **2 :** to have or experience too much of something — used with on ⟨afraid I'm beginning to OD on the girl-show fad —Robert MacKenzie⟩

odd–lot·ter \'äd'lät-ə(r)\ n **:** a speculator or an investor who habitually buys and sells stock in less than round lots

odd per·mu·ta·tion \-,pərmyü'tāshən, -,pām-, -,pȯim-, -yə'tā-\ n **:** a permutation that is produced by the successive application of an odd number of interchanges of pairs of elements — compare EVEN PERMUTATION

odont·o·log·i·cal \(,)ō,dänt²l'äjəkəl\ adj **:** of or relating to odontology

off \'ȯf, also 'äf\ vt, slang **:** to kill or murder ⟨if you want to off a pig, off him. Don't rap about it —Berkeley Barb⟩

⟨offed over 20 souls, none of them with a machine gun —Molly Ivins⟩

off Broad·way \-,brȯd,wā\ n, often cap O [fr. its usu. being produced in smaller theaters outside of the Broadway theatrical district] **:** a part of the New York professional theater stressing fundamental and artistic values and formerly engaging in experimentation — **off-Broadway** adj or adv, often cap O

off–cam·era \'ȯf,kam(ə)rə, also 'äf-\ adv or adj **1 :** out of the range of a motion-picture or television camera ⟨chided me off-camera during a commercial break — W.H. Manville⟩ **2 :** in private life ⟨if she won critical kudos on the entertainment pages, her performances off⁼ camera were met with less enthusiasm on the front pages —Arthur Knight & Hollis Alpert⟩

offering price* n **:** the price at which an open-end mutual fund is sold consisting of its asset value usu. plus a specified load

of·fi·ci·a·lis \ə,fishē'älⱥs, -'al-\ n, pl **-a·les** \-'ä(,)lās, -'a(,)lēz\ [NL, fr. ML, official] **:** the presiding judge of the matrimonial court of a Roman Catholic diocese

off–line \'ȯf,līn, also 'äf-\ adj **1 a :** not being in continuous direct communication with a computer ⟨an off-line scanner⟩ **b :** operating or done independently of a computer ⟨off-line storage of data⟩ **2 :** of, relating to, or being a cryptographic system in which encryption and decryption are independent of telecommunication machines — compare ON-LINE 3 — **off–line** adv

off–off–Broad·way \(')ȯf,ȯf,brȯd,wā, also (')äf,äf-\ n, often cap both Os [fr. its relation to off-Broadway being analogous to the relation of off-Broadway to Broadway] **:** an avant-garde theatrical movement in New York that stresses untraditional techniques and radical experimentation — **off–off–Broadway** adj or adv, often cap both Os

off–put·ting \'ȯf,pu̇d·iŋ, also 'äf-\ adj **:** that puts one off **:** repellent, disagreeable ⟨anything new is always off⁼ putting and upsetting —Dwight Macdonald⟩

offshore fund n **:** an investment fund based outside the U.S., not subject to registration with the Security and Exchange Commission, and barred by law from selling its shares within the U.S.

off–speed \'ȯf,spēd, also 'äf-\ adj **:** being slower than usual or expected ⟨throwing off-speed pitches⟩

off–the–peg \,ȯfthə',peg, also ,äf-\ adj, chiefly Brit **:** not made to order **:** ready-made, ready-to-wear ⟨off-the-peg clothes —The People⟩

off–the–rack \-',rak\ adj **:** ready-made, ready-to-wear ⟨off-the-rack suits⟩

off–the–shelf \-',shelf, -',sheúf\ adj **:** available as a stock item **:** not specially designed or custom-made ⟨off-the⁼ shelf computer peripherals⟩

off–the–wall \-',wȯl\ adj **:** highly unusual **:** bizarre ⟨an off-the-wall sense of humor⟩ ⟨the off-the-wall outcast who likes things that don't appeal to the masses —W.O. Johnson⟩

off·track \\'óf¦trak, *also* ¦äf-\ *adv or adj* **:** away from a racetrack ⟨betting *offtrack*⟩ ⟨*offtrack* bookies⟩

offtrack betting *n* **:** pari-mutuel betting that is carried on away from the racetrack

OJT *abbr* on-the-job training

Ok·to·ber·fest \äk'tōbə(r)ˌfest\ *n* [G, fr. *Oktober* October + *fest* festival] **:** a fall festival usu. featuring the drinking of beer

old lady*n **:** a girlfriend; *esp* **:** one with whom a man cohabits

old man*n **:** a boyfriend; *esp* **:** one with whom a woman cohabits

old–mon·ey \'ōl(d)ˌmənē, -ni\ *adj* **:** possessing wealth that has been inherited through several generations ⟨insists on protecting the names of his clients, a large number of whom are *old-money* and sensitive to publicity — Joanne Winship⟩

ole·an·do·my·cin \ˌōlēˌandə'mīsᵊn\ *n* [prob. fr. *oleand*er + connective *-o-* + *-mycin* substance obtained from a fungus, fr. *streptomycin*] **:** an antibiotic C₃₅H₆₁NO₁₂ produced by a streptomyces (*Streptomyces antibioticus*)

ol·fac·tron·ics \ˌäl.fak'träniks, ˌōl-\ *n pl but sing in constr* [*olfac*tion + *-tronics* (as in *electronics*)] **:** a branch of physical science dealing with the detection and identification of odors

ol·i·gid·ic \ˌälə'gidik, ˌōl-, -'ji-\ *adj* [*olig*- few (deriv. of Gk *oligos*) + *-idic* (as in *meridic*)] **:** having the active constituents with the exception of water undefined chemically ⟨*oligidic* growth medium⟩ — compare HOLIDIC, MERIDIC

oligo·mer \ō'ligəmə(r), ə'l-\ *n* [*oligo*- few (deriv. of Gk *oligos*) + *-mer* member of a class, fr. Gk *meros* part] **:** a polymer or polymer intermediate that contains relatively few structural units — **oligo·mer·ic** \ˌō'ligə'merik, ə¦l-, ˌäləgō'merik, -mir-\ *adj* — **oligo·mer·iza·tion** \-ˌligəˌmerə'zāshən, -mir-\ *n*

oli·go·my·cin \ˌäligō'mīsᵊn, ˌōli-\ *n* [*oligo*- + *-mycin*] **:** any of several antibiotic substances produced by a streptomyces (of a species similar to *Streptomyces diastatochromogenes*) and used esp. in biochemical research to inhibit oxidative phosphorylation

oli·go·nu·cle·o·tide \ˌäləgō'n(y)üklēəˌtīd, əˌligə-\ *n* **:** a chain of usu. from 2 to 10 nucleotides

olin·go \ō'liŋˌgō\ *n, pl* **-gos** [AmerSp, howling monkey] **:** any of a genus (*Bassaricyon*) of long-tailed slender-bodied carnivores of Central and South America that are related to the raccoon

om·buds·man \'äm,bùdzmən, 'óm-, -(ˌ)bəd-, äm'b-, óm'b-, -ˌman\ *n, pl* **om·buds·men** \-mən, -ˌmen\ [Sw, lit., representative, commissioner, fr. ON *umbothsmathr*, fr. *umboth* commission (fr. *um* around + *bjótha* to command) + *mathr* man] **1 :** a government official (as in Sweden or New Zealand) appointed to receive and investigate complaints made by individuals against abuses or capricious acts of public officials **2 :** one that investigates complaints (as from students or customers), reports findings, and helps to achieve equitable settlements — **om·buds·man·ship** \-mənˌship\ *n*

om·buds·wom·an \-ˌwùmən\ *n, pl* **om·buds·wom·en** \-ˌwimən\ **:** a woman who is an ombudsman

ome·ga*\ō'megə, ō'mēgə, ō'mägə\ *n* **1** *or* **omega par·ticle :** a negatively charged elementary particle that has a mass 3280 times the mass of an electron and that is an unstable baryon decaying into a xi and a pion with an average lifetime of about 10⁻¹⁰ second **2** *or* **omega me·son** \-'mez,än, -'mes,än, -'mā-, -'mē-\ **:** a very short-lived unstable meson with mass 1532 times the mass of an electron

om·ni·fo·cal \ˌämnə¦fōkəl, -nē-\ *adj* [*omni*- all (fr. L *omnis*) + *focal*] **:** of, relating to, or being a bifocal eyeglass that is so ground as to permit smooth transition from one correction to the other

on–board \ˌän¦bō(ə)rd, -¦bó(ə)rd, -¦bōəd, -¦bó(ə)d\ *adj* **:** carried within a vehicle (as a rocket, satellite, or spacecraft) ⟨an *onboard* computer⟩

on–cam·era \-¦kam(ə)rə\ *adv or adj* **:** within the range of a motion-picture or television camera ⟨is eager to do it *on-camera* —Robert Kotlowitz⟩

on·co·gen·e·sis \ˌäŋkō'jenəsəs\ *n* [NL, fr. *onco*- tumor (fr. Gk *onkos* bulk, mass) + *genesis*] **:** the induction or formation of tumors

on·co·ge·nic·i·ty \ˌäŋkōjə'nisəd-ē\ *n* **:** the capacity to induce or form tumors

on·cor·na·vi·rus \ˌän¦kórnə'vīrəs, äŋ-\ *n* [*onco*- + *RNA* + *virus*] **:** any of a group of RNA-containing viruses that produce tumors

one–lin·er \'wən'līnə(r)\ *n* **:** a very succinct joke or witticism ⟨turns away hard questions with easy *one-liners* — Andy Logan⟩

one–night stand*n* **:** a sexual encounter limited to a single occasion

one–off \'wən¦äf, -¦óf\ *adj, Brit* **:** limited to a single time, occasion, or instance **:** one-shot — **one–off** *n, Brit*

¹one–on–one \'wɔnän¦wən\ *adj or adv* **1 :** playing directly against a single opposing player ⟨pro basketball's most spectacular *one-on-one* player —Steve Cady⟩ ⟨everyone tends to go *one-on-one* because he thinks he can do it all by himself —Dave Cowens⟩ **2 :** involving a direct encounter between one person and another ⟨*one-on-one* counseling is still the only effective way of dealing with stress problems —Kathy Slobogin⟩

²one–on–one *n* **:** a game or an aspect of a game which pits one offensive player against a single defender; *esp* **:** an informal basketball game between two players who alternate at offense and defense

one–tailed test \'wənˌtā(ə)l(d)-\ *n* **:** a statistical test for which the critical region consists of all values of the test statistic greater than a given value or less than a given value but not both — called also *one-sided test*, *one-tail test;* compare TWO-TAILED TEST

one–time pad \'wənˌtim-\ *n* [prob. fr. its original form's being a pad of keys whose sheets were torn off and discarded after a single use] **:** a random-number additive or mixed keying sequence to be used for a single coded message and then destroyed

one–up \'wən'əp\ *vt* **-upped; -up·ping** [back-formation fr. *one-upmanship*] **:** to practice one-upmanship on ⟨intellectual argument is a serious business in our day and age; hopefully, we are trying to do something other than *one-up* each other —Nicholas Thompson⟩

one–world·ism \ˌwən'wər(ə)lˌdizəm, -'wōl-\ *n* **:** a belief in world government

onion dome *n* **:** a dome (as of a church) having the general shape of an onion — **on·ion–domed** \ˈȯnyən-ˌdōmd\ *adj*

on–line \ˈȯnˌlīn, ˈän-, *South sometimes* ˈȯn-\ *adj* **1 :** located at a point served directly by a particular railroad ⟨*on-line* industry⟩ **2 a :** being under the direct control of or in continuous direct communication with a computer ⟨*on-line* memory devices⟩ **b :** operating or done in real time ⟨*on-line* analysis of data⟩ **3 :** of, relating to, or being a cryptographic system whose telecommunication machines automatically encipher, transmit, receive, and decipher messages in a single instantaneous operation — compare OFF-LINE 2 — **on–line** *adv*

on–the–job \-thəˈjäb\ *adj* **:** of or relating to something (as training) learned, gained, experienced, or done while working at a job and often under supervision

on–the–scene \-thəˈsēn\ *adj* **:** being at the place of an action or occurrence ⟨an *on-the-scene* witness⟩

onto*prep* — used as a function word which precedes a word or phrase denoting a set each element of which is the image of at least one element of another set ⟨a function mapping the set *S onto* the set *T*⟩

on·to \ˈȯn(ˌ)tü, ˈän-\ *adj* **:** mapping in such a way that every element in one set is the image of at least one element in another set ⟨a function that is one-to-one and *onto*⟩

OOB \ˌō͞oˌōˈbē\ *n* [*off-off-Broadway*] **:** OFF-OFF-BROADWAY

op \ˈäp\ *or* **op art** *n* [by shortening] **:** OPTICAL ART — **op artist** *n*

op–ed page \ˈäpˌed-\ *n* [*op*posite + *ed*itorial] **:** the page opposite the editorial page of a newspaper that features by-lined articles (as by columnists) reflecting individual points of view

open*adj* **1 :** being a mathematical interval that contains neither of its endpoints **2 :** being a set each point of which has a neighborhood all of whose points are contained in the set ⟨the interior of a sphere is an *open* set⟩

open admission *n*, *pl* **open admissions** *usu sing in constr* **:** OPEN ENROLLMENT 2

open bar *n* **:** a bar (as at a wedding reception) at which drinks are served free — compare CASH BAR

open–cir·cuit \ˈōpənˈsərkət, ˈōpᵊmˈ-, -ˌsäk-, -ˈsȯik-\ *adj* **:** of or relating to an open circuit; *specif* **:** being or relating to television in which programs are broadcast so that they are available to all receivers within range

open classroom *n* **1 :** an informal flexible system of elementary education in which open discussions and individualized activities replace the traditional subject-centered studies **2 :** a classroom in an open classroom system

open enrollment *n* **1 :** the voluntary enrollment of a student in a public school other than the one he is assigned to on the basis of his residence **2 :** enrollment on demand as a student in an institution of higher learning irrespective of formal qualifications

open–heart \ˈōpənˈhärt, ˈōpᵊmˈ-, -ˈhȧt\ *adj* **:** of, relating to, or performed on a heart temporarily relieved of circulatory function and laid open for inspection and treatment ⟨*open-heart* surgery⟩

open loop *n* **:** a control system for an operation or process in which there is no self-correcting action

open marriage *n* **:** a marriage in which the partners agree to let each other have sexual partners outside the marriage

open season *n* **:** a time during which someone or something is the object of strong and continued attack or criticism ⟨during the last few years there has been an *open season* on the . . . school system —Sidney Hook⟩

open sentence *n* **:** a statement (as in mathematics) that contains at least one blank or unknown and that becomes true or false when the blank is filled or a quantity is substituted for the unknown

op·er·and\ˈäpəˌrand\ *n* **:** the part of a computer instruction that indicates the quantities to be operated on; *also* **:** one of these quantities

operating system *n* **:** software that supports or complements the hardware of a computer system (as by keeping track of the different programs in multiprogramming)

operation*n* **:** a single step performed by a computer in the execution of a program

op·er·a·tion·al·is·tic \ˌäpəˈrāshnᵊlˈistik, -shənᵊl-\ *adj* **:** of or relating to operationalism

op·er·a·tion·a·lize \ˌäpəˈrāshnᵊlˌīz, -shənᵊl-\ *vt* **-lized; -liz·ing :** to make operational ⟨*operationalize* a program⟩ — **op·er·a·tion·al·iza·tion** \äp(ə)ˌrāshnᵊləˈzāshən, -shənᵊl-, -ˌlˌi'zāshən\ *n*

op·er·a·tion·ist \ˌäpəˈrāsh(ə)nəst\ *n* **:** an advocate or adherent of operationalism

operator*or* **operator gene** *n* **:** a chromosomal region that triggers formation of messenger RNA by one or more structural genes and is itself subject to inhibition by a genetic repressor — compare OPERON

opera window *n* **:** a small window on each of the rear side panels of an automobile

op·er·on \ˈäpəˌrän\ *n* [ISV *operator* + *-on* basic hereditary component; prob. orig. formed in F] **:** the closely linked combination of an operator and the structural genes it regulates

opi·oid \ˈōpēˌȯid\ *adj* [*opiate* + *-oid* having the form of] **1 :** possessing some properties characteristic of opiate narcotics but not derived from opium **2 :** of, involving, or induced by an opioid substance or an opioid peptide

opioid peptide *also* **opioid** *n* **:** any of a group of endogenous neural polypeptides (as an endorphin or enkephalin) that bind esp. to opiate receptors and mimic some of the pharmacological properties of opiates

op·son·iza·tion \ˌäpsənəˈzāshən, -ˌnīˈz-\ *n* [*opson-* opsonin + *-ization* process] **:** the process of opsonizing

optical*adj* **1 :** being or relating to objects that emit light in the visible range of frequencies ⟨an *optical* galaxy⟩ ⟨*optical* astronomy⟩ **2 a :** of, relating to, or utilizing light ⟨an *optical* emission⟩ ⟨an *optical* telescope⟩ ⟨*optical* microscopy⟩ **b :** involving the use of light-sensitive devices to acquire information for a computer ⟨*optical* character recognition⟩ **3 :** of or relating to optical art ⟨*optical* painting⟩

optical art *n* **:** nonobjective art characterized by the use of straight or curved lines or geometric patterns often for an illusory effect (as of perspective or motion)

optical fiber *n* **:** a single fiber-optic strand

optic tec·tum \-ˈtektəm\ *n* **:** the visual projection area of fish and amphibians homologous to the mammalian superior colliculus; *also* **:** the superior colliculus

op·to·elec·tron·ic \ˌäp(ˌ)tōəˌlek'tränik, -ēˌlek-\ adj [optical + connective -o- + electronic] **:** being or related to a device in which light energy and electrical energy are coupled — **op·to·elec·tron·ics** \-iks\ n pl but sing in constr

OR \'ȯ(ə)r, 'ȯ(ə)\ n **:** a logical operator equivalent to the sentential connective or ⟨OR gate in a computer⟩

OR*abbr operations research

or·a·cy \'ȯrəsē, 'ȯr-, 'är-, -si\ n [oral + -acy (as in literacy)] **:** the capacity for oral expression and for understanding spoken language ⟨teaching literacy in the conventional form, and oracy with as acceptable an accent as may happen to have been spoken into the teaching tapes —James Pitman⟩

oral history n **1 :** tape-recorded historical information obtained in interviews with persons who often have led significant lives; also **:** the study of such information **2 :** a written work based on oral history — **oral historian** n

order*n **1 :** the number of elements in a finite mathematical group **2 :** a class of mutually exclusive linguistic forms any and only one of which may occur in a fixed definable position in the permitted sequence of items forming a word

ordered*adj **:** having elements succeeding according to rule: as **a :** having the property that every pair of different elements is related by a transitive relationship that is not symmetric **b :** having the elements arranged in a specified order ⟨a set of ordered pairs⟩ ⟨a set of ordered triples⟩

ordinal number*n **:** a number that designates both the order of the elements of an ordered set and the cardinal number of the set

or·ga·no \'ȯrgə(ˌ)nō, ȯr'ga(ˌ)nō\ adj [short for organometallic] **:** of, relating to, or being an organic compound that usu. contains a metal or metalloid bonded directly to carbon ⟨an organo derivative of mercury⟩

or·gano·chlo·rine \ȯrˌganə'klōrˌēn, -'klȯr-, ˌȯrgənō-, -rən\ adj [organo- organic + chlorine] **:** of, relating to, or belonging to the chlorinated hydrocarbon pesticides (as aldrin, DDT, or dieldrin) — **organochlorine** n

or·ga·nol·o·gy \ˌȯrgə'näləjē, ˌȯ(ə)g-, -ji\ n [organ + connective -o- + -logy study] **:** the study of the structure, history, and use of musical instruments — **or·ga·nol·o·gist** \-jəst\ n

or·gano·phos·phate \-'fäsˌfāt\ n **:** an organophosphorus pesticide — **organophosphate** adj

or·gano·phos·pho·rus \-'fäsf(ə)rəs\ also **or·gano·phos·pho·rous** \-'fäsf(ə)rəs; -fäs'fōrəs, -'fȯr-\ adj **:** of, relating to, or being a phosphorus-containing organic compound and esp. a pesticide (as malathion) that acts by inhibiting cholinesterase — **organophosphorus** n

Oriental Shorthair n **1 :** a breed of slender short-haired domestic cats resembling the Siamese in conformation but having a solid-colored coat in a wide range of colors and usu. green eyes **2** often not cap S **:** a cat of the Oriental Shorthair breed

ori·en·teer·ing \ˌȯrēən'ti(ə)riŋ, -ēˌ)en-\ n [prob. modif. (influenced by -eer, n. suffix) of Sw orientering, fr. orient-era to orient, fr. F orienter] **:** a cross-country race in which each participant uses a map and compass to navigate his way between checkpoints along an unfamiliar course

oro·so·mu·coid \ˌȯrəsō'myüˌkȯid\ n [Gk oros whey + E connective -o- + mucoid mucoprotein] **:** a mucoprotein found in blood and in nephrotic urine

or·thog·o·nal*\ȯr(r)'thägənᵊl\ adj **1 :** having a sum of products or an integral that is zero or sometimes one under specified conditions: as **a** of real-valued functions **:** having the integral of the product of each pair of functions over a specific interval equal to zero **b** of vectors **:** having the scalar product equal to zero **c** of a square matrix **:** having the sum of products of corresponding elements in any two rows or any two columns equal to one if the rows or columns are the same and equal to zero otherwise **:** having a transpose with which the product equals the identity matrix **2** of a linear transformation **:** having a matrix that is orthogonal **:** preserving length and distance **3 :** composed of mutually orthogonal elements ⟨an orthogonal basis of a vector space⟩

or·thog·o·nal·iza·tion \ȯr(r)ˌthägənᵊlə'zāshən, -gnəl-, -lˌi'z-\ n **:** the replacement of a set of vectors by a linearly equivalent set of orthogonal vectors

or·tho·mo·lec·u·lar \ˌȯr(r)thəmə'lekyələ(r), -thō-\ adj [ortho- straight, right, perpendicular (deriv. of Gk orthos straight) + molecular] **:** relating to or being a theory according to which disease and esp. mental illness may be cured by restoring the optimum amounts of substances normally present in the body ⟨an orthomolecular psychiatrist⟩ ⟨orthomolecular therapy⟩

or·tho·nor·mal \-'nȯrməl, -'nȯ(ə)m-\ adj **1** of real-valued functions **:** orthogonal with the integral of the square of each function over a specified interval equal to one **2 :** being or composed of orthogonal elements of unit length ⟨orthonormal basis of a vector space⟩

or·thot·ic \ȯr'thädˌik\ n **:** a support or brace for weak or ineffective joints or muscles

or·thot·ics \-iks\ n pl but sing in constr [fr. Gk orthōsis straightening; after such pairs as E prosthesis: prosthetics] **:** a branch of mechanical and medical science dealing with the support and bracing of weak or ineffective joints or muscles — **or·thot·ic** \-ik\ adj — **or·tho·tist** \'ȯrthətəst\ n

or·tho·tro·pic* \ˌȯ(r)thə'träpik, -ˌtrō-\ adj **1 :** being, having, or relating to properties (as strength, stiffness, and elasticity) that are symmetric about two or three mutually perpendicular planes ⟨a piece of straight-grained wood is an orthotropic material⟩ **2** of a bridge **:** designed so that the roadway serves as an orthotropic structural member **:** constructed with a steel-plate deck as an integral part of the support structure

Or·well·ian \ȯ(r)'welēən\ adj [George Orwell, pseudonym of Eric Blair †1950 Eng. writer] **:** of, relating to, or suggestive of George Orwell or his writings ⟨almost an example of Orwellian newspeak; revolution is transformed, at least for propaganda purposes, from a beginning into an end —Richard Schickel⟩ ⟨an Orwellian dystopia working away full blast —John Simon⟩

or·zo \'ȯr(ˌ)zō\ n [prob. modif. of NGk oryza rice, fr. Gk] **:** rice-shaped pasta

os·cu·lat·ing circle \ˌäskyə'lädˌiŋ-\ n **:** a circle which is tangent to a curve at a given point, which lies in the limiting plane determined by the tangent to the curve and a point moving along the curve to the point of tangency, which has its center situated on the normal to the curve at the given point and, also, on the concave side of the projection of the curve onto the limiting plane, and which has a radius equal to the radius of curvature

os·mol \'äz₁mōl, 'ä₁smōl\ n [blend of osmosis and mol] : a standard unit of osmotic pressure based on a one molal concentration of an ion in a solution — **os·mo·lal** \(')äz₁mōlǝl, (')ä₁smō-\ adj — **os·mo·lal·i·ty** \₁äzmǝ'laląd-ē, ₁äsm-\ n

os·mo·lar \(')äz₁mōlǝ(r), (')ä₁sm-\ adj : of, relating to, or having the properties of osmosis : osmotic — used chiefly of biological fluids — **os·mo·lar·i·ty** \₁äzmǝ'larąd-ē, ₁äsm-\ n

os·mot·ic shock \äz₁mäd·ik-, äs₁m-\ n : a rapid change in the osmotic pressure (as by transfer to a medium of different concentration) affecting a living system

os·so bu·co also **os·so buc·co** \₁ōsō'bü(₁)kō\ n [It ossobuco marrowbone] : a dish of veal shanks braised with vegetables, white wine, and seasoned stock

os·teo·gen·ic sarcoma \₁ästēǝ₁jenik-\ n : a sarcoma derived from bone or containing bone tissue : osteosarcoma

ost·mark \'ōst₁märk, 'äs-\ n [G, lit., East mark] : the East German mark

os·to·my \'ästǝmē\ n, pl **-mies** [colostomy] : an operation (as a colostomy) to create an artificial passage for bodily elimination

OTB*abbr offtrack betting

OTC abbr over-the-counter

oto·tox·ic \₁ōd·ǝ'täksik\ adj [oto- ear (fr. Gk ōt-, ous) + toxic] : producing, involving, or being adverse effects on organs or nerves involved in hearing or balance (ototoxic drugs) — **oto·tox·i·ci·ty** \-(₁)täk'sisǝd-ē, -i\ n

ou·gui·ya \ü'g(w)ē(y)ǝ\ n, pl **ouguiya** [native name in Mauritania] **1** : the basic monetary unit of Mauritania **2** : a coin or note representing one ouguiya

out*adj : not approved of or accepted by those who are keenly aware of and responsive to what is new and smart : not in (who decrees that pants are out and skirts back in —James Brady) (keep their ears open to discover what's in and what's out in the world of literary classics —Ray Walters)

out–front \'aút'frǝnt\ adj : being frank and open (an out⸗ front activist . . . signing peace petitions, testifying in Congress against the war —Frank Donner)

out–of–sight \₁aúd·ǝ(v)'sīt\ adj, slang : wonderful (one of the devious maneuvers was an out-of-sight kickoff return —Sports Illustrated)

out–of–stat·er \₁aúd·ǝ(v)'städ·ǝ(r), -ätǝ-\ n [fr. the phrase out of state + er, agent suffix] **1** : a visitor from another state **2** : a person whose legal domicile is in one state but who lives for an extended time in another state (as to attend college)

out–of–town·er \-'₁taúnǝ(r)\ n [fr. the phrase out of town + -er] : a visitor from out of town

out·reach*\'aút₁rēch\ n : the extending of services or activities beyond current or conventional limits (to provide what is called community outreach, new facilities were needed —Ada L. Huxtable); also : the extent of such services or activities (the international communications systems . . . are going to continue to expand their outreach —Harold Taylor)

outside*adj : made or done from the outside or from a distance (borrowed a basketball and practiced his outside shot all day)

ovals of Cas·si·ni \-kǝ'sēnē, -ka-, -ká-\ [G. D. Cassini †1712 Fr. astronomer] : a curve that is the locus of points of the vertex of a triangle whose opposite side is fixed and the product of whose adjacent sides is a constant and that has the equation $[(x + a)^2 + y^2)][(x - a)^2 + y^2] - k^4 = 0$ where k is the constant and a is one half the length of the fixed side

ov·en·proof \'ǝvǝn₁prüf\ adj : capable of withstanding the heat normally produced in a kitchen oven (ovenproof glass)

over·achiev·er \ ₁ōvǝrǝ₁chēvǝr, ₁ōvǝ(r)ǝ₁chēvǝ(r\ n : one who achieves success over and above a standard or expected level (tended to be overachievers, doing better in school than their IQs would indicate —The Sciences) — **over·achieve** \-ǝ₁chēv\ vi

over·book \₁ōvǝ(r)'búk\ vt : to issue reservations for (as an airplane flight) in excess of the space available ~ vi : to issue reservations in excess of the space available

over·dom·i·nance \₁ōvǝ(r)'däm(ǝ)nǝn(t)s\ n : the property of having a heterozygote that produces a phenotype more extreme or better adapted than that of the homozygote — **over·dom·i·nant** \₁ōvǝ(r)'däm(ǝ)nǝnt\ adj

¹over·dub \'ōvǝ(r)₁dǝb\ vt : to transfer (recorded sound) onto a recording that bears sound recorded earlier in order to produce a combined effect (what we did then was to put down all the tracks first and then I would overdub the vocal later —Carly Simon)

²overdub n **1** : the act or an instance of overdubbing (the last big album it took them eight months of overdubs to produce —Lester Bangs) **2** : recorded sound that is overdubbed (vocal overdubs)

over·fa·tigue \₁ōvǝ(r)fǝ₁tēg, chiefly dial -₁tig\ n : excessive fatigue esp. when carried beyond the recuperative capacity of the individual

over·ground \'ōvǝ(r)₁graúnd\ n [over above + ground] : ESTABLISHMENT (the underground medium as it grows often takes on the characteristics of the overground —R. J. Glessing) (the overground press)

over·kill \'ōvǝ(r)₁kil\ n [overkill, v.] **1** : the capability of destroying an enemy or target with a nuclear force larger than is required (thirty more Poseidons are to follow in this insane race for overkill —I. F. Stone) **2** : an excess of something (as a quantity or an action) beyond what is required or suitable for a particular purpose (an overkill in weaponry) (the failures of that tone—the satirical overkill in Dickens, the facetiousness of Thackeray —John Fowles) (the overkill was unbearable: none of the recipes seemed to contain one cup of sugar when two would do — Nora Ephron) **3** : killing in excess of what is intended or required : excessive killing (the overlong seasons and punishing overkill that brought ducks to the thin edge of extinction —Zack Taylor) — **over·kill** \'ōvǝ(r), ₁ōvǝ(r)'kil\ vb

overnight*n : an overnight stay

over·nu·tri·tion \₁ōvǝ(r)n(y)ü'trishǝn\ n : excessive food intake esp. when viewed as a factor in pathology

over·re·spond \₁ōvǝ(r)rǝ'spänd\ vi : to react excessively or too strongly

over·shoot \'ōvǝ(r)₁shüt\ n : the action or an instance of overshooting; esp : a going beyond an intended point (a pinpoint landing instead of another off-the-mark touchdown like the four-mile *overshoot* experienced on Apollo 11 —Richard Witkin⟩

over·steer \-ˌ'sti(ə)r, -ˌ'stiə\ *n* : the tendency of an automobile to steer into a sharper turn than the driver intends sometimes with the result that the vehicle's rear end swings to the outside; *also* : the action or an instance of oversteer

over·win·ter \ˌōvə(r)ˌ'wintə(r)\ *adj* : occurring during the period spanning the winter ⟨*overwinter* mortality of small game⟩

over·with·hold \ˌōvə(r)with'hōld, -wiᵗh-\ *vt* : to deduct a greater amount of (money) from an employee's pay for withholding tax than the employee is legally required to pay

Ovon·ic \ō'vänik\ *n* [short for *ovonic device*] : a device that operates in accordance with the Ovshinsky effect

Ovon·ics \-iks\ *n pl but usu sing in constr* [*Ov*shinsky effect + electr*onics*] : a branch of electronics that deals with applications of the Ovshinsky effect — **ovonic** *adj, often cap*

Ov·shin·sky effect \äv'shin(t)skē-, ȯv-\ *n* [Stanford R. *Ovshinsky* b1923 Am. inventor] : the change from an electrically nonconducting state to a semiconducting state shown by glasses of special composition upon application of a certain minimum voltage

OW* abbr one way

ox·a·cil·lin \ˌäksə'silən\ *n* [is*oxazole*, a compound C₃H₃NO + penic*illin*] : a semisynthetic penicillin that is esp. effective in the control of infections caused by penicillin resistant staphylococci

ox·az·e·pam \äk'sazə,pam\ *n* [hydr*oxyl* + di*azepam*] : a tranquilizing drug C₁₅H₁₁ClN₂O₂

Ox·bridge \'äks(ˌ)brij\ *adj* [*Ox*ford University, England + Cam*bridge* University, England] : of, relating to, or characteristic of Oxford and Cambridge universities ⟨ex-

acted an *Oxbridge* degree in order to ensure that its members had had the education of gentlemen —*Times Lit. Supp.*⟩ — compare PLATEGLASS, REDBRICK

ox·i·da·tive phos·phor·y·la·tion \'äksə,dād·iv-ˌfäsfərə'lāshən\ *n* : the synthesis of ATP by phosphorylation of ADP for which energy is obtained by electron transport and which takes place in the mitochondria during aerobic respiration

oxo·trem·o·rine \ˌäksō'tremə,rēn, -ərən\ *n* [*oxo*- oxygen + *tremor* + *-ine* chemical substance] : a cholinergic agent C₁₂H₁₈N₂O that induces tremors and is used to screen drugs for activity against Parkinson's disease

oxy·ac·id \'äksē,asəd\ *n* [*oxy*- oxygen + *acid*] : an acid (as sulfuric acid) that contains oxygen — called also *oxygen acid*

ox·y·gen·ase \'äksə,jā,nās, -,nāz\ *n* [*oxygen* + *-ase* enzyme] : an enzyme that catalyzes the reaction of an organic compound with molecular oxygen

oxygen cycle *n* : the cycle whereby atmospheric oxygen is converted to carbon dioxide in animal respiration and regenerated by green plants in photosynthesis

oxy·phen·bu·ta·zone \ˌäksē,fen'byüd·ə,zōn, -ütə-\ *n* [*-oxy*- containing hydroxyl + *phenylbutazone*] : a phenylbutazone derivative C₁₉H₂₀N₂O₃ used for its anti-inflammatory, analgesic, and antipyretic effects

oxy·some \'äksə,sōm\ *n* [*oxy*- + *-some* body, deriv. of Gk *sōma*] : one of the structural units of mitochondrial cristae that are observed by the electron microscope usu. as spheres or stalked spheres and that are prob. sites of fundamental energy-producing reactions

oysters Rocke·fel·ler \-'räk(ə),felə(r)\ *n pl* [John Davison *Rockefeller* †1937 Am. oil magnate] : a dish of oysters baked with chopped spinach and a seasoned sauce

ozone·sonde \'ō,zōn,sänd\ *n* : a balloon-borne instrument that measures the concentration of ozone at various altitudes and broadcasts the data by radio

P

p*abbr pico-

p*symbol **1** momentum of a particle **2** often cap the probability of obtaining a result as great as or greater than the observed result in a statistical test if the null hypothesis is true

pa*abbr pascal

PA*abbr physician's assistant

pa·'anga \pä-'äŋ(g)ə\ n, pl pa'anga [Tongan, lit., seed] **1 :** the basic monetary unit of Tonga **2 :** a coin or note representing one pa'anga

pace car n **:** an automobile that leads the field of competitors through a pace lap but does not participate in the race

pace lap n **:** a lap of an auto racecourse by the entire field of competitors before the start of a race to allow the engines to warm up and to permit a flying start

pad*— on the pad of a police officer **:** receiving money in exchange for ignoring illegal activities **:** taking graft ⟨getting on the pad in an area of high gambling activity ... he said, could bring a corrupt cop a tidy $1500 a month tax free —Richard Dougherty⟩

page*n **:** a sizable subdivision of computer memory; also **:** a block of information that fills a page and can be transferred as a unit between the internal and external storage of a computer

page*vi paged; pag·ing **:** to proceed through matter displayed on a CRT display as if turning pages

paging*n **:** the movement of blocks of information between internal storage and the external storage of a computer

pail·lard \pī'yär\ n [origin unknown] **:** a piece of beef or veal usu. pounded thin and grilled

pair–bond \'pa(ə)r,bänd, 'pe(ə)r-, 'paə,-, 'peə,-\ n **:** an exclusive union with a single mate at any one time **:** a monogamous relationship — pair–bond·ing \-iŋ\ n

paired–as·so·ci·ate learning \,pa(ə)rdə,sōs(h)ēət-, ,pe(ə)rd-, -shət-, -s(h)ē,āt-\ n **:** the learning of syllables, digits, or words in pairs (as in the study of a foreign language) so that one member of the pair evokes recall of the other

Pak \'pak, 'päk, 'pák\ n [by shortening] **:** a Pakistani — sometimes taken to be offensive

Paki \'páki, 'pak-, -ē\ n, pl Pakis [short for Pakistani] chiefly Brit **:** a Pakistani immigrant — usu. used disparagingly

pa·laz·zo pants \pə'lät(,)sō-\ n pl **:** extremely wide-legged pants for women

pa·leo·bio·ge·og·ra·phy \,pālēō,bīōjē'ägrəfē, -i\ n [paleo- + bio- life + geography] **:** a study that deals with the geographical distribution of plants and animals of former geological epochs — pa·leo·bio·geo·graph·i·cal \-jēə,grafəkəl\ adj

pa·leo·cli·mate \'pālēō,klīmət\ n **:** the climate during a past geological age

pa·leo·mag·ne·tism \,pālēō'magnə,tizəm, chiefly Brit ,pal-\ n [paleo- ancient (fr. Gk palaios ancient, fr. palai long ago) + magnetism] **1 :** the intensity and direction of residual magnetization in ancient rocks **2 :** a study that deals with paleomagnetism — pa·leo·mag·net·ic \-(,)mag'ned·ik\ adj — pa·leo·mag·net·i·cal·ly \-ək(ə)lē\ adv — pa·leo·mag·ne·tist \-(,)magnəd·əst\ n

pa·leo·tem·per·a·ture \-'tempə(r),chü(ə)r, -p(ə)rə-, -chə(r), -,t(y)ü(ə)r, -,chùə, -,t(y)ùə; rapid -'tem(p)chə(r)\ n **:** the temperature (as of the ocean) during a past geological age

Palestinian*n **:** a usu. Muslim or Christian member of an Arab people living in what was formerly Palestine

pal·i·mo·ny \'palə,mōnē, -ni\ n [blend of pal and alimony] **:** a court-ordered allowance paid by one member of a couple formerly living together out of wedlock to the other

pal·yno·morph \'palənə,mȯrf, -,mȯ(ə)f\ n [fr. palyn- (as in palynology) + connective -o- + -morph one having such a form] **:** a microscopic fossil composed esp. of pollen or spores

Pan–Af·ri·can·ism \,pan'afrəkə,nizəm\ n **:** a movement for the political union of all the African nations — Pan–Af·ri·can \-kən\ adj — Pan–Af·ri·can·ist \-kənəst\ n or adj

Panama Red n **:** marijuana of a reddish tint that is of Panamanian origin and is held to be very potent

pan·chres·ton \pan'krestən, -,tän\ n [Gk panchrēston panacea, fr. neut. of panchrēstos good for all work, fr. pan- all (fr. pan, neut. of pant-, pas all, every) + chrēstos good] **:** a broadly inclusive thesis that is intended to cover all possible variations within an area of concern and that in practice usu. proves to be an unacceptable oversimplification

pan·cu·ro·ni·um bromide \,pankyə'rōnēəm-\ or pancuronium n [perh. fr. pan- all + -cur- (prob. as in tubocurarine) + -onium an ion having a positive charge] **:** a neuromuscular blocking agent $C_{35}H_{60}Br_2N_2O_4$ used as a skeletal muscle relaxant

panda car \'pandə,ká(r\ n [so called fr. its black and white coloration] Brit **:** a police patrol car

p and h abbr postage and handling

pan·en·ceph·a·li·tis \,pan(,)en,sefə,līd·əs\ n [NL, fr. pan- + encephalitis] **:** inflammation of the brain affecting both white and gray matter and thought to be caused by a virus — see SUBACUTE SCLEROSING PANENCEPHALITIS

pan·gram \'pangrəm, -aŋg-, -,gram\ n [pan- all + Gk grammat-, gramma letter] **:** a short sentence (as "The quick brown fox jumps over the lazy dog") containing all 26 letters of the English alphabet — pan·gram·mat·ic \,pangrə'mad·ik, -aŋg-\ adj

pan·sex·u·al \(')pan,seksh(ə)wəl, -shəl\ adj **:** exhibiting or implying many forms of sexual expression — pan·sex·u·al·i·ty \,pan,seksho'waləd·ē, -i\ n

pant·dress \'pant,dres\ *n* **1 :** a garment having a divided skirt **2 :** a dress worn over matching shorts

Panther*n* **: BLACK PANTHER

pant·suit *or* **pants suit** \'pant,süt\ *n* **:** a woman's ensemble consisting usu. of a long jacket and tailored pants of the same material — **pant·suit·ed** *or* **pants–suit·ed** \'pant,süd·ǝd\ *adj*

panty hose *also* **panti·hose** \'pantē,hōz\ *n* **:** a one-piece undergarment for women consisting of hosiery combined with a panty

panty raid *n* **:** a raid on a women's dormitory by male college students to obtain panties as trophies

Pa·pa·ni·co·laou smear \,päpǝ'nēkǝ,laü-, ,papǝ'nik-\ *n* [George N. Papanicolaou †1962 Am. medical scientist] **: PAP SMEAR

pa·pa·raz·zo \,päpǝ'rät(,)sō\ *n, pl* **-raz·zi** \-sē\ [It, fr. It dial., a buzzing insect] **:** a free-lance photographer who aggressively pursues celebrities for the purpose of taking candid photographs ⟨the New York *paparazzi* were out in great numbers, and their flashbulbs were going off in flickering succession —John Corry⟩

paper factor *n* **:** a substance orig. isolated from pulpwood of the balsam fir that is a selectively effective insecticide with activity like that of juvenile hormone

paper gold *n* **: SDRS

pa·per–train \'pāpǝ(r),trān\ *vt* **:** to train (as a dog) to defecate and urinate on paper in the house

pa·po·va·vi·rus \pǝ'pōvǝ,vīrǝs\ *n* [*papilloma* + *polyoma* + *vacuolation* + *virus*] **:** any of a group of viruses that have a capsid with 42 protuberances resembling knobs and that are associated with or are responsible for various neoplasms (as some warts) of mammals

Pap smear *also* **Pap test** \'pap-\ *n* [*Pap* short for *Papanicolaou*, fr. George N. Papanicolaou †1962 Am. medical scientist] **:** a method for the early detection of cancer employing exfoliated cells and a special staining technique that differentiates diseased tissue

par·a·dor \,pärä'thór\ *n* [Sp; akin to Sp *parar* stop, prepare, fr. L *parare* prepare] **:** a government-operated hostelry in Spain often located in a renovated historic building (as a castle or monastery)

par·a·dox·i·cal sleep \,parǝ'däksǝkǝl-\ *n* **: REM SLEEP

para·foil \'parǝ,fóil\ *n* [*parachute* + *-foil* (as in *airfoil*)] **:** a self-inflating fabric device that resembles a parachute, behaves in flight like an airplane wing, is maneuverable, is capable of landing a payload at slow speed, and can be launched from the ground in a high wind like a kite

para·glid·er \'parǝ,glīdǝ(r)\ *n* [*parachute* + *glider*] **:** a triangular device on a spacecraft or rocket that consists of two flexible sections, that resembles a kite, and that is deployed when needed for guiding and landing a spacecraft after reentry or for recovering a launching rocket

para·in·flu·en·za virus \,parǝ,inflü,enzǝ-\ *n* [*para-* beside, closely resembling the true form (deriv. of Gk *para* beside) + *influenza*] **:** any of several myxoviruses that are associated with or are responsible for some respiratory infections in children

para·jour·nal·ism \-'jǝrnǝl,izǝm, -'jōn-, -'jain-\ *n* [*para-* beyond, outside of + *journalism*] **:** journalism that is heavily colored by the opinions of the reporter ⟨a mini epoch of ego-tripping *parajournalism* —Herbert Gold⟩ — **para·jour·nal·ist** \-ǝlǝst\ *n* — **para·jour·nal·is·tic** \-ǝl,istik\ *adj*

para·kite \'parǝ,kīt\ *n* [*parachute* + *kite*] **:** a parachute with slits that is towed against the wind by an automobile or motorboat so that a person harnessed to the parachute is lifted and pulled along through the air — **para·kit·ing** \-,kīd·iŋ\ *n*

para·lan·guage \-,laŋgwij, -wēj, *sometimes* -ŋw-\ *n* **:** optional vocal effects (as tone of voice) that accompany or modify the phonemes of an utterance and may communicate meaning

para·le·gal \-,lēgǝl\ *adj* [*para-* associated in a subsidiary capacity + *legal*] **:** of, relating to, or being a paraprofessional who assists a lawyer ⟨a *paralegal* counselor⟩ — **paralegal** *n*

para·lin·guis·tics \,parǝ,liŋ'gwistiks\ *n pl but usu sing in constr* **:** the study of paralanguage — **para·lin·guis·tic** \-ik\ *adj*

para·mag·net·ic resonance \,parǝ(,)mag,ned·ik-\ *n* **: ELECTRON SPIN RESONANCE

para·med·ic \,parǝ,medik\ *also* **para·med·i·cal** \-ǝkǝl\ *n* **:** one who works in a health field in an auxiliary capacity to a physician (as by treating common complaints, taking X rays, or giving injections)

pa·ram·e·ter*pǝ'ramǝd·ǝ(r)\ *n* **1 :** any of a set of physical properties whose values determine the characteristics or behavior of a system ⟨*parameters* of the atmosphere such as temperature, pressure, and density⟩ **2 :** something represented by a parameter; *broadly* **:** characteristic, element, factor ⟨still, by the *parameters* that count, I am among the more liberated women in my zip code —Gael Greene⟩ **3 :** a limit or boundary ⟨still operated within the *parameters* of the classical Western culture —E. B. Fiske⟩

pa·ram·e·ter·ize \pǝ'ramǝd·ǝ,rīz, 'pram-\ *or* **pa·ram·e·trize** \-mǝ,trīz\ *vt* **-ter·ized** *or* **-trized; -ter·iz·ing** *or* **-triz·ing :** to express in terms of parameters — **pa·ram·e·ter·iza·tion** \-,ramǝd·ǝrǝ'zāshǝn, ,pram-, -mǝ·trǝ-, -,ì'zā-\ *or* **pa·ram·e·tri·za·tion** \-mǝ·trǝ-\ *n*

para·met·ric amplifier \,parǝ,me·trik-\ *n* **:** a high-frequency amplifier whose operation is based on time variations in a parameter (as reactance) and which converts the energy at the frequency of an alternating current into energy at the input signal frequency in such a way as to amplify the signal

parametric equation *n* **:** any of a set of equations that express the coordinates of the points of a curve as functions of one parameter or that express the coordinates of the points of a surface as functions of two parameters

para·my·o·sin \,parǝ,mīǝsǝn\ *n* **:** a fibrous protein that is found in molluscan muscle

para·myxo·vi·rus \-,miksǝ,vīrǝs\ *n* **:** any of a group of RNA-containing viruses (as the mumps virus) that are larger than the related myxoviruses

para·po·lit·i·cal \-pǝ,lid·ǝkǝl\ *adj* **:** existing alongside a political structure or group in a professedly nonpolitical capacity ⟨*parapolitical* jobs like university presidencies — Adam Hochschild⟩

para·pro·fes·sion·al \-prǝ,feshnǝl, -ǝnǝl\ *n* **:** a trained aide who assists a professional person (as a teacher or physician) ⟨numbers of *paraprofessionals* serving more of the population at a lower technical level —E.Z. Friedenberg⟩ — **paraprofessional** *adj*

para·pro·tein \-'prō͟tēn, -'prōd·ēͻn\ *n* **:** any of various abnormal serum globulins with unique physical and electrophoretic characteristics

para·pro·tein·emia \͟parͻ͟prō͟tē'nēmēͻ, -ōd·ēͻ'n-\ *n* [*paraprotein* + *-emia* blood condition, deriv. of Gk *haima* blood] **:** the abnormal presence of a paraprotein in the blood

para·quat \'parͻ͟kwät\ *n* [*para-* + *quat*ernary] **:** an herbicide containing a salt of a cation $C_{12}H_{14}N_2$ that is used esp. as a weed killer

para·sex·u·al \͟parͻ͟seksh(ͻ)wͻl, -shͻl\ *adj* **:** relating to or being reproduction that results in recombination of genes from different individuals but does not involve meiosis and formation of a zygote by fertilization as in sexual reproduction ⟨the *parasexual* cycle in some fungi⟩

para·sex·u·al·i·ty*\-͟sekshͻ'walͻd·ē, -i\ *n* **:** the state of being parasexual

para·ven·tri·cu·lar nucleus \͟parͻ(͟)ven·͟trikyͻlͻ(r)-\ *n* **:** a nucleus in the hypothalamus that produces vasopressin and esp. oxytocin and that innervates the neurohypophysis

para·wing \'parͻ͟wiŋ\ *n* [*para*chute + *wing*] **:** PARAGLIDER

par·ent·ing \'parͻntiŋ, 'per-\ *n* [fr. gerund of *parent*, vb.] **:** the giving of guidance, care, and affection to a child by its parents ⟨felt *parenting* was his wife's job more than his —Virginia Satir⟩

par·gy·line \'pärjͻ͟lēn\ *n* [*pro*pargyl, an alcohol + *-ine* chemical substance] **:** a monoamine oxidase inhibitor $C_{11}H_{13}N$ whose hydrochloride is used as an antihypertensive and antidepressant agent

pa·ri·etals \pͻ'rīͻd·ͻlz\ *n pl* **:** the regulations governing the visiting privileges of members of the opposite sex in campus dormitories

par·i·ty*\'parͻd·ē, -i, *also* 'per-\ *n* **1 a :** the property of an integer with respect to being odd or even ⟨3 and 7 have the same *parity*⟩ **b :** the property of oddness or evenness of an odd or even function (as certain functions in quantum mechanics) **c** (1) **:** the state of being odd or even used as the basis of a method of detecting errors in binary-coded data (2) **:** PARITY BIT **2 :** the property of an elementary particle or physical system that indicates whether or not its mirror image occurs in nature

parity bit *n* **:** a bit added to an array of bits (as on magnetic tape) to provide parity

parking orbit *n* **:** the orbit of an artificial satellite or a space vehicle traveling around a body (as the earth) in such a way as to serve as a station from which another vehicle is launched or as to be itself propelled later into a new trajectory

Par·kin·son's Law \͟pärkͻnsͻnz-, ͟päk-\ *n* [C. Northcote *Parkinson* b1909 Eng. historian] **1 :** an observation in office organization: the number of subordinates increases at a fixed rate regardless of the amount of work produced **2 :** an observation in office organization: work expands so as to fill the time available for its completion

par·o·mo·my·cin \͟parͻmō'mīsᵊn\ *n* [Gk *paromoios* closely resembling (fr. *para-* beside + *homoios* like) + E connective *-o-* + *-mycin* substance obtained from a fungus, fr. *streptomycin;* fr. its similarity to neomycin] **:** a broad-spectrum antibiotic $C_{23}H_{45}N_5O_{14}$ that is obtained from a streptomyces (*Streptomyces rimosus* subspecies

paromycinus) and is used against intestinal amebiasis esp. in the form of its sulfate

Par·so·ni·an \pär'sōnēͻn, pͻ's-\ *adj* [Talcott *Parsons* †1979 Am. sociologist] **:** of or relating to the sociological theories of Talcott Parsons

Parsons table *n* [prob. fr. the name *Parsons*] **:** a rectangular table having straight legs that form the four corners

partially ordered *adj* **:** having some but not all mathematical elements connected by a relation that is transitive and not symmetric

partial product *n* **:** a product obtained by multiplying a multiplicand by one digit of a multiplier with more than one digit

par·ti·cle·board \'pärd·ͻkͻl͟bō(ͻ)rd, -͟bȯ(ͻ)rd; 'pȧd-, -͟bȯͻd, -͟bȯ(ͻ)d\ *n* **:** a composition board made of very small pieces of wood bonded together (as with a synthetic resin)

particle physics *n* **:** HIGH-ENERGY PHYSICS

partition*n **1 :** any of the expressions that for a given positive integer consist of a sum of positive integers equal to the given integer ⟨1 + 2 + 3 is a *partition* of 6⟩ **2 :** the separation of a set (as the points of a line) into subsets such that every element belongs to one set and no two subsets have an element in common

par·ton \'pär͟tän\ *n* [*part* + *-on* elementary particle] **:** a hypothetical particle (as a quark or a gluon) that is held to be a constituent of hadrons

party poop·er \-͟püpͻ(r)\ *n* **:** one who refuses to join in the fun at a party; *broadly* **:** one who refuses to go along with everyone else ⟨I hate to be a *party pooper* but I did not find it "dazzling" or "a smash" or "a milestone in TV entertainment"—Goodman Ace⟩

parv·al·bu·min \͟pärval͟byümͻn, -͟min, ͟pȧv-, *sometimes* -͟albyͻ-\ *n* [*parv-* small + *albumin*] **:** a small calcium-binding protein in vertebrate skeletal muscle

par·vo·vi·rus \͟pärvō͟vīrͻs, ͟pȧv-\ *n* [*parvo-* small + *virus*] **:** any of a group of small DNA-containing viruses that are thought to include the virus causing infectious hepatitis

par·y·lene \'parͻ͟lēn\ *n* [contr. of *paraxylene*] **:** any of several thermoplastic crystalline materials that are polymers of paraxylene and are used esp. as electrical insulation coating

pas·cal \pas'kal, pȧs'kȧl\ *n* [Blaise *Pascal* †1662 Fr. scientist and philosopher] **1 :** a unit of pressure in the mks system equivalent to one newton per square meter **2** *cap P or all cap* **:** a computer programming language developed from Algol and designed to process both numerical and textual data

pas de deux*\͟pädͻ'dā, -'dͻr, -'dü\ *n* **:** an intricate relationship or activity involving two parties or things ⟨every play written for the stage is . . . a *pas de deux* between language and action —Hilton Kramer⟩

pass–fail \'pas'fā(ͻ)l\ *n* **:** a system of grading whereby the grades "pass" and "fail" replace the traditional letter grades — **pass–fail** *adj*

passive*adj **1 :** not involving expenditure of chemical energy ⟨*passive* transport across a cell membrane⟩ **2 a :** exhibiting no gain or control — used of an electronic device (as a capacitor or resistor) **b :** operating solely by means of the power of an input signal ⟨a *passive* communication satellite that reflects television signals⟩ **c :** relating to the detection of or to orientation by means of an object through its emission of energy ⟨a *passive* microwave radiometer⟩ **3 :** making direct use of the sun's heat usu. without the intervention of mechanical devices ⟨a *passive* solar house⟩

passive immunization *n* **:** the process of conferring passive immunity

passive restraint *n* **:** a restraint (as an air bag or self=locking seat belt) that acts automatically to protect an automobile passenger during a crash

pasteurization*n **:** partial sterilization of perishable food products (as fruit or fish) with radiation (as gamma rays)

past·ies \'pāstēz\ *n pl* [*paste* to stick + *-ie*, dim. suffix] **:** small usu. round coverings for a woman's nipples worn esp. by a stripteaser ⟨she popped out of a birthday cake, wearing only *pasties* and a black garter —Timothy Ferris⟩

pas·ti·na \pä'stēnə\ *n* [It *pastina*, dim. of *pasta*] **:** very small bits of pasta used in soup or broth

pas·tis \pa'stis, -ēs\ *n* [F] **:** a French liqueur flavored with aniseed that is usu. drunk mixed with water

pata·phys·ics \ˌpad-ə¦'fiziks\ *n pl but sing in constr* [F *pataphysique*] **:** intricate and whimsical nonsense intended as a parody of science — **pata·phys·i·cal** \-əkəl\ *adj* — **pata·phy·si·cian** \-fə¦'zishən\ *n*

patch*n **:** a temporary correction in a faulty computer program

patch*vt **1 :** to make a patch in (a computer program) **2 :** to connect (as circuits) by a patch cord

patch·board \'pach̩bō(ə)rd, -̩bȯ(ə)rd, -̩bōəd, -̩bȯ(ə)d\ *n* **:** a plugboard in which circuits are interconnected by patch cords

patch panel *n* **:** PATCHBOARD

path*n **:** a sequence of arcs in a network that can be traced continuously without retracing any arc

patho·mor·phol·o·gy \ˌpathō(̩)mȯr¦'fäləjē\ *n* [*patho-* disease (deriv. of Gk *pathos*, lit., suffering) + *morphology*] **:** morphology of abnormal conditions — **patho·mor·pho·log·i·cal** \-ˌmȯrfə¦'läjəkəl\ *or* **patho·mor·pho·log·ic** \-jik\ *adj*

pa·tri·fo·cal \ˌpa·trə¦'fōkəl, ¦pä-\ *adj* [*patri-* father (fr. L *pater*) + *focal*] **:** gravitating toward or centered on the father **:** patricentric ⟨a *patrifocal* family structure⟩

patterning*n **:** physiotherapy that is designed to improve malfunctioning nervous control by means of feedback from muscular activity imposed by an outside source or induced by other muscles

pat·zer \'pätsə(r), 'pat-\ *n* [G *patzer* blunderer, fr. *patzen* to blunder] **:** an inept chess player

pau·piette \pō'pyet, (̩)pōpē'et\ *n* [F] **:** a thin slice of meat or fish wrapped around a forcemeat filling

pay*vb — **pay one's dues** *also* **pay dues** **1 :** to experience life's hardships **:** earn a right or position through experience, suffering, or hard work ⟨the importance of hard work, long hours — the *dues* they've *paid* to get where they are today —Laurence Bergreen⟩ **2 :** to suffer the consequences of or penalty for an act ⟨beware of the potential juror who has had unpleasant encounters with the law . . . having *paid his dues* he may be determined that you won't avoid yours —Robert Wieder⟩

pay–ca·ble \(')pā¦kābəl\ *n* **:** pay-TV sending programs through a cable television system to customers provided

with a special signal decoder — compare SUBSCRIPTION TV

pay·load*\'pā̩lōd\ *n* **:** the load that is carried by a spacecraft and that consists of things (as passengers or instruments) which relate directly to the purpose of the flight as opposed to things (as fuel) which are necessary for operation; *also* **:** the weight of such a load

pay·out ratio \'pā̩aùt-\ *n* **:** a ratio relating dividend payout of a company to its earnings or cash flow

pay television *n* **:** PAY-TV

pay–TV \'pā(̩)tē¦vē\ *n* **:** a service providing special noncommercial television programming (as recent movies or entertainment specials) by means of a scrambled signal over the air or through a cable system to subscribers who are provided with a signal decoding device — compare PAY-CABLE, SUBSCRIPTION TV

pazazz *var of* PIZZAZZ

PC*abbr professional corporation

PCB \ˌpē(̩)sē'bē\ *n* [*p*olychlorinated *b*iphenyl] **:** POLYCHLORINATED BIPHENYL

PCP \ˌpē(̩)sē'pē\ *n* **1** [prob. fr. *p*hencyclidine + *pill*] **:** PHENCYCLIDINE **2 :** a crystalline compound C_6Cl_5OH **:** pentachlorophenol

PCV valve *n* [*p*ositive *c*rankcase *v*entilation] **:** an automotive-emission control valve that recirculates gases (as from blow-by) through the combustion chambers to permit more complete combustion

PE*abbr physical education

peaceful co·ex·is·tence \-ˌkōəg'zistən(t)s\ *n* **:** a living together in peace rather than in constant hostility ⟨the *peaceful coexistence* of states with different social systems —A.P. Mendel⟩

peace·nik \'pē¦snik\ *n* [*peace* + *-nik* one connected with] **:** an opponent of war ⟨none are all the *peaceniks* in Israel young —Georgiana G. Stevens⟩; *specif* **:** one who participates in antiwar demonstrations ⟨pictures of protesting social workers, schoolteachers, *peaceniks* or whoever marching around carrying signs —*Wall Street Jour.*⟩

peace sign *n* **:** a sign made by holding the palm outward and forming a V with the index and middle fingers that is used to indicate the desire for peace or as a greeting or farewell

peace symbol *n* **:** the symbol ⊕ used to signify peace

peaches–and–cream *adj* **:** of, relating to, or having a smooth wholesome complexion

pearl**vi, of a surfboard* **:** to make a nose dive into the trough of a wave

peat·land \'pēt̩land\ *n* **:** land rich in peat

Peck's bad boy \ˌpeks-\ *n* [fr. the book *Peck's Bad Boy and his Pa* (1883) by George Wilbur Peck †1916 Am. journalist, humorist, and politician] **:** one whose bad behavior is a source of embarrassment or annoyance ⟨industry, the *Peck's bad boy* of environmentalism —*Newsweek*⟩

pedal steel *or* **pedal steel guitar** *n* **:** a box-shaped musical instrument with legs that has usu. 10 strings which are plucked with metal finger picks and of which the pitch may be adjusted either by sliding a steel bar along them or by using foot pedals to change their tension

pe·des·tri·an·ize*\pə'destrēə̩nīz\ *vt* **-ized; -iz·ing :** to convert into a walkway or mall — **pe·des·tri·an·iza·tion** \pə̩destrēənə'zāshən, -ˌnī'z-\ *n*

pe·do·phile \'pēdə,fīl\ *n* [back-formation fr. *pedophilia*] **:** one affected with pedophilia

peek–a–boo \'pēkə,bü\ *adj* **:** of, relating to, or being a document retrieval system in which desired documents are identified by light shining through matching holes in index cards

peel*vi **:** to break away from a group or formation — often used with *off*

Pe·king duck \,pē,kiŋ-, pā-\ *n* [*Peking*, China] **:** a Chinese dish consisting of roasted duck meat and strips of crispy duck skin topped with scallions and sauce and wrapped in thin pancakes

Pe·king·ol·o·gy \,pē(,)kiŋ'äləjē, pē',kiŋ-\ *n* [*Peking* + connective -*o*- + -*logy* theory, science, deriv. of Gk *logos* word] **:** the study of the policies and practices of Communist China — **Pe·king·ol·o·gist** \-jəst\ *n*

pel·o·ton \,pelə'tän, *F* plȯtōⁿ\ *or* **peloton glass** *n* [prob. fr. *F peloton* ball, ball of string] **:** a European ornamental glass often with a variegated metallized and satinized surface and usu. overlaid with strands of contrasting color

pem·o·line \'pemə,lēn, -ələn\ *n* [perh. fr. *phenyl* + *imino* + oxa*zolidinone*, a derivative of oxazolidine] **:** a synthetic organic drug $C_9H_8N_2O_2$ that is usu. mixed with magnesium hydroxide, is a mild stimulant of the central nervous system, and is used experimentally to improve memory

pen·ta·gas·trin \,pentə'gastrən\ *n* [*penta*peptide + *gastrin*, a hormone that induces secretion of gastric juice] **:** a pentapeptide $C_{37}H_{49}N_7O_9S$ that stimulates gastric acid secretion

pen·ta·pep·tide \,pentə'pep,tīd\ *n* [*penta*- five (deriv. of Gk *pente*) + *peptide*] **:** a polypeptide that contains five amino acid residues

pen·taz·o·cine \pen'tazə,sēn, -əsən\ *n* [*pent*- five + -*azocine* (as in *phenazocine*)] **:** an analgesic drug $C_{19}H_{27}NO$ that is less addictive than morphine

pen·to·bar·bi·tone \,pentō'bärbə,tōn\ *n* [*pent*- + connective -*o*- + *barbitone*] *Brit* **:** a granular barbiturate $C_{11}H_{18}N_2O_3$ used esp. in the form of its sodium or calcium salt as a sedative, hypnotic, and antispasmodic **:** pentobarbital

people mover *n* **:** any of various rapid-transit systems (as of moving sidewalks or automated driverless cars) for shuttling people (as within an airport or to and from it)

people's republic *n*, *often cap P&R* **:** a republic organized and controlled by a national Communist party

pepper steak *n* **1 :** thin-sliced steak cooked with green peppers, onions, tomatoes, and soy sauce **2 :** STEAK AU POIVRE

pep·ti·do·gly·can \,pep,tīdō'glī,kan\ *n* [*peptide* + connective -*o*- + *glycan*] **:** a polymer that is composed of polysaccharide and peptide chains and is found esp. in bacterial cell walls — called also *murein*

per·cen·tile*\pə(r)'sen,tīl\ *n* **:** a value on a scale of one hundred that indicates the percent of a distribution that is equal to or below it (as in performance) ⟨a score in the 95th *percentile* is a score equal to or better than 95 percent of the scores⟩

per·cia·tel·li \,perchə'te(l)lē, ,pər-\ *n* [It] **:** long tubular pasta slightly larger than spaghetti

pe·re·on·ite \pə'rēə,nīt\ *n* [*pereon* (var. of *pereion*) + -*ite* segment] **:** any of the segments of a pereion

per·fec·ta \pə(r)'fektə\ *n* [AmerSp (*quiniela*) *perfecta* perfect quiniela] **:** a betting pool in which the bettor wins by picking the first and second finishers in a specified race or contest in the correct order — called also *exacta*

performance*n **:** linguistic behavior — contrasted with *competence*

per·for·ma·tive \pər'fȯrməd·iv, -'fȯ(ə)m-\ *n* [*perform* + -*ative* (as in *imperative*)] **:** an expression that serves to effect a transaction or that constitutes the performance of the specified act by virtue of its utterance ⟨many *performatives* are *contractual* ("I bet") or *declaratory* ("I declare war") utterances —J.L. Austin⟩ — **performative** *adj*

peri·ap·sis \,perē'apsəs\ *n*, *pl* **-ap·si·des** \-'apsə,dēz\ [NL, fr. *peri*- around, near (deriv. of Gk *peri*) + *apsis*] **:** the apsis least distant from the center of attraction

peri·car·dio·cen·te·sis \,perə',kärdēō(,)sen',tēsəs\ *n* [NL, fr. *pericardi*- pericardium + *centesis*] **:** surgical puncture of the pericardium esp. to aspirate pericardial fluid

peri·cyn·thi·on \,perə'sin(t)thēən\ *n* [NL, fr. *peri*- + *Cynthia*, goddess of the moon (fr. Gk *Kynthia*) + -*on* (as in *aphelion*)] **:** PERILUNE

peri·lune \'perə,lün\ *n* [*peri*- + L *luna* moon] **:** the point in the path of a body orbiting the moon that is nearest to the center of the moon

peri·nu·cle·ar \,perə'n(y)üklēə(r), ÷ -kyələ(r)\ *adj* **:** situated around or surrounding the nucleus of a cell ⟨*perinuclear* structures⟩

pe·riph·er·al*\pə'rif(ə)rəl\ *adj* **:** auxiliary, supplementary ⟨a computer's *peripheral* equipment⟩; *also* **:** of or relating to computer peripherals

peripheral *n* **:** a device connected to a computer to provide communication (as input and output) or auxiliary functions (as additional storage)

peri·se·lene \'perəsə,lēn\ *n* [ISV *peri*- + -*selene*, fr. Gk *selēnē* moon] **:** PERILUNE

peri·se·le·ni·um \,perəsə'lēnēəm\ *n* [NL, fr. Gk *peri- peri*- + *selēnē* moon + NL -*ium*, alter. of -*ion* (as in *aphelion*)] **:** PERILUNE

peri·stal·tic pump \,perə'stȯltik-, -'stal-\ *n* **:** a pump in which fluid is forced along by waves of contraction produced mechanically on flexible tubing

pe·ri·tus \pə'rēd·əs\ *n*, *pl* **pe·ri·ti** \-ēd·ē, -ē,tē\ [NL, fr. L *peritus*, adj., skilled, experienced] **:** an expert (as in theology or canon law) who advises and assists the hierarchy (as in the drafting of schemata) at a Vatican council

per·lo·cu·tion·ary \,pərlō'kyüsh(ə),nerē, 'pāl-\ *adj* [*per*- by means of + *locutionary*] **:** of or relating to an act (as persuading, frightening, or annoying) performed by a speaker upon a listener by means of an utterance — compare ILLOCUTIONARY, LOCUTIONARY — **per·lo·cu·tion** \-shən\ *n*

¹perm \'pərm, 'pām, 'pəim\ *vt* [*perm* permanent wave] **:** to give (hair) a permanent wave

²perm \'pām, 'pərm\ *n* [short for *permutation*] *Brit* **:** an arrangement of all possible combinations of a selected number of competitors for wagering on predicted winners (as in a football pool) or the order of finish (as in a horse race)

³perm *vt*, *Brit* **:** to select (a number of competitors) for a betting perm

permanent press *n* **1 :** the process of treating a fabric with a chemical (as a resin) and heat for setting the shape and for aiding wrinkle resistance **2 :** material treated by permanent press **3 :** the condition of material treated by permanent press — **permanent–press** *adj*

per·me·ase \'pərmē̠ās, 'pōm-, 'pəim-, -āz\ *n* [ISV *perme-* (fr. *permeate*) + *-ase* enzyme] **:** an enzyme that catalyzes the transport of another substance across a cell membrane

per·oxi·some \pə'räksə̠sōm\ *n* [*perox*ide + *-some* body, deriv. of Gk *sōma*] **:** a cytoplasmic cell organelle containing enzymes for the production and decomposition of hydrogen peroxide — **per·oxi·som·al** \-̠räksə̠'sōməl\ *adj*

per·phe·na·zine \(̠)pə(r)'fēnə̠zēn, -'fen-\ *n* [*piperazine* + *phen*yl] **:** a phenothiazine tranquilizer $C_{21}H_{26}ClN_3OS$ that is used to control tension, anxiety, and agitation esp. in psychotic conditions

persistent*adj **1 :** degraded only slowly by the environment ⟨*persistent* pesticides⟩ **2 :** remaining infective for a relatively long time in a vector after an initial period of incubation ⟨*persistent* viruses⟩

personality inventory *n* **:** any of several tests that attempt to characterize the personality of an individual by objective scoring of replies to numerous questions concerning his or her own behavior and attitudes — see MINNESOTA MULTIPHASIC PERSONALITY INVENTORY

personal tax *n* **:** a tax exacted directly from the person on whom the ultimate burden of the tax is expected to fall **:** a direct tax

per·son·hood \'pərsⁿn̠hu̇d, 'pās-, 'pəis-\ *n* **:** the fact or state of being a person ⟨even while infringing these rights, we recognize them as rights. They are the privileges of *personhood* —Willard Gaylin & Marc Lappé⟩; *esp* **:** one's distinctive personal identity ⟨the brave, awkward attempts made . . . to assert their pride and *personhood* — Dotson Rader⟩

PERT \'pərt\ *n* [*program evaluation and review technique*] **:** a technique for planning, scheduling, and monitoring a complex project esp. by graphically displaying the separate tasks and showing how they are interconnected

pe·se·wa \pə'säwə\ *n* [native name in Ghana] **1 :** a monetary unit of Ghana equal to ¹/₁₀₀ cedi **2 :** a coin representing one pesewa

Pe·ter Principle \'pēd-ə(r)-\ *n* [Laurence Johnston *Peter* b1919 Am. (Canad.-born) educator, its formulator] **:** an observation: in a hierarchy every employee tends to rise to the level of his incompetence

pe·tit bour·geois \̠ped-ē̠'bu̇(ə)rzh̠'wä, pə̠tē(t)-; -̠bu̇(ə)zh̠'wä, -̠wà; *sometimes* -'bu̇zh̠-\ *adj* **:** of, relating to, or characteristic of the petite bourgeoisie

pet·nap·ping \'pet̠napiŋ\ *n* [*pet* + *-napping* (as in *kidnapping*)] **:** the act of stealing a pet (as a cat or dog) usu. for profit

pet·ro·dol·lar \̠pe·trō̠dälə(r)\ *adj* **:** of, relating to, or involving petrodollars

pet·ro·dol·lars \'pe·trō̠dälə(r)z\ *n pl* [*petro*leum + *dollars*] **:** foreign exchange obtained by petroleum-exporting countries through sales abroad; *esp* **:** the part in excess of domestic needs that constitutes a pool of potential foreign investment

pet·ro·pol·i·tics \-̠pälə̠tiks\ *n pl* [*petro*leum + *politics*] **:** the strategy of controlling petroleum sales as a way of achieving international political goals

petting zoo *n* **:** a collection of farm animals (as baby goats and pigs) or gentle exotic animals (as llamas) for children to pet and feed

PF**abbr, usu not cap* personal foul

pg*abbr picogram

PG \(̠)pē'jē\ *adj* [*parental guidance*] *of a motion picture* **:** of such a nature that persons of all ages may be allowed admission but parental guidance is suggested — compare G, R, X

phago·some \'fagə̠sōm\ *n* [*phago-* eating, feeding (fr. Gk *phagein* to eat) + *-some* body, deriv. of Gk *sōma*] **:** a membrane-surrounded vesicle that encloses materials taken into the cell by endocytosis

phal·lic**\'falik\ *adj* **:** of, relating to, or being the stage of psychosexual development in psychoanalytic theory during which a child becomes interested in his own sexual organs — **phal·li·cal·ly** \'falək(ə)lē\ *adv*

phar·ma·co·ge·net·ics \̠färməkōjə'ned·iks\ *n pl but sing in constr* [ISV *pharmaco-* medicine, drug (fr. Gk *pharmakon*) + *genetics*] **:** the study of the interrelation of hereditary constitution and variation in response to drugs — **phar·ma·co·ge·net·ic** \-ik\ *adj*

phase·down \'fāz̠dau̇n\ *n* **:** a gradual reduction (as in size or operation) **:** a slowing down by phases

phase·out \'fā̠zau̇t\ *n* **:** a gradual stopping of operations or production **:** a closing down by phases

phe·naz·o·cine \fə'nazə̠sēn, -əsə̠n\ *n* [*phenyl* + *-azocine* (perh. irreg. fr. *azoic* containing an azo group + *-ine* chemical substance)] **:** a drug $C_{22}H_{27}NO$ related to morphine that has greater pain-relieving and slighter narcotic effect

phen·cy·cli·dine \(')fen'siklə̠dēn, -'sīk-, -ədə̠n\ *n* [*phenyl* + *cyc*lic + *-idine* related compound] **:** a piperidine derivative $C_{17}H_{25}N$ used medicinally as an anesthetic and sometimes illicitly as a psychedelic drug to induce vivid mental imagery — called also PCP

phen·el·zine \'fenᵊl̠zēn\ *n* [*phenyl* + *ethyl* + *hydrazine*] **:** a monoamine oxidase inhibitor $C_8H_{12}N_2$ used esp. as an antidepressant drug

phe·neth·i·cil·lin \fə̠nethə'silən\ *n* [*phenyl* + *ethyl* + *penicillin*] **:** a synthetic penicillin administered orally and used esp. in the treatment of less severe infections caused by bacteria that do not produce penicillinase

phe·net·ic \fə'ned·ik\ *adj* [*phenotype* + *-etic* (as in *genetic*)] **:** of, relating to, or being classificatory systems and procedures that are based on overall similarity usu. of many characters without regard to the evolutionary history of the organisms involved — compare CLADISTIC

phe·net·ics \-iks\ *n pl but sing in constr* **:** biological systematics based on phenetic relationships — **phe·net·i·cist** \-'ned·əsəst\ *n*

phen·met·ra·zine \(')fen'me·trə̠zēn\ *n* [*phenyl* + *meth*yl + *tetra-* four + *oxazine*] **:** a sympathomimetic stimulant $C_{11}H_{15}NO$ used in the hydrochloride as an appetite suppressant

phe·no·thi·azine**\fēnō'thīə̠zēn\ *n* **:** any of various phenothiazine derivatives (as chlorpromazine) that are used as tranquilizing agents esp. in the treatment of schizophrenia

phe·noxy·ben·za·mine \fə;näksē;benzə,mēn\ *n* [ISV *phen-* phenyl + *oxy-* oxygen + *benz-* containing a benzene ring + *amine*] **:** a drug $C_{18}H_{22}ClNO$ that blocks the activity of alpha-receptors and is used as the hydrochloride esp. to produce peripheral vasodilatation

phen·tol·amine \fen'tälə,mēn, -əmən\ *n* [*phenyl* + *tolui*dine + *amine*] **:** an adrenergic blocking agent $C_{17}H_{19}N_3O$ that is used esp. in the diagnosis of hypertension due to pheochromocytoma

phe·ren·ta·sin \fə'rentəsən\ *n* [Gk *pherein* to carry + *entasis* tension, stretching + E -*in* chemical compound] **:** a pressor amine present in the blood in severe hypertension

pher·o·mone \'ferə,mōn\ *n* [ISV *phero-* (fr. Gk *pherein* to carry) + -*mone* (as in *hormone*); orig. formed as G *pheromon;* fr. its conveying information from one individual to another] **:** a chemical substance that is produced by an animal and serves as a specific stimulus to other individuals of the same species for one or more behavioral responses — **pher·o·mon·al** \-nᵊl\ *adj* — **pher·o·mon·al·ly** \-nᵊlē, -i\ *adv*

Phil·lips curve \,filəps-\ *n* [A.W.H. *Phillips b*1914 Brit. economist] **:** a graphic representation of the relation between inflation and unemployment which indicates that as the rate of either increases that of the other declines

phil·lu·men·ist \fə'lümənəst\ *n* [*phil-* loving (deriv. of Gk *philos* beloved, loving) + L *lumen* light + E -*ist*, n. suffix] **:** one who collects matchbooks or matchbox labels

phle·bol·o·gy \flə'bäləjē\ *n* [ISV *phlebo-* vein (deriv. of Gk *phleb-, phleps*) + -*logy* theory, science, deriv. of Gk *logos* word] **:** a branch of medicine concerned with the veins — **phle·bol·o·gist** \-jəst\ *n*

phone–in \'fō,nin\ *adj* **:** CALL-IN

pho·no·car·dio·graph \;fōnə;kärdēə,graf\ *n* **:** a recording instrument used in phonocardiography

pho·no·car·dio·graph·ic \-,kärdēə;grafik\ *also* **pho·no·car·dio·graph·i·cal** \-əkəl\ *adj* **:** of, relating to, or involving phonocardiography or a phonocardiogram — **pho·no·car·dio·graph·i·cal·ly** \-ək(ə)lē, -i\ *adv*

pho·no·rec·ord \'fōnō,rekə(r)d, *also* -k,ó(ə)rd *or* -k,ó(ə)d\ *n* [*phono*graph + *record*] **:** a phonograph record

pho·no·tac·tics \,fōnə'taktiks\ *n pl but sing in constr* [*phono-* sound, voice (deriv. of Gk *phōnē*) + *tactics*] **:** the area of phonology concerned with the analysis and description of the permitted phoneme sequences of a language — **pho·no·tac·tic** \;fōnə;taktik\ *adj*

phor·ate \'fó(ə)r,āt, 'fó(ə)r-\ *n* [*phosphor*us + *thio*n*ate*] **:** a very toxic organophosphate systemic insecticide $C_7H_{17}O_2PS_3$ that is used esp. to treat seeds

phos·pham·i·don \fäs'famə,dän\ *n* [*phosphor*us + *am*ide + -*on* chemical compound] **:** a contact and systemic organophosphorus insecticide and miticide $C_{10}H_{19}ClNO_5P$

phos·pha·ti·dyl·cho·line \,fäsfə;tīdᵊl;kō,lēn, fäs-;fad-əd²l-\ *n* [*phosphatidyl* + *choline*] **:** any of several waxy hygroscopic phosphatides that are widely distributed in animals and plants, form colloidal solutions in water, and have emulsifying, wetting, and antioxidant properties **:** lecithin

phos·pha·ti·dyl·eth·a·nol·amine \-,ethə;nōlə,mēn, -;nōl-\ *n* [*phosphatidyl* + *ethanolamine*] **:** any of a group

of phospholipids that occur esp. in blood plasma and in the white matter of the central nervous system **:** cephalin

phos·pho·enol·pyr·uvate \'fäs,fōə,nólpī'rü,vāt, -,nōl-, -,pī(ə)r'yü-\ *n* [*phosphoenolpyruv*ic (acid) + -*ate* salt or ester] **:** a salt or ester of phosphoenolpyruvic acid

phos·pho·fruc·to·ki·nase \'fäs(,)fō,frəktō'kī,nās, -frük-, -frük-, -,nāz\ *n* [*phosphor*us + *fruct*ose + *kinase*] **:** an enzyme that functions in carbohydrate metabolism and esp. in glycolysis by catalyzing the transfer of a second phosphate (as from ATP) to fructose

phos·pho·glyc·er·al·de·hyde \;fäs(,)fō,glisə'raldə,hīd\ *n* **:** a phosphate of glyceraldehyde $C_3H_5O_3(H_2PO_3)$ that is formed esp. in anaerobic metabolism of carbohydrates by the splitting of a diphosphate of fructose

phos·pho·ki·nase \-;kī,nās, -,nāz\ *n* **:** an enzyme that catalyzes the transfer of phosphate groups from ATP or ADP to a substrate

phos·pho·pyr·uvate \-pī'rü,vāt, -(,)pī(ə)r'yü-\ *n* **:** PHOS-PHOENOLPYRUVATE

phos·pho·trans·fer·ase \;fäs(,)fō;tran(t)sfə,rās, -āz, -;tranzf-\ *n* **:** any of several enzymes that catalyze the transfer of phosphorus-containing groups from one compound to another

pho·to·bi·ol·o·gist \'fōd·(,)ōbī;älə,jəst\ *n* **:** a specialist in photobiology

¹pho·to·chro·mic \;fōd·ə;krōmik\ *adj* [*photo-* light (fr. Gk *phōt-, phōs*) + *chrom-* color (deriv. of Gk *chrōma*) + -*ic*, adj. suffix] **1 :** capable of changing color on exposure to radiant energy (as light) ⟨*photochromic* glass⟩ ⟨*photochromic* proteins⟩ **2 :** of, relating to, or utilizing the change of color shown by a photochromic substance ⟨a *photochromic* process⟩ — **pho·to·chro·mism** \-,mizəm\ *n*

²photochromic *n* **:** a photochromic substance

pho·to·co·ag·u·la·tion \;fōd·ō(,)kō,agyə'lāshən\ *n* **:** surgical coagulation of tissue by means of a precisely oriented high-energy light source (as a laser beam) — **pho·to·co·ag·u·la·tive** \-kō;agyə,lād·iv, -ēv\ *adj* — **pho·to·co·ag·u·la·tor** \-kō;agyə,lād·ə(r)\ *n*

pho·to·di·ode \;fōd·ō;dī,ōd\ *n* **:** a semiconductor device for detecting and measuring radiant energy (as light) by means of its conversion into an electric current

pho·to·es·say \;fōd·ō'es,ā\ *n* **:** an analytic or interpretive photographic presentation usu. dealing with its subject from a personal point of view

pho·to·fab·ri·ca·tion \;fōd·(,)ō,fabrə;kāshən\ *n* [*photo*-photograph, photographic + *fabrication*] **:** a process for manufacturing components (as microcircuits) in which a design is photographed, reduced, and chemically etched on a surface (as of a semiconductor)

pho·to·in·duced \-ən;d(y)üst\ *adj* **:** induced by the action of light ⟨*photoinduced* color changes⟩

pho·to·isom·er·iza·tion \;fōd·ō(,)ī,sämərə'zāshən, -,rī-'zā-\ *n* **:** the light-initiated process of change from one isomeric form of a compound, radical, or ion to another

photolithography* *n* **:** a process involving the photographic transfer of a pattern to a surface for etching (as in producing an integrated circuit)

pho·to·mor·pho·gen·e·sis \;fōd·ə,mòrfə'jenəsəs\ *n* **:** plant morphogenesis controlled by radiant energy (as light) — **pho·to·mor·pho·gen·ic** \-'jenik\ *adj*

pho·to·phos·phor·y·la·tion \ˌfōd·ō‚fäs‚fȯrəˈlāshən\ *n* **:** the conversion of AMP and ADP to ATP in photosynthesis using radiant energy

pho·to·plate \ˈfōd·ō‚plāt\ *n* **:** a photographic plate

pho·to·po·la·rim·e·ter \ˌfōd·ō‚pōləˈrimәd·ә(r)\ *n* **:** a polarimeter combined with a telescope for producing an image (as of a planet) by means of polarized light

pho·to·poly·mer \ˌfōd·ōˈpäləmə(r)\ *n* **:** a photosensitive plastic used esp. in the manufacture of printing plates

pho·to·re·ac·ti·va·tion \-rē‚aktәˈvāshən\ *n* **:** repair of DNA (as of a bacterium) esp. by a light-dependent enzymatic reaction after damage by ultraviolet irradiation — **pho·to·re·ac·ti·vat·ing** \-ˈaktә‚vād·iŋ\ *adj*

pho·to—re·al·ism \ˌfōd·ōˈrēә‚lizәm, -ˈriә-\ *n* [*photo-* photographic + *realism*] **:** realism in painting characterized by extremely meticulous depiction of detail — **pho·to·re·al·ist** \-ˈәlȯst\ *n or adj*

pho·to·re·sist \-rәˈzist\ *n* **:** a photosensitive resist that polymerizes when exposed to ultraviolet light and that is used in chemical etching

pho·to·res·pi·ra·tion \-‚respәˈrāshәn\ *n* **:** oxidation involving production of carbon dioxide during photosynthesis

pho·to·scan \ˈfōd·ō‚skan\ *n* [*photoscan,* v.] **:** a photographic representation of variation in tissue state (as of the kidney) determined by gamma ray emission from an injected radioactive substance — **photoscan** *vb* — **pho·to·scan·ner** \-‚skanә(r)\ *n*

pho·to·sys·tem \-‚sistәm\ *n* **:** either of two photochemical reactions occurring in chloroplasts: **a :** one that proceeds best in long wavelength light — called also *photosystem I* \-ˈwәn\ **b :** one that proceeds best in short wavelength light — called also *photosystem II* \-ˈtü\

pho·to·tox·ic \ˌfōd·ōˈtäksik\ *adj* **1** *of a substance ingested or brought into contact with skin* **:** rendering the skin susceptible to damage (as sunburn or blisters) upon exposure to light and esp. ultraviolet light **2 :** induced by a phototoxic substance ⟨a *phototoxic* response⟩ — **pho·to·tox·i·oi·ty** \-täk‚sisәd·ē, -i\ *n*

phrase marker *n* **:** a representation of the immediate constituent structure of a linguistic construction

phrase structure *n* **:** the arrangement of the constituents of a sentence

phyl·lo \ˈfē(‚)lō, ˈfi(-\ *n* [modif. of NGk *phyllon* leaf, sheet (of pastry); akin to L *folium* leaf] **:** extremely thin pastry dough that is layered to produce a flaky pastry

phy·tane \ˈfī‚tān\ *n* [*phyt-* plant (deriv. of Gk *phyton*) + *-ane* saturated carbon compound] **:** an isoprenoid hydrocarbon $C_{20}H_{42}$ that is found esp. associated with fossilized plant remains from the Precambrian and later eras

phy·to·alex·in \ˌfid·ōәˈleksәn\ *n* [*phyto-* plant + *alexin*] **:** a chemical substance produced by a plant to combat infection by a pathogen (as a fungus)

phy·to·chem·i·cal \-ˈkemәkәl\ *adj* **:** of, relating to, or being phytochemistry — **phy·to·chem·i·cal·ly** \-k(ә)lē, -li\ *adv*

phy·to·chem·is·try \-ˈkemәstrē\ *n* **:** the chemistry of plants, plant processes, and plant products — **phy·to·chem·ist** \-ˈkemәst\ *n*

phy·to·chrome \ˈfid·ә‚krōm\ *n* [*phyto-* + *-chrome* coloring matter, deriv. of Gk *chrōma* color] **:** a chromoprotein that is present in traces in many plants and that plays a role in initiating floral and developmental processes when activated by red or far-red radiation

phy·to·he·mag·glu·ti·nin *also* **phy·to·hae·mag·glu·ti·nin** \ˌfid·ō‚hēmәˈglütᵊnәn\ *n* **:** a proteinaceous hemagglutinin of plant origin used esp. to induce mitosis (as in lymphocytes)

phy·to·tron \ˈfid·ә‚trän\ *n* [*phyto-* + *-tron* (as in *cyclotron*)] **:** a laboratory with facilities for growing plants under various combinations of strictly controlled environmental conditions

PI*abbr programmed instruction

Pia·get·ian \pyäˈzhäәn\ *adj* [Jean *Piaget* †1980 Swiss psychologist] **:** of, relating to, or dealing with Jean Piaget or his writings, theories, or methods

piano bar *n* **:** a cocktail bar that features live piano music

pic·ca·ta \pәˈkäd·ә, -ätә\ *n* [It *piccata* fried meat interlarded with bacon, fr. *piccare* to prick] **:** thin slices of meat (as veal) sautéed and served in a lemon and butter sauce

pick*n **:** a comb with long widely spaced usu. metal teeth used in grooming an Afro

pi·clo·ram \ˈpiklә‚ram, ˈpik-\ *n* [*picoline* + *chlorine* + *amine*] **:** a systemic herbicide $C_6H_3Cl_3N_2O_2$ that breaks down only very slowly in the soil

pi·co·far·ad \ˌpēkōˈfar‚ad, -ˈfarәd\ *n* [ISV *pico-* one trillionth, very small (perh. fr. It *piccolo* small) + *farad*] **:** one trillionth of a farad

pi·co·gram \ˈpēkә‚gram\ *n* **:** one trillionth of a gram

pi·co·mole \-‚mōl\ *n* **:** one trillionth of a mole

pi·cor·na·vi·rus \pәˈkȯrnә‚vīrәs\ *n* [*pico-* + *RNA* + *virus*] **:** any of a group of RNA-containing viruses that includes the enteroviruses and rhinoviruses

pi·co·sec·ond \ˈpēkō‚sekәnd, -әnt\ *n* **:** one trillionth of a second

piece*n — **piece of the action :** a share in activity or profit ⟨managers and agents and producers and all the others that had a *piece of the action* — Charlie Frick⟩

piece of cake : something easily done **:** cinch, breeze ⟨I tried to put him at ease. "A *piece of cake,*" I said — George Plimpton⟩

piece·wise \ˈpē‚swīz\ *adv* **:** with respect to a number of discrete intervals, sets, or pieces ⟨*piecewise* continuous functions⟩

pig*n **:** a policeman — usu. used disparagingly

piggyback*adj **1 :** of, relating to, or being something (as a capsule or package) carried into space as an extra load by a vehicle (as a spacecraft or rocket) **2 :** of, relating to, or being a radio or television commercial that is presented in addition to other commercials during one commercial break **3 :** supplemental, additional — **piggyback***adv

piggyback**vt :** to set up or cause to function in conjunction with something larger or more important ⟨school bus drivers' union is *piggybacking* its demand for recognition ... on the teachers' strike — *New Orleans (La.) Times-Picayune*⟩ ~ *vi* **:** to function or be carried as if on the back of another

pig out *vi, slang* **:** to eat greedily **:** eat a lot **:** gorge ⟨at dinner I can really *pig out* — Fred Ebb⟩

Pil·i·pi·no \ˌpilәˈpē(‚)nō\ *n* [Pilipino, fr. Sp *Filipino* Philippine] **:** the Tagalog-based official language of the Republic of the Philippines

pill**n, often cap* **:** an oral contraceptive — usu. used with *the*

pill·head \'pil,hed\ *n* **:** a person who takes pills or capsules (as of amphetamines) for nonmedicinal reasons

pillow talk *n* **:** intimate conversation between lovers in bed

pill pool *n* [fr. the drawing of small numbered balls from a bottle to determine order of play] **:** a pocket billiards game in which each player before playing draws from a bottle little numbered balls that are essential to the scoring of the game **:** Kelly pool

pimp·mo·bile \'pimpmō,bēl, -mə,-, *sometimes* -,bil\ *n* **:** an ostentatious customized luxury car that is used by a pimp or looks as if it would be used by a pimp

pi·ña co·la·da \,pēnyəkō'ládə, -kə'-\ *n* [Sp, lit., strained pineapple] **:** a tall drink made of rum, coconut cream, and pineapple juice mixed with ice

pi·ne·a·lec·to·mize \,pinēə'lektə,mīz, ,pī-\ *vt* **-mized; -miz·ing** [*pinealectomy* + *-ize*, vb. suffix] **:** to perform a pinealectomy on

pi·ne·a·lec·to·my \-təmē, -mi\ *n, pl* **-mies** [NL, fr. *pineal body* + *-ectomy* cutting out] **:** surgical removal of the pineal body

ping–pong \'piŋ,päŋ, -,pȯŋ\ *vb* [fr. *Ping-Pong*, a trademark] **:** shift, bounce ⟨avid faces, mostly women's faces whose eyes were rapidly *ping-ponging* back and forth —Grover Lewis⟩

pin·hold·er \'pin,hōldə(r)\ *n* **:** a flower holder that consists of a substantial base topped with projecting pins

pink–col·lar \,piŋk,kälə(r)\ *adj* **:** of, relating to, or constituting a class of employees in occupations traditionally held by women ⟨mature women tend to gravitate toward *pink-collar* jobs as secretaries, nurses, teachers and saleswomen —Emily Greenspan⟩

pi·no·cy·tot·ic \,pinō(,)sī,tä̇d·ik, ,pīn-, -ōsə̇'t-\ *adj* **:** of, relating to, or being pinocytosis — **pi·no·cy·tot·i·cal·ly** \-ək(ə)lē\ *adv*

pinta \'pintə\ *n* [*pint* + *-a* (as in *cuppa*)] *Brit* **:** a pint of milk ⟨if you want to reduce your chance of becoming intoxicated . . . then get down to your *pinta* before the party —*News of the World*⟩

Pin·ter·esque \,pintə'resk\ *adj* [Harold *Pinter* b1930 Eng. dramatist] **:** of, relating to, or characteristic of the writings of Harold Pinter ⟨the dialogue aims mostly for the *Pinteresque* pause-ridden innuendo —John Simon⟩

pin·yin \'pin'yin\ *n, often cap* [Chin (Pek) *p'in*¹ *yin*¹ to spell phonetically, fr. *p'in*¹ to arrange + *yin*¹ sound, pronunciation] **:** a system for romanizing Chinese ideograms

Pis·ce·an \'pisēən, 'pis-, *also* 'piskēən, 'pēsēən\ *n* [*Pisces* + *E* *-an* one belonging to] **:** PISCES

Pisces*n **:** one born under the astrological sign Pisces

pi·sci·cide \'pīsə,sīd, 'pisə-, 'piskə-\ *n* [*pisci-* fish (fr. L *piscis*) + *-cide* killer, deriv. of L *caedere* to cut, kill] **:** a substance used to kill fish — **pi·sci·ci·dal** \-'sīd·l\ *adj*

piss·er \'pisə(r)\ *n* **:** one that is inferior, difficult, or unpleasant — sometimes considered vulgar

piss off \'pis'äf, -'ȯf\ *vi, Brit* **:** to leave forthwith **:** get out — usu. used as a command; sometimes considered vulgar ⟨"How's it going, Michael?" "Piss off," he says. He was losing —Spike Milligan⟩ ~ *vt* **:** to make angry — sometimes considered vulgar

pis·tou \pēstü\ *n* [F] **:** a vegetable soup served with a puree of garlic, herbs, oil, and cheese and often tomatoes

pi·ta \'pēd·ə, -ētə\ *n* [NGk *pita* pie, cake] **:** a thin flat bread that can be separated easily into two layers

pits \'pits\ *n pl* **:** the worst imaginable — used with *the* ⟨the fans were the *pits* —Phil Villapiano⟩ ⟨that'd look the *pits* on me —Jacqueline Bisset⟩ ⟨a package tour that is the *pits* of tourism —Martin Levin⟩ ⟨the material written for me was really the *pits* —Joan Pringle⟩

pit stop *n* **1 :** a stop at a pit during an automobile race **2 :** a stop during a trip (as to get food or fuel or use the rest room); *also* **:** a place where such a stop can be made

pivot*n **:** a key player or position; *specif* **:** an offensive player position in basketball that is occupied by a player (as a center) who stands usu. with his back to his own basket to relay passes, shoot, or provide a screen for teammates

piv·ot·man \'pivət,man, 'pivətmən\ *n* **:** one who plays the pivot; *specif* **:** a center on a basketball team

pix·el \'piksəl, -,sel\ *n* [*pix*, plural of *pic* + *el*ement] **:** any of the numerous small discrete photographic elements that together constitute a picture (as a television image)

piz·zazz *or* **pi·zazz** *also* **pa·zazz** \pə'zaz\ *n* [origin unknown] **:** the quality of being exciting or attractive: as **a :** glamour, showiness ⟨bemoans the lack of color and provocative *pizzazz* in today's stars —Vernon Scott⟩ **b :** spirit, vitality ⟨we had four numbers with *pizzazz* and the rest of the show died around them —Gower Champion⟩

pk*abbr pike

PKU *abbr* phenylketonuria

pla·ce·bo effect \plə'sē(,)bō-\ *n* **:** improvement in the condition of a sick person that occurs in response to treatment but cannot be considered due to the specific treatment used

place value *n* **:** the value of the location of a digit in a numeral ⟨in 425 the location of the digit 2 has a *place value* of ten while the digit itself indicates that there are two tens⟩

¹plane·side \'plān,sīd\ *n* **:** the area adjacent to an airplane ⟨speaking briefly at *planeside* —*Christian Science Monitor*⟩

²planeside *adj* **:** engaged in or made at planeside ⟨paused first for a *planeside* interview —*Time*⟩ ⟨his *planeside* remark —*Newsweek*⟩

plan·e·tol·o·gy \,planə'täləjē\ *n* [*planet* + connective *-o-* + *-logy* science, theory, deriv. of Gk *logos* word] **:** a study that deals with the condensed matter (as the planets, natural satellites, comets, and meteorites) of the solar system — **plan·e·to·log·i·cal** \-ətᵊl'äjəkəl\ *adj* — **plan·e·tol·o·gist** \-'täləjə̇st\ *n*

plaque*n **:** a clear area in a bacterial culture produced by destruction of cells by a virus

plasma*n **:** a collection of charged particles (as in a metal) containing about equal numbers of positive ions and electrons that is a good conductor of electricity

plasma jet *n* **1 :** a stream of very hot gaseous plasma; *also* **:** a device for producing such a stream **2** *or* **plasma engine :** a rocket engine designed to derive thrust from the discharge of a magnetically accelerated plasma

plas·ma·pause \'plazmə,pȯz\ *n* **:** the outer boundary of a plasmasphere

plas·ma·sphere \-ˌsfi(ə)r, -ˌsfiə\ *n* ꞉ a region of a planet's atmosphere containing electrons and highly ionized particles that rotate with the planet

plasma torch *n* ꞉ a device that heats a gas by electrical means to form a plasma for high-temperature operations (as melting metal)

plas·mid \'plazməd\ *n* [*plasma* + *-id* structure, particle] ꞉ an extrachromosomal ring of DNA that replicates autonomously and is found usu. in bacteria

plas·mon \'plaz,män\ *n* [*plasma* + *-on* elementary particle] ꞉ a quantum of energy that propagates through a plasma as a result of charge density fluctuation

plastic*adj* ꞉ not genuine or sincere ꞉ artificial, phony ⟨this is the *plastic* age, the era of the sham and the bogus —Logan Gourlay⟩ ⟨having a speech writer would be definitely too *plastic* —Mark Spitz⟩ — often used as a generalized term of disapproval ⟨takes a positive effort of will ... to avoid *plastic* food, *plastic* living, and *plastic* entertainment —L.E. Sissman⟩

plas·to·cya·nin \ˌplastō'sīənən\ *n* [*plasto-* formation, development (fr. Gk *plastos* formed, molded) + *cyanin*] ꞉ a copper-containing protein that acts as an intermediary in photosynthetic electron transport

plas·to·qui·none \ˌplastōkwə'nōn, -ˌkwin,ōn\ *n* [*plasto-* + *quinone*] ꞉ a plant substance that is related to vitamin K and plays a role in photosynthetic phosphorylation

plate*n* **1** ꞉ a license plate (as for an automobile) **2** ꞉ a schedule of work to be done **3** ꞉ any of the large movable segments into which the earth's crust is divided according to the theory of plate tectonics

plate*vt* **plat·ed; plat·ing** [fr. the crossing of home plate by the scoring runner] ꞉ to cause (as a run) to score in baseball ⟨hit his triple and *plated* two runs —*Sporting News*⟩

plated am·ber·i·na \-ˌambə'rēnə\ *n* ꞉ an ornamental glass consisting of an amberina casing over a fiery opalescent or white lining

plate-glass \'plāt,glas, *in attributive position also* ˌplāt-ˌglas\ *adj* [fr. the common use of plate glass in constructing the buildings of modern British universities] ꞉ of, relating to, or being the British universities founded in the latter half of the twentieth century — compare OXBRIDGE, REDBRICK

plate-mak·er \'plāt,mākə(r)\ *n* ꞉ a machine for making printing plates and esp. offset printing plates — **plate-mak·ing** \-kiŋ\ *n*

plate tec·ton·ics \-tek'täniks\ *n pl but sing in constr* ꞉ a theory that the lithosphere of the earth is divided into a small number of plates which float on and travel independently over the mantle and that much of the earth's seismic activity occurs at the boundaries of these plates as a result of frictional interaction; *also* ꞉ the process and dynamics of plate movement

platform tennis *n* ꞉ a variation of paddle tennis that is played on a platform enclosed by a wire fence

platoon*n* ꞉ two or more players (as in baseball) who alternate in playing the same position

platoon*vt* ꞉ to alternate (one player) with another player in the same position ⟨if I can't play him every day, I'll *platoon* him in left field —Leo Durocher⟩ ~ *vi* **1** ꞉ to alternate with another player in the same position **2** ꞉ to use alternate players at the same position

play*vt* **1** ꞉ to catch or pick up (a batted ball) ꞉ field ⟨*played* the ball bare-handed⟩ **2** ꞉ to direct the course of (as a ball) ꞉ hit ⟨*played* a wedge shot to the green⟩; *also* ꞉ to cause (a ball or puck) to rebound ⟨*played* the ball off the backboard⟩ — **play by ear** ꞉ to deal with (as a situation) without previous planning or instructions — **play games** ꞉ to try to hide the truth from someone by deceptive means — **play one's cards** ꞉ to act with the means available to one

play–ac·tion pass \ˌplāˌakshən-\ *n* ꞉ a pass play in football in which the quarterback fakes a hand-off before passing the ball

play·book*\'plā,bůk\ *n* ꞉ a notebook containing diagramed football plays

play·date \'plā,dāt\ *n* ꞉ a scheduled showing of a production (as a movie)

play·list \-ˌlist\ *n* ꞉ a list of recordings to be played on the air by a radio station

plaza*n* ꞉ an open area often featuring pedestrian walkways and shops and usu. located near urban buildings

plea bargaining *n* ꞉ the negotiation of an agreement between a prosecutor and a defendant whereby the defendant is permitted to plead guilty to a reduced charge ⟨sometimes the prisoner helps delay his own trial because he realizes that the longer he is in prison the greater are the chances for *plea bargaining* and a reduced sentence — *Encore*⟩ — **plea–bargain** *vi* — **plea bargain** *n*

plench \'plench\ *n* [*pliers* + *wrench*] ꞉ a combination pliers and wrench operated by squeezing the handle and used to make pulling and turning motions under zero gravity

PL/1 \(ˌ)pēˌel'wən\ *n* [*programming language* (version) *1*] ꞉ a general purpose language for programming a computer

plot*vi* **plot·ted; plot·ting** ꞉ to be located by means of coordinates ⟨the data *plot* at a single point⟩

plug*vb* — **plug into** ꞉ to connect or become connected to by or as if by means of a plug ⟨the entire school is *plugged into* a ... computer system —Patricia Linden⟩ ⟨pay up to $100 a month to *plug into* these agencies — Elliott McCleary⟩ ⟨*plugged into* the major currents of celebrity socializing —*Women's Wear Daily*⟩

plug·ola \plə'gōlə\ *n* [*plug* + pay*ola*] **1** ꞉ payola given to broadcasters for favorably mentioning or displaying a product other than that of the sponsor of the program aired **2** ꞉ bias in news reporting ⟨unlike most of the smoothies that transmit the news, he unwittingly telegraphs his *plugola* —Philip Nobile⟩

plume*n* ꞉ a hypothetical column of molten rock rising continuously from the earth's lower mantle that is held to be the driving force in plate movement in the theory of plate tectonics

plus*prep* ꞉ besides — chiefly in oral use ⟨*plus* which, we were traveling in an area exposed to few blacks —Linda Harris⟩

¹plus *adv* ꞉ besides — chiefly in oral use ⟨hang around it because it's an open building with no lock on the door. *Plus* they go in there to hang out, out of the cold — Barbara Lamont⟩

²plus *conj* ꞉ and — chiefly in oral use ⟨if you want to make a super investment, *plus* you don't happen to be rich —*advt*⟩

P marker *n* [*P*, symbol for *phrase*] ꞉ PHRASE MARKER

pocket*n* **:** an area formed by blockers from which a football quarterback attempts to pass

pocket bread *n* **:** PITA

pod*n* **:** a detachable compartment (as for personnel, a power unit, or an instrument) on a spacecraft

po·go·noph·o·ran \ˌpōgə'näfərən\ *n* **:** a marine worm belonging to the phylum or class Pogonophora — **pogonophoran** *adj*

point estimate *n* **:** the single value assigned to a parameter in point estimation

point estimation *n* **:** estimation in which a single value is assigned to a parameter

point man*n* **:** a soldier who goes ahead of a patrol; *broadly* **:** one who is in the forefront ⟨establishing himself as *point man* for the new Republican foreign policy — R.L. Strout⟩

**point of accumulation : ** LIMIT POINT

point of no return **1 :** the point in the flight of an aircraft (as over an ocean) beyond which the remaining fuel will be insufficient for a return to the starting point **2 :** a critical point (as in development or a course of action) at which turning back or reversal is not possible

point–of–sale *or* **point–of–sales** *adj* **:** of or relating to the place (as a check-out counter) where an item is purchased ⟨*point-of-sale* advertising⟩ ⟨electronic *point-of-sale* terminals⟩

points *n pl* **1 :** a percentage of the face value of a loan often added as a placement fee or service charge **2 :** credit accruing from creating an advantageous impression ⟨a cocktail party liberal out to score sexual *points* via political erudition —*Rolling Stone*⟩ ⟨he gets *points* for courage —Sally Quinn⟩ ⟨if originality per se makes *points* for a filmmaker —Judith Crist⟩

point set *n* **:** a collection of points in geometry or topology

point set to·pol·o·gy \-tə'päləjē, -tō-, -tä-\ *n* **:** a branch of topology concerned with the properties and theory of topological spaces and metric spaces developed with emphasis on set theory

Pois·son distribution \pwä'sōⁿ-\ *n* [Siméon D. *Poisson* †1840 Fr. mathematician] **:** a probability density function that is often used as a mathematical model of the number of outcomes (as traffic accidents, atomic disintegrations, or organisms) obtained in a suitable interval of time and space, that has the mean equal to the variance, that is used as an approximation to the binomial distribution, and that has the form

$$f(x) = \frac{e^{-\mu}\mu^x}{x!} \text{ where } \mu$$

is the mean and *x* takes on nonnegative integral values

polar*adj* **1 a :** passing over a planet's north and south poles ⟨a satellite in a *polar* orbit⟩ **b :** traveling in a polar orbit ⟨a *polar* satellite⟩ **2 :** of, relating to, or expressed in polar coordinates ⟨*polar* equations⟩; *also* **:** of or relating to a polar coordinate system

pole*or* **pole position** *n* **:** the front-row position nearest the infield in the starting lineup of an automobile race

pole*n* **:** the point of origin of two tangents to a conic section that determine a polar

pole lamp *n* **:** a lamp that consists of a pole to which light fixtures are attached and that usu. extends from floor to ceiling

po·le·mol·ogy \(ˌ)pōlə'mäləjē\ *n* [Gk *polemos* war + E -*logy* science, theory, deriv. of Gk *logos* word] **:** the study of war

po·lio·vi·rus \ˌpōlē(ˌ)ō'vīrəs\ *n* [NL, fr. *poliomyelitis* + *virus*] **:** an enterovirus that occurs in several antigenically distinct forms and is the causative agent of human poliomyelitis

po·lit·i·ci·za·tion \pəˌlid·əsə'zāshən\ *n* **:** the act or process of politicizing ⟨the *politicization* of art is typical of totalitarian tyranny —B.W. Garfield⟩ ⟨*politicization* of campus leaders⟩

poll*vt* **:** to test (as several computer terminals sharing a single line) in sequence for messages to be transmitted

po·loi·dal \pō'loid°l, pə'-\ *adj* [*pole* + -*oidal* having the form of] **:** relating to or being a magnetic field that extends between the poles of a magnetic body (as the earth) into surrounding space

Po·lo·nia \pə'lōnēə\ *n* [ML, Poland] **:** people of Polish descent living outside Poland

poly·acryl·amide \ˌpälē'krilə,mīd\ *n* [*poly-* many, much (deriv. of Gk *polys*) + *acrylamide*] **:** a polyamide (–CH₂CHCONH₂–)ₓ of acrylic acid

polyacrylamide gel \-'jel\ *n* **:** hydrated polyacrylamide that is used esp. for electrophoresis

poly·ad·e·nyl·ic acid \ˌpälē'ad°n'ilik-\ *n* [*poly-* + *adenylic acid*] **:** RNA or a segment of RNA that is composed of a polynucleotide chain consisting entirely of adenylic-acid residues and that codes for polylysine when functioning as messenger RNA in protein synthesis

poly·al·co·hol \ˌpälē'alkə,hól, -ˌaúk-\ *n* **:** an alcohol (as ethylene glycol) that contains more than one hydroxy group

poly·car·bo·nate \ˌpälē'kärbə,nāt, -lə-, -'káb-\ *n* **:** any of various tough thermoplastics characterized by high impact strength and high softening temperature

poly·cen·trism \ˌpälē'sen·ˌtrizəm, -lə-\ *n* [ISV *poly-* + *centric* + -*ism*, prob. orig. formed in It] **:** the existence of a plurality of centers of Communist thought and leadership — **poly·cen·trist** \-n·trəst\ *n or adj*

poly·chlo·ri·nat·ed bi·phe·nyl \ˌpälē'klórə,nād·əd·ˌbi'fen°l, ˌpälə-, -'klór-, -'fēn-\ *n* **:** any of several compounds that are produced by replacing hydrogen atoms in biphenyl with chlorine, have various industrial applications, and are poisonous environmental pollutants which tend to accumulate in animal tissues

poly·chro·mat·ic*\-krō'mad·ik\ *adj* **:** being or relating to radiation that is composed of more than one wavelength

poly·cis·tron·ic \-sis'tränik\ *adj* **:** containing the genetic information of a number of cistrons ⟨*polycistronic* messenger RNA⟩

poly·clo·nal \ˌpälē'klōn°l, -ləˌk-\ *adj* [*poly-* + *clone* + -*al*, adj. suffix] **:** produced by or being cells derived from two or more cells of different ancestry or genetic constitution ⟨*polyclonal* antibody synthesis⟩

poly·cyt·i·dyl·ic acid \-ˌsid·ə'dilik-\ *n* [*poly-* + *cytidylic acid*] **:** RNA or a segment of RNA that is composed of a polynucleotide chain consisting entirely of cytidylic-acid residues and that codes for a polypeptide chain consisting of proline residues when functioning as messenger RNA in protein synthesis — see POLY I:C

poly·ether \ˌpälē'ēthə(r)\ *n* **1 :** a polymer in which the repeating unit contains a carbon-oxygen bond derived esp. from an aldehyde or an epoxide **2 :** a polyurethane foam made by use of a polyether

poly I:C \ˌpälēˌiˈsē\ or **poly I·poly C** \ˌpälēˈiˌpälēˈsē\ n [poly- + inosinic acid + poly- + cytidylic acid] **:** a synthetic 2-stranded RNA composed of one strand of polyinosinic acid and one strand of polycytidylic acid that induces interferon formation and has been used experimentally as an anticancer and antiviral agent

poly·imide \ˈpälēˌimˌid\ n **:** any of a class of polymeric synthetic resins resistant to high temperatures, wear, and corrosion and used esp. for coatings and films

poly·ino·sin·ic acid \ˈpälēˌinəˈsinik-, -ˌīn-\ n [poly- + inosinic acid] **:** RNA or a segment of RNA that is composed of a polynucleotide chain consisting entirely of inosinic-acid residues — see POLY I:C

poly·ly·sine \ˈpälēˈlīˌsēn\ n **:** a protein whose polypeptide chain consists entirely of lysine residues

poly·mer·ase \ˈpäləməˌrās, -āz\ n [polymer + -ase enzyme] **:** any of several enzymes that catalyze the formation of DNA or RNA from precursor substances in the presence of preexisting DNA or RNA acting as a template

poly·oma \ˌpälēˈōmə\ or **polyoma virus** n [NL polyoma, fr. poly- + -oma tumor] **:** a papovavirus of rodents that is associated with various kinds of tumors

poly·ri·bo·some \ˈpälēˌrībəˌsōm, -lə-\ n **:** a cluster of ribosomes held together by a molecule of messenger RNA and forming the site of protein synthesis — **poly·ri·bo·som·al** \-ˌrībəˈsōməl\ adj

poly·some \ˈpälēˌsōm, -lə-\ n [poly- + ribosome] **:** POLYRIBOSOME

poly·sor·bate \ˈpälēˈsòrˌbāt, -lə-\ n **:** any of several emulsifiers used in the preparation of some pharmaceuticals and foods

poly·syn·ap·tic \-səˈnaptik\ adj **:** involving two or more synapses in the central nervous system ⟨polysynaptic reflexes⟩ — **poly·syn·ap·ti·cal·ly** \-ək(ə)lē\ adv

poly·un·sat·u·rat·ed \ˈpälēˌənˈsachəˌrād-əd\ adj, of a fat or oil **:** rich in unsaturated bonds — **poly·un·sat·u·rate** \-ˌənˈsachəˌrāt, -ərət\ n

poly·uri·dyl·ic acid \-ˌyùrəˈdilik-\ n [poly- + uridylic acid] **:** RNA or a segment of RNA that is composed of a polynucleotide chain consisting entirely of uridlyic-acid residues and that codes for a polypeptide chain consisting of phenylalanine residues when functioning as messenger RNA in protein synthesis

pony car n [fr. the relatively small size of the cars and the fact that one of this group was named Mustang] **:** one of a group of 2-door hardtops of different makes that are similar in sporty styling, high performance characteristics, and price range

-poo \ˌpü\ suffix [origin unknown] — used as a disparaging diminutive ⟨cutesy-poo⟩

poof \ˈpüf, ˈpúf\ or **poove** \ˈpüv, ˈpúv\ n, pl **poofs** or **pooves** \ˈpüvz, ˈpúvz\ [prob. alter. of puff, n.] Brit **:** a homosexual

poo–poo \ˈpüˌpü\ n [redupl. of poop] slang **:** excrement

poor·boy \ˈpúr(ˌbòi, ˈpúə,-, esp South, NE, & Brit ˈpōə,- or ˈpó(ə),-\ n [prob. fr. its resemblance esp. in fit to the sort of outgrown sweater a poor child might wear] **:** a close-fitting ribbed sweater

poor–mouth \-ˌmaùth, -th\ vi **:** to plead poverty as a defense or excuse ⟨usually poor-mouths when it's his turn

to contribute⟩ ~ vt **:** to speak disparagingly of ⟨likes to poor-mouth his candidate's chances so that the candidate will appear to have pulled an astonishingly strong victory —Timothy Crouse⟩

pop*vt **popped; pop·ping :** to take (drugs) orally or by injection ⟨keeps popping pills⟩

pop*adj **:** of, relating to, or constituting popular mass culture ⟨pop culture⟩ ⟨pop clothes⟩ ⟨users of pop forms like nightclub comedy and folk-rock preaching —Seymour Krim⟩ ⟨a pop journalist carrying the aromas of discotheque and boutique —Irving Howe⟩

pop*or **pop art** n **:** art in which commonplace objects (as road signs, hamburgers, comic strips, or soup cans) are used as subject matter and are often physically incorporated in the work — **pop artist** n

popper*n, slang **:** a vial of amyl nitrite esp. when illicitly used as an aphrodisiac

pop·ster \ˈpäpstə(r)\ n **:** a practitioner of pop art

pop–top \ˈpäpˌtäp\ adj **:** having a tab that can be pulled off to make an opening ⟨a pop-top beer can⟩ — **pop–top** \ˈpäpˈtäp\ n

population explosion n **:** a pyramiding of numbers of a biological population; esp **:** the recent great increase in human numbers resulting from both increased survival and exponential population growth

pop wine n [perh. fr. pop carbonated beverage] **:** an inexpensive sweet wine and esp. a fruit wine or a fruit-flavored wine

pork belly n **:** an uncured side of pork

porn \ˈpó(ə)rn, ˈpó(ə)n\ or **por·no** \ˈpòr(ˌ)nō, ˈpó(ə)(ˌ)nō\ n [by shortening] **:** PORNOGRAPHY ⟨countless sex offenders, when caught, turn out to possess large libraries of porn —E.A. Roberts, Jr.⟩ ⟨grudgingly admits that there is no evidence to show that porno incites the viewer to anything but erotic feelings and expressions —P.M. McGrady, Jr.⟩ — **porn** or **porno** adj

por·nog·ra·phy*\pó(r)ˈnägrəfē, -fi\ n **1 :** material (as a book) that is pornographic **2 :** the depiction or portrayal of acts in a sensational manner so as to arouse (as by lurid details) a quick intense emotional reaction ⟨the pornography of violence⟩

porny \ˈpòrnē, ˈpó(ə)n-, -ni\ adj **porn·i·er; -est** [porn + -y, adj. suffix] **:** pornographic ⟨porny films⟩

po·ro·mer·ic \ˈpōrəˌmerik, ˈpòr-\ n [poro- pore (fr. Gk poros) + polymeric] **:** any of a class of tough porous synthetic materials used as a substitute for leather (as in shoe uppers)

POS abbr point-of-sale

posi·grade \ˈpäzəˌgrād\ adj [positive + -grade (as in retrograde)] **:** being an auxiliary rocket used for imparting additional thrust to a spacecraft in the direction of motion

posit*vt **:** to propose as an explanation **:** suggest ⟨many of these men, even at the nadir of their despair, posited ways out of the situation as they perceived it —Alan Heineman⟩ ⟨this syndrome is the only explanation I can posit for good reviews given to many bad musicals —Gene Lees⟩

po·si·tion·al notation \pəˈzishnəl-, -shənəl-\ n **:** a system of expressing numbers in which the digits are arranged in succession, the position of each digit has a place value, and the number is equal to the sum of the products of each digit by its place value

position paper *n* **:** a detailed report that recommends a course of action on a particular issue ⟨new *position papers,* press releases and speeches came out in an unfocused mass telling of corruption, bad police-community relations, pollution and the other standards of a reform campaign today —R.L. Maullin⟩

post code *n* **:** a code (as of numbers and letters) used similarly to the zip code esp. in the United Kingdom and Australia

post–de·ter·min·er \'pōs(t)də̇'tərməṅər, -dē-; -'təməṅə(r, -'təim-\ *n* [*post-* after (deriv. of L *post*) + *determiner*] **:** a limiting noun modifier (as *first* or *few*) characterized by occurrence after the determiner in a noun phrase

pos·ter·iza·tion \,pōstətə'zāshən, -rī'z-\ *n* [*poster* + *-ization* process of making or causing to resemble) **:** the obtaining of posterlike reproductions having solid tones or colors and little detail from photographs or other continuous-tone originals by means of separation negatives — **pos·ter·ize** \'pōstə,rīz\ *vb*

post·ir·ra·di·a·tion \,pōstir,ādē'āshən\ *adj* **:** occurring after irradiation ⟨mutations in *postirradiation* cell divisions⟩

post·mar·i·tal \(')pōs(t)'marəd·ᵊl, *Brit also* ,pōs(t)mə-'rit²l\ *adj* **:** occurring after a marriage has been terminated

post·mod·ern \(')pōs(t)'mädərn, ÷ -'mäd(ə)rən, -dən, -dᵊn\ *adj* **:** of or relating to any of several artistic movements that are reactions against the philosophy and practices of modern arts or literature

post·pro·duc·tion \,pōs(t)prə'dəkshən\ *n* **:** the period following filming in which a motion picture or television show is readied (as by editing and scoring) for public presentation

post·test \'pōs(t),test\ *n* **:** a test given to students after the completion of an instructional program to measure their achievement and the effectiveness of the program

post·tran·scrip·tion·al \,pōs(t)tran(t)'skripshnəl, -shən²l\ *adj* **:** occurring, acting, or existing after genetic transcription ⟨*posttranscriptional* control of messenger= RNA production⟩

post·trans·fu·sion \,pōs(t)tran(t)s'fyüzhən, -tranz'-\ *adj* **1 :** caused by transfused blood ⟨malpractice suits for *posttransfusion* hepatitis⟩ **2 :** occurring after blood transfusion ⟨induction of *posttransfusion* shock⟩

post·trans·la·tion·al \-tran(t)s'lāshnəl, -shən²l\ *adj* **:** occurring or existing after genetic translation

post·treat·ment \(')pōs(t)'trētmənt\ *adj* **:** relating to, typical of, or occurring in the stage following treatment ⟨*posttreatment* examinations⟩ — **posttreatment** *adv*

po·tas·si·um–ar·gon \pə,tasēəm'är,gän, -'à,gän\ *adj* **:** of, relating to, or being a method of dating archaeological or geological materials based on the radioactive decay of potassium to argon that has taken place in a specimen

pot·head \'pät,hed\ *n* **:** one who smokes marijuana

pot sticker *n* **:** a crescent-shaped dumpling filled with a spicy pork mixture, steamed, and then fried, and usu. served as an appetizer

pouil·ly–fuis·sé \pü'yēfw'ʸē'sā\ *n* [Solutré-*Pouilly* and *Fuissé,* Fr. villages] **:** a dry white Burgundy

pow·der–puff \'paùdə(r),pəf\ *adj* **:** intended or designed for females ⟨she played *powder-puff* football —

Sports Illustrated⟩ ⟨the home-and-husband syndrome of the *powder-puff* press —*New York*⟩

power *n* **:** the probability of rejecting the null hypothesis in a statistical test when a particular alternative hypothesis happens to be true

power broker *n* **:** a person (as in politics) able to exert strong influence because of votes or individuals that he controls ⟨is a cross between a professional trade association and a collection of *power brokers,* opinion leaders and fixers —Elizabeth B. Drew⟩

power function *n* **1 :** a function of a parameter under statistical test whose value for a particular value of the parameter is the probability of rejecting the null hypothesis if that value of the parameter happens to be true **2 :** a function (as $f(x) = ax^k$) that equals the product of a constant and a power of the independent variable

power series *n* **:** an infinite series whose terms are successive integral powers of a variable multiplied by constants

power structure *n* **1 :** a group of persons having control of an organization **:** ESTABLISHMENT ⟨the white *power structure*⟩ ⟨how the *power structure* in your local school district operates —R.N. Sheridan⟩ **2 :** the hierarchical interrelationships existing within a controlling group ⟨the *power structure* of the American educational establishment —Paul Woodring⟩

power sweep *n* **:** an end run in football in which one or more linemen pull out and run interference for the ball-carrier

pox·vi·rus \'päks,vīrəs\ *n* **:** any of a group of relatively large round, brick-shaped, or ovoid animal viruses (as the causative agent of smallpox) that have a fluffy appearance caused by a covering of tubules and threads

PPLO \,pē(,)pē,el'ō\ *n, pl* **PPLO** [pleuropneumonia-*l*ike organism] **:** any of a genus (*Mycoplasma*) of minute pleomorphic gram-negative nonmotile microorganisms without cell walls that are intermediate in some respects between viruses and bacteria and are mostly parasitic usu. in mammals **:** mycoplasma

pre·ag·ri·cul·tur·al \,prē,agrə'kəlch(ə)rəl\ *adj* [*pre-* before (deriv. of L *prae*) + *agricultural*] **:** existing or occurring before the practice of agriculture ⟨*preagricultural* domestication of mammals⟩

pre·bi·o·log·i·cal \-,bīə'läjə̇kəl\ *also* **pre·bi·o·log·ic** \-jik\ *adj* **:** of, relating to, or being chemical or environmental precursors of the origin of life ⟨*prebiological* molecules⟩ ⟨*prebiological* chemical evolution⟩

pre·bi·ot·ic \-,(,)bī'äd·ik\ *adj* **:** PREBIOLOGICAL

pre·cal·cu·lus \(')prē'kalkyələs\ *adj* **:** relating to or being mathematical prerequisites for the study of calculus ⟨*pre-calculus* mathematics⟩ — **precalculus** *n*

pre·cap·il·lary \(')prē'kapə,lerē, *Brit usu* ,prēkə'pilərē, -ri\ *adj* **:** being on the arterial side of and immediately adjacent to a capillary

precision *n* **1 :** the accuracy (as in binary or decimal places) with which a number can be represented usu. expressed in terms of computer words ⟨double *precision* arithmetic permits the representation of an expression by two computer words⟩ **2 :** RELEVANCE

pre·con·fer·ence \'prē,känfər(ə)n(t)s, -frən(t)s\ *n* **:** a conference held before the start of another conference or convention

pre·cop·u·la·to·ry \(')prē¦käpyələ¸tōrē, -¸tȯr-\ *adj* **:** preceding copulation ⟨*precopulatory* behavior⟩

pre·de·ter·min·er \¦prēdə¦tərmənər, -dē-; -¦tāmənə(r, -¦tȯim-\ *n* **:** a limiting noun modifier (as *both* or *all*) characterized by occurrence before the determiner in a noun phrase

pre·di·a·be·tes \-¸diə'bēd·ēz, -'bēd·əs\ *n* **:** an inapparent abnormal state that precedes the development of clinically evident diabetes — **pre·di·a·bet·ic** \-'bed·ik\ *adj or n*

predominantly*adv* **:** for the most part **:** mainly ⟨a Senator from a state with a *predominantly* agricultural economy —*Current Biog.*⟩

pre·emer·gent \-ə¦mərjənt, -ē¦m-, -¦mōj-, -¦məij-\ *adj* **:** used or occurring before emergence of seedlings aboveground ⟨a *preemergent* crabgrass control⟩

preempt*vt* **1 :** to take the place of **:** take precedence over ⟨the busing issue has *preempted* discussion of more basic problems —William Serrin⟩ **2 :** to gain a commanding or preeminent place in ⟨lost the 1970 congressional race ... but ran so well that he *preempted* the Democratic field for a rematch two years later —R. M. Williams⟩

pre·emp·tive*\pre'em(p)tiv\ *adj* **:** marked by the seizing of the initiative; *specif* **:** being or relating to a first military strike made to gain an advantage when a strike by the enemy is believed imminent ⟨a new policy of vigorous *preemptive* attacks against the ... guerrilla organizations —Terence Smith⟩ ⟨a *preemptive* strike⟩

pre–en·gi·neered \¦prē¸enjə¦ni(ə)rd, -¦niəd\ *adj* **:** constructed of or employing prefabricated modules ⟨a *pre‡ engineered* building⟩

preg·gers \'pregə(r)z\ *adj* [by alter.] *chiefly Brit* **:** pregnant — used as a predicate adjective

prehistoric*adj* **:** of or relating to a language in a period of its development from which contemporary records of its actual sounds and forms have not been preserved

pre·his·to·ry*\(')prē¦hist(ə)rē, -rī\ *n* **:** the prehistoric period of man's evolution

pre·im·plan·ta·tion \¦prē¸im(¸)plan¦tāshən\ *adj* **:** of, involving, or being an embryo before uterine implantation

pre·in·cu·ba·tion \¦prē¸iŋkyə¦bāshən, -¸ink-\ *n* **:** incubation (as of a biochemical) prior to a process (as a reaction)

prelate nul·li·us \-nü'lēəs\ *n, pl* **prelates nullius** [part trans. of NL *praelatus nullius dioecesis* prelate of no diocese] **:** a Roman Catholic prelate having ordinary jurisdiction over a district independent of any diocese

pre·launch \(')prē¦lȯnch, -¦länch\ *adj* **:** preparing for or preliminary to launch (as of a spacecraft) ⟨the *prelaunch* countdown⟩

pre·mei·ot·ic \¸prēmī'äd·ik\ *adj* **:** of, occurring in, or typical of a stage prior to meiosis ⟨*premeiotic* DNA synthesis⟩ ⟨*premeiotic* tissue⟩

pre·ovi·po·si·tion \¸prē¸ōvəpə'zishən\ *adj* **:** of, relating to, or being the period before oviposition of the first eggs by an adult female (as of an insect)

pre·plant \'prē¦plant, ¸prē¸plant\ *also* **pre·plant·ing** \-iŋ\ *adj* **:** occurring or used before planting a crop ⟨*preplant* soil fertilization⟩

¹prep·py *or* **prep·pie** \'prepē, -i\ *n, pl* **preppies** [*prep* + *-y* or *-ie* one associated with] **1 :** a student at or a gradu- ate of a preparatory school **2 :** a person deemed to dress or behave like a preppy

²preppy *or* **preppie** *adj* **prep·pi·er; -est** **1 :** relating to, characteristic of, or being a preppy **2 :** relating to or being a style of dress characterized esp. by classic clothing and neat appearance ⟨a pronounced *preppy* look ... with clothes in better repair than during the shopworn look of the radical era —Jon Nordheimer⟩ — **prep·pi·ly** \'prepəlē, -li\ *adv* — **prep·pi·ness** \'prepēnəs, -pin-\ *n*

pre·preg \'prē¦preg\ *n* [*pre-* + *impregnated*] **:** a reinforcing or molding material (as paper or glass cloth) already impregnated with a synthetic resin

pre·pro·cess \(')prē¦präs¸es, -¸prōs-, -əs\ *vt* **:** to do preliminary processing of (as data) — **pre·pro·ces·sor** \-s¸esə(r), -səsə(r), -sə¸sȯ(ə)r, -sə¸sȯ(ə)\ *n*

¹pre·pro·duc·tion \¦prēprə¦dəkshən\ *adj* **:** involving, existing, or taking place in the period before production begins ⟨*preproduction* planning⟩; *esp* **:** relating to or being a prototype ⟨designing *preproduction* cars — new models in an existing line or first models of a new line —Caroline Donnelly⟩

²preproduction *n* **:** the period in the development of a play or motion picture prior to staging or filming that usu. involves casting, hiring production crews, constructing sets, and finding a suitable theater or location for filming ⟨currently he's in *preproduction* on two new movies —*People*⟩

pre·pro·gram \(')prē¦prō¸gram, -¦prōgrəm\ *vt* **:** to program in advance of some anticipated use ⟨*preprogram* a computer⟩

pre·punch \(')prē¦pənch\ *vt* **:** to punch in advance of some anticipated use ⟨paper *prepunched* for a 3-ring binder⟩

pre·quel \'prēkwəl\ *n* [*pre-* + *-quel* (as in *sequel*)] **:** a literary or dramatic work whose story precedes that of an earlier work

pre·screen \(')prē¦skrēn\ *vt* **1 :** to screen beforehand ⟨*prescreen* schoolchildren for potential learning and behavior problems —Robert Reinhold⟩ **2 :** to view (as a television show) before public release ⟨many mass advertisers *prescreen* TV shows and pull ads from episodes they don't find appropriate for their products —J. H. Birnbaum *et al*⟩

pres·en·tism \'prezən¸tizəm\ *n* [*present* + *-ism*] **:** an outlook dominated by present-day attitudes and experiences ⟨conversations with students about their experiences with American history have persuaded me that *presentism* feeds less on deliberate personal myopia than on the historians' inability to make the past come alive —F.M. Hechinger⟩

¹pre·soak \(')prē¦sōk\ *vt* **:** to soak beforehand ⟨*presoak* stained clothes⟩ ⟨*presoaked* seeds⟩

²pre·soak \'prē¦sōk\ *n* **1 :** a cleaning agent used in presoaking clothes **2 :** an instance of presoaking

pre·sort \(')prē¦sȯ(ə)rt, -¦sȯ(ə)t\ *vt* **:** to sort (outgoing mail) by zip code usu. before delivery to a post office

press*vb* — **press the flesh :** to greet and shake hands with people esp. while campaigning for political office ⟨to win votes ... you have to get out in the streets and *press the flesh* —Susan Margolies⟩ ⟨says his running days are over, but show the four-time ... governor a crowd, and he reflexively begins *pressing the flesh* —People⟩

press kit *n* **:** a collection of promotional material for distribution to the press

pre·stress \'prē¦stres\ *n* **1 :** the process of prestressing **2 :** the stresses introduced in prestress **3 :** the condition of being prestressed

pre·syn·ap·tic \¦prēsə¦naptik\ *adj* **:** situated or occurring just before a nerve synapse 〈a *presynaptic* nerve ending〉 — **pre·syn·ap·ti·cal·ly** \-tək(ə)lē\ *adv*

pre·tax \(')prē¦taks\ *adj* **:** existing before provision for taxes 〈*pretax* earnings〉

¹pre·teen \'prē¦tēn\ *n* **:** a boy or girl not yet 13 years old

²preteen *adj* **1 :** relating to or produced for children younger than 13 〈*preteen* fashions〉 **2 :** being younger than 13 〈*preteen* youngsters〉

pre·treat·ment \(')prē¦trētmənt\ *adj* **:** occurring in or typical of the period prior to treatment 〈*pretreatment* population estimates made prior to spraying〉

pre·vent de·fense \'prē¸vent'dē¸fen(t)s; prē'vent-, prə'-, *also* -də'fen(t)s\ *n* **:** a football defense in which linebackers and backs play deeper than usual in order to prevent the completion of a long pass

pre·ven·tive detention*\prəventiv-, prē-\ *n* **:** imprisonment without the right to bail of an arrested person who is awaiting trial for a felony and who is considered dangerous to society

pre·writ·ing \'prē¸rīd·iŋ, -ītiŋ\ *n* **:** the formulation and organization of ideas preparatory to writing

price–earn·ings ratio \'prīs'ərniŋz-\ *n* **:** a measure of the value of a common stock determined as the ratio of its market price to its earnings per share and usu. expressed as a simple numeral **(price–earnings multiple)**

primal scream therapy *or* **primal therapy** *or* **primal scream** *n* **:** psychotherapy in which the patient recalls and reenacts a particularly disturbing past experience and expresses normally repressed anger or frustration esp. through spontaneous and unrestrained screams, hysteria, or violence

primary*adj **1 :** of, relating to, or being the amino acid sequence in proteins 〈*primary* protein structure〉 **2 :** of, relating to, involving, or derived from primary meristem 〈*primary* tissue〉 〈*primary* growth〉 **3 :** of, relating to, or involved in the production of organic substances by green plants 〈*primary* productivity〉

primary consumer *n* **:** a plant-eating organism **:** herbivore

primary derivative *n* **:** a word (as *telegram*) whose immediate constituents are bound forms

primary structure *n* **:** sculpture in the idiom of minimal art — **primary struc·tur·ist** \-'strəkchərəst, -ksh(ə)rəst\ *n*

pri·ma·to·log·i·cal \¸prīməd·əl'äjəkəl\ *adj* **:** of or relating to primatology 〈*primatological* research〉

prim·er*\'prīmə(r)\ *n* **:** a molecule (as of DNA) whose presence is required for formation of more molecules of the same kind

prime rate *n* **:** an interest rate at which preferred customers can borrow from banks and which is the lowest commercial interest rate available at a particular time and place

prime time \(')prīm'tīm\ *n* **:** the evening period generally from 7 to 11 p.m. during which television has its largest number of viewers — **prime–time** \¦prīm¦tīm\ *adj*

pri·mi·done \'prīmə¸dōn\ *n* [alter. of *pyrimidinedione* (chemical name)] **:** an anticonvulsant phenobarbital derivative $C_{12}H_{14}N_2O_2$ used esp. to control epileptic seizures

principal diagonal *n* **:** the diagonal in a square matrix that runs from upper left to lower right

principial*adj **:** of, relating to, or based on principle **:** principled 〈the difficulties may not be so much *principial* as psychological —William LaFleur & John Trimmer〉

print out *vt* **:** to make a printout of **:** produce in the form of a printout 〈I could just punch the right buttons on my computer, and it would *print out* the material I needed —Joseph Napolitan〉

print·out \'print¸aút\ *n* [*print out,* v.] **:** a printed record produced automatically (as by a computer)

pri·or·i·tize \prī'órə¸tīz, prī'är-, 'prīər-\ *vt* **-tized; -tiz·ing :** to list or rate (as projects or goals) in order of priority 〈expects his underlings to *prioritize* their work and their personal goals —*Newsweek*〉 〈said . . . that the party should *prioritize* its platform. It should establish the cost, feasibility and time frame of promised programs, he added —Charles Mohr〉

pri·va·tism \'prīvə¸tizəm\ *n* **:** the attitude of being uncommitted to or avoiding involvement in anything beyond one's immediate interests 〈the collapse of the mass political movements of the 60's into the narcissistic *privatism* of the 70's —Greil Marcus〉 — **pri·va·tis·tic** \¸prīvə'tistik\ *adj*

pro·ac·tive \(')prō¦aktiv\ *adj* [L *pro-* forward (fr. *pro* before, for) + E *active*] **:** involving modification by a factor which precedes that which is modified 〈*proactive* inhibition of memory〉

probability density *n* **:** DISTRIBUTION 3; *also* **:** a particular value of a probability density function

probability distribution *n* **:** DISTRIBUTION 2; *also* **:** DISTRIBUTION 3

pro·ben·e·cid \prō'benəsəd\ *n* [*propyl* + *benzoic* + *-e-* (arbitrary infix) + *acid*] **:** a drug $C_{13}H_{19}NO_4S$ that acts on renal tubular function and is used to increase the concentration of some drugs (as penicillin) in the blood by inhibiting their excretion and to increase the excretion of urates in gout

pro·bus·ing \'prō'bəsiŋ\ *adj* [*pro-* favoring + *busing*] **:** favoring busing as a means of establishing racial balance in the schools 〈could not condone what could be interpreted as a segregationist stand, and the organization adopted a *probusing* position —John Walsh〉

pro·car·ba·zine \prō'kärbə¸zēn, -äb-, -əzən\ *n* [*iso*propyl + *carb*amoyl + *hydra*zine] **:** an antineoplastic drug $C_{12}H_{19}N_3O$ that is a monoamine oxidase inhibitor used as the hydrochloride esp. in the palliative treatment of Hodgkin's disease

pro·cess·ible *or* **pro·cess·able** \'prä¸sesəbəl, 'prō-\ *adj* **:** suitable for processing **:** capable of being processed — **pro·cess·ibil·i·ty** *or* **pro·cess·abil·i·ty** \¸prä¸sesə'biləd·ē, ¸prō-, -əd·ē, -i\ *n*

pro·ces·sor*\'präs¸esə(r), 'prō-\ *n* **1 a :** a computer **b :** the part of a computer system that operates on data — called also *central processing unit* **2 :** a computer program (as a compiler) that puts another program into a form acceptable to the computer

pro–choice \'prō'chóis\ *adj* **:** favoring legalized abortion — **pro–choic·er** \-ə(r)\ *n* pro·co·ag·u·lant \ˌprōkōˈagyələnt\ adj **:** promoting the coagulation of blood ⟨procoagulant activity⟩ — **procoagulant** n

producer*n **:** any of various organisms (as a green plant) which produce their own organic compounds from simple precursors (as carbon dioxide and inorganic nitrogen) and many of which are food sources for other organisms — compare CONSUMER

pro·duc·tiv·i·ty*\(ˌ)prōˌdəkˈtivəd·ē, ˌpräd(ˌ)ək-, prə-ˌdək-\ n **:** rate of production esp. of food by the utilization of solar energy by producer organisms

professional corporation n **:** a corporation organized by one or more licensed individuals (as a doctor, lawyer, dentist, or physical therapist) esp. for the purpose of providing professional services and obtaining tax advantages

profile*n **:** degree or level of public exposure ⟨trying to keep a low profile⟩ ⟨a job with a high profile⟩ ⟨the Administration's modest profile contributed to a honeymoon with the press —Russell Watson⟩

pro·ges·to·gen \prōˈjestəjən, -ˌjen\ n [progestational + -ogen (as in estrogen)] **:** any of several progestational steroids (as progesterone) — pro·ges·to·gen·ic \(ˌ)prō-ˌjestəˈjenik\ adj

pro·grade \ˈprōˈgrād\ adj **:** being or relating to orbital or rotational motion of a body that is in the same direction as that of another celestial body ⟨prograde orbit of a satellite⟩

program*n **:** a sequence of coded instructions that is part of an organism ⟨the animal does have a program of reactions to stimuli arising in its external and internal worlds —W. G. Van der Kloot⟩

program*vt -grammed or -gramed; -gram·ming or -gram·ing 1 **:** to code in an organism's program ⟨the death of cells and the destruction of tissues, organs, and organ systems are programmed as normal morphogenetic events in the development of multicellular organisms —J. W. Saunders, Jr.⟩ 2 **:** to provide with a biological program ⟨cells that have been programmed to synthesize hemoglobin⟩ 3 **:** to direct or predetermine completely as if by computer programming; esp **:** to direct or predetermine the thinking or behavior of ⟨those who . . . programmed him to kill —Jim Hougan⟩ ⟨children are programmed into violence —Lisa A. Richette⟩

pro·gram·ma·ble or pro·gram·able \ˈprōˌgraməbəl\ adj **:** capable of being programmed ⟨a programmable calculator⟩ — pro·gram·ma·bil·i·ty \ˌprōˌgramə-ˈbiləd·ē\ n

programmed instruction n **:** instruction through information given in small steps with each requiring a correct response by the learner before going on to the next step

pro·gram·mer* or pro·gram·er \ˈprōˌgramə(r), ˈprō-grəm-\ n **:** one that prepares an instructional program

pro·gram·ming* or pro·gram·ing* \-ˌgramiŋ, -grə-miŋ\ n 1 **:** the process of instructing or learning by means of an instructional program 2 **:** the process of preparing an instructional program

progressive rock n **:** rock music characterized by relatively complex phrasings and improvisations and intended for a sophisticated audience

pro·in·su·lin \(ˈ)prōˈin(t)s(ə)lən\ n [pro- rudimentary + insulin] **:** a single-chain pancreatic polypeptide precursor of insulin that gives rise to the double chain of insulin by loss of the middle part of the molecule

projection*n **:** the process or technique of reproducing a spatial object upon a plane or curved surface by projecting its points; also **:** the graphic reproduction so formed

pro·jec·tu·al \prəˈjekchəwəl, prōˈ-\ n [project + -ual (as in visual)] **:** a usu. instructional material (as a transparency) to be projected (as onto a screen) by a projector

pro·kary·ote also pro·cary·ote \(ˈ)prōˈkarē,ōt\ n [pro-before, for + kary- cell nucleus (deriv. of Gk karyon nut, kernel) + -ote (as in zygote)] **:** a cellular organism (as a bacterium or a blue-green alga) that does not have a distinct nucleus — pro·kary·ot·ic also pro·cary·ot·ic \(ˌ)prōˌkarēˈäd·ik\ adj

pro–life \ˈprōˈlīf\ adj **:** opposed to legalized abortion ⟨pro-life candidate⟩ ⟨pro-life demonstration⟩ — pro–lif·er \-ˈ(r)\ n

¹pro·mo \ˈprō(ˌ)mō\ adj [short for promotional] **:** serving to advertise **:** promotional ⟨promo leaflets⟩

²promo n, pl promos **:** a promotional announcement, film, recording, blurb, or appearance ⟨shot some promos for his syndicated TV show —New Yorker⟩

pro·nase \ˈprōˌnās, -āz\ n [perh. fr. protein + -ase enzyme] **:** a protease from an actinomycete (Streptomyces griseus)

pro·neth·a·lol \prōˈnethəˌlól, -ˌlōl\ n [propyl + amine + methyl + naphthalene + methanol] **:** a drug C₁₅H₁₉NO that is a beta-adrenergic blocking agent

pro·nu·cle·ar \(ˈ)prōˈn(y)üklēə(r), ÷ -kyələ(r)\ adj **:** advocating the use of nuclear-powered generating stations

pro·pa·nil \ˈprōpəˌnil\ n [propionic + anilide] **:** a herbicide C₉H₉Cl₂NO used esp. to control weeds in rice fields

pro·phase*\ˈprōˌfāz\ n **:** the initial stage of meiosis in which the chromosomes become visible, homologous pairs of chromosomes undergo synapsis and become shortened and thickened, individual chromosomes become visibly double as paired chromatids, chiasmata occur, and the nuclear membrane disappears

pro·pio·phe·none \ˌprōpēōˈfē,nōn, -ˈfen,ōn\ n [ISV propio- propionic acid + phenyl + -one ketone] **:** a flowery-smelling compound C₉H₁₀O used in perfumes and in the synthesis of pharmaceuticals (as ephedrine) and organic compounds

pro·poxy·phene \prōˈpäksəˌfēn\ n [propi- propionic acid + oxy- containing hydroxyl + phene (alter. of phenyl)] **:** an analgesic C₂₂H₂₉NO₂ structurally related to methadone but less addicting that is administered in the form of its hydrochloride — called also dextropropoxyphene

pro·pran·o·lol \prōˈpranəˌlól, -ˌlōl\ n [prob. alter. of earlier propanolol, fr. propanol + -ol chemical compound] **:** a beta-adrenergic blocking agent C₁₆H₂₁NO₂ used as the hydrochloride in the treatment of abnormal heart rhythms and angina pectoris

pross \ˈpräs\ also pros·sie \ˈpräsē, -si\ or pros·tie or pros·ty \ˈprästē, -ti\ n, pl prosses also prossies or prosties [by shortening & alter.] slang **:** a prostitute

pros·ta·glan·din \ˌprästəˈglandən\ n [ISV prostate gland + -in chemical compound; fr. its occurrence in the sexual glands of mammals] **:** any of various oxygenated unsaturated cyclic fatty acids of animals that may perform a variety of hormonelike actions (as in controlling blood pressure or smooth muscle contraction)

pro·tein·oid \'prō,tē,nóid, 'prōt°n,óid, 'prōd·ēə,nóid\ *n* [*protein* + *-oid* something similar] **:** any of various polypeptides which can be obtained by suitable polymerization of mixtures of amino acids and some of which may represent an early stage in the evolution of proteins

Protestant ethic *n* **:** an ethic that stresses the virtue of hard work, thrift, and self-discipline ⟨the *Protestant ethic*, which holds that work is the way to salvation and worldly achievement the sign of God's favor —J.A. Lukas⟩

pro·the·tel·ic \,prōthə'telik\ *adj* **:** of, relating to, or characterized by prothetely ⟨a *prothetelic* larva⟩ ⟨*prothetelic* malformations⟩

pro·tho·rac·ic gland \,prōthə'rasik-\ *n* **:** one of a pair of thoracic endocrine organs in some insects that control molting

protocol*n **:** a set of characters at the beginning and end of a message that enables one machine (as a computer) to communicate with another

pro·to·con·ti·nent \,prōd·ō'känt°nənt, -'käntnənt\ *n* [*proto-* first, beginning (deriv. of Gk *prōtos*) + *continent*] **:** SUPERCONTINENT

pro·to·por·ce·lain \,prōd·(,)ō'pōrs(ə)lən, -'pòr-\ *n* [prob. trans. of G *urporzellan*] **:** a porcelaneous ware lacking some of the qualities of a true porcelain; *specif* **:** a hard-fired gray kaolinic Chinese stoneware known since Han times

protract*vt **:** to extend forward or outward ⟨the mandible is *protracted* and retracted in chewing⟩

pro·vi·ral \,prō'vīrəl\ *adj* **:** of, relating to, or being a provirus ⟨*proviral* DNA⟩

Pro·vo \'prō(,)vō\ *n, pl* **Provos** [by shortening & alter. fr. *provisional* (wing), name of the faction] **:** a member of the extremist faction of the Irish Republican Army

prox·e·mics \präk'sēmiks\ *n pl but sing in constr* [*proximity* + *-emics* (as in *phonemics*)] **:** the study of the personal and cultural spatial needs of man and his interaction with his environing space — **prox·e·mic** \-ik\ *adj*

pseud \'süd\ *n* [short for *pseudo-intellectual*] *Brit* **:** a person who is affectedly intellectual ⟨age-old clash between *pseuds* and philistines —E.S. Turner⟩

pseu·do·cho·lin·es·ter·ase \,südō,kōlə'nestə,rās, -,räz\ *n* [*pseudo-* false (deriv. of Gk *pseudēs*) + *cholinesterase*] **:** an enzyme that hydrolyzes choline esters and that is found esp. in blood plasma

pseu·do–event \,südōə',vent, -ē,-\ *n* **:** an event (as a press conference) that is designed primarily to attract attention

pseu·do·ran·dom \,südō'randəm\ *adj* **:** being or involving entities (as numbers) that are selected by a definite computational process (as one involving a computer) but that satisfy one or more standard tests for statistical randomness

pseu·do·uri·dine \,südō'yùrȧ,dēn, -ȯdȧn\ *n* [ISV *pseudo-* isomer or related compound + *uridine*] **:** a nucleoside $C_9H_{12}O_6N_2$ that is a uracil derivative incorporated as a structural component into transfer RNA

psi·lo·cin \'sīləsən\ *n* [NL *Psilocybe mexicana*, fungus from which it is obtained + E *-in* chemical compound] **:** a hallucinogenic tertiary amine $C_{12}H_{16}N_2O$ obtained from a fungus (*Psilocybe mexicana*)

psi·lo·cy·bin \,sīlə'sībən\ *n* [NL *Psilocybe mexicana*, fungus from which it is obtained + E *-in* chemical com-

pound] **:** a hallucinogenic indole $C_{12}H_{17}N_2O_4P$ obtained from a fungus (*Psilocybe mexicana*)

psi·lo·phyt·ic \,sīlə'fid·ik\ *adj* **:** of, relating to, or being plants of the order Psilophytales

psi particle \,sī-, ,psī-\ *n* **:** J PARTICLE

pso·ra·len \'sōrələn, 'sòr-\ *n* [alter. of *psorlea*] **:** a substance $C_{11}H_6O_3$ found in some plants that photosensitizes mammalian skin

psych*also **psyche** \'sīk\ *vt* **psyched; psych·ing 1** **:** to make (oneself) psychologically ready for performance — usu. used with *up* ⟨*psyched* himself up for the race⟩ **2 :** to make psychologically uneasy **:** intimidate, scare ⟨pressure doesn't *psych* me —Jerry Quarry⟩ — often used with *out* ⟨the enemy are completely *psyched* out by this unorthodox move —Kathleen Karr⟩

psych *also* **psyche** *n* **:** the state of being psyched up ⟨spoiled his *psych* for the race —Patricia N. Warren⟩

psy·che·de·lia \,sīkə'dēlyə\ *n* [NL, fr. E *psychedelic* + L *-ia*, *n.* suffix] **:** the world of people, phenomena, or items associated with psychedelic drugs

¹psy·che·del·ic \,sīkȧ,delik, *also* -,dil- *or* -,dēl-\ *adj* [Gk *psychē* soul + *dēloun* to show, revel (fr. *dēlos* evident) + E *-ic*, adj. suffix] **1 a :** of, relating to, or causing an exposure of normally repressed psychic elements ⟨*psychedelic* drugs⟩ **b :** of, relating to, involving, or resulting from the use of psychedelic drugs ⟨*psychedelic* indulgences⟩ ⟨a *psychedelic* experience⟩ ⟨experimental *psychedelic* therapy⟩ **c :** of, relating to, or concerned with psychedelics ⟨hippies escaping to their *psychedelic* lairs —T.E. Mullaney⟩ ⟨*psychedelic* medicine designed to help LSD users⟩ **2 a :** imitating or reproducing the effects (as distorted or heightened sense perception) of psychedelic drugs ⟨*psychedelic* light show⟩ ⟨*psychedelic* art⟩ **b** (1) **:** brightly colored ⟨ferryboats soon will take on a *psychedelic* look, with an overall coat of international orange and touches of red and yellow —N.Y. Times⟩ (2) *of colors* **:** fluorescent **c :** making use of electronically distorted sounds ⟨*psychedelic* rock⟩ **3 :** of, relating to, dealing in, or being the culture associated with psychedelic drugs ⟨*psychedelic* shops⟩ — **psy·che·del·i·cal·ly** \-lȧk(ə)lē\ *adv*

²psychedelic *n* **1 :** a psychedelic drug (as LSD) **2 a** **:** a user or an advocate of psychedelic drugs **b :** a person with psychedelic social and cultural interests and orientation

psy·che·del·i·cize \,sīkə'delȧ,sīz\ *vt* **-cized; -ciz·ing** **:** to make psychedelic ⟨the general reluctance of suburbia to be *psychedelicized* —Hendrik Hertzberg⟩

psy·chic en·er·giz·er \,sīkik'enə(r),jīzə(r)\ *n* **:** an antidepressant drug

psy·cho·ac·tive \,sīkō'aktiv\ *adj* [*psycho-* soul, spirit, mind, psychological (fr. Gk *psychē* breath, life, soul) + *active*] **:** affecting the mind or behavior ⟨*psychoactive* drugs⟩

psy·cho·bi·og·ra·phy \,sī(,)kōbī'ägrəfē, -fi\ *n* **:** a character analysis **:** a biography written from a psychodynamic point of view ⟨chilling *psychobiographies* of sadists Stalin and Himmler —*Time*⟩ — **psy·cho·bi·og·ra·pher** \-fə(r)\ *n* — **psy·cho·bio·graph·i·cal** \-,bīə,grafəkəl\ *adj*

psy·cho·chem·i·cal \,sīkō'kemȧkəl\ *n* **:** a psychoactive chemical; *esp* **:** a chemical warfare agent (as a war gas) that acts on nervous centers and makes affected individuals temporarily helpless — **psychochemical** *adj*

psy·cho·his·to·ry \'sīkō͵hist(ə)rē, -ri\ *n* **:** an analysis of an historical person or issue by psychoanalytic methods ⟨everybody these days is writing *psychohistory* (which has the great blessing of being both irrefutable and unprovable) —John P. Roche⟩ — **psy·cho·his·to·ri·an** \͵sīkō(h)is͵tōrēən, -'tȯr-, -'tär-\ *n* — **psy·cho·his·tor·i·cal** \-(h)is'tȯrəkəl, -'tär-\ *adj*

psy·cho·phar·ma·ceu·ti·cal \͵sīkō͵färmə'süd·əkəl\ *n* **:** a drug having an effect on the mental state of a person

psy·cho·phar·ma·col·o·gist \-mə'käl9jəst\ *n* **:** a specialist in psychopharmacology

psy·cho·quack \'sīkō͵kwak\ *n* **:** an unqualified psychologist or psychiatrist — **psy·cho·quack·ery** \͵sīkō-'kwak(ə)rē-, -ri\ *n*

psy·cho·sur·geon \'sīkō͵sərjən, -͵sȯj-, -͵sȯij-\ *n* **:** a surgeon specializing in psychosurgery

psy·chot·o·gen \sī'käd·əjən\ *n* [*psychotic* + connective *-o-* + *-gen* producer] **:** a chemical agent (as a drug) that induces a psychotic state — **psy·chot·o·gen·ic** \(͵)sī͵käd·ə'jenik\ *adj*

psy·choto·mi·met·ic \sī͵käd·ōmə'med·ik, -mī'm-\ *adj* [*psychotic* + connective *-o-* + *mimetic*] **:** of, relating to, or involving psychotic alteration of behavior and personality ⟨*psychotomimetic* drugs⟩ — **psychotomimetic** *n* — **psy·choto·mi·met·i·cal·ly** \-ək(ə)lē, -li\ *adv*

psy·cho·tox·ic \'sīkə'täksik\ *adj* **:** of, relating to, or being an habituating drug (as amphetamine) which is not a true narcotic but the abuse of which may be correlated with deleterious personality and behavioral changes

psych–out \'sī͵kaȯt\ *n* **:** an act or an instance of psyching out ⟨in a *psych-out* you always make a show of confidence, while you work to undermine the confidence of your competition —Don Schollander & Duke Savage⟩

PTV *abbr* public television

public access *n* **:** the provision of access by the public to television broadcasting facilities (as a cable television channel) for the presentation of programs

public television *n* **:** television that provides cultural, informational, and instructional programs for the public and that does not promote the sale of a product or service but does identify the donors of program funds **:** noncommercial television

puff*n* **:** an enlarged region of a chromosome that is associated with intensely active genes involved in RNA synthesis

pu·gil stick \'pyüjəl-\ *n* [prob. fr. *pugilist* boxer, fr. L *pugil*] **:** a heavy pole with padded ends used in training in the armed services to simulate bayonet fighting

pu·la \'p(y)ülə\ *n, pl* **pula** [native name in Botswana] **1** **:** the basic monetary unit of Botswana **2 :** a coin or note representing one pula

pull*vi* **1** *of an offensive lineman in football* **:** to move back from the line of scrimmage toward one flank to provide blocking for a ballcarrier **2 :** to work together to achieve a goal ⟨*pulling* with them to get the bill passed⟩ — **pull one's coat** *slang* **:** to provide information — **pull out all the stops :** to use all one's resources without restraint ⟨the company *pulled out all the stops* in applying anti-union pressure —Irving Kahan⟩ — **pull the rug from under** *or* **pull the rug out from under :** to remove support or assistance from

pull date *n* **:** a date stamped on perishable products (as baked goods or dairy products) after which they should not be sold

pullman*n, often cap* **:** a large suitcase

pullman*adj, sometimes cap* **:** being long and square-shaped ⟨a *pullman* loaf of bread⟩

pul·sar \'pəl͵sär\ *n* [*pulse* + *-ar* (as in *quasar*)] **:** a celestial source of pulsating radio waves, X rays, or visible light characterized by a short relatively invariable interval (as .033 second) between pulses that is held to be a rotating neutron star

pulse*n* **:** a dose of a substance esp. when applied over a short period of time ⟨*pulse*-labeled DNA⟩ ⟨*pulses* of colchicine applied to the cells⟩

pump*n* **1 :** electromagnetic radiation for pumping atoms or molecules **2 :** the process of pumping atoms or molecules **3 :** a mechanism (as the sodium pump) for pumping atoms, ions, or molecules

pump*vt* **1 :** to transport (as ions) against a concentration gradient by the expenditure of energy **2 a :** to raise (atoms or molecules) to a higher energy level by exposure to usu. electromagnetic radiation at one of the resonant frequencies so that reemission may occur at another frequency resulting in amplification or sustained oscillation **b :** to expose (as a laser, semiconductor, or crystal) to radiation in the process of pumping **pump iron :** to lift weights as a means of exercise or body building

pumped storage *n* **:** a hydroelectric system in which electricity is generated during periods of greatest consumption by the use of water that has been pumped into a reservoir at a higher altitude during periods of low consumption

pump jockey *n, slang* **:** a gasoline station attendant

punch–up \'pən͵chəp\ *n, Brit* **:** a fight ⟨take your children to the park and try to get them a turn on the swings. Do not get involved in *punch-ups* with other fathers — *Punch*⟩

punk rock *n* **:** a form of new-wave rock music characterized by extreme and often deliberately offensive expressions of alienation and social discontent

puppy dog *n* **:** a domestic dog; *esp* **:** one having the lovable attributes of a puppy

purse crab *n* [fr. the resemblance of the abdomen to a purse] **:** any of the family Leucosiidae of crabs characterized by a granular carapace and long claws and by an adult female having the abdomen formed into a hemispherical cup that snaps shut against the sternum to form a brood chamber for the eggs; *esp* **:** one (*Persephona mediterranea*) that occurs in shallow water along the Atlantic coast of Mexico and of the U.S. as far north as New Jersey

push·down \'püsh͵daȯn\ *n* **:** a store of data (as in a computer) from which the most recently stored item must be the first retrieved — called also *pushdown list, pushdown stack*

push·out \'püsh͵aȯt\ *n* **:** one who is dismissed (as from a school or job)

pussycat*n* **:** one that is weak, compliant, or amiable **:** softy ⟨he's slender and will really get banged around. Still, he's not a *pussycat* —Bruce Newman⟩

put*vb* — **put the make on :** to make sexual advances toward ⟨on a trip to the . . . Naval Station, the men spent most of their time *putting the make on* a cute young Wave who was their guide —David Wellman⟩ — **put the screws on** *also* **put the screws to :** to exert extreme pressure on ⟨*putting the screws on* their people, pushing them to maximum effort —M. R. Weisbrod⟩

put down**vt** **1 a :** to belittle or disparage ⟨many writers want to *put down* not only their interviewers but their critics —Melvin Maddocks⟩ **b :** to disapprove or criticize ⟨*put down* for the way he dressed⟩ **2 :** to deflate or squelch ⟨a legendary step-parent: rigid, oppressive, untrue, ever ready to *put down* the honest feeling and sound thought that arise within the individual —R.B. Heilman⟩

put–down \'pùt‚daùn\ *n* **:** an act or instance of putting down; *esp* **:** a deflating remark ⟨the bright quips and devasting *put-downs* they wish they'd thought of on the air —Max Gunther⟩

put–on*\-‚òn, -‚än\ *n* **:** an instance of putting someone on ⟨couldn't decide whether the question was serious or just a *put-on*⟩; *also* **:** a parody or spoof ⟨a kind of *put-on* of every pretentious film ever made —C.A. Ridley⟩

putz \'pəts\ *n* [Yiddish; perh. akin to G *putz* plaster, adornment] **1** *slang* **:** penis **2** *slang* **:** a stupid, foolish, or ineffectual person **:** jerk

py·re·throid \pī'rē‚thròid, -'re‚-\ *n* [*pyreth*rin + *-oid* something similar] **:** any of various synthetic compounds related to and resembling in insecticidal properties the pyrethrins — **pyrethroid** *adj*

py·ri·meth·amine \‚pīrə'methə‚mēn, -əmə̇n\ *n* [*pyrimi*dine + *ethyl* + *amine*] **:** a folic acid antagonist $C_{12}H_{13}ClN_4$ used in the treatment of malaria and of toxoplasmosis

Q

qi·vi·ut \'kēvēət, -vē‚üt\ *n* [Esk] **:** the wool of the undercoat of the musk-ox

QSO \‚kyü(‚)e'sō\ *n* [quasi-stellar object] **:** QUASAR

Quaa·lude \'kwā‚lüd\ *trademark* — used for methaqualone

¹quad \'kwäd\ *n* [by shortening] **:** QUADRIPHONY

²quad *adj* [by shortening] **:** QUADRIPHONIC

³quad *n* [short for *quadrillion*] **:** a unit of energy equal to one quadrillion British thermal units

quad·ra·phon·ic \‚kwädrə'fänik\ *adj* [*quadra*- (modif. of *quadri*-) + *phonic*] **:** of or relating to quadriphony

quadratic form *n* **:** a homogeneous polynomial of the second degree $\langle x^2 + 5xy + y^2$ is a *quadratic form*$\rangle$

quad·ri·phon·ics \‚kwädrə'fäniks\ *n pl but sing in constr* [*quadriphonic* + -*s*, pl. suffix] **:** QUADRIPHONY

qua·dri·pho·ny \'kwädrə‚fänē, -‚fōnē; -ni\ *n* [*quadri*- four (fr. L) + -*phony* sound, deriv. of Gk *phōnē* sound] **:** the transmission, recording, or reproduction of sound by techniques that utilize four transmission channels — **quad·ri·phon·ic** \‚kwädrə'fänik\ *adj*

quan·ta·some \'kwäntə‚sōm\ *n* [prob. fr. *quanta*, pl. of *quantum* + -*some* body, deriv. of Gk *sōma*] **:** one of the chlorophyll-containing spheroids found in the grana of chloroplasts

quan·tized \'kwän‚tīzd\ *adj* **:** characterized by the property of taking on only discrete values $\langle$*quantized* angular momentum$\rangle$

quantum chromodynamics *n pl but sing in constr* **:** CHROMODYNAMICS

quan·tum electronics \‚kwäntəm-\ *n pl but sing in constr* **:** a branch of physics that deals with the interaction of radiation with discrete energy levels in substances (as in a maser or laser)

quantum jump*or* **quantum leap** *n* **:** an abrupt and usu. significant change or increase $\langle$represents a *quantum jump* in daytime television programming quality — Benjamin Stein$\rangle$ $\langle$prices are making *quantum leaps* — Terry Robards$\rangle$

quark \'kwärk, 'kwȯrk\ *n* [coined by Murray Gell-Mann *b*1929 Am. physicist] **:** a hypothetical particle that carries a fractional electric charge, is thought to come in several types (as up, down, strange, charmed, and bottom), and is held to be a constituent of known hadrons

quartz heater *n* **:** a portable electric radiant heater that has heating elements sealed in quartz-glass tubes in front of a reflective backing

quartz–io·dine lamp \‚kwȯ(ə)rts‚ī·ə‚dīn-, -əd²n-, -ə‚dēn-\ *n* **:** an incandescent lamp that has a quartz bulb and a tungsten filament and that contains iodine which reacts with the vaporized tungsten to prevent excessive blackening of the bulb

qua·sar \'kwā‚zär, *also* -‚sär\ *n* [*quasi*-stellar radio source] **:** any of various celestial objects that resemble stars but are apparently far more distant and emit copious quantities of radiation usu. as bright blue and ultraviolet light and powerful radio waves

qua·si·par·ti·cle \‚kwā‚zi‚pärtəkəl, 'kwā‚sī-, ‚kwäzē-, ‚kwäsē-, ‚kwäzē-\ *n* [*quasi*- as if, in some sense (fr. L *quasi* as if) + *particle*] **:** a composite entity (as a vibration in a solid) that is analogous in its behavior to a single particle

qua·si–stel·lar object \-‚stelər-\ *n* **:** QUASAR

quasi–stellar radio source *n* **:** QUASAR

quas·qui·cen·ten·ni·al \‚kwäskwē(‚)sen'tenēəl, -skwə-\ *n* [fr. L *quadrans* quarter, after L *semis* half: E *sesquicentennial*] **:** a 125th anniversary — **quasquicentennial** *adj*

queen·side \'kwēn‚sīd\ *n* **:** the side of the chessboard containing the file on which both queens sit at the beginning of the game

queen–size *adj* **1 :** having dimensions of approximately 60 inches by 80 inches — used of a bed **2 :** of a size that fits a queen-size bed $\langle$a *queen-size* bedspread$\rangle$

queen substance *n* **:** a pheromone that is secreted by queen bees, is consumed by worker bees, and inhibits the development of their ovaries; *also* **:** the same or a similar substance secreted by termites

queue*n* **:** a sequence of messages or jobs held in auxiliary storage awaiting transmission or processing

queue*vt* **queued; queu·ing** *or* **queue·ing :** to send to or place in a queue

queuing theory *n* **:** the mathematical and statistical theory of queues and waiting lines (as in heavy traffic or in the use of telephone circuits)

quiche lor·raine \-lə'rän, -lȯ'-, -lō'-\ *n, often cap L* [*Lorraine*, region of western Europe] **:** a quiche containing cheese and crisp bacon bits

quick kick *n* **:** a punt in football made on first, second, or third down from a running or passing formation and designed to take the opposing team by surprise

quick opener *n* **:** an offensive play in football in which a back takes a direct handoff and runs straight to a hole in the line

qui·nu·cli·di·nyl ben·zi·late \kwə‚n(y)üklə‚dēn²l'ben-zə‚lāt\ *n* [*quinuclidine* + -*yl* chemical radical + *benzil* + -*ate* derivative compound] **:** BZ

quotient group *n* **:** a group whose elements are the cosets of a normal subgroup of a given group

quotient ring *n* **:** a ring whose elements are the cosets of an ideal in a given ring

R

r*abbr* **1** repeat **2** rerun
R *adj* [restricted] *of a motion picture* **:** of such a nature that admission is restricted to persons over a specified age (as 17) unless accompanied by a parent or guardian — compare G, PG, X
rabbit*n* **:** a runner on a track team who sets a fast pace for a teammate in the first part of a long-distance race
rab·bit \'rabət\ *vi* [perh. fr. ON *rabba* to chatter] *Brit* **:** to talk idly or incessantly — often used with *on* ⟨look at the way we go *rabbiting* on about our wonderful system of justice —*The People*⟩
rabbit ears *n pl* **:** an indoor dipole television antenna consisting of two usu. extensible rods connected to a base to form a V shape
race walking *n* **:** racing at a fast walk in track-and-field competition with each competitor required to maintain continuous foot contact with the ground and to keep the supporting leg straight — **race walker** *n*
rack car*n* **:** a railroad flatcar equipped with a 2-level or 3-level framework for transporting motor vehicles
rac·lette \ra'klet\ *n* [F, lit., scraper, fr. F *racler* to scrape] **:** a dish of Swiss origin consisting of melted cheese traditionally served with tiny boiled potatoes and sour pickles; *also* **:** a firm cheese suitable for use in this dish
rac·quet·ball \'rakət,ból\ *n* **:** a game similar to handball that is played on a 4-walled court with a short-handled racket and a ball larger than a handball
radar astronomy *n* **:** astronomy dealing with investigations of celestial bodies in the solar system by analyzing radar waves directed toward and reflected from the object being studied
radar telescope *n* **:** a radar transmitter-receiver with an antenna for use in radar astronomy
ra·di·al* \'rādēəl\ *n* **:** RADIAL TIRE
ra·di·al·ly symmetrical \,rādēəlē-\ *adj* **:** of, relating to, or characterized by radial symmetry
radial tire *or* **radial–ply tire** \'rādēəl;'plī-\ *n* **:** a pneumatic tire in which the ply cords that extend to the beads are laid at right angles to the center line of the tread
radical chic *n* **:** a fashionable practice among socially prominent people of associating with radicals or members of minority groups
ra·di·es·the·sia \,rādē(,)es'thēzh(ē)ə\ *n* [NL, fr. L *radius* ray + NL *esthesia* feeling, sensitiveness] **1 :** sensitiveness held to enable a person with the aid of divining rod or pendulum to detect things (as the presence of underground water, the nature of an illness, or the guilt of a suspected person); *also* **:** dowsing, divining **2 :** a study that deals with radiesthesia
ra·dio·car·bon dating \,rādēō;kärbən-, -;káb-\ *n* **:** CARBON DATING
ra·dio·chro·mato·gram \,rādē(,)ōkrō'mad·ə,gram, -krə'-\ *n* **:** a chromatogram revealing one or more radioactive substances

ra·dio·chro·ma·tog·ra·phy \,rādē(,)ō,krōmə'tägrəfē\ *n* [*radio-* radiation, radioactive + *chromatography*] **:** the process of making a quantitative or qualitative determination of a radioisotope-labeled substance by measuring the radioactivity of the appropriate zone or spot in the chromatogram — **ra·dio·chro·mato·graph·ic** \-,mad·ə-'grafik\ *adj*
ra·dio·ecol·o·gy \-ə'käləjē, -ē'k-\ *n* **:** the study of the effects of radiation and radioactive substances on ecological communities — **ra·dio·eco·log·i·cal** \-,ēkə'läjəkəl, -,ek-\ *adj* — **ra·dio·ecol·o·gist** \-ə'käləjəst, -ē'k-\ *n*
radio galaxy *n* **:** a galaxy that includes a source from which radio energy is detected
ra·dio·im·mu·no·as·say \'rādē,ō,imyənō'as,ā, -im,yü-, -,nōa'sā\ *n* **:** immunoassay of a substance (as insulin) that has been radioactively labeled — **ra·dio·im·mu·no·as·say·able** \-a'sāəbəl\ *adj*
ra·dio·im·mu·no·log·i·cal \-,imyənə'läjəkəl, -im,yünə-\ *also* **ra·dio·im·mu·no·log·ic** \-'läjik\ *adj* **:** of, relating to, or involving radioimmunoassay ⟨*radioimmunological* detection of a hormone⟩
ra·dio·iso·to·pic \,rādē(,)ō,īsə'täpik, -'tō-\ *adj* **:** of, relating to, or being a radioisotope ⟨*radioisotopic* techniques⟩ — **ra·dio·iso·to·pi·cal·ly** \-ək(ə)lē\ *adv*
ra·dio·phar·ma·ceu·ti·cal \-,färmə'süd·ə·kəl, -,fäm-\ *n* **:** a radioactive drug used for diagnostic or therapeutic purposes — **radiopharmaceutical** *adj*
ra·dio·pro·tec·tive \-prə'tektiv\ *adj* **:** serving to protect or aiding in protecting against the injurious effect of radiations ⟨*radioprotective* drugs⟩ — **ra·dio·pro·tec·tion** \-prə'tekshən\ *n*
ra·dio·pro·tec·tor \-'tektə(r)\ *also* **ra·dio·pro·tec·tor·ant** \-'tektərənt\ *n* **:** a radioprotective chemical agent
ra·dio·re·sis·tance \-rə'zistən(t)s\ *n* **:** resistance (as of a cell or a mutation) to the effects of radiant energy — **ra·dio·re·sis·tant** \-tənt\ *adj*
ra·dio·sen·si·tiz·er \-'sen(t)sə,tīzə(r)\ *n* **:** a substance or condition capable of increasing the radiosensitivity of a cell or tissue — **ra·dio·sen·si·ti·za·tion** \-,sen(t)sədə'zāshən, -ə,tī'z-\ *n* — **ra·dio·sen·si·tiz·ing** \-'sen(t)sə,tiziŋ\ *adj*
ra·dio·ster·il·ized \-;sterə,līzd\ *adj* **:** sterilized by irradiation (as with X rays or gamma rays) ⟨*radiosterilized* mosquitoes⟩ ⟨*radiosterilized* syringes⟩ — **ra·dio·ster·il·iza·tion** \-,sterələ'zāshən, -,li-\ *n*
ra·dio·te·lem·e·try \-tə'lemə,trē\ *n* **1 :** TELEMETRY 1 **2 :** BIOTELEMETRY — **ra·dio·tele·met·ric** \-,telə;me·trik\ *adj*
ra·dio–ul·na \-'əlnə\ *n* [NL, fr. *radius* (fr. L) + connective *-o-* + *ulna*] **:** a single bone in the forelimb of an amphibian (as a frog) that represents fusion of the separate radius and ulna of higher forms
Rag·doll \'rag,däl, -,dól\ *trademark* — used for a breed of domestic cats
rag·top \'rag,täp\ *n* **:** a convertible automobile

rail***n** : a specialized drag-racing vehicle with very large wide tires in the rear and tiny bicycle tires in the front and with a chassis that consists essentially of two long braced rails

rainbow*or **rainbow pill** *n, slang* : a drug in a tablet or capsule of several colors; *esp* : a combination of the sodium derivatives of amobarbital and secobarbital in a blue and red capsule

rain date *n* : an alternative date set aside for use if a scheduled outdoor event (as a ball game or concert) must be postponed because of rain

rain-suit \'rān,süt\ *n* : a suit of waterproof material consisting of pants and a usu. hooded jacket for wear in the rain usu. over ordinary clothes

raised ranch *n* : BI-LEVEL

ral·ly·mas·ter \'ralē,mastə(r), -li-\ *n* : one who organizes and conducts an automobile rally

ralph \'ralf, 'raúf\ *vb* [imit.] *slang* : to vomit

RAM *abbr* random-access memory

ramaki *var of* RUMAKI

rancher***n** : a one-story dwelling typically having an open plan and a low-pitched roof : ranch house

ranch·ette \,ran'chet\ *n* : a small ranch

rand \'rand, *In So. Africa usu* 'ránd *or* 'ránt *or* 'ränt (*the last is usual in Afrikaans*)\ *n, pl* **rand** *or* **rands** [fr *The Rand* (Witwatersrand), gold-producing district in South Africa] **1 a** : the basic monetary unit of the Republic of So. Africa **b** : the basic monetary unit of Lesotho **2** : a coin or note representing one rand

R and B *n* : RHYTHM AND BLUES

R and D *n* : research and development — usu. written *R&D* ⟨pharmaceutical houses decided the *R&D* of cancer drugs wouldn't pay its way in profits —Philip Nobile⟩

ran·dom–ac·cess \,randə'mak,ses\ *adj* : permitting access to stored data in any order the user desires ⟨*random-access* computer memory⟩

ran·dom·iz·er \'randə,mīzə(r)\ *n* : a device or procedure used for randomization ⟨a spinner with 10 positions can be used as a *randomizer* for the 10 digits⟩

rank***n** **1** : the number of linearly independent rows in a matrix **2** : a unit of wood cut for fuel equal to a stack 4 × 8 feet with lengths of pieces from about 12 to 16 inches : face cord

¹rap \'rap\ *n* [perh. by shortening & alter. fr. *repartee*] : talk, conversation, chat ⟨has long, disjointed philosophical *raps* with his closest friend —Chandler Brossard⟩

²rap *vi* **rapped; rap·ping** : to talk freely and frankly ⟨down at the corner bar *rapping* —Newsweek⟩ — **rap·per** \'rapə(r)\ *n*

rapid eye movement *n* : rapid conjugate movement of the eyes associated esp. with REM sleep

rapid eye movement sleep *n* : REM SLEEP

rap session *n* : a small usu. informal group discussion ⟨*rap sessions* in college dorms —J.S. Bruner⟩

rap sheet *n* : a police arrest record esp. for an individual

rapture of the deep *n* : NITROGEN NARCOSIS

Ras·ta \'rastə\ *also* **Ras·ta·man** \-mən, -,man\ *n, pl* **Rastas** *also* **Ras·ta·men** \-mən, -,men\ [*Rasta* by shortening; *Rastaman* fr. *Rasta* + *man*] : RASTAFARIAN

Ras·ta·fa·ri·an \,rastə'farēən, -'fer-\ *n* [*Ras Tafari*, before coronation name of Haile Selassie †1975 Ethiopian emperor + E *-an*] : an adherent of Rastafarianism

Ras·ta·fa·ri·an·ism \-ə,nizəm\ *n* : a religious cult among black Jamaicans that teaches the eventual redemption of blacks and their return to Africa, employs the ritualistic use of marijuana, forbids the cutting of hair, and venerates Haile Selassie as a god

raster***n** : a pattern of sequentially and closely laid out parallel scanning lines or rows of dots that form the image on a cathode-ray tube (as in a television or computer display)

rate of change : a value that results from dividing the change of a function of a variable by the change in the variable ⟨velocity is the *rate of change* of distance with respect to time⟩

rat fink \'rat',fiŋk\ *n* : FINK

ratio *vt* **1** : to express as a ratio **2** : to enlarge or reduce the size of (a photograph) in accordance with a ratio

rational*adj : relating to, consisting of, or being one or more rational numbers

rat's ass *n* : a minimum amount or degree of care or interest : hoot, damn — usu. used in the phrase *don't give a rat's ass*; often considered vulgar

raunch \'rónch, 'ränch\ *n* [back-formation fr. *raunchy*] : vulgarity, bawdiness, smuttiness ⟨Rabelais without the *raunch* would be a drag —Milton Mayer⟩

rave–up \'rā,vəp\ *n, Brit* : a wild party : bash ⟨go away for the weekend leaving the teenagers to have an all-night *rave-up* —Rosalie Shann⟩

raw bar *n* : a self-service counter in a restaurant featuring an array of raw shellfish

Ray·naud's phenomenon \(')rā'nōz-\ *also* **Raynaud's syndrome** *n* [Maurice *Raynaud* †1881 Fr. physician] : the symptoms associated with Raynaud's disease

RBE *abbr* relative biological effectiveness

read*vt **1** : to sense the meaning of (information) in recorded and coded form (as in storage) : acquire (information) from storage — used of a computer or data processor **2** : to read the coded information on (as tape or a punch card)

read*\'rēd\ *n* : something that is read ⟨an old-fashioned good *read*, bursting with characters and drama and emotion —Jane Clapperton⟩

read–only memory \,rēd'onlē-, -li-\ *n* : a small computer memory that cannot be changed by the computer and that contains a special-purpose program

read-out*\'rēd,aút\ *n* **1** : the process of reading **2 a** : the process of removing information from an automatic device (as an electronic computer) and displaying it in an understandable form **b** : the information removed from such a device and displayed or recorded (as by magnetic tape or printing device) **c** : a device used for readout **3** : the radio transmission of data or pictures from a space vehicle either immediately upon acquisition or later by means of playback of a tape recording

ready–made \'redē,mād, -di-\ *n* : an artifact (as a comb or a pair of ice tongs) selected and displayed as a work of art ⟨what the objet trouvé was to Dada: a perfect *ready-made* —John Simon⟩

re·ag·gre·gate \(')rē'agrə,gāt\ *vt* : to cause to re-form into an aggregate or a whole ⟨*reaggregate* the subunits of a macromolecule⟩ ~ *vi* : to re-form into an aggregate or whole ⟨the cells *reaggregated* into organized tissue⟩ — **re·ag·gre·gate** \-'agrə,gāt, -əgət\ *n* — **re·ag·gre·ga·tion** \,rē,agrə'gāshən\ *n*

real*_adj_ **:** REAL-VALUED ⟨functions of a _real_ variable⟩

real time _n_ **:** the actual time during which something takes place ⟨the computer may partly analyze the data in _real time_ (as it comes in) —R.H. March⟩ ⟨here's how it looked in _real time_ and in slow motion —J.W. Chancellor⟩ — **real–time** _adj_

real–valued \ˌrē(ə)lˈval(ˌ)yüd, -ˌvalyəd\ _adj_ **:** taking on only real numbers for values ⟨a _real-valued_ function⟩

re·branch \(ˈ)rēˈbranch\ _vi_ **:** to form secondary branches

recall*_n_ **1 :** a public call by a manufacturer for the return of a product that may be defective or contaminated **2 :** the ability (as of an information retrieval system) to retrieve stored material

re·ca·mier \ˌrākəˈmyā\ _n_ [so called fr. its appearance in a well-known portrait of Mme. Récamier by Jacques-Louis David †1825 Fr. painter] **:** a usu. backless couch with a high curved headrest and low footrest

re·can·a·li·za·tion \(ˌ)rēˌkanᵊləˈzāshən, -ˌīˈz-\ _n_ **:** the process of reuniting an interrupted channel of a bodily tube (as a vas deferens) — **re·ca·nal·ize** \ˈrēkəˈnalˌīz, (ˈ)rēˈkanᵊlˌīz\ _vt_

receptor*_n_ **:** a cellular entity (as a beta-receptor or alpha-receptor) that is a postulated intermediary between a chemical agent (as a neurohumor) acting on nervous tissue and the physiological or pharmacological response

re·charge·able \(ˈ)rēˈchärjəbəl, -ˌaj-\ _adj_ **:** capable of being recharged ⟨_rechargeable_ batteries⟩

re·char·ter \(ˈ)rēˈchärtər, -ˌchảd·ə(r\ _vt_ **:** to grant a new charter to ⟨_rechartered_ the national bank⟩ — **recharter** _n_

reciprocal*_n_ **:** MULTIPLICATIVE INVERSE

re·cla·ma \rāˈklāmə, -ämə\ _vi_ **re·cla·maed; re·cla·ma·ing** [perh. fr. L _reclamare_ to contradict loudly] **:** to request the reconsideration of a decision or a change in policy — used esp. in the military

recombinant DNA _n_ **:** DNA prepared in the laboratory by breaking up and splicing together DNA from several different species of organisms

re·cur·sion*\rəˈkərzhən, rēˈ-, -ˈkōzh-, -ˈkəizh-, _chiefly Brit_ -ˈkōshən\ _n_ **:** the determination of a succession of elements (as numbers or functions) by operation on one or more preceding elements according to a rule or formula involving a finite number of steps

re·cur·sive \rəˈkərsiv, rēˈ-, -ˈkōs-, -ˈkəis-\ _adj_ [_recursion_ + _-ive_, adj. suffix] **1 :** of, relating to, or involving mathematical recursion **2 :** of, relating to, or constituting a procedure that can repeat itself indefinitely or until a specified condition is met ⟨a _recursive_ rule in a grammar⟩ — **re·cur·sive·ly** \-lē, -li\ _adv_ — **re·cur·sive·ness** \-nəs\ _n_

re·cy·cle*\(ˈ)rēˈsīkəl\ _vt_ **1 :** to process (as liquid body waste, glass, or cans) in order to regain material for human use ⟨automobiles should be _recycled_ by melting and manufacturing into new products —J.S. Poliskin⟩ **2 :** to cause (as an electric generator) to accelerate gradually in bringing up to full power production **3 :** to adapt to a new use **:** alter, transform ⟨_recycle_ recent real events into prime time entertainment —Karl Meyer⟩ **4 :** to bring back **:** reuse, repeat ⟨a light, chatty tribute that _recycles_ a number of good anecdotes —Larry McMurtry⟩ **5 :** to make ready for reuse **:** restore ⟨the move to _recycle_ unused gas stations —Robert Frausto⟩ ∼ _vi_ **1 :** to stop the counting and return to an earlier point in a count-

down **2 :** to return to an original condition so that operation can begin again — used of an electronic device — **re·cy·cla·ble** \-k(ə)ləbəl\ _adj_ — **re·cy·cler** \-k(ə)lə(r)\ _n_

recycle*_n_ **:** the process of recycling

red·brick \ˈredˈbrik, _in attributive position also_ ˌredˌbrik\ _adj_ **1 :** built of red brick **2** [fr. the common use of red brick in constructing the buildings of relatively modern British universities] **:** of, relating to, or being the British universities founded in modern times — compare OXBRIDGE, PLATEGLASS

re·de·scribe \ˌrēdəˈskrīb\ _vt_ **:** to describe anew or again; _esp_ **:** to give a new and more complete description to (as a biological taxon)

re·de·scrip·tion \-dəˈskripshən\ _n_ **:** a new and more complete description (as of a biological taxon)

red–eye*_n_ **1 :** the phenomenon of a subject's eyes appearing red in color flash photography **2 :** a late night or overnight flight ⟨catch the _red-eye_ to New York —Lowell Cohn⟩

Red Guard _n_ [_red_ communist + _guard_] **:** a member of a teenage activist organization in China serving the Maoist cause

re·dis·tri·bu·tion·ist \(ˈ)rēˈdistrəˈbyüsh(ə)nəst\ _n_ **:** one that believes in or advocates a welfare state

red·line*\(ˈ)redˈlīn\ _vi_ **:** to withhold home-loan funds or insurance from neighborhoods considered poor economic risks ∼ _vt_ **:** to discriminate against in housing or insurance — **red·lin·ing** \-ˌlīniŋ\ _n_

red·line \(ˈ)redˈlīn\ _n_ **:** a recommended safety limit **:** the fastest, farthest, or highest point or degree considered safe; _also_ **:** the red line which marks this point on a gauge

reds _n pl, slang_ **:** red drug capsules containing the sodium salt of secobarbital — called also _red devils_

red·shirt*\ˈredˈshərt, -ˌshət, -ˌshəit\ _n_ [fr. the red jersey commonly worn by such a player in practice scrimmages against the regulars] **:** a college athlete who is kept out of varsity competition for a year in order to extend the period of his eligibility — **redshirt** _vb_ — **red·shirt·ing** \-ˌshərd·iŋ, -ˌshōd·iŋ, -ˌshəid·iŋ\ _n_

re·duc·tion·ism*\rəˈdəkshəˌnizəm\ _n_ **:** the attempt to explain all biological processes by the same explanations (as by physical laws) that chemists and physicists use to interpret inanimate matter; _also_ **:** the theory that complete reductionism is possible

redundant*_adj_ **1 :** serving as a duplicate for preventing failure of an entire system (as a spacecraft) upon failure of a single component **2** _Brit_ **:** being out of work **:** laid off **:** discharged ⟨he appeared in successive shows . . . before being made _redundant_ —The Guardian (London)⟩ ⟨hang on and hope not to be _redundant_ — Juliana Bland⟩

re·du·pli·cate*\rəˈd(y)üpləˌkāt, (ˈ)rē-\ _vi_ **:** to undergo reduplication ⟨chromosomes _reduplicate_⟩

re·dux \(ˈ)rēˈdəks\ _adj_ [L, lit., brought back, returned, fr. L _reducēre_ to bring back, fr. _re-_ re- + _ducēre_ lead] **:** brought back — used postpositively

reel–to–reel \ˌrē(ə)ltəˌrē(ə)l, -də-\ _adj_ **:** of, relating to, or utilizing magnetic tape that requires threading on a take-up reel ⟨a _reel-to-reel_ tape recorder⟩

reflection*_n_ **1 :** a transformation of a figure in which each point is replaced by a point symmetric with respect to a line   **2 :** a transformation that involves reflection in more than one axis of a rectangular coordinate system

re·fried beans \(')rē¦frīd-\ *n pl* [trans. of Sp *frijoles refritos*] **:** FRIJOLES REFRITOS

re·fuse·nik *or* **re·fus·nik** \rə'fyüz(ˌ)nik, rē-\ *n* [*refuse* + -*nik* one connected with] **:** a Soviet scientist who is refused permission to emigrate

reg·gae \'rä(ˌ)gā, 're-; re'gā, rā-; 'regē, -gi\ *n* [origin unknown] **:** popular music of Jamaican origin that combines indigenous styles with elements of rock 'n' roll and soul music and is performed at moderate tempos with the accent on the offbeat

region*n* **:** an open connected set together with none, some, or all of the points on its boundary ⟨a simple closed curve divides the plane into two *regions*⟩

re·gion·al \'rējənˀl, -jnəl\ *n* **:** something or someone regional

register*n*   **1 :** a device in a computer or calculator for storing small amounts of data; *esp* **:** one in which data can be both stored and operated on   **2 :** a variety of a language that is appropriate to a particular subject or occasion

regulator gene *or* **regulatory gene** *n* **:** a gene controlling the production of a genetic repressor

re·hab \'rē¦hab\ *n, often attrib* [by shortening]   **1 :** rehabilitation   **2 :** a rehabilitated dwelling ⟨over 1,000 *rehabs* sold as condominiums —*Civil Engineering*⟩ — **rehab** *vt* — **re·hab·ber** \-ə(r)\ *n*

reinforce*vb* **-forced; -forc·ing** *vt* **:** to stimulate (as an experimental animal or a student) with a reinforcer following a correct or desired performance — **re·in·force·able** \ˌrēən'fo(ə)rsəbəl, -'fo(ə)r-, -'foəs-, -'fo(ə)s-\ *adj*

re·in·forc·er\-sə(r)\ *n* **:** a stimulus (as a reward or the removal of discomfort) that is effective esp. in operant conditioning because it regularly follows a desired response

rejection*n* **:** the immunological process of sloughing off foreign tissue or an organ (as a transplant) by the recipient organism

re·jec·tive art \rə¦jektiv-\ *n* **:** MINIMAL ART

relative biological effectiveness *n* **:** the relative capacity of a particular ionizing radiation to produce a response in a biological system — abbr. *RBE*

rel·a·tiv·is·tic\ˌreləd-ə'vistik\ *adj*   **1 :** moving at a velocity such that there is a significant change in mass and other properties in accordance with the theory of relativity ⟨a *relativistic* electron⟩   **2 :** of or relating to a relativistic particle

released time*n* **:** time off from regular duties (as teaching) granted for taking part in some specific activity (as research or committee work)

relevance*n* **:** the ability (as of an information retrieval system) to retrieve material that satisfies the needs of the user

relocate*vi* **:** to move to a new location

reluctant dragon *n* **:** a leader (as a politician or military officer) who avoids confrontation or conflict

REM \ˌär(ˌ)ē'em, 'rem\ *n* **:** RAPID EYE MOVEMENT

re·mas·ter \(')rē¦mastə(r)\ *vt* **:** to create a new master of esp. by altering or enhancing the sound quality of an older recording

remote*adj* **:** acting, acted on, or controlled indirectly or from a distance ⟨time-sharing and other *remote* computing services —*GT&E Annual Report*⟩; *also* **:** relating to the acquisition of information about a distant object (as by radar or photography) without coming into physical contact with it ⟨*remote* sensing instruments⟩

REM sleep *n* **:** a state of sleep that recurs cyclically several times during a normal period of sleep and that is characterized by increased neuronal activity of the forebrain and midbrain, by depressed muscle tone, and esp. in man by dreaming, rapid eye movements, and vascular congestion of the sex organs — called also *paradoxical sleep, rapid eye movement sleep*

re·new·able\rə'n(y)üəbəl, rē'-\ *adj* **:** capable of being replaced by natural ecological cycles or sound management practices ⟨a *renewable* natural resource⟩

ren·min·bi \'ren'min'bē\ *n pl* [Chin *ren²min²* (fr. *ren²* human + *min²* people) people's + *bi⁴* currency] **:** the currency of the People's Republic of China **:** yuan

re·no·gram \'rēnəˌgram\ *n* [*reno-* kidney, renal (fr. L *renes* kidneys) + -*gram* drawing, writing, record, deriv. of Gk *gramma* letter, writing] **:** a photographic depiction of the course of renal excretion of a radioactively labeled substance — **re·no·graph·ic** \ˌrēnə'grafik\ *adj* — **re·nog·ra·phy** \rē'nägrəfē, rə'-\ *n*

re·no·vas·cu·lar \ˌrēnō¦vaskyələ(r)\ *adj* **:** of, relating to, or involving the blood vessels of the kidneys ⟨*renovascular* hypertension⟩

rent strike *n* **:** a refusal by a group of tenants to pay rent (as in protest against poor service)

reo·vi·rus \ˌrēō¦vīrəs\ *n* [respiratory enteric orphan *virus*] **:** any of a group of rather large, widely distributed, and possibly tumorigenic viruses with double-stranded RNA

repertoire*n* **:** a list or supply of capabilities ⟨the instruction *repertoire* of a computer⟩

rep·li·ca·ble \'repləkəbəl\ *adj* [LL *replicabilis* worth repeating, fr. *replicare* to repeat, reply + L -*abilis* capable of] **:** capable of replication ⟨*replicable* experimental results⟩

rep·li·case \'repləkās, -āz\ *n* [*replication* + -*ase* enzyme] **:** a polymerase that promotes synthesis of a particular RNA in the presence of a template of RNA — called also *RNA replicase*

rep·li·cate\'repləˌkāt\ *vi* **-cat·ed; -cat·ing :** to undergo replication **:** produce a replica of itself ⟨*replicating* virus particles⟩

replicate*n* **:** something (as a gene, DNA, or a cell) produced by replication

rep·li·ca·tive \'repləˌkād·iv\ *adj* **:** of, relating to, involved in, or characterized by replication ⟨the *replicative* form of tobacco mosaic virus⟩

re·po \'rē(ˌ)pō\ *n* [by shortening & alter. of *repurchase*] **:** a contract giving the seller of securities (as treasury bills) the right to repurchase after a specified period and the buyer the right to retain interest earnings

re·po·lar·iza·tion \ˌrē¦pōlərə'zāshən, -ə¦rī'z-\ *n* **:** polarization of a muscle fiber, cell, or membrane following depolarization

repress*vt* **:** to inactivate (a gene or formation of a gene product) by allosteric combination at a DNA binding site

re·press·ible \rə'presəbəl\ *adj* **:** capable of being repressed ⟨*repressible* enzymes controlled by their end products⟩ — **re·press·ibil·i·ty** \-,presə'biləd·ē\ *n*

re·pres·sor*\rə'presə(r)\ *n* **:** a protein that is determined by a regulator gene and that inhibits the function of a genetic operator

re·pro·cess \(')rē'prās,es, -,'prō-, -səs\ *vt* **:** to subject to a special process or treatment in preparation for reuse; *specif* **:** to extract uranium and plutonium from the spent fuel rods of a nuclear reactor for use again as fuel

re·pro·gram \(,)rē'prō,gram, -'prōgrəm\ *vt* **:** to program anew; *esp* **:** to write new programs for (as a computer) ~ *vi* **:** to rewrite a computer program

re·prog·ra·phy \rə'prägrəfē, rē'p-\ *n* [ISV *repro*duction + *-graphy* writing, representation, deriv. of Gk *graphein* to write] **:** the facsimile reproduction (as by photocopying) of graphic matter (as books or documents) — **re·prog·ra·pher** \-fə(r)\ *n* — **re·pro·graph·ic** \,rēprə-,grafik, ,rep-\ *adj* — **re·pro·graph·ics** \-iks\ *n pl but sing in constr*

re–re·fine \,'rērə'fīn, -rē'-\ *vt* **:** to refine (used motor oil) in order to produce a clean usable lubricant — **re–re·fin·er** \-ə(r)\ *n*

re·seg·re·ga·tion \(,)rē,segrə'gāshən\ *n* **:** a return (as of a school) to a state of segregation after a period of desegregation

re·ser·pi·nized \rə'sərpə,nīzd, rē-\ *adj* **:** treated or medicated with reserpine or a reserpine derivative ⟨*reserpinized* animals⟩ — **re·ser·pin·iza·tion** \-,sərpənə-'zāshən, -,nī'z-\ *n*

reserve*n **:** the lowest price that a seller agrees to accept for an item offered at auction

reserve clause *n* **:** a clause formerly common in contracts of professional athletes reserving for the club the exclusive right automatically to renew the contract and binding the athlete to the club for his entire playing career or until traded or released

re·sid \rə'zid\ *n* [by shortening] **:** RESIDUAL OIL

residence*n **:** the persistence of a substance that is suspended or dissolved in a medium ⟨the *residence* time of a pollutant⟩

residual*n **:** a payment (as to an actor or writer) for each rerun esp. of a commercial

residual oil *n* **:** fuel oil that remains after the removal of valuable distillates (as gasoline) from petroleum and that is used esp. by industry — called also *resid*

residual security *n* **:** common stock or a security convertible into common stock

residue*n **:** the remainder after subtracting a multiple of a modulus from an integer or a power of the integer which can appear as the second of two terms in a congruence ⟨2 and 7 are *residues* of 12 modulo 5⟩ ⟨9 is a quadratic *residue* of 7 modulo 5 since $7^2 - 8 \times 5 = 9$⟩

residue class *n* **:** the set of elements (as integers) that leave the same remainder when divided by the same modulus

resilience*n **:** an ability to recover from or adjust easily to misfortune or change ⟨marvellous *resilience* and courage in recovering from setbacks —*Times Lit. Supp.*⟩

resistance*n **:** RESISTANCE LEVEL

resistance level *or* **resistance area** *n* **:** a price level on a rising market at which a security resists further advance due to increased attractiveness of the price to potential sellers

re·sis·to·jet \rə'zistō,jet, rē'z-\ *n* [*resist*ance + connective *-o-* + *jet*] **:** a small reaction engine that uses electrically heated hydrogen or ammonia as a propellant and that produces small thrust (as for satellite control)

resonance*n **1 a :** the enhancement of an atomic, nuclear, or particle reaction or a scattering event by excitation of internal motion in the system **b :** magnetic resonance **2 :** an extremely short-lived elementary particle

res·pi·ro·met·ric \,respərō'me·trik, rə,spīrə'-\ *adj* **:** of or relating to respirometry or to the use of a respirometer ⟨*respirometric* studies⟩

re·spon·dent*\rə'spändənt\ *n* **:** a reflex that occurs in response to a specific external stimulus ⟨the knee jerk is a typical *respondent*⟩

respondent*adj **:** relating to or being behavior or responses to a stimulus that are followed by a reward ⟨*respondent* conditioning⟩

res·sen·ti·ment \rə,sän̄tē'män\ *n* [G, fr. F, resentment] **:** deep-seated resentment, frustration, and hostility accompanied by a sense of being powerless to express these feelings directly

re·start·able \(')rē'stärtəbəl, -'städ·əbəl\ *adj* **:** capable of being restarted ⟨*restartable* rocket engines⟩

restriction enzyme *also* **restriction endonuclease** *n* **:** any of various enzymes that break double-stranded DNA into fragments at specific sites in the interior of the molecule

re·tic·u·lo·sis \rə,tikyə'lōsəs, re-\ *n, pl* **-lo·ses** \-ō,sēz\ [*reticul-* reticulum + *-osis* abnormal condition] **:** an abnormal increase in cells of the reticuloendothelial system

ret·i·nal \'retən,al, -,ȯl\ *n* [*retina* + *-al* aldehyde] **:** a yellowish to orange aldehyde $C_{20}H_{28}O$ derived from vitamin A that in combination with proteins forms the visual pigments of the retinal rods and cones

ret·i·ni·tis pig·men·to·sa \,retən,īd·ə,spigmən-,'tōsə, -(,)men-, -ȯzə\ *n* [*pigmentosa* fr. NL, fem. of *pigmentosus* pigmented, fr. L *pigmentum* pigment + *-osus*, adj. suffix] **:** any of several hereditary progressive degenerative diseases of the eye marked by night blindness in the early stages, atrophy and pigment changes in the retina, constriction of the field of vision, and eventual blindness

ret·i·nol \'retən,ȯl, -,ōl\ *n* [*retina* + *-ol* chemical compound; fr. its being the source of retinal] **:** the chief and typical vitamin A

ret·ro–en·gine \'re·trō,enjən, *sometimes* 'rē-·-\ *n* [*retro-* backward, back (fr. L *retro*) + *engine*] **:** a rocket engine on a spacecraft that produces thrust in the direction opposite to that of the motion of the spacecraft and that is used to reduce speed

ret·ro·fire \-,fi(ə)r\ *vi, of a retro-engine or retro-rocket* **:** to become ignited ~ *vt* **:** to cause to retrofire — **retrofire** *n*

ret·ro·fit \,re·trō'fit, 're·trō,fit\ *vt* **-fit·ted; -fit·ting** [*retrofit*, n.] **:** to furnish with new parts or equipment not available or in place at the time of manufacture or construction ⟨subway systems must *retrofit* key stations to make them accessible to wheelchair users —*Wall Street Jour.*⟩

ret·ro·grade*\'re·trə,grād\ *adj* **:** being or relating to the rotation of a satellite in a direction opposite to that of the body being orbited

ret·ro·pack \'re·trō͵pak, *sometimes* 're̅·\ *n* **:** a system of auxiliary rockets on a spacecraft that produces thrust in the direction opposite to the motion of the spacecraft and that is used to reduce speed

ret·ro·re·flec·tion \͵re·trōrə͵flekshən, *sometimes* ͵re̅·\ *n* **:** the action or use of a retroreflector

ret·ro·re·flec·tor \-rə͵flektə(r)\ *n* **:** a device that reflects radiation (as light) so that the paths of the rays are parallel to those of the incident rays

Reu·ben sandwich \'rübən-, *in rapid speech also* ͵rübᵊm-\ *n* [fr. the name *Reuben*] **:** a grilled sandwich consisting of corned beef, Swiss cheese, and sauerkraut usu. on rye bread

re·vanch·ism \rə'vän͵shizəm\ *n* **:** a usu. political policy designed to recover lost territory or status **:** revanche ⟨a policy of nationalistic *revanchism* —Bernard Fall⟩

re·vas·cu·lar·iza·tion \(͵)rē͵vaskyələrə'zāshən, -͵rī'z-\ *n* **:** a surgical procedure for the provision of a new, additional, or augmented blood supply to a body part or organ

revenue sharing *n* **:** the dispensing of a portion of federal tax revenue to state and local governments to assist in meeting their monetary needs

re·verb \rə'vərb, 're̅·, -͵vōb, -vəib\ *n* [short for *reverberation*] **:** an electronically produced echo effect in recorded music; *also* **:** a device for producing reverb

reverse discrimination *n* **:** discrimination against whites or males (as in employment or education)

reverse osmosis *n* **:** the flow of fresh water through a semipermeable membrane when pressure is applied to a solution (as seawater) on one side of it

reverse tran·scrip·tase \-͵tran'skrip(͵)tās, -āz\ *n* [*transcription* + *-ase* enzyme] **:** a polymerase that catalyzes the formation of DNA using RNA as a template and that is found in many tumor-producing viruses containing RNA

re·ver·tant \rə'vərtᵊnt, rē'-, -vōt-, -vəit-\ *n* **:** a mutant gene, individual, or strain that regains a former capability (as the production of a particular protein) by undergoing further mutation ⟨yeast *revertants*⟩ — **revertant** *adj*

Reye's syndrome \͵rīz-, ͵rāz-\ *also* **Reye syndrome** \͵rī-, ͵rā-\ *n* [R. D. K. *Reye* †1977 Australian pathologist] **:** an often fatal encephalopathy esp. of childhood characterized by fever, vomiting, fatty infiltration of the liver, and swelling of the kidneys and brain

R factor *n* [*resistance*] **:** a group of genes present in some bacteria that provide a basis for resistance to antibiotics and can be transferred from cell to cell by conjugation

rhab·do·vi·rus \͵rabdō͵vīrəs\ *n* [*rhabdo*- rod, rodlike + *virus*] **:** any of a group of RNA-containing rod- or bullet= shaped viruses found in plants and animals and including the causative agents of rabies and vesicular stomatitis

rheu·ma·toid factor \'rümə͵tóid, 'rüm-\ *n* **:** an autoantibody of high molecular weight that is usu. present in rheumatoid arthritis

rhi·no·tra·che·i·tis \͵rīnō͵trāke̅'id·əs\ *n* [NL, fr. *rhino*- nose, nasal + *tracheitis*] **:** inflammation of the nasal cavities and trachea; *esp* **:** a disease of the upper respiratory system in cats that is characterized by sneezing, conjunctivitis with discharge, and nasal discharges and that affects esp. young kittens — see INFECTIOUS BOVINE RHINOTRACHEITIS

rhi·no·vi·rus \͵rīnō͵vīrəs\ *n* [NL, fr. *rhino*- nose (fr. Gk *rhin-, rhis*) + *virus*] **:** any of a group of picornaviruses that are related to the enteroviruses and associated with upper respiratory tract disorders

RHIP *abbr* rank has its privileges

rho*\'rō\ *or* **rho particle** *n* **:** a very short-lived unstable meson with mass 1490 times the mass of an electron

rhythm and blues *n* **:** blues orig. performed by black musicians for a black audience and marked by a strong simple beat and often an electronically amplified accompaniment

rial*\rē'(y)ȯl, -'(y)äl\ *n* **1 :** the basic monetary unit of the Yemen Arab Republic **2 :** a coin representing one rial

ri·bo·nu·cle·o·side \͵rī(͵)bō͵n(y)üklēə͵sīd\ *n* [*ribose* + *nucleoside*] **:** a nucleoside that contains ribose

ri·bo·nu·cle·o·tide \-͵tīd\ *n* [*ribose* + *nucleotide*] **:** a nucleotide that contains ribose and occurs esp. as a constituent of RNA

ribosomal RNA \-͵ä(͵)re'nā\ *n* **:** RNA that is a fundamental structural element of the ribosome

ri·bo·some \'rībə͵sōm\ *n* [*ribonucleic acid* + *-some* body, deriv. of Gk *sōma*] **:** any of the RNA-rich cytoplasmic granules that are sites of protein synthesis — **ri·bo·som·al** \͵rībə͵sōməl\ *adj*

rib·tick·ler \'rib͵tik(ə)lə(r)\ *n* **:** something said or done to provoke laughter **:** a joke

Rich·ter scale \'riktə(r)-\ *n* [Charles F. *Richter* b1900 Am. seismologist] **:** a logarithmic scale for expressing the magnitude of a seismic disturbance (as an earthquake) in terms of the energy dissipated in it with 1.5 indicating the smallest earthquake that can be felt, 4.5 an earthquake causing slight damage, and 8.5 a very devastating earthquake

ricky–tick \'rike̅͵tik, -ki͵-\ *n* [imit.] **:** sweet jazz of a style reminiscent of the 1920s — **ricky–ticky** \-͵tike̅\ *adj*

ride*vb — **ride shotgun** **1 :** to guard someone or something while in transit ⟨the armed security forces that have *ridden shotgun* on every Israeli civilian flight since the Athens raid —*Newsweek*⟩ **2 :** to ride in the front passenger seat of a motor vehicle ⟨a front-seat passenger *riding shotgun* and calling out road conditions ahead — P.J.C. Friedlander⟩

rid·er·ship \'rīdə(r)͵ship\ *n* **:** the number of persons who ride a particular system of public transportation ⟨total transit *ridership* in the United States has declined since World War II —Tom Wicker⟩

Rie·mann integral \͵rē͵män-, ͵rēmən-\ *n* [G.F.B. *Riemann* †1866 Ger. mathematician] **:** a number that is the difference between the values of the indefinite integral of a given function for two values of the independent variable **:** definite integral

ri·fam·pin \rī'fampən\ *or* **ri·fam·pi·cin** \rī'fampəsən\ *n* [*rifampin*, fr. *rif*amycin (from which it is derived) + *am*picillin (which it resembles in efficacy); *rifampicin* fr. *rifa*mycin + *ampicillin*] **:** a semisynthetic antibiotic $C_{43}H_{58}N_4O_{12}$ that acts against some viruses and bacteria esp. by inhibiting RNA synthesis

ri·fa·my·cin \͵rīfə'mīsᵊn\ *n* [alter. of earlier *rifomycin*, fr. *rif-* (fr. *replication inhibiting fungus*) + connective *-o-* + *-mycin* substance obtained from a fungus, fr. *streptomycin*] **:** any of several antibiotics that are derived from a bacterium of the genus *Streptomyces* (*S. mediterranei*)

righteous* *adj, slang* **:** genuine ⟨when we hear, 'Officer needs help,' we know it's no phony call, it's really *righteous* —Peter Torres⟩

right on *interj* — used to express agreement or to give encouragement ⟨and if you live communally, well, *right on*! —*Great Speckled Bird*⟩

right–on \ˌrīd-'òn, -'än\ *adj* **1 :** exactly correct ⟨the *right-on* naturalism of a writer with a perfect pitch for dialogue —L.E. Sissman⟩ **2 :** attuned to the spirit of the times ⟨rather than not be considered avant-garde, with it, *right-on*, or gung ho, I improvise several reasons for not having seen any of the new films —Goodman Ace⟩

right–to–work law \ˌrī(t)tə'wərk, -'wók-, -'wəik-\ *n* **:** any of various state laws banning the closed shop and the union shop

ring·git \'riŋgət\ *n* [native name in Malaysia] **1 :** the basic monetary unit of Malaysia **2 :** a coin or note representing one ringgit

¹rinky–dink \ˌriŋkē¸diŋk, -ki¸-\ *adj* [origin unknown] **1 :** not modern or up-to-date **:** backward, old-fashioned, out-of-date ⟨a *rinky-dink* town with its shacks and shanties —D.M. Milligan⟩ ⟨old-timers say it was truly a *rinky-dink* railroad in those days —Jules Loh⟩ **2 :** small-time ⟨he was a *rinky-dink* dope dealer mostly — V.E. Smith⟩

²rinky–dink *n* **1 :** one that is rinky-dink ⟨if the Senate Majority Leader's blood brother couldn't get through, how was a *rinky-dink* to make connections? —L.L. King⟩ **2 :** RICKY-TICK

rinky–tink \-¸tiŋk\ *n* [perh. by alter.] **:** RICKY-TICK — **rinky–tinky** \-¸tiŋkē, -ki\ *adj*

rio·ja \rē'ō(¸)hä\ *n, often cap* **:** a wine from the Rioja region of Spain; *esp* **:** a dry red wine from this region

ripe* *adj* **1 :** smelly or stinking **2 :** sexually or scatalogically suggestive ⟨*riper* video fiction for adults —Les Brown⟩

rip off *vt* **1 :** to rob ⟨assume that the visitor is more interested in *ripping off* the store than in quietly browsing —Janet Malcolm⟩; *also* **:** to steal ⟨$5-million worth of goods *ripped off* at various merchandise-loading . . . spots —*New York*⟩ **2 :** to exploit esp. financially **:** cheat ⟨being *ripped off* by . . . bakers who give us zero nutritional value for our money —Mary Daniels⟩

rip–off \'rip¸óf\ *n* **1 :** an act or an instance of stealing **:** theft ⟨site of a famous gem theft, among other *rip-offs* — R.R. Lingeman⟩; *also* **:** an instance of financial exploitation **:** gyp ⟨don't waste your money on this book . . . it's a *rip-off* —Peter Stollery⟩ **2 :** something (as a story or motion picture) that is obviously based on or imitative of something else ⟨this kaleidoscopic fantasy, a *rip-off* on everything from spy novels to the Oedipus complex — Barbara A. Bannon⟩

ripple effect *n* **:** a spreading, pervasive, and usu. unintentional effect or influence ⟨the whole industry would be forced to close down, which would have a *ripple effect* on other industries —Joe Klein⟩ — compare DOMINO EFFECT

rip·stop \'rip¸stäp\ *adj* **:** of or relating to a fabric that is woven with a double thread at regular intervals so that small tears do not spread ⟨*ripstop* nylon⟩

rise·time \'rīz¸tīm\ *n* **:** the time required for a pulse on an electronic display (as of an oscilloscope) to increase

from one specified value (as 10 percent) of its amplitude to another (as 90 percent)

ris·to·ce·tin \ˌristə¸sēt³n\ *n* [origin unknown] **:** either of two antibiotics or a mixture of both produced by an actinomycete of the genus *Nocardia* (*N. lurida*)

Ri·tal·in \rə'talən, rī'-\ *trademark* — used for methylphenidate

RNA polymerase *n* **:** an enzyme that promotes the synthesis of RNA using DNA or RNA as a template

RNA replicase *n* **:** REPLICASE

RNase \ˌä'ren¸äs, -äz\ *or* **RNAase** \ˌä(¸)re'nä¸äs, -¸äz\ [*RNA* + *-ase* enzyme] **:** an enzyme that catalyzes the hydrolysis of RNA **:** ribonuclease

road·hold·ing \(')rōd¦hōldiŋ\ *n, chiefly Brit* **:** the qualities of an automobile that tend to make it hold the road

road·ie \'rōdē\ *n* **1 :** one who manages the activities of entertainers on the road — called also *road manager* **2 :** one who works (as by moving heavy equipment) for traveling entertainers

road racing *n* **:** racing (as in automobiles or on motorcycles) over public roads or over a closed course designed to simulate public roads (as with left and right turns, sharp corners, and hills)

Rob·ert·so·ni·an \ˌräbə(r)t'sōnēən\ *adj* [prob. after W. *Robertson* fl 1916 Am. physician] **:** relating to or being a reciprocal translocation that takes place between two acrocentric chromosomes, between two metacentric chromosomes having one arm of each composed of heterochromatin, or between two chromosomes including one of each kind, that involves a break close to the centromere in one and just to the other side of the centromere in the other, and that is sometimes a mechanism in evolution for the reduction of chromosome number

ro·bot·ics \rō'bäd·iks\ *n pl but sing in constr* **:** technology dealing with the design, construction, and operation of robots in automation

rock·a·bil·ly \'räkə¸bilē, -li\ *n* [*rock* and roll + hill*billy*] **:** pop music marked by features of rock and country and western styles

rocker* *n* **:** a rock performer, song, or enthusiast ⟨not a shred of the showman about him, none of the erotic frenzy of the *rockers* —Herb Russcol⟩ ⟨shifting into a nice laid-back *rocker* —Loraine Alterman⟩

ro·la·mite \'rōlə¸mīt\ *n* [*roll* + *-amite*, ending coined by Donald Fancher Wilkes *b*1931 Am. engineer, inventor of the rolamite] **:** a nearly frictionless elementary mechanism consisting of two or more rollers inserted in the loops of a flexible metal or plastic band with the band acting to turn the rollers whose movement can be directed to perform various functions

role model *n* **:** a person whose behavior in a particular role is imitated by others ⟨the hero of two generations, and a *role model* for aspiring organic chemists everywhere —F.H. Westheimer⟩

role–play \'rōl¦plä\ *vt* **:** to act out ⟨students were asked to *role-play* the thoughts and feelings of each character —R. G. Lambert⟩ ~ *vi* **:** to play a role

rolf·ing \'rólfiŋ *also* 'róf-\ *n* [Ida *Rolf* †1979 Am. biochemist and physiotherapist] **:** a systematic massage of deep muscles intended to serve as both physical and emotional therapy

roll bar *n* **:** an overhead metal bar on an automobile designed to protect an occupant in case of a turnover

roll cage *n* : a protective framework of metal bars encasing the driver of a racing car

roller hockey *n* : a variation of ice hockey played on roller skates

Rolle's theorem \'rólz-, 'rōlz-\ *n* [Michel *Rolle* †1719 Fr. mathematician] : a theorem in mathematics: if a curve is continuous, crosses the x-axis at two points, and has a tangent at every point between the two intercepts, its tangent is parallel to the x-axis at some point between the intercepts

roll out *vi* : to run toward one flank usu. parallel to the line of scrimmage esp. before throwing a pass ⟨the quarterback would either hand off to the fullback or fake to him and *roll out* —Arthur Sampson⟩

roll·out \'rō,laùt\ *n* : a football play in which the quarterback rolls out

ROM *abbr* read-only memory

Ror·schach \'rò(ə)r,shäk, 'rò(ə),shäk\ *adj* : of, relating to, used in connection with, or resulting from the Rorschach test ⟨*Rorschach* blots⟩

rose *n* : a plane curve which consists of three or more loops meeting at the origin and whose equation in polar coordinates is of the form $\rho = a \sin n\,\theta$ or $\rho = a \cos n\,\theta$ where n is an integer greater than 1

rose medallion *n* : a chiefly 19th century enamel-decorated Chinese porcelain with medallions of oriental figures surrounded and separated by panels of flowers and butterflies

rosette *n* : a rose-shaped cluster of cells

rough trade *n* : male homosexuals who are or affect to be rugged and potentially violent; *also* : a homosexual of this sort

rouille \rüy\ *n* [F., lit., rust] : a peppery garlic sauce of Mediterranean French origin usu. served with fish soups and stews

round file *n* : a wastebasket

RP *abbr* received pronunciation

RPG \,är(,)pē'jē\ *n* [*r*eport *p*rogram *g*enerator] : a computer language that generates programs from the user's specifications esp. to produce business reports

rub *vb* — **rub one's nose in** : to bring forcefully or repeatedly to one's attention ⟨the satirist's business is to *rub our noses in* the mess, without relief —R.B. Heilman⟩

rubber–chicken circuit *n* : a series of social gatherings (as dinners) before which a traveling celebrity (as a campaigning politician) gives speeches

ru·go·la \'rügələ\ *n* [by alter.] : ARUGULA

ru·ma·ki *also* **ra·ma·ki** \rə'mäkē\ *n* [origin unknown] : a cooked appetizer consisting of pieces of usu. marinated chicken liver wrapped together with sliced water chestnuts in bacon slices

running dog *n* [trans. of Chin (Pek) *tsou²kou³* hunting dog, lackey, lit., running dog, fr. *tsou³* to go, walk, run + *kou³* dog] : one who does someone else's bidding : lackey ⟨charge the missionaries with being *running dogs* for the imperialistic foreign powers —*Living Age*⟩

rush *n* **1** : the immediate pleasurable feeling produced by a drug (as heroin or amphetamine) — called also *flash* **2** : a feeling of pleasure or euphoria : thrill, kick ⟨finding the sudden *rush* of success a little hard to get used to — Vince Aletti⟩

RV \,är've\ *n* : a recreational vehicle

R–value *n* [prob. fr. thermal *r*esistance] : a measure of the ability of a substance or combination of substances (as building material or insulation) to retard the flow of heat with higher numbers indicating better insulating properties

rya \'rēə, 'rīə\ *n* [*Rya*, village in southwest Sweden] : a Scandinavian handwoven rug with a deep resilient comparatively flat pile; *also* : the weave typical of this rug

S

s*abbr siemens

sac·cade*\sa'käd, sə'-\ n [saccade a quick check of a horse by a twitch of the reins, fr. F, lit., jerk, twitch] **:** a small rapid jerky movement of the eye esp. as it jumps from fixation on one point to another (as in reading)

sacred mushroom n **:** any of various New World hallucinogenic fungi (as genus Psilocybe) used esp. in some Indian ceremonies

saddled prominent n [fr. the hump or prominence on the back of the larva] **:** a moth (Heterocampa guttivitta) whose larva is a serious defoliator of hardwood trees in the eastern and midwestern U.S.

safari jacket n **:** a belted shirt jacket with bellows pockets

safari suit n **:** a safari jacket with matching pants

safe house n **:** a place where one may take refuge or engage in secret activities

safety net n [fr. the nets used to break the fall of circus high-wire performers or persons leaping from burning buildings] **:** something that provides security (as from financial loss) ⟨art became an act of constantly weaving a safety net under experience —William Stafford⟩ ⟨a treasured safety net which guarantees that their monthly checks will be inflation proof —H.B. Ellis⟩

Sag·it·tar·ian \ˌsajə'tarēən\ n [Sagittarius + E -an one belonging to] **:** SAGITTARIUS

Sagittarius*n **:** one born under the astrological sign Sagittarius

Sa·hel \sə'hā(ə)l, -'hē(ə)l\ n [F, fr. Ar sāḥil coast, shore] **:** a savanna or steppe region bordering a desert — **Sa·hel·ian** \-'hālēən, -'hēl-\ adj

sail·board \'sā(ə)l,bō(ə)rd, -,bȯ(ə)rd, -,bōəd, -,bȯ(ə)d\ n **:** a small flat sailboat that is designed for one or two passengers

sai·min \'sī'min\ n [prob. fr. Chin (Cantonese) sai mìn, lit., fine noodles] **:** an Hawaiian noodle soup

Saint Emi·lion \ˌsa͏ⁿtämēl'yȯⁿ\ n [Saint-Émilion, village in southwestern France] **:** a red Bordeaux wine

salad bar n **:** a self-service counter in a restaurant featuring an array of salad makings and dressings

sal·bu·ta·mol \sal'byüd·ə,mȯl, -ütə-, -ȯl\ n [salicyl- related to salicylic acid + butyl + amino + -ol hydrocarbon of the benzene series] **:** a xylene derivative $C_{13}H_{21}NO_3$ used as a bronchodilator

sal·sa \'sȯlsə, 'säl-\ n [Sp, lit., sauce] **:** popular music of Latin-American origin that has absorbed characteristics of rhythm and blues, jazz, and rock

sal·tim·boc·ca \ˌsȯltim'bä(k)kə, -'bȯ(-\ n [It] **:** scallops of veal prepared with sage, slices of ham, and sometimes cheese and served with a wine sauce

sal·uret·ic \ˌsalyə'red·ik\ n [L sal salt + E diuretic] **:** a drug that facilitates the urinary excretion of salt and esp.

of sodium ion — **saluretic** adj — **sal·u·ret·i·cal·ly** \-ˌred·ək(ə)lē\ adv

SAM \'sam, ˌe(ˌ)sā'em\ n **:** SURFACE-TO-AIR MISSILE

sam·bo \'sam(ˌ)bō, 'säm-\ n [Russ, fr. samozashchita bez oruzhiya self-defense without weapons] **:** an international style of wrestling employing judo techniques

sa·miz·dat \'sämēz,dät\ n [Russ, fr. sam self + izdatel'stvo publisher, fr. izdat' to publish, fr. iz out, from + dat' to give; akin to L dare to give] **:** the system in the U.S.S.R. by which government-suppressed literature is clandestinely printed and distributed; also **:** such literature

sampling distribution n **:** the distribution of a statistic (as a sample mean)

San·cerre \sänser\ n [Sancerre, France] **:** a white wine from the Loire valley of France

San·da ware \'sandə-, 'sän-\ n [Sanda, town in western Honshu, Japan, where it originated] **:** a Japanese pottery and esp. porcelain ware produced since the late 17th century and noted for its celadons

S and L \ˌesən'(d)el\ n **:** a savings and loan association

S and M abbr sadism and masochism; sadist and masochist

sandwich coin n **:** a clad coin

sandwich shop n **:** a restaurant serving light meals **:** luncheonette

san·gria \ saŋ'grēə, san-, säŋ-, sän-\ n [Sp sangría, lit., bleeding, fr. sangre blood, modif. of L sanguin-, sanguis blood] **:** a punch made of red wine, fruit juice, sugar, and usu. brandy, sliced fruit, and soda water

san·i·tize*\'sanə,tīz\ vt **-tized; -tiz·ing :** to make more acceptable by removing unpleasant or undesired features ⟨the heroine became a dance-hall hostess and she and her milieu have been further sanitized for the movies so that not even the properest Bostonian would suspect that dance-hall floozies aren't Radcliffe girls —Judith Crist⟩

Sapir–Whorf hypothesis \sə,pi(ə)r'(h)wȯ(ə)rf-\ n [Edward Sapir †1939 and Benjamin Lee Whorf †1941 Am. anthropologists] **:** WHORFIAN HYPOTHESIS

sa·ran·gi \'särən,gē, -əŋ,g-\ n [Skt sāraṅgī] **:** a stringed musical instrument of India that is played with a bow and that has a tone similar to that of the viola

SASE abbr self-addressed stamped envelope

Sas·quatch \'sas,kwach, -,kwäch\ n [prob. fr. some American Indian language of British Columbia] **:** a large hairy manlike animal that is reported as existing in the Pacific Northwest — called also bigfoot

satellite*n **:** a usu. independent urban community situated on the outskirts of a large city

satellite DNA n **:** a DNA fraction differing in density from most of an organism's DNA as determined by centrifugation that apparently consists of repetitive nucleotide sequences, does not undergo transcription, and is found in some organisms (as the mouse) esp. in centromeric regions

saturated diving *n* : SATURATION DIVING — **saturated diver** *n*

sat·u·ra·tion diving \\,sachə',rāshən-\ *n* : diving in which a person remains underwater at a certain depth breathing a mixture of gases under pressure until his body becomes saturated with the gases so that decompression time remains the same regardless of how long he remains at that depth — **saturation dive** *n*

Saturday night special *n* : an inexpensive easily concealed handgun

sau·vi·gnon blanc \\,sōvēn,yōnˈbläⁿ\ *n* [F, white sauvignon (variety of grape)] : a dry white California wine made from a grape orig. grown in France

saxi·tox·in \'saksə,'täksən\ *n* [NL *Saxidomus giganteus,* species of butter clam from which it is isolated + E *toxin*] : a potent nonprotein poison $C_{10}H_{17}N_7O_4 \cdot 2HCl$ that originates in a causative agent (*Gonyaulax catenella*) of red tide and sometimes occurs in normally edible mollusks

scag \'skag\ *n* [prob. alter. of *skag* cigarette butt, cigarette, of unknown origin] *slang* : heroin

sca·lar* \'skālə(r), -,lär, -,lá(r)\ *adj* : of or relating to a scalar or scalar product (*scalar* multiplication)

¹scam \'skam\ *n* [origin unknown] : a confidence scheme in which an established business is taken over, merchandise is purchased on credit and quickly sold, and then the business is abandoned or bankruptcy is declared; *broadly* : a fraudulent or deceptive practice (insurance swindles, credit-card rackets, and practically every *scam* devised by man —Joe Flaherty) (scenes and characters in the drug underworld that make your skin crawl, smuggling *scams* like boat drops and coke-loaded "souvenirs" —A.H. Johnston)

²scam *vt* **scammed; scam·ming** *slang* : to deceive or defraud (*scams* his senile grandmother out of $3 million worth of crucial shares —Jane Clapperton) — **scam·mer** \-ə(r)\ *n, slang*

scam·pi \'skampē, -pi\ *n, pl* **scampi** [It, pl. of *scampo* Norway lobster] : shrimp; *esp* : large shrimp prepared with a garlic-flavored sauce

scan* *vt* **scanned; scan·ning** : to make a detailed examination of (as a human body) for the presence or localization of radioactive material

scan* *n* **1** : a depiction (as a photograph) of the distribution of radioactive material in something (as a body organ) **2** : the usu. bright line or spot that moves across the screen of a cathode-ray tube (as in a radar set); *also* : the path taken by such a line or spot

scanning electron micrograph *n* : a micrograph made by scanning electron microscopy

scanning electron microscope *n* : an electron microscope in which a beam of focused electrons moves across the object with the secondary electrons produced by the object and the electrons scattered by the object being collected to form a three-dimensional image on a cathode-ray tube — called also *scanning microscope;* compare TRANSMISSION ELECTRON MICROSCOPE — **scanning electron microscopy** *n*

scarf \'skärf, 'skáf\ *vt* [perh. alter. of *scoff*] : to eat or consume esp. rapidly or greedily (swilling sangria and *scarfing* chile and chicken wings —Rex Weiner)

scattering matrix *n* : S MATRIX

sce·nar·io* \sə'narē(,)ō, -'ner-, -'när-, *sometimes* shə'när- *or* shə'när-\ *n* : a sequence of events esp. when imagined (pry . . . into the mind of the rapist, tune in on the obscene *scenarios* unreeling inside his head —W.H. Manville) (if you've been busted, then you know the *scenario* all too painfully —Joe Eszterhas); *esp* : an account or synopsis of a projected course of action or events (had drawn up a number of possible *scenarios* in which nuclear weapons would be used —Martin Mayer)

scene* *n* : a sphere of activity : a way of life (the social *scene*) (the drug *scene*) (thinks the performing arts *scene* here is great —Ellen Phillips) (leading figures of the German porno *scene* —*Times Lit. Supp.*)

schizy *or* **schiz·zy** \'skitsē\ *adj* [*schizoid* + *-y,* adj. suffix] : schizoid (the gap between his private and public selves was making him feel *schizy* —Peter Schjeldahl)

schlepp* *or* **schlep** *or* **shlep** *vi* **schlepped** *or* **shlepped; schlep·ping** *or* **shlep·ping** : to proceed or move slowly, tediously, or awkwardly (*schlepped* through ridiculous crosstown traffic and arrived an hour late — Philip Nobile)

schlepp \'shlep\ *or* **schlep·per** *or* **shlep·per** \'shlepə(r)\ *n* [Yiddish *shlep, shleper,* fr. *shlepen* to drag, pull, jerk, fr. MHG *sleppen, slēpen,* fr. MLG *slēpen*] : an awkward or incompetent person : jerk (I'm really quite helpless at a cocktail party, a real *schlepper* —G.L. Rogin)

schlock \'shläk\ *also* **shlocky** \'shläkē, -i\ *or* **shlock** \'shläk\ *adj* [Yiddish *shlak,* lit., blow, apoplectic stroke, curse, fr. MHG *slag, slac,* fr. OHG *slag,* fr. *slahan* to strike] : of low quality or little worth (*schlock* merchandise) (more *schlock* suburbs, maybe dolled up with a few fountains —Jack Rosenthal) (he was no longer scorned as a *schlock* artist: instead he was celebrated —Mordecai Richler) — **schlock** *n*

schlock·meis·ter \-'mīstə(r)\ *n* [*schlock* + G *meister* master] : one who makes or sells schlock products (Hollywood's *schlockmeisters,* meanwhile, are busily grinding out a dozen cookie-cutter copies —*Newsweek*)

schmear *also* **schmeer** *or* **shmear** \'shmi(ə)r, -iə\ *n* [Yiddish *shmir* smear, fr. *shmiren* to smear, fr. MHG *smiren, smirwen,* fr. OHG *smirwen*] : an aggregate of related things — usu. used in the phrase *the whole schmear*

schmuck *or* **shmuck** \'shmək\ *n* [Yiddish *shmok* penis, fool, fr. G *schmuck* adornment, fr. MLG *smuck;* akin to OE *smoc* smock] : a stupid, naïve, or foolish person (the all-American fan, the downtrodden *schmuck* who slumps in his $10 seat behind an immutable support column, quaffing overpriced beer and cold hot dogs —Charles Farley); *also* : one who is mean or nasty (sometimes, sure, I am too hard on somebody. Afterward I think, 'Povich, you are such a *schmuck'* —Maury Povich)

schtick *var of* SHTICK

schuss·boom·er \'shus,bümə(r), 'shüs-\ *n* [*schuss* straight high-speed run on skis (fr. G, lit., shot) + *boomer* one that booms] : one who skis usu. straight downhill at high speed

Schwarz·schild radius \'s(h)wò(ə)rts,chīld-; 'shfärt,-shilt-, 'shvä-\ *n* [Karl *Schwarzschild* †1916 Ger. astronomer] : the value of the radius of a collapsing celestial body beyond which gravitational forces are so strong that they prevent the escape of matter and energy with the result that the body becomes a black hole

sci-fi \'sī,fī\ *adj* [*science fiction*] **:** of, relating to, or being science fiction ⟨*sci-fi* writers⟩ ⟨*sci-fi* stories⟩

scin·ti·scan \'sintə,skan\ *n* [*scinti*llation + *scan*] **:** a two-dimensional representation of radioisotope radiation from a bodily organ (as the spleen or kidney)

scin·ti·scan·ning \-,skaniŋ\ *n* **:** the action or process of making a scintiscan

scle·ro·tes·ta \,sklirō'testə, ,sklerō-\ *n* [NL, fr. *sclero-* hard (deriv. of Gk *sklēros* + *testa*] **:** the middle stony layer of the testa in various seeds — compare ENDOTESTA — **scle·ro·tes·tal** \-'test⁹l\ *adj*

score*n, slang **:** a purchase or sale of narcotics

score*vb scored; scor·ing *vt* **1 :** to have sexual relations with ⟨adventuress who . . . *scores* the dude and splits —Elizabeth Ashley⟩ **2 :** to be successful in obtaining ⟨his buddies had *scored* a kilo and were busily breaking it down into lids —Robert Courtney⟩ ⟨should be able to *score* a ham sandwich —Glenn O'Brien⟩ ∼ *vi* **:** to succeed in having sexual relations ⟨college roommates who . . . *score* with the same girl —L. H. Lapham⟩

Scorpio*n **:** one born under the astrological sign Scorpio

Scorpion*n **:** SCORPIO

Scotch egg *n* **:** a hard-boiled egg wrapped in sausage meat, covered with bread crumbs, and fried

Scouse \'skaùs\ *n* [back-formation fr. *Scouser*] **1 :** SCOUSER **2 :** a dialect of English spoken in Liverpool

Scous·er \'skaùsə(r)\ *n* [*scouse* lobscouse + *-er*, n. suffix; fr. the popularity of lobscouse in Liverpool] **:** a native or inhabitant of Liverpool

scramble*vi scram·bled; scram·bling *of a football quarterback* **:** to run with the ball after the pass protection breaks down

scramble*n **:** a motorcycle race over a rough hilly course

scram·jet \'skram,jet\ *n* [*supersonic combustion ramjet*] **:** a ramjet airplane engine in which thrust is produced by burning fuel in a supersonic airstream after the airplane has attained supersonic speed by other means of propulsion

scratch*adj **:** made from scratch **:** made with basic ingredients ⟨a *scratch* cake⟩ ⟨*scratch* cooking⟩

scratch·pad \'skrach,pad\ *n* **:** a small fast auxiliary computer memory

screening test *n* **:** a preliminary or abridged test intended to eliminate the less probable members of an experimental series

screw up*vi **:** to botch an activity or undertaking ⟨if I *screwed up*, I was going to be benched —Terry Bradshaw⟩

screw–up \'skrü,əp\ *n* **1 :** one who screws up ⟨what each platoon leader was asked to do was get rid of his *screw-ups* —Frank Mankiewicz⟩ **2 :** an instance of screwing up **:** blunder ⟨the more people there are, the more chance there is for a *screw-up* —Adam Kennedy⟩

Scripture cake *n* **:** a fruitcake whose recipe refers to biblical passages where the ingredients are mentioned

scroll*vi **:** to move text across a display screen as if by unrolling a scroll

scu·ba diver \'sk(y)übə-\ *n* **:** one who swims under water with the aid of scuba gear — **scuba dive** *vi*

scum·bag \'skəm,bag\ *n* **1** *slang* **:** a condom **2** *slang* **:** a dirty or unpleasant person — used as a generalized term of abuse

scuz·zy \'skəzē, -zi\ *adj* scuz·zi·er; -est [perh. alter. of *disgusting*] *slang* **:** dirty, shabby, or foul in condition or character ⟨a bunch of *scuzzy* dope-crazed hippies —Maureen Orth⟩ ⟨the *scuzziest* stories have yet to be told publicly —Library Jour.⟩

SDRs \,es(,)dē'ärz, -'äz\ *n pl* [*special drawing rights*] **:** an international means of exchange created under the auspices of the International Monetary Fund for use by governments in settling their international indebtedness

SE*abbr Standard English

sea–grant college \'sē,grant-\ *n* **:** an institution of higher learning that receives federal grants for research in oceanography

seat*n **:** a precise or accurate contact between parts or surfaces

secondary*or **secondary offering** *n* **:** the sale of a large block of an already outstanding stock through dealers but off the floor of an exchange **:** secondary distribution

secondary derivative *n* **:** a word (as *teacher*) whose immediate constituents are a free form and a bound form

secondary recovery *n* **:** the process of obtaining oil (as by waterflood) from a well that has stopped producing

second–strike *adj* **:** being or relating to a weapons system capable of surviving a nuclear attack and then striking enemy targets

second world *n, often cap S&W* **:** the Communist nations as a political and economic bloc

security blanket *n* **1 :** a blanket carried by a child as a protection against anxiety **2 :** a usu. familiar object or person whose presence dispels anxiety ⟨he's America's old shoe. He's the national *security blanket* —Nicholas Von Hoffman⟩

sedimentation coefficient *n* **:** a measure of the rate at which a molecule (as a protein) suspended in a colloidal solution sediments in an ultracentrifuge usu. expressed in svedbergs

seed money *n* **:** money used for setting up a new enterprise ⟨has supplied six hundred thousand dollars of *seed money* for a combination land-planning and urban-renewal project —L.B. Sager⟩

see–through \,sē'thrü\ *adj* **:** transparent or translucent ⟨a *see-through* jacket⟩ ⟨*see-through* characters in a novel⟩ — **see-through** \'sē'thrü\ *n*

sel·e·nod·e·sy \,selə'nädəsē\ *n* [*selen-* moon (deriv. of Gk *selēnē*) + *-odesy* (as in *geodesy*)] **:** a branch of physical science that deals with determination of the shape and size of the moon and of the exact positions of points on it and with variations of lunar gravity — **sel·e·no·det·ic** \,selənō,ded·ik\ *adj*

self–ac·tu·al·ize \,sel'fakch(əw)ə,līz, ,seü'-, -'fakshwə,-, *South often* ,se(ə)'f-\ *vi* **:** to realize fully one's potential ⟨use it as a feedback to help students *self-actualize* —H.C. Lindgren⟩ — **self–ac·tu·al·iza·tion** \-,fakch(əw)ələ'zāshən, -,fakshwə-, -,lī'z-,\ *n* — **self–ac·tu·al·iz·er** \-'fakch(əw)ə,līzə(r), -'fakshwə-\ *n*

self–as·sem·bly \,selfə'semblē, ,seüf-, *South often* ,se(ə)f-\ *n* **:** the process by which a complex macromolecule (as collagen) or a supramolecular system (as a virus) spontaneously assembles itself from its components

self–con·cept \'self'kän,sept, 'seǔf-, *South often* 'se(ə)f-\ *n* **:** the mental image one has of oneself ⟨helped the boy revise his *self-concept* so that he would no longer consider himself defenseless against his acquisitive impulses —C.K. Aldrich⟩

self–deal·ing \-'dēliŋ\ *n* **:** financial dealing that is not at arm's length; *esp* **:** borrowing from or lending to a company by a controlling individual primarily to his own advantage

self–de·struct \'selfdə'strəkt, 'seǔf-, *South often* 'se(ə)f-\ *vi* **:** to destroy itself ⟨the endless opportunites have *self-destructed* —W.H. McAllister⟩ ⟨marriage that *self-destructed* after four years —Lois Armstrong⟩ — **self-destruct** *adj*

self–per·cep·tion \-pə(r)'sepshən\ *n* **:** SELF-CONCEPT

self–rep·li·cat·ing \-'replə,kād·iŋ\ *adj* **:** reproducing itself autonomously ⟨DNA is a *self-replicating* molecule⟩ — **self–re·pli·ca·tion** \-,replə'kāshən\ *n*

self–re·pro·duc·ing \-(,)rēprə'd(y)üsiŋ, *sometimes* -(,)rep-\ *adj* **:** SELF-REPLICATING

self–stim·u·la·tion \-,stimyə'lāshən\ *n* **:** stimulation of oneself as a result of one's own activity or behavior ⟨electrical *self-stimulation* of the brain in rats⟩ — **self–stim·u·la·to·ry** \-'stimyələ,tōrē, -,tȯr-, -i\ *adj*

selling climax *n* **:** a sharp decline in stock prices for a short time on very heavy trading volume followed by a rally

semi·au·to·mat·ed \'semē'ȯd·ə,mād·əd, 'se,mī-, 'semi-\ *adj* [*semi-* half, partly, partial (fr. L, half) + *automated*] **:** partly automated ⟨a *semiautomated* process⟩

semi·axis \-'aksəs\ *n* **:** a line segment that has one endpoint at the center of a geometric figure (as an ellipse) and that forms half of an axis

semi·co·ma·tose \'semē'kōmə,tōs, 'se,mī-, 'semə-\ *adj* **:** lethargic and disoriented but not completely comatose

semi·con·ser·va·tive \-kən'sərvəd·iv, -'sȯv-, -'sȯiv-\ *adj* **:** relating to or being replication (as of DNA) in which the original separates into parts each of which is incorporated into a new whole and serves as a template for the formation of the missing parts — **semi·con·ser·va·tive·ly** \-d·əvlē, -li\ *adv*

semi·group \'semē,grüp, 'se,mī-, 'semə-\ *n* **:** a mathematical set that is closed under an associative binary operation

semi·le·thal \'semē'lēthəl, 'se,mī-, 'semə-\ *n* **:** a mutation that in the homozygous condition produces more than 50 percent mortality but not complete mortality — **semile·thal** *adj*

sen*n* [*sen* Indonesian monetary unit] **:** a monetary unit of Malaysia equivalent to ¹/₁₀₀ ringgit

send up**(')sen'dəp\ *vt* **:** to make fun of **:** satirize, parody

send–up \'sen,dəp\ *n* [*send up*] **:** a parody or takeoff ⟨an affectionate *send-up* of the fluffy romantic musicals of the '30s —Frank Rich⟩ ⟨mixes suspense and mystery with some puckish *send-ups* of the genre —Hollis Alpert⟩

sene \'senē, -nə\ *n, pl* **sene** *or* **senes** [Samoan, fr. E *cent*] **1 :** a monetary unit of Western Samoa equivalent to ¹/₁₀₀ tala **2 :** a coin representing one sene

sen·gi \'seŋgē, -gi\ *n, pl* **sengi** [native name in the Congo] **:** a monetary unit of Zaire equal to ¹/₁₀₀ likuta or ¹/₁₀,₀₀₀ zaire

senior citizen *n* **:** an elderly person ⟨one more indignant *senior citizen* penning complaints about the universal

decay of virtue —John Updike⟩; *esp* **:** one who has retired ⟨now that I am a *senior citizen* and retired from routine daily business —F.P. Sherry⟩

sen·i·ti \'senətē, -ti\ *n, pl* **seniti** [Tongan, modif. of E *cent*] **1 :** a monetary unit of Tonga equal to ¹/₁₀₀ pa'anga **2 :** a coin representing one seniti

sen·ryu \'senrē(,)ü\ *n, pl* **senryu** [Jp] **:** a 3-line unrhymed Japanese poem structurally similar to haiku but treating human nature usu. in an ironic or satiric vein

sensitivity training *n* **:** training in a small interacting group that is designed to increase each individual's awareness of his own feelings and the feelings of others and to enhance interpersonal relations through the exploration of the behavior, needs, and responses of the individuals making up the group

sen·so·ri·neu·ral \'sen(t)s(ə)rē'n(y)ürəl\ *adj* [*sensori,* alter. of *sensory* + *neural*] **:** of, relating to, or involving the aspects of sense perception mediated by nerves ⟨*sensorineural* hearing loss⟩

sen·ti \'sentē, -ti\ *n, pl* **senti** [Swahili, modif. of E *cent*] **:** the cent of Tanzania

sen·ti·mo \'sentə,mō\ *n, pl* **-mos** [Pilipino, fr. Sp. *céntimo,* a monetary unit, modif. of F *centime,* fr. *cent* hundred, fr. L *centum*] **1 :** a monetary unit of the Republic of the Philippines equal to ¹/₁₀₀ peso **:** centavo **2 :** a coin representing one sentimo

sequence**vt* **:** to determine the sequence of chemical constituents (as amino-acid residues) in ⟨*sequenced* biological macromolecules⟩

se·quen·tial \sə'kwenchəl, (')sē'k-\ *n* **:** an oral contraceptive in which the pills taken during approximately the first three weeks contain only estrogen and those taken during the rest of the cycle contain both estrogen and progestogen

se·ri·al·ism \'sirēə,lizəm, 'sēr-\ *n* **:** serial music; *also* **:** the theory or practice of composing serial music

serial section *n* **:** any of a series of sections cut in sequence by a microtome from a prepared specimen (as of tissue) — **serially sectioned** *adj* — **serial sectioning** *n*

se·ro·con·ver·sion \'si(,)rōkən'vərzhən, -'vēzh-, -'vəizh-, *sometimes* 'se(-\ *n* [*sero-* serum + *conversion*] **:** the production of antibodies in response to an antigen administered as a vaccine

se·ro·ep·i·de·mi·o·log·ic \-,epə,dēmēə'läjik, -,dem-\ *or* **se·ro·ep·i·de·mi·o·log·i·cal** \-jəkəl\ *adj* **:** of, relating to, or being epidemiologic investigations involving the identification of antibodies to specific antigens in populations of individuals — **se·ro·ep·i·de·mi·ol·o·gy** \-mē'äləjē, -ji\ *n*

se·ro·to·ner·gic \,sirətə'nərjik\ *also* **se·ro·to·nin·er·gic** \,sirə,tōnə'nərjik, -,tän-\ *adj* [*serotonin* + *-ergic* stimulating activity] **:** liberating, activated by, or involving serotonin in the transmission of nerve impulses ⟨*serotonergic* pathways⟩

se·ro·type \'sirə,tīp, 'ser-\ *vt* **:** to determine the serotype of

service break *n* **:** a game won on an opponent's serve (as in tennis)

service mod·ule \-'mäj(,)ü(ə)l\ *n* **:** a space vehicle module containing propellant tanks, fuel cells, and the main rocket engine

session man *n* **:** a studio musician who backs up a performer at a recording session

set back *n* **:** an offensive back in football who usu. lines up behind the quarterback

Se·to ware \'sā,tō-, 'se-\ *also* **Seto** *n* [*Seto,* city in central Honshu, Japan, where it originated] **:** a Japanese ceramic ware traditionally produced since the 10th century comprising in its earlier period earthenwares often based on contemporaneous Chinese and Korean porcelains, later high-fired stonewares sometimes with notable brown, black, yellow, or celadon glazes, and from the end of the 18th century chiefly porcelain often decorated with underglaze blue

sex*n **:** the external genital organs of a human being

sex chromatin *n* **:** BARR BODY

sex·i·dec·i·mal \,seksə'des(ə)məl, -ksē-\ *adj* [*sexi-* six (fr. L *sex*) + *-decimal* (as in *duodecimal*)] **:** HEXADECIMAL

sex·ism \'sek,sizəm\ *n* [*sex* + *-ism* (as in *racism*)] **1** **:** prejudice or discrimination based on sex ⟨she liked to beat boys but not girls in an early version of sadistic *sexism* —Richard Fuller⟩; *esp* **:** discrimination against women ⟨trains female students to deal with the chauvinism and *sexism* of most of their teachers and fellow students —Ruth C. Benson⟩ **2** **:** behavior, conditions, or attitudes that foster stereotypes of social roles based on sex — **sex·ist** \'seksəst\ *adj or n*

sex kitten *n* **:** a woman with conspicuous sex appeal

sex·ploi·ta·tion \,sek,splói'tāshən\ *n* **:** the exploitation of sex in the media and esp. in film

sexy*adj **:** generally attractive or interesting **:** appealing ⟨big *sexy* matters of secrecy and national defense —Taylor Branch⟩ ⟨these are colorless benefits, *sexy* only to economists —Howard Felsher⟩

Sey·fert galaxy \,sēfə(r)t-, ,sī-\ *n* [Carl K. *Seyfert* †1960 Am. astronomer] **:** any of a class of spiral galaxies that have small compact bright nuclei exhibiting variability in light intensity, emission of radio waves, and spectra which indicate hot gases in rapid motion

shades \shādz\ *n pl* **:** tinted glasses **:** sunglasses ⟨looks the way Ben Franklin would look if Franklin had worn bangs and purple *shades* —Catherine Breslin⟩

shake·out \'shā,kaút\ *n* **:** a sharp break in a particular industry that usu. follows overproduction or excessive competition and tends to force out weaker producers

sha·ku·ha·chi \,shäkə'hächē\ *n, pl* **shakuhachi** [Jp, fr. *shaku* measure, foot + *hachi* eight] **:** a Japanese bamboo flute

sham·a·teur·ism \'shamə,tər,izəm, -əd-ə,ri-, -ə-,t(y)ú(ə)r,i-, -ə,chú(ə)r,i-, -əchə,ri-\ *n* [blend of *sham* and *amateurism*] **:** the practice of treating certain athletes as amateurs so that they will be eligible for amateur competition while subsidizing them with illegal payments or with excessive expense money

shape*vt **shaped; shap·ing :** to modify (behavior) by rewarding changes that tend toward a desired response

shatter cone *n* **:** a conical fragment of rock that has striations radiating from the apex and that is formed by high pressure (as from volcanism or meteorite impact)

sha·zam \shə'zam\ *interj* [incantation used by the comic-strip hero Captain Marvel, fr. Solomon, *H*ercules, *A*tlas, *Z*eus, *A*chilles, and *M*ercury, on whom he called] — used to indicate an instantaneous transformation or appearance

shell*n **1 :** a plain usu. sleeveless overblouse **2** *or* **shell company :** a business that exists without assets or independent operation as a legal entity through which another company can conduct certain dealings

shell*vt **:** to score heavily against (as an opposing pitcher in baseball)

shi·at·su \shē'ät(,)sü\ *n, often cap* [short for Jp *shiatsuryōhō,* lit., finger-pressure therapy, fr. *shi* finger + *atsu*-pressure + *ryōhō* treatment] **:** a massage with the fingers applied to those specific areas of the body used in acupuncture — called also *acupressure*

shield law *n* **:** a law that protects journalists from forced disclosure of confidential news sources

shift*n **1 :** a movement of bits in a computer register a specified number of places to the right or left **2 :** the act or an instance of depressing the shift key (as on a typewriter)

Shih Tzu \'shēd'zü\ *n* [Chin (Pek) *shih*[1] *tzu kou*[3] Pekingese dog, fr. *shih*[1] *tzu* lion + *kou*[3] dog] **1 :** an old Chinese breed of dogs that have a square short unwrinkled muzzle, short muscular legs, massive amounts of long dense hair, and a face that is sometimes compared to a chrysanthemum esp. because of hair that grows upward on the muzzle **2** *pl* **Shih Tzus :** a dog of the Shih Tzu breed

shil·in·gi \'shilingē, -gi\ *n, pl* **shilingi** [Swahili, fr. E *shilling*] **1 :** the basic monetary unit of Tanzania **2 :** a coin representing one shilingi

ship*n **:** a spacecraft ⟨the separation system for the Apollo command and lunar *ships* —Springfield (Mass.) Daily News⟩

shirt-dress \'shərt,dres, 'shət-, 'shəit-\ *n* **:** a dress that is patterned after a shirt and has buttons down the front and a collar

shirt-jac \'shərt,jak, 'shət-, 'shəit-\ *n* [by shortening] **:** SHIRT JACKET

shirt jacket *n* **:** a jacket having an open shirtlike collar and usu. long sleeves with cuffs **:** a shirt designed to be worn over another shirt or blouse

shirt suit *n* **:** a clothing ensemble consisting of a shirt or shirt jacket and matching pants

shirt-waist-er \'shōt,wāstə(r, 'shərt,wāstər\ *n* [*shirtwaist* + *-er*] *Brit* **:** a shirtwaist dress **:** SHIRTDRESS

shit*n **:** any of several intoxicating or narcotic drugs; *esp* **:** heroin — usu. considered vulgar

shit·head \'shit,hed\ *n* **:** a contemptible person — usu. considered vulgar

shit·kick·er \-,kikə(r)\ *n* **1** *slang* **:** an unsophisticated person from a rural area **2** *slang* **:** a fan or performer of country and western music

shit·less \'shitləs\ *adv* **:** to an extreme degree — used as an intensive ⟨scared *shitless*⟩; usu. considered vulgar

shlep, shlepper *var of* SCHLEPP

shlock *var of* SCHLOCK

shmear *var of* SCHMEAR

shmuck *var of* SCHMUCK

shock troops*n pl **:** a group of people militant in pressing for a cause ⟨corporate lobbyists, lawyers, . . . and other *shock troops* installed by business and industry —Philip Shabecoff⟩

shoot*vt **:** to inject (an illicit drug) esp. into the bloodstream — **shoot from the hip :** to act or speak hastily without consideration of the consequences ⟨second thoughts about letting their man *shoot from the hip* quite as much as his nature prompted him to —R.L. Maullin⟩ — **shoot the curl** *or* **shoot the tube** **:** to surf into or through the curl of a wave — **shoot the pier** **:** to surf between the pilings of an ocean pier

shoot down*vt* **1 :** to put an end to **:** make ineffective or void **:** defeat ⟨the measure was *shot down* on the floor of the legislature⟩ **2 :** to deflate or ridicule; *also* **:** to reprove **3 :** to expose weakness or inaccuracy in **:** discredit ⟨as soon as they come up with a nice, pat generalization, something *shoots* it *down* —P.B. Benchley⟩

shoot-'em-up \'shüd·ə¦məp\ *n* **:** a movie or television show with much shooting and killing

shopper*n* **:** a usu. free paper carrying advertising and sometimes local news

shopping bag *n* **:** a bag (as of strong paper or plastic) that has handles and is intended for carrying purchases

shopping-bag lady *n* **:** a homeless woman who roams the streets of a large city carrying her possessions in a shopping bag

shopping mall *n* **1 :** a pedestrian mall lined with shops **2 :** a shopping center with stores facing an enclosed pedestrian walkway

short*adj* **:** near the end of one's tour of duty

short*\\'shò(ə)rt, 'shò(ə)t\ *vt* **:** to sell (as stocks) short

short fuse *n* **:** a tendency to become angry quickly **:** a quick temper ⟨had a *short fuse* and would be the most likely to confront the President directly —Pierre Salinger⟩

short·list \'shò(ə)t¦list, 'shò(ə)rt-\ *n, Brit* **:** a list of candidates for final consideration (as for a position or a prize)

short-list \(')shò(ə)t¦list, (')shò(ə)rt-\ *vt, Brit* **:** to place on a shortlist ⟨time spent by management sorting out the replies and *short-listing* the candidates —Anthony Dambridge⟩

short position*n* **:** the market position of a trader who has made but not yet covered a short sale

short-term*\\'shòrt¦tərm; 'shò(ə)t¦tām, -¦təim\ *adj* **:** generated by assets held six months or less ⟨*short-term* capital gains⟩

shot*n* **:** an act, instance, or result of hitting: as **a :** a blow ⟨the boxer took a hard *shot* to the body⟩ **b :** a home run ⟨a three-run *shot* over the left-field wall⟩

shotgun* *n* **:** an offensive football formation in which the quarterback plays a few yards behind the line of scrimmage and the other backs are scattered as flankers or slotbacks

shot·mak·ing \'shät¦mākiŋ\ *n* **:** the ability to make accurate or successful shots (as in golf or basketball)

shoulder belt *or* **shoulder harness** *n* **:** an automobile safety belt worn across the torso and over the shoulder

showboat*n* **:** one who tries to attract attention by conspicuous behavior

showboat *vi* **:** to show off

shrink*\\'shriŋk\ *n* **1** [short for *headshrinker*] **:** a psychiatrist ⟨the personae are just those who would patronize a *shrink* —John Thompson⟩ **2 :** a woman's short usu. sleeveless sweater often worn over a long-sleeved blouse or sweater

shrink-wrap \-¦rap\ *vt* **:** to wrap (as a book or meat) in tough clear plastic film that is then shrunk (as by heating) to form a tightly fitting package

shtick *or* **schtick** *also* **shtik** \'shtik\ *n* [Yiddish *shtik,* lit., piece, fr. MHG *stücke,* fr. OHG *stucki*] **1 :** a show-business routine, gimmick, or gag **:** bit ⟨his familiar *shticks* — his comic shuffle, his stream-of-consciousness mumble, his mournful sheepdog glances —Stephen Farber⟩ **2 :** one's special trait, interest, or activity **:** BAG, THING ⟨an uneven . . . World War II shoot-'em-up, is viable if explosions and clichés are your *shtick* —Judith Crist⟩ ⟨yet another group in the educational bureaucracy dedicated to the preservation of its own *schtick* — Richard De Lone⟩

¹shuck \'shək\ *n* [origin unknown] **:** a wily deception **:** fraud, sham ⟨a public relations *shuck*⟩ ⟨a Return to Elegance . . . the latest clothing industry *shuck* —Tom Wolfe⟩

²shuck *vi* **:** to talk or act deceptively ∼ *vt* **:** to deceive, mislead, or swindle ⟨was trundled out at cocktail parties . . . to *shuck* the moneyed liberals —John Leonard⟩

shun·pik·er \'shən¦pīkə(r)\ *n* **:** one who engages in shunpiking

shun·pik·ing \-kiŋ\ *n* [*shun* + *pike* turnpike + *-ing*] **:** the practice of avoiding superhighways esp. for the pleasure of driving on back roads — **shun·pike** \-¦pīk\ *vi*

shunt*n* **:** a minor collision in auto racing

shuttle*n* **:** SPACE SHUTTLE

shuttle diplomacy *n* **:** negotiations esp. between nations carried on by an intermediary who shuttles back and forth between the disputants

SI [F *Système International d'Unités*] *abbr* International System of Units

sick·ie *also* **sick·ee** \'sikē, -ki\ *n* **:** a person who is morally or mentally sick

sick-out \'sik¦aùt\ *n* **:** an organized absence from work by workers on the pretext of sickness in order to apply pressure to management without an actual strike ⟨plan to stage mass *sick-outs* today in their contract dispute with the city —Emanuel Perlmutter⟩

side-dress \'sī(d)¦dres\ *n* **1 :** plant nutrients used to side-dress a crop **2 :** the act or process of side-dressing a crop

side-strad·dle hop \'sīd¦stradᵊl-\ *n* **:** JUMPING-JACK

SIDS *abbr* sudden infant death syndrome

sie·mens \'sēmənz, 'zē-\ *n, pl* **siemens** [Werner von *Siemens* †1892 Ger. electrical engineer and inventor] **:** a unit of conductance in the mks system equivalent to one ampere per volt

sig·ma* *\\'sigmə\ *or* **sigma particle** *n* **:** an unstable elementary particle of the baryon family existing in positive, negative, and neutral charge states with masses respectively 2328, 2343, and 2333 times the mass of an electron

sigma factor *n* **:** a detachable polypeptide subunit of RNA polymerase that is held to determine the genetic material which undergoes transcription

sign·age \'sīnij, -ēj\ *n* [*sign* + *-age* aggregation, collection] **:** signs (as of identification, warning, or direction) or a system or design of such signs

significance level *n* **:** LEVEL OF SIGNIFICANCE

signifier*n* **:** one who engages in signifying

sig·ni·fy·ing \'signə¦fiiŋ\ *n* **:** a good-natured needling or goading esp. among urban blacks by means of indirect gibes and clever often preposterous put-downs; *also* **:** DOZENS

sign on*vi **:** to announce the start of broadcasting for the day — **sign–on** \'sī͟ͅnȯn, -ˌnän\ *n*

si·jo \'sē(ˌ)jō\ *n* [Korean] **:** an unrhymed Korean verse form appearing in Korean in 3 lines of 14 to 16 syllables and usu. in English translation in 6 shorter lines

Si·las·tic \sə'lastik, sī-\ *trademark* — used for a soft pliable plastic

silky terrier *also* **silky** *n* **:** a low-set toy terrier that weighs 8 to 10 pounds, has a flat silky glossy coat colored blue with tan on the head, chest, and legs, and is derived from crosses of the Australian terrier with the Yorkshire terrier

sil·vex \'silˌveks\ *n* [prob. fr. L *silva* wood + E exterminator] **:** a selective herbicide $C_9H_7Cl_3O_3$ esp. effective in controlling woody plants but toxic to animals

sil·vi·chem·i·cal \ˌsilvə'keməkəl\ *n* [L *silva* wood + E connective *-i-* + *chemical*] **:** any of numerous chemicals derived from wood

si·ma·zine \'sīməˌzēn\ *n* [*sim-* (prob. alter. of *sym-* symmetrical) + tri*azine*] **:** a selective herbicide $C_7H_{12}N_5Cl$ used to control weeds among crop plants

simple**adj, *of a statistical hypothesis* **:** specifying exact values for one or more statistical parameters — compare COMPOSITE

simple closed curve *n* **:** a closed plane curve (as a circle or an ellipse) that does not intersect itself **:** Jordan curve

simply connected *adj* **:** being or characterized by a surface which is divided into two separate parts by every closed curve it contains

simply ordered *adj* **:** having any two elements equal or connected by a relationship that is not symmetric and any three elements transitively related

simulate*vt **-lat·ed; -lat·ing** **:** to make a simulation of (as a physical system) — **sim·u·la·tive** \'simyəˌlād·ȯv\ *adj*

sim·u·la·tion*\ˌsimyə'lāshən\ *n* **1 :** the imitative representation of the functioning of one system or process by means of the functioning of another ⟨a computer *simulation* of an industrial process⟩ **2 :** examination of a problem often not subject to direct experimentation by means of a simulator (as a programmed computer)

sing–along \'siŋəˌlȯŋ\ *n* **:** an informal session of group singing esp. of popular songs

single*n **:** an unmarried person and esp. one young and socially active — usu. used in pl. ⟨swinging *singles*⟩ ⟨the New York *singles* scene⟩ ⟨a way of life for young *singles* —Norman Mailer⟩

sin·gle–blind \ˌsiŋgəlˌblīnd\ *adj* **:** of, relating to, or being an experimental procedure in which the experimenters but not the subjects know the makeup of the test and control groups during the actual course of an experiment — compare DOUBLE–BLIND

single–cell protein *n* **:** protein produced by microorganisms cultured on organic material and used esp. as a source of food

singles bar *n* **:** a bar that caters esp. to young unmarried men and women

sin·glet*\'siŋglət\ *n* **:** an elementary particle not part of a multiplet

sin·gle·ton*\'siŋgəltən\ *n* **:** a mathematical set that contains exactly one element

singlar*adj **1** *of a matrix* **:** having a determinant equal to zero **2** *of a linear transformation* **:** having the property that the matrix of coefficients of the new variables has a determinant equal to zero

sin·gu·lar·i·ty*\ˌsiŋgyə'larəd·ē, *also* -'ler-\ *n* **1 :** a point at which the derivative of a given function of a real or complex variable does not exist but every neighborhood of which contains points for which the derivative exists **2** **:** a point at which space and time are infinitely distorted by gravitational forces and which is held to be the final state of matter falling into a black hole

singular point *n* **:** SINGULARITY 1

sin tax *n* **:** a tax on substances or activities traditionally considered sinful (as tobacco, liquor, or gambling)

sir·ta·ki \sir'täkē\ *n* [NGk; perh. akin to Turk *sirto* a kind of dance] **:** a Greek circle dance similar to a hora

sis·sy bar \'sisē-, -si-\ *n* **:** a narrow inverted U-shaped bar rising from behind the seat of a motorcycle or bicycle that is designed to support a driver or passenger

sisterhood*n* **:** a relationship of women united by a common cause or motivation ⟨*sisterhood* of feminists⟩ ⟨gay *sisterhood*⟩; *also* **:** women united in a sisterhood

sit·com \'sitˌkäm\ *n* [*situation* com*edy*] **:** SITUATION COMEDY

situation comedy *n* **:** a radio or television comedy series that involves a continuing cast of characters in a succession of unconnected episodes

situation ethics *n pl but sing or pl in constr* [trans. of G *situationsethik*] **:** a system of ethics which is based on what is consistent with brotherly love and by which acts are judged within their contexts instead of by categorical principles

ska \'skä\ *n* [origin unknown] **:** popular music of Jamaican origin that combines elements of traditional Caribbean rhythms and jazz

skag*var of SCAG

skate·board \'skātˌbō(ə)rd, -ˌbō(ə)rd, -ˌbōəd, -ˌbȯ(ə)d\ *n* **:** a narrow board about two feet long mounted on roller-skate wheels — **skate·board·er** \-ə(r)\ *n* — **skate·board·ing** \-iŋ\ *n*

skew field \'skyü-\ *n* **:** a mathematical field in which multiplication is not commutative

skew lines *n pl* **:** straight lines that do not intersect and are not in the same plane

skibob \'skēˌbäb\ *n* [*ski* + *bob* bobsled] **:** a vehicle that has two short skis one behind the other, a steering handle attached to the forward ski, and a low upholstered seat over the rear ski and that is used for gliding downhill over snow by a rider wearing miniature skis for balance — **ski·bob·ber** \-ə(r)\ *n* — **ski·bob·bing** \-iŋ\ *n*

skid pad *n* **:** a large usu. circular area of asphalt that is oiled to make it slick and that is used for testing automobiles and motorcycles with controlled skids and spins

skif·fle \'skifəl\ *n* [perh. imit.] **:** jazz or folk music played by a group all or some of whose members play nonstandard instruments or noisemakers (as jugs, washboards, or jew's harps)

skim*vt **skimmed; skim·ming** **:** to remove or conceal (as income) to avoid payment of taxes ⟨indicted by a Federal grand jury on charges they *skimmed* casino money to avoid full tax payment to the Federal Government — *Wall Street Jour.*⟩

skim\\'skim\ *n* **:** the concealing of income (as from gambling) to avoid payment of taxes

ski mask *n* **:** a knit fabric mask worn esp. by skiers for protection from the cold

skim·mer\\'skimə(r)\ *n* **:** a fitted sleeveless usu. flaring sheathlike dress

skin*n\ **:** a mutual touching or slapping of the palms that takes the place of a handshake — used chiefly in the phrases *give skin* or *give me skin*

skin \\'skin\ *adj* **:** involving subjects who are nude ⟨expected to conduct *skin* searches for weapons —Diane K. Shah⟩; *specif* **:** devoted to showing nudes ⟨*skin* magazines⟩

skin flick *n* **:** a motion picture characterized by nudity and explicit sexual situations

Skin·ner·ian \skə'nirēən, -'ner-\ *adj* [Burrhus Frederick *Skinner* b1904 Am. psychologist] **:** of, relating to, or suggestive of the behavioristic theories of B.F. Skinner ⟨*Skinnerian* behaviorism⟩ ⟨a *Skinnerian* world filled with conditioned people —Caryl Rivers⟩ — **Skinnerian** *n*

¹skin·ny–dip \\'skinē,dip\ *vi* [*skin* + *-y,* adj. suffix + *dip*] **:** to swim in the nude ⟨a male preserve surrendered last winter when a group of nude women invaded a swimming pool where men traditionally *skinny-dipped* alone —*Newsweek*⟩ — **skin·ny–dip·per** \-ə(r)\ *n* — **skin·ny–dip·ping** \-iŋ\ *n*

²skinny–dip *n* **:** a swim in the nude

skin–pop \\'skin,päp\ *vt* **:** to inject (a drug) subcutaneously rather than into a vein ⟨I started *skin-popping* heroin, and then I started mainlining —*Amazon Quarterly*⟩

skint \\'skint\ *adj* [perh. alter. of *scant*] *Brit* **:** being penniless **:** broke

skirt steak *n* **:** a narrow boneless strip of tender beef from the plate that is usu. broiled

ski touring *n* **:** cross-country skiing for pleasure — **ski tourer** *n*

ski·wear \\'ski,wa(ə)r, -,we(ə)r, -,waə, -,weə\ *n* **:** clothing suitable for wear while skiing

sky·div·ing \\'ski,dīviŋ\ *n* **:** the sport of jumping from an airplane at a moderate altitude (as 6000 feet) and executing various tumbles and dives before pulling the rip cord of a parachute — **sky diver** *n*

sky·jack \\'ski,jak\ *vt* [*sky* + *jack* (as in *hijack*)] **:** to commandeer (an airplane in flight) by the threat of violence — **sky·jack·er** \-ə(r)\ *n* — **sky·jack·ing** \-iŋ\ *n*

sky marshal *n* **:** an armed federal plainclothesman assigned to prevent skyjackings

sky·walk \\'ski,wòk\ *n* **:** a usu. enclosed aerial walkway connecting two buildings

slack–fill \\'slak,fil\ *n* **:** the part of the interior of a package or container (as of dry cereal) that is not filled by the product

slam*n\ **:** SLAMMER

slam dunk *n* **:** DUNK SHOT — **slam–dunk** \(')slam,dəŋk\ *vb*

slam·mer \\'slamə(r)\ *n* **:** a jail or prison ⟨the penalty for interstate real estate fraud can now send perpetrators to the *slammer* —Carter Shorr⟩

slap shot *n* **:** a shot in ice hockey that is made with a swinging stroke so that the puck often flies through the air

sleaze \\'slēz\ *n* [back-formation fr. *sleazy*] **:** a sleazy quality or appearance ⟨running the gamut from tacky *sleaze* to chi-chi elegance —Catherine Kellison⟩

sleep around *vi* **:** to engage in sex promiscuously ⟨suggesting that, in order to gain her information, she had *slept around* with several politicians —Robert Brustein⟩

sleeping pill *also* **sleeping tablet** *n* **:** a drug and esp. a barbiturate that is taken as a tablet or capsule to induce sleep

slide guitar *n* **:** BOTTLENECK

slim·mer \\'slimə(r)\ *n* [*slim,* vb. + *-er,* n. suffix] *chiefly Brit* **:** one who is on a diet

slim·nas·tics \,slim'nastiks\ *n pl but sing in constr* [blend of *slim* and *gymnastics*] **:** exercises designed to reduce one's weight

slingshot*n\ **1 :** a maneuver in auto racing in which a drafting car accelerates past the car in front by taking advantage of reserve power **2 :** a dragster in which the driver sits behind the rear wheels

slip·stream*\\'slip,strēm\ *n* **1 :** an area of reduced air pressure and forward suction immediately behind a rapidly moving vehicle (as a racing car) **2** *chiefly Brit* **:** conditions resembling those resulting from the slipstream of a rapidly passing vehicle ⟨my childhood, which was passed in the *slipstream* of an erratic father —John le Carré⟩

slipstream *vi* **:** to drive in the slipstream of a racing car

slit card *n* **:** a display card with a slit whereby it is attached to a book

slope*n\ **:** the slope of the line tangent to a plane curve at a point ⟨find the *slope* of the curve at the point *x*⟩

sloppy joe*\-'jō\ *n* **:** ground beef cooked in a seasoned sauce (as chili) and usu. served on a bun

sloshed \\'släsht\ *adj, slang* **:** drunk, intoxicated

slot*n\ **:** a gap between an end and a tackle in an offensive line in football

slot·back \\'slät,bak\ *n* **:** an offensive halfback in football who lines up just behind the slot between an offensive end and tackle

slot car *n* **:** an electric toy racing automobile that has an arm underneath fitting into a groove for guidance and metal strips alongside the groove for supplying electricity and that is remotely controlled by the operator's hand-held rheostat

slot racing *n* **:** the racing of slot cars — **slot racer** *n*

slow–pitch *also* **slo–pitch** \\'slo,pich\ *n* **:** softball played with 10 players on each side in which each pitch must travel in an arc from 3 to 10 feet high in order to be legal and in which base stealing is not permitted

slow virus *n* **:** a virus with a long incubation period between infection and development of the degenerative disease (as multiple sclerosis, rheumatoid arthritis, or kuru) associated with it

slugging average *n* **:** the ratio expressed as a 3-place decimal of the total number of bases reached on base hits to official times at bat for a baseball player — called also *slugging percentage*

slum·lord \\'sləm,lȯ(ə)rd, -,lȯ(ə)d\ *n* [*slum* + *landlord*] **:** a landlord who receives unusually large profits from substandard properties

slump·fla·tion \,sləm(p)'flāshən\ *n* [*slump* + *inflation*] **:** a state or period of combined economic decline and rising inflation

slurb \'slərb\ *n* [*sl-* (as in *sloppy, sleazy, slovenly, slipshod*) + sub*urb*] **:** a suburb characterized by wearisomely uniform and usu. poorly constructed houses ⟨the aerospace *slurb* that stretches through the ghosts of fruit groves from the L.A. basin toward the Mexican border —Herbert Gold⟩ ⟨blighting the whole northwestern corner of the state with sprawling *slurbs* —John Fischer⟩

Slur·vian \'slərvēən, ˌsləv-, 'sləiv-\ *n* [irreg. fr. *slur* + *-ian*, n. suffix] **:** speech characterized by slurring

smack \'smak\ *n* [perh. fr. Yiddish *shmek* sniff, whiff, pinch (of snuff)] *slang* **:** heroin

smaller European elm bark beetle *n* **:** a European beetle (*Scolytus multistriatus*) that is established in eastern North America

smart*adj **1 :** being a guided missile ⟨a laser-guided *smart* bomb⟩ **2 a :** operating by automation ⟨a *smart* machine tool⟩ **b :** INTELLIGENT ⟨a *smart* computer terminal⟩

smarts \'smärts, 'smàts\ *n pl, slang* **:** intelligence or know-how ⟨went to show that intellectual heavies could be beautiful in spite of all those *smarts* —Cyra McFadden⟩ ⟨figured they had political *smarts* —Kate Haracz⟩

smashed \'smasht\ *adj, slang* **:** drunk, intoxicated

S ma·trix \'esˌmā·triks\ *n* [scattering *matrix*] **:** a unitary matrix in quantum mechanics the absolute values of the squares of whose elements are equal to probabilities of transition between different states — called also *scattering matrix*

smog·less \'smägləs, *also* 'smóg-\ *adj* **1 :** marked by the absence of smog ⟨a *smogless* city⟩ **2 :** emitting no fumes that would contribute to the production of smog ⟨*smogless* cars of the future⟩

smoke detector *n* **:** an alarm that activates automatically when it detects smoke

smoke–in \'smō·kin\ *n* [*smoke* + *-in* organized public protest] **:** a large gathering of people publicly smoking marijuana usu. in support of its legalization

Smok·ey \'smōkē, -ki\ *n, pl* **Smokeys** [*Smokey* the Bear, advertising symbol of U.S. Forest Service who wears a hat shaped like a state trooper's] *slang* **:** a police officer on highway patrol ⟨truckers soon discovered they could warn one another of cruising or hidden *Smokeys* via the citizens' band —L.L. King⟩

smoking gun *n* **:** something that serves as conclusive evidence or proof esp. of a crime ⟨in most murders there are eyewitnesses, clear motives, *smoking guns* —John Sansing⟩ ⟨while the testimony . . . did not contain a *smoking gun*, it nevertheless did cast doubt on the overall propriety of the transaction —Frank Reynolds⟩

snake oil*n **:** empty talk **:** poppycock, bunkum ⟨this kind of analysis is subject to a considerable adulteration with *snake oil*, and there are plenty . . . who scoff at it —*Business Week*⟩

SNG *abbr* substitute natural gas; synthetic natural gas

snow**n, slang* **:** heroin

snow·belt \'snōˌbelt\ *n, often cap* **:** a region that receives an appreciable amount of annual snowfall ⟨a state in the *snowbelt*⟩

snowbird*n **:** one who travels to warm climes for the winter ⟨the *snowbirds*, who winter in Florida and go north with the swallows —Harriet Van Horne⟩

snow·mak·er \'snōˌmākə(r)\ *n* **:** a device for making snow artificially

snow·mak·ing \-kiŋ\ *adj* **:** used for the production of artificial snow usu. for ski slopes ⟨*snowmaking* machines⟩

snow·mo·bil·ing \'snō(ˌ)mō,bēliŋ\ *n* **:** the sport of driving or racing a snowmobile — **snow·mo·bil·er** \-lə(r)\ *also* **snow·mo·bil·ist** \-ləst\ *n*

soap*n **1 :** a serial drama performed usu. on a daytime radio or television program **:** soap opera **2 :** the melodrama and sentimentality characteristic of a soap opera; *also* **:** something (as a novel) having such qualities ⟨very superior *soap*, the kind of skillful fiction that would have made a wonderful . . . movie —J.A. Avant⟩

Soa·ve \'swävā, sə'w-, -ve\ *n* **:** a dry white wine from the area about Soave, Italy

so·cial·ist realism \ˌsōsh(ə)ləst-\ *n* [trans. of Russ *sotsialisticheskiĭrealizm*] **:** a theory of Soviet art, music, and literature that calls for the didactic use of artistic work to develop social consciousness in an evolving socialist state — **socialist re·al·ist** \-'rēələst\ *n*

sociobiology*n **:** the comparative study of social organization in animals and man esp. with regard to its genetic basis and evolutionary history — **so·cio·bi·ol·o·gist** \ˌsōs(h)ē(ˌ)ōbïˌäləjəst\ *n*

so·cio·lin·guis·tic \ˌsōs(h)ē(ˌ)ōliŋ'gwistik\ *adj* [*socio-*society, social, sociological + *linguistic*] **1 :** of or relating to the social aspects of language **2 :** of or relating to sociolinguistics

so·cio·lin·guis·tics \-tiks\ *n pl but usu sing in constr* **:** the study of linguistic behavior as determined by sociocultural factors (as social class or educational level)

so·ci·ol·o·gese \ˌsōsē,älə'jēz *also* ˌsōshē-\ *n* [*sociology* + *-ese* particular language or style] **:** a style of writing held to be characteristic of sociologists

so·cio·re·li·gious \ˌsōs(h)ēōrəˌlijəs, -rēˌl-\ *adj* **:** of, relating to, or involving a combination of social and religious factors

sodium do·de·cyl sulfate \-ˌdōdəˌsil-\ *n* **:** the crystalline sodium salt of sulfated lauryl alcohol **:** sodium lauryl sulfate

sodium pump *n* **:** the process by which sodium ions are actively transported across a cell membrane; *esp* **:** the process by which the appropriate internal and external concentrations of sodium and potassium ions are maintained in a nerve fiber and which involves the active transport of sodium ions outward with movement of potassium ions to the interior

sodium stea·rate \-'stēəˌrāt, -'sti(ə)rˌāt\ *n* **:** a white powdery salt $C_{17}H_{35}COONa$ that is soluble in water, is the chief constituent of some laundry soaps, and is used esp. in cosmetics and toothpaste

soft*adj **1 :** occurring at such a speed and under such circumstances as to avoid destructive impact ⟨*soft* landing of a spacecraft on the moon⟩ **2 :** not protected against enemy attack ⟨a *soft* aboveground launching site⟩ **3** *of a detergent* **:** BIODEGRADABLE **4** *of a drug* **:** considered less detrimental than a hard narcotic ⟨marijuana is usually regarded as a *soft* drug⟩ **5 a :** being low due to sluggish market conditions ⟨*soft* prices⟩ **b :** sluggish or slow ⟨a *soft* market⟩ **6 :** not firmly committed **:** irresolute, undecided ⟨there is still an abundance of *soft* votes around to make it anyone's or no one's ball game —Louis Harris⟩ **7 :** SOFT-CORE ⟨*soft* pornography⟩ **8 a :** being or based on interpretive or speculative data ⟨*soft* evidence⟩ ⟨*soft* data⟩ **b :** utilizing or based on soft data ⟨*soft* science⟩

softbound \'sȯf(t)'baúnd\ *adj* **:** not bound in hard covers ⟨*softbound* books⟩

soft–core \'sȯf(t)'kō(ə)r, -'kȯ(ə)r, -'kȯə, -'kȯ(ə)\ *adj* [*soft* + *-core* (as in *hard-core*)] *of pornography* **1 :** containing descriptions or scenes of sex acts that are less explicit than those in hard-core material ⟨just another *soft-core* exploitation film designed for those who like their sex simulated —Judith Crist⟩ **2 :** relatively mild **:** moderate ⟨this is a network for sports junkies. It's not for *soft-core* fans who like to watch an NFL game, then switch to the news —Scott Rasmussen⟩

soft–land \'sȯft'land\ *vb* [back-formation fr. *soft landing*] *vi* **:** to make a soft landing on a celestial body (as the moon) ~ *vt* **:** to cause to soft-land — **soft–land·er** \-ə(r)\ *n*

soft landing *n* **:** the aversion of a major economic decline through a gradual slowing of the economy

soft–lin·er \('')sȯft'linə(r)\ *n* [*soft* + *-liner* (as in *hard-liner*)] **:** an advocate of a flexible course of action

soft paste*n* **1 :** a fine-grained opaque Chinese ceramic ware related to true porcelain but having part of the kaolin replaced by pegmatite and usu. being fired twice **2 :** a lightweight soft opaque clay body (as of early Staffordshire)

soft rock *n* **:** rock music that is less driving and gentler sounding than hard rock

soft–top \'sȯf'täp\ *n* **:** an automobile or motorboat having a top that may be folded back

soft·ware \'sȯft,wa(ə)r, -,we(ə)r, -,waə, -,weə\ *n* **1 :** the entire set of programs, procedures, and related documentation associated with a system and esp. a computer system; *specif* **:** computer programs **2 :** something used or associated with and usu. contrasted with hardware; *esp* **:** materials for use with audiovisual equipment

soil·borne \'sȯi(ə)l,bō(ə)rn, -,bȯ(ə)rn, -,bōən, -,bȯ(ə)n\ *adj* **:** transmitted by or in soil ⟨*soilborne* fungi⟩ ⟨*soilborne* diseases⟩

So·ka Gak·kai \,sōkä'gä'kī\ *n* [Jp *Sōka Gakkai*, fr. *sōka* value-creation + *gakkai* learned society] **:** a Japanese sect of Buddhism that emphasizes active proselytism and the use of prayer for the solution of all human problems

solar cell *n* **:** a photovoltaic cell (as one including a junction between two types of silicon semiconductors) that is able to convert sunlight into electrical energy and is used (as in artificial satellites) as a power source

solar panel *n* **:** a battery of solar cells (as in a spacecraft)

solar pond *n* **:** a pool of salt water heated by the sun; *esp* **:** one that lies under a layer of fresh water and warms sufficiently to be used either as a direct source of heat or to provide power for a turbine electric generator

solar sail *n* **:** a propulsive device that consists of a flat material (as aluminized plastic) designed to receive thrust from solar radiation pressure and that can be attached to a spacecraft

solar wind *n* **:** plasma continuously ejected from the sun's surface into and through interplanetary space

soldier*n* **:** BUTTON MAN

sol·id–state \'sälǝd,stāt\ *adj* **1 :** relating to the properties, structure, or reactivity of solid material; *esp* **:** relating to the arrangement or behavior of ions, molecules, nucleons, electrons, and holes in the crystals of a sub-

stance (as a semiconductor) or to the effect of crystal imperfections on the properties of a solid substance **2 a :** utilizing the electric, magnetic, or photic properties of solid materials ⟨a *solid-state* component⟩ **b :** utilizing solid-state circuitry as opposed to electron tubes ⟨a *solid-state* stereo system⟩

sol·i·tons \'sälǝ,tänz\ *n pl* [*solitary* + *-on* elementary particle] **:** solitary waves (as in a gaseous plasma) that retain their shape and speed after colliding with each other

solution set *n* **:** the set of values that satisfy an equation; *also* **:** TRUTH SET

So·ma·li*\sō'mälē, sǝ'-\ *n* **1 :** a breed of domestic cat that prob. originated as a spontaneous mutation of the Abyssinian and closely resembles it but has a long silky coat and plumelike tail **2 :** a cat of the Somali breed

so·mato·me·din \,sōməd·ǝ'mēdⁿn\ *n* [*somato-* body, soma (deriv. of Gk *sōmat-*, *sōma* body) + *-medin* (perh. as in *intermedin*)] **:** any of several endogenous peptides produced esp. in the liver and dependent on and mediating growth hormone activity (as in sulfate uptake by epiphyseal cartilage)

so·mato·sen·so·ry \,sōmǝd·ǝ'sen(t)s(ǝ)rē\ *adj* **:** of, relating to, or being sensory activity having its origin elsewhere than in the special sense organs (as eyes or ears) and conveying information about the state of the body proper and its immediate environment ⟨neuromuscular spindles and touch receptors are typical of the systems making *somatosensory* inputs to the brain⟩

so·mato·ther·a·py \-'therǝpē, -pi\ *n* **:** therapy for psychological problems that uses physiological intervention (as drugs or surgery) to modify behavior — **so·mato·ther·a·pist** \-pǝst\ *n*

so·mato·tro·pic hor·mone \-,trōpik'hȯr,mōn, -'hȯ(ə)-\ *n* **:** a vertebrate polypeptide hormone that is secreted by the anterior lobe of the pituitary gland and regulates growth

so·mato·stat·in \,sōmǝd·ǝ'statⁿn\ *n* [*somato-* + *-stat* growth inhibitor + *-in* chemical compound] **:** a polypeptide neurohormone composed of a chain of 14 amino-acid residues that inhibits the secretion of several hormones (as growth hormone, insulin, and gastrin)

something*pron* — **something else :** something or someone special or extraordinary ⟨the solos . . . were *something else* —Thomas Pynchon⟩ ⟨this guy is *something else* —Claude Brown⟩

son et lumière \sōnälūēmyer\ *n* [F, lit., sound and light] **:** an outdoor spectacle at an historic site consisting of recorded narration with light and sound effects

son·i·cate \'sänǝ,kāt\ *vt* **-cat·ed; -cat·ing :** to disrupt (as bacteria) by treatment with high-frequency sound waves — **son·i·ca·tion** \,sänǝ'kāshǝn\ *n*

so·no·chem·is·try \,sänō'kemǝstrē, 'sōnō-\ *n* [*sono-* sound (fr. L *sonus*) + *chemistry*] **:** a branch of chemistry that deals with the chemical effects of ultrasound — **so·no·chem·i·cal** \-'kemǝkǝl, -mēk-\ *adj*

so·no·gram \'sōnǝ,gram\ *n* **:** an image produced by sonography

so·nog·ra·phy \sō'nägrǝfē, -fi\ *n, pl* **-phies :** ULTRASONOGRAPHY — **so·no·graph·ic** \,sōnǝ'grafik\ *adj*

sorghum web·worm \-'web,wǝrm, -,wǝm, -,wǝim\ *n* **:** a noctuid moth (*Celama sorghiella*) whose hairy green-ish larva is sometimes a destructive pest of the seed heads of sorghum

sort***n** **:** an instance of sorting ⟨an alpha *sort* done by computer⟩

soul***n** **1 :** a strong positive feeling (as of intense sensitivity and emotional fervor) conveyed esp. by black American performers ⟨feel that white rock singers lack *soul* —Rita Kramer⟩ **2 :** NEGRITUDE **3 :** SOUL MUSIC **4 :** SOUL FOOD **5 :** SOUL BROTHER

soul *adj* **1 :** of, relating to, or characteristic of black Americans or their culture ⟨vocals are delivered in a raspy, *soul* style —Ellen Sander⟩ **2 :** designed for or controlled by blacks ⟨*soul* radio stations⟩

soul brother *n* **:** a black male — used esp. by blacks

soul food *n* **:** food (as chitterlings, hogs' jowls, ham hocks, collard greens, catfish, and cornbread) traditionally eaten esp. by southern black Americans

soul music *n* **:** music that originated with black American gospel singing, is closely related to rhythm and blues, and is characterized by intensity of feeling and earthiness

soul sister *n* **:** a black woman or girl — used esp. by blacks

sounding***n** **:** SIGNIFYING

sound pollution *n* **:** NOISE POLLUTION

sound·scape \'saún(d),skāp\ *n* **:** a mélange of musical and often nonmusical sounds

soup***n** **:** the fast-moving white water that moves shoreward after a wave breaks

source language *n* **:** a language which is to be translated into another language — compare TARGET LANGUAGE

southern pea *n* **:** a cowpea or black-eyed pea

southwestern corn borer *n* **:** a pyralid moth (*Diatraea grandiosella*) whose larva causes serious damage esp. to corn crops by boring in the stalks

soybean cyst nem·a·tode \-'nemə,tōd\ *n* **:** a nematode (*Heterodera glycines*) that is a pest of legumes and esp. soybeans and that causes stunting and yellowing of the plants and reduction in yield

soy·milk \'sȯi,milk, -,miúk\ *n* **:** a milk substitute based on soybeans esp. as a protein source and usu. supplemented (as with calcium and vitamins)

spa*\'spä, 'spȯ, 'spá\ *n* **:** HEALTH SPA

space***n** **:** a set of mathematical entities (as points or vectors) with a collection of axioms of geometric character — see METRIC SPACE, TOPOLOGICAL SPACE, VECTOR SPACE

space·borne \',späs,bō(ə)rn, -,bȯ(ə)rn, -,bōən, -,bȯ(ə)n\ *adj* **1 :** carried in or moving through space external to the atmosphere ⟨*spaceborne* satellites⟩ **2 :** involving the use of spaceborne equipment ⟨*spaceborne* television⟩

spaced–out \'spä,staut\ *adj* **:** dazed or stupefied by or as if by a narcotic substance ⟨a *spaced-out* addict dances by, bumping into people —Marcia Chambers⟩

space shuttle *n* **:** a reusable rocket-launched vehicle that is designed to go into an earth orbit, to shuttle people and cargo to and from an orbiting spacecraft, and to glide to a landing

space sickness *n* **:** unpleasant physiological effects occurring under the conditions of sustained spaceflight

space walk *n* **:** an extravehicular venture made by an astronaut in space — **space walk** *vi* — **space-walk·er** \'spä,swȯkə(r)\ *n* — **space·walk·ing** \-,kiŋ\ *n*

space·wom·an \'spä,swúmən\ *n, pl* **space·wom·en** \'spä,swimən\ **:** a woman astronaut

spac·ey *also* **spacy***\'spāsē, -sí\ *adj* **spa·ci·er; -est** **1 :** SPACED-OUT **2 :** odd, weird, offbeat

spa·ghet·ti·ni \spə,ge'tēnē\ *n* [It, dim. of *spaghetti*] **:** a pasta thinner than spaghetti but thicker than vermicelli

spaghetti western *n, often cap W* **:** a western motion picture produced by Italians

span***vt** **spanned; span·ning :** to be capable of expressing any element of under given operations ⟨a set of vectors that *spans* a vector space⟩

Span·glish \'spaŋ(g)lish\ *n* [blend of *Spanish* and *English*] **:** Spanish marked by a considerable number of borrowings from English

spark chamber *n* **:** a device usu. used to detect the path of a high-energy particle that consists of a series of charged metal plates or wires separated by a gas (as neon) in which observable electric discharges follow the path of the particle

spatial sum·ma·tion \-(,)sə'māshən\ *n* **:** sensory summation that involves stimulation of several spatially separated neurons at the same time

spatter glass *n* **:** END-OF-DAY GLASS

speak·er·phone \'spēkə(r),fōn\ *n* **:** a combination microphone and loudspeaker device for two-way communication by telephone lines

spear·ing \'spi(ə)riŋ\ *n* **:** an illegal check in hockey in which one player jabs another in the body with the end of a hockey stick

special drawing rights *n pl* **:** SDRS

special situation *n* **:** an exceptional corporate condition or prospect that offers unusual chances for capital gains

special theory of relativity : a theory that is based on the two postulates (1) that the speed of light in a vacuum is constant and independent of the source or the observer and (2) that the mathematical forms of the laws of physics are invariant in all inertial systems and which leads to the assertion of the equivalence of mass and energy and of change in mass, dimension, and time with increased velocity

spe·cies·ism \'spē(,)s(h)ē,zizəm\ *n* [*species* + *-ism* (as in *racism*)] **:** prejudice or discrimination based on species; *esp* **:** discrimination against animals

spec·ti·no·my·cin \,spektənō'mīsᵊn\ *n* [NL, fr. *spectabilis* (species name) + *-in* chemical compound + connective *-o-* + *-mycin* substance obtained from a fungus, fr. *streptomycin*] **:** a white crystalline antibiotic $C_{14}H_{24}N_2O_7$ produced by a bacterium of the genus *Streptomyces* (*S. spectabilis*) that is effective against a broad spectrum of bacteria and is used clinically primarily to treat gonorrhea esp. in the form of its hydrochloride

speed***n** **:** methamphetamine; *also* **:** a related drug

speed freak *n* **:** one who habitually misuses amphetamines and esp. methamphetamine

speedo \'spē(,)dō\ *n, pl* **speedos** [by shortening] *chiefly Brit* **:** a speedometer

speed–read·ing \'spēd,rēdiŋ\ *n* **:** a method of reading rapidly by skimming — **speed–read** \-,rēd\ *vt* — **speed–read·er** \-ə(r)\ *n*

speed shop *n* **:** a shop that sells custom automotive equipment esp. to hot rodders

S phase *n* [synthesis] **:** the period in the cell cycle during which DNA replication takes place — compare G₁ PHASE, G₂ PHASE, M PHASE

sphe·ro·plast \'sfirə‚plast, 'sfer-\ *n* [*sphero-* sphere, spherical + *-plast* particle, granule, cell, deriv. of Gk *plastos* molded] **:** a modified gram-negative bacterium that is characterized by major alteration and partial loss of the cell wall and by increased osmotic sensitivity and that can result from various nutritional or environmental factors or be induced artificially by use of a lysozyme

spider hole *n* **:** a camouflaged foxhole

spi·e·di·no \‚spēō'dē(‚)nō\ *n, pl* **-ni** \-(‚)nē\ [It, lit., skewer, fr. *spiedo* spit, spear, fr. OF *espiet* lance, fr. (assumed) Frankish *speut* lance; akin to G *spies* spit, Sp *espeto* skewer] **:** a dish of meat rolled around a filling or minced and formed into balls then usu. batter-dipped and cooked on a skewer; *also* **:** slices of bread and mozzarella prepared in a similar way and served with an anchovy sauce

spike*n* **:** ACTION POTENTIAL

spin·ner\'spinə(r)\ *n* **:** a surfing feat in which a standing surfer makes a complete turnaround while the board continues to move straight ahead

spin–off\'spin‚óf\ *n* **1 :** the distribution by a business to its stockholders of particular assets and esp. of stock of another company **2 :** a collateral or derived product or effect **:** by-product ⟨new household products that are *spin-offs* from missile research⟩; *also* **:** a number of such by-products ⟨the *spin-off* from defense research⟩ **3 :** something that is imitative or derivative of an earlier work; *esp* **:** a television show starring a character who was popular in a secondary role in an earlier show

spin·out \-‚aůt\ *n* **:** a rotational skid by an automobile that usu. causes it to leave the roadway

spin resonance *n* **:** ELECTRON SPIN RESONANCE

spin·to \'spēn-(‚)tō, 'spin-‚\ *adj* [It, lit., pushed, fr. past part. of *spingere* to push] *of a singing voice* **:** having both lyric and dramatic qualities ⟨her sumptuous *spinto* soprano has never sounded so firmly under control —D.J. Henahan⟩ — **spinto** *n*

spin wave *n* **:** a wave of quantized energy that propagates through a substance as a result of magnetic field shifts within an atom in response to an outside stimulus (as a variable magnetic field or radio waves)

spiny–head·ed worm \‚spīnē‚hedəd-\ *n* **:** a parasitic worm belonging to the taxon Acanthocephala

spi·ro·no·lac·tone \spī‚ränə'lak‚tōn, spə‚rōnō-\ *n* [*spiro-* chemical compound with one or more two-ring systems (deriv. of L *spira* coil) + *-no-* (prob. arbitrary infix) + *lactone*] **:** an aldosterone antagonist that promotes diuresis and sodium excretion and is sometimes used to relieve ascites

splash·down \'splash‚daůn\ *n* **:** the landing of a manned spacecraft in the ocean — **splash down** \(')splash'daůn\ *vi*

spliff \'splif\ *n* [origin unknown] **:** a marijuana cigarette

spline \'splīn\ *also* **spline function** *n* **:** a function that is defined on an interval, is used to approximate a given function, and is composed of pieces of simple functions defined on subintervals and joined at their endpoints with a suitable degree of smoothness

split*vt* **:** to leave ⟨*split* the scene⟩ ~ *vi* **:** to leave ⟨the women *split* for New York on Tuesday —Linda Francke⟩

⟨*split* from the train and headed for the depot restroom — Ben Fong-Torres⟩

split–brain \'split'brān\ *adj* **:** having the optic chiasma and corpus callosum severed ⟨behavior in *split-brain* animals⟩

split end *n* **:** an offensive end in football who lines up usu. several yards to the side of the formation

spo·do·sol \'spädə‚sol, 'spōd-\ *n* [Gk *spodos* wood ash + L *solum* ground, soil] **:** any of various podzols esp. of cool humid regions that have a horizon below the surface composed of an illuvial accumulation of humus with iron or aluminum or both

spoil·er\'spóilə(r)\ *n* **1 :** an air deflector on the front or on the rear deck of an automobile and esp. a racing car for reducing the tendency to lift off the road at high speeds **2 :** a political candidate who has little chance of winning but whose candidacy may deprive one of the leading candidates of a victory

spokes·per·son \'spōk‚spərsən, -pəs-, -pəis-\ *n* [*spokes-* (as in *spokesman*) + *person*] **1 :** one who speaks as the representative of another; *esp* **:** one delegated by others to express or present their views or opinions publicly ⟨a frequent State House *spokesperson* —J.R. Dorsey⟩ **2 :** one that is or becomes an interpreter (as of an era) or an outstanding advocate (as of a cause) ⟨an effective *spokesperson* for higher education —Paul Lacey⟩ ⟨an especially powerful and influential *spokesperson* for what had become a cultural change in attitudes toward female relationships —Janet Cooper⟩

sponge·ware \'spənj‚wa(ə)r, -‚we(ə)r, -‚waə, -‚weə\ *n* **:** a typically 19th century earthenware with background color spattered or dabbed (as with a sponge) and usu. a freehand central design

spook*n* **:** an undercover agent **:** spy ⟨the feeling persists that there's no such thing as a former intelligence officer . . . once a *spook*, always a *spook* —H.E. Meyer⟩

spoon·er \'spünə(r)\ *n* **:** a container that is designed to hold extra teaspoons and forms part of a 19th century table service

spo·ro·pol·len·in \‚spōrə'pälənən, ‚spór-\ *n* [ISV *sporo-* seed, spore + *pollen* + *-in* chemical compound] **:** a chemically inert polymer that makes up the outer layer of pollen grains and spores of higher plants

spotted alfalfa aphid *n* **:** a highly destructive Old World aphid (*Therioaphis maculata*) that is established in the U.S. from coast to coast in warmer areas and that injects a toxic saliva in feeding esp. on alfalfa and causes yellowing and stunting of affected plants

sprang \'sprań\ *n* [prob. fr ON *sprang* lace-weaving; akin to Norw *sprang* fringes, strands, D *sprank* pattern, ornament] **:** a weaving technique in which threads or cords are intertwined and twisted over one another to form an openwork mesh

spread end *n* **:** SPLIT END

sprech·stim·me \'shprek‚shtimə, -ek‚-\ *n, often cap* [G, lit., speaking voice] **:** a vocal passage or performance in which a declamation is delivered with rhythmic inflections

sprint car *n* **:** a typically open-wheel open-cockpit rugged racing automobile powered by a large production model engine and usu. raced on a dirt track

spritz \'sprits\ *n* [prob. fr. G *spritze* squirt, injection] **:** an improvised usu. humorous harangue

square one *n* **:** the initial stage or starting point of a process ⟨had to start all over again, from *square one* —H.C. McDonald⟩

square out *n* **:** a pass pattern in football in which a receiver runs downfield a short distance and then breaks at a 90-degree angle for the sideline

squib kick \'skwib-\ *n* **:** a kickoff in football in which the ball bounces along the ground

sr*abbr steradian

Sri Lan·kan \(')srē'läŋkən\ *n* **:** a native or inhabitant of Sri Lanka — **Sri Lankan** *adj*

sRNA \,es,är(,)e'nā\ *n* [*s*oluble *RNA*] **:** TRANSFER RNA

SSL *abbr* Licentiate of Sacred Scriptures

SST \,e(,)se'stē\ *n* **:** SUPERSONIC TRANSPORT

stack*n **1 :** a memory or a section of memory in a computer for temporary storage **2 :** a computer memory consisting of arrays of memory elements stacked one on top of another

stacked heel *n* **:** a shoe heel made of layers of leather

stadium coat *n* **:** a coat of medium length designed for casual winter wear

staff*n, *pl* **staff** **:** a member of a staff

stag·fla·tion \'stag'flāshən\ *n* [blend of *stagnation* and *inflation*] **:** persistent inflation combined with stagnant consumer demand and relatively high unemployment — **stag·fla·tion·ary** \-shə,nerē, -i\ *adj*

staging*n **:** the disengaging and discarding of a burned≠ out rocket unit from a space vehicle during flight

stand–alone *adj* **:** operating or capable of operating independently of a computer ⟨a *stand-alone* word processing system⟩ ⟨a *stand-alone* line printer⟩

standing crop*n **:** the total amount or number of living things (as an uncut farm crop, the fish in a pond, or the organisms in an ecosystem) in a particular situation at any given time

stand·off\'stan,dóf\ *n* **:** a standoff insulator

stan·nous flu·o·ride \'stanəs'flü(ə),rīd\ *n* **:** a white compound SnF2 of tin and fluorine used in toothpaste to combat tooth decay

sta·pe·dec·to·my \,stāpə'dektəmē, -pē'd-\ *n*, *pl* **-mies** [ISV *staped-* (fr. NL *staped-, stapes* stapes) + *-ectomy* surgical removal] **:** surgical removal and prosthetic replacement of the stapes to relieve deafness — **sta·pe·dec·to·mized** \-tə,mīzd\ *adj*

stark·ers \'stärkərz, 'stäkəz\ *adj* [*stark* stark-naked + *-ers* (Oxford University slang suffix)] *chiefly Brit* **:** completely unclothed **:** nude ⟨a red flannel nightdress which would bring surrogate dignity to his otherwise *starkers* consort —John Taylor⟩

star·quake \'stär,kwāk, 'stá,-\ *n* **:** a seismic event on a star

state of the art **:** the level of development (as of a device, procedure, process, technique, or science) reached at a particular time usu. as a result of modern methods

state–of–the–art *adj* **:** made or done with the most up≠ to-date methods and technology available ⟨a *state-of-the≠ art* computer⟩

static*n **:** heated opposition or criticism ⟨he takes no *static* from anyone —David Wellman⟩

station*n **:** a pocket with its automatic signature-feeding equipment in a gathering machine in a book bindery

sta·tis·tic\'stə'tistik\ *n* **:** a random variable that takes on the possible values of a statistic

stave church *n* **:** a church of medieval Nordic origin that is made of wooden staves and has gables, a cupola, and often a series of pitched roofs

STD \,e(,)stē'dē\ *n* [*s*exually *t*ransmitted *d*isease] **:** a disease (as syphilis, gonorrhea, or the genital form of herpes simplex) usu. or often transmitted by direct sexual contact

steady state theory *n* **:** a theory in astronomy: the universe has always existed and has always been expanding with hydrogen being created continuously and spontaneously — compare BIG BANG THEORY

steak au poivre \-(,)ō'pwävr(ə), -v(rə)\ *n* [F *au poivre* with pepper] **:** a steak that has had coarsely ground black pepper pressed into it before cooking, is served with a seasoned sauce, and is often flambéed with cognac — called also *pepper steak*

steak Diane \-(')dī,an\ *n* [prob. fr. the name *Diane*] **:** a steak that is served with a seasoned butter sauce and is often flambéed with cognac

steak tar·tare \-(,)tär'tär, -(,)tä'tá(r\ *n* [F *tartare* Tartar] **:** highly seasoned ground beef eaten raw

stel·lar·a·tor \'stelə,räd·ə(r)\ *n* [*stellar* + *-ator* (as in *generator*); fr. its use of temperatures approaching those occurring in some stars] **:** a toroidal device for producing controlled nuclear fusion that involves the confining and heating of a gaseous plasma by means of an externally applied magnetic field

stel·lar wind \,stelə(r)-\ *n* **:** plasma ejected at varying rates from a star's surface into interstellar space

ste·re·ol·o·gy \,sterē'äləjē, ,stir-\ *n* [ISV *stereo-* solid, stereoscopic, dealing with three dimensions (deriv. of Gk *stereos* solid) + *-logy* theory, science, deriv. of Gk *logos* word] **:** a branch of science concerned with inferring the three-dimensional properties of objects or matter ordinarily observed two-dimensionally — **ste·reo·log·i·cal** \-rēə'läjəkəl\ *adj* — **ste·reo·log·i·cal·ly** \-k(ə)lē\ *adv* — **ste·re·ol·o·gist** \-rē'äləjəst\ *n*

ste·reo·phone \'sterēə,fōn, 'stir-\ *n* [*stereo* stereophonic + *phone*] **:** a stereophonic headphone

ste·reo·tape \-,tāp\ *n* **:** a stereophonic magnetic tape

ste·reo·tax·ic \'sterēə'taksik, 'stir-\ *adj* [NL *stereotaxis* stereotaxic technique (fr. *stereo-* solid, dealing with three dimensions + Gk *taxis* arrangement) + E *-ic*, adj. suffix] **:** of, relating to, involving, or being a technique or apparatus used in neurological research or surgery for directing the tip of a delicate instrument (as a needle or an electrode) in three planes in attempting to reach a predetermined locus in the nervous system — **ste·reo·tax·i·cal·ly** \-ək(ə)lē\ *adv*

ste·reo·tax·is\-,taksəs\ *n* **:** a stereotaxic technique or procedure

ste·roi·do·gen·e·sis \stə,róidə'jenəsəs, ,stir,óidə-, *also* ,ster-\ *n* [NL, fr. *steroid* + connective *-o-* + *genesis*] **:** synthesis of steroids

ste·roi·do·gen·ic \stə,róidə'jenik, ,stir,óidə-, *also* ,ster-\ *adj* **:** of, relating to, or involved in steroidogenesis ⟨*steroidogenic* cells⟩ ⟨*steroidogenic* response of ovarian tissue⟩

Ste·ven·graph \'stēvən,graf\ *or* **Ste·vens·graph** \-nz,g-\ *n* [Thomas *Stevens*, 19th cent. Am. weaver + E *-graph* something written, recording instrument, deriv. of Gk *graphein* to write] **:** a picture woven in silk

stick*vb — **stick it to :** to treat harshly or unfairly ⟨he *sticks it* mercilessly to the phonies —Wilfred J.J. Sheed⟩

stick shift n **:** a manually operated gearshift mounted esp. on the floor of an automobile

sticky wicket n **:** a difficult or delicate problem or situation ⟨several *sticky wickets* have cropped up that promise to take years to resolve —Ron Scherer⟩

stiletto heel n **:** a high thin heel on women's shoes that is narrower than a spike heel

still bank \'stil,baŋk\ n [*still* stationary] **:** a bank (as in the shape of an animal or a ship) with a slot for inserting coins — compare MECHANICAL BANK

sting*n **:** an elaborate confidence game; *specif* **:** such a game worked by undercover police in order to trap criminals

¹**stir–fry** \(')stər,frī, (')stə,-\ vt **:** to fry quickly over high heat in a lightly oiled pan (as a wok) while stirring continuously

²**stir–fry** n **:** a dish of something stir-fried

stish·ov·ite \'stishə,vīt\ n [S.M. *Stishov*, 20th cent. Russ. mineralogist] **:** a dense tetragonal mineral SiO_2 consisting of silicon dioxide that is a polymorph of quartz and that is formed under great pressure

sto·chas·tic*\stə'kastik\ adj **1 :** involving a random variable ⟨a *stochastic* process⟩ **2 :** involving chance or probability **:** probabilistic ⟨a *stochastic* model of radiation-induced mutation⟩

stoked \'stōkt\ adj [fr. past part. of *stoke* stir up (a fire)] slang **:** being in an enthusiastic or exhilarated state

STOL abbr short takeoff and landing

stone*adj **:** absolute, complete ⟨a zeal that might be called pure *stone* craziness —Edwin Shrake⟩

stone \'stōn\ adv **:** absolutely, completely — used as an intensive ⟨it is a *stone* positive fact, a scientific certainty —R.A. Aurthur⟩

stone·wall*\'stōn,wól\ vi **:** to be uncooperative, obstructive, or evasive ⟨possible that the Soviet Union will gradually abandon the *stonewalling* obstruction of the past quarter century —Lord Cavadon⟩ ⟨he can go in and *stonewall* and say, "I don't know anything about what you are talking about" —J.W. Dean III⟩ ~ vt **:** to refuse to comply or cooperate with ⟨intention to *stonewall* further requests for . . . evidence —Newsweek⟩

stop*vb — **stop a stock** of a stock-market specialist **:** to agree to a later sale or purchase of a specified number of shares at the price current when the agreement is made

stop out*\(')stäp'aút\ vt **:** to sell securities of (a shareowner) on a stop order ~ vi **:** to withdraw temporarily from enrollment at a college or university

stop–out \'stäp,aút\ n [*stop out*] **:** a person who stops out of a college or university

storage ring n **:** a device for storing a beam of high-energy particles collected from an accelerator until needed for collision with a second beam

stove·pipe \'stōv,pīp\ adj, of trousers **:** having creaseless legs with the same circumference at the cuff as at the hip

STP \,e(,)stē'pē\ n [fr. *STP*, trademark for a motor fuel additive] **:** a psychedelic drug chemically related to mescaline and amphetamine — called also *DOM*

straight*adj **1 :** of, relating to, or characterized by heterosexuality ⟨living in two worlds: the *straight* world of his work, and the gay world of his friends and lovers — Robert Athanasiou, Phillip Shaver, & Carol Tavris⟩ ⟨division persists between gay and *straight* feminists — Myrna Lamb⟩ **2 :** not high on drugs or alcohol

straight*n **1 :** one who adheres to conventional attitudes and mores ⟨the hippie who cadged a dime from a *straight* —Milton Mayer⟩ **2 :** a nonuser of illicit drugs ⟨everybody coming here on wings from the whole world, *straights* and heads both —Hank Heifetz⟩ **3 :** one who is heterosexual ⟨*straights* and gays⟩

straight–ahead \,sträd·ə,hed\ adj **:** relating to or being music performed in an unembellished manner typical of the idiom or of the performer ⟨*straight-ahead*, searching jazz with no gimmicks —David Spitzer⟩; *broadly* **:** straightforward, unadorned ⟨applauded Hollywood people's *straight-ahead* love for their work —Sheila Weller⟩

straight–arrow \,sträd·'arō, -arə(w)\ adj **:** rigidly proper and conventional ⟨the *straight-arrow* guy and his girl, the latter a believer in early marriage and eternal obligation —Time⟩ — **straight arrow** n

straight–leg \'strāt,leg, -,lāg\ adj **:** being a garment with legs having essentially the same diameter throughout their length ⟨*straight-leg* jeans⟩

strain·me·ter \'strän,mēd·ə(r), -ētə-\ n **:** a mechanical, electrical, or optical instrument for measuring deformation of a body or a change in length over a given length under stress

strand·ed \'strandəd\ adj **:** having a strand or strands esp. of a specified kind or number — usu. used in combination ⟨the double-*stranded* molecule of DNA⟩ — **strand·ed·ness** \-nəs\ n

strange*adj **:** of or relating to a particle (as the kaon) having a strangeness quantum number different from zero ⟨*strange* quark⟩

strangeness*n **:** a quantum characteristic of a quark or strongly interacting fundamental particle indicated by a number equal to its hypercharge minus its baryon number that is conserved in strong interactions with other fundamental particles

strat·e·gize \'strad·ə,jīz, -atə-\ vi **-gized; -giz·ing :** to develop a plan or strategy ⟨while the bird-watcher is wasting time in peace and solitude, our birder is busy *strategizing* to add "exclusives," or rare birds, to his embossed record book —J.E. Maslow⟩

strategy*n **:** an adaptation or complex of adaptations (as of behavior, metabolism, or structure) that serves or appears to serve an important function in achieving evolutionary success ⟨the reproductive *strategies* of beech and yellow birch —L.K. Forcier⟩

strat·i·fi·ca·tion·al grammar \,strad·əfə,kāshnəl-, -shənᵊl-\ n **:** a grammar based on the theory that language consists of a series of hierarchically related strata linked together by representational rules

strat·i·fied charge engine \,strad·ə,fīd·\ n **:** an internal-combustion engine in which the fuel charge is divided into two layers of differing concentration within the cylinder with a rich mixture in a small section close to the spark plug and a lean mixture in the remainder of the cylinder so that the engine runs on an overall leaner mixture

Stra·vin·ski·an or **Stra·vin·sky·an** \strə'vin(t)skēən\ adj [Igor Fëdorovich *Stravinsky* †1971 Am. (Russ.-born) composer] **:** of, relating to, or suggestive of Igor Stravinsky or his music ⟨mixture of pungent dissonance,

Stravinskian rhythms and French chic —H.C. Schonberg⟩

strawberry jar *n* [prob. fr. their original use as strawberry planters] **:** a ceramic planter with pocketed openings in the sides into which small plants can be inserted for growing

streak*n **:** an act or instance of streaking

streak*vi **:** to run naked through a public place

streak·er \'strēkə(r)\ *n* **:** a person who engages in streaking

streak·ing \'strēkiŋ\ *n*   **1 :** the lightening (as by chemicals) of a few long strands of hair to produce a streaked effect — compare FROSTING   **2 :** the act or practice of running naked through a public place

stream**n, Brit* **:** one of several curricula of study to which students are assigned according to their needs or levels of ability **:** track

streaming**n, Brit* **:** TRACKING

street*n **:** the streets of a city seen as the home of ruffians and derelicts and as the scene of crime, violence, and drug trafficking ⟨caught with heroin worth about $25,000 on the *street* —Loudon Wainwright⟩

street·scape \'strēt,skāp\ *n* [*street* + *-scape* (as in *landscape*)]   **1 :** the appearance or view of a street ⟨the first major high-rise incursion in that cherished *streetscape* — William Marlin⟩   **2 :** a work of art depicting a view of a street

street–smart \',strēt¦smärt, -¦smȧt\ *adj* **:** STREETWISE

street theater *n* **:** drama or mime often dealing with controversial social and political issues usu. performed in an informal setting outdoors (as on streets or in parks) — called also *guerrilla theater*

street·wise \'strēt¦wīz\ *adj* **:** familiar with the life and attitudes of street people ⟨kid, if you don't know what a peteman is . . . run along and get *streetwise* —John Crosby⟩; *esp* **:** wise and resourceful in surviving and getting what one wants on the street ⟨a *streetwise* child-hustler determined to survive —Elaine Landau⟩

strep·to·ni·grin \,streptə'nīgrən\ *n* [NL *strepto-* (fr. *Streptomyces flocculus,* actinomycete from which it is produced) + L *nigr-, niger* black + E *-in* chemical compound; prob. fr. its dark color] **:** a toxic antibiotic $C_{25}H_{22}N_4O_8$ from an actinomycete of the genus *Streptomyces* (*S. flocculus*) that interferes with DNA metabolism and is used as an antineoplastic agent

strep·to·zo·toc·in \,streptə(,)zō'täkən\ *n* [*strepto-* + *zo-* animal, animal life + *tocin* (alter. of *toxin*)] **:** a broad-spectrum antibiotic $C_8H_{15}N_3O_7$ with antineoplastic and diabetogenic properties that has been isolated from a bacterium of the genus *Streptomyces* (*S. achromogenes*)

stretch receptor *n* **:** a sensory end organ in a muscle that is sensitive to stretch in the muscle, consists of small striated muscle fibers richly supplied with nerve fibers, and is enclosed in a connective tissue sheath **:** muscle spindle

stretch reflex *n* **:** a spinal reflex involving reflex contraction of a muscle in response to stretching

strewn field *n* **:** an area in which tektites are found

stri·a·tion*\strī'āshən\ *n* **:** one of the alternate dark and light cross bands of a myofibril of striated muscle

stride piano *n* [fr. *stride bass,* left-hand part characterized by a rhythmic back and forth striding movement] **:** a style of jazz piano playing in which the right hand plays the melody while the left hand alternates between a single note and a chord played an octave or more higher

strike*n **:** a perfectly thrown ball ⟨fired a *strike* to first base⟩

striking price *n* **:** a price agreed upon as that at which an option contract (as a put or call) can be exercised

strip*n **:** a commercially developed area esp. along a highway

strip city *n* **:** an urban area forming a long narrow strip

stroke*vt **stroked; strok·ing :** to flatter or pay attention to in a manner designed to reassure or persuade ⟨works hard at *stroking* the interest groups that are likely contributors to his campaign —David Ignatius⟩

stro·mat·o·lite \strō'mad-əl,īt\ *n* [L *stromat-, stroma* bed covering + E connective *-o-* + *-lite* mineral, rock, fossil, deriv. of Gk *lithos* stone] **:** a laminated sedimentary fossil formed from layers of blue-green algae — **stro·mat·o·lit·ic** \-,mad-əl'id·ik\ *adj*

strong interaction *also* **strong force** *n* **:** a fundamental interaction experienced by elementary particles (as hadrons) that is more powerful than any other known force and is responsible for the binding together of neutrons and protons in the atomic nucleus and for processes of particle creation in high-energy collisions

stro·phoid \'strō,fȯid\ *n* [F *strophoïde,* fr. Gk *strophos* twisted band (fr. *strephein* to twist) + *-oïde* something similar] **:** a plane curve that is generated by a point whose distance from the y-axis along a variable straight line which always passes through a fixed point is equal to the y-intercept and that has the equation $\rho = \alpha$ (sec $\theta \pm tan$ θ) in polar coordinates

strop·py \'sträpē, -pi\ *adj* [by alter. and shortening of *obstreperous*] *Brit* **:** inclined to take offense **:** touchy, belligerent ⟨Scotch is the drink but Scots are the people, and very *stroppy* they get about it, too —Leslie Sellers⟩

structural gene *n* **:** a gene determining the amino acid sequence of a protein (as an enzyme) through a specific messenger RNA

strung out *adj*   **1 :** addicted to a drug ⟨Butch, Danny, and Kid were all *strung out.* They were junkies all the way —Claude Brown⟩   **2 :** physically debilitated from or as if from long-term drug addiction ⟨dreaming of himself as a footloose cowboy, although he was to spend much of his life (and end it) *strung out,* ill, and living with his mother —*New Yorker*⟩   **3 :** intoxicated or stupefied from drug use ⟨two girls were *strung out* on one of the benches —Barbara Lamont⟩   **4** *slang* **:** infatuated **:** HUNG UP ⟨if I had've got *strung out* over one of these guys —Diana Ross⟩

student's t distribution *n, often cap S* [*Student,* pen name of W. S. Gossett †1937 Brit. statistician] **:** T DISTRIBUTION

student union *n* **:** a building on a college campus that is devoted to student activities and that usu. contains lounges, auditoriums, eating facilities, offices, and game rooms

stuff*n   **1 :** STUFF SHOT   **2 :** any of several habit-forming or narcotic drugs; *specif* **:** heroin ⟨I got wrecked every night on booze, pills, pot — everything except *stuff* —Art Pepper⟩

stuff*vt **:** to throw or drive (a ball or puck) into a goal from very close range

stuff shot *n* **:** DUNK SHOT

Sty·ro·foam \'stīrə,fōm\ *trademark* — used for an expanded rigid polystyrene plastic

subacute scle·ros·ing pan·en·ceph·a·li·tis \-sklə-ˌrōsiŋˌpanen,sefə'lid-əs\ *n* [*sclerosing* (pres. part. of *sclerose*) + *panencephalitis*, fr. *pan-* whole, general + *encephalitis*] **:** a central nervous system disease of children and young adults caused by infection of the brain by measles virus or a closely related virus and marked by intellectual deterioration, convulsions, and paralysis

sub·cel·lu·lar \ˌsəb'selyələ(r)\ *adj* [*sub-* under, less or smaller than full or normal (fr. L *sub*) + *cellular*] **:** of less than cellular scope or level of organization ⟨*subcellular* particles⟩ ⟨*subcellular* studies⟩

sub·com·pact \'səbˌkäm,pakt\ *n* **:** an automobile smaller than a compact

sub·dis·ci·pline \ˌsəb'disəplən, -,plin\ *n* **:** a subdivision of a branch of learning

sub·duc·tion*\səb'dəkshən\ *n* **:** the action or process of the edge of one crustal plate descending below the edge of another — **sub·duct** \səb'dəkt\ *vb*

sub·em·ployed \ˌsəbəmˈploid\ *adj* **:** subjected to subemployment ⟨a more relevant approach to understanding social conditions . . . would be to measure those who have been *subemployed* for any significant period of time —Michael Marien⟩

sub·em·ploy·ment \-'ploimənt\ *n* **:** inadequate employment including unemployment, part-time employment, and full-time employment that does not provide a living wage

sub·field \'səb,fēld\ *n* **1 :** a subset of a mathematical field that is itself a field **2 :** a subdivision of a field (as of study) ⟨each of the 12 *subfields* in physics that are discussed in the report —*Chem. & Engineering News*⟩

sub·gov·ern·ment \ˌsəb'gəvə(r)mənt, -və(r)nm-, -v(ə)m-, -ˌgəb(ə)m-\ *n* [*sub-* subordinate + *government*] **:** an informal or unofficial association of persons or institutions that exercises considerable influence on a formal government or organization

sub·group*\'səb,grüp\ *n* **:** a subset of a mathematical group that is itself a group

sub·gum \'səb'gəm\ *n* [Chin (Cant) *shâp kám*, lit., mixture] **:** a dish of Chinese origin prepared with a mixture of vegetables (as peppers, water chestnuts, and mushrooms)

sub·li·cense \ˌsəb'līsən(t)s\ *vt* [*sublicense*, n.] **:** to grant to another a sublicense for

sub·man·dib·u·lar gland \ˌsəbman'dibyələ(r)-\ *also* **submandibular** *n* **:** a salivary gland inside of and near the lower edge of the mandible on each side **:** submaxillary gland

sub·mil·li·me·ter \ˌsəb'milə,mēd-ə(r)\ *adj* **:** being less than a millimeter in a specified measurement ⟨a *submillimeter* wave⟩

sub·mi·to·chon·dri·al \-,mīd-ə'kändrēəl\ *adj* **:** of, relating to, composed of, or being parts and esp. fragments of mitochondria ⟨*submitochondrial* membranes⟩ ⟨*submitochondrial* particles⟩

sub·nu·cle·ar \ˌsəb'n(y)üklēə(r), ÷ -kyələ(r)\ *adj* **:** of, relating to, or being a particle smaller than the atomic nucleus

sub·or·di·na·tor \sə'bórdᵊn,ād-ər, -'bȯ(ə)d-\ *n* **:** one that subordinates; *esp* **:** a subordinating conjunction

sub·pro·gram \'səb,prō,gram, -prōgrəm\ *n* **:** a semiⁱⁿdependent portion of a program (as for a computer)

sub·ring \-,riŋ\ *n* **:** a subset of a mathematical ring which is itself a ring

sub–Sa·ha·ran \ˌsəbsə'haran, -ˈher-, -ˈhär-\ *adj* [*sub-* next lower than + *Saharan*] **:** of, being, or relating to the part of Africa south of the Sahara desert

sub·sat·el·lite \ˌsəb'sad-ᵊl,īt\ *n* **1 :** a political entity within the sphere of influence of another entity that is itself a satellite of a stronger power **2 :** an object carried into orbit in and subsequently released from an artificial satellite

subscription TV *n* **:** pay-TV that broadcasts programs directly over the air to customers provided with a special receiver — called also *subscription television;* compare PAY-CABLE

sub·se·quence \'səb,sēkwən(t)s, -,kwen-\ *n* **:** a mathematical sequence that is part of another sequence

sub·shell \'səb,shel\ *n* **:** any of the one or more orbitals making up an electron shell of an atom

substance P *n* **:** a mammalian polypeptide present esp. in the gastrointestinal tract and pituitary gland that causes reduction in blood pressure and contraction of smooth muscle and that is thought to function as a neurotransmitter esp. in the transmission of pain impulses

sub·stan·tia gel·a·ti·no·sa \(ˌ)səb'stanch(ē)ə,jelət°n-ˈōsə, -ˈōzə\ *n* [NL, lit., gelatinous substance] **:** a mass of gelatinous tissue that lies on the dorsal surface of the dorsal column and extends the entire length of the spinal cord into the medulla oblongata and that functions in the transmission of painful sensory information

sub·text \'səb,tekst\ *n* **:** the implicit or metaphorical meaning of a text as opposed to its literal meaning — **sub·tex·tual** \ˌsəb'teksch(əw)əl\ *adj*

sub·til·i·sin \ˌsəb'tiləsən\ *n* [NL *subtilis*, specific epithet of *Bacillus subtilis*, species to which *Bacillus amyloliquefaciens* was once thought to belong + E *-in* chemical compound] **:** an extracellular protease produced by a soil bacterium of the genus *Bacillus* (*B. amyloliquefaciens*)

sub·to·pia \ˌsəb'tōpēə\ *n* [*suburbs* + *-topia* (as in *utopia*)] *chiefly Brit* **:** the suburbs of a city ⟨those who can happily shoot a pheasant on a nursery farm in *subtopia* — Christopher Wordsworth⟩ — **sub·to·pi·an** \-ēən\ *adj, chiefly Brit*

sub·top·ic \'səb,täpik\ *n* **:** a secondary topic **:** one of the subdivisions into which a topic may be divided

sub·vi·ral \ˌsəb'vīrəl\ *adj* **:** relating to, being, or caused by a piece or a structural part (as a protein) of a virus ⟨*subviral* infection⟩

suc·ci·nate de·hy·drog·e·nase \ˌsəksə,nāt,dē(ˌ)hī-ˈdräjə,nās, -āz\ *n* **:** an iron-containing flavoprotein enzyme **:** succinic dehydrogenase

suc·cor·ance*\'səkərən(t)s\ *n* **:** a dependence on or an active seeking for nurturant care — **suc·cor·ant** \'səkərənt\ *adj*

suck**vt* **:** to perform fellatio upon — often used with *off;* usu. considered vulgar ∼ *vi, slang* **:** to be extremely objectionable or inadequate ⟨our life-style *sucks* —*Playboy*⟩ ⟨people who went said it *sucked* —H. S. Thompson⟩

sudden infant death syndrome *n* **:** death of an infant in apparently good health due to unknown causes that occurs usu. before one year of age — called also *crib death*

suicide pact *n* **:** an agreement between two or more individuals wherein they commit suicide together or one kills the other or others and then commits suicide

suicide squad *n* [fr. the fact that kickoffs are more dangerous than other plays] **:** a special squad used on kickoffs in football

sui·cid·ol·o·gy \ˌsüəˌsīˈdäləjē\ *n* [*suicide* + connective *-o-* + *-logy* science, theory, deriv. of Gk *logos* word] **:** the study of suicide and suicide prevention — **sui·cid·ol·o·gist** \-jəst\ *n*

sul·fa·meth·ox·a·zole \ˌsəlfəˌmethˈäksəˌzōl\ *n* [*sulfa*-sulfonamide + *meth*- methyl + *oxazole*] **:** a sulfonamide $C_{10}H_{11}N_3O_3S$ used as an antibacterial (as in the treatment of urinary tract infections)

sul·fin·py·ra·zone \ˌsəlfənˈpīrəˌzōn\ *n* [*sulfinyl* + *pyrazole* + *-one* ketone or analogous compound] **:** a uricosuric drug $C_{23}H_{20}N_2O_3S$ used in long-term treatment of chronic gout

sul·fo·bro·mo·phtha·lein \ˌsəlfəˈbrō(ˌ)mōˈthaleēn, -ˈthalˌēn, -ˈthäˌlēn\ *n* [ISV *sulfo*- containing a sulfonic acid group + *bromo*- containing bromine in place of hydrogen + *phthalein*] **:** a diagnostic material used in the form of its disodium salt $C_{20}H_8Br_4Na_2O_{10}S_2$ in a liver function test

sul·fo·nyl·urea \ˌsəlfəˌnilˈ(y)ùrēə\ *n* [NL, fr. ISV *sulfonyl* + NL *urea*] **:** any of several hypoglycemic compounds related to the sulfonamides and used in the oral treatment of diabetes

sul·phide*\ˈsəlˌfīd\ *n* **:** a ceramic form and esp. a portrait bas-relief enclosed in clear glass where it glitters like silver

sum*n **:** UNION 1

su·mi–e \ˈsümēˈä\ *n* [Jp *sumie;* akin to Jp *sumi* India ink] **:** the Japanese art of monochromatic ink painting

sum up*vt, Brit **:** to determine the importance, value, or size of **:** assess ⟨that skilled, professional inspection . . . with which we *sum* each other *up* —Doris Lessing⟩

sun·belt \ˈsənˌbelt\ *n, often cap* **:** the southern and southwestern states of the U.S.

sun·roof \ˈsənˌrüf, -ˌrûf\ *n* [fr. its letting in the sunlight] **:** an automobile roof having a panel that can be opened

sun·seek·er \ˈsənˌsēkə(r)\ *n* **1 :** a person who travels to an area of warmth and sun esp. in winter ⟨the cream of cruising comfort for the winter *sunseekers* —B.D. Walker⟩ **2 :** a photoelectric device on a spacecraft or artificial satellite that maintains a constant fix on the sun and forms a part of the navigational system of the vehicle

sun·set \ˈsənˌset\ *adj* **:** stipulating the periodic review of government agencies and programs in order to continue their existence ⟨*sunset* laws⟩ ⟨the *sunset* plan to force review of major federal programs —*Wall St. Jour.*⟩

sunshine*adj **:** forbidding or restricting closed meetings of legislative or executive bodies and sometimes providing for public access to records ⟨*sunshine* laws⟩ ⟨a *sunshine* requirement to be disregarded only when there is a need for private discussions of personnel matters —K. E. Meyer⟩

su·per·al·loy \ˈsüpərˌalȯi, -rəˌlȯi\ *n* [*super*- over, exceeding the norm (fr. L *super*) + *alloy*] **:** any of various high-strength often complex alloys having resistance to high temperature

su·per·city \ˈsüpə(r)ˌsidˌē, -i\ *n* **:** a very large and sprawling city **:** megalopolis

su·per·clus·ter \ˈsüpə(r)ˌkləstə(r)\ *n* **:** a large cluster of galaxies

su·per·coil \ˈsüpə(r)ˌkȯi(ə)l\ *n* **:** SUPERHELIX — **supercoil** \ˌsüpə(r)-\ *vi* — **su·per·coiled** \-ˌkȯild\ *adj*

su·per·con·ti·nent \ˈsüpə(r)ˌkänt(ə)nənt\ *n* **:** a hypothetical former large continent from which other continents broke off and drifted away — called also *protocontinent*

su·per·cur·rent \-ˈkərənt\ *n* **:** a current of electricity flowing in a superconductor

su·per·dense \-ˈden(t)s\ *adj* **:** of extremely great density; *specif* **:** relating to or being a highly compact state of matter in which electrons and protons are pressed together to form neutrons ⟨a *superdense* neutron star⟩

su·per·fec·ta \ˈsüpə(r)ˌfektə\ *n* [blend of *super* and *perfecta*] **:** a variation of the perfecta in which a bettor wins by selecting the first four finishers of a race in the correct order of finish — compare TRIFECTA

su·per·graph·ics \ˈsüpə(r)ˈgrafiks\ *n pl but sing or pl in constr* **:** billboard-sized graphic shapes usu. of bright color and simple design

su·per·group \ˈsüpə(r)ˌgrüp\ *n* **:** a rock group made up of former members of other rock groups

su·per·heavy \ˈsüpə(r)ˈhevē, -i\ *adj* **:** relating to or being a chemical element with a greater atomic mass than that of any known element; *also* **:** being an atomic nucleus with a higher atomic number than any known — **superheavy** *n*

su·per·he·lix \-ˈhēliks\ *n* **:** a helix (as of DNA) which has its axis arranged in a helical coil — **su·per·he·li·cal** \-ˈheləkəl, -ˈhēl-\ *adj* — **su·per·he·lic·i·ty** \-helˈisədˌē, -i\ *n*

su·per·jet \-ˌjet\ *n* [*supersonic* + *jet*] **:** a supersonic jet airplane

su·per·mas·sive \ˈsüpə(r)ˌmasiv\ *adj* **:** having extraordinarily great mass; *esp* **:** having a hypothetical mass over 50,000 times that of the sun ⟨a *supermassive* black hole⟩

su·per·mol·e·cule \-ˈmäləˌkyü(ə)l\ *n* **:** a large molecule (as of protein or rubber) built up from smaller chemical structures **:** macromolecule — **su·per·mo·lec·u·lar** \ˈsüpə(r)məˈlekyələ(r)\ *adj*

su·per·plas·ti·ci·ty \ˈsüpə(r)ˌplastˈisədˌē\ *n* **:** the quality or state of having enhanced ductility as a result of microstructural change brought about by heat and mechanical treatment — used of an alloy — **su·per·plas·tic** \-ˈplastik\ *adj or n*

su·per·po·ten·cy \-ˈpōtᵊn(t)sē\ *n* **:** the quality or state of being superpotent

su·per·po·tent \-ˈpōtᵊnt\ *adj* **:** of greater than normal or acceptable potency ⟨in regard to safety, assays are available which are intended to ensure that tablets are not *superpotent* —L.C. Lasagna⟩

supersonic transport *n* **:** a supersonic transport airplane

su·per·star \ˈsüpərˌstär, ˈsüpəˌstä(r\ *n* **:** a star (as in sports or the movies) who is considered extremely talented, has great public appeal, and can usu. command a high salary; *broadly* **:** one that is very prominent or a prime attraction ⟨a diplomatic *superstar*⟩ ⟨a *superstar* among growth stocks⟩ — **su·per·star·dom** \ˈsüpərˌstärdəm, ˈsüpəˌstä(rdəm\ *n*

sup·ply–side \səˌplīˈsīd\ *adj* **:** of, relating to, or being an economic theory that recommends the reduction of tax rates esp. in the highest brackets to encourage more earning, savings, and investment to expand economic activity and therefore the total taxable national income — **sup·ply–sid·er** \-ˌsīdə(r)\ *n*

support*n **:** SUPPORT LEVEL

support hose *n* **:** elastic stockings

support level *or* **support area** *n* **:** a price level on a declining market at which a security resists further decline due to increased attractiveness to traders and investors

sup·press*\sə'pres\ *vt* **:** to inhibit the genetic expression of ⟨*suppress* a mutation⟩

sup·pres·sant \sə'presᵊnt\ *n* **:** an agent (as a drug) that tends to suppress or reduce in intensity rather than eliminate something (as appetite)

su·pra·cel·lu·lar \ˌsüprə'selyələ(r)\ *adj* [*supra*- over, transcending (fr. L *supra* above, beyond) + *cellular*] **:** of greater than cellular scope or level of organization

su·pre·mo \sə'prē(ˌ)mō, sü'p-\ *n, pl* **-mos** *often cap* [Sp & It, fr. *supremo*, adj., supreme, fr. L *supremus*] *Brit* **:** one who is highest in rank or authority ⟨the Russians ... have just appointed a new energy *supremo* —*London Times*⟩

surf·able \'sərfəbəl, 'sōf-, 'səif-\ *adj* **:** suitable for surfing

sur·face–ef·fect ship \'sərfəsə̣ˌfekt-, 'sōf-, 'səif-\ *n* **:** a ground-effect machine that operates over water

surface feeder *n* **:** a duck (as a mallard or shoveler) that feeds by dabbling

surface structure *n* **:** a formal representation of the phonetic form of a sentence; *also* **:** the structure which such a representation describes

surface–to–air missile \ˌsərfəstə̣'a(ə)r-, ˌsōf-, ˌsəif-, -ˌ(e(ə)r-\ *n* **:** a usu. guided missile launched from the ground against a target in the air — called also *SAM*

surf and turf *n* **:** seafood (as lobster tails or shrimp) and a beefsteak (as filet mignon) served as a single course

surf·er's knot \'sərfə(r)z-, 'sōf-, 'səif-\ *n* **:** a knobby lump just below a surfer's knee or on the upper surface of his foot caused by friction and pressure between surfboard and skin

sur·jec·tion \ˌsər'jekshən, sə(r)'-, ˌsə̄-\ *n* [F, fr. *sur* over, on, onto + *-jection* (as in *projection* projection)] **:** a mathematical function that is an onto mapping — compare BIJECTION, INJECTION

sur·jec·tive \-'jektiv\ *adj* [F, fem. of *surjectif*, fr. *sur* onto + *-jectif* (as in *projectif* projective)] **:** ONTO ⟨a set of *surjective* functions⟩

sur·ro·ga·tion \ˌsərə'gāshən\ *n* [*surrogate* + *-ation* action, process] **:** the use of surrogates (as abstracts) in place of longer items (as documents) in an information= retrieval system

sur·veil \ˌsər'vā(ə)l, sə(r)'-, ˌsə̄-\ *vt* **sur·veilled; sur·veil·ling** [back-formation fr. *surveillance*] **:** to subject to surveillance ⟨will enable us to *surveil* almost any point on earth —Stansfield Turner⟩

sur·viv·al·ist \sə(r)'vīvələst\ *n* **:** one that views survival of a catastrophic event as a primary objective — **survivalist** *adj*

su·shi \'sü‚shē, -(ˌ)shi\ *n* [Jp] **:** a dish consisting of a cake of rice with raw fish, vegetables, and a vinegar sauce

suss out \(')səsˌaút\ *vt* **sussed out; suss·ing out** [perh. short for *suspect*] *Brit* **:** to inspect or study so as to gain more knowledge **:** figure out ⟨when people phone in

you've only got five seconds to *suss out* whether they're going to be obscene —Simon Williams⟩

sweat equity *n* **:** an owner's labor on improvements that increase the value of a property

sweep*n* **:** a television ratings period during which four consecutive one-week surveys are taken to determine advertising rates for local stations — usu. used in pl.

sweeper*or* **sweeper back** *n* **:** a lone back in soccer who plays between the line of the defenders and the goal

swing*vi* **1 :** to be lively and up-to-date ⟨he digs the hip scene and *swings* —Stan Sauerhaft⟩ **2 :** to engage in sex freely ⟨couples who *swing* are incapable of intimate relationships even with each other, and use wife-swapping as a safety valve —*Time*⟩

swing*also* **swing pass** *n* **:** a play in football in which a backfield receiver runs to the outside to take a short pass

swing–by \'swiŋˌbī\ *n, pl* **swing–bys :** an interplanetary mission in which a space vehicle utilizes the gravitational field of a planet near which it passes for changing course

swing·er*\'swiŋə(r)\ *n* **1 :** a lively and up-to-date person who indulges in what is considered fashionable ⟨reputation as a *swinger* since coming to Washington, where ... he is everybody's prize catch for a dinner party —Martin Mayer⟩ **2 :** one who engages freely in sex ⟨one of the *swingers*, who, ironically, is at this moment too sexually exhausted to take advantage of the compliance of the woman he most wants —Henry Hewes⟩

swing·ing*\-iŋ\ *n* **:** the practice of engaging in sex freely; *specif* **:** the exchanging of sex partners

swinging*adj* **:** being lively and up-to-date ⟨*swinging* moderns⟩; *also* **:** abounding in swingers and swinging entertainment ⟨a mod photographer in *swinging* London town —Andrew Sarris⟩

swing·man \'swiŋˌman\ *n* **:** a player capable of playing effectively in two different positions and esp. of playing both guard and forward on a basketball team

swing–wing \ˌswiŋˌwiŋ\ *adj* **:** having an airplane wing whose outer portion folds back along the fuselage to give the plane an arrowlike planform at high speeds

swipe*n* **:** a sharp often critical remark ⟨taking a few *swipes* at the phony model heroes —J. K. Fairbank⟩

switched–on \(')swichtˈȯn, -ˈän\ *adj* **:** attuned to what is new and exciting ⟨with-it in the *switched-on* world of psychedelic art —Elenore Lester⟩

switch–hitter*n, slang* **:** a bisexual person

symmetric group *n* **:** a permutation group that is composed of all of the permutations of *n* things

symmetric ma·trix \-'mā-triks\ *n* **:** a matrix that is its own transpose

symmetry*n* **:** a rigid motion of a geometric figure that determines a one-to-one mapping onto itself

sym·pa·tho·lyt·ic \ˌsimpəthō'lid·ik\ *n* **:** a sympatholytic agent

sym·pa·tho·mi·met·ic \ˌsimpə(ˌ)thōmə'med·ik, -mī'm-\ *n* **:** a sympathomimetic agent

syn·an·throp·ic \ˌ(ˌ)sinən'thräpik, -an'th-\ *adj* [*syn*- with (deriv. of Gk *syn*) + *anthropic*] **:** ecologically associated with man ⟨*synanthropic* flies⟩ — **syn·an·thro·py** \sə'nan(t)thrəpē\ *n*

syn·ap·to·ne·mal complex *or* **syn·ap·ti·ne·mal complex** \sə̣ˌnaptə‚nēməl-\ *n* [*synaptic* + connective *-o-*

or -*i*- + -*nema* one having, being, or resembling a thread (deriv. of Gk *nēma* thread) + -*al*, adj. suffix] **:** a complex tripartite protein structure that spans the region between synapsed chromosomes in meiotic prophase

syn·ap·to·some \sə'naptə,sōm\ *n* [*synaptic* + connective -*o*- + -*some* body, deriv. of Gk *sōma*] **:** a nerve ending that is isolated from homogenized nerve tissue ⟨noradrenaline uptake by *synaptosomes* prepared from rat brain —*Current Contents*⟩ — **sy·nap·to·so·mal** \sə,naptə'sōməl\ *adj*

syn·chro·tron radiation \'siŋk(r)ə,trän-, 'sin-\ *n* [from its having been first observed in a synchrotron] **:** electromagnetic radiation emitted by high-energy charged relativistic particles (as electrons) when they are accelerated by a magnetic field (as in a nebula)

syn·di·cate*vt -**cat·ed; -cat·ing :** to sell (as a series of television programs) directly to local stations

syn·ec·tics \sə'nektiks\ *n pl but usu sing in constr* [perh. fr. Gk *synektiktein* to bring forth together (fr. *syn*- together, with + *ektiktein* to bring forth, fr. *ex*- out + *tiktein* to beget) + E -*s* (as in *dialectics*)] **:** a theory or system of problem-stating and problem-solving based on creative thinking that involves free use of metaphor and analogy in informal interchange within a carefully selected small group of individuals of diverse personality and areas of specialization — **syn·ec·tic** \-tik\ *adj* — **syn·ec·ti·cal·ly** \-tək(ə)lē\ *adv*

syn·er·gism*'sinə(r),jizəm\ *n* **:** interaction of discrete agencies (as of industrial firms or physical equipment) in combination such that the total effect is greater than the sum of the individual effects ⟨neither of these vocalists has very high-class equipment and no *synergism* occurs when they team up —Noel Coppage⟩

syn·fuel \'sin,fyü(ə)l\ *n* [*synthetic fuel*] **:** a liquid or gaseous fuel derived from a fossil fuel that is solid (as coal) or part of a solid (as tar sand or oil shale) or from fermentation (as of grain)

syn·gas \-,gas\ *n* [*synthesis gas*] **:** a mixture of carbon monoxide and hydrogen used esp. in chemical synthesis

syn·ge·ne·ic \,sinjə'nēik\ *adj* [Gk *syngeneia* kinship (fr. *syn*- together, with + *genos* kind, kin) + E -*ic*] **:** sufficiently alike genetically to have similar antigens or immunological reactions ⟨*syngeneic* grafts between members of an inbred strain⟩ ⟨*syngeneic* rats⟩ — compare ALLOGENEIC, XENOGENEIC

syn·tac·tic foam \sən'taktik-\ *n* [*syntactic*, fr. Gk *syntaktikos* putting together] **:** a plastic in which preformed cells (as tiny hollow glass spheres) have been incorporated, which can withstand great pressures (as at ocean depths), and which floats

syn·thase \'sin,thās, -āz\ *n* [*synthesis* + -*ase* enzyme] **:** any of various enzymes that catalyze the synthesis of a substance without involving the breaking of a high-energy phosphate bond (as in ATP)

synthesizer*n **:** a usu. computerized electronic apparatus for the production and control of sound (as for producing music)

synthetic*adj **:** of or relating to a synfuel

synthetic division *n* **:** a simplified method of dividing one polynomial by another of the first degree by writing down only the coefficients of the several powers of the variable and changing the sign of the constant term in the divisor so as to replace the usual subtractions by additions

systems analysis *n* **:** the act, process, or profession of studying an activity (as a procedure, a business, or a physiological function) typically by mathematical means in order to define its goals or purposes and to discover operations and procedures for accomplishing them most efficiently

systems analyst *n* **:** a specialist in systems analysis

T

T*n : T-shirt

T*abbr **1** tera- **2** tesla

TA \(₁)tē'ā\ *n* : a teaching assistant ⟨appointed several *TA*s to grade papers for the professors⟩

TA *abbr* transactional analysis

tab·bou·leh \tə'bülə\ *n* [Ar *tabbūla;* akin to Ar *taubala* to spice, season] : a salad of Lebanese origin that includes among its ingredients cracked wheat, onions, parsley, and tomatoes

tab·bou·li *or* **tab·bu·li** *or* **ta·boo·ley** *or* **ta·boo·li** \tə'bülē, -li\ *n* : TABBOULEH

ta·bla \'täblə, 'təb-\ *n* [Hindi *tabla,* fr. Ar *ṭabla*] : a pair of small different-sized hand drums used esp. in Hindu music

ta·can \'ta₁kan\ *n* [*ta*ctical *a*ir *n*avigation] : a system of navigation employing ultra-high frequency signals to determine the distance and bearing of an aircraft from a transmitting station

tach \'tak\ *n* [short for *tach*ometer] : a device for indicating speed of rotation : tachometer

tach·ism \'ta₁shizəm\ *n, often cap* [F *tachisme,* fr. *tache* stain, spot, blob + *-isme* -ism (action, state)] : ACTION PAINTING — **tach·ist** \'tashəst\ *adj or n, often cap*

tachy·ar·rhyth·mia \₁takēā₁ri(th)mēə\ *n* [*tachy*- rapid + *arrhythmia*] : arrhythmia characterized by a rapid irregular heartbeat

tachy·on \'takē₁än\ *n* [*tachy*- rapid (fr. Gk *tachys*) + *-on* elementary particle] : a hypothetical particle that travels faster than light and behaves in a manner opposite to that of ordinary particles so that with an increase in velocity its energy decreases

tad**'tad\ *n* : a very small or insignificant amount or degree : bit ⟨could inject at least a *tad* more variety into their work —Richard Cromelin⟩ ⟨one perhaps a *tad* more liberal than the other but not essentially different —Steve Wise⟩

tae kwon do \'tī'kwän'dō\ *n, often cap T&K&D* [Korean] : a Korean martial art

ta·gli·a·tel·le \₁tälyä'tel(₁)ā\ *n* [It, fr. *tagliato* cut, past part. of *tagliare* to cut, trim, fr. LL *taliare* to split] : pasta in the shape of noodles

tag·me·mic \(₁)tag'mēmik\ *adj* [*tagmeme* + *-ic,* adj. suffix] : of or relating to a grammar that describes language in terms of the relationship between grammatical function and the class of items which can perform that function — **tag·me·mi·cist** \-'mēməsəst\ *n* — **tag·me·mics** \-'mēmiks\ *n pl*

tag question *n* : a question (as *isn't it* in "it's fine, isn't it?") added to a statement or command to gain the assent of the person addressed

tag sale *n* [fr. the tag on each item indicating its price] : GARAGE SALE

ta·hi·ni \tə'hē(₁)nē, tä-\ *n* [Turk *tāhin* sesame flour or oil] : a smooth paste made from sesame seeds

tai chi *or* **t'ai chi** \'tī'jē, -'chē\ *also* **tai chi chuan** *or* **t'ai chi ch'uan** \-'chü'än\ *n, often cap T & Cs* [Chin (Pek) *t'ai⁴ chi² ch'uan²* Chinese shadowboxing, fr. *t'ai⁴* greatest, highest + *chi²* reach + *ch'uan²* boxing] : an ancient Chinese discipline practiced as a system of exercises for attaining bodily or mental control and well-being

tail·gate**'tā(₁)l₁gāt\ *vi* **tail·gat·ed; tail·gat·ing** : to hold a tailgate picnic (as before a football game)

tail·gate \'tā(₁)l₁gāt\ *adj* [*tailgate,* n.] : served from or set up on the tailgate esp. of a station wagon ⟨a *tailgate* picnic⟩

ta·ka \'täkə\ *n, pl* **taka** *or* **takas** [Bengali *ṭākā,* fr. Skt *ṭaṅka* coin] **1** : the basic monetary unit of Bangladesh **2** : a coin or note representing one taka

take*vb — **take a bath** : to suffer a heavy financial loss — **take a position** *of a security dealer* : to hold in his own account stock bought in the course of trading — **take the mickey** *chiefly Brit* : to joke or kid ⟨he was making out he was only *taking the mickey,* but I could see he meant it —Bill Naughton⟩ — **take the mickey out of** *chiefly Brit* : to tease or make fun of ⟨a machine-gun barrage of one-liners and jokes that *took the mickey out of* everyone there —Peter Bogdanovich⟩

take*n — **on the take** : paid for illegal favors ⟨crooked county commissioners . . . *on the take* —Aaron Latham⟩

take–home \'täk₁hōm, 'tā₁kōm\ *adj* : that may be worked on without supervision outside the classroom ⟨a *take-home* exam⟩

take off*vi **1** : to start rapid activity, development, or growth ⟨the business *took off* and has been flying high ever since —R.H. Jones⟩ **2** : to spring into wide use or popularity ⟨a liquid dentifrice which . . . *took off* like a rocket when first introduced —Martin Mayer⟩

take·out**'tā₁kaut\ *n* : an intensive study or report ⟨one of the best *takeouts* on urban welfare —Brock Brower⟩

take–out \'tā(₁)kaut\ *adj* : designed for the sale of or being food that is not to be consumed on the premises ⟨a *take-out* counter in a restaurant⟩

¹ta·la \'tälə\ *n* [Skt *tāla* hand-clapping, musical beat, alter. of *tāḍa* beating, fr. *tāḍayati* he beats] : one of the ancient traditional metrical patterns of Hindu music

²tala *n, pl* **tala** [Samoan, fr. E *dollar*] **1** : the basic monetary unit of Western Samoa **2** : a coin or note representing one tala

talking head *n* : the televised image of the head of a person who is talking ⟨bored by a set of *talking heads* discoursing more or less dispassionately —H.S. Ashmore⟩

talk show *n* : a radio or television program in which usu. well-known persons engage in discussions or are interviewed

tam·ba·la \(₁)täm'bälə\ *n, pl* **tambala** *or* **tambalas** [native name in Malawi, lit., cockerel] **1** : a monetary unit of Malawi equal to $^1/_{100}$ kwacha   **2 :** a coin representing one tambala

tan·door \tän'dů(ə)r\ *n, pl* **tan·doo·ri** \-'dů(ə)rē, -ri\ [Punjabi *tandoor* clay oven; akin to Turk *tandir* oven] **:** a cylindrical clay or earthenware oven in which food is cooked over charcoal

tan·doo·ri \tän'dů(ə)rē, -ri\ *adj* [*tandoor*] **:** cooked in a tandoor ⟨*tandoori* chicken⟩

tank suit *n* **:** a one-piece bathing suit with shoulder straps

tank top *n* [fr. its resemblance to a tank suit] **:** a sleeveless collarless shirt with shoulder straps and no front opening

tape deck *n*   **1 a :** a mechanism that moves a tape past a magnetic head (as of a tape recorder)   **b :** a device that contains such a mechanism and provisions usu. for the recording as well as the playback of magnetic tapes and that usu. has to be connected to a separate audio system   **2 :** TAPE PLAYER

tape player *n* **:** a self-contained device for the playback of recorded magnetic tapes

tar·dive dys·ki·ne·sia \'tärdiv,diskə'nēzh(ē)ə, -kī-\ *n* **:** a central nervous system disorder characterized by twitching of the face and tongue and involuntary motor movements of the trunk and limbs and occurring esp. as a side effect of prolonged use of antipsychotic drugs (as phenothiazine)

tar·dy \'tärdē, 'tád-, -di\ *n, pl* **tardies** [*tardy*, adj.] **:** an instance of being tardy (as for class) ⟨three unexcused *tardies* are equivalent to one absence⟩

tar·get·able \'tärgəd-əbəl\ *adj* **:** capable of being aimed at a target ⟨missiles with *targetable* warheads⟩

target language *n*   **1 :** a foreign language that is the subject of study   **2 :** a language into which a translation (as by machine) is made — compare SOURCE LANGUAGE

tar pit *n* **:** an area in which natural bitumens collect and are exposed at the earth's surface and which tends to trap animals and preserve their hard parts

tart up *vt* [*tart* (prostitute) + *up*] *chiefly Brit* **:** to add superficial adornment to ⟨*tarted up* pubs and restaurants for the spenders —Arnold Ehrlich⟩

Tas·lan \'tas,lan\ *trademark* — used for thread and textured yarn

tau particle \'taů-, 'tó-\ *n* **:** a short-lived fundamental particle of the lepton family that exists in positive and negative charge states and has a mass about 3500 times heavier than an electron

Taurean* *n* **:** TAURUS

Taurus* *n* **:** one born under the astrological sign Taurus

ta·ver·na \tä'vе(ə)rnə\ *n* [modif. (prob. influenced by E *tavern*) of NGk *taberna* tavern] **:** a café in Greece

tax base *n* **:** the wealth (as real estate or income) within a jurisdiction that is liable to taxation

tax haven *n* **:** a country or territory in which taxes are low or nonexistent and which is thus attractive to foreign investors

taxi squad *n* [fr. the practice of a former owner of a professional team who employed such surplus players as drivers for a taxi fleet which he also owned] **:** a group of professional football players under contract who practice with a team but are ineligible to participate in official games

taxon *abbr* taxonomic; taxonomy

tax selling *n* **:** concerted selling of securities late in the year to establish gains and losses for income-tax purposes

tax shelter *n* **:** a strategy (as formation of a philanthropic foundation), an investment (as in a venture capital enterprise or tax-free municipal bonds), or a tax code provision (as for a depreciation allowance) that reduces one's tax liability

tax–shel·tered \'tak(s),sheltə(r)d\ *adj*   **1 :** characterized or produced by a tax shelter ⟨a *tax-sheltered* investment⟩ ⟨*tax-sheltered* income⟩   **2 :** of, relating to, or involving investments relieved by law from the payment of tax on income often for a particular period or under particular circumstances ⟨*tax-sheltered* retirement plans⟩

Tay·lor's series *also* **Taylor series** \'tālə(r)-\ *n* [Brook *Taylor* †1731 Eng. mathematician] **:** a power series that gives the expansion of a function $f(x)$ in the neighborhood of a point a provided all derivatives exist and the series converges and that has the form

$$f(x) = f(a) + \frac{f^{[1]}(a)}{1!}(x-a) + \frac{f^{[2]}(a)}{2!}(x-a)^2 + \ldots + \frac{f^{[n]}(a)}{n!}(x-a)^n + \ldots$$

where $f^{[n]}(a)$ is the derivative of nth order of $f(x)$ evaluated at a

Tay–Sachs disease \'tä,saks-\ *also* **Tay–Sachs** *n* [Waren *Tay* †1927 Eng. physician and Bernard P. *Sachs* †1944 Am. neurologist] **:** a fatal hereditary disorder of lipid metabolism characterized by the accumulation of sphingolipid esp. in nervous tissue due to an enzyme deficiency

T–bill \'tē,bil\ *n* [Treasury] **:** a U.S. treasury note

TCDD \,tē,sē(,)dē'dē\ *n* [*tetra*- containing four atoms, radicals, or groups + *chlor*- containing chlorine + *dibenzo*- containing two benzene rings + *dioxin*] **:** DIOXIN

T cell *n* [thymus-derived *cell*] **:** a lymphocyte differentiated in the thymus, characterized by specific surface antigens, and specialized for cell-mediated immunity (as in the defense against viruses and cancer and the rejection of foreign tissues) or for cooperation with B cells in immunoglobulin synthesis — compare B CELL

t distribution *n* **:** a probability density function that is used esp. in testing hypotheses concerning means of normal distributions whose standard deviations are unknown and that is the distribution of a random variable

$$t = \frac{u \sqrt{n}}{v}$$

where u and v are themselves independent random variables and u has a normal distribution with mean 0 and a standard deviation of 1 and v^2 has a chi-square distribution with n degrees of freedom — called also *student's t distribution*

tea break *n, chiefly Brit* **:** a short rest period during the working day for the drinking of tea

tea ceremony *n* **:** a Japanese ceremony consisting of the serving and taking of tea in accordance with an elaborate ritual **:** chanoyu

teach–in \'tē,chin\ *n* **:** an extended meeting usu. held on a college campus for lectures, debates, and discussions on important issues (as U.S. foreign policy)

teaching machine *n* **:** any of various mechanical devices for presenting a program of instructional material

team foul n : one of a designated number of personal fouls the players on a basketball team may commit during a given period of play before the opposing team begins receiving bonus free throws

team handball n : a game developed from soccer which is played between two teams of seven players each and in which the ball is thrown, caught, and dribbled with the hands

tear*vb — tear a strip off Brit : to bawl out : scold

tear·gas \'ti(ə)r,gas, 'tiə,-\ vt : to use tear gas on ⟨tired of being maced and clubbed and teargassed by the police — R.J. Glessing⟩

tearoom*n : a men's room used as a site for homosexual activity

tease*n : an advertisement meant to arouse curiosity sometimes by withholding part of the material information

tech·ne·tron·ic \,teknə·'tränik\ adj [technological + electronic] : shaped or influenced by the changes wrought by advances in technology and communications ⟨our modern technetronic society⟩

tech·nol·o·gize \tek'nälə,jīz\ vt -gized; -giz·ing : to affect or alter by technology ⟨technologized American society⟩

tech·nop·o·lis \tek'näpələs\ n [techno- art, craft, technical, technological (fr. Gk technē art, craft) + -polis city, deriv. of Gk polis] : a society strongly influenced by and heavily dependent on technology ⟨we must civilize technopolis, where barbarism and anonymity are well entrenched —M. W. Fishwick⟩ — tech·no·pol·i·tan \(,)teknə'pälət°n, -tən\ adj

tech·no·struc·ture \'teknō,strəkchə(r)\ n : a large-scale corporation or system of corporate enterprises; also : a group of professionals who control a technostructure

teeny \'tēnē, -ni\ n, pl teen·ies : a teenager

teeny·bop \'tēnē,bäp, -ni-\ adj [back-formation fr. teenybopper] : of, relating to, or being a teenybopper

teeny·bop·per \-,bäpə(r)\ n : a teenager and esp. a teen-aged girl; esp : one who is enthusiastically devoted to pop music and to current fads

TEFL \'tefəl\ abbr teaching English as a foreign language

tei·cho·ic acid \tā,kōik-, tī,-\ n [teichoic, fr. Gk teichos wall + E -ic, adj. suffix] : any of a class of strongly acidic polymers found in the cell walls, capsules, and membranes of all gram-positive bacteria and containing residues of the phosphates of glycerol and adonitol

tele·con·fer·ence \'telə,känfər(ə)n(t)s, -frən(t)s\ n : a conference among people remote from one another who are linked by telecommunication devices (as telephones, televisions, or computer terminals) — tele·con·fer·enc·ing \-iŋ\ n

Tele·copi·er \'telə,käpēə(r)\ trademark — used for transmitting and receiving equipment for producing facsimile copies of documents

tele·di·ag·no·sis \,telə,dīəg'nōsəs\ n [tele- distant (deriv. of Gk tēle far off) + diagnosis] : the diagnosis of physical or mental ailments based on data received from a patient by means of telemetry and closed-circuit television

tele·fac·sim·i·le \-fak'simə(,)lē, -əli\ n : a system for the transmission and reproduction of fixed graphic matter (as printing) by means of signals transmitted (as between libraries) over telephone wires

tele·lec·ture \'telə,lekchə(r)\ n 1 : a loudspeaker connected to a telephone line for amplifying voice communication 2 : a lecture delivered to an audience by telelecture

te·lem·e·try \tə'lemə·trē, -ri\ n 1 : the science or process of telemetering data 2 : data transmitted by telemetry 3 : BIOTELEMETRY

tele·on·o·my \,telē'änəmē, -mi\ n [teleo- complete + -nomy system of laws governing a field] : the quality of apparent purposefulness in living organisms that derives from their evolutionary adaptation

tele·pro·cess·ing \'telə,präs,esiŋ, -,prōs-, -səsiŋ\ n : computer processing via remote terminals

tele·text \'telə,tekst\ n : an electronic system in which printed information (as news items) is broadcast over an unused portion of a television signal and displayed on a viewer's television set that is equipped with a decoder

tel·ex \'te,leks\ n [teleprinter + exchange] : a communication service involving teletypewriters connected by wire through automatic exchanges — telex vt

te·lo·phase*\'telə,fāz, 'tēl-\ n : a stage in meiosis that is usu. the final stage in the first and second meiotic divisions but may be missing in the first and that is characterized by formation of the nuclear membrane and by changes in coiling and arrangement of the chromosomes

temp*n : a temporary worker

tem·peh \'tem,pā\ n [Indonesian témpé] : an Asian food prepared by fermenting soybeans with a rhizopus

tem·plate*\'templət\ n : a molecule (as of DNA) in a biological system that serves as a pattern for the generation of another macromolecule (as messenger RNA)

temporal sum·ma·tion \-(,)sə'māshən\ n : sensory summation that involves the addition of single stimuli over a short period of time

ten·der·om·e·ter \,tend(ə)'räməd·ə(r)\ n [tender + connective -o- + -meter instrument for measuring, deriv. of Gk metron measure] : a device for determining the maturity and tenderness of samples of fruits and vegetables

-tene \,tēn\ adj comb form [-tene, n. comb. form, deriv. of Gk tainia ribbon, band] : having (such or so many) chromosomal filaments ⟨polytene⟩ ⟨pachytene⟩

ten·seg·ri·ty \ten(t)'segrəd·ē, -rətē, -i\ n [tension + integrity] : the property of a skeletal structure having continuous tension members (as wires) and discontinuous compression members (as metal tubes) so that each member performs efficiently in producing a rigid form

ten·sio·met·ric \,ten(t)sēə'metrik\ adj [tension + -metric measuring, deriv. of Gk metron measure] : of, relating to, or involving the measurement of tension or tensile strength — ten·si·om·e·try \,ten(t)sē'ämə·trē\ n

ten–speed \'ten,spēd\ n : a bicycle with a 10-speed derailleur

tent trailer n : a 2-wheeled automobile-drawn trailer having a canvas shelter that can be opened up above the body to provide camping facilities

ten·ured \'tenyə(r)d, -,yu̇(ə)rd, -,yu̇əd\ adj : having tenure ⟨tenured faculty members⟩

tenure–track \'tenyə(r),trak, also -,yu̇r-, -,yu̇(ə)-\ adj : relating to or being a teaching position that may lead to one's being granted tenure

teo·na·na·catl \,tāō,nänə'kätəl\ n [Nahuatl, fr. teotl god + nanacatl mushroom] : any of several New World mushrooms (*Psilocybe* and related genera of the family Agaricaceae) that are sources of hallucinogens

te·pa \'tēpə\ *n* [*tri-* three (fr. L & Gk) + ethylene + phosphorus + *a*mide] **:** a soluble crystalline compound $C_6H_{12}N_3OP$ that is related to ethylenimine and that is used esp. as a chemosterilant of insects, an alleviant in some kinds of cancer, and in finishing and flame-proofing textiles

teph·ra \'tefrə\ *n* [Gk *tephra* ashes; akin to L *favilla* ashes] **:** solid material ejected during the eruption of a volcano and transported through the air

tequila sunrise *n* **:** a cocktail consisting chiefly of tequila, orange juice, and grenadine

tera- \'terə\ *comb form* [ISV, fr. Gk *teras* monster] **:** a trillion of ⟨*tera*ton⟩ ⟨*tera*hertz⟩

te·rato·car·ci·no·ma \'terəd-ō,kärs°n,ōmə\ *n* [*teratoma* + *carcinoma*] **:** a malignant teratoma; *esp* **:** one involving germinal cells of the testis

te·rato·gen \tə'rad-əjən, 'terəd-əjən, -,jen\ *n* [*teratomonster* (fr. Gk *teret-, teras*) + *-gen* producer, deriv. of Gk *genēs* born] **:** a teratogenic agent (as a drug or virus)

ter·i·ya·ki \,terē'(y)äkē\ *n* [Jp, fr. *teri* sunshine + *yaki* roast] **:** a dish of Japanese origin consisting of meat, chicken, or shellfish that is grilled or broiled after being marinated in a spicy soy sauce

terminal*n **:** a device (as a video display unit) by which data can enter or leave a communication network

ter·ra \'terə\ *n, pl* **ter·rae** \-r(,)ē, -r,ī\ [NL, fr. L, land] **:** any of the relatively light-colored highland areas on the surface of the moon or a planet

Ter·ran \'terən\ *n* [*Terra*, the planet Earth (fr. L *terra* Earth) + E *-an* one belonging to] **:** an inhabitant of the earth ⟨the way *Terrans* may appear to inhabitants of outer space —Jane Manthorne⟩

tertiary*adj **1 :** being or relating to the recovery of oil and gas from old wells by means of the underground application of heat and chemicals **2 :** being or relating to the purification of wastewater by removal of fine particles, nitrates, and phosphates

TESL \'tesəl\ *abbr* teaching English as a second language

tes·la \'teslə\ *n* [ISV, fr. Nikola *Tesla* †1943 Am. electrician and inventor] **:** a unit of magnetic flux density in the mks system equivalent to one weber per square meter

TESOL \'tē,sòl, -ōl\ *abbr* teachers of English to speakers of other languages; teaching of English to speakers of other languages

test ban *n* **:** a self-imposed ban on the atmospheric testing of nuclear weapons that is mutually agreed to by countries possessing such weapons

test–drive \'tes(t),drīv\ *vt* **-drove; -driv·en; -driv·ing** **:** to drive (a motor vehicle) in order to evaluate performance

tet·ra·ben·a·zine \,te·trə,benə,zēn\ *n* [*tetra-* four (deriv. of Gk *tetra-*) + *benzo*[*a*]quinolizine, fr. *benzo-* related to benzene or benzoic acid + *a* (an indicator of position) + *quinoli*ne + *azine*] **:** a serotonin antagonist $C_{19}H_{27}NO_3$ that is used esp. in the treatment of psychosis and anxiety

tet·ra·func·tion·al \,te·trə,fəŋ(k)shnəl, -shənəl\ *adj* **:** of, relating to, or being a compound with four sites in the molecule that are highly reactive (as in polymerization)

tet·ra·hy·dro·can·nab·i·nol \,te·trə,hīdrəkə'nabə,nól\ *n* [*tetrahydro-* combined with four hydrogen atoms + *cannabinol*, a phenol obtained from hemp] **:** a physiologically active liquid from hemp plant resin that is the chief intoxicant in marijuana — called also *THC*

tet·ra·hy·me·na \,te·trə'hīmənə\ *n* [NL, fr. *tetra-* + Gk *hymēn* membrane] **1** *cap* **:** a genus of free-living ciliate protozoans much used for genetic and biochemical research **2 :** a member of the genus *Tetrahymena* and esp. *T. pyriformis*

tet·ra·pyr·role *also* **tet·ra·pyr·rol** \,te·trə,pi,rōl, -òl, -əpə,r-\ *n* **:** a chemical group consisting of four pyrrole rings joined either in a straight chain (as in phycobilins) or in a ring (as in chlorophyll)

Tet·raz·zi·ni \,te·trə,zēnē, -ni\ *adj* [Luisa *Tetrazzini* †1940 Ital. opera singer] **:** prepared with pasta and a white sauce seasoned with sherry and served au gratin ⟨chicken *Tetrazzini*⟩ ⟨turkey *Tetrazzini*⟩

Texas citrus mite *n* **:** a red spider (*Eutetrarychus banksi*) that causes leaf injury to citrus trees

Tex–Mex \'tek,smeks\ *adj* [*Tex*as + *Mex*ico] **:** of, relating to, or being the Mexican-American culture or cuisine existing or originating esp. in southern Texas ⟨*Tex-Mex* cooking⟩ ⟨*Tex-Mex* music⟩

text*n **:** matter chiefly in the form of words captured by computer-based equipment ⟨a *text*-editing typewriter⟩

tex·tur·ize \'tekschə,rīz\ *vt* **-ized; -iz·ing** [*texture* + *-ize*, vb. suffix] **:** to give a particular texture to ⟨the flat thermoplastic yarn is fed into the unit and is *texturized* as it approaches the knitting needles —*Technical Survey*⟩

TG*abbr **1** transformational-generative **2** transformational grammar

T–group \'tē,grüp\ *n* [*training group*] **:** a group of people under the leadership of a trainer who seek to develop self≠ awareness and sensitivity to others by verbalizing feelings uninhibitedly at group sessions — compare ENCOUNTER GROUP

thal·as·se·mic \,thalə'sēmik\ *adj* **:** of, relating to, or affected with thalassemia — **thalassemic** *n*

tha·lid·o·mide \thə'lidə,mīd, -əməd\ *n* [ph*thalimide* + connective *-o-* + *imide*] **:** a sedative and hypnotic drug $C_{13}H_{10}N_2O_4$ that has been the cause of malformation in infants born to mothers using it during pregnancy

thatch*n **:** a mat of undecomposed plant material (as grass clippings) accumulated next to the soil in a grassy area (as a lawn)

THC \,tē(,)āch'sē\ *n* [*tetrahydrocannabinol*] **:** TETRAHYDROCANNABINOL

the·ater \'thēəd-ə(r), 'thiə-, *oftenest in South* 'thē,ād-ə(r) *also* thē'ā-\ *adj* **:** tactical ⟨*theater* nuclear weapons⟩

theater of the absurd : theater that seeks to represent the absurdity of human existence in a meaningless universe by bizarre or fantastic means (as senseless or repetitious dialogue)

the·be \'tā(,)bā\ *n, pl* **thebe** [native name in Botswana] **1 :** a monetary unit of Botswana equal to $1/100$ pula **2 :** a coin representing one thebe

theme \'thēm\ *adj, of a restaurant or hotel* **:** having an elaborate, specialized, or fantasy decor and setting ⟨*theme* restaurants that look like railroad cars or Polynesian villages⟩

theme park *n* **:** an amusement park in which the structures and settings are based on a central theme

theorem*n **1 :** a stencil **2 :** a painting produced esp. on velvet by the use of stencils for each color

therapeutic index *n* **:** a measure of the relative desirability of a drug for the attaining of a particular medical end that is usu. expressed as the ratio of the largest dose producing no toxic symptoms to the smallest dose routinely producing cures

thermal*adj* **:** designed (as with insulating air spaces) to prevent dissipation of body heat ⟨*thermal* underwear⟩

thermal pol·lu·tion \-pə'lüshən\ *n* **:** the discharge of heated liquid (as wastewater from a factory) into natural waters at a temperature detrimental to existing ecosystems

ther·mo·form \'thərmə,form\ *vt* [*thermo*- heat (fr. Gk *thermē*) + *form*] **:** to give a final shape to (as a plastic) with the aid of heat and usu. pressure — **thermoform** *n* — **ther·mo·form·able** \,'thərmə,'förməbəl\ *adj*

ther·mo·gram*\'thərmə,gram\ *n* **1 :** a photographic record made by thermography **2 :** a temperature-weight change graph obtained in thermogravimetry

ther·mo·graph*\-,graf\ *n* **1 :** THERMOGRAM **2 :** the apparatus used in thermography

ther·mo·gra·vim·e·try \,thər(,)mōgrə'vimə·trē\ *n* [ISV *thermo*- + *gravimetry;* prob. orig. formed in F] **:** the determination (as with a thermobalance) of weight changes in a substance at a high temperature or during a gradual increase in temperature — **ther·mo·grav·i·me·tric** \-,gravə'me·trik\ *adj*

ther·mo·phys·i·cal \,thərmō'fizəkəl, -mə-\ *adj* **:** of, relating to, or concerned with the physical properties of materials as affected by elevated temperatures

ther·mo·rem·a·nent \-,remənənt\ *adj* [*thermo*- heat + *remanent*] **:** being or relating to magnetic remanence (as in a rock cooled from a molten state or in a baked clay object containing magnetic minerals) that indicates the strength and direction of the earth's magnetic field at a former time — **ther·mo·rem·a·nence** \-,nən(t)s\ *n*

ther·mo·sphere \'thərmə,sfi(ə)r\ *n* **:** the part of the earth's atmosphere that begins at about 50 miles above the earth's surface, extends to outer space, and is characterized by steadily increasing temperature with height — **ther·mo·spher·ic** \,thərmə'sfi(ə)rik, -'sfer-\ *adj*

the·ta rhythm \'thād-ə-, 'thēd-ə-\ *n* **:** a relatively high amplitude brain wave pattern between approximately 4 and 9 hertz that is characteristic esp. of the hippocampus but occurs in many regions of the brain including the cortex

thia·ben·da·zole \,thīə'bendə,zōl\ *n* [*thiazole* + *benzimidazole*] **:** a drug $C_{10}H_7N_3S$ used in the control of parasitic roundworms and fungus infections and as an agricultural fungicide

thi·a·zide \'thīə,zīd, -əzəd\ *n* [*thi*- sulfur (deriv. of Gk *theion*) + *diazine* + *oxide*] **:** any of several drugs used as oral diuretics esp. in the control of high blood pressure

thing*n* **:** a personal choice of activity — often used with *do* ⟨letting students do their own *thing* —*Newsweek*⟩

think tank *also* **think factory** *n* **:** an institute, corporation, or group organized for interdisciplinary research (as in military strategy or technological and social problems) ⟨corporate wise men who ponder others' problems, for a stiff fee, in the seclusion of *think tanks* —Leonard Iaquinta⟩ — **think tank·er** \-,taŋkə(r)\ *n*

thin–lay·er chro·ma·tog·ra·phy \,thin,lāər,krōmə-'tägrəfē, -,le(ə)r-\ *n* **:** chromatography in which the solution containing the substances to be separated migrates

through a thin layer of the absorbent medium (as silica gel, alumina, or cellulose) arranged on a rigid support — compare COLUMN CHROMATOGRAPHY — **thin–layer chro·ma·to·gram** \-krō'mad-ə,gram\ *n* — **thin–layer chro·ma·to·graph·ic** \-krō,mad-ə'grafik, -,krōməd-ə-\ *adj*

thi·o·rid·a·zine \,thīə'ridə,zēn, -əzən\ *n* [*thio*- sulfur (deriv. of Gk *theion*) + *piperidine* + *phenothiazine*] **:** a phenothiazine tranquilizer used as the hydrochloride $C_{21}H_{26}N_2S_2 \cdot HCl$ for relief of anxiety states and in the treatment of schizophrenia

third market *n* [fr. its distinction from the organized exchanges and the market in unlisted securities] **:** the over-the-counter market in listed securities — compare FOURTH MARKET

third–stream \,'thərd,strēm, ,'thəd-, ,'thəid-\ *adj* **:** of, relating to, or being music that incorporates elements of classical music and jazz

third world *n, often cap T&W* [trans. of F *tiers monde*] **1 :** a group of nations esp. in Africa and Asia that are not aligned with either the Communist or the non-Communist blocs ⟨wants Greece to stay in the *Third World*, away from Russian or American influence —Christopher Sharp⟩ **2 :** an aggregate of minority groups within a larger predominant culture ⟨Community High, for example, has 65 *Third World* students and 120 whites —*Time*⟩ **3 :** the aggregate of the underdeveloped nations of the world ⟨the *Third World* consists, by definition, of poor rural societies —J.K. Galbraith⟩ — **third world·er** \-,'wər(ə)ldə(r), -,'wōl-, -,'wəil-\ *n, often cap T&W*

ThM *abbr master of theology*

tho·rac·ic gland \thə'rasik-\ *n* **:** PROTHORACIC GLAND

threads *n pl* **:** clothes ⟨specializing in *threads* to fit the fashion-conscious soul brother —*Newsweek*⟩

thrift shop *n* **:** a shop that sells secondhand articles and esp. clothes and is often run for charitable purposes

throm·box·ane \thräm'bäk,sān\ *n* [*thrombocyte* + *ox*- containing oxygen + *-ane* saturated carbon compound] **:** any of several potent regulators of cellular function that are formed from endoperoxides and were first isolated from thrombocytes

through·put*\'thrü,pùt\ *n* **:** output, production ⟨the *throughput* of a computer⟩

throw·away \,'thrōə,wā\ *adj* **1 a :** that may be thrown away **:** disposable ⟨*throwaway* containers⟩ ⟨this flashlight is sturdy and well made for a *throwaway* item —*Consumer Reports*⟩ **b :** accustomed to or depending on the discarding rather than the reusing or recycling of materials after initial use ⟨our *throwaway* society⟩ ⟨a *throwaway* economy⟩ **2 :** written or spoken (as in a play) in a low-key or unemphasized manner ⟨*throwaway* lines⟩ **3 :** nonchalant, casual ⟨all put together with such style, such *throwaway* chic —Peter Buckley⟩

throw pillow *n* **:** a small pillow used esp. as a decorative accessory

thrust chamber *n* **:** a jet engine that consists of a combustion chamber in which solid or liquid fuel is ignited and that is used for the propulsion of a missile or vehicle (as an airplane)

thrust·or *also* **thrust·er***\'thrəstə(r)\ *n* **:** an engine (as a jet engine) that develops thrust by expelling a jet of fluid or a stream of particles **:** reaction engine

thrust stage *n* **:** a theater stage surrounded on three sides by the audience; *also* **:** a forestage that is extended into the auditorium to increase the stage area

thumb piano *n* **:** any of various musical instruments of African origin (as the kalimba, mbira, or zanza) that consist essentially of a resonator and a set of tuned metal or wooden strips that are plucked with the thumbs or fingers

thy·la·koid \'thīlə,kȯid\ *n* [ISV *thylak-* (fr. Gk *thylakos* sack) + *-oid* one that resembles; prob. orig. formed in G] **:** any of the membranous lamellae of protein and lipid in plant chloroplasts that are the sites of the photochemical reactions of photosynthesis

thy·mec·to·mize \thī'mektə,mīz\ *vt* **-mized; -miz·ing** **:** to subject to thymectomy (studies in rats *thymectomized* at birth)

thy·mi·co·lym·phat·ic \,thīmə(,)kōlim,'fad·ik\ *adj* [*thymic* + connective *-o-* + *lymphatic*] **:** of, relating to, or affecting both the thymus and the lymphatic system

thy·mo·sin \'thīməsən\ *n* [fr. Gk *thymos* thymus + E *-in* chemical compound] **:** a polypeptide thymic hormone that influences the maturation of T cells destined for an active role in cell-mediated immunity

thy·ris·tor \thī'ristə(r)\ *n* [*thyra*tron + trans*istor*] **:** any of several semiconductor devices that act as switches, rectifiers, or voltage regulators

thy·ro·cal·ci·to·nin \,thīrō,kalsə,'tōnən\ *n* [*thyro*id + *calcitonin*] **:** CALCITONIN

thy·roid–stim·u·lat·ing hor·mone \,thī,rȯid,'stimyə-,lād·iŋ'hȯr,mōn, -'hȯ(ə),mōn\ *n* **:** a hormone secreted by the anterior pituitary that regulates the formation and secretion of thyroid hormone **:** thyrotrophin

thy·ro·tro·pin–releasing hormone \,thīrə,'trōpən-\ *also* **thyrotropin–releasing factor** *n* **:** a tripeptide hormone synthesized in the hypothalamus that stimulates secretion of thyrotropin by the anterior lobe of the pituitary gland

tic* *n* **:** a frequent usu. unconscious quirk of behavior or speech (it appears that the word "like" has replaced "you know" as vocalized pause and verbal *tic* —G. B. Dearing)

ticked* *adj* **:** angry, upset

ticket pocket *n* **:** a small pocket within or just above the outside pocket of a man's suit jacket

tick off* *vt* **:** to make angry or indignant (a casual, personal meditation on . . . whatever happens to tickle or *tick off* the writer at the moment —Robert MacKenzie)

¹ticky–tacky \'tikē,takē\ *also* **ticky–tack** \-,tak\ *n, pl* **ticky–tack·ies** *also* **ticky–tacks** [redupl. of *tacky*] **:** sleazy or shoddy material used esp. in the construction of look-alike tract houses (sprawling suburbs are filled with more than enough neon, plastic and *ticky-tacky* — J.P. Sterba); *also* **:** something built of ticky-tacky

²ticky–tacky *also* **ticky–tack** *adj* **1 :** being of an uninspired or monotonous sameness or commonness (*ticky-tacky* suburbs which the architects are preparing for them to live in —Edward Hoagland) **2 :** tacky (feared that *ticky-tacky* souvenir shops and hot-dog stands would invade his privacy —*U.S. News & World Report*) (mishmash of pictures, potted history and *ticky-tacky* recipes —R. A. Sokolov) **3 :** built of ticky-tacky (the houses aren't *ticky-tacky* but they're not posh —A. P. Sanoff)

tight* *adj* **1 :** marked by friendliness and compatibility **:** close (the Men's Alpine Ski Team is a *tight* bunch, surprisingly free of backbiting —Herbert Burkholz) (*tight* ethnic neighborhoods) **2 :** being or performing music in a polished style with precise arrangements (some favor *tight* playing, with crisply articulated notes, others open playing, generally faster and more flowing —Eleanor Blau)

tight–assed \,'tid-,ast, *also* -,ȧst\ *adj, slang* **:** rigidly proper, conventional, or inhibited (*tight-assed* social climbers obsessed with consumer goods —Ellen Willis)

tight end *n* **:** an offensive end in football who lines up within two yards of the tackle

time di·la·tion \-di'lāshən\ *also* **time di·la·ta·tion** \-,dilə'tāshən, -,dīlə-\ *n* **:** a slowing of time on a system moving at a velocity approaching that of light relative to an observer as predicted by the theory of relativity

time frame *n* **:** a period of time esp. with respect to some action or project (mandatory *time frames* within which committees must act —Guy Halverson)

time reversal *n* **:** a formal operation in mathematical physics that reverses the order in which a sequence of events occurs

time reversal in·var·i·ance \-(')in,'verēən(t)s, -,'var-\ *n* **:** a principle in physics: if a given sequence of events is physically possible the same sequence in the opposite order is also possible

time–shar·ing \'tīm,she(ə)riŋ, -,sha(ə)riŋ\ *n* **1 :** simultaneous use of a central computer by many users at remote locations **2** *or* **time–share :** joint ownership or rental of a vacation lodging (as a condominium) by several persons with each occupying the premises in turn for short periods — **time–share** *vt* — **time–shared** \-,she(ə)rd, -,sha(ə)rd, -,sheəd, -,shaəd\ *adj*

times sign *n* **:** the symbol × used to indicate multiplication — called also *multiplication sign*

time–test·ed \'tīm,testəd\ *adj* **:** having effectiveness that has been proved over a long period of time (*time-tested*, universally accepted ideas that are set forth in school and college texts —J.S. Trefil)

time trial *n* **:** a competitive event (as in auto racing) in which individuals are successively timed over a set course or distance

time–trip \(')tīm,'trip\ *vi* **:** to experience nostalgia (*time-tripping* into a more glamorous past —*N.Y. Times*)

time warp *n* **:** an anomaly, discontinuity, or suspension held to occur in the progress of time

ting ware \'ting-\ *also* **ting yao** \-'yaù\ *n, often cap T* [*Ting* fr. *Ting Chou*, town southwest of Peking, China, where it was originally made; *Ting yao* fr. *Ting* + Chin (Pek) *yao*² pottery] **:** a Chinese porcelain ware known since Sung times that is typically expertly potted, often decorated with engraved underglaze designs, and characteristically glazed with a milk-white to creamy white or less often an iron-red glaze

Tin·ker·toy \'tiŋkə(r),tȯi\ *trademark* — used for a construction toy of fitting parts

tip of the iceberg [fr. the fact that most of an iceberg is submerged] **:** the earliest, most obvious, or most superficial manifestation of some phenomenon

tis·sue* *vt* **tis·sued; tis·su·ing :** to remove (as cleansing cream) with a tissue

tis·su·lar \'tish(y)ələ(r)\ adj [tissue + -lar (as in cellular)] : of, relating to, or affecting organismic tissue ⟨tissular lesions⟩ ⟨tissular grafts⟩

tit·fer \'titfə(r\ n [by shortening & alter. fr. tit for tat, rhyming slang for hat] Brit : a hat

T lym·pho·cyte \'tē'lim(p)fə,sīt\ n [thymus-derived lymphocyte] : T CELL

TM*abbr transcendental meditation

toea \'tóiə\ n, pl toea also toeas [prob. Pidgin English, modif. of E dollar] 1 : a monetary unit of Papua New Guinea equal to $1/100$ kina 2 : a coin representing one toea

together adj 1 : appropriately prepared, organized, or balanced ⟨a super-delicious, beautifully together album —Clayton Riley⟩ 2 : composed in mind or manner : self-possessed ⟨a warm, sensitive, reasonably together girl —East Village Other⟩ — often used as a generalized term of approval ⟨don't let the out-of-the-way location put you off, it's every bit as together as any place downtown —Jay Hoffman⟩

to·ka·mak \'tōkə,mak, 'täk-\ n [Russ] : a toroidal device for producing controlled nuclear fusion that involves the confining and heating of a gaseous plasma by means of an internal electric current and its attendant magnetic field

toke \'tōk\ n [origin unknown] 1 slang : a puff on a marijuana cigarette ⟨every well-bred person passes a joint to his nearest neighbor and waits for it to come back before taking a second toke —R.A. Sokolov⟩ 2 slang : a tip given esp. by a gambler to the dealer at a casino — **toke** vb, slang

token*n : a token member of a group; esp : a token employee

token*adj : serving or intended to show absence of discrimination

to·ken·ism \'tōkə,nizəm\ n : the policy or practice of making only a token effort (as to desegregate or provide equal employment opportunities) ⟨creeping tokenism but little more . . . the top woman in every bank is outranked by at least 100 men —Carol Greitzer⟩ — **to·ken·is·tic** \-istik\ adj

to·laz·o·line \tō'lazə,lēn\ n [tol- toluene + azole + -ine chemical substance] : a weak alpha-adrenergic blocking agent $C_{10}H_{12}N_2$ used as the hydrochloride to produce peripheral vasodilatation

Tom*\'täm\ n : an Uncle Tom ⟨I don't see why he wants to talk that I'm a Tom, that I don't stand up for the black man —Joe Frazier⟩ ⟨it had always proven sufficient for him to label his opponent a Tom and read the New York Times editorials supporting the hapless fellow from a sound truck to back up the charge —R.M. Levine⟩

tom vi **tommed; tom·ming** often cap : UNCLE TOM ⟨the history of the American Negro from a tomming laughing boy to a fierce enduring militant —Pete Hamill⟩

ton*n 1 Brit : a speed of 100 miles per hour — often used in the phrase do the ton or do a ton ⟨the first cars were doing the ton barely ten years after Victoria's Diamond Jubilee —London Times⟩; called also ton-up \'tən,əp\ 2 Brit : a score of 100 runs in cricket : a century

tone block n : a rhythm band instrument consisting of a usu. slotted block of wood held in one hand and struck by a rod or drumstick

Tonkinese*\'täŋkə,nēz, -ēs\ n 1 : a breed of short-haired cat developed in the U.S. by crossing the Siamese with the Burmese that has a brown or bluish gray body coat with darker points and blue-green eyes 2 pl **Tonkinese** : a cat of the Tonkinese breed

tool n : a design (as on the binding of a book) made by tooling

toothpick*n : a small often elaborate container for a supply of toothpicks at table

¹top 40 n pl, often cap T : the 40 best-selling phonograph records for a given period

²top 40 adj : constituting, playing, or listing the top 40 ⟨top 40 tunes⟩ ⟨top 40 stations⟩

to·po·cen·tric \'täpə,sen·trik, 'tōp-\ adj [topo- place (deriv. of Gk topos) + -centric centered] : relating to, measured from, or as if observed from a particular point on the earth's surface : having or relating to such a point as origin ⟨topocentric coordinates⟩

to·po·log·i·cal*\,täpə'läjəkəl, ,tōp-\ adj : being or involving properties unaltered under a homeomorphism ⟨continuity and connectedness are topological properties⟩

topological group n : a mathematical group which is also a topological space, whose multiplicative operation is continuous such that given any neighborhood of a product there exist neighborhoods of the elements composing the product with the property that any pair of elements representing each of these neighborhoods form a product belonging to the given neighborhood, and whose operation of taking inverses is continuous such that for any neighborhood of the inverse of an element there exists a neighborhood of the element itself in which every element has its inverse in the other neighborhood

to·po·log·i·cal·ly equivalent \,täpə'läjək(ə)lē-, ,tōp-\ adj : related by a homeomorphism ⟨two topologically equivalent figures can be made to coincide if subjected to a suitable elastic motion⟩

topological space n : a set with a collection of subsets satisfying the conditions that both the empty set and the set itself belong to the collection, the union of any number of the subsets is also an element of the collection, and the intersection of a finite number of the subsets is an element of the collection

topological transformation n : a one-to-one mapping in topology between two figures that is continuous in both directions : homeomorphism

top·on·o·mas·tic \(,)täp'anə,mastik, təp-\ adj [top- place + onomastic] : of or relating to place-names ⟨toponomastic study⟩

to·pos \'tō,pōs, 'tä,p-\ n, pl **to·poi** \-,pói\ [Gk, place, commonplace, topic] : a stock rhetorical theme or topic

TOR abbr third order regular

torpedo*n, pl **-does** : HOAGIE

torque \'tó(ə)rk, 'tó(ə)k\ vt **torqued; torqu·ing** : to impart torque to : cause to twist (as about an axis) ⟨after a day the spinning satellite is magnetically torqued into a new orientation so that another great circle can be scanned —W.D. Metz⟩ — **torqu·er** \-ə(r)\ n

toss–up*n : something that offers no clear basis for choice ⟨it's a toss-up as to which of the two cities has the worst urban problems —S.H. Robock⟩

total*vt : to make a total wreck of (a car) : demolish ⟨had totaled a couple of cars and had been involved in a few motorcycle accidents —Anthony Mancini⟩

total environment *n* : ENVIRONMENT

tote*n* : a large handbag : tote bag

tot lot *n* : a small playground for young children

Tot·ten trust \‚tät³n-\ *n* [fr. the name *Totten*] : a trust created by a depositor who opens a savings account in another person's name but retains the right to revoke the trust and to withdraw and use the money

touch*vb* — **touch base** : to come in contact or communication ⟨coming in from the cold to *touch base* with civilization —Carla Hunt⟩

tough*adj, slang* : excellent, splendid, great — used as a generalized term of approval ⟨the barbecue . . . was well attended, and judged "real *tough* " . . . by boys as well as girls —Judy Van Vliet Cook⟩

touring car*n* : a usu. 2-door sedan as distinguished from a sports car or grand touring car

tourist trap *n* : a place (as a shop, restaurant, or resort area) that exploits tourists ⟨advised us to get out of a lousy *tourist trap* like Paris —Alexander King⟩

tow–away zone \'tōə‚wā-\ *n* : a no-parking zone from which parked vehicles may be towed away

tow·el·ette \‚taù(ə)‚let\ *n* [*towel* + *-ette*, dim. suffix] : a usu. premoistened small piece of material used for personal cleansing (as of the hands)

town house*n* : a single-family house of two or sometimes three stories connected to another house by a common sidewall

toxic shock syndrome *n* : an acute disease that is characterized by fever, sore throat, and diffuse erythema, that is associated esp. with the presence of a bacterium (*Streptomyces aureus*), and that occurs esp. in menstruating females using tampons

tra·cheo·esoph·a·ge·al \‚trākē(‚)ōə‚säfə'jēəl, trə‚kēō-\ *adj* [*tracheo-* tracheal and + *esophageal*] : relating to or connecting the trachea and the esophagus ⟨a *tracheoesophageal* fistula⟩

track*n* 1 : one of a series of parallel or concentric paths along which material (as music or information) is recorded (as on a phonograph record or magnetic tape) 2 : a group of grooves on a phonograph record containing recorded sound : band

track*vt* : to assign (students) to a curricular track ~ *vi* : to move or progress in accordance with or be consistent with an expected or reasonable pattern

track·ing \'trakiŋ\ *n* : the policy or practice of assigning students to a curricular track

track record *n* : a record of accomplishments ⟨a modern university president is expected to have practical vision, a good *track record* in administration, and national prominence —W.G. Bennis⟩ ⟨he had to reestablish his commercial credibility, an irony indeed for a man whose moneymaking *track record* had once been incomparable —Martin Gottfried⟩

track·suit \'trak‚süt\ *n* : a suit of clothing consisting usu. of a jacket and pants and often worn by athletes (as runners) when working out

tract house *n* : one of many similarly designed houses built on a tract of land

trade*n* 1 *slang* : male homosexuals who are prostitutes and often of aggressively masculine manner; *also* : a homosexual of this sort 2 : a passive partner in a male homosexual relationship

trade–off \'trā‚dȯf\ *n* 1 : a balancing of desirable considerations or goals all of which are not attainable at the same time ⟨the education versus experience *trade-off* which governs personnel practices —H.S. White⟩ 2 : a giving up of one thing in return for another : exchange ⟨the shipper is willing to make a *trade-off*, paying more for freight service to pay less for handling and for carrying inventory —J.F. Spencer⟩

trail bike *n* : a small motorcycle designed for uses other than on highways and for easy transport (as on an automobile bumper)

trail·er·able \'trālərəbəl\ *adj* : able to be conveyed by a trailer ⟨there are over 100 *trailerable* sailboat models to choose from —Robert Black⟩

trail·head \'trā(ə)l‚hed\ *n* : the point at which a trail begins

train·ee·ship \trā'nē‚ship\ *n* : the position or status of a trainee; *specif* : one involving a program of advanced training and study esp. in a medical science and usu. bearing a stipend and allowances (as for travel)

tramp art *n* : a style of wood carving flourishing in the U.S. from about 1875 to 1930 that is characterized by ornate layered whittling often of cigar boxes or fruit crates; *also* : an object of wood carved in this style

tram·po·lin·ing \‚trampə‚lēniŋ\ *n* : the sport of jumping and tumbling on a trampoline

trans·ac·tion·al analysis \tran(t)'sakshnəl-, -shən³l-, -n'za-\ *n* : a system of psychotherapy involving analysis of individual episodes of social interaction for insight that will aid communication (as by the substitution of constructive mature verbal exchanges for destructive immature ones)

trans·am·i·nate \tran(t)'samə‚nāt, -n'za-\ *vb* -**nat·ed;** -**nat·ing** [back-formation fr. *transamination*] *vi* : to induce or catalyze a transamination ~ *vt* : to induce or catalyze the transamination of

trans·ax·le \'tran(t)‚saksəl\ *n* [*trans*mission + *axle*] : a unit consisting of a combination of transmission and front axle used in front-wheel-drive automobiles

trans·car·ba·myl·ase \(‚)tran(t)‚skärbə‚mil‚ās, -nz‚k-, -‚āz\ *n* [*trans-* across (fr. L *trans*) + *carbamyl* + *-ase* enzyme] : any of several enzymes that catalyze the addition of a carbamoyl radical to a molecule (as ornithine to form citrulline in urea synthesis)

transcendental meditation *n* : a technique of meditation in which the mind is released through the use of a mantra

trans·cor·tin \(')tran(t)s‚kȯrt³n, -nz‚k-\ *n* : an alpha globulin produced in the liver that binds with and transports hydrocortisone in the blood

transcribe*vt* -**scribed;** -**scrib·ing** : to cause (as DNA) to undergo genetic transcription

transcript*n* : a sequence of RNA produced by transcription from a DNA template

tran·scrip·tase \tran'skrip‚tās, -āz\ *n* [*transcript*ion + *-ase*] : REVERSE TRANSCRIPTASE

tran·scrip·tion*\tran(t)s'kripshən\ *n* : the process of constructing a messenger RNA molecule using a DNA molecule as a template with resulting transfer of genetic information to the messenger RNA — compare TRANS-LATION

tran·scrip·tion·ist \tran'skripsh(ə)nəst\ *n* : one that transcribes (as dictation)

trans·duce \tran(t)s'd(y)üs, -nz'-\ *vt* **-duced; -duc·ing** [L *transducere* to lead across, transfer, fr. *trans-* + *ducere* to lead] **1 :** to convert (as energy or a message) into another form **2 :** to bring about the transfer of (as a gene) from one microorganism to another by means of a viral agent

trans·earth \'tran,zǝrth, -,zōth, -,zǝith\ *adj* **:** of or relating to the entry of a spacecraft into a trajectory between a celestial body (as the moon) and the earth and to the travel of the spacecraft in the direction of the earth ⟨*transearth* injection⟩ ⟨*transearth* burn⟩

trans·fec·tion \tran(t)s'fekshǝn, -nz'f-\ *n* [*trans-* + in*fection*] **:** infection of a cell with isolated viral nucleic acid followed by production of the complete virus in the cell — **trans·fect** \-'fekt\ *vt*

transfer factor *n* **:** a polypeptide that is produced and secreted by a lymphocyte functioning in cell-mediated immunity and that upon incorporation into a lymphocyte which has not been sensitized confers upon it the same immunological specificity as the sensitized cell

transfer RNA *n* **:** a relatively small RNA that transfers a particular amino acid to a growing polypeptide chain at the ribosomal site of protein synthesis during translation — compare MESSENGER RNA

transform*n **1 :** a mathematical element obtained from another by transformation **2 :** a linguistic structure (as a sentence) produced by means of a transformation ⟨"the duckling is killed by the farmer" is a *transform* of "the farmer kills the duckling"⟩

transform*vt **:** to cause (a cell) to undergo genetic transformation

transformation*n **1 :** genetic modification of a bacterium by incorporation of free DNA from another ruptured bacterial cell **2 :** one of an ordered set of rules that specify how to convert the deep structures of a language into surface structures; *also* **:** the process or relation specified by such a rule

trans·for·ma·tion·al \'tranzfǝ(r)'māshǝnǝl, -n(t)sf-, -shnǝl\ *adj* **:** of, relating to, characterized by, or concerned with transformation and esp. linguistic transformation ⟨*transformational* theory⟩ ⟨*transformational* rules⟩

transformational grammar *n* **:** a grammar that generates the deep structures of a language and relates these to the surface structures by means of transformations

trans·for·ma·tion·al·ist \,tranzfǝ(r),māshǝnǝlǝst, -n(t)sf-, -shnǝl-\ *n* **:** an exponent of transformational grammar

trans·fu·sion·al \tranz'fyüzhǝnǝl, -n(t)s'f-, -zhnǝl\ *adj* **:** of, relating to, or caused by transfusion ⟨*transfusional* shock⟩ ⟨*transfusional* reactions⟩

transistor*or **transistor radio** *n* **:** a transistorized radio ⟨conversations always seemed to be carried on over a background of *transistors* or record machines —George Plimpton⟩

transition*n **:** a genetic mutation in RNA or DNA that results from the substitution of one purine base for the other or of one pyrimidine base for the other

trans·ke·tol·ase \,tran(t)skē'tól,ās, -nzk-, -'tō,lās, -āz\ *n* [*trans-* + *ketol* + *-ase*] **:** an enzyme that catalyzes the transfer of the ketonic residue CH_3COH — O — from the phosphate of xylulose to that of ribose to form the phosphate of sedoheptulose

translate*vt **-lat·ed; -lat·ing :** to subject (as genetic information) to translation in protein synthesis

translation*n **:** the process of forming a protein molecule at a ribosomal site of protein synthesis from information contained in messenger RNA — compare TRANSCRIPTION

trans·lu·nar \(')tran(t)s'lünǝ(r), -nz'l-\ *adj* **:** of or relating to the entry of a spacecraft into a trajectory between a celestial body (as the earth) and the moon and to the travel of the spacecraft in the direction of the moon ⟨*translunar* injection⟩ ⟨*translunar* burn⟩

trans·mem·brane \-'mem,brān\ *adj* **:** taking place, existing, or arranged from one side to the other of a membrane ⟨a *transmembrane* potential⟩

transmission electron microscope *n* **:** a conventional electron microscope which produces an image of a cross-sectional slice of a specimen all points of which are illuminated by the electron beam at the same time — compare SCANNING ELECTRON MICROSCOPE — **transmission electron mi·cros·co·py** \-mī'kräskǝpē, -i\ *n*

transmitter*n **:** NEUROTRANSMITTER

trans·moun·tain \(')tran(t)'smaúnt°n, -nz'm-\ *adj* **:** crossing or extending over or through a mountain ⟨*transmountain* road⟩ ⟨a *transmountain* tunnel⟩

trans·mu·ta·tion**\,tran(t)smyü'tāshǝn, ,tranzm-\ *n* **:** the effect of controlled reduction firing on certain chiefly oriental copper-containing and/or iron-containing ceramic glazes (**transmutation glazes**) that is typically a variegation of colors (as purple, blue, and red) and a thick often bubbly consistency

trans·pep·ti·dase \\(')tran(t)'speptǝ,dās, -nz'p-, -āz\ *n* **:** an enzyme that catalyzes the transfer of an amino acid residue or a peptide residue from one amino compound to another

transport*n **:** a mechanism for moving tape and esp. magnetic tape past a sensing or recording head

trans·pose**\'tran(t)s,pōz, -nz,p-\ *n* **:** a matrix formed by interchanging the rows and columns of a given matrix

trans·po·son \tran(t)s'spō,zän, -nz'pō-\ *n* [*transpose* + *-on* basic hereditary component] **:** a segment of DNA that is capable of producing copies of itself which can be inserted at random within the genome and that is sometimes used to introduce genes into an organism from an exogenous source (as an individual of another species)

trans·ra·cial \(')tran(t)s'rāshǝl, -nz'r-\ *adj* **:** involving two or more races ⟨*transracial* adoption⟩

trans·sex·u·al \(')tran'seksh(ǝ)wǝl, -shǝl\ *n* **:** a person with a psychological urge to belong to the opposite sex that may be carried as far as surgical modification of the sex organs to mimic the other sex — **transsexual** *adj* — **trans·sex·u·al·ism** \tran'seksh(ǝ)wǝ,lizǝm, -shǝ,lizǝm\ *n* — **trans·sex·u·al·i·ty** \,tran,sekshǝ'walǝd-ē, -i\ *n*

trans·tho·rac·ic \,tran(t)sthǝ'rasik, -nzth-\ *adj* **1 :** performed or made by way of the thoracic cavity **2 :** crossing or having connections that cross the thoracic cavity ⟨a *transthoracic* pacemaker⟩ — **trans·tho·rac·i·cal·ly** \-'rasǝk(ǝ)lē\ *adv*

trans·ve·nous \(')tran(t)s'vēnǝs, -nz'v-\ *adj* **:** relating to or involving the use of an intravenous catheter containing an electrode carrying electrical impulses from an extracorporeal source to the heart ⟨*transvenous* pacing of the heart⟩

tran·yl·cy·pro·mine \,tran^əl'sīprə,mēn, -əmən\ *n* [*trans*- + phen*yl* + *cy*clic + *propyla*min*e*] **:** an antidepressant drug C9H11N that is an inhibitor of monoamine oxidase and is administered as the sulfate

trash*vt **1 :** to vandalize or wreck ⟨*trash* a college ROTC building —Susan Brownmiller⟩ ⟨beer and food stands had been liberated and then *trashed* —Larry Sloman⟩ **2 :** to smash or destroy ⟨*trashing* store windows⟩ ⟨a career politician finally smelling the White House is not much different from a bull elk in the rut. He will stop at nothing, *trashing* anything that gets in his way —H.S. Thompson⟩ **3 :** to spoil or ruin ⟨*trashing* the environment⟩ ⟨so-called developers have already *trashed* several other good streets in Montreal —J.W. Maclellan⟩ ⟨*trash* his own lumpish songs by bawling in a voice that is both ear-splitting and off-pitch —Stephen Holden⟩ ~ *vi* **:** to trash something esp. as a form of protest ⟨those who stopped marching when marching turned to *trashing* — Elinor Langer⟩ — **trash·er** \'trashə(r)\ *n*

travel trailer *n* **:** a trailer drawn esp. by a passenger automobile and equipped for use (as while traveling) as a dwelling

treat·abil·i·ty \,trēd·ə'biləd·ē\ *n* **:** the condition of being treatable ⟨an interpretation of the law based on *treatability* of felonious behavior⟩

trend·set·ter \'trend,sed·ə(r), -etə-\ *n* **:** one that sets a trend ⟨they must risk their bankrolls on the sort of stylish merchandise that lives or dies at the whim of the *trendsetter* —Marilyn Bethany⟩

trendy \'trendē, -di\ *adj* **trend·i·er; -est 1 :** very fashionable **:** up-to-date, chic ⟨he's a *trendy* dresser —*Sunday Mirror* (London)⟩ **2 :** faddish ⟨a newspaper of *trendy* triviality —J. H. Plumb⟩ ⟨I hear *trendy* clergymen asking God to attend to our balance of payments —Malcolm Muggeridge⟩ — **trend·i·ly** \-dəlē, -dəlē\ *adv* — **trend·i·ness** \-dēnəs, -dən-\ *n* — **trendy** *n*

trial*n **:** one of a number of repetitions of an experiment ⟨what is the probability of getting k successes in n *trials*⟩

tri·am·cin·o·lone \,trīam'sinə,lōn\ *n* [*tri*- three + *am*yl + *cine*ne, a terpene + prednis*olone*] **:** a corticoid drug C21H27FO6 used esp. in treating psoriasis and allergic skin and respiratory disorders

triangle inequality *n* [fr. its application to the distances between three points in a coordinate system] **:** an inequality stating that the absolute value of a sum is less than or equal to the sum of the absolute value of the terms

tri·bol·o·gy \trī'bäləjē, trə'-, -ji\ *n* [*tribo*- friction + *-logy* theory, science, deriv. of Gk *logos* word] *Brit* **:** a study that deals with the design, friction, wear, and lubrication of interacting surfaces in relative motion to each other (as in bearings or gears) — **tri·bo·log·i·cal** \,trībə'läjəkəl, ,trib-\ *adj*, *Brit* — **tri·bol·o·gist** \trī'bäləjəst, trə'-\ *n*, *Brit*

tri·chlor·fon *also* **tri·chlor·phon** \(')trī'klō(ə)r,fän, -'klō(ə)r-\ *n* [*tri*- three + *chlor*ine + *-fon* (irreg. fr. *phosphonate*) or *-phon* (fr. *phosphonate*)] **:** a crystalline compound C4H8Cl3O4P that is used as an insecticide and anthelmintic

trick·le–down \'trikəl'daun\ *adj* **:** relating to or working on the principle of trickle-down theory ⟨are we going to emphasize the *trickle-down* techniques, such as lower

taxes for the rich that are supposed to eventually lead to more jobs for the middle class —L. C. Thurow⟩

trickle–down theory *n* **:** an economic theory that financial benefits given to big business will in turn pass down to smaller businesses and consumers

tri·fec·ta \(')trī'fektə\ *n* [*tri*- + per*fecta*] **:** a variation of the perfecta in which a bettor wins by selecting the first 3 finishers of a race in the correct order of finish — called also *triple;* compare SUPERFECTA

tri·fluo·per·a·zine \,trī,flüö'perə,zēn, -əzən\ *n* [*tri*- + *fluo*rine + pi*perazine*] **:** a phenothiazine tranquilizer C21H24F3N3S used esp. in the treatment of psychotic conditions (as schizophrenia)

tri·flu·ra·lin \trī'flürələn\ *n* [*tri*- + *fluo*rine + a*niline*] **:** an herbicide C13H16F3N3O4 used in the control of weeds (as pigweed and annual grasses)

tri·func·tion·al \(')trī'fəŋ(k)shnəl, -shənəl\ *adj* **:** of, relating to, or being a compound with three sites in the molecule that are highly reactive (as in polymerization)

tri·jet \'trī,jet\ *n* **:** an aircraft powered with three jet engines — **tri·jet** \'trī,jet\ *adj*

tri·lev·el \'trī,levəl\ *adj* **:** having three levels or floors ⟨a *tri-level* house⟩ — **tri–level** *n*

tri·ma·ran \'trīmə,ran\ *n* [*tri*- + *-maran* (as in *catamaran*)] **:** a fast pleasure sailboat with three hulls side by side

tri·meth·o·prim \trī'methə,prim\ *n* [*tri*- + *metho*methyl + *-prim* (by shortening & alter. fr. *pyrimidine*)] **:** a synthetic antibacterial and antimalarial drug C14H18N4O3

trip*n **1 :** an intense visionary experience undergone by a person who has taken a psychedelic drug (as LSD); *broadly* **:** an exciting experience ⟨orgasm . . . is the ultimate *trip* —D.R. Reuben⟩ **2 :** pursuit of an absorbing or obsessive interest **:** kick ⟨he's on a nostalgia *trip*⟩ **3 :** way of life **:** SCENE ⟨the whole super-star *trip* —Joe Eszterhas⟩

trip *vi* **tripped; trip·ping :** to get high on a drug **:** TURN ON — often used with *out* ⟨the pot generation (roughly, those who use marijuana frequently and *trip* out occasionally) —Pauline Kael⟩ — **trip·per** \'tripə(r)\ *n*

triple*n **:** TRIFECTA

triple jump *n* **:** a jump for distance in track-and-field athletics usu. from a running start and combining a hop, a stride, and a jump in succession **:** hop, step, and jump

triplet*n **1 :** a group of three elementary particles (as positive, negative, and neutral pions) with different charge states but otherwise similar properties **2** *or* **triplet state :** any state of an elementary particle having one quantum unit of spin

tri·umph·al·ism \(')trī'əm(p)fə,lizəm, *also* 'trīəm-\ *n* **:** the doctrine, attitude, or belief that one religious creed is superior to all others ⟨a form of *triumphalism* which should have died with the ecumenical decrees —P. S. McGarry⟩ — **tri·umph·al·ist** \-fələst\ *n or adj*

trivia**n pl but sing in constr* **:** a quizzing game involving obscure facts ⟨good *trivia* players are obsessive about detail, and in *trivia* they find a rewarding way to deal with it —Lee Pulos⟩

trivial*adj **:** relating to or being the mathematically simplest case; *specif* **:** characterized by having all variables equal to zero ⟨a *trivial* solution to an equation⟩

triv·i·al·ist \'trivēələst\ *n* [*trivial* + *-ist* specialist] **:** one who takes a special interest in trivia or trivial matters

tRNA \\'tē,är,en¦ā\ *n* [*transfer RNA*] **:** TRANSFER RNA

trog·lo·bite \\'träglə,bīt\ *n* [alter. (influenced by *troglodyte*) of *troglobiont*] **:** an animal living in or restricted to caves; *esp* **:** one occurring in the lightless waters of caves **:** troglobiont — **trog·lo·bit·ic** \\,träglə¦bid·ik\ *adj*

troi·ka* \\'troika\ *n* **1 :** an administrative or ruling body of three ⟨replaced by a *troika* of three coequal secretaries-general —*Newsweek*⟩ **2 :** a group of three ⟨astrology, yoga, and poetry are the *troika* of humanities that most interest him —A.J. Liebling⟩

Trombe wall \\'tróm,bwól, 'träm-, 'trōⁿ-\ *n* [Felix *Trombe* 20th cent. Fr. designer] **:** a south-facing masonry wall that is usu. glazed on the exterior and is designed to absorb solar heat and release it into the interior of a building

tro·phic level \\'trōfik-\ *n* **:** one of the hierarchical strata of a food web characterized by organisms which are the same number of steps removed from the primary producers

tro·po·col·la·gen \\,träpə¦käləjən, ¦trōp-\ *n* [*tropo-* turn, change, tropism (fr. Gk *tropos* turn) + *collagen*] **:** a soluble substance whose elongated asymmetrical molecules are the fundamental building units of collagen fibers

tro·po·nin \\'trōpənən, 'träp-, -,nin\ *n* [*tropo-* + *-n-* (arbitrary infix) + *-in* chemical compound] **:** a protein component of skeletal muscle myofibrils that is held to initiate muscle contraction by regulating calcium sensitivity of actomyosin

trouser* *adj* **:** of or relating to a male dramatic role played by a woman ⟨a *trouser* character in opera⟩

trouser suit *n, chiefly Brit* **:** PANTSUIT

truck* *vi* **:** to roll along esp. in an easy untroubled way ⟨keep on *trucking*⟩

trust fund* *n* **:** a governmental fund consisting of moneys accepted for a specified purpose (as civil service retirement) that is administered as a trust separately from other funds and is expended only in furthering the specified purpose

truth set *n* **:** a mathematical or logical set containing all the elements that make a given statement of relationships true when substituted in it ⟨the equation $x + 7 = 10$ has as its *truth set* the single number 3⟩

tryp·sin·iza·tion \\,tripsənə¦zāshən, trəp,sin-, -,ī¦z-\ *n* **:** the action or process of trypsinizing

T–time \\'tē,tim\ *n* [prob. fr. *t* (abbr. for *time*)] **:** the time of initial firing of a rocket vehicle or missile

tube* *n* **1 :** picture tube; *broadly* **:** television ⟨hardly a moment next fall when gunplay can't be found somewhere on the *tube* —R.K. Doan⟩ ⟨no politician can lightly offend the men who govern the *tube* —Leonard Ross⟩ **2 :** CURL **3 :** an article of clothing usu. of knitted material in the shape of a tube ⟨denim *tubes*⟩ ⟨*tube* top⟩ ⟨*tube* socks⟩ — **down the tube** *or* **down the tubes** **:** into a state of collapse, deterioration, or ruin ⟨I know what it means to see a crop go *down the tubes* —B. S. Bergland⟩

tu·be·rous scle·ro·sis \\,t(y)üb(ə)rə(s)sklə¦rōsəs\ *n* **:** a dominant genetic anomaly in man marked by multiple tumor formation **:** epiloia

tu·bu·lin \\'t(y)übyələn\ *n* [*tubule* + *-in*] **:** a globular protein that polymerizes to form microtubules

tu·fo·li \\t(y)ü'fōlē, -lǐ\ *n, pl* **tufoli** [It (Sicilian), pl. of *tufolo* duct, fr. LL *tubulus*, dim. of L *tubus* tube] **:** a macaroni shell large enough for stuffing (as with meat or cheese)

tu·mori·gen·e·sis \\,t(y)ümərə¦jenəsəs\ *n* [*tumor* + connective *-i-* + *genesis*] **:** the formation of tumors

tu·mor·i·gen·ic \\,t(y)ümərə¦jenik\ *adj* **:** producing or tending to produce tumors; *also* **:** carcinogenic ⟨*tumorigenic* cells⟩ — **tu·mor·i·ge·nic·i·ty** \\,t(y)ümərəjə¦'nisəd-ē\ *n*

tune out *vt* **:** to become unresponsive to **:** ignore ⟨these findings . . . give the lie to the assumption that a mass audience will *tune out* a program that deals provocatively with uncomfortable social realities —K. E. Meyer⟩ ∼ *vi* **:** to dissociate oneself from what is happening ⟨when things get a bit too much, she simply *tunes out* temporarily —Ann Nietzke⟩

tunnel* *n* **:** CURL

tunnel di·ode \\-'dī,ōd\ *n* **:** a semiconductor device that has two stable states when operated in conjunction with suitable circuit elements and a source of voltage, is capable of extremely rapid transformations between the two by means of the tunnel effect of electrons, and is used for amplifying, switching, and computer information storage and as an oscillator

tunnel vision* *n* **:** extreme narrowness of viewpoint **:** narrow-mindedness ⟨computer specialists develop a type of *tunnel vision* consisting of statistical-empirical-digital thinking —L.J. Peter⟩ — **tun·nel vi·sioned** \\,tənᵊl¦vizhənd\ *adj*

-tu·ple \\,təpəl, ,tüp-\ *n comb form* [quintuple, sextuple] **:** set of (so many) elements — often used of sets with ordered elements ⟨the ordered 2-*tuple* (a, b)⟩

tur·bi·dite \\'tərbə,dīt\ *n* [*turbid* + *-ite* rock] **:** a sedimentary deposit consisting of material that has moved down the steep slope at the edge of a continental shelf; *also* **:** a rock formed from this deposit

tur·bo·elec·tric \\,tərbō¦lektrik, -ē¦l-\ *adj* [*turbo-* turbine + *electric*] **:** involving or depending as a power source on electricity produced by turbine generators ⟨ships with *turboelectric* drive⟩

tur·bo·fan \\'tərbō,fan, -bə-\ *n* **1 :** a fan that is directly connected to and driven by a turbine and is used to supply air for cooling, ventilation, or combustion **2 :** a jet engine having a turbofan

tur·bo·pump \\-,pəmp\ *n* **:** a pump that is driven by a turbine

tur·bo·shaft \\-,shaft\ *n* **:** a gas turbine engine that is similar in operation to a turboprop engine but instead of being used to power a propeller is used through a transmission system for powering other devices (as helicopter rotors and pumps)

Tu·ring machine \\'t(y)ùriŋ-\ *n* [A. M. *Turing* †1954 Eng. mathematician] **:** a hypothetical computing machine that has an unlimited amount of information storage

tu·ris·ta \\tü(ə)r'ēstə\ *n* [Sp, lit., tourist] **:** intestinal sickness and diarrhea commonly affecting a tourist in a foreign country; *esp* **:** MONTEZUMA'S REVENGE

turkey* *n* **:** a stupid, foolish, or inept person ⟨pay your scouting people chicken feed and you'll wind up with *turkeys* in your infield —Alvin Dark⟩

turn·around* \\'tərnə,raùnd, 'tən-, 'tə̇in-\ *n* **:** the readying of a pad and the installation of the booster for the next spacecraft launching

Tur·ner's syndrome \'tərnər-, 'tānə-, 'tainə-\ *n* [Henry Herbert *Turner* †1970 Am. physician] **:** a genetically determined condition that is associated with the presence of one X chromosome and no Y chromosome and that is characterized by an outwardly female phenotype with incomplete and infertile gonads

turn·key \'tərn,kē, 'tən-, 'təin-\ *adj* **:** supplied or installed complete and ready to operate ⟨a *turnkey* nuclear plant⟩ ⟨*turnkey* project⟩ ⟨a *turnkey* computer system⟩; *also* **:** of or relating to a turnkey installation ⟨a *turnkey* contract⟩ ⟨*turnkey* vendors⟩

turn off*vi **:** to lose interest **:** withdraw ⟨the kids *turn off* or drift into another world —Edwin Sorensen⟩ ~ *vt* **:** to cause to turn off ⟨dropouts who are *turned off* by . . . political phoniness —Hendrik Hertzberg⟩ — **turn–off** \'tər,nȯf, 'tə,nȯf, 'təi,nȯf\ *n*

turn on*vt **1 :** to cause to undergo an intense visionary experience esp. by taking a drug (as LSD or marijuana); *broadly* **:** to cause to get high **2 :** to move pleasurably **:** stimulate ⟨the ballet . . . was *turning* the audience *on* like magic —Clive Barnes⟩; *also* **:** to excite sexually **3 :** to cause to gain knowledge or appreciation of something specified ⟨*turned* his siblings *on* to black music —Fred Bernstein⟩ ~ *vi* **1 :** to undergo an intense visionary experience esp. as a result of taking a drug; *broadly* **:** to get high **2 :** to become pleasurably excited ⟨*turns on* instead with classical music or jazz —Julie M. Heldman⟩ — **turn–on** \'tər,nȯn, 'tə,n-, 'təi,n-, -än\ *n*

turn·over**\'tər,novər; 'tə,nōvə, 'təi,n-\ *n* **:** the act or an instance of a team's losing possession of a ball through error or a minor violation of the rules (as in basketball or football)

tush \'tùsh\ *n* [Yiddish *toches*] *slang* **:** the buttocks

tushy *also* **tush·ie** \'tùshē, -shi\ *n, pl* **tushies** [*tush* + *-y* or *-ie,* dim. suffix] *slang* **:** the buttocks

tutorial*n **:** a paper and esp. a technical paper written to give practical information on a specific subject

TV \(₌)tē'vē\ *n* [*transvestite*] **:** a transvestite

TV dinner *n* [fr. its saving the television viewer from having to interrupt his viewing to prepare a meal] **:** a quick-frozen packaged dinner that requires only heating before it is served

twee \'twē\ *adj* [baby talk for *sweet*] *chiefly Brit* **:** affectedly or excessively dainty, delicate, cute, or quaint ⟨such a theme might sound *twee* or corny —*Times Lit. Supp.*⟩

twin double *n* **:** a system of betting (as on horse races) in which the bettor wins by selecting the winners of two consecutive pairs of races

two–tailed test \,tü,tā(ə)l(d)-\ *n* **:** a statistical test for which the critical region consists of all values of the test statistic greater than a given value plus the values less than another given value — called also *two-sided test, two≈ tail test;* compare ONE-TAILED TEST

ty·lo·sin \'tīləsən\ *n* [origin unknown] **:** an antibacterial antibiotic $C_{45}H_{77}NO_{17}$ from an actinomycete of the genus *Streptomyces* (*S. fradiae*) used in veterinary medicine and as a feed additive

type I error \,tīp'wən-\ *n* **:** rejection of the null hypothesis in statistical testing when it is true

type II error \,tīp'tü-\ *n* **:** acceptance of the null hypothesis in statistical testing when it is false

ty·ro·sine **hy·drox·y·lase** \,tīrə,sēnhī'dräksə,lās, ,tir-, -əsən-, -āz\ *n* [*hydroxyl* + *-ase* enzyme] **:** an enzyme that catalyzes the first step in the biosynthesis of catecholamines (as dopamine and noradrenaline)

U

U \'yü\ adj [upper class] **:** characteristic of the upper classes ⟨the deference that the *U* British accent creates — Gershon Legman⟩

ubi·qui·none \yü'bikwə̯,nōn; ˌyübəkwə̯'n-, -'kwi̯,n-\ n [blend of L *ubique* everywhere and E *quinone*; fr. its occurrence in nature] **:** a quinone that functions as an electron transfer agent between cytochromes in the Krebs cycle — called also *coenzyme Q*

UDP \ˌyü(ˌ)dē'pē\ n [uridine *d*iphosphate] **:** a diphosphate of uridine $C_9H_{14}N_2O_{12}P_2$ that functions esp. as a glycosyl carrier in the synthesis of glycogen and starch and is used to form polyuridylic acid

ufol·o·gy \yü'fäləjē\ n, *often cap* UFO [*UFO* + -*logy* theory, science, deriv. of Gk *logos* word] **:** the study of unidentified flying objects — **ufo·log·i·cal** \ˌyüfə'läjəkəl, -fō'-\ adj, *often cap* UFO — **ufol·o·gist** \yü'fäləjəst\ n, *often cap* UFO

ULCC \ˌyü,cl(ˌ)sē'sē\ n [*ultra-large crude carrier*] **:** a crude-oil tanker with an extremely large capacity

ul·tra·fiche \'əltrə,fēsh, *also* -,fish\ n [*ultra-* beyond, extremely (fr. L *ultra* beyond) + *fiche*] **:** a microfiche of printed matter that is very greatly reduced (as 100 to 1)

ul·tra·high \ˌəltrə'hī\ adj **:** very high **:** exceedingly high ⟨*ultrahigh* vacuum⟩ ⟨at *ultrahigh* temperatures⟩

ul·tra·mi·cro·fiche \ˌəltrə̯'mīkrō,fēsh, *also* -,fish\ n **:** UL-TRAFICHE

ul·tra·mi·cro·tome \-ˌmīkrə,tōm\ n **:** a microtome for cutting extremely thin sections for electron microscopy — **ul·tra·mi·crot·o·my** \-(ˌ)mī'kräd·əmē, -mi\ n

ul·tra·min·ia·ture \-ˌminēə,chü(ə)r, -ˌminə̯-, -ˌminyə-, -əchə(r), -ˌchùə, -ˌt(y)ù(ə)r, -ˌt(y)ùə\ adj **:** very small **:** subminiature ⟨*ultraminiature* cameras⟩ — **ul·tra·min·ia·tur·iza·tion** \-ˌminēə,chùrə'zāshən, -ˌminə̯-, -ˌminyə-, -əchər-, -ˌt(y)ùr-\ n

ul·tra·pure \ˌəltrə'pyü(ə)r, -ˌpyùə\ adj **:** of the utmost purity ⟨an *ultrapure* reagent⟩

ul·tra·so·nog·ra·phy \ˌəltrəsə'nägrəfē, -sō'n-, -fi\ n [*ultrasonic* + connective -*o-* + -*graphy* writing, representation, deriv. of Gk *graphein* to write] **:** a diagnostic technique for the examination of internal body structures that involves the formation of a two-dimensional image by ultrasonic waves — **ul·tra·so·no·graph·ic** \-ˌsōnə'grafik, -ˌsän-\ adj

ul·tra·thin \-ˌthin\ adj **:** exceedingly thin ⟨*ultrathin* sections for use in electron microscopy⟩

umbilical n [short for *umbilical cord*] **1 :** a cable conveying power to a rocket or spacecraft before takeoff **2 :** a tethering or supply line (as for an astronaut outside a spacecraft or an aquanaut underwater) ⟨he is to be connected to the craft by a 30-foot *umbilical* —Neal Stanford⟩

una·ry \'yünərē, -ri\ adj **:** having or consisting of a single element, item, or component **:** monadic

un·bun·dling \ən'bənd(ə)liŋ\ n **:** separate pricing of products and services ⟨*unbundling* left … customers free to shop around for bargains in systems-engineering, programming and employee education —*Time*⟩ — **un·bun·dle** \(ˌ)ən'bəndəl\ vb

Un·cle Tom \ˌəŋkəl'täm\ vi **Un·cle Tommed; Un·cle Tom·ming :** to behave like an Uncle Tom ⟨I didn't sell out or *Uncle Tom* when I got famous —Muhammad Ali⟩

Uncle Tom·ism \-'tä,mizəm\ n **:** behavior or attitudes characteristic of an Uncle Tom ⟨has taken the trouble … to disguise his *Uncle Tomism* in a profusion of African garb —N.J. Loftis⟩ — **Uncle Tom·ish** \-'tämish\ adj

un·con·ju·gat·ed \ˌən'känjə,gäd·əd\ adj [*un-* + *conjugated*] **:** not chemically conjugated

un·cool \ˌən'kül\ adj **1 :** lacking in assurance, sophistication, or self-control ⟨they got lost and didn't want to look *uncool* by asking directions —F. C. Klein⟩ **2 :** failing to accord with the mores of a particular group ⟨protest, to this generation of college students, is not only dead — it is *uncool* —Jon Nordheimer⟩

un·der·achieve \ˌəndərə'chēv\ vi **:** to perform below an expected level of proficiency ⟨the intellectually capable but *underachieving* youngster —*Children's House*⟩ — **un·der·achieve·ment** \-mənt\ n — **un·der·achiev·er** \-ə(r)\ n

un·der·class \'əndə(r)ˌklas\ n [prob. trans. of Sw *underklass*] **:** the lowest stratum of society usu. composed of disadvantaged minority groups ⟨the problems of the black *underclass* —Godfrey Hodgson⟩ ⟨copy editors and other *underclasses* of the publishing community —V.S. Navasky⟩

un·der·coat·ing \'əndə(r)ˌkōd·iŋ\ n **:** a usu. asphalt-based waterproof coating applied to the undersurface of a vehicle

un·der·fund \ˌəndə(r)'fənd\ vt **:** to provide insufficient funds for ⟨Congress has *underfunded* the program⟩

underground* adj **:** existing, produced, or published outside the establishment esp. by the avant-garde ⟨*underground* movies⟩ ⟨the *underground* press⟩; *also* **:** of or relating to the avant-garde underground ⟨the *underground* life-style, once intended to be a shocking fist in the face of the Establishment, is now predictable —John Lahr⟩

underground* n **:** a usu. avant-garde group or movement that functions outside the establishment

underground vt **:** to place underground ⟨*undergrounding* power lines⟩

un·der·kill \'əndə(r)ˌkil\ n [*under* + -*kill* (as in *overkill*)] **:** lack of the force required to defeat an enemy ⟨models in which human sacrifice is weighed impersonally in a calculation of *underkill* and overkill —Kingman Brewster, Jr.⟩

un·der·pop·u·la·tion \ˌəndə(r)ˌpäpyə'lāshən\ n **:** the state of being underpopulated

un·der·steer \'əndər‚sti(ə)r, -də‚stiə(r\ *n* **:** the tendency of an automobile to turn less sharply than the driver intends; *also* **:** the action or an instance of understeer — **un·der·steer** \‚əndər'sti(ə)r, -də‚stiə(r\ *vi*

un·der·whelm \‚əndə(r)'(h)welm, -eŭm\ *vt* [*under* + *-whelm* (as in *overwhelm*)] **:** to fail to impress or stimulate ⟨then the movie opened, and the critics were *underwhelmed* —Lee Dembart⟩

un·dock* \‚ən'däk\ *vt* **:** to disconnect or uncouple ⟨*undock* the lunar module from the command module⟩

un·flap·pa·ble \‚ən'flapəbəl\ *adj* **:** marked by assurance and self-control **:** imperturbable ⟨trying very hard to remain cool and *unflappable* —E.V. Cunningham⟩ — **un·flap·pa·bil·i·ty** \-‚flapə'biləd·ē\ *n* — **un·flap·pa·bly** \-'flapəblē\ *adv*

un·flapped \‚ən'flapt\ *adj* [*un-* + *flapped*, past part. of *flap*] **:** emotionally undisturbed **:** calm, unruffled

un·glued \‚ən'glüd\ *adj* [fr. past part. of *unglue*] **:** being in a confused or agitated state or condition ⟨by the semifinals, everyone had come a little *unglued* —John Duka⟩ ⟨could trigger civil disturbance, even insurrection. Things seemed on the verge of becoming totally *unglued* — *Worcester Junior Coll. Quarterly*⟩

un·hip \‚ən'hip\ *adj* **:** not hip **:** UNCOOL

union* *n* **1 :** the set of all elements belonging to one or more of a given collection of two or more sets — called also *join, sum* **2 :** the mathematical or logical operation of converting separate sets to a union ⟨does set multiplication distribute... over *union* —*School Mathematics Study Group: Introd. to Matrix Algebra*⟩

¹**uni·sex** \'yünə‚seks, -nē‚-\ *n* [*uni-* one, single (deriv. of L *unus* one) + *sex*] **:** the quality or state of not being distinguishable (as by hair or clothing) as to sex ⟨is *unisex* the ideal or will the New Woman be molded into a wholly new human pattern unleashing unprecedented torrents of feminine energy? —John Cogley⟩

²**unisex** *adj* **1 :** not distinguishable as male or female ⟨a *unisex* face⟩ ⟨how *unisex* the Chinese appeared to be — Jonathan Mirsky⟩ **2 :** suitable or designed for both males and females ⟨*unisex* clothes⟩ ⟨a *unisex* boutique⟩

uni·sex·u·al* \‚yünə'‚sekshə(ə)wəl, -shəl\ *adj* **:** UNISEX ⟨the *unisexual* badly-needs-a-bath bunch was in deep trouble —Jerry Hopkins⟩

uni·tar·i·ly \‚yünə'terəlē\ *adv* **:** in a unitary manner

uni·tar·i·ty \‚yünə'terəd·ē\ *n* **:** the requirement in quantum mechanics that the S matrix be a unitary transformation between initial and final states of motion

uni·tary ma·trix \‚yünə‚terē'mā·triks\ *n* **:** a matrix that has an inverse and a transpose whose corresponding elements are pairs of conjugate complex numbers

unitary transformation *n* **:** a linear transformation of a vector space that leaves scalar products unchanged

unit circle *n* **:** a circle whose radius is one unit of length long

uni·term \'yünə‚tərm, -‚tōm, -‚təim\ *n* **:** a single term used as a descriptor in document indexing

unit membrane *n* **:** a 3-layered membrane that consists of an inner lipid layer surrounded by a protein layer on each side

unit pricing *n* **:** the pricing of products (as packaged foods) whereby the unit price is indicated along with the total price

uni·trust \'yünə‚trəst\ *n* **:** a trust from which the beneficiary receives annually a fixed percentage of the fair market value of its assets

unit train *n* **:** a railway train that transports a single commodity directly from producer to consumer

unit trust *n* **1** *Brit* **:** a mutual fund **2 :** an investment company whose portfolio consists of long-term bonds that are held to maturity

Universal Product Code *n* **:** a bar code that identifies a product's type and price

universal set *n* **:** a set that contains all elements relevant to a particular discussion or problem **:** universe of discourse

un·lead·ed* \‚ən'‚ledəd\ *adj* **:** not treated or mixed with lead or lead compounds ⟨*unleaded* fuels⟩

un·linked \‚ən'liŋkt\ *adj* [*un-* + *linked*] **:** not belonging to the same genetic linkage group ⟨*unlinked* genes⟩

un·per·son \'ən‚pərsən, -‚pōs-, -‚pəis-\ *n* **:** an individual who usu. for political or ideological reasons is removed completely from recognition, consideration, or memory ⟨became an *unperson* when he was removed from the Lenin Mausoleum —Henry Tanner⟩

up* *n* **1 :** a feeling of contentment, excitement, or euphoria **2 :** UPPER

up·date \'əp‚dāt\ *n* **1 :** the act or an instance of updating ⟨this roseate-faced institution ... has come through successive *updates* with its gentility intact —Creighton Whitmore⟩ **2 :** current information for updating something ⟨navigational *update* for a spacecraft computer⟩ **3 :** an up-to-date version, account, or report ⟨*updates* of a machine-readable catalog ... can be produced easily by a simple sorting operation —Concetta N. Sacco⟩

up·field \'əp‚fē(ə)ld\ *adv or adj* **:** in or into the part of the field toward which the offensive team is headed ⟨pushed *upfield* on a 74-yard scoring drive⟩

up–front \‚əp'frənt\ *adj* **1 :** uninhibitedly honest **:** candid ⟨the most sensitive, open, *up-front*, uninhibited ... student in the class —L.J. Peter⟩ **2 :** made, sent, or furnished ahead of time **:** advance ⟨offered $2 million in *upfront* cash plus 10 percent of the gross —Tommy Thompson⟩ **3 a :** given emphasis ⟨she appears on *up-front* leads on only about half the album's tunes —David Logan⟩ **b :** readily seen or perceived **:** obvious

up front *adv* **:** in advance ⟨actors demanding $1 million *up front*⟩

up·man·ship \'əpmən‚ship\ *n* [short for *one-upmanship*] **:** the art or practice of going a friend or competitor one better or keeping one jump ahead of him **:** one-upmanship ⟨real-estate people believe that social *upmanship* has much to do with the suburban boom —Tris Coffin⟩

up·mar·ket \'əp‚märkət, -‚mak-\ *adj* **:** appealing to affluent consumers ⟨basic two-door model ... lacks many of the fine features we appreciate in the *upmarket* models — *Consumer Reports*⟩

upper* *n* **1 :** a stimulant drug; *esp* **:** amphetamine — compare DOWNER **2 :** something that induces a state of good feeling or exhilaration

up quark *n* **:** a quark having an electric charge of $+\frac{2}{3}$, a baryon number of $\frac{1}{3}$, zero charm, and zero strangeness

up·scale \'əp‚skāl\ *adj* **:** of, being, relating to, or appealing to affluent consumers ⟨the *upscale* audience so attractive to advertisers —K. E. Meyer⟩ ⟨*upscale*, two-income, often childless couples —Laurie Johnston⟩

upsilon particle *n* **:** any of a group of unstable electrically neutral fundamental particles of the meson family that have a mass about 10 times that of a proton and are held to consist of a bottom quark-antiquark pair

up·tick \'əp,tik\ *n* **1 :** a stock market transaction at a price above the last previous transaction in the same security — compare DOWNTICK **2 :** an increase in business or prosperity **:** upbeat 〈building of new theaters is on the *uptick* —M.J. Edmands〉

up·tight \,əp'tīt\ *adj* **1 :** being in financial difficulties **:** broke 〈surtax was another blow to an industry already *uptight* —*Chem. & Engineering News*〉 **2 a :** showing signs of tension or uneasiness **:** apprehensive 〈I was a little *uptight* about it at first —Phyllis Craig〉 **b :** angry, indignant 〈I've been doing that voice in Negro theaters for years. Nobody ever got *uptight* —Flip Wilson〉 **3 :** rigidly conventional 〈*uptight* and antiseptic white community —J.M. Culkin〉 — **uptight** *n* — **up·tight·ness** \-nəs\ *n*

up·time \'əp,tīm\ *n* **:** the time during which a piece of equipment (as a computer) is functioning or is able to function 〈*uptime* as a percentage of scheduled machine time was better than 99% —*Datamation*〉

up·val·ue \'əp,val(,)yü, -,valyə(w)\ *vt* **:** to assign a higher value to; *specif* **:** to officially revalue (a currency) upward — **up·val·u·a·tion** \-,valyə'wāshən\ *n*

upward mo·bil·i·ty \-mō'bilòd-ē\ *n* **:** the capacity or facility for rising to a higher social or economic class of society 〈the lives of quiet desperation so many couples live in the rat race of *upward mobility* —Judith Crist〉 — **upwardly mobile** *adj*

ura·nia \yù'rānēə, -nyə\ *n* [NL, fr. *uranium* + -*a* oxide] **:** URANIUM DIOXIDE

uranium di·ox·ide \-(')dī,äk,sīd\ *n* **:** a dioxide UO₂ of uranium obtained as a brown to black crystalline powder by heating uranium trioxide or tri-uranium oct-oxide in hydrogen or carbon monoxide and formerly used in gas mantles and in ceramic glazes

uranium tri·ox·ide \-(')trī,äk,sīd\ *n* **:** a brilliant orange compound UO₃ that is formed in the course of refining uranium and that has been used as a coloring agent for ceramic wares

uranium 238 *n* **:** an isotope of uranium of mass number 238 that absorbs fast neutrons to form a uranium isotope of mass number 239 which then decays through neptunium to form plutonium of mass number 239

ur·ban·ol·o·gist \,ərbə'näləjəst, ,āb-, ,əib-\ *n* [fr. *urban*-*ology* (fr. *urban* + connective -*o*- + -*logy* theory, science, deriv. of Gk *logos* word) + -*ist* specialist] **:** one who specializes in the problems of cities 〈the slow death of an urban community — one whose case history is all too familiar to *urbanologists* —Seth King〉 — **ur·ban·ol·o·gy** \-jē\ *n*

urban renewal *n* **:** a construction program to replace or restore substandard buildings in an urban area

urban sprawl *n* **:** the spreading of urban developments (as houses and shopping centers) on undeveloped land near a city 〈the *urban sprawl* which is rapidly devouring the remaining green spaces of the populous eastern seaboard —L.W. Cassels〉

ureo·tel·ic \yə,rēə,telik, ,yùr-\ *adj* [*urea* + connective -*o*- + *tel*- end, complete (deriv. of Gk *telos* end) + -*ic*, adj. suffix; fr. the fact that urea is the end product] **:** excreting nitrogen mostly in the form of urea 〈mammals are *ureotelic* animals〉 — **ureo·te·lism** \-l,izəm, ,yùrē'ät³l,-\ *n*

uri·co·tel·ic \,yùrəkō,telik\ *adj* [*uric* (acid) + connective -*o*- + *tel*- + -*ic*; fr. the fact that uric acid is the end product] **:** excreting nitrogen mostly in the form of uric acid 〈birds are *uricotelic* animals〉 — **uri·co·te·lism** \-l,izəm, ,yuri'kat³l,-\ *n*

uro·ki·nase \,yùrə,kī,nās, -,nāz\ *n* [*urine* + connective -*o*- + *kinase*] **:** an enzyme that is similar to streptokinase, is found in human urine, and is used to dissolve blood clots (as in the heart)

ur·ti·car·io·gen·ic \,ərd·ə,karēə,jenik, -,ker-\ *adj* [*urticaria* + connective -*o*- + -*genic* produced by, producing] **:** being an agent or substance that induces or predisposes to urticarial lesions (as wheals on the skin)

U-value *n* [unit] **:** a measure of the overall heat transmission of the materials in a building section including air films and air spaces expressed as the number of British thermal units transmitted through one square foot per hour per degree Fahrenheit temperature difference

V

vac·ci·nee \ˌvaksəˈnē\ n [*vaccinate* + *-ee* recipient of an action] **:** a vaccinated individual

val·in·o·my·cin \ˌvalə(ˌ)nōˈmīsᵊn\ n [*valine*, a crystalline amino acid + connective *-o-* + *-mycin* substance obtained from a fungus, fr. *streptomycin*] **:** an antibiotic $C_{54}H_{90}N_6O_{18}$ produced by a bacterium of the genus *Streptomyces* (*S. fulvissimus*)

Val·ium \ˈvalēəm, -lyəm\ *trademark* — used for a preparation of diazepam

val·ue–add·ed tax \ˌvalˌyüˈadəd-, ˌvalyəˈwadəd-\ n **:** an incremental excise that is levied on the value added at each stage of the processing of a raw material or the production and distribution of a commodity

van*n **:** a multipurpose enclosed motor vehicle having a boxlike shape, rear or side doors, and side panels often with windows

van·co·my·cin \ˌvaŋkəˈmīsᵊn, ˌvan-\ n [*vanco-* (arbitrary prefix) + *-mycin*] **:** an antimicrobial agent from an actinomycete of the genus *Streptomyces* (*S. orientalis*) that is effective against spirochetes

va·nil·la \vəˈnilə, -nel-\ adj [fr. the fact that vanilla ice cream is considered the plainest flavor] **:** lacking distinction **:** ordinary, plain ⟨there's nothing fancy about this design. It's just plain *vanilla* —*Newsweek*⟩ ⟨convinced her that sunny outdoor California was a big *vanilla* void compared with the intellectual East —Judith Sims⟩

vanity plate n **:** an automobile registration plate bearing letters, numbers, or a combination of these chosen by the owner

vanner*n **:** one who drives a usu. customized van

van·pool \ˈvanˌpül\ n **:** an arrangement by which a group of people commute to work in a passenger van

van·pool·ing \-ˌpüliŋ\ n [*vanpool* + *-ing*] **:** the act or practice of commuting in a vanpool

va·rac·tor \vəˈraktər, (ˈ)vaˌr-, (ˈ)veˌr-\ n [*varying* + *reactor*] **:** a semiconductor device whose capacitance varies with the applied voltage

variable annuity n **:** an annuity contract which is backed primarily by a fund of common stocks and the payments on which fluctuate with the state of the economy

vas·cu·li·tis \ˌvaskyəˈlīd-əs\ n, pl **-li·ti·des** \-ˈlīd-əˌdēz\ [NL, fr. *vascul-* vascular (fr. L *vasculum* small vessel) + *-itis* disease, inflammation] **:** inflammation of a blood or lymph vessel

va·so·ac·tive \ˌvā(ˌ)zōˈaktiv, ˌvā(ˌ)sō-, ˌva(ˌ)zō-\ adj [*vaso-* vessel (fr. L *vas*) + *active*] **:** affecting the blood vessels esp. in respect to the degree of their relaxation or contraction — **va·so·ac·tiv·i·ty** \-(ˌ)akˌtivəd-ē\ n

VAT abbr value-added tax

Vatican roulette n, slang **:** the rhythm method of birth control

VC*abbr Vietcong

VCR \ˌvē(ˌ)sēˈär, -ˈä(r\ n [*videocassette recorder*] **:** a video tape recorder that uses videocassettes

vector*n **:** an element of a vector space

vector space n **:** a set representing a generalization of a system of vectors and consisting of elements which comprise a commutative group under addition, each of which is left unchanged under multiplication by the multiplicative identity of a field, and for which multiplication under the multiplicative operation of the field is commutative, closed, distributive such that both $c(A + B) = cA + cB$ and $(c + d)A = cA + dA$, and associative such that $(cd)A = c(dA)$ where A, B are elements of the set and c, d are elements of the field

vee·na \ˈvēnə\ n [alter. of *vina*] **:** a stringed instrument of India having usu. four strings on a long bamboo fingerboard with movable frets and a gourd resonator at each end

ve·gan \ˈvejən, ˈvēgən\ n [by contraction fr. *vegetarian*] **:** a strict vegetarian **:** one that consumes no animal food or dairy products

ve·gan·ism \ˈvejəˌnizəm, ˈvēgə-\ n **:** strict vegetarianism

vege·bur·ger \ˈvejēˌbərgər; -ˌbəgə(r, -ˌbəig-\ n [*vegetable* or *vegetarian* + *-burger* patty, sandwich] **:** a patty of vegetable protein used as a meat substitute; *also* **:** a sandwich containing such a patty

Vel·cro \ˈvelˌkrō\ *trademark* — used for a fastening tape

ventriculo- comb form [NL, fr. L *ventriculus* stomach, ventricle of the heart] **1 :** ventricle ⟨*ventriculo*tomy⟩ **2 :** ventricular and ⟨*ventriculo*atrial⟩

ve·ra·pam·il \ˌvi(ə)rəˈpaməl, ˌver-, -mˌil\ n [*veratryl* + *propyl* + *amino*] **:** a coronary vasodilator $C_{27}H_{38}N_2O_4$ used esp. in the form of its hydrochloride

ver·dic·chio \(ˌ)vərˈdē(k)kyō, ver-, -kē(ˌ)ō\ n, often cap [It, fr. the name of the grape] **:** a light dry white wine from Italy

ve·ris·mo \vāˈrēz(ˌ)mō, veˈr-, -ˈriz-\ n [It, fr. *vero* true, fr. L *verus*] **:** artistic use of contemporary everyday material in preference to the heroic or legendary esp. in grand opera **:** verism

ver·ni·er*\ˈvərnēər, ˈvōnēə(r, ˈvəinēə(r\ also **vernier engine** n **:** any of two or more small supplementary rocket engines or gas nozzles mounted on a missile or rocket vehicle and designed to make fine adjustments in the speed or course or to control the attitude

Vé·ro·nique also **Ve·ro·nique** \vārônēk\ adj [F, fr. *Véronique* Veronica] **:** prepared or garnished with usu. white seedless grapes ⟨chicken *Véronique*⟩ ⟨sole *Véronique*⟩

vesico- comb form [NL, fr. L *vesico* bladder] **:** of or relating to the urinary bladder and ⟨*vesico*ureteral⟩

veto–proof adj **:** having enough potential votes to be passed over a veto or to override vetoes consistently ⟨a *veto-proof* bill⟩ ⟨a *veto-proof* Congress⟩

vex·il·lol·o·gy \ˌveksəˈläləjē\ n [L *vexillum* flag + E connective *-o-* + *-logy* theory, science, deriv. of Gk *logos* word] **:** the study of flags — **vex·il·lo·log·i·cal** \ˌveksə-lōˈläjəkəl, (ˈ)vekˈsiləˈlä-\ *adj* — **vex·il·lol·o·gist** \ˌveksə-ˈläləjəst\ *n*

vibe \ˈvīb\ *n* [by shortening and alter. fr. *vibration*] **:** a characteristic aura, spirit, or atmosphere **:** vibration ⟨there was a beautiful *vibe* about them —Yoko Ono⟩ — usu. used in pl. ⟨the good guy is someone who radiates good *vibes* . . . to others and is not psychotic about doing his own thing —Franklin Chu⟩

vi·bra·harp \ˈvībrəˌhärp, -ˌhåp\ *n* [fr. *Vibra-Harp*, a former trademark] **:** a vibraphone — **vi·bra·harp·ist** \-pəst\ *n*

vi·bron·ic \(ˈ)vīˈbränik\ *adj* [*vibr*ation + electr*onic*] **:** of or relating to transitions between molecular energy states when modified by vibrational energy

vic·tim·less \ˈviktəmləs\ *adj* **:** having no victim ⟨*victimless* crimes such as drunkenness, drug use, gambling, consensual illicit sex —Jonathan Kwitny⟩

vic·tim·ol·o·gy \ˌviktəˈmäləjē\ *n* [*victim* + connective *-o-* + *-logy*] **:** the study of the ways in which the behavior of a victim of a crime may have led to or contributed to his victimization — **vic·tim·ol·o·gist** \-jəst\ *n*

Vic·to·ri·ana \(ˌ)vikˌtōrēˈänə, -tȯr-, -ˈanə\ *n* [NL, neut. pl. of *Victorianus* Victorian] **:** materials concerning or characteristic of the Victorian age ⟨at home in his favorite armchair surrounded by assorted *Victoriana*, newspapers, and shaggy fur throws —Margaret R. Weiss⟩

vid·eo·cas·sette \ˌvidēˌōkəˈset\ *n* **:** a videotape recording mounted in a cassette

vid·eo·con·fer·ence \-ˌkänfər(ə)n(t)s, -frən(t)s\ *n* **:** a teleconference conducted by television — **vid·eo·con·fer·enc·ing** \-iŋ\ *n*

vid·eo·disc *or* **vid·eo·disk** \-ˌdisk\ *n* **:** a disc recording of a motion picture or a television production for playback through a home television set

video game *n* **:** an electronic game played by means of images on a video screen

vid·eo·land \ˈvidē(ˌ)ōˌland\ *n* **:** television as a medium or industry

vid·eo·phone \ˈvidēəˌfōn, -ēōˌ\ *n* **:** a telephone equipped for transmission of video as well as audio signals so that users can see each other

video recorder *n* **:** VIDEO TAPE RECORDER

¹vid·eo·tape \-ˌtāp\ *n* **1 :** a recording of a television production on magnetic tape **2 :** the magnetic tape used in a video tape recording

²videotape *vt* **:** to make a videotape of ⟨*videotaping* their classroom work in order to undertake the most exacting self-scrutinization —T.J. Cottle⟩

video tape recorder *n* **:** a device for making a videotape recording

vid·eo·tex \ˈvidēōˌteks\ *also* **vid·eo·text** \-ˌtekst\ *n* [*video* + *tex* (alter. of *text*) or *text*] **:** an interactive electronic system in which data is transmitted from a computer network over telephone or cable-television lines and is displayed on a subscriber's television or computer terminal screen

video vé·ri·té *or* **video ve·ri·te** \-ˌverəˈtā\ *n* [*video* + *verité* or *verite* (as in *cinéma vérité*)] **:** the art or technique of filming or videotaping a television program (as a documentary) so as to convey candid realism

Vi·et·nam·iza·tion \vē͜ˌetnəməˈzāshən, ˌvyet-, -ˌmīˈz-, *also* ˌvēat- *or* ˌvēt-\ *n* **:** the act or process of transferring war responsibilities from U.S. to Vietnamese hands — **Vi·et·nam·ize** \vē͜ˈetnəˌmīz, ˈvyet-, *also* ˈvēat-, ˈvēt-\ *vb*

view·da·ta \ˈvyüˌdädə, -ˌdad·ə, -ˌdädˌə\ *n* **:** VIDEOTEX

view·er·ship \ˈvyüərˌship, ˈvyů(ə)r-; ˈvyüə,-, ˈvyůə,-\ *n* **:** a television audience esp. with respect to size or makeup ⟨increased *viewership* of network news broadcasts — Desmond Smith⟩

-ville \ˌvil, *esp South* vəl\ *n suffix* [*-ville*, suffix occurring in names of towns, fr. F, fr. OF, fr. *ville* farm, village] **:** place or category of a specified nature ⟨squares*ville*⟩ ⟨dulls*ville*⟩

VIN *abbr* vehicle identification number

vin·blas·tine \vinˈblaˌstēn, -ˈblastən\ *n* [contr. of *vincaleukoblastine*] **:** an alkaloid $C_{46}H_{58}N_4O_9$ from Madagascar periwinkle used esp. in the form of its sulfate to treat human neoplastic diseases

vin·ca·leu·ko·blas·tine \ˌviŋkəˈlükəˈblaˌstēn, -ˈblastən; -ˌlükə(ˌ)blaˈstēn\ *n* [NL *Vinca* periwinkle + E *leukoblast* + *-ine* chemical substance] **:** VINBLASTINE

vin·cris·tine \vinˈkriˌstēn, viŋˈk-, -ˈkristən\ *n* [NL *Vinca* + L *crista* crest + E *-ine*] **:** an alkaloid $C_{46}H_{56}N_4O_{10}$ from Madagascar periwinkle used esp. in the form of its sulfate to treat some human neoplastic diseases (as leukemias)

vin·da·loo \ˈvindəˌlü\ *n* [prob. fr. Pg *vin d'alho* wine and garlic sauce, fr. *vinho* wine + *alho* garlic] **:** a curried meat dish made with garlic and wine or vinegar

vine*n*, *slang* **:** an article of clothing; *esp* **:** a man's suit

vi·ol·o·gen \ˈvīələjən\ *n* [*viol-* (as in *violet*) + connective *-o-* + *-gen* one that generates] **:** a chloride of any of several bases used as an oxidation-reduction indicator because color is exhibited in the reduced form

Virgo*n* **:** one born under the astrological sign Virgo

Vir·go·an \ˈvərˌgōən, ˈvä,-, ˈvəi,-\ *n* [*Virgo* + E *-an* one belonging to] **:** VIRGO

vi·ri·on \ˈvīrēˌän, ˈvir-\ *n* [ISV *viri-* (fr. NL *virus*) + *-on* particle, unit] **:** a complete virus particle that consists of an RNA or DNA core with a protein coat sometimes with external envelopes and that is the extracellular infective form of a virus

virtual*adj* **:** of, relating to, or being a hypothetical fundamental particle whose energy, momentum, and mass are not related as they would be for a real particle and whose transitory existence is inferred from indirect evidence ⟨*virtual* photon⟩

virtual memory *n* **:** external memory (as magnetic disks) for a computer that can be used as if it were an extension of the computer's internal memory

visual lit·er·a·cy \-ˌlid·ərəsē, -ˈliˌtrəsē, -si\ *n* **:** the ability to recognize and understand ideas conveyed through visible actions or images (as pictures)

vital signs *n pl* **:** signs of life; *specif* **:** the pulse rate, respiratory rate, body temperature, and sometimes blood pressure of a person

vi·ta·min·iza·tion \ˌvīd·əmənəˈzäshən, *Brit also* ˌvitə-\ *n* **:** the action or process of vitaminizing

vit·rec·to·my \vəˈtrektəmē, -miˈ\ *n, pl* **-mies** [NL, fr. *vitreous humor* + *-ectomy* surgical removal] **:** surgical removal of all or part of the vitreous humor

VLCC \ˌvēˌelˌ(ˌ)sēˈsē\ *n* [*very large crude carrier*] **:** a crude oil tanker with a very large capacity

vocabulary*n, pl* **-lar·ies :** a list or collection of terms or codes available for use (as in an indexing system)

voice–over \'vȯi͜ˌsōvə(r)\ *n* **:** the voice of an unseen narrator heard in a motion picture or television program ⟨narrates in *voice-over,* explaining how to make both maple syrup and maple sugar —*Booklist*⟩; *also* **:** the voice of a visible character indicating his thoughts but without motion of his lips ⟨it's cheating to have the Bard's soliloquies recited as *voice-overs* while the camera lingers on still faces —Liz Smith⟩

voice-print \'vȯis͟ˌprint\ *n* **:** a spectrographically produced individually distinctive pattern of certain voice characteristics that is an effective agent of identification

VOLAR *abbr* volunteer army

vol·ca·no·ge·nic \ˌvälkənəˈjenik, ˌvȯl-\ *adj* [*volcano* + *-genic* produced by, producing] **:** of volcanic origin ⟨*volcanogenic* sediments⟩

vol·tam·met·ry \vȯl'tamə·trē, -ri\ *n* [*volt-ammeter* + *-y* activity] **:** the detection of minute quantities of chemicals (as metals) by measuring the currents generated in electrolytic solutions when known voltages are applied — **vol·tam·met·ric** \ˌvȯltə'me·trik\ *adj*

-vol·tine \'vȯlˌtēn, 'vȯl-\ *adj comb form* [F, fr. It *volta* time, occasion, lit., turn, fr. *voltare* to turn, fr. (assumed) VL *volvitare,* freq. of L *volvere* to roll] **:** having (so many) generations or broods in a season or year ⟨multi*voltine*⟩

vol·un·teer·ism \ˌvälən·ˈti(ə),rizəm\ *n* **:** the act or practice of doing volunteer work in community service

vom·it·ous \'vämə̇d·əs, -ətəs\ *adj* [*vomit* + *-ous,* adj. suffix] **:** sickening, disgusting

von Wil·le·brand's disease \fȯnˈvilə̇ˌbrän(t)s-\ *n* [E. A. *von Willebrand* †1949 Finnish physician] **:** a genetic disorder that is inherited as an autosomal recessive trait and is characterized by deficiency of a plasma clotting factor and by mucosal and petechial bleeding due to abnormal blood vessels

voucher*n **:** a form or check indicating a credit against future purchases or expenditures

VP*abbr verb phrase

VSO *abbr* very superior old — usu. used of brandy 12 to 17 years old

VSOP *abbr* very superior old pale — usu. used of brandy 18 to 25 years old

V/STOL \'vēˌstȯl, -ȯl\ *abbr* vertical short takeoff and landing

VTOL \'vēˌtȯl, -ȯl\ *abbr* vertical takeoff and landing

VVSOP *abbr* very very superior old pale — usu. used of brandy 25 to 40 years old

W

¹wacko \'wak(ₐ)ō\ *adj* [alter. of *wacky*] *slang* **:** absurdly or amusingly eccentric or irrational **:** wacky

²wacko *n, slang* **:** a person who is or who acts wacky

wafer*n **:** a thin slice of material (as silicon or gallium arsenide) used as a base for an electronic component or components (as an integrated circuit)

wafer*vt **1 :** to prepare (as hay or alfalfa) in the form of small compressed cakes suggestive of crackers **2 :** to divide (as a silicon rod) into wafers

waffle*vi **waf·fled; waf·fling :** to talk indecisively or evasively **:** equivocate ⟨has *waffled* miserably in his economic and foreign affairs stances —*Christian Science Monitor*⟩

waffle *n* **:** empty or pretentious words ⟨a lot of rather vague *waffle* about how nice he was —Dan Davin⟩

wa·hi·ne**\wä'hēnē, -(ₐ)nā\ *n* [*wahine* a Polynesian woman, fr. Maori & Hawaiian, woman] **:** a girl surfer

wake surfing *n* **:** the sport of riding (as on a surfboard) the wake of a powerboat

walking catfish *n* **:** an Asian catfish of the genus *Clarius* (*C. batrachus*) that is able to move about on land and has been inadvertently introduced into Florida waters

walk–up*\'wȯ,kəp\ *adj* **:** designed to allow pedestrians to be served without entering a building ⟨the *walk-up* window of a bank⟩

wall*n — **up against the wall :** in or into a tight or difficult situation ⟨high costs ... have finally driven a ghastly number of colleges and universities *up against the wall* —G. W. Bonham⟩ — **up the wall** *slang* **:** into a state of intense agitation, annoyance, or frustration ⟨the steady crunch-crunch drove [him] *up the wall* —Cyra McFadden⟩

wall system *n* **:** a set of shelves often with cabinets or bureaus that can be variously arranged along a wall

¹wall–to–wall *adj* **1 :** covering the entire floor ⟨*wall-to-wall* carpeting⟩ **2 a :** covering or filling the entire space or time ⟨a disco crammed with *wall-to-wall* bodies —*Women's Wear Daily*⟩ ⟨relying too heavily on *wall-to-wall* action —Karla Kuskin⟩ **b :** occurring or found everywhere **:** ubiquitous ⟨the *wall-to-wall* comforts that the current affluence made available —W. H. Jones⟩

²wall–to–wall *n* **:** a wall-to-wall carpet

Wan·kel engine \'väŋkəl-, ¦waŋ-\ *n* [Felix *Wankel* *b*1902 Ger. engineer, its inventor] **:** an internal-combustion rotary engine that has a rounded triangular rotor functioning as a piston and rotating in a space in the engine and that has only two major moving parts

war–game \'wȯ(ə)r,gām, 'wȯ(ə),-\ *vt* **:** to plan or conduct in the manner of a war game ⟨*war-gamed* an invasion —*Newsweek*⟩ ∼ *vi* **:** to conduct a war game — **war–gam·er** \-ə(r)\ *n*

warning track *or* **warning path** *n* **:** a usu. dirt or cinder strip around the outside edge of a baseball outfield to warn a fielder running to make a catch that he is approaching a wall, a fence, or bleachers

wash·a·te·ria *also* **wash·e·te·ria** \,wȯshə'tirēə, -ēr-\ *n* [*wash* + *-ateria* or *-eteria* (as in *cafeteria*)] *chiefly South* **:** a self-service laundry usu. with coin-operated machines

WASP *or* **Wasp** \'wäsp, 'wȯsp\ *n* [white Anglo-Saxon Protestant] **:** an American of northern European and esp. British stock and of Protestant background; *esp* **:** a member of the dominant and most privileged class of people in the U.S. ⟨some are *WASP*s with names that sound like banks and colleges —Jesse Kornbluth⟩ — **Wasp·dom** \-spdəm\ *n* — **Wasp·ish** \-spəsh\ *adj* — **Wasp·ish·ness** \-spəshnəs\ *n*

waste*vt **wast·ed; wast·ing :** to kill or severely injure ⟨comes back and *wastes* one of the ushers with a kick that opens up one side of his face —Robert Greenfield⟩ ⟨demanding that he hurry and ... *waste* the Vietnamese so that the attack could press forward —*Time*⟩

wasted**adj, slang* **:** intoxicated from drugs or alcohol

waste·wa·ter \'wäst,wȯd·ə(r), -,wä-\ *n* **:** water that has been used (as in a manufacturing process) **:** sewage

water bed *n* **:** a bed whose mattress is a plastic bag filled with water

wa·ter·flood \'wȯd·ə(r),fləd, 'wä-\ *vi* **:** to pump water into the ground around an oil well nearing depletion in order to force out additional oil

wa·ter·fowl·er \'wȯd·ə(r),faủlə(r), 'wä-\ *n* **:** a hunter of waterfowl

wa·ter·fowl·ing \-liŋ\ *n* **:** the occupation or pastime of hunting waterfowl

Wa·ter·gate \'wȯd·ə(r),gāt, 'wȯtə(-, 'wä-\ *n* [fr. The *Watergate*, apartment and office complex in Washington, D.C.; fr. the scandal following the break-in at the Democratic National Committee headquarters there in 1972] **:** a scandal usu. involving abuses of office, skullduggery, and a cover-up ⟨are we observing a reflection of the many *Watergate*s in society, at the lower levels — state, county, city, town? —C. R. Gadaire⟩

water toothpick *or* **water pick** *n* **:** a tooth-cleaning device that cleans by directing a jet of water over and between teeth

Wat·son–Crick \¦wätsən¦krik, *also* -,wȯt-\ *adj* **:** of or relating to the Watson-Crick model ⟨*Watson-Crick* helix⟩ ⟨*Watson-Crick* structure⟩

Watson–Crick model *n* [J. D. *Watson b*1928 Am. biologist and F.H.C. *Crick b*1916 Eng. biologist] **:** a model of DNA structure in which the molecule is a cross-linked double-stranded helix, each strand is composed of alternating links of phosphate and deoxyribose, and the strands are cross-linked by pairs of purine and pyrimidine bases projecting inward from the deoxyribose sugars and joined by hydrogen bonds with adenine paired with thymine and with cytosine paired with guanine — compare DOUBLE HELIX

wave function*n **:** a quantum-mechanical function whose absolute value squared represents the relative probability of finding a given elementary particle within a specified volume of space

waxing*n **:** the process of removing body hair with a depilatory wax

way–out \'wā¦aut\ adj **:** FAR-OUT ⟨perhaps a little closer to reality than some of the weird, way-out designs created by Detroit automakers —Ed Janicki⟩ — **way–out·ness** \(')wā'aútnəs\ n

weak interaction or **weak force** n **:** a fundamental interaction experienced by elementary particles that is responsible for some particle decay processes, for nuclear beta decay, and for emission and absorption of neutrinos

weath·er·ize \'wethə,rīz\ vt **-ized; -iz·ing :** to make (as a house) better protected against winter weather esp. by adding insulation and by caulking joints — **weath·er·iza·tion** \,wethərə'zāshən, -ə,rī'z-\ n

we·del \'vādəl, 'we-\ vi [back-formation fr. wedeln] **:** to ski downhill by means of wedeln

we·deln \'vādəl(ə)n, 'wed-\ n, pl **wedelns** or **wedeln** [G, fr. wedeln to fan, wag the tail, fr. wedel fan, tail, fr. OHG wadal; akin to ON vēl bird's tail] **:** a style of skiing in which the skier moves the rear of the skis from side to side making a series of short quick turns while following the fall line

weirdo \'wi(ə)r(¸)dō, 'wiə(¸)dō\ n, pl **weir·dos :** one that is unusually strange, eccentric, or queer ⟨small-town bigots who hate pacifists, pot smokers and long-haired weirdos —Vincent Canby⟩ ⟨reported backstage that a real weirdo was waiting outside in the line wearing a bizarre outfit —George Malko⟩

well–formed \'wel¦fó(ə)rmd, -¦fó(ə)md\ adj **:** produced by the correct application of a set of transformations **:** grammatical ⟨grammar . . . specifies the infinite set of well-formed sentences —Jerry Fodor & Jerrold J. Katz⟩ — **well–formed·ness** \,wel'fó(ə)rm(¸)dnəs, -'fó(ə)m-\ n

well–or·dered \'wel¦órdərd, -¦ó(ə)dəd\ adj **:** partially ordered with every subset containing a first element and exactly one of the relationships "greater than", "equal to", or "less than" holding for any given pair of elements

well–or·der·ing \-'órd(ə)riŋ, -'ó(ə)d-\ n **:** an instance of being well-ordered

western omelet n **:** an omelet made usu. with diced ham, green pepper, and onion

wet*adj — **wet behind the ears :** immature, inexperienced ⟨I was a little offended. I thought they shouldn't betray their extreme youthfulness. Maybe, I thought, they were a little wet behind the ears —Walter Cronkite⟩

wet bar n **:** a bar for mixing drinks (as in a home) that contains a sink with running water

wet look n **:** a glossy effect on fabrics that is produced by coating with urethane

WF \'dəbə(l)yü'ef, -b(ə)yə'(w)ef\ n [withdrawn failing] **:** a grade assigned by a teacher to a student who withdraws from a course with a failing grade

whacked out \'wak¦daút\ adj [fr. past part. of whack] **1 :** exhausted, worn-out **2 :** WACKO **3 :** intoxicated from drugs or alcohol **:** stoned

whack off vb **:** to masturbate — usu. considered vulgar

wheeler and dealer n **:** WHEELER-DEALER

wheel·er–deal·er \'hwēlə(r)¦dēlə(r), 'wē-\ n [irreg. fr. wheel and deal] **:** a shrewd operator esp. in business or politics ⟨rich but rickety conglomerates thrown together overnight by some high-stepping wheeler-dealer —Tom Wicker⟩

wheel·ie \'hwē(ə)lē, 'wē-\ n [wheel + -ie one of such a kind] **:** a maneuver in which a wheeled vehicle (as a motorcycle, bicycle, or dragster) is balanced momentarily on its rear wheel or wheels

wheels n pl, slang **:** a wheeled vehicle; esp **:** automobile ⟨no chick ever got hot pants for a guy who didn't have his own wheels —William Jeanes⟩

where*n — **where it's at 1 a :** a place of central interest or activity ⟨downtown is where it's at, and the . . . money machine is putting its funding into downtown development —Horace Sutton⟩ **b :** something (as a topic or field of interest) of primary concern or importance ⟨they realized vocals were where it's at —C. M. Young⟩ **2 :** the true nature of things ⟨would be a lot better off if someone would grab them by the collar and tell them where it's at —Paul Mazursky⟩

whip·sawed \'hwip,sód, 'wip-\ adj **:** subjected to a double market loss through trying inopportunely to recoup a loss by a subsequent short sale of the same security

whisker*n **:** a thin hairlike crystal (as of sapphire or a metal) of great strength used esp. to reinforce composite structural material

whis·tle–blow·er \'hwisəl¦blō(ə)r\ n **:** one who reveals something covert or who informs against another ⟨unless whistle-blowers can bring problems to lawmakers' attention . . . democracy inevitably breaks down —Michael Nelson⟩ — **whis·tle–blow·ing** \-¦blōiŋ\ n

white amur \-(')ä¦mù(ə)r, -ə'm-, -úə\ n [amur, fr. Amur river, NE Asia] **:** GRASS CARP

white backlash n **:** the hostile reaction of white Americans to the advances of the civil rights movement

white flight n **:** the departure of white families usu. from neighborhoods undergoing racial integration or from cities implementing school desegregation

white hole n **:** a hypothetical extremely dense celestial object that radiates enormous amounts of energy and matter — compare BLACK HOLE 1

white knight n **:** one that comes to the rescue (as of a failing business) **:** savior, rescuer; also **:** one that champions a cause

white room \'hwīt,rüm, 'wīt-, -,rùm\ n **:** CLEAN ROOM ⟨an artist was also in the white room on top of the Pad 14 gantry as the astronaut was buttoned into his tiny Mercury spacecraft —R.N. Watts, Jr.⟩

whit·ey \'hwīd·ē, 'wī-\ n, often cap [white + -y one of such a kind] **:** the white man **:** white society ⟨Negro leaders who are seen as stooges for Whitey —Times Lit. Supp.⟩ — usu. used disparagingly

whiz kid also **whizz kid** n [whiz + kid] **:** a person who is unusually intelligent, clever, or successful esp. at an early age ⟨a 19-year-old whiz kid . . . could read at 2, turned out a historical novel at 14 and entered Oxford at 16. She speaks 11 languages and can read 22 —People⟩

wholesale price index n **:** an index measuring the change in the aggregate wholesale price of a large number of commodities in the primary market expressed as a percentage of this price in some base period

Whorf·ian hypothesis \'hwȯrfēən-, 'w-, -ȯr-\ n [Benjamin Lee *Whorf* †1941 Am. anthropologist] **:** a theory in linguistics: an individual's language determines his conception of the world

Wic·ca \'wikə\ n [OE *wicca* wizard; akin to OE *wicce* witch, *wiccian* to practice witchcraft] **:** the cult or religion of witchcraft — **Wic·can** \'wikən\ adj or n

wide·band \'wīd,'band\ adj **:** BROADBAND

wide receiver n **:** a football receiver who normally lines up several yards to the side of the offensive formation

wig·gy \'wigē, -i\ adj **:** wacky, crazy 〈shrinks . . . to straighten out *wiggy* pets —Parker Hodges〉

wig·let \'wiglət\ n **:** a small wig used esp. to enhance a hairstyle

wild card n **1 :** one picked to fill a leftover tournament berth after regularly qualifying competitors have all been seeded **2 :** an unknown or unpredictable factor

Wild·ean \'wī(ə)ldēən\ adj [Oscar Fingal O'Flahertie Wills *Wilde* †1900 Eng. (Irish-born) writer] **:** of, relating to, or suggestive of Oscar Wilde or his writings 〈a *Wildean* wit and dandy —*Times Lit. Supp.*〉

Wil·son's disease \'wilsənz-\ n [Samuel A. K. *Wilson* †1937 Eng. neurologist] **:** a hereditary disease that is determined by an autosomal recessive gene and is marked esp. by cirrhotic changes in the liver and severe mental disorder due to a ceruloplasmin deficiency and resulting inability to metabolize copper

wimp \'wimp\ n [perh. fr. Brit. slang *wimp* girl, woman, of unknown origin] **:** a weak or ineffectual person 〈are such *wimps* that they will take just about anything we dish out —Barney Matthews〉 — **wimpy** \-pē, -pi\ adj

Win·ches·ter \'win,chestə(r)\ adj [fr. the code name used by the original developer] **:** relating to or being computer disk technology that permits high-density storage by sealing the rigid metal disks against dust

wind·blast \'win(d),blast\ n **1 :** a gust of wind **2 :** the destructive effect of air friction on a pilot ejected from a high-speed airplane

wind·chill \'win,chil\ or **windchill factor** or **wind·chill index** n **:** a still-air temperature with the same cooling effect on exposed human flesh as a given combination of temperature and wind speed

wind down vt **:** to cause a gradual lessening of usu. with the intention of bringing to an end **:** DE-ESCALATE 〈*wind down* a war〉 〈anti-inflation action to *wind down* federal spending —*Amer. Libraries*〉 ~ vi **1 :** to draw gradually toward an end 〈the dress strike appears to be *winding down* —Sandy Parker〉 **2 :** relax, unwind 〈inside, amid the odor of sweat and cigaret smoke and beer and whisky, perhaps 20 auto workers are *winding down* after their work turn —Everett Groseclose〉

wind farm n **:** an area of land with a cluster of wind turbines for driving electrical generators

window *n **1 :** a range of wavelengths in the electromagnetic spectrum to which a planet's atmosphere is transparent **2 :** an interval of time within which a rocket or spacecraft must be launched to accomplish a particular mission **3 :** an area at the limits of the earth's sensible atmosphere through which a spacecraft must pass for successful reentry

windowpane *n **:** tattersall

wind turbine n **:** a turbine driven by the wind

wing *vb — **wing it :** to act or perform without preparation or guidelines **:** improvise 〈an excellent speaker who seems to be proud of his ability to *wing it* without notes or text —Charles Mohr〉

win·kle·pick·er \'wiŋkəl,pikə(r)\ n [*winkle* + *picker;* fr. the notion that the point is sharp enough to be used for picking winkles out of their shells] **:** a shoe with a sharp-pointed toe

win·less \'winləs\ adj **:** being without a win 〈had a *winless* season his first year coaching〉

win·ter·im \'wintə,rim\ n [blend of *winter* and *interim*] **:** an intersession at some colleges and universities that falls chiefly in January

wipe·out \'wī,paȯt\ n **1 :** the act or an instance of wiping out; *esp* **:** complete destruction **2 :** a fall from a surfboard caused usu. by losing control, colliding with another surfer, or being knocked off by a wave

wired *adj **:** feverishly excited **:** HYPER 〈was *wired* and fighting everyone who got in his way —Tony Sanchez〉

wishbone *n **:** a variation of the T formation in which the halfbacks line up farther from the line of scrimmage than the fullback does

witch of Agne·si \-än'yāzē, -zi\ or **witch** n [Maria Gaetana *Agnesi* †1799 Ital. mathematician; *witch* (transl. of It *avversiera* female devil, by confusion with It *versiera,* lit., turning, Agnesi's name for the curve)] **:** a plane cubic curve that is symmetric about the y-axis and approaches the x-axis as an asymptote, that is constructed by drawing lines from the origin intersecting an upright circle tangent to the x-axis at the origin and taking the locus of points of intersection of pairs of lines parallel to the x-axis and y-axis each pair of which consists of a line parallel to the x-axis through the point where a line through the origin intersects the circle and a line parallel to the y-axis through the point where the same line through the origin intersects the line parallel to the x-axis through the point of intersection of the circle and the y-axis, and that has the equation $x^2y = 4a^2(2a-y)$

withhold *vt **:** to deduct (withholding tax) from income

wok \'wäk\ n [Chin (Cant) *wôk*] **:** a bowl-shaped cooking utensil used esp. in the preparation of Chinese food

Wolf–Ra·yet star \'wu̇lfrī'ā-\ n [Charles *Wolf* †1918 & Georges *Rayet* †1906 Fr. astronomers] **:** any of a class of white stars which are found mainly in the Milky Way and Magellanic Clouds and whose spectra are characterized by very broad bright lines esp. of hydrogen, helium, carbon, and nitrogen that indicate very hot unstable stars

wom·an·pow·er \'wu̇mən,paȯ(ə)r, -,pau̇ə\ n **:** the supply of women available and fitted for service 〈huge and growing waste of gifted, educated *womanpower* in contemporary American society —*Current Biog.*〉

won \'wȯn, 'wän\ n, pl **won** [Korean *wǎn*] **1 :** the basic monetary unit of Korea **2 :** a coin or note representing one won

wooden rose n **:** a tuberous half-hardy trailing vine (*Ipomoea tuberosa*) grown in warm regions esp. for its hard showy yellow rose-shaped calyx and seed capsule

woodshed *n **:** a place, means, or session for administering discipline

woody *or **wood·ie** \'wu̇dē, -i\ n, pl **woodies :** a wood-paneled station wagon

214 • word

word*n **:** a combination of electrical or magnetic impulses conveying a quantum of information in communications and computer work

word processing *n* **:** a system for the production of typewritten documents (as business letters) with automated typing and text-editing equipment

word processor *n* **:** a keyboard-operated terminal usu. with a video display and a magnetic storage device for use in word processing; *also* **:** software (as for a computer system) to perform word processing

words·man·ship \'wərdzmən͵ship, 'wȯd-, 'wȯid-\ *n* [*word* + work*manship*] **:** the art or craft of writing

work·a·hol·ic \͵wərkə'hȯlik, ͵wōk-, ͵wȯik-, *sometimes* -'häl-\ *n* [*work* + connective *-a-* + *-holic* (as in *alcoholic*)] **:** a compulsive worker ⟨*workaholics* . . . are possessed of vast energy, many self-doubts and a consuming will to work —Marilyn M. Machlowitz⟩

work·a·hol·ism \'wərkə͵hȯ͵lizəm, 'wōk-, 'wȯik-, *sometimes* -͵hä͵l-\ *n* **:** an obsessive need to work ⟨informs us that *workaholism* increased markedly "since layoffs became widespread" —*East Village Other*⟩

work ethic *n* **:** a belief in work as a moral good

work·fare \'wərk͵fa(ə)r, 'wōk-, 'wȯik-, -͵fe(ə)r, -͵faə, -͵feə\ *n* [*work* + wel*fare*] **:** a welfare program in which recipients are required to perform usu. public service work

work·load \-͵lōd\ *n* **:** the amount of work performed or capable of being performed (as by a mechanical device) usu. within a specified period

work release *n* **:** a corrections program that releases prisoners daily to work at full-time jobs

work·sta·tion \'wərk͵stāshən, 'wōk-, 'wȯik-\ *n* **:** an area with equipment for a single worker; *also* **:** a usu. intelligent terminal connected to a data-processing or word≈ processing network

work–to–rule \͵wərktə'rül, ͵wōk-, ͵wȯik-\ *n, chiefly Brit* **:** the practice of working according to the strictest interpretation of the rules so as to slow down production and force employers to comply with demands ⟨local hospitals have banned the admission of non-urgent cases because of the *work-to-rule* which has closed some operating theatres —*Evening Post (Nottingham)*⟩ — **work–to–rule** *vi, chiefly Brit*

world line *n* **:** the aggregate of all positions in space-time of any individual particle that retains its identity

worry beads *n pl* [fr. the belief that the fingering releases nervous tension] **:** a string of beads to be fingered so as to keep one's hands occupied

WP \͵dəbə(l)yü'pē, -b(ə)yə'-\ *n* [withdrawn passing] **:** a grade assigned by a teacher to a student who withdraws from a course with a passing grade

W particle *n* [*W,* abbr. for *weak*] **:** a hypothetical fundamental particle that is over 50 times heavier than a proton, has positive and negative charge states, and is thought to transmit the weak force between particles in nuclei

wrap·around \͵rapə͵raund\ *adj* **1 :** of or relating to a flexible printing surface wrapped around a plate cylinder **2 :** made to be wrapped around something and esp. the body ⟨a *wrap-around* skirt⟩ **3 :** shaped to follow a contour; *esp* **:** made to curve from the front around to the side ⟨*wraparound* sunglasses⟩

wrecked \'rekt\ *adj* [fr. past part. of *wreck*] *slang* **:** being under the influence of alcohol or drugs **:** stoned

wrecker's ball *n* **:** a heavy iron or steel ball swung or dropped by a derrick to demolish buildings

wrist wrestling *n* **:** a form of arm wrestling in which opponents interlock thumbs instead of gripping hands

write*vt **:** to give up (property) to another for money or other valuable consideration **:** sell

writer's block *n* **:** a psychological inhibition preventing a person from proceeding with a piece of writing

wu–ts'ai \'wüt'sī\ *n* [Chin (Pek) *wu³ts'ai³* five colors] **:** a 5-colored overglaze enamel decoration used on Chinese porcelain since the Ming period

X

X \'eks\ *adj, of a motion picture* **:** of such a nature that admission is denied to persons under a specified age (as 17) — compare G, PG, R

Xan·a·du \'zanə‚d(y)ü\ *n* [*Xanadu,* locality in *Kubla Khan* (1798) poem by Samuel T. Coleridge †1834 Eng. poet] **:** a place of idyllic beauty ⟨this is a *Xanadu* only about half an hour by electric train from the . . . hum of the parent city —William Sansom⟩

xe·nate \'zē‚nāt, 'ze-\ *n* [ISV *xenon* + *-ate* salt or ester of an acid] **:** a salt of xenic acid

xe·nic \'zēnik, 'zen-\ *adj* [*xen-* guest, foreigner, strange (deriv. of Gk *xenos* stranger, guest, host) + *-ic,* adj. suffix] **:** of, relating to, or employing a culture medium containing one or more unidentified organisms ⟨*xenic* cultivation of insect larvae⟩ — **xe·ni·cal·ly** \-ək(ə)lē\ *adv*

xe·nic acid \‚zēnik-, ‚ze-\ *n* [*xenic* fr. ISV *xenon* + *-ic,* adj. suffix] **:** a weak acid known only in the form of its hydrate ($XeO_3 \cdot xH_2O$) and obtained by hydrolysis from xenon fluorides

xe·no·bi·ol·o·gy \‚zenō(‚)bī'äləjē, ‚zē-, -ji\ *n* [*xeno-* guest, stranger, strange (deriv. of Gk *xenos* stranger, guest, host) + *biology*] **:** EXOBIOLOGY

xe·no·bi·ot·ic \-(‚)bī'äd‚ik\ *n* **:** a chemical compound (as a drug, pesticide, or carcinogen) that is foreign to a living organism — **xenobiotic** *adj*

xe·no·ge·ne·ic \-jə‚nēik\ *also* **xe·no·gen·ic** \-'jenik\ *adj* [*xeno-* + *-geneic,* alter. of *-genic* producing, produced by] **:** derived from, originating in, or being a member of another species ⟨a *xenogeneic* antibody⟩ ⟨*xenogeneic* hosts⟩ — compare ALLOGENEIC, SYNGENEIC

xe·no·graft \'zenə‚graft, 'zē-\ *n* **:** a tissue graft carried out between members of different species

xe·non hexa·flu·o·ride \'zē‚nän‚heksə'flu(ə)r‚īd, 'zen-\ *n* **:** a highly reactive colorless crystalline compound XeF_6

xenon te·tra·flu·o·ride \-‚te·trə-\ *n* **:** a colorless crystalline compound XeF_4 that sublimes readily in air and is formed by heating xenon with fluorine under pressure

xe·no·tro·pic \‚zēnə'träpik, -'trōp-\ *adj* **:** replicating or reproducing only in cells other than those of the host species ⟨*xenotropic* viruses⟩

xe·ro·der·ma pig·men·to·sum \'zirə‚dərmə‚pigmən‚tōsəm, -‚men‚-\ *n* [NL *pigmentosum,* fr. L *pigmentum* pigment + L *-osum,* neut. of *-osus -ose*] **:** a genetic condition inherited as a recessive autosomal trait that is caused by a defect in mechanisms that repair DNA mutations (as those caused by ultraviolet light) and is characterized by the development of pigment abnormalities and multiple skin cancers in body areas exposed to the sun

Xe·rox \'zi(ə)r‚äks, 'zē‚räks\ *trademark* — used for a xerographic copier

xi*\'zī, 'ksī\ *or* **xi particle** *n* **:** an unstable elementary particle existing in negative and neutral charge states with masses respectively 2585 and 2572 times the mass of an electron

X–ray astronomy *n* **:** astronomy dealing with investigations of celestial bodies by means of the X rays they emit

X–ray dif·frac·tion \-də'frakshən\ *n* **:** a scattering of X rays by the atoms of a crystal that produces an interference effect so that the diffraction pattern gives information on the structure of the crystal or the identity of a crystalline substance

X–ray star *n* **:** a luminous starlike celestial object emitting a major portion of its radiation in the form of X rays

xu \'sü\ *n, pl* **xu** [Vietnamese, fr. F *sou* sou] **:** a former coin of South Vietnam equivalent to the cent

Y

YA *abbr* young adult

YAG \'yag\ *n* [*y*ttrium *a*luminum *g*arnet] **:** a synthetic yttrium aluminum garnet of marked hardness and high refractive index that is used esp. as a gemstone and in laser technology

ya·ki·to·ri \ˌyäki'tȯrē, -ri\ *n* [Jp, lit., grilled chicken, fr. *yaki* roasting + *tori* bird, chicken] **:** bite-sized marinated chicken pieces grilled on small bamboo skewers

Ya·ma·to–e \yä'mätə‚wä\ *also* **Ya·ma·to** \-'mä(‚)tō\ *n* [Jp *yamato-e*, fr. *Yamato* Japan + *e* picture, painting] **:** a movement in Japanese art arising in medieval times and marked by the treatment of Japanese themes with Japanese taste and sentiment

yard sale *n* **:** GARAGE SALE

ya·yoi \(')yä‚yȯi\ *adj, often cap* [*Yayoi,* site in Tokyo, Japan, where remains of the period were discovered] **:** of, relating to, or being typical of a Japanese cultural period extending from about 200 B.C. to A.D. 200, being generally neolithic but including the beginning of work in metal, and characterized esp. by unglazed wheel-thrown pottery **(Yayoi ware)** usu. without ornamentation but often of florid shape

yech *or* **yecch** \'yək, 'yək\ *interj* [imit.] — used to express rejection or disgust

Yellow Pages *n pl* **:** the section of a telephone directory that lists business and professional firms alphabetically by category and that includes classified advertising; *also* **:** a listing of products or services that is independently published

yen·ta \'yen·tə\ *n* [Yiddish *yente* vulgar and sentimental woman, fr. the name *Yente*] **:** a talkative, gossipy, or meddlesome person and esp. such a woman ⟨a head floor nurse — a *yenta* whose own vocal equipment could drown out the brass section of the Hamburg Philharmonic —Robert Craft⟩

yé–yé \ˌyā(‚)yā\ *adj* [F, fr. E *yeah-yeah,* exclamation often interpolated in rock 'n' roll performances] **:** of, relating to, or featuring rock 'n' roll as it developed in France ⟨op-art boutiques crowding the elegant Parisian boulevards, . . . *yé-yé* discotheques in quaint old houses —*Newsweek*⟩

yield to maturity **:** the total rate of return to an owner holding a bond to maturity expressed as a percentage of cost

YIG \'yig\ *n* [*y*ttrium *i*ron *g*arnet] **:** a synthetic yttrium iron garnet having ferrimagnetic properties that is used esp. as a filter for selecting or tuning microwaves

Yi–hsing ware \'yē'shiŋ‚-\ *also* **Yi–hsing** *or* **Yi–hsing yao** \ˌyē‚shiŋ'yaù\ *n* [*Yi-hsing* fr. *Yi-hsing* (*Ihing*), town in southern Kiangsu province, China; *Yi-hsing yao* fr. *Yi-hsing* + Chin (Pek) *yao*[2] pottery] **:** reddish yellow pottery made at Ihing in Kiangsu, China, and introduced into Europe by the Portuguese **:** boccaro

Yin·glish \'yiŋ(g)lish\ *n* [blend of *Yiddish* and *English*] **:** English marked by a considerable number of borrowings from Yiddish

yob·bo \'yäb(‚)ō\ *n, pl* **yobbos** *or* **yobboes** [*yob* + *-o* one having such qualities] **1** *Brit* **:** lout, yokel **2** *or* **yob*** *Brit* **:** hoodlum

yock \'yək, 'yäk\ *or* **yuck** \'yək\ *or* **yuk** *vi* **yocked** *or* **yucked** *or* **yukked; yock·ing** *or* **yuck·ing** *or* **yuk·king** [imit.] **:** to laugh esp. in a boisterous or unrestrained manner

youth·cult \'yüth‚kəlt\ *n* **:** public preoccupation and bias in favor of youth

youth·quake \-ˌkwāk\ *n* **:** the impact of the values, tastes, and mores of youth on the established norms of society

yo-yo*\'yō(‚)yō\ *n, pl* **yo–yos :** a stupid or foolish person ⟨you don't want to look like a *yo-yo* in front of a hundred guys —B.R. Brown⟩

yo-yo *vi* **yo–yoed; yo–yo·ing :** to move from one position to another repeatedly ⟨I'll be *yo-yoing* back and forth from the Coast —Telly Savalas⟩: as **a :** to vacillate ⟨the Supreme Court has *yo-yoed* on the issue of the right to travel —F.P. Graham⟩ **b :** to fluctuate ⟨bond prices will *yo-yo* —W.S. Pinkerton, Jr.⟩

¹yuck *also* **yuk***n **1** *slang* **:** laugh **2** *slang* **:** joke, gag

²yuck \'yək, 'yək\ *also* **yuk***interj [imit.] — used to express rejection or disgust ⟨spending hours over some new dish and saying "*yuck,* I hate that" —Anne Dowie⟩

yucky \'yəkē, 'yəkē, -i\ *adj* [*yuck* + *-y,* adj. suffix] *slang* **:** offensive, distasteful ⟨not even a decent pool, unless you counted the *yucky* old bathtub in the phys ed building —W.F. Reed⟩

Z

zaf·tig also **zof·tig** \'zäftig, 'zȯf-\ adj [Yiddish zaftik juicy, succulent, fr. G saftig, fr. saft juice, sap, fr. OHG saf] of a woman : having a full rounded figure : pleasingly plump ⟨nice-looking, sort of zaftig, Jewish girl. A little thick in the thighs and ankles, but definitely one of your look-back ladies —Albert Goldman⟩

zai·bat·su \(')zī'bät(,)sü\ n pl [Jp, fr. zai money, wealth + batsu clique, clan] : the powerful financial and industrial conglomerates of Japan ⟨the zaibatsu . . . countered military influence to a substantial extent before 1937 — Vera M. Dean⟩

zaire \'zī(ə)r, zä'i(ə)r\ n [F zaïre, fr. Zaïre (formerly Congo), country in west central Africa, fr. Zaïre, former name of the Congo river] **1** : the basic monetary unit of Zaire **2** : a note representing one zaire

Zair·ian or **Zair·ean** \'zī(ə)rēən, zī'i(ə)r-\ n : a native or inhabitant of Zaire — **Zairian** or **Zairean** adj.]

¹zap \'zap\ interj [imit.] **1** — used to express the sound made by or as if by a gun ⟨we would go through lists of names, pointing our fingers and saying, "Zap, you're sterile" —Sally Kempton⟩ **2** — used to indicate a sudden or instantaneous occurrence ⟨you hold the wires in place and zap — it's done —Gary Scott⟩

²zap vb **zapped; zap·ping** vt **1 a** : to destroy or kill by or as if by shooting ⟨cartoon heroes were zapping cartoon villains and monsters —Edith Efron⟩ ⟨zapped the crocodile with a bullet right through the eye —Time⟩ **b** : to hit suddenly and forcefully ⟨can zap him with long or short alarm sounds —Esquire⟩ ⟨the vibes given off by a contented pair . . . zap prospective interlopers like poison darts —Miranda Hostler⟩ **2** : to propel suddenly or speedily ⟨film can instantly zap us anywhere in time — Jacob Brackman⟩ ~ vi : to go speedily : zoom, zip ⟨zap off on a jet to someplace like Miami —H.S. Thompson⟩

³zap n : something that imparts interest or excitement : kick ⟨will add a certain zap to a steak tartare —Nathaniel Benchley⟩; also : a sudden forceful blow or attack ⟨a zap or two from a satellite-mounted death ray —Harvey Ardman⟩

ze·atin \'zēətən, -t⁰n\ n [NL Zea, generic name of maize + E -tin (as in kinetin)] : a cytokinin first isolated from maize endosperm

zebra crossing n, Brit : a crosswalk marked by a series of broad white stripes

zel·ko·va* \'zelkəvə, zel'kōvə\ n : a plant of the genus Zelkova; esp : a tall widely spreading Japanese tree (Z. serrata) resembling the American elm and replacing the latter as an ornamental and shade tree because of its resistance to Dutch elm disease

Zen·do \'zen(,)dō\ n, pl **zendos** [Jp zendō, fr. zen Zen sect + -do shrine] : a place used for Zen meditation

ze·ner di·ode \,zēnə(r)'dī(,)ōd, 'zen-\ n, often cap Z [Clarence Melvin Zener b1905 Am. physicist] : a silicon semiconductor device used esp. as a voltage regulator

zep·po·le \(t)se(p)'pō(,)lā, ze-\ also **zep·po·li** \-(,)lē\ n, pl **zeppole** also **zeppoli** [It] : a doughnut made from deep-fried cream puff dough

zero–based \'zērō¦bäst, ¦zir-\ or **zero–base** \-¦bās\ adj : having each item justified on the basis of cost or need ⟨zero-based budgeting⟩

zero vector n : a vector which is of zero length and all of whose components are zero

zilch \'zilch, 'ziùch\ n [origin unknown] : nothing, zero ⟨right now the credibility of the Administration is zilch —R.J. Dole⟩ ⟨overnight, my desirability as a commercial voice dropped from sky-high to zilch —Orson Bean⟩

zill \'zil\ n [prob. fr. Turk zil cymbals] : a small metallic cymbal used in pairs with one worn on the thumb and the other on the middle finger

zing* vt **1** : to hit suddenly and forcefully : ZAP ⟨zing you with a . . . service fee every time you step out on the court —Barry Tarshis⟩ **2** : to attack in words : satirize, criticize ⟨politicians who are zinged in his columns —Ron Nessen⟩ ~ vi **1** : zip, speed ⟨movie zings right along — Playboy⟩ **2** : to be alive : bubble over ⟨zinging with raw energy and ambition —David Bellamy⟩

zing·er \'ziŋə(r)\ n **1** : a pointed witty remark or retort ⟨the critics got in their zingers —Caryl Rivers⟩ **2** : something causing or meant to cause interest, surprise, or shock ⟨a muddled performance — but with a zinger of a finish —Mark Kram⟩

zingy \'ziŋē, -ŋi\ adj **zing·i·er; -est 1** : enjoyably exciting ⟨a zingy musical⟩ **2** : strikingly attractive or appealing ⟨wore a zingy new outfit⟩

zinj·an·thro·pine \zin'jan(t)thrə,pīn\ n [zinjanthropine adj., fr. zinjanthropus + -ine, adj. suffix] : any of several closely related primitive extinct African hominids including zinjanthropus — **zinjanthropine** adj

¹zip \'zip\ n [by shortening] : ZIP CODE

²zip n [prob. alter. of zero] : zero, nothing ⟨a score of 21 – zip⟩ ⟨so far we have zip to show for our efforts —Susan Zirinsky⟩

zip code \'zip-\ n, often cap Z&I&P [ZIP fr. zone improvement plan] : a number that identifies each postal delivery area in the U.S.

zip–code \'zip,kōd\ vt : to furnish with a zip code

zip–out \'zip,aùt\ adj : attached by means of a zipper ⟨a zip-out liner in a trench coat⟩

zir·ca·loy \'zərkə¦lȯi\ n [zirconium + alloy] : any of several zirconium alloys notable for corrosion resistance and stability over a wide range of radiation and temperature exposures

zit \'zit\ n [origin unknown] slang : a pimple ⟨searching his face for zits in a cosmetic mirror —Charles Young⟩

zi·ti \'zēd-ē, -ē(,)tē\ n, pl **ziti** [It, lit., boys, pl. of zito, modif. of citto, boy, youth] : medium-sized tubular pasta

Z line n : any of the dark bands across a striated muscle fiber that mark the junction of actin filaments in adjacent sarcomeres

zoftig *var of* ZAFTIG

Zol·ling·er–El·li·son syndrome \ˌzäliŋəˈreləsən-\ *n* [R.M. *Zollinger b*1903 Am. surgeon & E.H. *Ellison* †1970 Am. surgeon] **:** a syndrome consisting of fulminating intractable peptic ulcers, gastric hypersecretion and hyperacidity, and hyperplasia of the pancreatic islet cells

zone*n **:** a designated area (as a row on a punch card or a channel on magnetic tape) in which bits signifying information other than digits are recorded (as in Hollerith code or EBCDIC)

zone melting *n* **:** a technique for the purification of a crystalline material and esp. a metal in which a molten region travels through the material to be refined, picks up impurities at its advancing edge, and then allows the purified part to recrystallize at its opposite edge

zone refine *vt* **:** to produce or refine by zone melting

Zon·ian \ˈzōnēən\ *n* [fr. Panama Canal *Zone* + *-ian* one belonging to] **:** a U.S. citizen who lives in the Panama Canal Zone

zonk \ˈzäŋk, ˈzȯŋk\ *vb* [back-formation fr. *zonked*] *vt* **:** to stun or stupefy ⟨tranquilizers *zonk* a person out —R.R. Fieve⟩; *also* **:** to hit suddenly and forcefully **:** ZAP ⟨being *zonked* by a wild surfboard is the biggest danger — Mary Lou Britton⟩ — often used with *out* ~ *vi* **:** to pass out from or as if from alcohol or a drug — often used with *out*

zonked \ˈzäŋkt, ˈzȯŋkt\ *also* **zonked–out** \ˈzäŋkˈdau̇t, ˈzȯŋk-\ *adj* [origin unknown] **:** being or acting as if under the influence of alcohol or a drug (as LSD) **:** high

zo·ri \ˈzōrē, ˈzȯrē\ *n, pl* **zori** [Jp, *zōri*, lit., straw sandals, fr. *sō-* grass, vegetation + *-ri* footwear] **:** a flat thonged sandal usu. made of straw, cloth, leather, or rubber

Zorn's lemma \ˈzȯ(ə)rnz-, ˈtsȯ-\ *n* [Max August *Zorn b*1906 Ger. mathematician] **:** a lemma in set theory: if a set S is partially ordered and if each subset for which every pair of elements is related by exactly one of the relationships "less than," "equal to," or "greater than" has an upper bound in S, then S contains at least one element for which there is no greater element in S

Z particle *n* **:** a hypothetical electrically neutral fundamental particle about 96 times heavier than a proton that is held to transmit the weak force between particles in nuclei

ZPG *abbr* zero population growth

zup·pa in·gle·se \ˈtsüpə·iŋˈglä(ˌ)zā, ˈzü-, -inˈg-, -(ˌ)sā, -ˈglāsē, -zē\ *n, often cap I* [It, lit., English soup] **:** a dessert consisting of sponge cake and custard or pudding that is flavored with rum, covered with cream, and garnished with fruit

zy·de·co \ˈzīdəˌkō\ *also* **zod·i·co** \ˈzädəkō\ *n, pl* **-cos** *often cap* [perh. modif. of F *les haricots* beans, fr. the Creole dance tune *Les Haricots Sont Pas Salé*] **:** popular music of southern Louisiana that combines dance tunes of French origin with elements of Caribbean music and the blues and that is usu. played by small groups featuring guitar, washboard, and accordion